Leo Strauss, the Straussians, and the American Regime

Leo Strauss
1899–1973

Leo Strauss, the Straussians, and the American Regime

Kenneth L. Deutsch
and
John A. Murley
Editors

ROWMAN & LITTLEFIELD PUBLISHERS, INC.
Lanham • Boulder • New York • Oxford

ROWMAN & LITTLEFIELD PUBLISHERS, INC.

Published in the United States of America
by Rowman & Littlefield Publishers, Inc.
4720 Boston Way, Lanham, Maryland 20706
http://www.rowmanlittlefield.com

12 Hid's Copse Road
Cumnor Hill, Oxford OX2 9JJ, England

British Library Cataloguing in Publication Information Available

Library of Congress Cataloging-in-Publication Data

Leo Strauss, the Straussians, and the American regime / Kenneth L. Deutsch
and John A. Murley, editors.
    p.   cm.
    Includes bibliographical references (p.) and index.
    ISBN 0-8476-8691-4 (cloth: alk. paper).—ISBN 0-8476-8692-2 (paper: alk. paper)
    1. Strauss, Leo—Contributions in political science. I. Deutsch, Kenneth L.
    II. Murley, John A. (John Albert)
    JC251.S8L454   1999
    320.53'0973—dc21   99-22578
                                                                              CIP

Printed in the United States of America

∞™ The paper used in this publication meets the minimum requirements of Amercian
National Standard for Information Sciences—Permanence of Paper for Printed Library
Materials, ANSI/NISO Z39.48-1992.

To the memory of Rose Bachem Alent—
colleague and friend.

—K. L. D.

For Dawn Legler Murley—
wife, friend, and companion of four decades.

—J. A. M.

Contents

vii

Preface

$\mathcal{M}$ore than four decades ago Willmoore Kendall announced "there is a new breed of political scientists abroad in the land, as different from the old breed as chalk from cheese." He was referring to the earliest members of the first generation of students of Leo Strauss. This new breed of political scientists, Kendall observed "are still *rara avis*, and come, for the most part, from a single institution, namely the University of Chicago, and for good reason. Most of them are pupils of one of the two or three great teachers of politics of our day, Professor Leo Strauss, who communicates to them, as if by magic, his own love of learning, his own sense of the gravity of the great problems of politics."[1] Kendall also noticed that "into the vocabulary of professionals in the field of political theory there has entered, in recent years, a new noun 'Straussian.'" It is, he observed, a noun that "does service . . . as an adjective (as in the sentence, 'Professor So-and-so is a 'Straussian')."[2] Since Kendall wrote, the influence of Leo Strauss has been extended through the first generation, including many not discussed in this book, to their students and to their students' students, into the third generation.

We wish to explore, upon the centenary of Leo Strauss's birth, his enduring legacy as a teacher and scholar, a legacy that has richly influenced the study of the American regime. In recent years academic and political criticisms have been lodged against Strauss and "Straussians" (those who acknowledge the influence of Leo Strauss on their work). It has been said that Strauss sought to organize a return to ancient Athens, or to defend liberal capitalism against its critics, or to affirm Nietzschean nihilism under cover of an esoteric natural right teaching. Critics such as Sheldon Wolin, Charles Larmore, Stephen Holmes, Shadia Drury, and George Kateb have accused him of founding an antidemocratic cult dedicated to maintaining orthodoxy within its elitist membership. Has any other contemporary academic political thinker been subjected to the rancor that Leo Strauss has? Thus, Brent Staples could actually write on the *New York Times* editorial page that Strauss thought philosopher-kings should rule in such a way as to keep the "rabble" in their place. Thus also Shadia Drury in her book *Leo Strauss and the American Right* blames him for the contemporary political agenda of the Republican Party, the suppression of women, and the pernicious influence of the phalocratic character of his political philosophy.

This book shows that the diverse academic and public activities of Strauss's students and followers in American politics have been profoundly influenced by the questions raised between ancient and modern republicanism, between reason and revelation, and between poetry and philosophy, as well as by the understanding of the theological-political problem and by the importance of the nonhistoricist reading of texts. Strauss taught that all of these questions must be taken seriously. He and his students, unto the third generation, share questions about the origins and health of the American regime rather than final answers or political orthodoxies. Strauss encouraged his students to explore the crisis of liberal democracy, the pervasive character of relativism in contemporary political science, the original intent of the Framers, the problems of statesmanship and political exigency, and the problem of the philosopher's relationship to a liberal democratic regime. He very much sought to provide his students and followers with that critical distance needed for judging the dominant opinions of our era, attempting thereby to draw them out of the "cave" of the contemporary American regime.

Actually, Strauss sought to free his followers from a "second cave," one much deeper than Plato's original cave. As he put it:

> Bearing in mind the classic representation of the natural difficulties in philosophizing, in other words, the Platonic allegory of the cave, one can say that today we are in a second, much deeper cave, than the fortunate ignorant persons with which Socrates was concerned. We need history first of all to reach the cave from which Socrates can lead us to the light. We need preparatory instruction—that is, precisely learning by reading.[3]

Liberation from the "second, much deeper cave" requires the radical questioning of the layer of ideas—positivism, modern rationalism, and historicism—that covers over all natural phenomena. Liberation from the second cave will enable some to pursue a serious study of the relationship between wisdom and consent found in the type of democracy identified with the self-understanding of the American Founders as well as in the study of the political problems of tyranny and the universal state. Strauss's paradox here is as follows: Only in a contemporary liberal democracy will the search for truth be permitted, yet it is necessary for us to begin leaving the depths of the second cave of contemporary American liberal democracy in order for that search to take place. In this manner Leo Strauss was both cautious and bold in his approach to the contemporary American liberal democratic regime.

In Part One George Anastaplo, Laurence Berns with Eva Brann, Joseph Cropsey, and Harry V. Jaffa offer, in alphabetical order, reflections for this volume. They describe various facets of Leo Strauss's extraordinary life as teacher and scholar in the United States. They draw upon their exposure to him at the New School for Social Research, the University of Chicago, Claremont Men's College, and St. John's College (Annapolis).

Part Two addresses "Taking Strauss Seriously." Kenneth L. Deutsch begins with
Leo Strauss's influence on the study of the American regime. Hadley Arkes describes
the teacher he encountered in Strauss's classes at the University of Chicago. Eugene
F. Miller documents the bold encounter between Strauss and American social science. Gregory Bruce Smith explores Strauss's political response to Friedrich
Nietzsche's and Martin Heidegger's teachings. Aryeh Botwinick makes a case with
reference to the American Founding, for reading Strauss as a "mitigated skeptic"
who embraces the American Founding because of its link between liberalism and
skepticism. Ronald J. Terchek locates Leo Strauss in the debate in which both liberalism and communitarianism are accepted in part and rejected in part as solutions
to political problems.

Part Three surveys how first-generation Straussians have established the
thought of the Founding generation and the thought of Abraham Lincoln as central to understanding the aspirations of the American regime. John A. Murley
explores the distinctive and wide-ranging constitutionalism of George Anastaplo.
Gary D. Glenn discusses Walter Berns's moderate constitutionalism. Walter Nicgorski
identifies Allan Bloom's debt to Leo Strauss on liberal education. Christopher A.
Colmo presents Joseph Cropsey's understanding of the modernity of the American
regime. Michael Zuckert examines Martin Diamond's work on *The Federalist*. Will
Morrisey explores Paul Eidelberg's analysis of the American Regime as a mixed
regime. Charles R. Kesler discusses the Lincolnian themes that have guided Harry
V. Jaffa's study of America. Miriam Galston addresses Ralph Lerner's study of the
independent and thoughtful deliberation of the Framers as a distinctive mode for
our time. Larry Arnhart explores Roger Masters's work on natural right and evolutionary biology. Murray Dry examines the work of Herbert Storing as teacher
and scholar of the Founding.

Although Strauss wrote very little directly on American political institutions,
one can discern Straussian themes in the research of those influenced by Strauss
who have studied Congress, the presidency, the Supreme Court, and the bureaucracy. Part Four suggests that research. John A. Murley discusses deliberation and
representation in Congress. Robert Eden addresses leadership and statesmanship in
the presidency. Ralph A. Rossum revisits the First Amendment and the role of the
Supreme Court as republican schoolmaster. John A. Marini explores the problems
of constitutionalism, tyranny, and the universal state.

Since the mid-1970s more than a few scholars influenced by Leo Strauss have
assumed a wide variety of significant positions in one or another Democratic or
Republican administrations in Washington. In Part Five Gary J. Schmitt and Abram
N. Shulsky, Carnes Lord, Susan Orr, William A. Galston, and Mark Blitz offer their
reflections from their various perspectives of practice, including their views on the
often tenuous yet challenging relationships between ancient and modern republican theory and contemporary political practice.[4]

With any project of this kind insightful suggestions can make all the difference. Helpful suggestions over the course of this book's progress have been made

by Walter Soffer as well as by several of the contributors. We wish also to acknowledge the extraordinary efforts of two editors, Jonathan Sisk and Steve Wrinn of
Rowman & Littlefield, who have contributed to the conversation that is political
philosophy. We wish to record as well our gratitude to the Earhart Foundation for
their generous support of this work.

Kenneth L. Deutsch and John A. Murley
December 1998

NOTES

1. Willmoore Kendall, *The Conservative Affirmation* (Chicago: Henry Regnery, 1963),
pp. 202–3. See also *ibid.* pp. 249–52, 257–60.

2. Willmoore Kendall, review of *Ancients and Moderns: Essays on the Tradition of Political
Philosophy*, ed. Joseph Cropsey, *American Political Science Review* 61 (September 1967),
pp. 783–84. See also Willmoore Kendall, "John Locke Revisited," in *Willmoore Kendall Contra
Mundum*, ed. Nellie D. Kendall (Lanham, Md.: University Press of America, 1994), pp. 418–56.

3. Jurgen Gebhardt, "Leo Strauss: The Quest for Truth in Times of Perplexity," in *Hannah
Arendt and Leo Strauss: German Émigrés and American Political Thought after World War II*, ed.
Peter Graf Kielmansegg *et al.* (Cambridge: Cambridge University Press, 1995), p. 98.

4. It is also worthy to note that many others influenced by Leo Strauss and his students
have assumed, at various times, responsible positions in Washington. Among these have been
the following: William B. Allen served as chairman of the U.S. Civil Rights Commission.
John T. Agresto served as deputy chairman and then as acting chairman of the National
Endowment for the Humanities. Joseph Bessette served as acting director of the Bureau of
Justice Statistics. Mark Blitz served as the associate director of the U.S. Information Agency.
David Epstein serves in the Office of Net Assessment in the Department of Defense. Robert
A. Goldwin served as special assistant to President Gerald R. Ford. Alan Keyes served as assis-
tant secretary of state for International Organization Affairs. William Kristol served as chief
of staff for Vice President Dan Quayle. Carnes Lord served on the National Security Council
and later as the chief foreign policy adviser of Vice President Quayle. Michael Malbin served
as the associate director of the House Republican Conference. John A. Marini and Ken
Masugi each served as special assistant to the chairman of the U.S. Equal Employment
Opportunity Commission. Gary L. McDowell served as adviser to Attorney General Edwin
Meese III. James H. Nichols served as a senior official at the National Endowment for the
Humanities. Charles Fairbanks served as assistant deputy secretary of state for human rights.
Ralph A. Rossum served as director of the Bureau of Justice Statistics. Gary J. Schmitt served
as head of President Ronald Reagan's National Advisory Board of Foreign Intelligence. Peter
W. Schramm served as a senior official in the Department of Education. Steven R. Schlesinger
served as Director of the Bureau of Justice Statistics. Abram N. Shulsky served as director of
strategic arms control policy at the Department of Defense. Nathan Tarcov served as a member of the State Department policy planning staff. Michael Uhlman served as Assistant
Attorney General in the Ford Administration and as special assistant to President Ronald
Reagan. Jeffrey D. Wallin served as Director of General Program at the National Endowment

for the Humanities. Bradford P. Wilson served as Administrative Assistant to the Chief Justice of the United States, Warren Burger.

Parts of this list can be found in Robert Devigne, *Recasting Conservatism: Oakeshott, Strauss, and the Response to Postmodernism* (New Haven: Yale University Press, 1994), pp. 221–22, n. 76. As Devigne points out, this kind of information is found in the short biographies of contributors to books and journals.

Part One

On Leo Strauss's American Career

· *1* ·

Leo Strauss at the University of Chicago

George Anastaplo

> But Jesus said unto them, "A prophet is not without honor except in his own country and in his own house." And he did not do many mighty works there because of their unbelief.
>
> —*Matthew 13:57–58*

I

Leo Strauss, who was born on September 20, 1899, left the country of his birth in 1932. His principal "house" thereafter was the University of Chicago, where he spent his most productive years. After leaving Germany (never to return except, in 1954, primarily for a visit to his father's grave) he lived in France and England before settling permanently in the United States, becoming an American citizen in 1944. In this country he taught principally at the New School for Social Research in New York from 1938 to 1949, in the Political Science Department of the University of Chicago from 1949 to 1967, at Claremont Men's College in 1968–1969, and then at St. John's College in Annapolis (where he was reunited with his fellow student and old friend, Jacob Klein) until his death there on October 18, 1973.[1]

During his two decades at Chicago he took leaves which permitted him to visit Israel (in 1954–1955) and to visit the Center for Advanced Study in the Behavioral Sciences at Palo Alto (in 1960–1961). On a couple of occasions during his Chicago years he was incapacitated somewhat by major illnesses, brought on in part perhaps by a neglect of his health related to his single-minded pursuit of his studies. He was notorious for a schedule that kept him at his desk through much of the night.

Mr. Strauss offered almost eighty courses during his Chicago tenure. He settled down, after a few years of experimentation in scheduling, to offering one or two courses each quarter, one at 3:30 on Tuesdays and Thursdays, the other (when

3

a second was given) at the same time on Mondays and Wednesdays.[2] The typical class ran much longer than the ninety minutes officially allocated to it, which could lead to the spouses of Mr. Strauss's students petitioning him to "release" them in time for supper with their families. Of course, so far as he personally was concerned, those students could go home whenever they chose.

The classes ran as long as they did because they were obviously addressing, in a way not available anywhere else on campus, the most important questions of a philosophical as well as of a political character. His classroom was often packed, perhaps with at least as many auditors as registered students. The following recent recollection by a then-mature student (a former Army officer), interested in American politics, could be endorsed by many others. He had come in the mid-1960s to the University of Chicago and hence to Mr. Strauss more or less by chance, but he was intrigued for two years thereafter by what he heard a very small man with a quiet voice saying for hours at a time. There was on exhibit, he recalls, a peculiar combination of a physical unimpressiveness and an awesomely powerful intellect. Even though the texts discussed in the classes were obviously long familiar to Mr. Strauss, he constantly probed them with a childlike freshness, always unearthing new things worthy of consideration. It was a revelation for this student to see how carefully a text could be read. Also a revelation to this and other students was a teacher's obvious joy in working things out and communicating them to the young. This was contagious, even though it was evident that Mr. Strauss had the advantage of being able to draw upon a vast storehouse of information and insights ("facts and values"?) to guide and illuminate what he was doing and saying. So contagious was this joy, and so enlightening was this scholarship, that I remain both puzzled and saddened by those quite talented young men who were personally exposed for some time to Leo Strauss at the University of Chicago and yet would not only turn away from him but could even incline toward his severest critics.

Roughly one-third of the Strauss courses at Chicago took ancient texts (primarily from Plato and Aristotle) as their announced points of departure, roughly one-third took modern texts (from Machiavelli and Vico on), with the remainder devoted to general topics (such as "Natural Right") during which Mr. Strauss would range across millennia. (None of the course titles, collected in the first appendix to this article, mentioned literary or theological texts. Aristophanes, however, was drawn upon considerably for the Winter 1960 course, anticipating the 1966 *Socrates and Aristophanes* book.) Mr. Strauss's last public appearance at the University of Chicago (December 1, 1967) was not on its main campus, but rather downtown (65 East South Water Street) at its adult education center (then known as University College) where he had more effective "political" support than he evidently did by that time on campus. That farewell lecture, by a mild-mannered scholar who could not help but antagonize many of his prestigious colleagues in the University, was entitled, appropriately enough, "The Socratic Question."[3]

II

Critical to understanding the University of Chicago experience in the 1950s and 1960s is the fact that most faculty and students lived close to the campus and hence to each other. The city itself is remarkably slow-paced for so large a population. It was fairly easy in Chicago, and especially in the Woodlawn-Hyde Park-Kenwood area, for faculty and students to stay in touch—and to have reliable notions about what "everyone" was doing. Thus, the spouse of a visiting professor from Paris recently remarked that it was nice that they did not have to get on the Metro to return home after an evening at a colleague's house in the University neighborhood. Thus, also, Mr. Strauss once told me, when I inquired whether I could pick up anything for him in Europe, that he could get whatever he wanted on 57th Street (that is, in Hyde Park).

It was characteristic of most of the young scholars that Mr. Strauss nurtured at Chicago, especially in American studies, that they had not come to the University to study with him. Insofar as they were interested primarily in American institutions, they were not naturally of a speculative turn of mind. Still, "metaphysical" interests became unavoidable for them once they came to see what Mr. Strauss was saying, and why. The responses among the students who would become "Straussians" ranged, as should be evident in the other articles in this Deutsch-Murley collection, from those whose sound inclinations were informed and thus reinforced by Mr. Strauss to those whose impassioned souls were radically "turned" by him.

Many of his better students had come to the University of Chicago as a school where works of the mind were believed to be taken seriously. This belief was reinforced by the luminous reputation of Robert Maynard Hutchins, whose generation-long tenure as President of the University was drawing to a close when he (perhaps at the urging of R. H. Tawney and with, it seems, a timely endorsement by Edward Shils) personally hired Mr. Strauss. (Mr. Strauss became, in 1959, the Robert Maynard Hutchins Distinguished Service Professor at the University of Chicago.)

Chicago was special, not least in that it (unlike other great universities in this country) did not then regard itself as training the political leaders and business executives of the next generation, but rather its educators. Moreover, the general academic tone at Chicago had traditionally been set by its graduate departments, not by its small college or by its professional schools. Even so, the graduate faculty teaching in the college could be readily challenged and otherwise stimulated by bright youngsters who tended to be interdepartmental in their interests. All this contributed to an intellectual intensity rarely seen even in the better universities on so broad a basis, at least in this country. The University of Chicago was also special in its relaxed openness (then as well as now) to Jewish faculty and students, even as it struggled to accommodate itself to the racially volatile urban setting in which it found itself soon after the Second World War. The most distinguished Jewish officer that the University of Chicago has had used to say, "At this University, you should assume someone is a Jew unless he denies it—and sometimes even if he denies it."

Of the ten men singled out in this book as of "the first generation" of Straussians working in American studies, all but two of them originally studied with Mr. Strauss at Chicago. And most of them taught at Chicago at one time or another. The Chicago influence is evident as well among the three dozen contributors to the Strauss-Cropsey *History of Political Philosophy* textbook.[4]

Of course, yet another score of equally competent scholars could be identified as "the first generation"—and they, too, are predominantly Chicago men. It is evident from any such inventory, by the way, that "the first generation" was massively male and white, perhaps even more so than American graduate schools generally were at that time (except in departments such as English, home economics, nursing, Romance languages, and social work). The specialness, if not exclusivity, of the Strauss circle was not lost upon spouses who sensed that they could no longer share the most important things with their husbands.[5]

III

What did political science look like at Chicago before Leo Strauss came? One can get some notion of this by examining the course offerings of the Political Science Department before 1949, by noticing which public men and political scientists have been awarded honorary degrees since the founding of the University in 1893, and by studying the biographies of the social scientists assembled in recollections of distinguished scholars brought together in 1991 for a centennial celebration of the University. (The roster of the Chicago political science faculty before Mr. Strauss joined it during the 1948–1949 academic year is set forth in Appendix B of this article. The roster of that faculty when he retired during the 1967–1968 academic year is set forth in Appendix C of this article.) These and other sources testify that the political science primarily in evidence at Chicago before Leo Strauss joined the faculty had been what was coming to be available also at the other great universities in the United States.[6]

The kind of dedication to old-fashioned political philosophy evident in Mr. Strauss's work had not been prized, even in "political theory" courses, in the Political Science Department at the University of Chicago before he came. Nor does such political philosophy seem destined to be as important in that department, ever more "scientific" in its orientation, once the Straussians now associated with the department retire. A "scientific" orientation was anticipated in the quotation attributed to Lord Kelvin with which the Social Science Research Building (known simply as Social Science) was adorned when it was built in 1929, "When you cannot measure, your knowledge is meager and unsatisfactory."

Of course, the University at large has long been interested in "the great books." Leo Strauss entered a community, therefore, which had already begun to be shaped in this respect by distinguished scholars. Some resentment developed in these circumstances, especially since "competitors" could believe that Mr. Strauss was "stealing" some of their best students. The Committee on Social Thought, to which the politically minded Straussians now on the Chicago campus have almost all retreated, was a reliable source of good students for Mr. Strauss. Eventually, his courses came to be cross-listed for a few years in the University *Time Schedules* by the Committee, but never by the Philosophy Department or by the Classics Department.

Leo Strauss did have a way of reading that suggested a depth of inquiry that tended to offend some of his brightest and most learned colleagues. He had heard that a professor in the University of Chicago Law School read the Constitution as carefully as Mr. Strauss himself read the best books. It should be noticed that that professor, too, failed to win many enduring converts among his own colleagues.[7]

IV

It is curious that someone as congenitally impractical as Leo Strauss became as influential with practical Americans as he did, teaching them how to be sensible (that is, truly practical) about the institutions, principles, and politics of their country. American studies were not critical to his own interests, as may be seen in the chapters commissioned for the *History of Political Philosophy* collection. For instance, Mr. Strauss probably knew better and respected more Winston Churchill (both as author and as politician) than he did any American statesman, living or dead.

Although Mr. Strauss did not create an interest in American political things among his students, he *could* enrich whatever interest students happened to have upon coming to the University. His students' views of politics were expanded and deepened, even as their tastes were refined. He thus opened them up to the best thinking in the Anglo-American political tradition, even as he reminded them of the Classical roots of that tradition, a tradition which his students could see adapted for modern conditions by artists such as William Shakespeare and John Milton. Taken by Mr. Strauss from Classical teachers such as Plato and Aristotle was the significance of the *regime* with its grounding in moral and political principles. (This is to look at the community and its institutions "from the top down," as Abraham Lincoln had done, rather than, as is common in most academic disciplines today, "from the bottom up.") Related to this empowerment by Mr. Strauss of his students was his ability to encourage them to take religious thought and institutions more seriously than they otherwise might have done, something which remains essential for understanding the work of the greatest American statesmen.

Mr. Strauss's "political teaching" has been summed up in this way by two younger scholars reviewing his career:

> [His] own teaching on politics, in the narrow sense, can best be understood as
> an attempt to revivify, adapt, and apply, in the dramatically new circumstances of
> our time, [the] centuries-old Socratic tradition. Having come to maturity in the
> unfortunate Weimar Republic, and having gratefully found in the United States
> a refuge and protection against Fascism, Strauss was a firm supporter and friend—
> but for this very reason, no flatterer—of liberal democracy.[8]

Or, as one of "the first generation" has aptly put it, recalling Mr. Strauss's youthful
political Zionist activities in Germany:

> [It] would be a mistake to conclude that Strauss cared about the fate of consti-
> tutional democracy only to the extent to which it was linked to the fate of phi-
> losophy. Like Socrates, he was just in more than one sense. His support of liberal
> democracy can be compared to his support of political Zionism. No one who
> knew Strauss ever doubted the depth and genuineness of his concern for Israel.
> Nor could anyone who knew him think that this concern was based on the
> belief that the fate of philosophy in some mysterious way depended on the sur-
> vival of Israel. He thought no such thing. His support of political Zionism was
> unhesitating even though his approval of it was not unqualified.[9]

This and like observations help correct the unfortunate argument, made even by
some apparent Straussians, that the moral virtues did not have, for Leo Strauss, any
intrinsic worth, whatever he might have personally found it prudent to say repeatedly both on behalf of nature as a guide and against moral relativism, historicism,
value-free social science, and the like.[10]

V

The profound effect that Leo Strauss had upon his students is obvious enough, helping them to "grow up." Far less obvious (and worthy of extended investigation) is
the effect his students and, partly through them, the United States had upon him
as a scholar. Would not his own studies in philosophy probably have been significantly different if he had not settled in the United States, a country where common sense and hence moderation remain vital to a stable regime? At the very least,
he might not have made as much elsewhere of *political* philosophy as he evidently
considered himself obliged to do at Chicago as a member of a political science faculty. Consider, for example, how he opened a course at Chicago on Plato's *Meno*
(and on Jacob Klein's *Commentary* on that dialogue) in the Spring of 1966 (Tuesdays
and Thursdays, at 3:30, in Social Science 305):

> This course is devoted to an introduction to political philosophy. . . . I'll begin at
> the beginning. What is political philosophy? A very simple reflection suffices to
> explain what political philosophy means. All political action is concerned with

either preservation or change. When it is concerned with change it is concerned with change for the better. When it is concerned with preservation, it is concerned with avoiding something worse [G.A.: and concerned also with enjoying properly and thereby reinforcing something good?]. Therefore all political action presupposes opinions of better and worse. But you cannot have an opinion of better and worse without having an opinion of good or bad. When you see that you follow an opinion, you are by this very fact driven to try to find knowledge, to replace opinion by knowledge. Therefore all political action points by itself toward knowledge of the good. Now the complete political good we call the good society and therefore all political action points to the question of the good society.

Bad enough as such talk of the good (echoing the opening of Aristotle's *Politics*, if not also Plato's Doctrine of the Ideas) may have seemed to the conventional academician, what immediately followed was even worse, commenting as it did upon specific opinions fashionable thirty years ago in the United States:

Today there are quite a few people who are doubtful whether one can speak of the good society because that would imply that there is a common good; and for some reason they think there couldn't be a common good. But quite a few of these people speak, for example, of the great society, which is another form of the good society—only one doesn't know why *great society* is preferable to *good society*. At least it has never been explained to us. Others speak of the open society, which is also a form of the good society—and again we are not told why *the open society* is a better term than *the good society*. Be this as it may, one can reject only verbally the quest for the good society. And this is the concern of political philosophy.

This was hardly the kind of talk to be expected from a political *scientist*—or, for that matter, from the most celebrated scholars in, say, the Classics Department, the History Department, the Law School, the Philosophy Department, or the Sociology Department of the University of Chicago during Mr. Strauss's two decades there. His credentials as a scholar were further jeopardized by his questioning of such intellectual icons as Max Weber and Hans Kelsen with respect to the "fact-value" problem and related issues.

We can perhaps see even better what Leo Strauss was truly like among us if we speculate further about what he would have been and what he might have done if he had never come to live in this country. Would he, without the Nazi experience, have been more of a "metaphysician" (and hence much more of a Heideggerean and hence also somewhat less outspoken against Nihilism) than we knew him? Is it not likely that if he had remained in Europe—whether in Germany or perhaps in England—his work would have been much more obviously "theoretical" than he ever allowed it to appear at Chicago, with Nietzsche (to whom he had an early attachment) becoming more critical to his thought? It is possible, therefore, that the United States, with its stable and productive liberal democracy, may have helped save Mr. Strauss from the liabilities of European intellectual life in the twentieth century.[11]

Or, suppose Mr. Strauss had been chosen to fill the post at Hebrew University for which it has been *said* he was considered in 1933?[12] He might have been obliged, from the outset there, to be concerned more about local politics and policies than he ever had to be in the United States. But could he, a rather timid man physically, have prospered in the war zone that the Middle East became?

And what would have happened there to that fruitful tension seen in his thought between Jerusalem and Athens? Would a Leo Strauss based in the Holy Land have been moved to be more overtly "Jewish"? Would even more have been heard from him about the Bible, Maimonides and the like? Certainly, the students eventually available to him in an independent Israel (or, for that matter, in a healthy Germany) would have been quite different from the students routinely available in Chicago. To Jewish intellectuals in Israel, or to German intellectuals in, say, Freiburg, Leo Strauss's ideas might have *sounded* too familiar for them to notice what was truly challenging in what he ventured to say.

VI

Would the suspicions engendered by Straussians, which became familiar at Chicago and elsewhere in American academic life, have been different in Israel—or in Freiburg? Are not these suspicions in part due to how some of Mr. Strauss's least politic students conducted themselves, coming to seem more of a "cult" than they might have been regarded among either the Israelis or the Germans?

Reservations, if not even outrage, can be heard in this country, from decent academicians, about any scholar who collects "disciples." Such "possessiveness," it is said by conscientious academicians, can be quite destructive, especially when it is transmitted to those of the scholar's students who become teachers in turn. One eminent scholar (who happens to be well-disposed to me personally, however much of a Straussian I may be because of what he calls my "piety towards a teacher whom [he] never admired") has recently put such reservations thus in a letter to me:

> [There was at the University of Chicago] a clique of Straussians who thought they knew a truth that lesser mortals failed to grasp and condescended accordingly. . . . A man who attracts disciples seems to me a bad man—stunting independent growth among his pupils by inviting them to surrender their own judgement to his superior insight. That is a kind of presumption no man has the right to make, according to my lights. Those who do, and the disciples who flock to follow them, are morally and intellectually deficient, unable or unwilling to stand on their own feet, relying on superior authority and all that. [This] is a personality trait that has a wide prevalence in Germany or did have in the 1930s. [It is] related to family patterns, I presume, and also to the historical-social-intel-

lectual traditions of central Europe. Strauss shared this pernicious tradition, and demanded/expected discipleship. A bad man therefore in my book.

Anyone who knew the first Straussians personally, however, should have been able to recognize them to be as high-minded and decent as they were talented and ambitious. This is not to deny that some Straussians failed to appreciate sufficiently, in their youth, the fact that one aspect of true superiority is a willingness, if not even a duty, not to dwell upon (however much one might have to take account of) the limitations of those who happen to be either inadequately trained or less talented. Certainly, condescension is to be avoided, especially by the ambitious. Consider the caution implicit in Mr. Strauss's observation, "To respect opinions is something entirely different from accepting them as true." But then, the more Socratic a thinker may be, the more likely it is that an irrepressible Alcibiades will be attached to him here and there. It is not surprising, although not always fair, that the shortcomings, including the presumptuousness, of disciples (especially those with a political bent and a spirited character) should be visited upon their master. Thus, another eminent scholar, who is generally easygoing and tolerant as well as quite learned, has recently been moved to write to me about one of the Straussians who had been at the University of Chicago that he was "a divisive figure on campus, and intent on proselytizing young people to his paranoid elitist views."

But these can be accidental matters and consequences, dependent in part upon the temperament, principles, and circumstances of observers. The enduring source of the opposition that Leo Strauss had to contend with, at least in a community in which he seemed to be establishing new modes and orders, was the kind of thinking he personally advocated and exhibited. One is not likely to be cherished, among the recognized elite of the academic profession (or anywhere else?), if one insists (however courteously) upon getting down to those fundamentals of which others may be barely aware. An instructive response to the academic critics of Leo Strauss I have just quoted is supplied us by a sober political scientist who probably learned as much from him as anyone else ever did. He recently recalled that the most important lesson taught by Mr. Strauss came from his repeatedly appearing in front of a class and venturing to minister to his own as well as to his students' ignorance by asking, "What *does* this mean?"

VII

The status of Leo Strauss at the University of Chicago these days is such that one rarely hears his "mighty works" referred to outside of a quite limited circle of faculty and students which does find a home (for the time being) in the Committee on Social Thought. Nor is his name officially associated there with a building (or even a room in a building), a professorship, or an award as are the names of scores of other former University of Chicago professors of note.

A dozen of Mr. Strauss's books *are* published currently by the University of Chicago Press. But this may reflect more what is happening elsewhere in this country as well as abroad with his reputation than it does any influence he has generally on the Chicago campus these days. This may reflect as well the years of competent service by a devoted Straussian as a member of the faculty governing board of the Press. There sometimes seems to be much more of a Leo Strauss "presence" at Boston College, Claremont-McKenna College, the University of Dallas, Dominican University, Fordham University, the University of Toronto, and St. John's College than there is *in political science* at the University of Chicago at this time.

The more prestigious a university is, the more likely it is that its professors will "have" to be on "the cutting edge" of the recognized disciplines of the day. In political science, we have noticed, the leading lights will be very much occupied with the innovations that dominate "scientific" political science from time to time, a preoccupation from which Mr. Strauss saved his grateful students.

But more important than what he was against was what he was for, and it is this which inspired the better students who happened upon him at the University of Chicago in the 1950s and 1960s. What he was truly *for*, in the American context, is suggested by the magisterial way he opened his *Natural Right and History*:

> It is proper for more reasons than the most obvious one that I should open this [University of Chicago lecture series] by quoting a passage from the Declaration of Independence. The passage has frequently been quoted, but, by its weight and its elevation, it is made immune to the degrading effects of the excessive familiarity which breeds contempt and of misuse which breeds disgust. "We hold these truths to be self-evident, that all men are created equal, that they are endowed by their Creator with certain unalienable Rights, that among these are Life, Liberty, and the pursuit of Happiness." The nation dedicated to *this proposition* has now become, no doubt partly as a consequence of this dedication, the most powerful and prosperous of the nations of the earth. Does this nation in its maturity still cherish *the faith* in which it was conceived and raised? Does it still hold those "truths to be self-evident"? [Emphasis added.][13]

The competent authoritativeness of the Strauss mind remained evident to the end of his life. One of my children remarked upon the uncompromising thoroughness with which Leo Strauss, by then quite feeble, would approach a text in his weekly seminar at St. John's College. He did not make big, spectacular points (I was reminded by this account of what I had myself observed at the University of Chicago a generation earlier) but rather accumulated, as he moved along, a considerable aggregate of many points (any one of which, it sometimes seemed, other scholars might have made). He somehow managed to keep these points in mind, all of them together, as he subjected the text to a deeper and deeper interpretation week after week, as if he could go on forever—which is, it can be said, what his *logos* is still doing in the University of our hearts.

APPENDIX A
Preliminary Roster of the Strauss Courses Scheduled
by the Political Science Department,
The University of Chicago, 1949–1967

This Roster has been culled primarily from the copies of the *University of Chicago Time Schedules* on file at the University of Chicago in the offices of the Registrar and the Department of Political Science. The term "Preliminary" is used here (1) because some of the entries are changed by hand in one or the other of the sets consulted of the *Time Schedules*, (2) because only the last name of the instructor is ever listed (and there were others by the name of "Strauss" teaching at the University of Chicago in the Social Sciences Division during the period reviewed), and (3) because there are odd features in some of the early entries (such as the quarter of the year or the time of day recorded for the course).

All of the courses, unless otherwise indicated, were scheduled for ninety minutes twice a week. Some courses are said to meet once a week (that is, for ninety minutes). Some of the entries collected below are supplemented by the sometimes unreliable information taken from the "Theory" (and later the "Political Theory") section of the Political Science Department listing in the annual *University of Chicago Announcements*. (This supplementary information and its source are provided in brackets.) The *Time Schedules*, which are issued on a quarterly basis, are more apt to be accurate, recording changes made after the annual *Announcements* are issued. (After Mr. Strauss's first half-dozen years at Chicago, the *Announcements* did not usually mention the quarters in which the courses listed would be given, sometimes making it difficult to determine what substitutions were made. Two Strauss courses which are listed several times in the *Announcements* never appear as such in the *Time Schedules*. They are (1) "History of Political Ideas: Its Nature and Function" [1952–1954, 1954–1955, 1955–1956]; (2) "Political Philosophy: Its Theme and History" [1964–1965, 1965–1966, 1967–1968].)

The titles of all texts listed in the entries below are italicized in this Roster, however presented in the *Time Schedules* or in the *Announcements*. Also, colons have been added to many of the entries (and removed from other entries) as part of my attempt to make the entries uniform in appearance. The cross-listings of the Strauss courses by other University of Chicago academic units, between 1957 and 1960, are noticed in this Roster. Those units were the Committee on Social Thought [S.T.] and the adult education division, known then as University College [U.C.].

The first course offered by Leo Strauss at the University of Chicago seems to have been on Rousseau, with only three students, beginning either in January or in March 1949. Both this course and any other offerings in the first half of 1949 may have been settled upon too late for inclusion not only in the annual *Announcements* but also in the quarterly *Time Schedules*.

Unedited, and sometimes partial, transcripts began to be made of many of Leo Strauss's courses in 1953, transcripts which he did not personally review. The existence of a transcript for a course is indicated in this Roster, with the subject of the transcript suggested whenever the course title is not specific enough. I cannot personally vouch for all of the transcripts or transcript-subjects recorded here. But I can affirm that there are many gems in those often ragged transcripts, long-neglected gems illuminating an abundance of authors and issues.

(There may be other transcripts not recorded here. Also, the transcript title page may indicate a different school term from that which I have usually taken from the *Time Schedules*. In several instances I have determined the term from remarks recorded in the transcripts. There should turn up from time to time sets of detailed notes by graduate students and others in the Strauss classes, some of which notes may be better in critical respects than the related transcripts. See, for Mr. Strauss's notes, note 11 (end), below.)

The Autumn Quarter at the University of Chicago begins each academic year in late September or early October; the Winter Quarter, in early January; the Spring Quarter, in late March or early April; the Summer Quarter, in June. The Autumn, Winter, and Spring Quarters run for eleven weeks each, with the last three weeks devoted to a reading period and examinations. The Summer Quarter is shorter.

This Roster is drawn upon at the end of this Appendix for a listing, in alphabetical order, of most of the authors to which Strauss courses may have been devoted at the University of Chicago.

—*G.A.*

WINTER QUARTER, 1949
(or perhaps SPRING QUARTER, 1949)
—Rousseau (not listed in either the *Time Schedules* or the *Announcements*)
SUMMER QUARTER, 1949
—History of Political Ideas: Its Nature and Functions [at 8:30–10 MW]
—Seminar in Political Theory [at 8:30–10 TT] [*Announcements*: "The Problem of Theory and Practice: Burke"]
AUTUMN QUARTER, 1949
—Natural Right
—The Roman Idea: Cicero [*Announcements*: "On Cicero's *Republic* and *Laws*"]
WINTER QUARTER, 1950
—Plato's Political Philosophy and Its Metaphysical Foundations
—Hobbes's *The Citizen* [*Announcements*: "Utopias and Political Science" (on More's Utopia and Harrington's *Oceana*)]
SPRING QUARTER, 1950
—Seminar in Aristotle's *Politics* [*Announcements*: "Medieval Political Doctrines" (on Marsilius of Padua's *Defender of the Peace*)]
AUTUMN QUARTER, 1950
—Basic Problems of Political Philosophy
—Seminar in Political Philosophy: Machiavelli's *Discourses*
WINTER QUARTER, 1951
—Principles of Classical Political Philosophy [*Announcements*: "On the fundamental concepts of Platonic and Aristotelian politics"]
—Seminar in Political Philosophy [*Announcements*: "On Locke's *Civil Government*"]
SPRING QUARTER, 1951
—Classical Natural Right Doctrines [*Announcements*: "Seminar on Political Philosophy" (on the Trial of Socrates)]
AUTUMN QUARTER, 1951
—Seminar in Political Philosophy: Rousseau's *Discourse on Inequality*
—Natural Right

WINTER QUARTER, 1952
—Plato's Political Philosophy and Its Metaphysical Foundations
—Seminar in Political Philosophy: Edmund Burke's Political Writings
SPRING QUARTER, 1952
—Seminar in Political Philosophy: Machiavelli's *Discourses*
SUMMER QUARTER, 1952
—Basic Problems of Political Philosophy: The Problem of Power [8:30–10 TT]
—Seminar in Political Philosophy: Nietzsche [9–12 F]
AUTUMN QUARTER, 1952
—Seminar in Politics and Policy Formation (with [Charles] Hardin) [Met once a week]
—Seminar in Political Philosophy: Aristotle's *Politics*
WINTER QUARTER, 1953
[No "Strauss" listing]
SPRING QUARTER, 1953
—Principles of Classical Political Philosophy
—Seminar in Political Philosophy [Probably on Machiavelli's *The Prince*]
AUTUMN QUARTER, 1953
—Seminar in Political Philosophy: Hobbes's *Leviathan* [changed from "Montesquieu's
   Spirit of Laws"] [Transcript available]
WINTER QUARTER, 1954
—Natural Right [Transcript available]
—Seminar in Political Philosophy: Montesquieu's *The Spirit of Laws*
SPRING QUARTER, 1954
—Plato's Political Philosophy and Its Metaphysical Foundations [Partial transcript avail-
   able on Plato's *Statesman*]
—Seminar in Political Philosophy: Rousseau
AUTUMN QUARTER, 1954 [Visit to Europe and Israel]
[No "Strauss" listing]
WINTER QUARTER, 1955 [Visit to Europe and Israel]
[No "Strauss" listing]
SPRING QUARTER, 1955 [Visit to Europe and Israel]
[No "Strauss" listing]
AUTUMN QUARTER, 1955
—Seminar in Political Philosophy
WINTER QUARTER, 1956
—Basic Problems of Political Philosophy [also U.C.]
—Seminar in Political Philosophy: Historicism and Modern Relativism [Transcript
   available, primarily on Collingwood and Nietzsche]
SPRING QUARTER, 1956 [Heart attack, May 1956]
—Seminar in Politics (with [Charles] Hardin) [Met once a week]
—Seminar in Political Philosophy: Kant
—Seminar: Reading of Aristotle's *Politics* [Partial transcript available] [Met once a week]
AUTUMN QUARTER, 1956
—Seminar in Political Philosophy: Hobbes
WINTER QUARTER, 1957
—Plato's Political Philosophy and Its Metaphysical Foundations [Transcript available
   on Plato's *Gorgias*]

—Seminar in Political Philosophy: Thucydides
SPRING QUARTER, 1957
—Seminar in Political Philosophy: Plato's *Republic* [Transcript available]
AUTUMN QUARTER, 1957
—Seminar in Political Philosophy: Aristotle's *Politics* [also S.T., U.C.]
WINTER QUARTER, 1958
—Basic Problems of Political Philosophy [also S.T.] [Cancelled?]
—Seminar in Political Philosophy: Locke's *Civil Government* [Transcript available]
SPRING QUARTER, 1958
—Basic Problems of Political Philosophy [also S.T.] [*Announcements*: "Principles of
    Classical Political Philosophy"]
—Seminar in Political Philosophy: Kant [also S.T.] [Transcript available]
AUTUMN QUARTER, 1958
—Principles of Classical Political Philosophy [also S.T.]
—Seminar in Political Philosophy: Hegel's *The Philosophy of History* [also S.T.]
    [Transcript available]
WINTER QUARTER, 1959
—Seminar in Political Philosophy: Plato's *Laws* [also S.T.] [Transcript available on
    Plato's *Minos* and *Laws*]
SPRING QUARTER, 1959
—Natural Right [also S.T.] [Transcript available on Nietzsche, primarily on *Thus Spake
    Zarathustra*]
—Seminar in Political Philosophy: Cicero [also S.T.] [Transcript available]
AUTUMN QUARTER, 1959
—Plato: Political Philosophy [also S.T.] [Transcript available on Plato's *Banquet*]
—Seminar in Political Philosophy: Spinoza [another offering is crossed out] [Transcript
    available]
WINTER QUARTER, 1960
—Seminar on the Origins of Political Science [Transcript available on The Problem
    of Socrates, primarily on Plato's *Apology* and *Crito* and on Aristophanes' *Clouds*,
    Birds, and *Wasps*]
SPRING QUARTER, 1960
—Introduction to Political Philosophy: Study of Aristotle's *Politics* [also S.T.] [Transcript
    available]
—Seminar in Political Philosophy: Karl Marx (with [Joseph] Cropsey) [also S.T.]
    [Transcript available]
AUTUMN QUARTER, 1960 [Visit to the Center for Advanced Study in the Behavioral
    Sciences]
    [No "Strauss" listing]
WINTER QUARTER, 1961 [Visit to the Center for Advanced Study in the Behavioral
    Sciences]
    [No "Strauss" listing]
SPRING QUARTER, 1961 [Visit to the Center for Advanced Study in the Behavioral
    Sciences]
    [No "Strauss" listing]

AUTUMN QUARTER, 1961
—[Basic] Principles of Classical [Political] Philosophy [Transcript available]
—Seminar in Political Philosophy: Plato's *Republic* [Transcript available]
WINTER QUARTER, 1962
—Seminar in Political Philosophy: Thucydides [Transcript available]
SPRING QUARTER, 1962
—Seminar in Political Philosophy: Nietzsche
AUTUMN QUARTER, 1962
—Natural Right [Transcript available]
—Seminar in Political Philosophy: Rousseau [Transcript available]
WINTER QUARTER, 1963
—Seminar in Political Philosophy: Xenophon [Transcript available]
SPRING QUARTER, 1963
—Seminar in Political Philosophy: Aristotle's *[Nicomachean] Ethics* [Transcript available]
AUTUMN QUARTER, 1963
—Plato: Political Philosophy [Transcript available on Plato's *Gorgias*]
—Seminar in Political Philosophy: Vico [Transcript available]
WINTER QUARTER, 1964
—Seminar in Political Philosophy: Hobbes [Transcript available on Hobbes's *De Cive*
    and *Leviathan*]
SPRING QUARTER, 1964
—Seminar in Political Philosophy: Aristotle [Transcript available on Aristotle's *Rhetoric*]
AUTUMN QUARTER, 1964
—Seminar in Political Philosophy: Grotius [Transcript available on Grotius's *On the
    Law of War and Peace*]
WINTER QUARTER, 1965
—Introduction to Political Philosophy [Transcript available, primarily on Aristotle's
    Politics, but also on (among others) Comte, Nietzsche, and Weber]
—Seminar in Political Philosophy: Hegel [Transcript available, primarily on *The
    Philosophy of History*]
SPRING QUARTER, 1965
—Plato's Political Philosophy [Transcript available on Plato's *Protagoras*]
AUTUMN QUARTER, 1965 [Hospitalized with heart trouble, October 8, 1965]
—Principles of Classical Political Philosophy [Cancelled?]
—Seminar in Political Philosophy [Cancelled?]
WINTER QUARTER, 1966
—Seminar in Political Philosophy: Montesquieu [Transcript available on *The Spirit of
    Laws*]
SPRING QUARTER, 1966
—Political Philosophy: Plato's *Meno* [and Klein's *Commentary*] [Transcript available]
—Political Philosophy: Montesquieu [Transcript available on *The Spirit of Laws* and
    Persian Letters]
AUTUMN QUARTER, 1966
—Plato's Political Philosophy [Transcript available, primarily on Plato's *Apology* and
    Crito, but also on Xenophon]
WINTER QUARTER, 1967
—Seminar in Nietzsche [Transcript available, primarily on *Beyond Good and Evil* and
    on *The Genealogy of Morals*]

SPRING QUARTER, 1967
—Kant [Transcript available:The Political Philosophy of Kant]
AUTUMN QUARTER, 1967
—Seminar in Political Philosophy [Transcript available on Aristotle's *Politics*].

Most of the authors to whom Strauss courses were, or were intended to be, devoted in whole or in major part at the University of Chicago are collected here. (Even cancelled courses suggest what was being thought about, and when, by Mr. Strauss.) The following entries are taken either from course titles in the *Time Schedules* and the *Announcements* (including cancelled courses) or from the transcripts of the courses:

Aristophanes (Winter, 1960)
Aristotle (Spring 1950,Winter 1951,Autumn 1952, Spring 1956,Autumn 1957, Spring 1960,
    Spring 1963, Spring 1964,Winter 1965,Autumn 1967)
Burke (Summer 1949,Winter 1952)
Cicero (Autumn 1949, Spring 1959)
Collingwood (Winter 1956)
Comte (Winter 1965)
Grotius (Autumn 1964)
Harrington (Winter 1950)
Hegel (Autumn 1958,Winter 1965)
Hobbes (Winter 1950,Autumn 1953, Spring 1956,Winter 1964)
Kant (Spring 1956, Spring 1958, Spring 1967)
Klein (Spring 1966)
Locke (Winter 1951,Winter 1958)
Machiavelli (Autumn 1950, Spring 1952, Spring 1953)
Marsilius of Padua (Spring 1950)
Marx (Spring 1960)
Montesquieu (Winter 1954,Winter 1966, Spring 1966)
More (Winter 1950)
Nietzsche (Summer 1952,Winter 1956, Spring 1959, Spring 1962,Winter 1965,Winter
    1967)
Plato (Winter 1950,Winter 1951, Spring 1951,Winter 1952, Spring 1954,Winter 1957,
    Spring 1957,Winter 1959,Autumn 1959,Winter 1960,Autumn 1961,Autumn 1963,
    Spring 1965, Spring 1966,Autumn 1966)
Rousseau (Winter 1949 (?),Autumn 1951, Spring 1954,Autumn 1962)
Spinoza (Autumn 1959)
Thucydides (Winter 1957,Winter 1962)
Vico (Autumn 1963)
Weber (Winter 1965)
Xenophon (Winter 1963,Autumn 1966)

Transcripts are also available for a course given by Leo Strauss at Claremont Men's College (1968) on Aristotle's *Nicomachean Ethics* and for courses given by him at St. John's College (1971–1973) on Nietzsche and on Plato's *Laws*. See, for transcripts of some of the lectures given by him at the University of Chicago, note 3, below.

APPENDIX B
Roster of the Faculty of the Political Science Department,
The University of Chicago, as Recorded in
The *University of Chicago Announcements, The College and the Divisions*,
1948–1949

Leonard Dupee White, Ph.D., Litt. D., Chairman of the Administrative Committee of the
Department of Political Science and Professor of Public Administration
Charles Herman Pritchett, Ph.D., Secretary of the Department of Political Science and
Associate Professor of Political Science [became Acting Chairman in 1948–49]
Roy Blough, Ph.D., LL.D., Professor of Economics and of Political Science
Melville C. Branch, Jr., Ph.D., Associate Professor of Political Science
David Easton, Ph.D., Assistant Professor of Political Science
Herman Finer, Sc.D., Professor of Political Science
Morton Melvin Grodzins, Ph.D., Assistant Professor of Political Science
Charles M. Hardin, Ph.D., Assistant Professor of Political Science
Robert Anderson Horn, Ph.D., Assistant Professor of Political Science
Walter Johnson, Ph.D., Assistant Professor of American History
Jerome Gregory Kerwin, Ph.D., LL.D., Professor of Political Science
Avery Leiserson, Ph.D., Assistant Professor of Political Science
Hans J. Morganthau, J.D., Associate Professor of Political Science
Floyd Wesley Reeves, Ph.D., Professor of Administration
Max Rheinstein, Dir. Utr. Iur., Max Pam Professor of Comparative Law
Clarence E. Ridley, Ph.D., Associate Professor of Political Science
Rexford Guy Tugwell, Ph.D., Professor of Political Science and Director of the Program of
Education and Research in Planning
Quincy Wright, Ph.D., LL.D., Professor of International Law
Charles Edward Merriam, Ph.D., LL.D., Morton D. Hull Distinguished Service Professor
Emeritus of Political Science.
An Instructor, six Lecturers, a Research Associate, and two Visiting Professors are not included
in this Roster. Typically, the tenured ranks at the University of Chicago are those of
Professor and Associate Professor.

APPENDIX C
Roster of the Faculty of the Political Science Department,
The University of Chicago, as Recorded in
The *University of Chicago Announcements, The College and the Divisions*,
1967–1968

Leonard Binder, Ph.D., Chairman of the Department of Political Science and Professor of
Political Science
Jeremy R. Azrael, Ph.D., Associate Professor of Political Science
Joseph Cropsey, Ph.D., Associate Professor of Political Science
David Easton, Ph.D., Professor of Political Science

Richard E. Flathman, Ph.D., Assistant Professor of Political Science and of the Social Sciences in the College

J. David Greenstone, Ph.D., Assistant Professor of Political Science

Morton A. Kaplan, Ph.D., Professor of Political Science

Nathan Leites, Ph.D., Professor of Political Science

Theodore J. Lowi, Ph.D., Associate Professor of Political Science

Duncan MacRae, Jr., Ph.D., Professor of Political Science

John Dickinson May, Ph.D., Assistant Professor of Political Science and of the Social Sciences in the College

Grant McConnell, Ph.D., Professor of Political Science [became Chairman in 1967–68]

Hans J. Morgenthau, J.D., LL.D., Albert A. Michelson Distinguished Service Professor of Political Science and of Modern History

Paul E. Peterson, Ph.D., Assistant Professor of Political Science and of Education

Kenneth Prewitt, Ph.D., Assistant Professor of Political Science and of the Social Sciences in the College

C. Herman Pritchett, Ph.D., Litt. D., Professor of Political Science

Lloyd I. Rudolph, Ph.D., Associate Professor of Political Science

Herbert J. Storing, Ph.D., Associate Professor of Political Science

Leo Strauss, Ph.D., LL.D., Robert Maynard Hutchins Distinguished Service Professor of Political Science

Tang Tsou, Ph.D., Professor of Political Science

George E. Von der Muhll, Ph.D., Assistant Professor of Political Science and of the Social Sciences in the College

Albert Wohlstetter, Ph.D., University Professor in Political Science

Aristide Zolberg, Associate Professor of Political Science

Herman Finer, Sc.D., Professor Emeritus of Political Science

Jerome Gregory Kerwin, Ph.D., LL.D., Litt.D., Professor Emeritus of Political Science

Rexford Guy Tugwell, Ph.D., Litt.D., Professor Emeritus of Political Science

Quincy Wright, Ph.D., LL.D., Professor Emeritus of International Law.

Two Lecturers and a Research Associate are not included in this Roster. Typically, the tenured ranks at the University of Chicago are those of Professor and Associate Professor.

NOTES

1. I have discussed, in the following places, Leo Strauss, American political science, the University of Chicago, and Straussians: (i) *The Artist as Thinker: From Shakespeare to Joyce* (Athens: Ohio University Press, 1983), pp. 250–72, 474–85, 497; (ii) *Human Being and Citizen: Essays on Virtue, Freedom, and the Common Good* (Chicago: Swallow Press, 1975), pp. 8f, 61f, 159, 331; (iii) "Jacob Klein of St. John's College," *The Newsletter*, Politics Department, The University of Dallas, Spring 1979, pp. 1–8; (iv) "To My Fellow Straussians," remarks in 1983 at the American Political Science Association annual convention (incorporated in Item viii, below, pp. 361–63); (v) Robert L. Stone, ed., *Essays on "The Closing of the American Mind"* (Chicago: Chicago Review Press, 1989), pp. 225–34, 267–84; (vi) "Shadia Drury on 'Leo Strauss,'" 1 *The Vital Nexus* 9–15 (Halifax, 1990) (see note 13, below); (vii) *The American Moralist: On Law, Ethics, and Government* (Athens: Ohio University Press, 1992), pp. 139–60,

622; (viii) five essays in Harry V. Jaffa, ed., *Original Intent and the Framers of the Constitution* (Washington, D.C.: Regnery Gateway, 1994), pp 167–234, 359–68; (ix) "Law & Politics," 25 *Political Science Reviewer* 127–50 (1996); (x) "First Impressions," 26 *Political Science Reviewer* 248–57 (1997); (xi) "'Racism,' Political Correctness, and Constitutional Law," 42 *South Dakota Law Review* 108f (1997); (xii) "The University of Chicago," *Academic Questions*, Spring 1998, pp. 74–77; (xiii) "'McCarthyism,' The Cold War, and Their Aftermath," 43 *South Dakota Law Review* 103, 111–13, 156–71 (1998); (xiv) "Leo Strauss and Judaism," 1998 *Great Ideas Today* 457 (1998) (also appended, in an expanded version, to Item xvi of this note); (xv) "Samplings," 27 *Political Science Reviewer* 345, 373f, 416f (1998); (xvi) "Law & Literature and the Bible: Explorations," 23 *Oklahoma City University Law Review* 515, Appendices B, D, F, G, and J (1998); (xvii) *The Thinker as Artist: From Homer to Plato & Aristotle* (Athens: Ohio University Press, 1997), pp. 182f, 303f, 402. See, also, notes 7, 10, and 13, below.

2. These courses, after the early years which had seen him hold forth in Classics, in Rosenwald, in Social Science, in Swift, and even in the Law School, usually met in Social Science 105, 302, or 305. Mr. Strauss reported, on January 6, 1964, that he had theretofore "devoted each seminar to a single text, and to each text in its entirety." Half of the Strauss courses in the *Time Schedules* are identified as "seminars."

Leo Strauss was originally identified in the *University of Chicago Directory* (and in the *Announcements*) as Professor of Political Philosophy (for a few years), then as Professor in the Department of Political Science, then as Robert Maynard Hutchins Distinguished Service Professor in the Department of Political Science, and finally as Robert Maynard Hutchins Distinguished Service Professor Emeritus in the Department of Political Science. By the time he left Chicago he had been awarded honorary degrees by Dropsie College, Hamburg University, St. John's University, and Union College. C. Herman Pritchett was the chairman of the department during most of Mr. Strauss's service, with his chairmanship interrupted by that of Morton M. Grodzins for a few years. (Thus, his principal department chairmen were primarily interested in American studies.)

Mr. and Mrs. Strauss's principal Chicago residences were at 1209 East 60th Street (for about six years) and then at 6019 South Ingleside (for about twelve years). The office he settled into for his last decade at the University was Social Science 309, a fact that the current occupant of this office (who is not a political scientist) was unaware of when recently asked. (The Political Science Department is now in the Albert Pick Hall for International Studies.)

3. See Anastaplo, *The Artist as Thinker*, pp. 259–62. A number of Mr. Strauss's Chicago students inaugurated their teaching careers by serving downtown in the University's Basic Program of Liberal Education for Adults. See *ibid.*, pp. 284–300 (including the Basic Program reading list). See, also, Anastaplo, "'McCarthyism,' The Cold War, and Their Aftermath," pp. 163–71. Graduate students who undertake to teach adults are likely to appreciate the importance of both common sense and the surfaces of texts. It is difficult to develop and sustain something like the Basic Program in this country at this time unless the intellectual resources and traditions of the University of Chicago can be drawn upon.

Leo Strauss's mild yet firm manner is reflected in the "concluding remark" of his 1953 Charles R. Walgreen Foundation Lectures on Machiavelli at the University of Chicago:

> It was inevitable that I should have hurt the feelings of some of you, partly by expounding without any reserve certain shocking thoughts of Machiavelli, but partly also by expressing certain views of my own, which could not well be to everyone's taste.

As for the former offense, I plead not guilty—not guilty even of bad company or bad association. We would make impossible freedom of historical inquiry if the historian were not permitted to set forth as clearly and thoughtfully as he can what he is certain was the view of the thinker he is studying. In addition, there are certain prodigious errors which, if arrived at and stated in a certain manner, are so far from lacking greatness that they illumine most impressively if unintentionally the greatness of the giver of all greatness.

As for my own offense, I can only say that I have the earnest desire to live in peace, and therefore to agree with the opinions of my fellow men. Through no fault of my own, my fellow men do not agree with each other. I was therefore forced to make a choice, or to take a stand. Once having been forced to do so, it would have been dishonorable, I thought, to becloud the issue or to beat around the bush. So I ask you not to take ill what to the best of my knowledge was not ill meant. Thank you.

(I have made adjustments in the paragraphing and punctuation of this passage taken from the unpublished transcript of Mr. Strauss's four Walgreen Lectures on Machiavelli. Six Walgreen Lectures on Natural Right and History had been delivered by him at the University of Chicago in 1949.) See, on Machiavelli and the American regime, note 11, below.

In addition to his 1967 farewell lecture, "The Socratic Question," Mr. Strauss gave at least four other talks for the Basic Program: (i) "On the Interpretation of *Genesis*" (January 25, 1957) (published in *L'Homme*, vol. 21, no. 1 [January–March 1981], pp. 5–20; also in Kenneth Hart Green, ed., *Jewish Philosophy and the Crisis of Modernity* [Albany: State University of New York Press, 1997], pp. 359–76); (ii) "What Is Liberal Education?" (June 6, 1959) (a graduation address, published in Leo Strauss, *Liberalism Ancient and Modern* [New York: Basic Books, 1968], pp. 3–8); (iii) "Plato's *Republic*" (December 1959) (transcript available); [iv] "Hobbes's *Leviathan*" (April 17, 1962) (transcript available). Mr. Strauss also gave a talk at the funeral of a Basic Program instructor, Jason Aronson (December 6, 1961) (published in Anastaplo, *The Artist as Thinker*, pp. 270–71; also in Green, ed., *Jewish Philosophy and the Crisis of Modernity*, pp. 475–76). See note 12, below.

Mr. Strauss was obliged to retire at the University of Chicago in 1967. Sixty-five was the critical age then, with a likelihood or at least the prospect of annual extensions for two or three years before retirement became "mandatory." The University of that day had means, however, for encouraging faculty members regarded by the authorities as truly distinguished to continue to serve the institution well into their seventies, if not even into their eighties. I do not believe that these means were ever attempted to be used in Mr. Strauss's case.

4. Of the three dozen contributors to the *History of Political Philosophy*, edited by Leo Strauss and Joseph Cropsey and first published by the Rand McNally Company in 1963, about two-thirds of them had studied at the University of Chicago. (I myself probably should have accepted the invitation to contribute to the *History* a chapter on Thomas Jefferson, especially if I could have added to it some thoughts on what Abraham Lincoln was able to do with the Declaration of Independence, culminating in the Emancipation Proclamation and the Gettysburg Address. See Anastaplo, *Abraham Lincoln: A Constitutional Biography* (Lanham, Md.: Rowman & Littlefield, 1999), chaps. 1, 2, 14, 15.) Of the fifteen contributors to the Leo Strauss Festschrift, *Ancients and Moderns* (published by Basic Books in 1964), half of us had studied at Chicago. See, also, Herbert J. Storing, ed., *Essays on the Scientific Study of Politics* (New York: Holt, Rinehart, and Winston, 1962). Critical to the development reflected in these three collections is what has been called, with some plausibility, Leo Strauss's "almost

single-handed recovery of classical political philosophy." His influence here can be said to be reflected in the American Political Science Association's "Leo Strauss Award," "for the best doctoral dissertation in the field of political philosophy."

5. I say "no longer" because many of the Strauss students, in his early days at Chicago, were Second World War veterans who had already settled into family lives of their own. All this is aside from the cultic implications of the *esotericism* issue developed by Mr. Strauss, an issue easily made too much of by some Straussians and made even more of by their critics. See, e.g., Plato, *Republic* 414D; Plutarch, *The Oracles at Delphi No Longer Given in Verse* 407C sq. (Loeb Classical Library edition, p. 329f);Victor Klemperer, *I Will Bear Witness: A Diary of the Nazi Years 1933–1941* (New York: Random House, 1998), p. 12 ("No one dares write a letter, no one dares make a telephone call, we visit one another and weigh up our chances.... Newspapers are read differently now ... Between the lines. Art of the eighteenth century, the art of reading and writing awakens again."). See, also, note 13, below. Conjectures about esotericism are sometimes used to present the mature Strauss as much more of a Nietzschean than he was. See, e.g., Laurence Lampert, *Leo Strauss and Nietzsche* (Chicago: University of Chicago Press, 1996). See, also, note 9, below.

See, on Leo Strauss and the erotic, Anastaplo, *The Artist as Thinker*, pp. 266–67. Some eminent scholars talked much more about the erotic experiences of the soul than Mr. Strauss ever did, but he managed, more than they could, actually to arouse *eros*, a real affection in students, without doing anything but read texts with them.

There were no women on the teaching faculty of the University of Chicago Political Science Department either when Mr. Strauss joined it in 1949 or when he left it in 1967. There *are* a few on that faculty today. See Appendices B and C of this article. See, on Mr. Strauss's male "puppies," note 6, below.

6. See The University of Chicago, *Honorary Degrees, 1891–1967* (1967); Edward Shils, ed., *Remembering the University of Chicago: Teachers, Scientists, and Scholars* (Chicago: University of Chicago Press, 1991). (The Shils chapter on Robert Maynard Hutchins in this *Remembering* collection describes, at page 192, the hiring of Leo Strauss by the University of Chicago.) See, for Edward G. Banfield on Leo Strauss, *ibid.*, pp. 490–501. (The Banfield chapter includes, at p. 498, the report, "There were no women among the [Strauss] 'puppies.'") See, on various of Mr. Strauss's distinguished Chicago predecessors in political science and related disciplines, *ibid.*, pp. 244–52 (Frank H. Knight), 276–86 (Harold D. Lasswell), 338–50 (Charles Edward Merriam), 383–96 (Robert E. Park), 413–29 (Robert Redfield), 558–67 (Quincy Wright). See, also, S. J. D. Green, "The Tawney-Strauss Connection: On Historicism and Values in the History of Political Ideas," 67 *Journal of Modern History* 255 (1995).

The Chicago School in political science was, well before Leo Strauss's two decades of service at the University of Chicago, influential nationwide:

> There was the Chicago blip in the interwar decades (1921–1940), introducing empirical research programs, emphasizing psychological and sociological interpretations of politics, and demonstrating the value of quantification.

> Gabriel A. Almond, "Political Science: The History of the Discipline," in Robert E. Goodin and Hans-Dieter Klingeman, eds., *The New Handbook of Political Science* (Oxford: Oxford University Press, 1996), p. 50. The Hutchins Administration at the University of Chicago is said to have "attacked the value of empirical research in the social sciences," because of which (it is also said) various prominent professors (such as George Herbert Mead, Harold Laswell, and Harold Gosnell) left the University. *Ibid.*, p. 68. See, for Mr. Hutchin's

unpredictability as an administrator (however good his intentions may have always been), Anastaplo, "Freedom of Speech and the First Amendment," 21 *Texas Tech Law Review* 1941, 2033f (1990).

7. See Anastaplo, "Mr. Crosskey, The American Constitution, and the Natures of Things," 15 *Loyola University of Chicago Law Journal* 181–260 (1984). See, also, Anastaplo, *The Constitution of 1787: A Commentary* (Baltimore: Johns Hopkins University Press, 1989), pp. ix, x, 333, 338; *The Amendments to the Constitution: A Commentary* (Baltimore: Johns Hopkins University Press, 1995), pp. ix, 457, 464; "Bar Examination Put Under Microscope," *Chicago Daily Law Bulletin*, November 6, 1998, pp. 20–21, November 25, 1998, p. 5.

Perhaps the most (if not the only) eminent "convert," among established political scientists in this country, to the Straussian persuasion was Willmoore Kendall. See, e.g., the review of Leo Strauss's *Thoughts on Machiavelli*, in *Willmoore Kendall Contra Mundum*, ed. Nellie D. Kendall (New Rochelle, N.Y.: Arlington House, 1971), pp. 449–56. See, also, Kendall, Book Review, 61 *American Political Science Review* 793 (1967); *The Political Thought of Willmoore Kendall*, eds. John Alvis and John A. Murley (including the Kendall-Strauss correspondence) (in course of preparation). See, as well, Green, "The Tawney-Strauss Connection," p. 264f.

See, for suggestions about how a first-class academic department can be built around prominent scholars, Marshall Stone, "Reminiscences of Mathematics at Chicago," in Shils, ed., *Remembering the University of Chicago*, pp. 483–89. Compare Banfield, "Leo Strauss," in *ibid.*, p. 497: "That he lived in an intellectual world that was foreign to most of his colleagues, a world that it was pointless for them to visit as tourists, meant that Strauss had remarkably little contact with other teachers at the University of Chicago." See, also, note 13, below. Among the senior Chicago faculty with whom Mr. Strauss did have considerable contact were Ludwig Bachhofer, Peter H. von Blanckenhagen, Morton M. Grodzins, Charles M. Hardin, Jerome G. Kerwin, and C. Herman Pritchett. He was somewhat familiar as well with, among others, Herman Finer, David Grene, Friedrich A. von Hayek, Christian W. Mackauer, Edward Shils, and Yves R. Simon.

Naturally, Leo Strauss's most intense social life was always with those who were most sympathetic to his thought—and, on the University of Chicago campus, that usually meant his graduate students and those former students of his who were on the Chicago faculty. See Xenophon, *Memorabilia*, I, vi, 14.

8. Nathan Tarcov and Thomas L. Pangle, "Epilogue: Leo Strauss and the History of Political Philosophy," in Leo Strauss and Joseph Cropsey, eds., *History of Political Philosophy*, Third Edition (Chicago: University of Chicago Press, 1987), p. 927. Perhaps more should have been said in that "Epilogue" about Mr. Strauss's remarkable Medieval studies. This 1987 "Epilogue" could well be supplemented by more of what Harry Jaffa has had to say about Mr. Strauss, the United States, and the Classics, such as the observation that he "thought that American politics, at its best, showed a practical wisdom that owed much to a tradition older than Locke." Jaffa, *The Conditions of Freedom* (Baltimore: Johns Hopkins University Press, 1975), p. 7. See, also, *ibid.*, p. 9f. Compare Tarcov and Pangle, "Epilogue," pp. 916f, 928f. Compare, also, Leo Paul S. de Alvarez, ed., *Abraham Lincoln, The Gettysburg Address, and American Constitutionalism* (Irving, Tex.: University of Dallas Press, 1976), pp. 165–68.

9. Hilail Gildin, "Leo Strauss and the Crisis of Liberal Democracy," in Kenneth L. Deutsch and Walter Soffer, eds., *The Crisis of Liberal Democracy: A Straussian Perspective* (Albany: State University of New York Press, 1987), pp. 92-93. See, also, *ibid.*, p. 100. See, as well, Anastaplo, *The Artist as Thinker*, p. 457 n. 283; note 11, below. Mr. Gildin has been primarily responsible, for decades now, for the publication of an invaluable journal, *Interpretation*.

Mr. Strauss's ability to come up with the apt qualification could be seen in an exchange he had, about a quarter of a century ago, with Raymond Aron, during a University of Chicago seminar (in Social Science 302 [now known as the Edward Shils Seminar Room]). The exchange went something like this: M. Aron had occasion to report that Charles de Gaulle spoke at times of the State as a cold monster, imitating Nietzsche in this respect. But, Mr. Strauss responded, Nietzsche despised the State, while de Gaulle tries to pet it. What made this exchange particularly memorable for me was Mr. Strauss's reaching out to pet de Gaulle's State in such a way as to conjure up the image of a dog having his head patted. Everyone present, including M. Aron, was delighted by the wonderful gesture. And M. Aron, upon his return home, related the episode around Paris. See, on Mr. Strauss and Nietzsche, note 3, above.

10. See, on intellectuals and morality, Anastaplo, "Lessons for the Student of Law: The Oklahoma Lectures," 20 *Oklahoma City University Law Review* 17, 179–87 (1996); "Natural Law or Natural Right?" 38 *Loyola of New Orleans Law Review* 915 (1993); "Teaching, Nature, and the Moral Virtues," 1997 *Great Ideas Today* 2, 23f (1997). See, also, Banfield, "Leo Strauss," pp. 495 (para. 2), 496 (para. 1). See, as well, Anastaplo, "On Freedom: Explorations," 17 *Oklahoma City University Law Review* 467, 666–707 (1992); *The American Moralist*, pp. 20–32, 125–38, 185–98, 327–37, 341–48, 407–21; *Campus Hate-Speech Codes, Natural Right, and Twentieth Century Atrocities* (Lewiston, N.Y.: Edwin Mellen Press, 1999), p. 127f.

The argument sometimes made on behalf of "philosophy"—that morality is *not* grounded in nature and hence is not choiceworthy for its own sake but is only "instrumental"—can be understood as a sophisticated form of Hobbesianism conjured up by would-be realists. I, partly on the basis of having seen Leo Strauss "in action" on a number of occasions, continue to believe that there was for him a basis in nature for the moral virtues. (One practical consequence of his genuine regard for morality was his alliance, in effect, with American Roman Catholics with respect to moral concerns. See, e.g., "Was Leo Strauss a Secret Enemy of Morality?" in Ernest L. Fortin, *Classical Christianity and the Political Order* [Lanham, Maryland: Rowman & Littlefield, 1996], pp. 317–27. See, as well, *ibid.*, pp. 329–36; Anastaplo "On How Eric Voegelin Has Read Plato and Aristotle," *Independent Journal of Philosophy*, vol. 5/6, pp. 85–91 [1988].) Special emphasis should perhaps be placed here upon prudence, the virtue that may be most susceptible to the guidance of political philosophy. See, on having to know what a literary character *should* have done in order truly to see what he *has* done, Anastaplo, *The Artist as Thinker*, p. 7f.

Mr. Strauss's openness to the virtue of prudence followed naturally, it could be said, upon the congenital physical wariness he exhibited. A testimonial to this wariness, it could also be said, was the copy he had on his office wall of Albrecht Dürer's famous watercolor, *Junger Feldhase (A Young Hare,* 1502). (This framed copy has been inherited by Joseph Cropsey.) Mr. Strauss, in referring to this picture, could speak of "nature, nature." Even more telling perhaps (if not disquieting for some) was that he particularly liked the picture because, he said, the hare sleeps with its eyes open. (Whether it really sleeps thus may be questioned.) One critic's description of this picture suggests what there is in it that Mr. Strauss may have instinctively responded to: "The hare, fearful, has cowered down, carefully testing the surroundings, ready to spring up and flee." Peter Strieder, ed., *Albrecht Dürer: Paintings, Prints, Drawings* (New York: Abaris Books, 1982), p. 203. And yet, it should be added, however fearful Mr. Strauss could at times be (something which may have helped him understand Thomas Hobbes), he soon came to have somehow for me the "look" of Socrates, who was (however wary) anything but fearful at heart. See, on Leo Strauss's shunning of the dishonorable, note 3, above.

See, also, Anastaplo, *The Artist as Thinker*, p. 260 ("He reminds me of a con about to make a break.").

11. These liabilities are evident in the Jacques Derrida vogue, a remarkable exercise in elegant obfuscation, of which much can be made on the University of Chicago campus these days. These liabilities are evident as well in the obtuseness exhibited by Martin Heidegger, to the very end of his life, about the American regime, especially when compared to the Soviet regime. See Anastaplo, *The American Moralist*, p. 161. See, for a refreshing contrast to the Heidegger approach in comparing regimes, Leo Strauss, *Thoughts on Machiavelli* (Glencoe, Ill.: Free Press, 1958), pp. 13–14:

> While freedom is no longer a preserve of the United States, the United States is now the bulwark of freedom. And contemporary tyranny has its roots in Machiavelli's thought, in the Machiavellian principle that the good end justifies every means. At least to the extent that the American reality is inseparable from the American aspiration, one cannot understand Americanism without understanding Machiavellianism which is its opposite.

See, also, the text at note 9, above. See, as well, note 3, above.

Another vogue at the University of Chicago turned around the personality and work of Hannah Arendt. It is *perhaps* indicative of Mr. Strauss's waning influence at Chicago toward the end of his service in the Political Science Department that one of her courses should have been listed by his department in both the 1966–1967 and the 1967–1968 *Announcements*. This course, "A Reconsideration of Basic Moral Propositions from Socrates to Nietzsche," was also listed by the Committee on Social Thought *and* (something that never happened to Mr. Strauss) by the Philosophy Department.

Of course, the metaphysical interests of Leo Strauss are evident both in his publications and in his course transcripts. His only explicitly "metaphysical" course offering at Chicago, where he took seriously his being based in a political science department, was an informal reading with a group of us at night of Hegal's *Logic*. This was, I believe, during the Winter of 1957–1958. (Also, he had a longstanding interest in Pierre Bayle which he did not publicize.)

The thought of Leo Strauss in the United States has recently been accounted for in this way by a distinguished political scientist at Stanford University:

> The Straussian version of the history of political science harkens back to the German intellectual polemics of the late 19th and early 20th centuries. As a young German Ph.D. in the immediate post-World War I years, Leo Strauss shared in the general admiration of Max Weber for "his intransigent devotion to intellectual honesty ... his passionate devotion to the idea of science ..." [Citing Strauss, *The Rebirth of Classical Political Rationalism* (1989), p. 27.] On his way north from Freiburg where he had heard the lectures of [Martin] Heidegger in 1922, Strauss describes himself as having experienced a Damascan disillusionment with Weber and a conversion to Heideggerean existentialism. Strauss's mode of coping with the pessimism of the Heidegger view of the nature of "being" was through an affirmative political philosophy, seeking the just society and polity through the recovery of the great exemplars of the canon of political philosophy, through dialogue and deliberation, and through the education of a civic elite.

Almond, "Political Science," p. 79. See, also, note 13, below. This Stanford (originally University of Chicago) political scientist then said,

> According to Strauss, Weber was the problematic intellectual figure who legitimated modern positivistic social science, its separation of fact and value, its "ethical neutrality," its effort to become "value free." Strauss attributes to Max Weber the belief that all value conflicts are unsolvable. [Citing Strauss, *What Is Political Philosophy?* (1959), p. 21f.]

Ibid., p. 79. The Strauss position is criticized by Mr. Almond, who calls the description of "the Weberian fact-value formulation" a "Straussian caricature." *Ibid.*, p. 81.

To what extent did the Nazi atrocities help expose what was dubious about the Nietzschean persuasion, just as the Stalinist terror (and thereafter the massive Chinese repression and the Pol Pot madness) helped expose what was dubious about the Marxist persuasion? What was the pre-Second World War status of political science as a discipline in German universities? And how was "political theory" regarded in those days? Consider, in this context, Leo Strauss's response in 1932 to the work of Carl Schmitt. Consider, also, an observation about Leo Strauss made by R. H. Tawney, in 1942, that "'America,' it seems, had made 'a new man of him,' transforming an intellect of delicate perfection into a personality 'tough enough' to be 'a successful professor.'" Green, "The Tawney-Strauss Connection," p. 264. See, also, "[Hans Georg] Gadamer on [Leo] Strauss: An Interview," in Ernest L. Fortin, *Human Rights, Virtue, and the Common Good* (Lanham, Md.: Rowman & Littlefield, 1996), pp. 175–89.

Hilail Gildin (see note 9, above) has authorized me to quote here from his letter to me of January 13, 1999 in which he comments in an instructive fashion on several points made by me in this article:

> I am glad your article will be one of those which introduce the Deutsch-Murley volume. What you write brings Strauss to life as a human being much as your [1974] *Yahrzeit* piece did .... [See Item i in note 1, above.]

> In early 1941 Strauss gave a lecture called "German Nihilism" in the General Seminar of the Graduate Faculty of the New School. It will soon appear in *Interpretation* ... The observations he makes about England on the last two pages will interest you ... Strauss found in England the very things that you suggest, in Section V [of your article], that America may have taught him. He also saw some things that are not as readily visible here. If he could have, he would have remained in England. I don't begrudge him that. This is not to deny that he was grateful to America for taking him in and for what he was able to do here. He also enjoyed the much easier relations between professor and student that he found in the United States.

> As for your remark regarding what might have become of him had he remained in Germany, Strauss says in the 1964 Preface to the German edition of his *Hobbes* book that the theologico-political problem remained *the* theme of his investigations from the time of his *Spinoza* book. In the first paragraph of the later Preface to his *Spinoza* book, he speaks of finding himself in the grip of the theologico-political predicament as a young man. [Jacob] Klein's characterization of him in the memorial meeting at St. John's [College] is not in conflict with Strauss's self-description ("His main interest throughout his life is the way *man* has to live here on earth."). Strauss was, to be sure, forever mindful of the ultimate presuppositions of what he was saying, as he

makes clear in the final paragraph of his *Restatement* on Xenophon's *Hiero*. Had he remained in Germany I don't think he would have been either more or less theoretical or metaphysical than he in fact was, though I am sure there would have been differences of all kinds.

The mere fact that, as his students, we rejected the fact/value distinction and historicism was enough to make people believe that we were brainwashed members of a fringe sect. Of course we did not think that we were the ones who were brainwashed. The [first] letter-writer you quote [in Section VI of your article] doesn't realize that being taught to take Socrates seriously as a philosopher is the very opposite of being brainwashed.

I do find Mr. Gildin's letter most instructive, however different our interpretations may seem to be of some of the evidence noticed by him. As for "the ultimate presuppositions of what he was saying": there are, in the Leo Strauss Archives in the University of Chicago Library's Special Collections, sets of sometimes detailed notes made by Mr. Strauss upon reading texts, upon preparing lectures, and perhaps upon giving courses. Some of these notes, which should illuminate his "presuppositions," precede his Chicago years.

12. See Yosef Goell and Jon Immanuel, "Slayer of Sacred Cows," *Jerusalem Post*, June 7, 1990. See, on Leo Strauss and Judaism, Ralph Lerner, "Leo Strauss (1899-1973)," *American Jewish Year Book*, p. 92 (1976); Green, ed., *Jewish Philosophy and the Crisis of Modernity*; Anastaplo, *The Artist as Thinker*, pp. 254, 268–71, 475 n. 285. "Being Jewish was a central fact of life for Strauss. He once confided that he could never feel completely comfortable with a non-Jew." Banfield, "Leo Strauss," p. 493. Even so, the memorial service conducted for Mr. Strauss at the University of Chicago was in a modest lecture hall on campus, not at the local Hillel House (where he had had a fruitful association with Rabbi Maurice Pekarsky and Rabbi Richard Winograd and where he had lectured on several occasions) or at any of the Jewish places of worship in the neighborhood.

My own assessment of Leo Strauss's Jewishness has been described in this fashion by a Jewish scholar (Green, ed., *Jewish Philosophy and the Crisis of Modernity*, p. 476):

> As a non-Jew and a careful observer, Anastaplo in his article [in *The Artist as Thinker*, pp. 250–72, 474–85] keenly appreciates what he regards as the twofold beneficial influence which Judaism exercised on Strauss, and through him on his students both Jewish and non-Jewish. First, it somehow helped make Strauss, as both a thinker and a careful reader, receptive to the premodern idea of philosophy and resistant to certain modern ideas. Second, it overflowed through him as a Jewish thinker and scholar so as to leave a deep and vivifying impression on those who encountered him, through his intellectual seriousness about Judaism, and through his human example of devotion to Judaism.

See, for my review of Mr. Green's useful book, items xiv and xvi in note 1, above.

13. Leo Strauss, *Natural Right and History* (Chicago: University of Chicago Press, 1953), p. 1. Jenny Strauss-Clay found herself obliged to recall this passage for the benefit of troubled critics who have condemned her father as an enemy of democracy, etc. See "Revisiting Leo Strauss," *New York Times*, Sept. 1, 1996, sec. 7, p. 4. Compare, e.g., Brent Staples, "Undemocratic Vistas," *New York Times*, Nov. 28, 1994, sec. A, p. 16. See, also, Laurence Berns, "Correcting the Record on Leo Strauss," 28 *PS: Political Science and Politics* 659–60 (1995);

Anastaplo, "Lessons for the Student of Law," p. 65, n. 134. See, for what I have considered salutary for students of liberal democracy to notice about the high and low in the work of Leo Strauss, Anastaplo, *Liberty, Equality & Modern Constitutionalism* (Newburyport, Mass.: Focus Publishing, 1999), Volume One, Section IV. 3.

Distortions with respect to the thought of Leo Strauss are, unfortunately, not confined to newspapers. Consider, for example, the Strauss entry in the recently issued *Routledge Encyclopedia of Philosophy* which asks readers to believe, "[Strauss] thought that in the *Republic* Thrasymachus, not Socrates, was Plato's true spokesman" (citing, for some reason, Strauss, *The City and Man* [1964, 1977], p. 77). This careless encyclopedia entry concludes with this judgment:

> Some find Strauss' elitism disconcerting. An elite that is radical, secretive and duplicitous, an elite that exempts itself from the moral principles it deems applicable to the rest of humanity, cannot be trusted with political power.

The author of this entry, if not also the encyclopedia editors, should simply have known better. See, e.g., Item vi in note 1, above. See, also, note 5, above. See, as well, note 11, above.

The responses to be made to the various critics of Leo Strauss I have noticed in this article could include and develop such sentiments as are included in a letter of mine (of August 24, 1976) to an eminent professor at an Eastern university:

> ... I do not believe you appreciate how special Mr. Strauss was. I suppose I sat in on more classes of his than anyone else—simply because I have been here at the University [of Chicago] since the Second World War and have not been much concerned about "keeping up appearances" in these matters—and I saw, year in and year out, a remarkable mind at work, a mind head and shoulders above the others around the University whom I had contact with and who were themselves widely acclaimed. . . .
>
> No doubt there is the talk you report at the end of your commentary about the [offensive] response of [the students of] "Straussian professors" to "non-Straussian professors." I say "no doubt" because I realize that you must have come across such talk. But the phenomena you describe there have not come to my personal attention, at least not in the extreme form you report. . . .
>
> No doubt, also, there are at times signs of what you call an "arrogant orthodoxy"— and yet the remarkableness of Mr. Strauss, even more remarkable than you acknowledge, is (it seems to me) a fact apparent to any sensitive, intelligent person privileged really to have known him. I can understand, I repeat, why you respond as you do to what you have encountered—but, I should add, a good deal of what you find offensive comes from people who, all too often and not without some basis, consider themselves very much on the defensive.
>
> I appreciate very much your characterization of my [1974] article on Mr. Strauss as "the most detached and yet sympathetic portrait [you've] seen so far." The article [which has been reprinted as the Epilogue in *The Artist as Thinker*] was intended to help people not already "captured" by Mr. Strauss to see him somewhat more clearly than he might otherwise be seen as a result of partisan maneuverings. That I can appreciate your response to certain manifestations of [Straussian] orthodoxy is due to such experiences of my own as the pained silence which has greeted my article on Mr.

Strauss—that is, the pained silence exhibited by those who consider themselves the inner circle (or perhaps more precisely, who are thus considered by many).

This is not a proper reply or comment upon your commentary. But it is, I hope, a useful caution. . . .

It is a mistake, in any event, to regard Leo Strauss as ordinary in his political opinions, whether or not "orthodox." See, e.g., Anastaplo, *The Artist as Thinker*, pp. 474–75, n. 282; Items iv and vi in note 1, above. See, also, the text at note 7 of John A. Murley, "*In re* George Anastaplo," in this Deutsch-Murley collection. It is unlikely that Mr. Strauss (whatever sympathies he might have had in Germany for decidedly conservative causes in the late 1920s or early 1930s) would have endorsed the recent "conservative" assault upon evolutionary biology, just as he had reservations about a free-market economy. See, e.g., Ronald Bailey, "Origin of the Specious: Why Do Neoconservatives Doubt Darwin?" *Reason Magazine*, July 1997. Consider, on the lessons to be learned from nature, revelation, and modern science, the work of such second-generation Straussians as John Alvis, Larry Arnhart, Christopher A. Colmo, and J. Harvey Lomax, Leonard R. Sorenson, Jules Gleicher, and Stephen Vanderslice. Consider, also, Mr. Strauss's 1956 identification, not altogether in jest, of Alexandre Kojève, Jacob Klein, and himself as the only ones "in the present generation who still believe in Reason." Consider, as well, his observations, in another 1956 letter: "I wish power and understanding were more united than they are. But I am afraid that the efforts which sensible men would have to make in order to acquire more power would detract from the most reasonable employment of their reason. So we have to go on trusting on occasional friendly gestures of *fortuna*, that loose woman."

Edward Banfield concluded his 1991 memoir of Leo Strauss at the University of Chicago with these salutary observations (Shils, ed., *Remembering the University of Chicago*, p. 501):

I hope enough has been said to convey some sense of the special greatness of Strauss as a teacher, scholar, and human being. Directly and through his writing he enabled many people to see more clearly what it means to be fully human. That such a man flourished for so many years in the United States and at the University of Chicago must be both a source of pride and grounds for hope. To paraphrase a few words of what he said in eulogy of Sir Winston Churchill (whom he thought the greatest man of this century), Strauss's life reminds us to see things as they are—to see them in their greatness as well as their misery, in their brilliance as well as their mediocrity.

I concluded my 1974 article on Mr. Strauss with these observations (reprinted, in 1983, in *The Artist as Thinker*, p. 271):

Thus ends my remembrance for this occasion of a most remarkable man, an intrepid stepson of the University of Chicago and its determined benefactor. Even if I should be destined to remain in this university community another twenty-six years, I for one do not expect to happen upon his like again.

See Plato, *Phaedo* 118.

· 2 ·

Leo Strauss at St. John's College (Annapolis)

Laurence Berns with Eva Brann

I

It was Robert Goldwin, then Dean of St. John's at Annapolis, who found the means to bring Leo Strauss to Annapolis as Scott Buchanan Distinguished Scholar in Residence in 1969. Goldwin was also responsible for organizing the remarkable talks, which have been printed as "A Giving of Accounts: Jacob Klein and Leo Strauss."[1] Strauss had been lecturing and answering questions at St. John's once almost every year for quite a few years. He did not have to go out of his way to make what he was trying to do understandable and appreciated. Furthermore, a good number of his better students had come to him from St. John's, and a small number of his former students were now teaching there. He sensed that it was a place where he could feel at home. One very important reason for that was that his old and very close friend, Jacob Klein, was at St. John's.

Strauss's residence at St. John's reraised for some students of both men the question of their differences. Eva Brann has put it as follows:

> Those of us who had not studied with Mr. Strauss were under the impression, which I am pretty sure but not absolutely certain came from Mr. Klein himself, that these two old friends, who in many ways stood together, differed in deep and significant ways. The gist of the difference was as follows: Mr Strauss believed that the central inquiry was political philosophy; he believed that modernity was grounded in a revolution in political theory and in a confrontation with questions of divinity; he had an increasing and by no means merely critical interest in religion. Mr Klein, on the other hand, regarded philosophy, that is, the inquiry into being, as the most fundamental human activity; he focused on mathematical physics as the determining feature of modernity, and his relation to religious studies was remote. I do know that it was a direct consequence of Mr. Strauss's sojourn here that the questions of Socrates's ultimate intention became a problem to some of us not in the Ciceronian version according to which Socrates

31

brought philosophy down from heaven to earth, but in the way in which the *Republic* induces the question whether contemplation is for the sake of the city or the converse, whether philosophy grounds politics or the opposite, whether the good is primarily a principle of being or of action.

It is also my impression that this was pretty much the way Jacob Klein saw the question: it is consistent with what he said in "A Giving of Accounts . . ." and in his Memorial Address for Strauss.[2] Many people share that view, and, I believe, Strauss is partly complicit in its being widespread; nevertheless, I think it is fundamentally mistaken. It is, however, close to, and easily taken for what I will try to articulate as the correct view of Strauss's position. As far as I understand it, there was no difference between Strauss and Klein about "philosophy, that is, the inquiry into being, as the most fundamental human activity." *Natural Right and History*, pp. 123–126, one place among a number of others, is a good place to begin:

> Let us then see what is implied by Socrates' turning to the study of human things. His study of human things consisted in raising the question "What is?" in regard to those things . . . But it was not limited to raising the question "What is?" in regard to specific human things, such as the various virtues. Socrates was forced to raise the question as to what the human things as such are, or what the *ratio rerum humanarum* is. But it is impossible to grasp the distinctive character of human things as such without grasping the essential difference between human things and the things which are not human, i.e., the divine or natural things. This, in turn, presupposes some understanding of the divine or natural things as such. *Socrates' study of the human things was then based on the comprehensive study of "all things." Like every other philosopher, he identified wisdom, or the goal of philosophy, with the science of all the beings: he never ceased considering "what each of the beings is."*

> . . . Socrates' turn to the study of human things was based, not upon disregard of the divine or natural things, but upon a new approach to the understanding of *all* things. That approach was indeed of such a character that it permitted, and favored, the study of the human things as such, *i.e., of the human things in so far as they are not reducible to the divine or natural things.*[3] Socrates deviated from his predecessors by identifying the science of the whole, or of everything that is, with the understanding of "what each of the beings is." For "to be" means "to be something" and hence to be different from things which are "something else"; "to be" means therefore "to be a part." Hence the whole cannot "be" in the same sense in which everything that is "something" "is"; the whole must be "beyond being." And yet the whole is the totality of the parts. To understand the whole then means to understand all the parts of the whole or the articulation of the whole. If "to be" is "to be something," the being of a thing, or the nature of a thing, is primarily its What, its "shape" or "form" or "character," as distinguished in particular from that out of which it has come into being. The thing itself, the completed thing, cannot be understood as a product of the process leading up to it, but, on the contrary, the process cannot be understood except in the light of the completed thing or of the end of the process.

This paragraph is based, it seems to me, primarily on what one might learn from Xenophon's *Memorabilia*, and Plato's *Sophist* and *Parmenides* with some help from Alfarabi. The next paragraph (*NRH*, 123) focuses on *eidos*. It is, I believe, Strauss's interpretation of the meaning of Socrates's "second sailing," *Phaedo*, 98 ff. and the theoretical parts of the *Republic*, as is also the end of the previous paragraph.

According to this understanding of being, each of the major parts, the major kinds of being, possesses, or is constituted by, an inner intelligible articulation of its own. They can then be studied best to begin with by attending directly to their own inner and articulable principles, rather than by trying to deduce them from (or to reduce them to) the alleged "metaphysical" or "scientific" principles out of which (e.g., "Matter in Motion") they could be said to have come into being. It is easy then from this point of view to come to think that one's own special field of interest stands separately by itself without connection to any broader understanding of being. As a Professor of Political Science Strauss had many good students with a keen natural interest in things political and little interest in more speculative questions. By liberating such students from methodological dogmas parading as science, he allowed them to follow up their own natural interests, to study political things in their own natural articulation, in their own terms, as political practitioners understand them. It is not difficult, and not particularly damaging, for such students to look away from the philosophic considerations that they sense are not within their own field of competence. Furthermore, if the reigning generally accepted opinions among scientific and philosophic authorities should be thought to be deleterious to sound morality and political life, there would be an additional reason for encouraging belief in the relatively independent status of different kinds of subject matters, especially in the field of "the human things." Aristotle would seem to have encouraged belief in this kind of "special relativity," more than Plato. Plato never allows one to forget the "general relativity" that they both share—the notion of being implicit in the "What is?" question—by never presenting any serious discussion apart from the presence of philosophy, or a philosopher.

The final paragraph of Strauss's "Restatement," his answer to Kojève's "Tyranny and Wisdom," (which is missing from the 1963 English version of *On Tyranny*, translated in the French version, and translated from the French in the revised English version of 1991) provides another way of seeing Strauss's agreement with what Eva Brann describes as Klein's view of "the most fundamental human activity."

> The utmost I can hope to have shown in taking issue with Kojève's thesis regarding the relation of tyranny and wisdom is that Xenophon's thesis regarding that grave subject is not only compatible with the idea of philosophy but required by it. This is very little. For the question arises immediately whether the idea of philosophy is not itself in need of legitimation. Philosophy in the strict and classical sense is quest for the eternal order or for the eternal cause or causes of all things. It presupposes then that there is an eternal and unchangeable order within which History takes place and which is not in any way affected by History. It presupposes in other words that any "realm of freedom" is not more than a

dependent province within "the realm of necessity." It presupposes, in the words of Kojève, that "Being is essentially immutable in itself and eternally identical with itself." This presupposition is not self-evident. Kojève rejects it in favor of the view that "Being creates itself in the course of History," or that the highest being is Society and History, or that eternity is nothing but the totality of historical, i.e., finite time. On the basis of the classical presupposition, a radical distinction must be made between the conditions of understanding and the sources of understanding, between the conditions of the existence and perpetuation of philosophy (societies of a certain kind, and so on) and the sources of philosophic insight. On the basis of Kojève's presupposition, that distinction loses its crucial significance: social change or fate affects being, if it is not identical with Being, and hence affects truth. On the basis of Kojève's presuppositions, unqualified attachment to human concerns becomes the source of philosophic understanding: man must be absolutely at home on earth, he must be absolutely a citizen of the earth, if not a citizen of a part of the inhabitable earth. On the basis of the classical presupposition, philosophy requires a radical detachment from human concerns: man must not be absolutely at home on earth, he must be a citizen of the whole. In our discussion, the conflict between the two opposed basic presuppositions has barely been mentioned. But we have always been mindful of it. For we both apparently turned away from Being to Tyranny because we have seen that those who lacked the courage to face the issue of Tyranny, who therefore *et humiliter serviebant et superbe dominabantur*, were forced to evade the issue of Being as well, precisely because they did nothing but talk of Being.[4]

Both Klein and Strauss, I have argued, chose to pursue philosophy in the classical sense as described above, each for himself. Strauss did not seriously study modern natural science, but did not minimize its importance. In his last years during a Plato's *Laws* course he was giving at St. John's a student asked him, "If you could speak now to Plato and Aristotle, what would you ask them?" Strauss paused to gather his thoughts and then said, "I think I would ask them whether the development from Galileo and Newton would cause them in any way to modify their teaching about the forms." He evidently did not think it would be a reasonable expenditure of his powers and time to pursue that subject in detail. He did study very carefully what Klein had written on the subject. There was no principled difference with Klein on that matter. Their different stances toward the study of religion, however, do, I believe, point to interesting and serious differences.

For Strauss, as the quotation from the "Restatement" indicates, the idea of philosophy is in need of legitimation. Philosophy, its origin, and its choice as a way of life, were philosophic problems for Strauss, the highest themes, perhaps, for that *part* of philosophy called political philosophy. For readers of his books they are known as the question of "The Origin of the Idea of Natural Right," or the question of the discovery of nature. Klein was interested in a related problem, but from a different angle, especially in connection with modern science, the problem of "sedimentation,"[5] but his problem was not thought of in any special connection with religion.

Very early in a review of a book by Julius Ebbinghaus Strauss refers to Socrates's remark that knowing that one does not know is the beginning of philosophy. He connects it up with the image of the cave in Plato's *Republic*: We find ourselves "in a second, much deeper cave than the lucky ignorant ones with whom Socrates had to deal." Our faith in the superiority of modern thought keeps us from even recognizing that we are in a cave, keeps us from seeing the universality, the permanence, of the problem that the image of the cave points to: "the actual not-knowing of present day philosophizing is not at all the natural not-knowing with which philosophizing must begin; . . . it requires a long detour, a great effort to come back. . . . to the state of natural ignorance."[6] If we do not adequately understand that from which our philosophizing begins or departs, we may, while we think that we are philosophizing, find ourselves unwittingly following principles serving ends very different from philosophic ends.

> Philosophy is the ascent from what is first for us to what is first by nature. This ascent requires that what is first for us be understood as adequately as possible in the manner in which it comes to sight prior to the ascent. . . . the city as it primarily understood itself [is] distinguished from the manner in which it was exhibited by classical political philosophy: the holy city in contradistinction to the natural city. . . . what is 'first for us' is not the philosophic understanding of the city but that understanding which is *inherent in the city as such*, in the prephilo-sophic city, according to which the city sees itself as subject and subservient to the divine in the ordinary understanding of the divine or looks up to it.[7]

If religion, especially since it is an intellectual as well as an emotional power, is one of the major powers constituting the prephilosophic "world," it becomes a major problem for that discipline, i.e., political philosophy, that studies the relations between the prephilosophic and the philosophic "worlds." That problem was deepened as a philosophic problem for Strauss by what he presents as the mutual irrefutability of reason and revelation.

II

Every Wednesday from 3:30 to 5:30 Strauss would conduct a class that would usually study one book per semester, or in the case of a large book like Plato's *Laws*, one book for the whole year. The classes were well-attended by students and, occasionally, Tutors.[8] They were much like classes I had attended at the University of Chicago, except that Strauss would occasionally mention that since he was at St. John's he did not need to present his usual apology for, or justification of, the study of old books.[9] He would usually speak for ten, fifteen or twenty minutes and then stop for questions and reasonably free-floating discussions. If my memory serves, there were classes on Thucydides, Xenophon, Plato's *Laws*, and Nietzsche's *Beyond Good and Evil*.

Different members of the faculty sought opportunities to chat with him. I saw him for at least a couple of hours almost every week. His relation to Klein was rather touching. They both seemed to enjoy and admire each other very much. Klein was something like a big brother to the somewhat more tempestuous Strauss, whose health was also going into a drastic decline during this time. It is difficult for anyone who did not experience it to fathom how impractical Strauss was in everything that did not pertain to his scholarly and academic pursuits. My wife and I were very moved when we learned from both Mrs. Strauss and Mrs. Klein how, when Strauss learned about the birth of our daughter, he decided that *he himself* would have to go to purchase an appropriate gift! Any old friend, or attendant, of Strauss knows that he was hardly capable of going by himself to buy anything. But this was an important matter, he was not going to ask just anyone to accompany him. This was a matter that called for Jacob Klein! So the two philosophers went on an expedition to Annapolis's baby clothes store and after, I assume, much deliberation bought a nicely wrapped, pretty, little, pink and white baby outfit, complete with beret. (Strauss usually wore a beret.)

On a number of occasions Strauss attended Friday night formal lectures at St. John's. I gave one once on Aristotle's *Politics*, entitled "Rational Animal-Political Animal." I felt a little funny about wasting his time, since I thought that just about everything I had to say on the subject had been learned in his classes or from his books. So, after the lecture as we walked to the Conversation Room for the customary question period, I said to him, "Well, this is all pretty old stuff for you." I was pleased to hear him reply, "No, no, I had never made the connection to *On Interpretation*."

In his last year his health and strength were almost gone; he would drag himself into the room for his classes on the arm of and strongly supported by his assistant and helper Ted A. Blanton, then a junior at St. John's.[10] He would collapse into his chair and be slumped together there silently for a few seconds, then we would hear something soft like "Thucydides says . . . " and then marvelously his voice would fill out, he would sit up, and for the next two hours we would be caught up by his usual fascinating discourse and conversation. After two hours he would announce the assignment for next time, then collapse again into his chair and be slowly taken away by Blanton. It is difficult to find words adequate to praise Blanton for the gracious way he served Strauss till the very end. That service was joined to a rather beautiful friendship. Some of Blanton's words at the St. John's Memorial Meeting for Strauss may be a fitting end for this essay:

> When I would leave his home he always took my hand and thanked me for everything I had done. But truly I was the one who owed the thanks. Upon leaving his home I was both restful and restless: restful because of the calmness and the sheer delight of his words to me and restless because he instilled in me an eagerness to think and to learn. Friendship appeared to me in a fuller light: friendship is not that relationship where all is relaxed but the relationship where

one's highest faculties are poised for graceful movement. I believe that in those moments I was more fully human than at any other time.

NOTES

1. First published in *The College*, (Annapolis: St. John's College, April 1970), pp. 1–5. Reprinted in Leo Strauss, *Jewish Philosophy and the Crisis of Modernity: Essays and Lectures in Modern Jewish Thought*, (Albany: SUNY Press, 1997), edited by Kenneth Hart Green, pp. 457–466.

2. The Memorial Meeting for Leo Strauss at St John's was held on October 31, 1973. The speakers were Jacob Klein, the Rev. J. Winfree Smith, Ted A. Blanton and Laurence Berns. The speeches were printed in *The College*, (Annapolis: St. John's College, January, 1974), pp. 1–5.

3. Emphasis added.

4. This, Strauss's own original English version, is taken from a copy of a typescript entitled *RESTATEMENT* (1950) given to me by Leo Strauss before the essay was printed. This paragraph has been printed in *op. cit.*, editor K. H. Green, note 1 above, pp. 471–473.

5. See *Jacob Klein: Lectures and Essays*, R. B. Williamson and E. Zuckerman, editors, (Annapolis: St John's College Press, 1985), pp. 72–78.

6. *Deutsche Literaturzeitung*, December 27, 1931, Heft 52, pp. 2451–2453. Translation from the German by L. Berns. Cf. Leo Strauss, *Persecution and the Art of Writing*, (Glencoe, Illinois: The Free Press, 1952), pp. 154–58.

7. Leo Strauss, *The City and Man*, (Chicago: Rand McNally, 1964), pp. 240–241. Emphasis supplied.

8. "Tutor" is the sole faculty rank at St. John's College.

9. I had mixed feelings about this compliment to St. John's. Strauss's "apologies" for reading old books usually involved very interesting critiques and analyses of modern philosophy and thought, pointing to why classical studies were needed for a more adequate understanding. We were missing those analyses.

10. Theodore A. Blanton is presently a Judge of the District Court in Salisbury, North Carolina.

Leo Strauss at the University of Chicago

Joseph Cropsey

$\mathcal{L}$eo Strauss was not quite fifty years old when early in 1949 he joined the faculty at the University of Chicago. His appointment was to a considerable extent negotiated between himself and Robert Maynard Hutchins, with the influential and perhaps primary intervention of Hans Morgenthau, then apparently a pro tem chairman of the Political Science Department. Strauss enjoyed a collegial friendship with such senior members of the department as Herman Pritchett, Morton Grodzins, Jerome Kerwin, and Charles Hardin, and with such juniors as Edward Banfield and Robert Osgood, as well, of course, as Herbert Storing. As Strauss became better known in the discipline for his criticism of "scientific" or "value-free" social science, as well as for whatever reservations he might have had or were attributed to him regarding liberal politics, the public reaction against his position found a parallel within the department, and divisions developed therein that persisted throughout the period of his residence. With the end of Herman Pritchett's chairmanship in the early 1960s, at a time when Strauss's retirement was approaching under the 65-year rule then in effect, the reaction to Strauss found expression in the administration of the department. Curiously, in roughly this same period, Strauss was finding favor in an unexpected quarter in the larger world, for this was the time when the radical movement was in protest against the moral vacuity that it denounced in the value-free behavioralism abroad at the time. This external vagary had no counterpart in the department.

Divisions among the faculty were inevitably repeated in the student body. Strauss's classrooms, however, were always full, and his influence as a teacher was resounding, not only within the Political Science Department but also among the students in the Committee on Social Thought, of which he was not a member. Of course his teaching, like his writing, might lean against such prevalent currents as historicism and positivism to the point of prompting a species of physiodicy at the same time that it moved to preserve a space for revelation in its contest with reason alone. Thus the intellectual atmosphere was vibrant, within political theory and

39

also in constitutional law and public administration, fields that engaged many of Herbert Storing's students.

Strauss was a towering presence in the department who neither sought nor had any discernible influence on what passes for the politics of the group. His reputation having grown to the international magnitude it now has, his bearing on the study of his subject in his late department is very much as it might be in any well-constituted academic community.

4

Strauss at One Hundred

Harry V. Jaffa

I

About ten years ago I had a letter from Dante Germino, asking why Strauss's students had paid so little attention to the work of Eric Voegelin. Earlier, Dante had asked me to lecture at Virginia. On that occasion he had been suddenly hospitalized. Although nothing serious had resulted, I did not see him during my visit. His students however had been models of hospitality, and in the seminars I conducted they showed themselves well trained, and highly motivated in right directions. Dante had taught political philosophy to Lawrence McGoldrick, my son-in-law to be. Dante and his wife and daughter had attended Lawrence and Karen's wedding in the University of Virginia Chapel in 1979. Dante's daughter had been a waitress at the rehearsal dinner at the Boar's Head Inn in Charlottesville (where Lawrence had been a waiter). For all these reasons I thought it fitting to respond in as friendly a manner as possible.

I wrote, in part,

> As to the "incomprehensibility" of the neglect of Voegelin by Straussians, some of it must be put down to the blinding power of the light that emanated from Strauss himself. For it is the paradoxical truth that light can at once enable one to see and, if sufficiently intense, to blind. I have often compared my encounter with Strauss, beginning in September 1944 to the experience of Saul on the road to Damascus. When one is in that kind of exalted consciousness, it is easy to neglect or dismiss other prophets (or to assume without inquiring that they must be false prophets!).

I went on to say that it was a mistake to continue to think of "Straussians" as a single class. As illustrative of this, I sent a copy of my critique of *The Closing of the American Mind*. Unfortunately, he took offense at my implied comparison—as he thought it—of Strauss and Jesus. But he took infinitely greater offense at what I had written about homosexuality in the Bloom review. He accused me of a lack of scholarly integrity for not taking as unqualified truth what John Boswell (of whom I had never heard!) had written in his book on Christianity and homosexuality. Boswell, as it happened, was a professor of history at Yale (he died of AIDS at the age of 47), and his book was a "revision" of all traditional morality concerning homosexuality, in the Old Testament as well as in the New. (The story of Sodom, for example, was about "inhospitality.") Dante's consuming preoccupation with homosexuality soon ended any further discussion of political philosophy.

I do not think my response about how my encounter with Strauss changed my life offended Christian piety. The paradigmatic account of the phenomenon of conversion—the source for Christianity itself—is the cave in Plato's *Republic*. No one's life, I believe, was "turned around" more completely than mine by my meeting with Strauss.

My five years at Yale were not wasted. They were, in fact, probably the best non-Straussian preparation for what followed. As an English major, I read only good books. For four years (sophomore year through graduate school) I attended an informal weekly Bible reading by my favorite professor, Alex Witherspoon. When *Crisis of the House Divided* was published, I sent him a copy, with an inscription that said truly that he was responsible for my sensitivity to the all-important biblical nuances and allusions in Lincoln. In my senior year I had a seminar on modern poetry and the then "new criticism," with Andrews Wanning, fresh from Oxford, and I. A. Richards. We used Brooks and Warrens' *Understanding Poetry*, a text I still find wonderful reading. I also had an invigorating introduction to the microanalysis of literary texts in Empson's *Seven Types of Ambiguity* and *Some Versions of Pastoral*. This seminar was memorable because I dragged Dick Ellmann into it, whence he went on to become the greatest literary scholar of our time on Yeats and Joyce. That year I also had an independent study in Plato and Aristotle with Eugene O'Neill, Jr., who showed great personal kindness to me. At the end of my time at Yale the three authors who had come to mean most to me were Plato, Aristotle, and Shakespeare. I had good instincts but no guide to unlock their mysteries.

Before Strauss, my greatest ambition was to write a history of Elizabethan drama. In my mind, this was the way to discover the secret of Shakespeare, which I assumed could be achieved only by the closest study of the soil out of which Shakespeare came. I was also greatly influenced by Marxist and Freudian interpretations. I recall being impressed by an interpretation of Shakespeare, in which Ariel was said to be the apotheosis of the free wage laborer! And Ernest Jones' Freudian book on Hamlet ranked very high. In all such accounts, the high was understood in the light of the low. It was Strauss who struck off the shackles in my cave, and set my feet in the upward path.

Little did I, or could I, have imagined in 1939 or 1940 that my ambition would be fulfilled—at least in part—in 1977, when I set forth the hypothesis that Shakespeare was the poet mentioned by Socrates at the end of the Symposium. Only Strauss could have led me to see that Shakespeare's inner and ultimate motivation was Platonic.

If I had any pre-Straussian theoretical framework, it was that of the sociology of knowledge. Later, Strauss would describe his own project—ironically—as the sociology of philosophy! From the perspective of the sociology of knowledge no distinction could be drawn between opinion and knowledge. Whatever believed itself to be true could be believed to be true only relative to the environment that "produced" it. This applied even to the most sophisticated literary criticism. Thus, what I later learned to be historicism (*the* idol of our modern cave) had permeated every atom of my mental existence. I had assumed that everything was relative except the proposition that everything was relative. The contradiction therein had not of course penetrated my consciousness before Strauss.

Strauss began *Natural Right and History* (1953) by quoting "We hold these truths to be self-evident . . ." and asking, "Does this nation in its maturity still cherish the faith in which it was conceived and raised? Does it still hold those truths to be self-evident . . ." He not only quoted from the Declaration, but used Lincoln's words, without quotation marks, to characterize it. Strauss clearly thought that the nation no longer dwelt within the precincts of the principles of the Declaration, and *Natural Right and History* goes a long way towards explaining why. But he never addressed directly the question of how the authority of those principles might be restored.

I claim no right to speak for Strauss in this matter. I can say however that it was a subject we discussed continuously in the late forties and early fifties. I believe that Strauss believed that my restoration of Lincoln was the most likely way to restore the aforesaid authority, and that this was the form in which the statesmanship of classical political philosophy might become authoritative in our world. While Strauss articulated the connection between Plato, biblical religion, and medieval political philosophy, to discover the presence of classical principles in the post-classical world, he propelled my articulation of the connection between Plato, biblical religion, Shakespeare, and Lincoln. And Lincoln's recovery of the Founding corresponded closely with the Maimonidean recovery of the rational origins of prophecy.

II

It is almost routine in the scholarship of greatness, whether philosophic or political, to discover fathomless complexity in its subjects. Certainly this has been true about Lincoln. Yet in the case of Lincoln, as in that of many others, the difficulty has been more in the mind of the observer rather than in the subject. Scholars who do not to believe in "an abstract truth applicable to all men and all time" either do not believe that Lincoln believed it, or think of him as unsophisticated. In either case, they embark on a quest for hidden motives because they cannot see the ones that lie plainly on the surface.

The recent torrent of literature about Strauss is not unlike that about Lincoln. No one would deny Strauss's complexity. Yet great minds are often, if not always, as great in their simplicities as in their complexities. Lincoln's statesmanship can always be explained in its relationship to "a central idea from which all its minor thoughts radiate." Strauss revealed himself perhaps more directly than anywhere else in his eulogy of Churchill.

> The tyrant stood at the pinnacle of his power. The contrast between the indomitable and magnanimous statesman and the insane tyrant—this spectacle in its clear simplicity was one of the greatest lessons which men can learn, at any time.

To the best of my recollection, in the political science of the 1930s neither Hitler nor Stalin was referred to as a tyrant. Their regimes were called dictatorships, or totalitarian, in deference to the quest for a "value free" objectivity. Yet this "objectivity" made it impossible to understand political reality. Strauss's *On Tyranny* was written in part to restore the classical term and with it the classical understanding. The centrality of "tyranny" in all its classical dimensions to the Declaration of Independence also demonstrates the essentially classical understanding of politics in the American Revolution. The magnanimity of those who pledged their lives, fortunes, and sacred honor directly parallels the contrast between Hitler and Churchill.

Strauss understood that modern tyranny was different from the tyrannies of the ancient world. But the identification of the species, or variety, depended upon recognizing the genus. The recognition of tyranny did however not come from books. It came from experience antecedent to books. The "spectacle" which Strauss says presents us with one of the greatest of all lessons, is therefore the ground of an education upon which great books can build, but without which they cannot instruct. The *Nicomachean Ethics* is addressed only to those who have sufficient experience of the moral phenomena, and who are well brought up. The greatest political books are those that reflect an original understanding of the moral and political phenomena, unmediated by ideology or philosophy. It was the corruption of that original understanding by modern philosophy that denied to the democracies the understanding of tyranny that nearly destroyed them.

In a letter to Löwith, Strauss once remarked that he had found great difficulty in understanding what Aristotle meant by magnanimity, until he realized that Churchill was a perfect example of it. That Churchill helped Strauss understand Aristotle illuminates profoundly how political philosophy depends upon the pre-philosophic experience of political life. The lesson embodied in the "clear simplicity" of the confrontation of Churchill and Hitler is that of the reality of evil, and the primacy of the good. It is also that the conflict of good and evil lies at the foundation of human experience. To reduce that experience to a subjective "value judgment" is not merely to trivialize it, but to blind one to objective reality. In Strauss's earlier work he referred to political philosophy as a part of philosophy. In his later years, I believe, he regarded it as the foundation of philosophy. So far are the moral distinctions from being merely subjective, they are the distinctions most knowable

"to us," and hence the starting points of reasoning about "the whole."
"A Summary View of the Rights of British America" is Jefferson's com-
pendium of the American position, written a year before the onset of the
Revolution, and two years before the Declaration of Independence. In it he tells
the King that "The great principles of right and wrong are legible to every reader . . ."
These are of course the principles we hold to be self-evident. They are the principles of a free people, the principles of good and lawful self-government, distinguished from the evil principles of tyranny or slavery. They are the principles of
Churchill as opposed to Hitler.

III

Everyone knows that Strauss ended his ever memorable lectures on "Progress or
Return" by asserting the categorical opposition of Reason and Revelation as ultimate principles, and the necessity to make a choice between them. I have come to
have doubts however as to whether this opposition is as categorical as Strauss made
it seem in that lecture. That it formed part of his peroration, and was therefore a
rhetorical conclusion does not, of itself, disqualify it as a dialectical conclusion. But
in his desire that classical political philosophy provide the moral foundation for constitutional government that modern philosophy had destroyed, he had particular
motives for absolutizing the difference of revelation and reason.

Modern philosophy was a rebellion against both classical rationalism and biblical religion. The skepticism that accompanied Socratic rationalism applied necessarily to the enterprise of Socratic rationalism. That is to say, Socratic rationalism
had to grant the premise that supplied the ground of faith. The reason in skepticism
for continuing an endless inquiry, and the reason for ending such inquiry by turning to biblical religion, was one and the same reason. Nor was there, in that very
reason, any ground for preferring the one alternative to the other. For Strauss, to
restore the authority of Socratic rationalism was of necessity to restore the authority of biblical faith.

The attempt to remove skepticism from philosophy had proved an utter failure. The project to infinitely enhance the power of reason over human life had culminated in the fact-value distinction, and the complete destruction of reason as a
guide to human life. Both the Bible and Socratic philosophy provided a firm basis
for moral choices, and the moral choices they endorsed were substantially the same.
Whether the ultimate reason for choosing the moral virtues was obedient love of
the living God, or the goodness of the life of autonomous reason, was less important than their agreement upon the moral order which must inform the life of
decent society. From this perspective revelation and reason, Jerusalem and Athens,
were in agreement. For this reason Strauss was committed no less to the defense of
Jerusalem than of Athens. For this reason, it would have been imprudent of him to

allow his own preferences to weaken the case for either of these cities, or the principles they represented.

The moral and political harmony of revelation and reason is reflected in the Declaration of Independence, in which rational moral truths, the truths of "the laws of nature and of nature's God," are enshrined within the order of Creation. Strauss was keenly aware, however, as were the American Founders, that those who had falsely claimed the authority either of reason or of revelation, as the basis of political authority, had done so in the interest of despotism. The absolutised claims of faith, stigmatizing opposition as heresy, supported the union of altar and throne, and the Inquisition. Modern rationalism, dismissing biblical faith as superstition, had led to the regimes of the Jacobins, the Bolsheviks, and the Nazis. Neither classical rationalism, nor genuine faith in a living God would claim political power in its own right. The true constitutional regime, shaped by the wisdom both of revelation and reason, formed the character of the citizens by the free and uncoerced dissemination of opinion.

Notwithstanding the foregoing, Strauss seems on occasion to have written to the contrary. The dialectical confrontation on page 75 of *Natural Right and History* ends with the assertion that "The mere fact that philosophy and revelation cannot refute each other would constitute the refutation of philosophy by revelation." However, in his autobiographical preface he remarks that ". . . Jewish orthodoxy based its claim to superiority to other religions from the beginning on its superior rationality (Deut.4:6)." In the passage in question, Moses tells the children of Israel that if they keep the laws that he has set before them, the nations which shall hear these laws will say "Surely this great nation is a wise and understanding people." In citing this, Strauss seems to impute to the Bible something like the doctrine of the *Meno*, that learning is recollection, and that the recognition of wisdom is a human potentiality common to all nations. The suggestion here, however slender, is that the Bible is a Platonic book, and that reason is the esoteric foundation of revelation. In the Introduction to *The City and Man* (1964), however, his remarks on this theme seem to point to the priority of revelation.

> It is not sufficient for everyone to obey and to listen to the Divine message of the City of Righteousness, the Faithful City. In order to propagate that message among the heathen, nay, in order to understand it as clearly and as fully as is humanly possible, one must also consider to what extent man could discern the outlines of that City if left to himself, to the proper exercise of his own powers. But in our age it is much less urgent to show that political philosophy is the indispensable hand maid of theology than to show that political philosophy is the rightful queen of the social sciences, the sciences of man and human affairs: even the highest lawcourt in the land is more likely to defer to the contentions of social science than to the Ten Commandments as the words of the living God.

Strauss—addressing the "crisis of the West"—says that is not sufficient to "obey and listen to the Divine message of the City of Righteousness, the Faithful City." (The capitals are Strauss's.) But what is not sufficient may nonetheless be necessary. Strauss will undertake to show "to what extent man could discern the outlines of that City if left to himself," i.e., without revelation. The purpose in so doing however is, to repeat, "to propagate that message—viz., the Divine message of the City of Righteousness, the Faithful City"—among the heathen. I do not recall Strauss speaking elsewhere of "heathen." What is most remarkable however is that the City whose outlines are sought by man's unaided powers, and which we want to understand as clearly and fully as is humanly possible, is the Faithful City. Jerusalem and Athens seem to have become one.

This appears to be confirmed by Strauss's saying that it is less urgent—but nonetheless urgent—to show that political philosophy is the indispensable hand-maid of theology. The reason it is less urgent than it otherwise would be is that "even the highest lawcourt in the land is more likely to defer to the contentions of social science than to the Ten Commandments as the words of the living God." Strauss is clearly referring to Warren's opinion for the Court in *Brown v. Board of Education*, the 1954 decision declaring school segregation to be unconstitutional. In that opinion Warren abandoned any attempt to ground his reading of the equal protection clause of the fourteenth amendment on the intent of its framers and ratifiers, preferring instead what he said modern psychology told us was the effect of segregation upon the "minds and hearts" of Negro children. His authority was Kenneth Clark's doll tests, which Thurgood Marshall, the attorney for the NAACP, had brought to his attention. But the aforesaid tests did not actually prove what they were said to prove, and it is unlikely that Warren (or his fellow justices) even knew that they were. Warren seized upon them because they constituted a license to disregard the genuine meaning of the equal protection clause. The "contentions of science" were nothing but a cynical device by which the court could emancipate itself from the restraints of the Constitution. The original meaning of the equal protection clause had been embodied in Justice Harlan's dissenting opinion in *Plessy* (1898), the case that had enshrined "separate but equal" in constitutional law. Harlan had declared that the Constitution was color-blind, and did not recognize different classes of citizens. Harlan's opinion, which should have been the opinion of the Court in *Brown*, was clearly based upon the proposition that all men are created equal. The actual alternative to the "contentions of social science" was therefore the Declaration of Independence, and of the Creator and author of "the laws of nature and of nature's God." To re-establish the authority of political philosophy as the architectonic social science meant therefore to reestablish both the natural and divine foundation of American constitutionalism. Clearly the crisis of the West could not be resolved apart from its biblical foundations interpreted by the kalam of political philosophy.

In the essay "What Is Liberal Education?" Strauss addresses the crisis of the West from the difference between mass democracy and "democracy as originally meant." For Jefferson, democracy was intended to provide more effectually than any other form of government for "a pure selection of [the] natural aristoi into the offices of government." Without liberal education, the natural aristoi have themselves become debased. The liberal education which was the ground and basis of the Founding was supremely expressed in the Declaration of Independence, and in the harmony of reason and revelation, in the support of the moral and political order.

Strauss concludes that essay with something that more nearly approaches a confession of faith, than anything in any other writing of which I am aware. It is an appeal to experience, the experience which accompanies the act of understanding, when we not only understand, but understand that we understand. This "noesis noeseos" is "so high, so pure, so noble an experience that Aristotle could ascribe it to his God." Strauss continued:

> This experience is entirely independent of whether what we understand primarily is pleasing or displeasing, fair or ugly. It leads us to realize that all evils are in a sense necessary if there is to be understanding. It enables us to accept all evils that befall us and which may well break our hearts in the spirit of good citizens of the city of God. By becoming aware of the dignity of the mind, we realize the true ground of the dignity of man and therewith of the goodness of the world, whether we understand it as created or uncreated, which is the home of man because it is the home of the human mind.

We are invited, on the basis of an experience available to man as man, to become "good citizens of the city of God." The realization of the dignity of man is independent of whether we understand the world to be "created or uncreated." Strauss says nothing here of the necessity to choose between these two opinions. The crisis of the West does not require us to make such a choice, and we do not know that Strauss himself ever made it. What it does require is to recognize the authority of the moral order based upon the dignity of man, supported both by reason and revelation. To secure that recognition was, I believe, the essential purpose of Leo Strauss's life and work.

Part Two

Taking Leo Strauss Seriously

Leo Strauss, the Straussians, and the American Regime

Kenneth L. Deutsch

$\mathcal{L}$eo Strauss was one of the most significant refugees from Nazi Germany who arrived in the United States in the 1930's. We are commemorating the centennial of Strauss's birth in 1999. Strauss's intellectual influence on the study of the American regime has been enormous. Since his death in 1973, Strauss has been both revered and reviled. Some see him as a savant for the perplexed leading them out of a contemporary liberalism devoid of purpose and a sense of duty, while others, often acrimoniously, view him as an elitist leader of a "Straussian" cult bent on containing the relativists and nihilists, and questioning contemporary forms of American egalitarianism and democratic practice.

Strauss considered modern liberal democracy to have abandoned the classical meaning of the good life and good society. At the root of modernity is the view that there is nothing independent of humanity which is superior in dignity to human artifice; the design of politics is rooted in human freedom and not divine or natural necessity. Though Strauss respected his modern American haven, he taught that contemporary American liberal democracy was losing its original sense of purpose and entering a modern condition of crisis. He was keenly aware of the alteration of the natural rights tradition in contemporary American law and politics, the pandering of political leaders to public passions, technological domination of the economic and political processes, and growing moral relativism. Compared to all other contemporary available alternatives, the American regime was decent but flawed. The best possible regime in our time is a liberal democratic regime which attempts to balance and disarm political tensions, and is cognizant of its inability to eradicate them.[1] Human beings will never create a society which is free of contradictions. Strauss's friendly criticism of modern American liberal democracy seeks, therefore, to give it a backbone as it struggles to harness the severity of political passions, sustain dialogue and intellectual diversity, and house the philosophic enterprise. Strauss's friendly criticism of American liberal democracy also recognizes that the American regime was rooted in three faiths in tension drawing sustenance from modern natural rights theory, from premodern beliefs in the Judeo-Christian God, and classical republican virtues. His great concern was that since 1950 the American commitment to modern natural right, shorn of strong religious counterbalance, has led to a greater emphasis on relativism and a corresponding loss of a moral compass.

The decay of an earlier American ethos of personal and social responsibility, a decline in moral education and the absence of statesmen capable of reviving a sense of public dedication have made it difficult for the American political process to contend effectively with such problems as delimiting the role of technology in the public and private realms, distinguishing the problems of discrimination in the public and private realms and countering the influence of perfectionist or liberationist ideologies that pose a threat to the conservation of limited government. According to Strauss, "True liberals today have no more pressing duty than to counteract the perverted liberalism which contends 'that just to live, securely and happily, and protected and unregulated, is man's simple but supreme goal' and which forgets quality, excellence or virtue."[2]

Leo Strauss's writings present a number of themes which have profoundly influenced his many students and followers when they consider the health of American liberal democracy. These political themes include: the question of natural right, the significance of the founders' texts and the importance of constitutional form, the seminal role of statesmen, liberal education and liberal democracy, the fecklessness of the American political science profession, religion and the city, and the vocation of the political philosopher in a liberal democratic regime.

THE PROBLEM OF NATURAL RIGHT AND CONSENT

The problem of natural right is an inquiry concerning whether humans have fixed natures that are not subject to fundamental change. For Strauss, though there may be a universally valid hierarchy of ends, there is no universal set of valid rules for action. Natural right is changeable and one must be prepared for extreme, dangerous and complex situations. The human being's attachment to one's own also makes a naturally just regime impossible. Politics requires an appropriate mixture or balance between wisdom and consent. As Strauss puts it, "The political problem consists in reconciling the requirements for wisdom with the requirement for consent."[3] Strauss distinguished the classic view in which wisdom takes precedence over consent from the modern view in which consent takes precedence over wisdom. The perennial challenge of politics is working out the tension between wisdom and consent or justice and law. For Strauss, the political is understood to be more than expediency, deference to decency or public safety. The best approach to politics is to develop a moral sense to the full "experiential amplitude of one's culture/political context."[4] Judgment is moral reasonableness which accepts the irreducible ambiguities and tensions of the human condition especially the tension between our bodies and souls and our own good and the common good. Given the complexities and irreducible ambiguities of the human condition, Strauss was dedicated to keeping alive the quarrels between classical and modern natural right (the Ancients and the Moderns), reason and revelation, and the philosopher and the city. Strauss does not give his followers a "philosophical kit" which enables them to solve all problems. Rather, he equips them with a set of fundamental alternatives challenging them and subsequent generations to explore the morally serious differences and relationships between the tyrant and the statesman, rights and duties, and constitutional form and political exigencies. Whether or not there is cosmic support for rights and justice, Strauss taught that certain actions or decisions are likely to be destructive to those individuals or nations that indulge in them. Strauss's students have engaged in considerable controversy about a number of political questions. Are there truths now, or have they ever been, self-evident in the Declaration of Independence? Is the equality of man one of those self-evident truths? What would be the political consequences of denying the equality of man? Such followers of Strauss as Harvey Mansfield and Harry Jaffa approach with great seriousness the matter of human equality. They also have disagreements as to whether the principle "all men are created equal" is indeed self-evident and the surest foundation for the rule of law.

THE FRAMERS' CONSTITUTIONAL FORM AND THE INTERPRETATION OF TEXTS

It is well known that Strauss taught that each text had to be approached on its own terms. One's own preconceptions must not be imposed on the text. Strauss's followers specializing in the American Constitution emphasize the dignity of the Constitution against contemporary liberal, behavioral, rational choice, and postmodern theorists. George Anastaplo, Ralph Lerner and Walter Berns are excellent examples of Strauss's students who read the texts of the Constitution and the Bill of Rights as if they are great works of political philosophy. As Anastaplo puts it, ". . . there is a sense to the whole of the Constitution that the document can be thought about, part by part as well as in terms of the relations among parts. This thinking about the Constitution—the very insistence that it can be thought about—is critical."[5] Harvey Mansfield insisting on the importance of constitutional form has been concerned with the fact that many political and constitutional commentators display a "willful disillusionment with a government that works." Mansfield claims that "Postmoderns do not as a rule recommend more democracy, claiming it to be a good even in unlimited amount; rather, they attack every obstacle standing in the way of popular will."[6] Because of their defense of the importance (but not absoluteness) of constitutional procedure, Strauss's students of the American constitution have often been referred to as constitutional fundamentalists, or, as Sheldon Wolin unfairly characterized their position, "misplaced biblicism."[7]

Martin Diamond, one of the most sympathetic of Strauss's students to the Framers' texts still understands them as lowering standards (in comparison to classic natural right). The American regime is a political system founded on the pursuit of interest—a "low but solid standard." The American regime is grounded in the first wave of modernity (Hobbes and Locke) and could very well begin to experience the second and third waves of modernity (Rousseau and Nietzsche). Even Diamond, the most committed Straussian to Madisonian teachings, recognized the risk that the regime could become engulfed by "the selfish, the interested, the narrow and the crassly economic."[8]

Other Straussians, though they may identify the American constitutional regime as a best possible one among available alternatives, emphasize the inherent "tensions" in the Constitution—namely the concern of the many for security to pursue private interests and the need of the few to pursue honor and fame. Joseph Cropsey describes the conflict within the American regime—between aspirations for greatness and for self-preservation—as "energetic tension." This "energetic tension" generated by the Founders can be found in the competition between the president and Congress over power.[9] Sometimes this tension produces prosperity and sometimes it produces corruption. The American Constitution, for Mansfield, is founded on both restraints on government and leadership that must keep the people secure. Strauss himself argued that "even good laws are harmful from the fact that they cannot see."[10] He claimed that what we need is responsible rule from leaders and at times "an active forbearance from governing" from the public.[11] To be sure, this position has been vigorously castigated by many scholars such as George Kateb when he refers to the Straussian position as "the authoritarianism of moral elitism" and a threat to democratic legitimacy leading in the end to a form of paternalism.[12]

THE ROLE OF STATESMEN

Strauss wrote a candid letter to Karl Löwith concerning his own political convictions: "I really believe . . . that the perfect political order, as Plato and Aristotle have sketched it, is the perfect political order."[13] The best regime is based on the teaching that human beings are unequal from the point of view of their perfection. The wise are better suited to rule over others. The realization of the best regime depends on the "chance" appearance of princes friendly to philosophy. The modern regime becomes the best regime possible by eliminating chance through a lowering of standards in which there is a compromise between wisdom and unwisdom, tyranny and consent. The best possible regime includes the rule of law under which the state entrusts its administration to "gentlemen." The gentleman is sufficiently wealthy, well-bred and public-spirited to be involved in noble pursuits. The gentleman is "a political reflection or imitation of the wise man."[14]

Strauss distinguishes between two different standards of human excellence—the virtue of the citizen best embodied in the moral excellence of the gentleman (the ruler or founder) and the excellence of the philosopher or the wise man. The outstanding statesman and founder possess practical wisdom, the proper ordering or synthesis of the moral virtues. By following the course of the mean (finding balance or moderation) is to grant each good thing its due whether it concerns the care of the body or the cultivation of the mind. This gentleman, founder or statesman lives by a rational principle signifying some order or hierarchy of goods in promoting the common good. There are no fixed rules in statesmanship; there is practical wisdom. The statesman is concerned with his own good which embraces the good of the community. He facilitates the coordination of the diverse purposes and pursuits of private persons. The unity or order that is achieved contains the mark of his own character. Strauss observes that the authors of *The Federalist Papers* clearly express some of these teachings, most especially "that diversity and inequality in the faculties of men which shows itself in the acquisition of property" (Strauss's "summary" of Madison's position). He also presents a rather positive view of Hamilton's teachings in *Federalist* #35. In a modern republic, says Strauss, Hamilton is quite right to teach that the best we can expect is an electorate not depraved who will elect as its representatives—landlords, merchants and members of the learned professions "'who possess most wisdom to discern, and most virtue to pursue, the common good of society,' or those who are most outstanding by 'merits and talents,' by 'ability and virtue.'"[15]

According to Thomas Pangle, Publius does project the need for statesman devoted to virtue and the common good. "Like Hume and Machiavelli before him, Hamilton dares to declare openly what the classical theorists only wondered about with caution: The noblest men, those who are presumably most familiar with the beauty of the moral virtues, are not ruled by the love of those virtues, but by the love of the reward they may bring."[16] Service in the three branches of government, especially the presidency, would provide opportunities for the "gentleman" to gain reputations for wisdom, patriotism and the love of justice.

Harry Jaffa also places great emphasis on the salutary role statesman can play in choosing to present what is "high" in American life such as Lincoln's teachings and rhetoric about the Declaration of Independence. Jaffa's presentation of Lincoln as a great statesman is an example of the tension between nature and convention in statesmanship—in which "the highest ambition can be concerned only in the highest service, that egotism and altruism ultimately coincide in that consciousness of superiority which is superiority in the ability to benefit others." The Declaration of Independence, to Lincoln, prescribed equality and consent of the governed obligating a statesman to include popular opinion in his political calculus—a principle grounded "in that consciousness of freedom which is also a consciousness of self-imposed restraints". Statesmanship, for Jaffa, at its profoundest "is the vindication of the people's cause on the highest grounds which had hitherto been claimed for aristocratic forms."[17]

THE ROLE OF LIBERAL EDUCATION

Leo Strauss observed that "the classics had no delusions about a genuine aristocracy's ever becoming actual."[18] They would be content with a regime in which the gentlemen share power with the people thereby empowering the people to elect the magistrates and the council from among the gentlemen and holding them accountable for their actions at the end of their term of office.[19] He argued that the responsibility of the people is "the most obvious crux of modern republicanism." Those called upon to be the people's representatives are to be prepared by a liberal education in "good breeding."[20] Strauss claimed that "Our present predicament appears to be caused by the decay of religious education of the people and the decay of liberal education of the representatives of the people."[21] Liberal education gives those who are receptive and willing to hear some examples of human greatness to found an "aristocracy within democratic mass society" by contributing qualities of dedication, of concentration, of breadth, and depth to democratic practice.[22] Strauss raises the possibility that the liberally educated could be heard in the marketplace.

Strauss is certainly very well known for his dauntless and spirited defense of the great books as central to liberal education. The great books were written by those who are no longer pupils—the greatest minds. In liberal education these great books are to be studied "with the proper care." A great book is not simply part of a canon. These books challenge us to pursue an adventure in self-discovery and an inquiry concerning the fundamental alternatives. A serious study of the great books, then, enables us to engage in a conversation and in disagreements in which we become aware of the inclinations toward these alternatives and the opposing positions. A liberally educated person displays both Socratic ignorance and an openness to the possibility of truth. A liberal education cannot provide a simple defense of natural right or refutation of historicism. For Strauss, it may be necessary to live in a tension between "natural right" and "history" in which we neither adopt natural right or the opinion that historical fate has superseded it. Rather, liberal education can contribute greatly to a person's struggle toward whatever knowledge that would come by transcending these alternatives. Natural right is a problem, not a doctrine.[23] Strauss calls upon others to hear themselves recreate in themselves this conversation or dialogue that is often suppressed in modern liberal democracies.

Allan Bloom and Thomas Pangle have applied and extended Strauss's teachings on the role liberal education can play in providing some "philosophic guidance" for thoughtful citizens of American democracy and "opening" the American mind. Bloom and Pangle inquire about the natural hierarchy of the soul and the description of the soul's pursuits by the institutions and culture of contemporary liberal democracy. Pangle, following Strauss, believes that "What most threatens us ... is not unsettling skepticism, or revolutionary discord, or the excesses of passionate diversity, but the deadening conformism to a bloodless and philistine relativism that saps the will and the capacity to defend or define any principled basis of life."[24] The classical regime of Plato and Aristotle is considered impracticable by the Straussians; a small society ruled by the landed gentry is no longer feasible once technology, advanced weaponry, and acquisitiveness have been unleashed. Given that liberal democracy is the only decent regime "viable in our age," it would be clearly imprudent to try to return to premodern conditions. Liberal democracy in giving freedom to all is giving freedom to philosophers. Liberal democracy, with its original commitment to the rule of law, freedom of inquiry and equal opportunity (in opposition to unjust privileges), must be now defended against the deadening conformism of mass culture, technical education producing "narrow and unprincipled efficiency," "specialists without spirit" attempting to satisfy the desires of "voluptuaries without heart." Strauss exhorted his students and others who have been influenced by him to be nuanced defenders of liberal democracy: "We are not permitted to be flatterers of democracy precisely because we are friends and allies of liberal democracy."[25] He urged them to use the freedom that exists in American liberal democracy to create "outposts" dedicated to excellence and liberal education.[26]

Strauss and his followers look upon liberal education as "the ladder by which we try to ascend from mass democracy to democracy as originally meant."[27] We judge the present day ills of American democracy by what democracy was "meant to be." According to Strauss, "democracy was meant to be an aristocracy that has broadened into a universal aristocracy." Even though Strauss can foresee the broadening of the aristocracy under proper conditions, he does not view equality of opportunity as mandating equal conditions; liberal education "will always remain the obligation and the privilege of a minority." In the final analysis, Strauss's understanding of the principles of classical political philosophy obligates us to take the view that "wisdom cannot be separated from moderation and hence to understand that wisdom requires unhesitating loyalty to a decent constitution even to the cause of constitutionalism."[28] We need to accommodate our need for a constitutional democracy with the necessity to establish outposts of excellence in order that we be protected from the twin dangers of visionary expectations from politics and unmanly contempt for politics.[29]

A fair characterization of Strauss's teachings on American democracy can be found in the following remarks of Horst Mewes:

> We have, I think gotten the overall impression that he [Strauss] is not a genuine democrat. I think ... that Strauss represented a type, and that is the Federalist's democratic republic. The type of democracy that is essentially based on a representative republic governed by an elected, natural aristocracy of merit. Now I regard that to be a genuine type of democracy in the self-understanding of the founders. Whether it is or not, he is providing the most profound theory at the

moment that is available for that type of democracy. Now, the fact that this is an extremely unpopular type of democratic theory right now is more than obvious. It is quite clearly a perfectionist theory as it provides a theory of human excellence.[30]

Perhaps we should change Mewes' word "perfectionist" for the word meritocratic in his characterization of Strauss's "democratic" politics.

THE FECKLESSNESS OF THE AMERICAN POLITICAL SCIENCE PROFESSION

Strauss began his career in the United States when the behavioral revolution in political science was in the ascendancy. His publications such as *Natural Right and History* and *Essays on the Scientific Study of Politics* (written in conjunction with a number of his students) were to become part of a counterrevolution seeking the renewal of interest in the pursuit of political philosophy. During the 1950's most political scientists were writing about the death of political philosophy or that political philosophy should be consigned to the doghouse.

Strauss's spirited rejection of modern political science is related to his view of the state of contemporary American democracy: "There exists a whole science . . . political science—which has so to speak no other theme than the contrast between the original concept of democracy, or what one may call the ideal of democracy, and democracy as it is."[31] Strauss's critique of behavioral political science centered on the inability of its proponents to recognize the difference between the ideal of democracy and democracy as it is. For that matter, they could not make a principled distinction between liberal democracy and tyranny.

Modern "value-free" political science has unreflectively accepted historicism and moral relativism in its denial of the human capacity to achieve objective knowledge about political things in a world devoid of moral purpose and moral responsibility. The historicist position reduces the study of political things to reflexes of the historical process. Any study of political things is simply based on social conditions, or the political state of affairs and is only relevant to a particular time, place or circumstance. For Strauss, this modern behavioral persuasion reduced human reasoning to a reflex of social and psychic structure.

Strauss was defiant in his claim that American political science was so lacking in understanding that it was unable to recognize the worst tyrannies for what they were: "when we were brought face to face with tyranny—with a kind of tyranny that surpassed the boldest imagination of the most powerful thinkers of the past— our political science failed to recognize it."[32] Modern political science finds itself unable to "speak of tyranny with the same confidence with which medicine speaks, for example, of cancer" and it "cannot understand social phenomena as what they are. It is therefore not scientific."[33]

A "value-free" political science, declaring such judgments methodologically out of bounds, simply seeking to describe political situations, is feckless. The human world cannot be understood with "value-free" categories. Strauss observed that:

> Political things are by their nature subject to approval or disapproval, to choice and rejection, to praise and blame. It is of their essence not to be neutral but to raise a claim to men's obedience, allegiance, decision, or judgment. One does not understand them as what they are, as political things, if one does not take seriously their explicit or implicit claims to be judged in terms of goodness or badness, or of justice, i.e., if one does not measure them by some standard of goodness or justice. To judge soundly one must know the true standards. If political philosophy wishes to do justice to its subject matter, it must strive for genuine knowledge of these standards.[34]

Genuine political science is political philosophy; it is the quest to replace opinion with knowledge of the nature of political things. Thomas Pangle states that this quest does not mean that the scientific analysis of political data should be relegated to the sidelines; "but that study must understand itself to be subordinate to or under the guidance of and in service to a higher study, a civic art or true science of politics devoted to the pursuit of knowledge of justice, or the common good, of virtuous citizenship and far-sighted statesmanship."[35]

RELIGION AND THE CITY

Strauss taught that political atheism is a modern phenomenon which is simply incompatible with a stable and just order. When trust exists in a providential order to which one's conduct conforms, the dignity of moral obligations is enhanced and duty is raised to the level of aspiration. Belief in the immortality of the soul along with eternal awards and punishments acts as a powerful support for morality. The law possesses a higher dignity if the universe is of divine origin. No other source of "modes and orders" could command such a great measure of assent and contribute to the stability of political life.[36]

Many students of Strauss claim there is a serious weakness in the American regime in its failure to provide for virtue. It "damps down" the highest aspirations of human beings, whether philosophic or religious. As Herbert Storing put it, "they [the Framers] took for granted a certain kind of public-spirited leadership, so they took for granted the republican genius of the people; but that cannot prudently be taken for granted."[37] Paul Eidelberg recognizes that ". . . the Constitution does not provide for the education of the rulers. And therein is the paramount failure of the Founding Fathers."[38] Wilmoore Kendall decries the fact that the Constitution fails to answer the question how the people will be kept virtuous thereby leaving the American polity unarmed before the threat of moral relativism.[39]

Martin Diamond ponders the question of how might Aristotle rank America. Is it a genuine political community with its own moral foundation nurturing in its citizens certain ethical excellences of what is advantageous and just or is it an association or place for the sake of compacts and trade? Or does America possess a unique ethos of ethics and politics?[40] Diamond readily admits that the Framers' new constitutional order removed the task of character formation from its "previously preeminent place" on the agenda of public life and perhaps above all they depoliticized religion relegating it to private discretion. The question Diamond and many other Straussians have asked Americans to consider is the following: is the *novo ordo seclorum* with its counterpoised use of ambitious interest as the principal security for the pubic good and its emancipation of acquisitiveness going to permit those with "better motives" to be able to attain their full natural height? Strauss's own repeated answer was to renew the religious education of the people and the liberal education of the representatives of the people in order to moderate the excesses of American liberal democracy with "better motives" and to consider "thought of better or worse."

These concerns have challenged a number of Strauss's students to become scholars of the First Amendment especially the religion clauses. These scholars generally present the case for nonpreferential support of religion. They concentrate on the debates about the ratification of the First Amendment claiming that interpretation of the religion clauses should be guided by the majority consensus of those supporting religion on a nonpreferential basis rather than on Jefferson and Madison who tend to be strict separationists. Much attention is given to Article III of the Northwest Ordinance which states that, "Religion, morality and knowledge being necessary to good government and the happiness of mankind, schools and other means of education shall forever be encouraged." Nonpreferential support for religion fosters in the citizenry self-restraint, social responsibility, reverence for the old, and an ennobling sense of self-restraining awe. The public practice of those virtues is particularly important for a society based on "ordered liberty."[41]

An example of a Straussian nonpreferentialist view can be found in the work of George Anastaplo. Anastaplo is particularly concerned about the health of church-sponsored schools. Anastaplo advances the view that "considerable financial help will be needed if these schools are to continue to perform the services for the entire community they do. Costs are going up, especially as expenditures for teachers' salaries and for equipment have to increase; tuition can hardly be expected to keep up with these costs."[42] Defending religious education for inner-city youths is an especially significant community benefit. Anastaplo argues that consideration should be given to "the Roman Catholic parochial schools in our inner cities, schools in which the student body can again and again be made up primarily of Southern Baptists. Poor minority students in inner-city parishes are subsidized by middle-class white parishes in the suburbs. How long can this be expected to continue? What may government properly do to help the considerable variety of sects that help make our lives civilized? It is short-sighted to try to provide for a community without being sensitive to the religious facets of most enduring enterprises."[43] Most Straussians consider the nonpreferential collaboration between "church and state" to be part of prudent statesmanship and sensible constitutional interpretation.

THE PHILOSOPHER AND THE AMERICAN CITY

Strauss teaches that there is a permanent and radical disproportion between philosophy and politics; there is always a "fundamental tension between the requirements of philosophy and the requirements of political society."[44] Political systems are closed—"the element of society is opinion."[45] In his autobiographical "A Giving of Accounts," Strauss tells us that "I arrived at a conclusion that I can state in the form of syllogism: Philosophy is the attempt to replace opinion by knowledge; but opinion is the element of the city, hence philosophy is subversive, hence the philosophers must unite in such a way that they will improve rather than subvert the city. In other words the virtue of the philosopher's thought is a certain kind of *mania* while the virtue of the philosopher's public speech is *sophrosyne*. Philosophy is as such transpolitical, trans-religious, trans-moral, but the city is and ought to be moral and religious."[46]

Philosophy dissolves opinion, the element in which society breathes, and thus "endangers" society. Genuine philosophy "is animated by the spirit of social responsibility."[47] It recognizes that not all truths are harmless, certain truths "must remain the preserve of a small minority . . ."[48] A cautious and discrete manner of writing and public speech is intended "to lead potential philosophers to philosophy, both by training them and by liberating them from the charms which obstruct the philosophic effort, as well as to prevent the access of philosophy to those who are not fit for it."[49]

There can only be closed societies, that is states "with their distinctive perspectives and foundations."[50] The philosopher seeks to question and perhaps even destroy those perspectives and foundations by demonstrating that the laws of the city based on those perspectives are merely authoritative opinion or agreements that are not necessarily grounded in nature. The philosopher's presence in the city is therefore problematic; it may even be dangerous. The true philosopher must be engaged, as we discussed above, in a politics of moderation—a politics concerned with securing the political conditions necessary for his own survival and for the philosophic life. Liberal democracy is the feasible regime best suited to provide those conditions which will permit the defense of philosophy. Liberal democracy can be ennobled by a true philosophy that increases the number of individuals who are most lucidly alive to fundamental and comprehensive problems and does no harm. But doing no harm is not quite good enough. Victor Gourevitch puts Strauss's position this way:

The philosopher will wish to participate in some way in the affairs of his city because, while agreeing with Strauss that a good man will not be a good citizen in a bad city, he also agrees with Socrates in holding that such a man is not as truly good as the good or excellent man who is a good citizen in a good city. He will then regard political action on behalf of his city and political action on behalf of his own good or excellence as converging on one and the same goal.[51]

For Strauss, the relationship between the philosopher and the city includes the tension between the philosophic enterprise and the care of the city. How does the Straussian political philosopher deal then with the question of American patriotism?

Strauss's own teachings concerning patriotism and the American regime are as follows:

The United States may be said to be the only country in the world which was founded in explicit opposition to Machiavellian principles. According to Machiavelli, the founder of the most renowned commonwealth of the world was a fratricide: the foundation of political greatness is necessarily laid to crime. If we can believe Thomas Paine, all governments of the Old World have an origin of this description; their origin was conquest and tyranny. But the Independence of America [was] accompanied by a Revolution on the principles and practices of Governments: "the foundation of the United States was laid in freedom and justice, Government founded on a moral theory, on a system of universal peace, on the indefeasible hereditary Rights of Man, is now revolving from west to east by a stronger impulse than the Government of the sword revolved from east to west." This judgment is far from being obsolete. While freedom is no longer a preserve of the United States, the United States is now the bulwark of freedom. A contemporary tyranny has its roots in Machiavelli's thought, in the Machiavellian principle that the good end justifies every means. At least to the extent that the American reality is inseparable from the American aspiration, one cannot understand Americanism without understanding Machiavellianism which is its opposite.[52]

Strauss the political philosopher acknowledges the conflict between the American aspiration and the American reality. For him, Machiavelli "would not hesitate to suggest a mischievous interpretation of the Louisiana Purchase and of the fate of the Red Indians."[53] Strauss's political analysis of the American founding accommodates the existence of the Framers' moral theory, the conflict between aspirations and realities, and the desire of Americans to re-assert the moral theory or ideals of their society against its inevitable disappointments or mistakes.

How do the followers of Strauss react to and develop Strauss's political analysis of the American founding and American realities? What should be the proper approach to American patriotism?

Here we find significant differences between the Straussians. Thomas Pangle argues that "our American tradition itself, and our authentic attachment to that tradition, compels us to re-enact within ourselves far-reaching debates over the most fundamental principles of political right."[54] Proper American patriotism, for Pangle, is a great challenge to the minds of citizens with no moral tests concerning "un-Americanism." Quoting Leo Strauss in *Natural Right and History*, Pangle argues that the proper foundations of patriotism must avoid "fanatical obscurantism."[55] Those who seek to create "thin poetry" and "compromised scholarship" are creating myths. "Those who seek to maintain the myth are compelled to obscure, with feverish zeal, the true roots of the nation. But their task is hopeless; the obscurantist fever intensifies; and from the fever spreads the germ of nihilism.[56]

Pangle identifies Harry Jaffa and a number of his followers as purveyors of "thin poetry" and compromised scholarship by creating "the myth of America-as-heir-to classical philosophy." Pangle is quite critical of Charles Kesler, one of those Jaffa followers, who attacks those who interpret America in the light of John Locke and the modern natural rights tradition as being "un-American," thereby "running down" the country. Pangle asks rather provocatively whether those who subscribe to the Jaffa position approach the debate about ancient and modern influences on the American regime "as if it were a morality play, a tale of a fight between the forces of good and the forces of evil." As Pangle puts it, "If—God forbid—Locke and his great [modern] predecessors were predominant sources of American principles, it would follow that American principles are 'base'. It is as if to step off the pedestal of Aristotle to sink irretrievably into muck."[57] Pangle rejects the Jaffa call to a "patriotism that claims to find in our national tradition the fulfillment of every high standard proposed by the theological and philosophical wisdom of the ages."[58] Such a call is untrue to our tradition, and it will "earn the distrust rather than the allegiance of America's best youth."[59]

Harry Jaffa takes strong umbrage at being "denounced as the deceptive purveyor of 'a new mythic Americanism' designed to subvert the truth about our origins as a nation."[60] Jaffa believes that he has an answer to explain the denunciation he has experienced, namely "I dared to contradict the assertion of Walter Berns (the doyen of Pangle's school) that the Founding Fathers were not Christian. The issue reduced to its simplest form, is this: Pangle and Walter Berns are convinced that the thought of the Founding Fathers (and Lincoln as well) is to be derived almost wholly from the thought of John Locke. But the John Locke they recognize is not the one who quoted Hooker and who led—or misled—his readers into thinking that his doctrines were well within the framework of traditional moral philosophy and moral theology. Their Locke is the one who, in the immortal words of Joseph Sobran, 'gave his tongue to Hooker and his heart to Hobbes.'"[61]

Jaffa rejects the notion that all the Framers were disciples of a Hobbesian Locke thereby subscribing to atheism. Jaffa claims that "Pangle and Berns insist that Hobbes was an atheist, and Locke a Hobbesian, therefore the American Revolution was atheistic in its intention as the Bolshevik Revolution."[62] Jaffa criticizes Berns for claiming natural rights doctrine is incompatible with Christian doctrine as understood by modern political thinkers and the Founders. Jaffa rejects the notion that Madison, Jefferson, and Washington were enemies of revealed religion creating in its place a hedonist atheist and materialist political order. Contrary to Berns, Jaffa argues that Washington et al. were not wearing "masks of piety over the sneer of contempt."[63]

Jaffa quotes Washington directly, who at the successful conclusion of the Revolution, declared that the greatest blessing we received was "the pure and benign light of revelation." When laying his sword, Washington delivered the nation into the promised land of freedom, making it his "earnest prayer that God would have [us] . . . in His holy protection . . . and that he would most graciously be pleased to dispose us all to do justice, to love mercy, and to demean ourselves with that charity, humility and pacific temper of mind which were the characteristics of the Divine Author of our blessed religion, and without a humble imitation of Whose example we can never hope to be a happy nation."[64]

Jaffa completes his rejection of the Pangle school's teachings by stating that "the Founding Fathers had their own purposes: They took from Locke what they wanted, and they interpreted what they took in the light of a freedom—loving, but also a moral and God-fearing people. Materialism, atheism and hedonism although they have certainly become part of our culture—are no part of what Abraham Lincoln called 'our ancient faith.'"[65] The "essential elements in American patriotism" are to be found in what Washington spoke of in his Inaugural Address as "the rules of order and right which Heaven itself has ordained."

As the above discussion of Pangle's and Jaffa's positions clearly shows, they are divided not only on the question of "true patriotism," but also on the more fundamental issues of the nature and purpose of the American founding as well as the import of Leo Strauss's teachings for understanding political philosophers and statesmen. We must still conclude that there is considerable consensus among the Straussians concerning Strauss's legacy as they seek to comprehend the complexities of the American founding, the crisis of contemporary liberal democracy, the quarrel between ancient and modern republicanism, the problem of natural right, the centrality of religious education and liberal education, and the crucial importance of political philosophy within the discipline of American political science. We must also conclude that for good or ill serious fissures have emerged among Strauss's followers which have produced a considerable amount of heat as well as light. This book will explore the consensus as well as the heat and the light.

Charles Larmore in his book *The Morals of Modernity* represents many mistaken critics of Strauss when he concludes his chapter on Strauss with this observation: "Strauss was a thinker of great learning and conviction, but his vision, historical and philosophical, was fundamentally flawed. The school of thought he founded, and which shows no sign of extinction, draws its inspiration, of course, more directly from the historical than the philosophical component of his thought. . . . No doubt, Strauss will continue to have faithful followers as long as the vogue of modernity bashing persists. They, too, will promise much and deliver little."[66] This book on Strauss's influence on the study of American politics will challenge whether Larmore's conclusions about Strauss and his followers are valid. Perhaps it is more sensible to approach

Strauss and his followers as *incontournable* (to cite George Steiner's use of this French term)—they are a presence and a provocation which one cannot avoid or circumvent in the study of the American regime.

NOTES

1. Leo Strauss, "Political Philosophy and the Crisis of Our Time," in *The Post-Behavioral Era: Perspectives on Political Science*, George J. Graham Jr. and George W. Carey (eds.) (New York: David McKay Co. Inc., 1972), pp. 22–23.

2. Leo Strauss, *Liberalism Ancient and Modern* (Foreword by Allan Bloom) (Ithaca: Cornell University Press, 1989), pp. 29, 64.

3. Leo Strauss, *Natural Right and History* (Chicago: University of Chicago Press, 1953), p. 141.

4. Peter C. Emberley, "Leo Strauss: Machiavellian or Moralist," *The Vital Nexus*, vol. 1, no. 1, p. 57.

5. Cited in John A. Murley, "Our Character Is Our Fate: The Constitutionalism of George Anastaplo," *The Political Science Reviewer*, vol. xvi, p. 50.

6. Harvey Mansfield, *America's Constitutional Soul* (Baltimore: Johns Hopkins University Press, 1991), pp. ix–x.

7. Sheldon Wolin, *The Presence of the Past* (Baltimore: John Hopkins University Press, 1989), p. 3.

8. Martin Diamond, "Ethics and Politics: The American Way," in *The Moral Foundations of the American Republic*, Robert H. Horowitz (ed.), 3rd edition (Charlottesville: University Press of America, 1986), p. 95.

9. Robert Devigne, "Strauss and 'Straussianism': From Ancient to Modern Liberalism," (unpublished paper), p. 21.

10. Leo Strauss, *On Tyranny* (Ithaca: Cornell University Press, 1983), p. 76.

11. Harvey Mansfield, *Taming the Prince* (New York: Free Press, 1989), pp. 289–290.

12. George Kateb, "On the Legitimization Crisis," *Social Research* (Winter, 1979), pp. 704–705.

13. Letter to Karl Löwith, 18 August 1946) "Correspondence Concerning Modernity: Karl Löwith and Leo Strauss," *Independent Journal of Philosophy*, vol. 4 (1983), p. 107.

14. Op. cit., *Natural Right and History*, p. 142.

15. Op cit., *Liberalism Ancient and Modern*, p. 16.

16. Thomas Pangle, *The Spirit of Modern Republicanism: The Moral Vision of the Founders and the Philosophy of John Locke* (Chicago: University of Chicago Press, 1988), p. 110.

17. Quotations cited in Thomas S. Silver and Peter W. Schramm (eds.), *Natural Right and Political Right: Essays in Honor of Harry V. Jaffa* (Durham: Carolina Academic Press, 1984), pp. 6–7.

18. Op cit., *Liberalism Ancient and Modern*, p. 15.

19. Ibid., p. 15.

20. Ibid., pp. 15–16.

21. Ibid.

22. Ibid., p. 5.

23. Op cit., *Natural Rights and History*. See the excellent discussion of these matters by Timothy Fuller, "Reflections on Leo Strauss and America," in *Hannah Arendt and Leo Strauss:*

German Émigrés and American Political Thought After WWII, Peter Graf Kielmansegg, et al. (eds.) (Cambridge: Cambridge University Press, 1995), pp. 72–76.

24. Thomas Pangle, *Ennobling of Democracy* (Baltimore: Johns Hopkins University Press, 1992), p. 213.

25. Op. cit., *Liberalism Ancient and Modern*, p. 24.

26. Ibid.

27. Ibid., p. 5.

28. Ibid., p. 24.

29. Ibid.

30. Op cit., Kielmansegg, et al., p. 189.

31. Op. cit., *Liberalism Ancient and Modern*, p. 5.

32. Cited in Leo Strauss, *On Tyranny*, Victor Gourevitch and Michael S. Roth (eds.) (New York: Free Press, 1991), p. x.

33. Ibid., p. 177.

34. Op. cit., *What is Political Philosophy?*, p. 12.

35. Op. cit., *Ennobling of Democracy*, p. 203.

36. Op. cit., *What is Political Philosophy?*, p. 229, and *Natural Right and History*, pp. 152–154.

37. Herbert Storing, *What the Anti-Federalists Were For* (Chicago: University of Chicago Press, 1981), p. 73.

38. Paul Eidelberg, *The Philosophy of the American Constitution* (New York: Free Press, 1968), pp. 248–249.

39. Willmoore Kendall, *Contra Mundum*, N. Kendall (ed.) (New Rochelle: Arlington House, 1971), pp. 399–402.

40. Op. cit., Diamond, p. 343.

41. See the excellent essay by Thomas Lindsay, "Religion and the Founders' Intentions," in *The American Experiment: Essays on the Theory and Practice of Liberty*, Peter Augustine Lawler and Robert Martin Schaefer (eds.) (Lanham, Md.: Rowman & Littlefield Pub., 1994), pp. 127–130.

42. George Anastaplo, *The American Moralist: On Law, Ethics and Government* (Athens: Ohio University Press, 1991), p. 451.

43. Ibid., pp. 451–452.

44. Op. cit., *What is Political Philosophy?*, p. 229.

45. Op. cit., *Natural Right and History*.

46. Leo Strauss, "A Giving of Accounts," *The College*, vol. 22, no. 1 (April 1970), p. 4.

47. Op. cit., *On Tyranny* (Cornell edition), p. 26.

48. Op. cit., *What is Political Philosophy?*, p. 222.

49. Op. cit., *On Tyranny* (Cornell edition), p. 26.

50. Leo Strauss, "An Unspoken Dialogue," *Interpretation*, vol. 7 (September 1978), p. 2.

51. Victor Gourevitch, "Philosophy and Politics I–II," *Review of Metaphysics*, vol. 22 (1968), pp. 312–313.

52. Leo Strauss, *Thoughts on Machiavelli* (Chicago: University of Chicago Press, 1959), pp. 13–14.

53. Ibid., p. 14.

54. Thomas Pangle, "Patriotism American Style," *National Review* (Nov. 29, 1985), p. 31.

55. Ibid., p. 32.

56. Ibid.

57. Ibid.

58. Ibid., p. 34.
59. Ibid.
60. Ibid.
61. Ibid., p. 36.
62. Ibid.
63. Ibid.
64. Cited in ibid.
65. Ibid.
66. Charles Larmore, *The Morals of Modernity* (Cambridge: Cambridge University Press, 1996), p. 76.

· *6* ·

Strauss on Our Minds

Hadley Arkes

$\mathcal{H}$e was a small man, with a small voice; in fact, he had to be fitted with a small microphone, and a cord draped around his neck, so that his voice could be heard from the well of the large lecture room by students gathered about him in a semi-circle. His former students, and now colleagues, Herbert Storing and Joseph Cropsey, seemed to be cast as gentle, solicitous giants, as they towered over him, helping to fit him with the cord and microphone. He would be attached then to a tape recorder, which would take down everything said in the next hour and a half, stretching into three hours. In fussing over him, taking care of him, Storing and Cropsey would look like nothing so much as sons. Every gesture implied a reverence for the father they were attending, who was not of course adept at handling mechanical things, like microphones. The one device he would handle, however, was his cigarette holder. He would fix the cigarette in the holder, and occasionally he would pause in his exploration of a text as he took a long draw on the mouth-piece. The interruption seemed to mark a deeper pause, to prolong his meditation on the passage in the text, and so it worked, overall, to enhance the effect. It also introduced accents of silence, set off against that slight voice, from the small frame, moving slowly, in a talmudic style, line by line, almost word by word, concentrat-ing his learning for the sake of extracting, from the text, every shade of meaning and intention.

That was how Leo Strauss appeared on the first day I saw him, at the University of Chicago. I was 22, a first-year graduate student, and he was a legend to be fathomed. One of the first puzzles to be pondered, though, was the question of how this small, unprepossessing man, should set off such large passions. How did he draw to himself this gathering of students of all ages, with people in their fifties, with a handful of Catholic priests, along with the expected crowd of smart, aggres-sive Jewish students in their twenties? And quite apart from the people who were drawn to him, why did he arouse such fierce hatred in the academy?

These scenes, and these questions, came flashing back just a couple of years ago when Strauss had suddenly become the target of a political attack, quite out of scale, on the part of a young editorial writer in the *New York Times*. What triggered the attack was an event that was taken, by liberals, as a political earthquake: In November 1994, the Republicans had won control of the House of Representatives for the first time since 1952, and Eisenhower's first landslide. In this extraordinary happening, not a single Republican incumbent had lost. Walter Dean Burnham, writing in the *Wall Street Journal*, had found, in this remarkable turn, the marks of a "critical election" and the possible emergence, finally, of a Republican majority.[1] That prospect, delivered with a jolt, seemed to concentrate the minds of many liberals—and send others off into flights of recrimination, flaring out into theories ever more inventive and bizarre. And so, the young writer in the *Times* sought to account for the deeper influences that were suddenly fueling political conservativism in our time; and in the throes of his inspiration, he made his way, of all things, to Leo Strauss. Strauss had hardly been a household word; he was a political philosopher known mainly in rather refined circles in the academy, and he had been dead for 21 years. Yet, he was now tagged as the evil genius behind the resurgence of American conservatism.

As far as I can recall, Strauss had never recommended any measure of public policy or sought to recruit the sentiments of his audience to the side of any faction or cause in the conflict of the political parties. But there was, no doubt, a conservative teaching, which manifested itself in a following that became, over the years, more and more conservative politically. The connection was enough apparently for this young writer to extrapolate, and draw out implications that were even more remarkable. Strauss was caricatured as "unapologetically elitist and anti-democratic," as a philosopher hostile to the "Enlightenment presumption that all men are created equal." He was described as deeply resistant to all change, a man who regarded "the status quo as an expression of divine will."[2] Strauss seemed to be charged with responsibility for every retrograde sentiment that liberals attach to the new, conservative militance. There were intimations that Strauss was the inspiration for the darker messages contained in the controversial book by Charles Murray and Richard Herrnstein, *The Bell Curve*, and as Michael Uhlmann remarked, in a commentary on this outburst, it was hard to see "how Strauss managed to avoid responsibiity for [the] baseball strike." The most bizarre criticism of all surely had to be the attack on Strauss for being an enemy of the Declaration of Independence. Strauss's most important book, *Natural Right and History*, begins with the Declaration, precisely because the Declaration reflected an older tradition that spoke seriously of moral "truths" grounded in the nature of human beings. Those truths promised then to endure in all times and places, where human nature remained the same, and human things could still be distinguished from the things that were subhuman and superhuman. For Strauss, the Declaration marked an understanding, on the part of the American Founders, that connected them to the classics and to the biblical tradition.

These things would be known instantly to anyone who had the remotest acquaintance with the writings of Strauss and his students. But the writer in the

Times had been liberated from any encumbrances of that kind. That detachment seemed to equip him now to render a more disinterested public service by sounding the alarm over Strauss.

But why a need to sound the alarm, more than 20 years after the death of Strauss? The most gifted students of Strauss's students, his academic grandchildren, have now been blocked out of the most prestigious universities, by a system of political screening as forbidding as any blacklist, and far more effective. Many of them, blocked from the academy, turned instead to the law or journalism. Some found refuge in the government, where they had the chance to write and sustain their interests while working as staffers for Republicans in Congress. The influence of Strauss then in the academy has never seemed to be at lower ebb. And yet, what sets off the alarms now is that Strauss and his followers have affected the understanding, and the furnishings of mind, of the conservatives who have been taking power. There have been students of Straussians, like William Kristol, or Paul Wolfowitz (in the State Department), or men who had themselves studied with Strauss, like Michael Uhlmann (counsellor to President Reagan) or Angelo Codevilla (in the Senate committee on Intelligence) who have put their impress on policy through their posts in the government. And then there are others, like Clarence Thomas, who have studied political theory with Straussian friends.

But then there is the deeper problem, which dare not speak its name: The Straussians may supply a direction to Republican leaders, precisely because the teachings of Strauss are far more in accord with the sentiments of that broad public which has been bringing forth now a conservative majority. Strauss recognized, with the classics, that the "multitude," the people at large, are not philosophers. But Strauss appreciated Machiavelli's sense that the people at large would be conservative in their reflexes. They would have an attachment to their own, to the things that were familiar and ancestral, and at the same time most people, anchored in the world, are not moral relativists. Beyond that, the moral sentiments of the public are given a further support from the fact that most Americans are religious. Whose teachings then are the American people likely to find more resonant with their own: the teachings of Strauss, or the doctrines of those liberals and postmodernists in the academy, who hold that God is dead, that there is no "nature" or truths about nature, including the nature that distinguishes men from women, and sexuality from homosexuality?

Hence the irony that may function now as political camouflage: No one is more contemptuous of the public, of its intelligence, its piety, its moral and political reflexes, than the liberals now dominant in the academy. Liberal critics accuse Strauss of the heresy of elitism, of aversion to the multitude, and yet Straussians would be far more likely than their liberal adversaries to affirm William Buckley's maxim: Straussians *know* that they would rather be ruled by the first two hundred names in the Boston telephone directory than by the Faculty of Harvard.

But there, in brief, was everything summarized. Strauss continued to elicit the hatred of the Left because he was the preeminent figure who had stood against the currents of moral relativism that had taken hold of the Left—and diverted the Left from the moral grounds of its own liberalism. The American Founders and Lincoln could vindicate the cause of freedom because they thought that the case for human freedom was anchored in a moral truth. The Left in American politics continued to proclaim the cause of liberation and human rights, but it no longer summoned the conviction that it could speak, seriously, of "nature," of "truths," and therefore of "rights" that were truly rightful.

Harry Jaffa was one of Strauss's first students in America, and one of the most devoted to his memory and his mission. In offering a summary account of that mission, he has written that Strauss sought to restore both reason and revelation against the tendency of modern science to deny them both. Against the insistence of social science that moral propositions cannot be knowable in the way that scientific propositions are—that they cannot be measured for their truth or falsity—Strauss sought to restore the conviction that we can indeed speak of moral truths, that we can have rational knowledge of right and wrong. And against that tendency in modernity to proclaim that God was dead, Strauss sought to reassert the tradition of revelation. There were two strands of ancient wisdom that moved him to return to the classics, to the beginning of political philosophy in Plato and Aristotle, and to the ancient sources of law as they could be found in the Hebrew Bible. Against the claims of modernity, he would return then to Athens and Jerusalem.

That he would be taken then as the adversary of modern relativism, and its political doctrines, should occasion no surprise. It would be a matter merely of truth in labelling. But how did it come about that a writer for the *Times*, by and large insulated from any knowledge of Strauss's writing, and blissfully delivered from literacy, should nevertheless deliver such emphatic judgments on the meaning of Strauss's work? Literary detectives who cast their eyes about might notice a striking similarity between the diatribe levelled at Strauss and the charges that were developed at length by Prof. Stephen Holmes of the University of Chicago in his recent book, *The Anatomy of Antiliberalism*.[3] Apart from the charges echoed in the *New York Times*, Holmes added the sting of others, as he took it upon himself to reveal to his own, privileged readers what Strauss himself had concealed. Behind the close reading of the Bible, and the intense study of Maimonides, Holmes found more than the evidence of doubt, or of a philosopher caught between Athens and Jerusalem. Without any direct personal knowledge of Strauss, Holmes was nevertheless sure enough to declare that Strauss was, in plain truth, an atheist. But more than that, a man with "a total cynicism about religion." Without a trace of equivocation, he attributes to Strauss this sentiment: "that most people are not merely inferior to the philosophical supermen. Their lives are utterly valueless and unjustifiable unless they serve to make philosophers more comfortable and secure."[4]

In a recent book, called *Leo Strauss and Nietzsche*, Prof. Laurence Lampert comes essentially to the same conclusion, but without the edge of hostility shown by Holmes. It should be said that Lampert treats Strauss, for the most part, with respect, in the sense that he reads Strauss, line by line, and in the style by which

Strauss read others. He may not treat Strauss fully with respect, because he does not respect Strauss's account of himself, or the reasons why Strauss might have chosen to cloak his own teachings with a bit of mystery. Still, the hostility is absent because Lampert was convinced that Strauss, behind the facade, was really, like himself a Nietzschean. Lampert was moved to say of Strauss that "he did not become a Straussian":

> He did not hold as timelessly true those twin pillars of a popular Straussianism alleged of him by both friends and enemies: he was not ultimately a loyalist to God and nation because he was not ultimately a loyalist at all.[5]

In this reading, Strauss's ultimate loyalty, if he had an ultimate loyalty, was to philosophy. But Lampert also attributes to Strauss a willingness to temper his teaching with prudence, and so he goes on to say that

> if Strauss was not a Straussian, he was responsible for Straussianism. He evidently believed that it was in the interests of philosophy here and now to encourage the appearance of shared loyalties with believers in God and nation—and the appearance of complete opposition to Nietzsche.[6]

These kinds of "interpretations" Strauss would have regarded as attacks or libels, and our reflex is to ask just where, in the writings of Strauss, could one find a single passage to justify these extravagant conclusions. And yet, this challenge to produce the source would be treated by Holmes and Lampert as disingenuous: For after all, did Strauss himself not teach about the art of "writing between the lines"? Many of us harbor thoughts that we would not readily speak in public, and in the case of Strauss it was evident that he was decorously holding something back, that he was not inclined to put into print everything he understood. And in Strauss's case, one had to suspect that there were serious reasons, political and therefore moral reasons, for the reticence. Lampert could make the fair, or tenable, point then that Strauss had ample means himself for dispelling some of the mystery that surrounds his own teaching. He could have said, with Nietzsche, "Hear me! For I am this and this and this. Above all, do not mistake me for someone else" (*Ecce Homo*). Lampert remarks that "the absence of any such essay pointing to himself and his real beliefs suggests on its own that Strauss had no intention of making himself clear in the way that popular or political Straussianism is clear."[7]

In this rejoinder, as I say, Lampert makes a fair point, and it might be said, in addition, that the readings of Strauss offered by his enemies, or by the people who would read him as a closet Nietzschean, find an echo in readings that have been offered even by some Straussians, or people who have been adherents to Strauss. Stanley Rosen, for example, has concluded that "there is no theoretical foundation or superstructure to Strauss's conception of philosophy." He finds clues then to suggest that "Strauss regarded philosophy as finally impossible because of the impossibility of furnishing the discursive validation of the foundations." If this reading is correct, then as Rosen remarks, "We are dangerously close to Nietzsche."[8] Rosen has not been alone in this reading; in fact, there has been a serious division among the followers of Strauss, and the students of his students, a division that Harry Jaffa has described as "the Crisis of the Strauss Divided."

In that division, my own understanding has aligned me with Harry Jaffa, whom I have taken as my own teacher in these matters, along with Mr. Strauss. And so I was surprised, to put it mildly, a couple of years ago, when I offered a commentary on Strauss writing between the lines and suddenly brought down on myself some pointed reproaches coming, we might say, from my side of the family. What occasioned the criticism was a short piece I had done for *National Review* in 1995, as a kind of introduction to the work of Strauss. I had remarked, in that essay, that parts of Strauss's teaching were indeed held back or concealed in layers of reticence and indirection, in the style he described in *Persecution and the Art of Writing*. As a fairly obvious case in point I offered that passage in *Natural Right and History*, in which Strauss touches on some rather harsh, inconvenient truths that it will be hard for a democracy to acknowledge—namely, that it may require methods not strictly in accord with the rules of constitutionalism to deal with the most "unscrupulous and savage" enemies of free government. But then Strauss quickly adds, in a telling passage, "Let us leave these sad exigencies covered with the veil with which they are justly covered."[9] For those interested in certain arcane arts, that passage occurs on p. 160, in a book of 323 pages.

What else had Strauss been holding back? I went on to say that Strauss's reticence may have reflected what was called, in the Declaration of Independence, a "decent respect for the opinions of mankind." Rather than showing a contempt for the public, this reserve on the part of a philosopher may reflect a proper caution about the things that philosophers may claim to know. And here is the passage that caused, as we say, the duck to fly down. I said that there are many subtleties packed into that terse proposition, "All men are created equal," but as Mr. Strauss seemed to understand, it was not prudent for the philosopher to inquire with a merciless honesty into the doubtful assumptions tucked away in that proposition, the proposition that Lincoln described as the father of all principles among us. A philosopher who saw the world rightly could never seriously hold that all men were born with an equal aptitude, say, for brain surgery, for physics or philosophy. Nor could he say that everyone was born with an equal aptitude for rendering justice or reasoning about matters of right and wrong. In fact, that cardinal principle of the American regime marked, for Strauss, the scaling down of natural justice. As Strauss wrote, "political society requires the dilution of the perfect and exact right, of natural right proper. . . . The principle governing the dilution is consent, that is, the democratic principle of simple equality according to which every citizen possesses the same title to rule as every other." If things were ordered rightly by nature, the wise would hold a natural mandate to direct the affairs of those who are notably less than wise. But political life would always require the acquiesence or consent of the mulititude as a practical matter. The principle of equality would be a rule then of *political jus-*

tice, a rule that could not give a strenuous justification for itself in natural justice. But as Strauss wrote, even the best of societies may be sustained with conventions that will not withstand a rigorous examination. The philosopher plays with a kind of political dynamite if he runs the risk of dislodging people from the wholesome prejudices, or the useful conventions, that support their own freedom.

It was at this point that one colleague and friend thought I was edging into heresy. For I ran the risk of suggesting that the "self-evident" truth of the Declaration of Independence was not in fact a truth after all. But that "proposition," as Lincoln called it, was indeed the anchoring principle in the American regime, and I have made it part of my own vocation, in writing and teaching, to expound the truth of that proposition as part of a curriculum of explaining how we can indeed know moral truths in the strictest sense.[10] In my own reckoning, that proposition in the Declaration could indeed be defended as a truth, along the lines that Harry Jaffa has indeed expounded it, though I would differ slightly from Jaffa and hold that it could not be merely an "inductive" truth. An inductive truth can yield no more than a generalization from experience, and yet the proposition "all men are created equal" really has the standing of an "axiom" or "first principle," as the Founders understood them. They are what Alexander Hamilton had in mind when he wrote, in the Federalist #31, that "In disquisitions of every kind, there are certain primary truths or first principles upon which all subsequent reasonings must depend."[11] As Jaffa himself has recalled, neither Lincoln nor the Founders thought that all men were equally virtuous, intelligent or beautiful, or that all people had an equal claim to our affections and respect. What they meant, rather, as Jaffa has explained, is that no man was by nature the ruler of other men in the way that men were by nature the ruler of dogs and horses.[12] To put it another way, beings who can give and understand reasons deserve to be ruled with the rendering of reasons, by a government that seeks their consent.

These understandings may be grounded in a common sense understanding of the things that separate human beings from animals. They are confirmed by experience, and yet they cannot strictly be dependent on experience. For we are dealing here with an axiom, or a necessary truth, and as Thomas Reid pointed out long ago, "propositions of this kind, from their nature, are incapable of proof by induction."[13] Induction depends on conclusions drawn from experience, and we cannot have the experience of a necessary truth. To speak of the things that must be true of necessity is to speak of things that will hold true in the future as well as the present, and if we can know things solely on the strength of experience, we cannot claim to have experienced the future. Or as Bertrand Russell once observed, we can know through induction that the future will resemble the past in many respects, but the "principle of induction" we cannot know through induction.[14]

But that is to say, we may be joined in our confidence in the central, defining "truth" of the Declaration, and yet we recognize that there is much yet, in that proposition, to be explained. As Aquinas reminded us, a self-evident truth is not necessarily evident to every self happening along the street. The axioms of geometry may be true *per se nota*, true in themselves, and yet they may not be obvious. In the same way, the proposition "all men are created equal" does not exactly explain itself, and indeed Harry Jaffa has taken it as part of his own mission to expound, in the most compelling way, the truth of that proposition. I did not mean to suggest, in my own commentary on Strauss, that Strauss would reach a judgment on this matter, or on the principles of the American regime, different from the judgment that Jaffa would reach. But I did mean to suggest that the philosopher would find, in that principle, layers of problems that would have to be explained, and claims that would have to be defended.

Beyond that point, however, I was mildly surprised to find a difference with my friend, Prof. Jaffa, in our reading of Strauss on *Persecution and the Art of Writing*. I took Strauss's commentary there to be indifferent to the nature of the regimes. Jaffa took it to mean that the need to cloak teaching between the lines is an expedient that arises under tyrannies; but that cloaking would not be necessary or desirable in a regime of constitutional freedom. Especially under the conditions of democracy in America, it was possible to teach openly, and therefore, in Jaffa's reading, Strauss sought in his writing to teach what he meant. I must confess that, in my own credulity, I usually take Strauss to say, in his writing, what he means to say; and yet, I cannot see how Strauss's admonition to philosophers would not apply in a democratic regime quite as well. For in this regime, as in any others, the polity is sustained by the opinions and prejudices of the multitude. Those opinions may be rather detached from the bedrock of reasons that support them, and floating aloft as opinions, unanchored, they may not withstand the polemic arts of a seasoned philosopher. But on this point, we are not left solely to inference, for Strauss's own words should be telling. As Strauss put it, in *Persecution and the Art of Writing*, Plato managed to evade, through his arts, the grave dangers that faced the philosopher, "but the success of Plato must not blind us to the existence of a danger *which, however much its forms may vary, is coeval with philosophy*."[15] The problem then, in principle, figures to be largely indifferent to the character of the regime.

Harry Jaffa and I happen to think that behind the patriotic slogans and conventions, in America, the regime is founded on real truths; but Strauss would still urge us, I think, to be cautious. Mr. Strauss regarded the American regime as a model of moderation, and perhaps even as the best practicable regime in the modern period. But there was something, after all, contained in Strauss's remark, echoing Locke, that the American Founders had built on "low but solid ground." This wonder of moderation was not to be disdained in a century that had cast up the passions of Nazism, and brought them forth in a country that had shown the deepest refinements of philosophy and culture. The notion of a "low but solid ground" suggested a compromise, a scaling down, and Strauss was acutely conscious of what had been lost in that scaling down.

That reading of Strauss has been supported, I think, by Kenneth Green in his book on Strauss and Maimonides.[16] As Green observed, a central point in esoteric teaching was to avoid corrupting the multitude. The philosophers and the people of more refined sensibility required "a properly disciplined society which tolerates philosophy." The enterprise needs to be sustained then by a "noble rhetoric" that rests precisely, as Green said, on "the need to defend the decent morality and its supporting religion in which most men believe."[17]

But with Green, this argument cuts against the grain: When commentators write about Strauss concealing, between the lines, his true understanding, they tend to assume that Strauss is concealing his doubts about moral absolutes, and therefore his doubts about revelation and God. With Green, however, the teaching is quite different: In Green's understanding, Strauss shared Maimonides's dubiety about "natural law," or the kinds of moral understanding accessible to men as men, through the gift of reason. In Green's construal, Maimonides did not think that natural law was either natural or truly rational. He was inclined to regard law as "entirely conventional until it is grounded by a lawgiver who issues the basic 'natural law' . . . as unconditional commandments, and who attaches to them appropriate sanctions."[18] Green is convinced that Strauss finally shared that judgment of Maimonides, but the consequence then, as Green says, is "devastating to all human societies not based solely on revealed morality and religion."[19]

And yet, what made the American regime a model of moderation was the fact that it was not based on revelation, and that is why America became the first polity in which Jews and Christians could stand together on a plane of common citizenship. If Green is correct, the cost of this moderate achievement for Strauss was that the American regime had no real moral ground on which to sustain itself. It could give a moral account of itself only on grounds that were diminished—the grounds that were understandable, alike, to Christians, Jews, and nonbelievers. But as Harry Jaffa has argued, the American Founding can be understood quite readily in terms that run back to the classics and to the differences in nature between human beings and animals. Jaffa would also follow Aquinas in holding that natural law reasoning is itself part of the nature wrought by God in the creation. Humans act at the highest pitch of their nature when they come to understand the laws of reason and morality, and when they order their lives by this understanding, they act in accord with the design of God. In that sense, there can be a critical convergence between the moral teachings of the classics and the teachings that come from the biblical tradition.[20]

But the question is whether that was also Strauss's understanding. If Green is correct, the question must be subject to doubt, for it is bound up with everything that was vexing and insoluble in the problem of reason versus revelation, the problem that lured Strauss ever more deeply into the study of the classics and became the central question that drove him on in his work.

America had become a refuge for religion; and yet Strauss had to understand that Christians and Jews could share the ground of a common citizenship only if there was nothing in the laws that favored Christianity over Judaism. Indeed, the laws would have to be purged of any traces that might accord, to Christianity, or to religion, a preeminent respect. As this logic has now worked itself out in our own time, the separation of church and state has fostered the conviction, in the circles of the educated, that there is something divisive and unsettling about religion in the life of a republic. It has become an urgent matter then to remove religion from the laws. But in that event, religion would be removed to a domain of privacy, at the periphery of our public life. It would be treated merely as another activity that excites personal passions or private interests, on the same plane as opera or baseball.

Under the terms of this political settlement, there would be tolerance for religion, but religion would be radically diminished in its standing. Strauss understood with a penetrating gravity just what was taking place here in the creation of a liberal democracy, for the alternatives had been crystallized sharply by Spinoza: The ground of the law, and of a common citizenship, would not be found in revelation or religion, but in a universal, "rational morality." But under these conditions, Jewish life could not be the same because Jewish "law" would no longer be law in the strictest sense. The Mosaic law might be followed among Jews, but it would no longer be what it was—not merely a code for all of those who attached themselves to Judaism, but a political law, a doctrine that could be imposed, with the moral conviction and authority of "law." By the logic of liberal democracy, the Mosaic law had to be displaced, decisively, as a governing doctrine. Something distinctive to Judaism would be lost. But what was held out to Jews now was the blessing of liberal society, a society in which "Jews and Christians can be equal members."

Strauss would never conceal to himself, in a benign haze, just what was being denigrated or lost in this arrangement of the modern, liberal regime. And once again, Spinoza could be taken as the key. Strauss pointed out, rather archly, that in Spinoza's new bible science, there was a willingness to read the Bible as we would read any other book. Strauss complained that Spinoza had put the Old and the New Testaments on the same plane; he treated them as documents, or teachings, of equal value. But when the attempt was made in this way to find the thread that linked these two traditions, that common thread turned out to be, as Strauss said, "rational morality."

Strauss would return, thirty years later, to that book of his youth on Spinoza, and he would write, in a new preface, that "I understood Spinoza too literally because I did not read him literally enough."[21] I would recall this line because I would say the same thing about Strauss now. And what moves me to these reflections are the arguments that have been collected and concentrated in recent years, on this matter of reason and revelation, on Strauss as a philosopher or a Jew. Prof. David Novak, who had studied with Strauss, organized a conference a few years ago, at the University of Virginia, on the subject of *Strauss and Judaism*. In the culminating paper of the conference, Novak argued finally that it was hard to make sense of Strauss except on the terms expounded by Jaffa.[22] By Strauss's own account, the "theologico-political" question was at the core of his life's work, and his straining over the problem made sense only as the strain experienced by a serious Jew. Jaffa's own student, Susan Orr, has brought forth a new book on *Jerusalem and Athens*,[23] in which she offers a truly Strauss-like reading of Strauss's essay

"Jerusalem and Athens." She offered, that is, an exceedingly close reading, in which she managed to draw in all of the other strands, in the works of Strauss, that bear on the problem of reason and revelation. In that respect, Susan Orr produced a kind of mirror image of Laurence Lampert's book *Strauss and Nietzsche*. Lampert had subjected to a comparable, close reading, Strauss's essay on Nietzsche ("Notes on the Plan of Nietzsche's Beyond Good and Evil"). Working in the same style, but from different perspectives, Orr and Lampert—to no one's surprise—came out with conclusions that are entirely at odds. I do not mean to be flippant about Mr. Lampert's work, for he has proceeded diligently, and makes some tenable points. But it seems to me that his inventiveness finally soars off into a realm of interpretation quite untethered. Susan Orr had evidently absorbed herself deeply in Strauss's writing, but I think she managed to find something quite critical, which she could not have found in the writing or the literature. That "something" should have been evident to us all along as a key to the problem; and with her book I think I have experienced myself a late epiphany: For it strikes me now that the key to the puzzle, or to this dispute over the work of Strauss, is something that runs back to that scene I described at the head of this essay; that first moment in which I saw Strauss, in his classroom, enveloped by his students.

In order to arrive at that moment, and the encounter with Strauss, I had been preparing for over a year. One of my professors in political theory was kind enough to work with me, in a reading course, and with his tutelage I immersed myself in the reading of Strauss. The writings were engaging, summoning, but, to me, dense and elusive—and so I was, at that first moment, fascinated but deeply fearful that all of this was quite over my head. And yet, what seems striking, in retrospect, is that the oddities or contrasts that were evident at once to the uninstructed youth that day, in Strauss's class, could still provide the best guides to the work of Strauss. What may emerge finally, as the most reliable guide to Strauss's teaching, are the things that could be grasped at once, on that first day, by that youngster of 22. And so I am inclined to say now about Strauss that perhaps we understood him too literally in the past because we did not understand himself literally enough: Perhaps certain commentators, who were trained and over-trained, fell into mistakes that would elude the less tutored, because they did not credit the most obvious things in his teaching, which were before us all the time.

The first thing that drew my own attention, on that first day with Strauss, was the presence of clerical collars, of Catholic priests, of varying ages. There were also gray-haired men, officers recently retired from the military, there to sit at the feet of Mr. Strauss, along with the Catholic priests and the young, aggressive Jewish students from Chicago. The class was supposed to last for an hour and a half, at the edge of the day. But it would go on for about three hours, into the dinner hour. It was clear that the deep interest could not be detached from the substance of what was being taught; the substance that had drawn priests and retired officers to Chicago to study with Strauss. What connected everyone in that room was the interest in standing against the current culture with its variants of moral relativism.

But that is to say:What connected the Christians and Jews in that room was the religion of reason, or "rational morality." And yet, if there was something admirable and compelling about the common study of Christians and Jews in that classroom, one had to wonder why the same shared understandings could not provide the ground of a common citizenship.Why could it not supply the foundation of a polity that would contain, as equal members, Christians and Jews?

Mr. Strauss had once pointed out, in an essay on Hermann Cohen, that Cohen had been writing with the freedom of the philosopher to express himself with a critical fulness; and he felt obliged to acknowledge that this freedom on the part of philosophers had not been common in the past in other regimes.That freedom was a defining feature only of a liberal democracy, the regime shaped by the thought of Spinoza. Strauss himself made use of that same franchise, to write fully. Surely he must have understood that he himself had been a beneficiary of that regime created by Spinoza; the regime whose deepest foundations he was exposing now to his own, serious questioning.The problem of Spinoza was complicated, of course, by the fact that Spinoza was an apostate. He had left the Jews; and afer the experience of the Nazis, Strauss made it clear, on several occasions, that it was unthinkable for Jews to defect and cease being Jewish. But with all of the serious quarrels that Strauss had with Spinoza, the matter of "rational morality" should not have been seriously at issue, for the cause of rational morality was, after all, part of Strauss's own mission in teaching and politics.

Or so at least it appeared to that 22-year-old, and to the people joining him in that classroom with Strauss in 1962. But if we are to credit Prof. Lampert's careful book, all of this was a facade and a deception.There was no unsaying Strauss's remark that no Jew who was honorable could detach himself from his people. But if Lampert is correct, that sentiment had to express a purely political judgment, for Strauss's attachment to Jews and Judaism could not depend on the substance of Judaism itself. In Lampert's reading, Strauss had turned discreetly away from Judaism as he came to absorb more deeply, with Nietzsche, the "idiocies of revealed religion."[24] To announce that recognition would have been, apparently, a gratuitous assault on his own people, simply not to be countenanced. In this reading, Strauss would feign his religiosity, as he would feign his teaching about the Ten Commandments and about moral truths holding in all times and places.

But let us suppose for a moment that Strauss was feigning all of these things, in the way of helping sustain for the public these wholesome prejudices. Still, we would have to ask,What was the purpose of this charade? What was being hidden behind this artifice of concealment? The answer, I gather, from Lampert, is that all of this was done to preserve a regime in which philosophers would be free to pursue their lives as philosophers. Of course, not all philosophers have thought it necessary to philosophy, or to their lives as philosophers, to preserve a regime built on the proposition that "all men are created equal." Nor have they have found their safety, as philosophers, in sustaining a government restrained by law. But even if the philosopher finds some reason to prefer a constitutional government, what is the nature of that philosophic life he is seeking to preserve? It is apparently a life of the most rigorous flexing of the mind—but directed toward what end? Toward the discovery that there is nothing to be known? But as Strauss said, the life of a philosopher was devoted to an inquiry into the "permanent things." Did that not rather presuppose that there was something to be known? Or that it was indeed possible for the life of philosophy to give an account, finally, of its own goodness or worth? If we followed Lampert, we would suspect that the hidden secret of the philosopher is the awareness that he cannot really explain why the life of philosophy merits the commitment of a lifetime. For that is the sober recognition that may emerge, once the urbane have come to understand, as Lampert says, "the idiocies of revealed religion." For they would sweep away then the nonsense of a Lawgiver, and deliver themselves from the pretense that there are real truths lying behind their moral judgments.

These are the kinds of recognitions that come flowing out with more candor at the end of Lampert's book, as he begins to settle his own judgments. Nietzsche, in his estimate, was the philosopher of first rank, and he had things compellingly right. Presumably, then, a life committed to philosophy would take as its purpose the progressive revelation of what Nietzsche so firmly knew, and so persuasively imparted. And what would those things be? Lampert sought to restate Nietzsche's view on "the religion of the future." With a Nietzschean flavor, he offered a list with a rhetorical sweep and aspiration—too sweeping to be contained here—but we can sample the tone and character. Heading the list of the things the philosopher would know was that

> the intelligible character of the whole shows itself to our best penetration as a process of relentless, surging energy in which every power draws its ultimate consequences at every moment—blind, meaningless, wasteful abundance that consumes whatever it generates and is lovable as it is;

> the highest ideal is a post-Platonic, post-modern loyalty to the earth that can learn how to assign limits to the human conquest of nature and human nature out of love of the natural order of which we are dependent parts; . . .

and that

> a proper physio-psychology can become aware of the unity of our species amid the whole array of species, and and aware that all species share the common fate on our planet of appearing, flourishing, and falling extinct.[25]

As the saying goes, let a candid world judge: Anyone who has even a middling acquaintance with Strauss's writing would probably be able to mark off at once the lines of Strauss's reactions to these kinds of claims. Certain powers that are blind and meaningless, without moral substance or direction, nevertheless command our love? On what grounds? By what standard could we regard them as worthy of our affection or respect? We would remind ourselves that love cannot be detached from the grounds of respect, and therefore from the grounds of a moral judgment. When we speak of an obligation to observe limits, we speak again in moral terms, and how could inanimate nature—a nature with no moral purpose—be the source of obligations for creatures who do possess the capacity to reason over matters of right and wrong? This construction of the problem covers a paganism that inverts the teaching of the Bible: As Strauss reminds us, the lifeless parts of creation came first, and the project ascended then to the living things. And preeminent among the living things—as the object of Creation—was man himself. The earth was made for men, not men for the earth.[26] Even from a more analytic perspective, it is only beings capable of moral purposes who are capable of imparting moral purposes to inanimate matter. On the same ground, Strauss would recoil at the notion that all living things are created equal, or that we would find the equality of all species in the cardinal fact that all of us—lawyers, outfielders, goldfish and rutabagas—that all of us, in time, die. That perspective manages a mindless, egalitarian sweep by putting everything on the same plane. It denies what sets human beings apart from animals and all living things; it denies what is distinctive and "higher" about human nature.

Anyone who knows the least thing about Strauss would know that this would be the line of his reaction. No doubt his argument would be attended by shades of subtlety that would not all be expressed, but could anyone doubt, even for a moment, that this would be the heart of Strauss's response? And could anyone have the least doubt that the convictions expressed in this way were anything other than Strauss's own, firmly settled understanding?

In a talk he gave, in February 1962, before the Hillel group at the University of Chicago, Strauss recalled that, as a youngster he had seen in his family's home Jews who had fled from the pogroms in Russia. The stories struck the child and his family as bizarre, for they lived in Germany, in a civilized country, and such things were inconceivable there.[27] But of course, before too long, they proved not so inconceivable after all. When Strauss wrote a second preface to that work, of his youth, on Spinoza, that book written when he was 25, he took account of events that intervened and put the problem of Jews and Spinoza's argument in a different register. The world had seen now something novel, "the only German regime—[indeed, as Strauss said] the only regime ever anywhere—which had no other clear principle than murderous hatred of the Jews." This searing fact seemed to make the most profound difference for Strauss by affecting with an even deeper significance the question of whether Jews continue to be Jews, or whether they defect, in the style of Spinoza. And they were in danger of defecting when they fell away to the lure of philosophy. At the end of his talk, at Hillel, on "Why We Remain Jews," one student, pulling together the strands, along with the things left unsaid, asked "am I correct that your answer is that we have no choice [but to remain Jews]?" And Strauss replied, "As honorable men, surely not."[28]

But apart from the significance of the German experience as it bore on Strauss's Judaism, it seems a wonder to me that its significance seems be easily passed by when it comes to the matter of fixing the critical points, or signposts, in Strauss's thought. Perhaps the point is overlooked because the Nazi regime is still within the span of our lifetimes, but that regime provided in itself a refutation of the claims of modernity and "progress." The Nazi regime offered the most dramatic descent into barbarism, but a barbarism allied with a society at the most advanced stage of science and technology. By any measures of learning and scholarship, Germany had to be reckoned one of the most cultivated and advanced of the so-called "civilized" countries. So much for the assurance that the progress of time and science would lift the level of civilization. So much, that is, for the facile assumption that education—especially an education liberated from superstition—would take the place of religion and bring society onto a steadier plane of moral improvement. The example of Germany is quite sufficient in itself to disprove all of those beamish expectations. And in disproving them, it would seem to install the plausibility of making a return to the more ancient sources: For it should be clear now, beyond cavilling, that later is not necessarily better. In that case, it must be entirely plausible that an earlier generation understood the enduring human questions as well as they may ever be understood, and perhaps even better.

The theme of an "eternal return" is critical in Strauss, as is the accent on the lessons to be gleaned from the experience of Germany. There is not the least doubt then—nothing hidden between the lines—to suggest that Strauss thought there was anything equivocal about the refutation of the claims of modernity and progress. And in that event, there does not seem to me the least reason to doubt that he returned to the classics, not to foster a wholesome piety for the multitude, but because he would find there the sources of wisdom for the kinds of questions that had to be at the center of our lives. At the same time, the experience of Germany had to confirm everything that was problematic in the modern tendency to convert "civilizations" into a plural: Instead of speaking about the moral requirements of a truly "civilized" country, writers would speak of different "civilizations," arising from different cultures, each demanding respect on its own terms. Prof. Melville Herskovits once explained, earnestly, that the doctrine of cultural relativism affirmed the rightness or "the validity of every set of norms for the people who have them."[29] By that reckoning, the Holocaust had to be morally right if it had sprung from the German culture, and any moral judgment cast from the outside had to be suspect. Nothing confirmed more fully the emptiness, or the terminal fatuity, of cultural relativism. Could anyone bear even the slightest doubt about the way in which Strauss was likely to have responded to the kind of "argument" offered by Herskovits? The concern with historicism and cultural relativism stands at the very beginning of *Natural Right and History*, and it is the concern that pervades that book. Indeed, it is hard to pick up any book of Strauss's, from the writings on Spinoza and Machiavelli, to the writings on Jerusalem and Athens, in which this question is not present. If it is not at the center, it is a concern that hovers over everything. If there is anything lurking between the lines of Strauss, it could hardly be a teaching on cultural relativism at odds with the position he had conveyed forcefully, persistently, luminously, on any occasion on which he was given the chance to write and speak. To use an old expression, this is a lesson that he taught going out and coming in, a lesson he taught morning and night, and it was an inseparable part of his teaching.[30]

Of course, Nietzsche too sought to transcend cultural relativism and speak on behalf of a nature that was universal. But the notion of nature, and the moral lessons arising from that nature, marked off a curriculum quite different from the things Strauss would teach. Nietzsche too would return to the classics, and it is a tangled matter to explain why Nietzsche and Strauss extracted such different lessons. One difference was suggested in an oblique manner by Strauss. The wisdom he sought, on returning to the ancients, had to bear on the question of the kind of life that was best for man. And when humans were joined by a concern for the terms of principle on which they lived, they would be facing the question of polity. Those terms of principle would express themselves in "the laws" and the character of political life. They would mark the deep, abiding importance of the political regime. In his essay "Liberal Education and Responsibility," Strauss reflected again on the hubris of those writers, in the nineteenth century, who fancied that education would take the place of religion and morality. Strauss remarked that "Karl Marx, the father of communism, and Friedrich Nietzsche, the step-grandfather of fascism, were liberally educated on a level to which we cannot even hope to aspire." The lesson drawn by Strauss was "that wisdom cannot be separated from moderation and hence . . . wisdom requires unhesitating loyalty to a decent constititution and even to the cause of constititutionalism."[31] I have taken Strauss to mean here that, if Marx and Nietzsche had been attentive to the things in their own thought that undermined a constitutional order, or a regime of legal restraint, they would have been led to the things that were most problematic, or fearful, in their own thought.

The American republic was the example, par excellence, of that moderate regime enhanced by a decent constitution. As I have noted, this was the first regime in which Jews and Christians would stand on a plane of civic equality. And yet, Strauss surely had to understand that something was sacrificed on the side of religion—and Judaism—in receiving this rare benefit. Kenneth Green caught the sense of this in his book on Strauss and Maimonides, where he felt compelled to temper his admiration by registering the concern of whether Maimonides and Strauss had achieved their reconciliation of philosophy and religion "ultimately from the side of philosophy." If so, he raised the question of whether their victories "have not been achieved at too dear a cost to the spirit and substance of Judaism."[32] In the American regime, a certain insulation or space for religion could be secured, but at the expense of putting religion at the periphery of our public lives. And once placed there, it would come to be seen, as Justice Scalia suggests, as something that could be decorously pursued only in private, rather like the savoring of pornography. On the other hand, in that other notion of separating Church and State, the understanding held by Roger Williams, the state and politicians would be kept out of the garden of religion. And so, religion still flourishes in the United States, more seriously than in other countries. Of course, those religions seem to be getting thinner on substance with each generation, but the wonder, nevertheless, is that they are there, that they endure, and they flourish in a manner that astonishes their adversaries. The Supreme Court has done little of late to sustain the cause of religion, but the vitality of churches in this country probably bears some connection to the freedom that was secured for religion under the American Constitution. Strauss might have seen this arrangement as Harry Jaffa has seen it, as the best practicable regime, especially in the modern period; on that basis the bargain could have seemed eminently sensible.

But that would have been the reckoning of a philosopher, or of a worldly man with a political sense. Not long after Mr. Strauss's death in 1973, Milton Himmelfarb was doing a commemorative piece, and as he tried to estimate Strauss's relation to Judaism he remarked that Strauss had not been seen often in the synagogue. I remember calling Himmelfarb at the time and recounting to him a story I had been told about Mr. Strauss's appearance for a lecture at Amherst—a few years before I had arrived at the College. After his lecture, he was approached by a professor of English, a man of Jewish ancestry who had managed, with a steady policy, to detach himself from things Jewish. He ran up to Strauss and said, "But if I follow what you've said, you would have to believe in revelation." To which Strauss replied, "But I'm a Jew." The professor of English said, "But what does *that* mean—these days?" To which Strauss said, "That's not *my* problem."

Milton Himmelfarb listened to this story and observed, "Well, it was Athens and Jerusalem, wasn't it? His heart was in Jerusalem, his head was in Athens, and the head is the organ of the philosopher." And after all the shadings and turns in the argument, after all of the ellipses and writing between the lines, that may be, in the end, the truth of the matter. But it cannot be such an unequivocal truth, since Strauss himself evidently strained to render the matter more complicated.

Still, for reasons thoroughly weighed, Strauss had not chosen to teach theology. He had deliberately taken as his vocation the study of political philosophy, and he wrote as a philosopher. His arguments in defense of revelation—his arguments about the limits of philosophy—were the arguments of a philosopher. He wrote books, which under the hazards of publication could be read by people who were not philosophers. But even more to the point, those books could be read by people who were both believers and nonbelievers. For all of his reverent gestures toward revelation, Strauss approached his project with the canons of reason, and with all of the formidable equipment, that we associate with the most accomplished philosopher. And the result might have been comparable to the effects produced by Spinoza: Strauss's own students, absorbing his temper and his style, might preserve their reverence for things ancestral, even as they detached themselves from Judaism. One of the most devoted students of Mr. Strauss remarked to me once that he had raised his children on the Nicomachean Ethics. His grown children share his interest in political philosophy, but almost needless to say, they do not put on *tallisim* (prayer shawls) and *daven* (pray) in the synagogue.

On the other hand, even Strauss's students who were not religious managed to preserve a certain reverence for religion. And of course many of them went on to become more deeply religious, or more deeply committed as Jews and Christians. By the fruit we shall know the tree, and it has become utterly clear, over the past thirty years, that the apostles of Nietzsche and Heidegger in the academy do not produce students who are serious Christians and Jews. These things stand among the plainest things before us, which makes it all the more remarkable to me that I had neglected myself to notice another side of the problem, which had been evident to me from those first days that I had been in the presence of Mr. Strauss. It required Susan Orr to give me a mild jolt on this matter and point out what I had known all along. Without any religious pleading—and indeed by purposely avoiding any appeal to religious attachments—Strauss had drawn to himself young students who had drifted from the Judaism and Christianity of their families. Strauss managed to draw them into a set of philosopohic problems that they found utterly compelling, and once drawn in that way, some of them would make their way back on their own to Christianity and Judaism. Paul Rahe once remarked of Allan Bloom that his appeal had been to students on the Left, with the most penetrating critique of bourgeois society. But after Bloom had drawn their interest, and led them back to Rousseau and then Plato and Aristotle, he had drawn them decisively away from the political Left.

In the same, curious way, Strauss emitted the signals of an accomplished philosopher who was tutored in his religious tradition, deeply reverent toward it, earnestly inclined to take seriously the questions it raised. And yet he conveyed a sense, also, of being detached from that religious tradition, not firmly or entirely committed. It was hardly a matter of inadvertence that, in his essay "Jerusalem and Athens," he referred to something that held "for all of us who cannot be orthodox."[33] Strauss was utterly disarming then; he posed no threats, he made no appeals for conversion, among people who were uncertain about their religious commitments. But in fact, his posture became all the more enticing: He would lure his students into a serious philosophic inquiry, demanding, intense, and affected with an edge of danger precisely because of an overhanging sense that something profoundly serious was at stake.

Susan Orr suggests, in this vein, that Strauss presented a religiosity far more muted than it actually was: He seemed to have sensed, as a matter of pedogogy, that he had to engage the students where he found them, and that he would find them detached and uncertain about their own religious commitments. And yet, it struck me, from my first moments in that classroom, that it had the feel of Hebrew School. There was a sense of religious engagement, or devotion, that filled the air. Susan Orr, who had never been in that room, or known Strauss, may have grasped, with a stunning accuracy, what she could not have known directly. She surmised that Strauss had muted the religious argument precisely "in order to convince 'those of who cannot be orthodox' to listen to him. Those who fall into that category," she said, "are not simply secular Jews but those Christians who have abandoned their religion as well. He speaks to the lost souls of both traditions."[34]

I do not think I would have counted as a lost soul, but those lines had a deeper resonance for me because I was there, and I can report that the truth of those lines was evident. I can also know it, from a distance of 35 years, because I know it to have been true in my own case. I had studied Hebrew as a youngster, as part of a religious education that had become a fading memory. What was most obvious and striking in Strauss, to me, was the example of a serious philosopher who was now drawing from Hebrew texts with the same facility with which he was drawing from the ancient Greek. I had not seen Hebrew used in this way, for anything but devotional purposes—which is to say, I had not seen Hebrew used for the sake of exploring a problem of philosophic consequence. The lesson, so obvious that it was inescapable, was that a serious philosopher thought that there was something there to be learned, something of an urgent significance for people apart from Jews. And it went without saying that, what was there to be learned, he evidently regarded as compelling and true. But now we may wonder, was it all so obvious that it has gone unnoticed? That Strauss was appealing to our religious sense—and appealing even more persuasively because he was appealing to us as apprentices in philosophy— was a matter so plain that it could hardly be treated as a matter of doubt by commentators who are overly clever in extracting the hidden teaching in Strauss. With theories running deep, people may persuade themselves that Strauss was a closet atheist, determined, in his heart of hearts, to live the life mapped out by Nietzsche. But it has to be said that this construction simply makes no contact with the teaching of Strauss, as that teaching was manifest—and manifest even to the newest, young student—who spent hours in his classroom.

These recollections came flowing back, as I say, after reading Susan Orr's book, and around the same time, I had received a letter from one of my favorite students, from the 1970's, who was now resident in Japan as a journalist. He recalled that he had been "a Catholic only in name during my school days, but I still felt a very strong attachment to the moral fundamentals. The 'mysteries' of faith left me cold," but in an odd, moving way, our work together on the American Founders and natural right seemed to confirm for him the ground of the Church's teaching. Those studies, into the ground of moral truths, had carefully avoided any appeal to faith or revelation. Nevertheless, as he wrote, they "amounted to a major step toward faith for me. I am a conscientious Catholic these days, far from perfect in my own life, of course, but very much at ease with the Church." As for myself, I became aware long ago that I could never pretend to understand the fuller teaching of Mr. Strauss or take on his vocation. And yet, with this letter from my student I could not help wondering whether I had absorbed some of Strauss's purpose even more than I knew, and imparted to my students the effect that Strauss, with the most conscious design, had imparted to his own.

But the letter from Japan confirmed—yet again, as Strauss understood—that reason was the handmaid of revelation. When we studied with Strauss, late into the winter afternoons, it felt, as I say, like nothing so much as Hebrew School. The concentration was riveting, the spirit pervasively religious. The text might have been

Plato's *Gorgias*, or Locke's *Second Treatise*, but none of us doubted that the curriculum in which we seemed to be immersed now with our hearts—with a far deeper conviction than we had ever summoned—was the religion of reason.

NOTES

1. See Walter Dean Burnham, "The Fourth American Republic?," *Wall Street Journal* (October 16, 1995).

2. Brent Staples, "Undemocratic Vistas: The Sinister Vogue of Leo Strauss," *New York Times* (November 28, 1994), editorial page.

3. (Cambridge: Harvard University Press, 1993), pp. 61–87.

4. *Ibid.*, pp. 87, 88, 70.

5. Laurence Lampert, *Leo Strauss and Nietzsche* (Chicago: University of Chicago Press, 1996), p. 130.

6. *Ibid.*, at 132.

7. *Ibid.*, at 130.

8. See Stanley Rosen, "Leo Strauss and the Quarrel Between the Ancients and the Moderns," in Alan Udoff (ed.), *Leo Strauss's Thought: Toward a Critical Engagement* (Boulder and London: Lynne Rienner Publishers, 1991), pp. 155–68, at p. 162; see also 164–66. Rosen finally draws the distinction between Strauss and Nietzsche in this way: "Nietzsche rejects theoretical truth in favor of art. Strauss rejects theoretical truth in favor of prudence. Nietzsche, like Strauss, defends the classical perception of nobility. But whereas Strauss associates this perception with an unstable blend of theory and practice, Nietzsche associates it with production" (p. 166).

9. Strauss, *Natural Right and History* (Chicago: University of Chicago Press, 1953), p. 160.

10. See, in this respect, my book *First Things* (Princeton: Princeton University Press, 1986).

11. *The Federalist Papers* (New York: Random House, n.d.).

12. See Harry Jaffa, *Equality and Liberty* (New York: Oxford University Press, 1965), pp. 176–78.

13. See Thomas Reid, *Essays on the Intellectual Powers of Man* (Cambridge; MIT Press, 1969 [1814–1815]), p. 654. For a fuller discussion of this problem, see *First Things, supra*, note 10, Ch. IV.

14. See his *Problems of Philosophy* (Oxford: Oxford University Press, 1958), pp. 66–68.

15. Strauss, *Persecution and the Art of Writing* (Glencoe: Free Press, 1952), p. 21; emphasis added.

16. Kenneth Hart Green, *Jew and Philosopher: The Return to Maimonides in the Jewish Thought of Leo Strauss* (Albany: State University of New York Press, 1993).

17. *Ibid.*, p. 125.

18. *Ibid.*, p. 132.

19. *Ibid.*, p. 133.

20. Jaffa, "Leo Strauss, the Bible, and Political Philosophy" in Kenneth L. Deutsch and Walter Nicgorski, *Leo Strauss: Political Philosopher and Jewish Thinker* (Lanham, Md.: Rowman & Littlefield, 1994), pp. 195–210.

21. Strauss, *Spinoza's Critique of Religion* (New York: Schocken Books, 1965; originally published in 1930), p. 31.

22. See David Novak, "Philosophy and the Possibility of Revelation: A Theological Response to the Challenge of Leo Strauss," in Novak (ed.), *Leo Strauss and Judaism: Jerusalem and Athens Critically Revisted* (Lanham, Md.: Rowman & Littlefield, 1996), pp. 173–92. To this conference I contributed a keynote address: Arkes, "Athens and Jerusalem: The Legacy of Leo Strauss," pp. 1–23.

23. (Lanham, Md.: Rowman & Littlefield, 1995).

24. Lampert, *supra*, note 5, p. 184.

25. *Ibid*, p. 180.

26. Strauss, "Jerusalem and Athens: Some Preliminary Reflections," in Orr, *supra*, note 23, pp. 179–207, at p. 185.

27. Strauss, "Why We Remain Jews: Can Jewish Faith and History Still Speak to Us?," in Deutsch and Nicgorski, *supra*, note 20, pp. 43–79, at p. 44.

28. *Ibid.*, p. 62.

29. Melville Herskovits, *Cultural Relativism* (New York: Vintage Books, 1972), p. 31.

30. It would be hard to find any collection of essays by Strauss, or indeed any lecture by Strauss, that did not contain some reference to the argument over moral relativism. If the concern were really remote—or altogether false—it would be hard to account for his willingness to strike off an essay to point up the moral relativism lurking in the popular writing of Isaiah Berlin, and in that fashionable liberalism that Berlin represented. See Strauss, "Relativism," in *The Rebirth of Classical Political Rationalism* (Chicago: University of Chicago Press, 1989), pp. 13–26. If these arguments did not reflect Strauss's true convictions, it would have to be said that he devoted, to the arts of feigning, an energy and acuity that were wholly out of scale.

31. Strauss, "Liberal Education and Responsibility," in *Liberalism Ancient and Modern* (New York: Basic Books, 1968), pp. 9–25, at p. 24.

32. Green, *supra*, note 16, at p. 138.

33. See Strauss in Orr, *supra*, note 26, at p. 182.

34. Orr, *supra*, note 23, pp. 149–150.

· 7 ·

Leo Strauss: Philosophy and
American Social Science

Eugene F. Miller

$\mathcal{F}$or social science in the United States after World War II, the encounter with Leo Strauss was doubly unsettling. Strauss insisted on reopening debate on the nature of social science, a question thought settled by the dominant behavioral movement, and in doing so he provoked that disquiet, vexation, and even hostility which arise when settled views are disturbed.

The social science that Strauss confronted was sure of several things: that the scientific enterprise was something distinct from philosophy; that its task was to explain actual behavior by close attention to facts and their causes or correlates; that moral judgments had no proper place in the theory required to explain behavior; and that its new approach promised results far superior to those that earlier philosophic inquiry had achieved. Some small space was grudgingly allowed for antiquaries to investigate the history of political philosophy, but merely as a discredited tradition whose study could illustrate the perils of a defective logic or, at best, suggest hypotheses for scientific testing. Strauss questioned these certitudes and insisted on restoring political philosophy as the comprehensive social science.

In formulating its new methodology, mid-century social science drew heavily from positivist writings in the philosophy of science. It believed that this methodology's key assumptions about knowing or meaning had been validated by post-Humean philosophy. Thus when Strauss maintained that positivism's flaws were fatal and that German historicism represented much the stronger philosophical force, social science was incredulous. Strauss seemed very much the ill-informed old fogy who had failed to keep track of the latest philosophical currents. The irony was that Strauss, while still a student in the early 1920s, had wrestled with positivism and historicism in their most powerful forms. Having studied Max Weber—a writer to whom he would return in the 1940s—he attended the Freiburg lecture course of Martin Heidegger, who at the time was an unknown young man in Edmund Husserl's entourage. Strauss would soon report to Franz Rosensweig that "com-

egger, Max Weber, till then regarded by me as the incarnation of the
.ce and scholarship, was an orphan child."[1] Heidegger's thought was
ɔwn to American social science in the 1940s, when Strauss came on
the scʋ..ʋ, ut later its force would become visible to all as Nietzschean and
Heideggerian "postmodernism" swept through American universities. Positivism's
collapse as a philosophic school or movement took social science largely by surprise, but Strauss's readers could have predicted it.

THE CRITIQUE OF POSITIVISM

Strauss's explicit critique of social science positivism appears in writings from *On
Tyranny* (1948) to *Liberalism Ancient and Modern* (1968)—a period that coincides
roughly with his tenure on the political science faculty at the University of Chicago
(1949–1968). This critique is intended to serve as a gateway to the serious study of
political philosophy (the critique of historicism is also part of this gateway). It aims
to show Strauss's readers that the reigning methodology prevents them both from
seeing political things as they are and from addressing questions that are of fundamental concern in political life. Once they have overcome current prejudices against
serious inquiry, Strauss invites them to enter into open-minded dialogue with the
great political philosophers, to approach them as thinkers from whom they might
learn the truth about the nature of political things and the good or just political
order.

Strauss's critique of social science positivism is highly complex, as we see in
his searching examination of Weber's thought,[2] but its design is sketched clearly in
a terse paragraph near the end of the Introduction to *The City and Man*.[3] What follows is commentary, drawn from Strauss's various writings, on key sentences (italicized) from this paragraph.

The paragraph begins: "*One can come to doubt the fundamental premise of present-
day social science—the distinction between values and facts—by merely considering the reasons advanced in its support as well as the consequences following from it.*" As we see, Strauss
regarded the fact-value distinction as "the fundamental premise" of the social science of his time, even though he acknowledged that some rejected this distinction
by holding that social scientists must practice "sympathetic understanding," i.e., actually embrace the values accepted by the societies or individuals that they study.[4]

Doubts arise about the fact-value distinction when we consider (1) the arguments for it, and (2) its consequences. Arguments for the fact-value distinction draw
on the idea that social science must be modelled on natural science: scientific objectivity is said to preclude moral evaluation. At the root of such arguments, however,
is a claim about the limitations of reason, namely, the claim that "conflicts between
different values or value-systems are essentially insoluble for human reason."[5] As
regards the merits of this claim, Strauss insists that no one has yet provided the critique of reason that would be required to prove it.

What "consequences" of the fact-value distinction lead Strauss to doubt it? Here we must distinguish between theoretical and practical consequences. The chief theoretical consequence of the fact-value distinction is to prevent its adherents from seeing social or human things as they are. Evaluation is indispensable to understanding social phenomena, and social science positivism, by attempting to purge scientific inquiry of so-called value judgments, makes the study of the important phenomena impossible. Even positivistic social science attests to the indispensability of value judgments by bringing them in through the back door. Strauss holds, contrary to positivist dogma, that the "Is," properly understood, does imply the "Ought." In defining something, in saying what it is, we necessarily imply some understanding of the proper shape of that thing, i.e., what it ought to be.[6] Positivism eventually undercuts itself as a theoretical position. Compelled finally to admit that modern science is merely "one historically relative way of understanding things which is not in principle superior to alternative ways of understanding," it "necessarily transforms itself into historicism."[7]

The ultimate practical consequence of the fact-value distinction is nihilism, which Strauss defines broadly as "the view that every preference, however evil, base, or insane, has to be judged before the tribunal of reason to be as legitimate as any other preference."[8] Nihilism manifests itself as the belief that since "our principles have no other support than our blind preferences, everything a man is willing to dare will be permissible"[9] or, less boldly, as "a state of indifference to any goal, or of aimlessness and drifting."[10] Although the social scientist might affirm the fact-value distinction, typically he does not take it to heart or live by it: "His 'ethical neutrality' is so far from being nihilism or a road to nihilism that it is not more than an alibi for thoughtlessness and vulgarity."[11] In other words, the social scientist in fact embraces "democratic values," but thoughtless or uncritically, so as to overlook inherent dangers that liberal democracy's greatest proponents have warned against: "Social science positivism fosters not so much nihilism as conformism and philistinism."[12] Nevertheless, for liberal democratic societies at large, value relativism can lead to aimlessness and drifting. When "self-evident truths" about natural justice or natural rights are reduced to "ideology," a civilization guided by those truths will find itself in crisis: "The crisis of the West consists in the West's having become uncertain of its purpose."[13] The new social or political science, however, is oblivious of the crisis of the West: "it fiddles while Rome burns."[14]

Having observed that the fact-value distinction constitutes the fundamental premise of present-day social science, Strauss now maintains that "*the issue concerning that distinction is part of a larger issue,*" namely, how social science stands in relation to the pre-scientific or common-sense understanding of political life. The fact-value distinction "*is alien to that understanding of political things which belongs to political life but it becomes necessary, it seems, when the citizen's understanding of political things is replaced by the scientific understanding.*"

One is reminded here of Strauss's early teacher, Husserl, who argued that by a process of "sedimentation," the modern sciences had lost touch with their experiential base in pre-scientific understanding and thus with the insights and questions that originally had animated them.[15] Following Descartes's path, positivistic social science defines knowledge in such a way as to depreciate all knowing that is pre-scientific. Consequently it forgets the questions most relevant to political life itself and comes to be preoccupied with the scientific proof of things known well enough, or better, to ordinary understanding. In abandoning the citizen's understanding of political life, social science loses sight of what it is that forms societies into wholes, i.e., the regimes. Political science, as the architectonic study of regimes, is now replaced by a plurality of social sciences with no intrinsic order.[16]

"*The scientific understanding implies then a break with the pre-scientific understanding, yet at the same time it remains dependent on the pre-scientific understanding.*" Positivistic social science is unable to carry through its attempted break with what can be called the common-sense view of political things. Unavoidably it takes distinctions vital to common life for granted, most notably, the very basic distinction between humans and non-humans.[17] While priding itself on a wholesale liberation from opinion, it ends up embracing opinions uncritically. Social or political science, properly understood, treats opinion as its "*basis or matrix.*" It has the character of an ascent from pre-scientific opinions about things to a more consistent and complete understanding than opinion can provide. This dialectical ascent begins by taking the citizen's perspective very seriously, even though it goes on to treat that opinion critically.[18]

The paragraph concludes: "*Classical political philosophy is the primary form of political science because the common sense understanding of political things is primary.*" Strauss suggests two reasons why social or political science must treat common-sense understanding as primary and try to recover it. First, as we have seen, the quest for political knowledge properly begins from this understanding, i.e., from civic opinion. Second, social science, to understand itself, must grasp the character of that pre-scientific understanding which it somehow modifies. Nevertheless, recovering the common-sense understanding of political things is now very difficult, because we view political life through the medium of concepts inherited from a complex tradition of political philosophy as well as the medium of the new natural science that emerged in early-modern times. The best path to such a recovery, Strauss concludes, is a return, albeit tentative or experimental, to classical political philosophy:

> Classical political philosophy attempted to reach its goal by accepting the basic distinctions made in political life exactly in the sense and with the orientation in which they are made in political life, and by thinking them through, by understanding them as perfectly as possible.[19]

The Greek Socratics—Aristotle, Plato, Xenophon—enjoyed a "direct relation to political life" that we can recover by returning to their writings. This is why classical political philosophy must be regarded as "*the primary form of political science.*"

In sum, social science must return from inherited constructs and methodologies to social reality, i.e., it must "look at social phenomena primarily in the perspective of the citizen and statesman." But this is not all. It must then view that reality "in the perspective of the citizen of the world, in the twofold meaning of 'world': the whole human race and the all-embracing whole."[20] This means, however, that social science must be developed as a branch of philosophy, understood as "quest for universal knowledge, for knowledge of the whole." Political philosophy—the inclusive social science—is the branch of philosophy "which is closest to political life, to non-philosophic life, to human life."[21] As regards the all-embracing whole, a question crucial for social science is whether man is a distinctive part of that whole who can be viewed as a being *sui generis*. Positivistic social science follows the path laid out by modern science, which is to deny essential or irreducible differences and to view things in terms of their genesis or conditions. This means, "humanly speaking, to understand the higher in terms of the lower: the human in terms of the sub-human, the rational in terms of the sub-rational, the political in terms of the sub-political."[22] Strauss acknowledges that a new approach to social science must eventually be supported by a non-reductionist science of nature:

> Social science, as the study of things human, cannot be based on modern science, although it may judiciously use, in a strictly subordinate fashion, both methods and results of modern science. Social science must rather be taken to contribute to the true universal science into which modern science will have to be integrated eventually.[23]

WHAT NEW DIRECTION FOR SOCIAL SCIENCE?

Strauss's discussion of social science has a constructive side as well as a critical side. That constructive side, which has yet to receive the attention it deserves, consists of proposals for reconstituting social science so as to make it truly empirical in character as well as properly reflective. Strauss's reexamination of the classics is intended to illuminate and advance those proposals. What direction would social science take, if it were reconstituted along the lines that he recommends?

Strauss can agree with positivists that social science should be grounded in experience, but he objects to their narrow way of defining human experience. Sense data, whether given immediately or filtered through scientific constructs, cannot disclose the social or political things. Such realities come to presence in speech, i.e., in the ordinary discourse of everyday life. Social or political things would not be visible at all if people did not talk about them. Since it cannot profitably get behind speech to unarticulated experience, social science must begin from speech, or from the opinions expressed in speech. More precisely, political science, as the comprehensive social science, begins from the opinion of citizens, especially the best-informed and most active citizens, and from the laws that formulate opinion authoritatively.[24]

In holding that political science properly begins from opinion, Strauss does not mean opinions of the kind elicited by scientific polls or questionnaires. He has in mind political opinion as voiced in its primary context, which is controversy over issues vital to the community's well-being. The chief issue, though often a latent one, in such controversies is how the community will be governed, or who will enjoy the full privileges of citizenship, or what type of human being will rule. In the political arena, citizens press rival claims, in the name of justice, that raise, directly or indirectly, the question of who should rule. By attentiveness to such debate, political scientists come to see that the choice of regimes is the most fundamental decision that a community can make. A community's way of life, its dominant patterns of thought, and its manners are shaped by its regime or ruling part. Political science is the study of regimes, and it is first among the social sciences because social phenomena cannot be understood apart from the regime that shapes them. In line with this principle, Strauss himself interprets American phenomena in light of our democratic regime. That regime today exhibits strong pressures towards permissive egalitarianism that initially were held in check by liberalism's founding principles or by older moral traditions, and these pressures shape all aspects of American society— our laws, our manners, our educational arrangements, our tastes. Even our social science is, in this respect, quite American. In characterizing positivistic social science, Strauss emphasizes its "democratism," i.e. the unavowed regime commitment that controls its analysis of social phenomena. The "tacit presupposition" of its data and its methodology is a highly permissive form of liberal democracy, and even its allegedly "value-free" stance can be seen to reflect the premise that all values or desires are equal.[25]

By starting from civic debate, political science comes to recognize not only the priority of regimes to other social phenomena, but also the existence of a variety of competing regimes. The classical writings in particular afford the broad perspective on civic debate that moderns need in order to glimpse the main types of regime—monarchy, aristocracy, democracy, oligarchy, tyranny, along with mixtures thereof—and their distinguishing characteristics. Central to any regime is some view of the best life for human beings, of the virtues that convey title to rule, and of the principle of justice by which goods are to be distributed. Having forsworn "value judgments," positivistic social science is unable to make distinctions of morality or justice that are required if one is to see regimes as they are. It is blind not only to the character of liberal democracy, but also to that regime's main competitor at mid-century: ". . . when we were brought face to face with tyranny—with a kind of tyranny that surpassed the boldest imagination of the most powerful thinkers of the past—our political science failed to recognize it."[26] Lacking a sense of "the essential differences or the heterogeneity of regimes," positivism tries to understand political life in terms of variables present in all systems or else in terms of the subpolitical, e.g., laws of sociology or of experimental psychology.[27]

The civic debate that brings the salience of regimes to light also serves to orient political science and give direction to its inquiries. What Strauss says here about the classical approach is crucial for understanding his own political science. Whereas today's social science favors the posture of a detached observer, the classics adopted the practical orientation that is inherent in political life itself. Mindful that communities are divided principally by disputes about regimes, the classics proposed to resolve such disputes "in the spirit not of the partisan but of the good citizen, and with a view to such an order as would be most in accordance with the requirements of human excellence."[28] As civic-minded arbitrators or umpires, they hoped to restore peace among warring factions by settling the most fundamental of all political controversies, the question of the best regime. Recognizing that regimes are matters for legislation, or for what we now call constitution-making, the classical political scientists addressed their teachings above all to legislators, i.e., to lawgivers undertaking to establish new regimes or to improve existing ones. They knew that improvement must be guided by some understanding of the form of rule that is best in itself, but at the same time, they saw that the conditions required to establish the simply best regime are seldom if ever present. Thus their teachings about the best regime were highly flexible and not at all doctrinaire. Besides considering what is simply best, they also gave attention to what is generally best for most communities, or best given available materials, or best where the aim is only to improve a regime without changing its basic form.[29]

For Strauss as for the classics, the guiding question of political science is "a subject of actual political controversy carried on in pre-philosophic political life," namely, how the community should be structured or who should rule it.[30] The classical teaching on the best regime addressed and attempted to resolve this controversy in a public-spirited way. To determine what form of rule is best, the classics were compelled to explore the question of what moral qualities best equip human beings to rule, or what virtue is. Starting from moral distinctions as made by decent people in everyday life, they concluded that the community should be ruled by "good men," namely, those who are wise and virtuous and who will prefer the common interest to private interests. This means that aristocracy, or rule of the truly virtuous, is the best regime. All regimes are to be measured by this standard and where possible brought closer to it, perhaps by some admixture of the aristocratic principle. Strauss reminds us that the classics' preference for true aristocracy was shared by the great minds who initiated modern democracy. Democracy was expected to broaden into an aristocracy as all or most men, through universal education, became virtuous and wise, or at least to provide for the selection of what Thomas Jefferson called the "natural *aristoi*" into offices of the government.[31] Today, with the degeneration of modern democracy into "mass culture," liberal education becomes "the necessary endeavor to found an aristocracy within democratic mass society."[32]

In sum, Strauss would have us recover the direct relation to political life that classical political science had enjoyed. Our political science should adopt the orientation that is natural to political life, along with the moral distinctions and the articulation of questions that such an orientation implies. Nevertheless, Strauss points out that political science, as a philosophical endeavor, must finally transcend the citizen's or statesman's horizon. By contrasting Socratic or Platonic political philosophy and Aristotelian political science, he shows us that different views are possible as to the integrity of the political horizon and the manner of transcending it.

According to Strauss, Socrates conceived of the whole in such a way that each part, including the political sphere, is somehow open to the whole. This means that the dialectical quest for political knowledge, which begins from opinions about political things, cannot be pursued independently of quest for knowledge of the whole. In transcending moral opinion, Socrates' dialectic depreciates it, so that the "good man" becomes the wise man or philosopher and right practice is made to depend on theoretical knowledge of the whole, or on cosmology. Aristotle, by contrast, separates the quest for the best political order from cosmology. He upholds the dignity of moral virtue, as it is exhibited in the life of the gentleman, and the capacity of moral virtue to illuminate the principles or ends of action. Refusing to make good practice dependent on theory, he maintains that practical wisdom or prudence, in pursuing ends of action disclosed by moral virtue, is sufficient to guide political action. By thus remaining within the limits of the gentleman's understanding of the moral life, Aristotle becomes the founder of political science as a distinct discipline. Of course, Aristotle's own understanding transcends the horizon of those to whom his political science is addressed. His broader understanding of the nature of things permits him to articulate, augment, and correct the gentleman's perspective and point beyond it to philosophy as the truly good and happy life, yet he does not depreciate that perspective in the Socratic way.[33] A full account of Strauss's political science would require us to consider whether he stands closer to the Socratic or to the Aristotelian position as regards transcending the political horizon, but such an undertaking lies beyond the scope of the present essay.

SOCIAL CRITIQUE AND THE PHILOSOPHIC LIFE

A word must be said finally about the rhetoric that Strauss employs in treating American social science, for this, too, reflects his understanding of the philosophic life. Strauss's critique of social science positivism may fairly be characterized as intransigent and caustic, although he is conciliatory toward that large body of social or political scientists who wish simply to investigate social phenomena but feel obliged to defer to positivism on methodological issues. If the positivist response is harsh and dismissive, it is also true that Strauss seems to go out of his way to be provocative. He does not attack the luminaries of American social science by name or directly review their works, but even this is belittling, for it underscores his judgment that Max Weber remains "the greatest social scientist of our century."[34] Strauss's critique of social science provides a rare instance where he claims to understand writers—and this includes Weber—better than they understood themselves. In most controversies that he reopened—reason vs. revelation, ancients vs. moderns, even historicism vs. natural right—it is difficult to say with certainty where Strauss himself stands (witness the interpretations that place him on both sides of these con-troversies), but so emphatic is his rejection of positivism that no one seems to have placed him in that camp. One wonders, however, if the very force of this rhetoric might not disguise some sense of kinship, some hope for rehabilitation.

To decide why Strauss chose to attack social science positivism so severely, one must first raise the more general question of why philosophers should wish to involve themselves at all in controversies of the day, if their primary concern is quest for knowledge of the eternal order. Strauss himself points out that many philoso-phers, in order to pursue their inquiries safely and without distraction, not only refrained from openly criticizing prevailing opinions, but even gave the appearance of adopting them. Why then do philosophers leave their secluded gardens to enter the marketplace and even involve themselves in political debate? Strauss rejects Alexandre Kojève's contention that the desire for recognition draws philosophers into public life, offering instead the following explanation. The natural attachment that human beings feel for each other, arising from the needs of the body, is felt too by philosophers, if in lesser degree than by non-philosophers. This leads philoso-phers to try to help others, to do what is possible to ameliorate their condition, even to advise lawgivers on how to establish good regimes or improve existing ones. Moreover, philosophers assist the political community by defending salutary opin-ions, as well as prudential judgments and sound practices, against challenges arising from misguided or pernicious theory. By serving this way as good citizens, philoso-phers also benefit themselves and, more broadly, the cause of philosophy itself by allaying suspicions that philosophic inquiry endangers the political community. Beyond this, philosophers are drawn into the marketplace by their admiration for well-ordered souls and their desire to produce good order in the souls of the best young people—the potential philosophers—through education. Philosophy is forced to become "political" both to protect and to perpetuate itself.[35]

Strauss's critique of social science positivism is designed to carry out these perennial tasks of philosophy, as they presented themselves under the circum-stances of his time. In the manner of a good citizen, he refutes theories that under-cut or demoralize liberal democracy by insisting that its core "values" or founding principles lack rational grounding. He defends the integrity of prudential state-craft against positivism's radical depreciation of pre-scientific knowing. He advances liberal education by showing that the fundamental questions of ethics or moral philosophy are not in fact "meaningless," but should of be of the utmost concern to us.

The severity of Strauss's critique is calibrated to the depth of the current cri-sis of the West, which engulfs liberal democracy and poses an unprecedented threat to the philosophic enterprise itself.[36] His critique proceeds from a calculation that the cause of philosophy and good government will best be served under current circumstances by a bold offense, not by stealth and indirection. Despite the intran-sigence of Strauss's attack on social science positivism, one may suppose that he was not unmindful of some common ground with that position, namely, a desire to uphold the possibility of scientific truth. Perhaps he judged that a bold assault might open the eyes of positivistic social scientists—if not the captains then their trusting followers—to the way that science itself was now imperiled and thereby force an alliance against a common foe that denied the possibility of objective science altogether. To some degree such an alliance did emerge in American political science following the turmoil of the 1960s.

Strauss's students and followers are not divided over the merits of Strauss's critique of mid-century social science, but they are at odds on what stance now to take towards the social sciences, especially political science, where many are housed. One group holds that political science remains positivist at heart, destructive of liberal democracy's moral foundations, and fundamentally antagonistic toward political philosophy, so that the uncompromising assault undertaken by Strauss must continue. It is wary in particular of apparent concessions that purport to honor Strauss or seem to make room for political philosophy. Another group insists that political science, in recent decades, has changed in important ways: positivism has lost its grip; increasingly the character of scientific knowledge and its relation to practical wisdom are treated as open questions; inquiry about the good or just life is accorded greater respect; Strauss's students have assumed positions of leadership and distinguished themselves through professional awards and achievements; and the importance of Strauss's own contribution is increasingly recognized. We do not propose to enter into this controversy here, but this point can be made: Strauss's example of relentless critique is not necessarily conclusive for us, since circumstances change and none of us is Leo Strauss.[37] Strauss's own account of the nature of the philosophic life indicates that one's proper stance towards political society and its intellectual currents cannot be settled apodictically, once and for all, but must be determined prudentially, here and now, with a view to what advances philosophy and in full appreciation of the uncertainty and variability of human affairs.

NOTES

1. "A Giving of Accounts" with Jacob Klein, *The College* (St. John's College at Annapolis and Santa Fe), 22 (April, 1970): 3; Compare *The Rebirth of Classical Political Rationalism*, ed. Thomas L. Pangle (Chicago: University of Chicago Press, 1989): 27–28.

2. Leo Strauss, *Natural Right and History* (Chicago: University of Chicago Press, 1953): 35–80.

3. See Leo Strauss, *The City and Man* (Chicago: Rand McNally, 1964): 11–12.

4. *The Rebirth of Classical Political Rationalism*, 8–9.

5. Leo Strauss, *What is Political Philosophy? and Other Studies* (Glencoe: The Free Press, 1959): 22; *Natural Right and History*, 64–74.

6. *What is Political Philosophy?*: 21–22, 259; "An Epilogue" in *Essays on the Scientific Study of Politics*, ed. Herbert J. Storing (New York: Holt, Rinehart and Winston, 1962): 325.

7. *What is Political Philosophy?*: 25–26; Today this conclusion is embodied in the widespread view that modern science is unavoidably "Eurocentric."

8. *Natural Right and History*: 42

9. *Natural Right and History*: 4–5.

10. *What is Political Philosophy?*: 18–19.

11. *What is Political Philosophy?*: 20.

12. *What is Political Philosophy?*: 20.

13. *The City and Man*: 3.

14. "An Epilogue": 327.

15. See Edmund Husserl, *The Crisis of European Sciences and Transcendental Phenomenology*, trans. David Carr (Evanston: Northwestern University Press, 1970); and Strauss's survey in *Studies in Platonic Political Philosophy* (Chicago: University of Chicago Press): 29–37.

16. *What is Political Philosophy?*: 17, 23–25, 34; "An Epilogue": 318–19; *Rebirth of Classical Political Rationalism*: 4–5.

17. *What is Political Philosophy?*: 23–24; "An Epilogue": 314–16.

18. *What is Political Philosophy?*: 23–25.

19. *What is Political Philosophy?*: 79–80; Strauss qualifies this statement somewhat by acknowledging that classical political philosophy, in focusing on the internal structure of the city, abstracts from two vital concerns of actual cities: "the omnipresence of War" and "the concern with the divine"; see *The City and Man*: 239–41; *What is Political Philosophy?*: 84–85.

20. *The Rebirth of Classical Political Rationalism*: 8.

21. *What is Political Philosophy?*: 10–11.

22. "An Epilogue": 311.

23. *The Rebirth of Classical Political Rationalism*: 8.

24. "An Epilogue": 314–16; *What is Political Philosophy?*: 11–12, 24–25; *The City and Man*: 19–21.

25. "An Epilogue": 326–27; *What is Political Philosophy?*: 20, 24; *The City and Man*: 34–35; *The Rebirth of Classical Political Rationalism*: 5–6.

26. *On Tyranny*, ed. Victor Gourevitch and Michael S. Roth (Revised and Expanded Edition: New York: The Free Press, 1963): 23.

27. "An Epilogue": 319–20.

28. *What is Political Philosophy?*: 90; stated differently, the classics' viewpoint was not that of "the ordinary partisan, but that of the partisan of excellence" (*The City and Man*: 47).

29. *What is Political Philosophy?*: 28, 33–36, 83–87; *The City and Man*: 45–49.

30. *What is Political Philosophy?*: 84.

31. *What is Political Philosophy?*: 84–86; Leo Strauss, *Liberalism Ancient and Modern* (New York: Basic Books, 1968): 3–25. Strauss notes that "modern democracy would have to be described with a view to its intention from Aristotle's point of view as a mixture of democracy and aristocracy," since offices are filled by voting for candidates, as distinguished from election by lot (*The City and Man*: 35).

32. *Liberalism Ancient and Modern*: 5; Cf. *What is Political Philosophy?*: 36–38; *The City and Man*: 31.

33. *The City and Man*: 13–49; *What is Political Philosophy?*: 38–40.

34. *Natural Right and History*: 36. Here Strauss observes that "no one since Weber has devoted a comparable amount of intelligence, assiduity, and almost fanatical devotion to the basic problem of the social sciences."

35. "Restatement on Xenophon's *Hiero*," in *On Tyranny*: 196–206; *What is Political Philosophy?*: 90–94.

36. Since the crisis of the West arises more from liberal democracy's demoralization—its loss of its original sense of purpose and its permissivist drift—than from the external danger

posed by Communism, this crisis would not, from Strauss's standpoint, be ended by Communism's recent collapse. Strauss indicates just how deep that moral crisis is by declaring, for example, that "Rome burns" ("An Epilogue": 327) or, as regards prospects for upholding liberal education and human excellence within mass democracy, that "we must realize that we must hope almost against hope" (*Liberalism Ancient and Modern*: 24).

37. In 1962, a young doctoral student presented Strauss with a prospectus for a dissertation on David Hume that began with a harsh indictment of positivistic social science. Strauss advised the student to tone that part down, whereupon the student, wishing to show his unswerving loyalty and courage, reminded Strauss of his own example. "Yes," replied Strauss in his often colloquial manner, "but I have one foot in the grave." On the larger issue raised here, consider Strauss's account of the form of rhetoric that Socrates chose to employ at his trial, including the prudential considerations governing that choice and the intended lesson for his followers; see *Studies in Platonic Political Philosophy*: 51–54, 65–66; and *Xenophon's Socrates* (Ithaca: Cornell University Press, 1972): 124–26, 129–40. To be sure, "one runs little risk in taking issue" with positivistic political science ("An Epilogue": 307), as compared to the grave danger of bodily harm that philosophers have faced in openly questioning some political or religious dogmas.

· 8 ·

Athens and Washington: Leo Strauss and the American Regime

Gregory Bruce Smith

"Every enhancement of the type "man" has so far been the work of an aristocratic society . . . that believes in the long ladder of an order of rank and differences. . . . Without that *pathos of distance* . . . that other, more mysterious pathos
could not have grown up either—the craving for an ever new widening of dis-
tances within the soul itself, the development of ever higher, rarer, more remote,
further-stretching, more comprehensive states." *Beyond Good and Evil*, #257

I

The one-hundredth anniversary of Leo Strauss's birth arrives one year before the
impending millennium. That year also marks the twenty-sixth anniversary of his
death. In the intellectual life span of significant thinkers, both are short periods of
time. But already we can look back at a very diverse group of interpretative con-
frontations with Strauss's thought. There is every reason to believe there will be
more diversity to come. It seems to me that Strauss fostered that diversity himself,
for example through the various, irresolvable tensions that he put forward on the
very surface of his work: Philosophy and the City, Athens and Jerusalem, Ancients
and Moderns. To the extent that he pursued a self-conscious "project," the interpretative diversity that has emerged is no doubt essential to Strauss's undertaking,
whatever that proves to be.

To date, various interpreters have asserted that Strauss's thought is a manifestation of everything from a naïve attempt to return to the Greek polis, to an elitist
teaching regarding the existence of a rigid natural hierarchy that must be given
direct political manifestation, to a conservative defense of modern, liberal capitalism, to a Nietzschean nihilism hiding behind an esoteric natural right teaching, to
a Machiavellian atheism, to the efforts of a medieval rabbi in disguise. In light of

103

this interpretative diversity—and there is some textual support for all these positions, and others besides—it is difficult to assess with any precision Strauss's precise relation to the present and future American regime. This is especially true if we are hoping for guidance on everyday policy decisions.

While it is altogether fair to call Strauss a supporter of American political life, if his thought is of any lasting significance it will be because it transcends the confines of any particular regime or time. Surely Strauss knew that everything that comes into being passes away, especially political dispensations. And Strauss would never have accepted the End of History thesis, as his exchange with Alexander Kojève makes clear.[1] Hence the ongoing need for both continuity and change remains the unavoidable given. Strauss was a proponent of *both* continuity and change.

Strauss once pointed toward the need for the "loyal and loving reshaping or reinterpretation of the inherited."[2] In short, what is needed is to plot a course into the future, which remains loyal to the spirit, if not always the letter, of the past. Hence Strauss, like all the serious thinkers he dealt with, was "untimely" in that his thinking was projected beyond the present and into the future, the only moment of temporality a thinker can in any way effect. It may or may not be true that philosophy is ultimately a contemplative activity, but Strauss of all people knew that when serious individuals write books they intend to accomplish more than to simply foster private reflection. Books are unavoidably public documents aimed at present and future generations.

It is clear from his many works that Strauss reflected upon the issue of *transitions* from past to future and how the thinker is implicated in them. He understood the unprecedented and untenable nature of our time. But again, if Strauss is a significant thinker, ultimately he was primarily a proponent of philosophy rather than any particular moral, political or religious dispensation past, present or future, although, as any reader of Strauss knows, these concerns are far from being mutually exclusive. My assertion will be that it is precisely because of his understanding of philosophy and its future prospects that Strauss could be a genuine, sympathetic supporter of the present-day American regime as well as someone capable of wishing it well into the future. Yet to my mind the most interesting issue that reflection on Strauss's thought opens for us as lovers of our own is: What is required to keep the American regime worthy of a serious philosophic defense into the future?

II

The title of this essay, "Athens and Washington," is intended to evoke two dichotomies simultaneously. The first is the dichotomy Athens and Jerusalem, which has gained a certain prominence in recent interpretations of Strauss's work. The other is the dichotomy Moscow and Washington which points toward the

Heideggerian, and more generally postmodernist, conclusion regarding the metaphysical equality and thereby questionableness of all modern political dispensations. Again, while I will stipulate that most of the prominent interpretative efforts to untangle Strauss's enigmatic corpus to date have rested on at least an element of the truth, I will argue that it is only through grasping the iconoclastic fashion in which Strauss was a proponent of "Athens" that one can understand his ultimate support for the American regime and thereby his most profound practical influence. It may be a very long time before we can begin to judge his ultimate philosophical influence.

Given the nature of Strauss's corpus, it is almost impossible to arrive at any apodictic conclusions. At some point a more or less well-founded speculative leap is required. But that leap must take off from substantial textual facts. On the assumption that it is true that the beginning is more than half the whole, let us on this occasion begin with the straightforward clues that Strauss gives us about the beginnings of his own thought. Strauss once observed that at the formative period of his thought he was totally absorbed in the reading of Nietzsche.[3] Strauss even makes the striking observation that he not only read the work of Nietzsche voraciously, but that he simply believed *everything* he thought he understood: "Nietzsche so dominated and charmed me between my 22nd and 30th years that I literally believed everything I understood of him."[4]

At the very end of his life Strauss returned to Nietzsche in an essay on *Beyond Good and Evil*. In that essay, Strauss prominently observed that Nietzsche's writings went out of their way to call attention to "Mr. Nietzsche." Strauss never did anything of the kind. He never wrote anything resembling *Ecce Homo* telling us about Mr. Strauss or how to interpret his various books. The rare occasions when Strauss calls attention to himself autobiographically are therefore doubly significant. They amount to an attempt to call attention to something Strauss thought had been overlooked. This, taken together with the series of indications Strauss gave of how to read other significant thinkers, gives us our present point of departure.

Was Strauss a Nietzschean? Yes and No. He was a Nietzschean in line with everything he thought he understood of Nieztsche. But Strauss's Nietzsche would not be recognizable as the Nietzsche presented in most contemporary scholarship. To take but one example, the postmodernist Nietzsche, Strauss could have cared less about who was more "metaphysical," Nietzsche or Heidegger. That would have been an utterly superficial, derivative and obscurantist issue for him. Nor would Strauss have accepted that at the heart of Nietzsche's thought lay only the will of an esoteric nihilist.[5] Strauss's Nietzsche intended a paradoxical "return" to Nature, not the customarily announced metaphysical emancipation from it. And perhaps even more iconoclastic, Strauss's Nietzsche was a Platonist.[6] Indeed, it is in understanding what Strauss meant by Platonism that we simultaneously grasp what he owes to Nietzsche.

Strauss discovered Nietzsche's Platonism before he turned to the systematic study of Jewish thought that occupied a good deal of his early scholarly efforts.[7]

Strauss discovered Nietzsche's Platonism before he systematically confronted the work of Farabi who allegedly so massively influenced his reading of Maimonides. My assertion is that before Strauss turned to Farabi, Maimonides, and ultimately Plato, he already had his understanding of Platonism in hand. Why he presented that Platonism through the lens of, for example, his Maimonides rather than Nietzsche is an open question. An equally important question is why Strauss made so much of the *tension* between Jerusalem and Athens in such a way that serious commentators think it reasonable to conclude that he ultimately chose Jerusalem. Before we can assess what to make of Strauss's work on various Jewish thinkers, and long before we can proclaim Strauss a "Jewish thinker" himself, we must attend to the Platonism Strauss found in Nietzsche.

We have only one text of Strauss's specifically addressed to a Nietzschean work. It is the late essay, "A Note on the Plan of Nietzsche's *Beyond Good and Evil.*"[8] It would be misleading to immediately assume that whatever is ultimately presented in that text represents what Strauss thought he understood 50 years earlier. But if there are central clues in that essay that point back to themes that were crucial in Strauss's works in the 1930's, 1940's and beyond, highlighting those convergences will prove to be valuable.

Strauss's late interpretation of Nietzsche comes into boldest relief when seen in the light of customary interpretations. Most noteworthy is the central position of God and religion as co-topics in Strauss's reading. Equally noteworthy is the importance given to the issue of "transition" to a future where man is translated "back" into nature albeit paradoxically becoming "natural" for the first time. Strauss's interpretation runs in the face of those attempts to use Nietzsche to pursue a perfectly straightforward modern desire for the autonomy afforded by the freedom from nature. Finally, Strauss brings into high relief Nietzsche's longing for a total transformation of philosophy—at least a transformation of its *public* persona. The future philosophers become the peak of existence in whose being all of existence is justified. Those new philosophers are said to rule in subtle and indirect ways as priests of a new religiosity. Behind these more public philosophers, however, lurks another breed of philosophers in the freedom of a high solitude. God, religion, the high solitude of future philosophy, "nature" and the need for a transition to a unique future become the central themes.

For Strauss's Nietzsche, at least as matters come to light in *Beyond Good and Evil,*[9] the central issue is whether philosophy will rule over religion or religion over philosophy. By comparison, Strauss asserts that for Plato and Aristotle the central issue was the rule of the city over philosophy or philosophy over the city. For Plato and Aristotle, religion is subsumed under the city. Strauss would have us believe that religion is taken to a higher plane by Nietzsche and in the process politics is transported to a lower plane. Yet the assertion is far from obvious. Indeed, Strauss goes to some pains to point out that the first chapters of *Beyond Good and Evil* are about philosophy and religion, while the later chapters are about politics and morals. Hence by Strauss's own reckoning, the organization of the book seems to point toward the confrontation between philosophy/religion on the one hand and politics/morals on the other.

Complicating matters further, religion is discussed in chapters whose titles make them appear to be about political matters and political matters are discussed in the chapter *Das Religiose Wesen*. The same can be said for the way the topic of philosophy is interspersed in all of the chapters. Further, just as *Beyond Good and Evil* criticizes all past philosophy while projecting a categorically different future philosophy, modern politics is criticized and a new, aristocratic, postmodern politics is held out as a redemptive possibility beyond the age-old spirit of revenge. It can easily be argued that the chasm between philosophy and the city, central to Strauss's conception of Platonism, was learned from Nietzsche. Yet Strauss seems determined to focus our attention on the future relation between philosophy and religion.

The mature Strauss's lifework on Aristophanes, Socrates, Xenophon, Thucydides, Plato, etc., seems to be built around the attempt to recover the experiences out of which philosophy initially grew. Those experiences are alternately designated prescientific, pre-theoretical or "natural." When Strauss is finished trying to articulate those natural experiences it turns out that philosophy initially emerged in the midst of the experience of an unavoidable antagonism between philosophy and the laws, customs and gods of particular cities. The city was seen as intrinsically closed and particular; philosophy as open, skeptical and longing for knowledge of the universal. There are places in his corpus where Strauss makes it appear that this is the central and untranscendable tension for all time—a "natural" tension.

But if the abolition of the political is at all thinkable, then this tension is not natural in the sense of always emerging on its own in all circumstances. One can speculate that what Strauss is signaling in his late piece on Nietzsche is the possibility or even expectation that religion will in the future rise in importance as the political wanes. Any consciously plotted transition to the future would have to take that into account, accentuating its positive possibilities, limiting its negative ones.

In the aftermath of the collapse of modern rationalism—and Strauss shares with Nietzsche, Heidegger and many others the understanding that this has already happened—perhaps there is a logic that takes over that gains powerful momentum. Perhaps part of what is implied in that momentum is that politics will wane and an ambiguous religiosity will become ascendant. I say ambiguous because the object of that religiosity remains an open question. For example, with Nietzsche there is an attempt to attach it to the god Dionysos who will be a manifestation of the eternal, this-worldly circularity of the Will to Power. With Heidegger it is attached to a vague longing for yet unseen gods. From Strauss we get a particular manifestation of Jerusalem, as brought forth by the Hebrew prophets, as lovingly reinterpreted by Strauss.

The possible rise of a new religiosity seems linked with Strauss's understanding that the modern longing to abolish the political could be successful even though the modern rationalism that fostered it has collapsed. Strauss repeatedly argued that the resulting World State would lend itself to the degradation and dehumanization of man and a possible tyranny of immense proportions because the abolition of the political would require that mankind cease to strive to understand the good, the just and the noble and pursue them in action.

At one point Strauss says in praise of Heidegger that he is the only man who has an inkling of what is implied in the technological world civilization that is coming.[10] Strauss tells us that Heidegger believed that every great civilization in the past had had a religious foundation. But according to Strauss, in his search for a new god to save us, Heidegger had gone over to the side of the gods of the poets. Philosophy had thereby abdicated. It was in Nietzsche that the desire to have philosophy rule over religion is to be found. In this, Strauss apparently took the side of Nietzsche.

Like both his Nietzsche and his Heidegger, Strauss points to the impending significance of religion in the age after the collapse of modern rationalism when a worldwide technological civilization looms. But unlike either his Nietzsche or his Heidegger, Strauss still points to the importance of retaining, indeed retrieving, the political. He also points to the need to retain ties with the traditions of the past even as we move to a unique future that will need to be confronted in unique ways. A loving reinterpretation of past traditions is needed to make a successful transition to the future. Strauss tries to make that unique future both religious and political. As we will see, the two converge in a way that allows continuity with the past. In this regard we have something resembling the eternal return of the same.

III

In the English translation of his early work on Spinoza, Strauss bookends his confrontation with the "theological-political problem" first published in 1930 with an autobiographical piece added in 1962 that confronts the nature of the "Jewish problem" and a respectful piece on Carl Schmitt's *Der Begriff Des Politischen*. The theological-political problem, while for many reasons not as publicly prominent, was a lifelong theme for Strauss as much as the more discussed tension between philosophy and the city. The "problem" concerns the irresolvable tension between the claims of philosophy and Revelation. Each claims to have the ultimate wisdom and the only genuine understanding of the good life. Strauss tried to show that Spinoza had not refuted Revelation, and by extension, neither had anyone else.

The autobiographical discussion that prefaces the Spinoza critique discusses the problem confronted by Jews in Nazi Germany. Because of their precarious situation, they were forced to question the essential nature of their fundamental identity and how to maintain it. For example, did its maintenance require the creation of a secular Jewish state, moving to a tolerant liberal state, assimilationism of one kind or another, a return to "cultural" principles, or a return to the traditional, orthodox faith in miracles, creation *ex nihilo*, and the existence of a mysterious, willful, voluntaristic God? In this autobiographical piece philosophy, politics and religion are brought together in a distinctive way.

In Strauss's account of Jerusalem, and this is true throughout his corpus, it is not the orthodox faith in miracles, creation ex nihilo and the existence of a willful mysterious God qua lawgiver that is central to Revelation, but the phenomenon of the prophet. Strauss's prophet is a human lawgiver who through his poetic speech orders a community. The prophets are depicted as philosophers in the city.[11] The primacy of the political is preserved in Strauss's rendition of Hebrew Revelation—law and lawgivers, obedience and law followers become central.[12]

Strauss eventually argued that the "Jewish problem" is identical to a universal human problem; in other words, there can be no contradiction-free society as the moderns hoped—least of all a global, technological state. Whenever Strauss turned to an explicit discussion of what was at the essential core of Jewishness, he never argued that it was to be found in membership in a particular tribe. And he never argued that it had anything to do with a return to traditional orthodoxy or Jewish "culture." In fact, in spite of his youthful fascination with Zionism, he came to argue that the existence of a specific Jewish state would in no way solve the "Jewish problem" as he articulated it. What Strauss defended is precisely the *rational* elements in the Jewish law, especially as interpreted by commentators like Maimonides. Strauss repeatedly argued that Judaism was always legalistic, hence rationalistic.[13] Further, Strauss argued that the Jewish God was always seen as the true God for all mankind, not merely the God of that particular tribe with which He initially covenanted. This is, to say the least, an argument not shared by all.[14]

Strauss repeatedly observed that in the Bible the beginning of wisdom is fear of the Lord, where for the Greeks it is wonder. The foundational necessity of fear was never in evidence in Strauss's work. And he knew perfectly well that all manner of dangerous nonsense could be advanced under the umbrella of divine inspiration or Revelation. The difference between true and false prophets had to be maintained and could only be discerned by the "intrinsic quality of revelation," i.e., its rationality.[15] Revelation needs philosophy. Granted, philosophy cannot give an apodictic proof of the impossibility of Revelation and hence of philosophy's superiority. But that incapacity to disprove Revelation is hardly a crippling blow for any philosophy which, like Revelation, knows its own limitations and realizes there is a mystery at the core of Being.

Strauss's longtime philosophic friend Jacob Klein once asserted that Strauss belonged to two worlds. The implication was that he was both a philosopher and a Jew. But in Strauss's terms that ultimately reduces to the fact that Strauss, like everyone else, had roots, belonged to a specific tradition and had a fated particularity: the love of one's own has its own beauty and fascination. Put another way, that meant no more than that Strauss was both a philosopher and a political man.

Having repeatedly rationalized Revelation and Judaism, Strauss nonetheless turned around and argued paradoxically that the Bible is "the East within us."[16] This is part of his argument that at the heart of Western Civilization lies the energizing tension between Athens and Jerusalem, at least his lovingly reinterpreted variants of them. But it is also a response to Heidegger's attempt to import an Eastern element to help save the West by turning toward either a "second beginning" that takes off from the pre-Socratics or by importing something like non-subjectivist Buddhism. Strauss responded that we already have, and always have had, an Eastern, which is to say non-rationalist, element in the very heart of the West.

Without presently trying to resolve the seeming contradiction between depicting Judaism, and hence Biblical Revelation, as both rational and irrational, Strauss seems to be trying to argue that after the collapse of modern rationalism, the West would be well served by the energizing tension of his own variants of Athens and Jerusalem. This is all part of Strauss's transition to a future that remains in touch with its past rather than having effected a radical break. Past and future are linked. We do not need a "destruktion" or "deconstruction" of the West in either a Nietzschean or Heideggerian variant. We need instead a loving reinterpretation of our tradition.[17]

We will return to Strauss's understanding of Athens in a moment, but we should note that Strauss makes it clear that he did not expect to ever see a perfect philosophic system that could explain the Whole. Hence we will never have perfect knowledge of man's place in the whole. Barring such a perfect philosophic system, Strauss asserted that it may be true that the world could never be perfectly intelligible without the premise of a mysterious God.[18] Thereby, Strauss publicly defended at least one of the tenets of orthodoxy and by extension, the life of the orthodox believer. He defended that life, just as he defended a substantive vision of the political against Schmitt's formalism, but he did not choose either for himself as the central venue of his life. His is the benevolent act of a man on behalf of some of his destiny-mates. But it is also an act of honesty on the part of a man who was committed to the philosophic life while understanding in a deep and penetrating fashion the limits of rationalism. Perhaps he understood those limits even more profoundly than Socrates, because Strauss had been a witness to the shipwreck of modern rationalism.

Despite his attempts to rationalize Judaism and Revelation, Strauss seems frequently to circle back in the direction of the mysterious, willful God of orthodoxy. At the heart of all that is, as with Heidegger, a mysterious absence that human logos cannot penetrate.[19] Yet Strauss could still remain committed to rationalism. Strauss left matters at saying that "it is unwise to say farewell to Reason."[20] Since modern reason had self-destructed, Strauss made it appear that we had to go back to a previous rationalism. But he was really looking forward to a future rationalism born of the novel tensions he proposed. The point at which Strauss stood in proposing those tensions—especially that between Athens and Jerusalem—was *outside* of both. His was a Platonism learned from Nietzsche, informed by theoretical insights taken from Heidegger, projected back on selected ancient and medieval authors as part of a loving reinterpretation that could foster a transition to a novel future. Therein lay Strauss's novelty.

IV

To return to Strauss's essay on *Beyond Good and Evil*, following Nietzsche's lead, Strauss calls attention to the differences between all past "prejudiced" philosophers, present "free spirits" and the so-called "philosophers of the future." All past philosophers were prejudiced and went astray in a variety of ways that need not detain us at present.[21] Present philosophers are free from past prejudices but as their precursors, they are not yet the philosophers of the future. The "philosophers of the future" will have the overall obligation to rule and will for all intents and purposes be priests of a new life and nature affirming religion. Strauss stresses that for Nietzsche, while belief in the old God is dead, religiosity itself is growing and will only continue to grow into the future. This is put forward as a consistent outcome following the collapse of faith in modern rationalism. But despite the growing religiosity, for an extended period into the future, mankind will be left in a transitional period of atheism, left, that is, to worship the Nothing.

Strauss asserts that worshiping the Nothing is not where Nietzsche wants to leave the matter. He wants to make a transition from the No-saying of the present and immediate future to a Yes-saying, affirmative stance toward reality in the more distant future. The growing religiosity must be made compatible with this affirmative stance. There must be a religion of the Will-to-Power—understood as a vindication of a this-worldly circular god—that will be administered by the philosophers of the future who will be religious in a way no past philosophers have been.

The curious fact about the philosophers of the future is that in many ways they will not be as free and clear-sighted—and certainly not as capable of freely chosen solitude—as the prejudice-free "free spirits" of the present. Those free spirits seem to occupy a privileged moment.[22] Their response to that moment is to be the precursors to a different kind of philosopher. But their kind of philosophy will survive into the future, hidden deep within the interstices of the world where the philosophers of the future will be far more visible.

As the epigram to this essay argues, the freest philosophers must not only be shielded from what elsewhere in *Beyond Good and Evil* is called the "necessary dirt of all politics," but from any public persona or public function whatsoever. They must freely choose solitude, unlike involuntary solitaries of the past such as Spinoza or Giordano Bruno. That is best accomplished by the existence of a long ladder of different types of individuals. To the extent that free-spirited philosophy becomes in the process a skeptical, questioning "way of life" without public responsibilities or fixed metaphysical doctrines, it will tend to withdraw into solitude ruling over the religious philosophers of the future in a subtle and indirect fashion, publicly allowing religion to rule over what remains of politics.[23] What is Strauss trying to signal by this unique interpretation?

One can only speculate about precisely what Strauss most appreciated in Nietzsche when he was young and reading him both voraciously and surreptitiously.

But I would point to two texts to which Strauss only rarely thematically alludes. They are two of Nietzsche's earliest works—*The Birth of Tragedy* and *Untimely Meditations*. In the latter, Nietzsche discusses at length the ways in which the will to truth—i.e., philosophy—is inimical to life. Nietzsche's assertion is that we should choose life over truth. The philosophic longing for truth must not be allowed to destroy life which requires all manner of tensions, contradictions and sheltering half-truths or outright myths and lies. One might note that for Nietzsche, the historical sense that contemporary man is so proud of, and Nietzsche is more than willing to use it, is one of the truths from which we should be shielded. Strauss was likewise a public opponent of what he called historicism.

Yet despite making this argument, Nietzsche never tired of praising the clear-sightedness of free-spirited philosophy. What he ends up doing is positing a great chasm between what is good for life for most and what is an unavoidable instinct for some. Fortunately, that instinct of the few is what gives meaning to life for others if it is exercised with discretion. This chasm between philosophy and life, or alternately put, between philosophy and the city, is what became central to what Strauss meant by Platonism.[24] I suggest that Strauss learned it from Nietzsche. One ramification for both Strauss and Nietzsche was the need for esoteric speech and philosophic solitude.

In *The Birth of Tragedy*, Nietzsche points out the ways in which Greek civilization was energized if not constituted by the tension between Apollonian and Dionysian tendencies. This was part of his critique of modern rationalist civilization which had attempted to overcome all the tensions and contradictions which healthy civilizations require. The Greeks gave this particular tension to themselves—Nietzsche goes so far as to assert that they invented both of the tendencies symbolized by Apollo and Dionysos—in the height of their spiritual strength. In a parallel fashion, Strauss repeatedly argued that at the heart of Western Civilization was to be found the energizing tension between Reason and Revelation, Athens and Jerusalem. Strauss asserted that as long as that tension remained in place Western Civilization need not die. Asserting the life giving need for a certain tension is not the same as asserting the simple truth of either of the participants in the tension.

We should recall the understanding Strauss attributes to Xenophon that even after the Socratic turn, the real Socrates continued to free-spiritedly think about all things, human, cosmic and presumably divine. That real philosopher need never show himself on the public stage if he is prudent like the Socratic Socrates made young and noble by Plato. As Nietzsche would have it, a public persona or mask can go forth into the world. Perhaps more to the point, the real philosopher may, for the first time, be able to withdraw and have no responsibility except to himself if things are arranged correctly. A present danger may point to a future possibility that has never yet existed.

It is in this light that we should look at Strauss's argument in favor of the plausibility of Revelation. Its possibility had to be defended *philosophically* and the wisdom of Athens had to be depicted as a rationalism that knew its limits. Beyond the collapse of modern rationalism lies the tension between a specific view of Jerusalem and a unique kind of rationalism allegedly exemplified by medieval and classical thought. I suggest that Strauss got the underlying idea for this necessary tension from Nietzsche, and long before he turned to Maimonides, Farabi, or Plato.

Apparently, what is required now is not to accentuate the original tension between philosophy and the city—although Strauss repeatedly returns to that theme—but primarily the tension between philosophy understood as a particular "way of life," and a somewhat untraditional variant of Biblical religion that can be seen to have a rational leaning. Both leave an element of the mysterious at the core of Being. In different ways, this mysteriousness is at the heart of the public teachings of both Nietzsche and Heidegger; it is not at the heart of the public teachings of either Farabi or Maimonides.

V

Once one begins to look closely, it becomes more difficult to say precisely what the metaphor Athens meant for Strauss than what he intended by Jerusalem. We cannot leave matters at the easy-going statement that Athens stands for rationalism. For Strauss there are different variants of rationalism and utter incommensurability between the modern and non-modern forms. For example, Strauss publicly rejected the premise, advanced by Heidegger among others, that modern rationalism descends in a direct line from Greek rationalism. "Athens" represents a specific variant of rationalism for Strauss. What I will assert is that there is a postmodern variant of rationalism toward which Strauss points. Athens is the metaphor for that postmodern rationalism as much as it is for the elements drawn from Greek thinkers.

In line with his depiction of the *Socratic* Socrates, Strauss initially presents the rationalism indicative of the metaphor Athens as a search for the "nature" or "natures" of the various categories or "tribes" of things visible to all via the senses. This is what follows from interrogating what is alternately called the pre-theoretical, pre-philosophic, "natural" or common sense experience of reality.[25] Strauss asserted that using this approach we could gain considerable knowledge regarding the heterogeneity of the multiplicity of tribes even if we could have at best limited knowledge of homogeneity, the ultimate One of the whole cosmos.

But according to Strauss, Greek philosophy, and thereby "Athens," is also connected with the discovery of the more generic (abstract?) philosophic concept "nature." According to this argument, the concept nature was discovered by reflecting upon such common sense experiences as the multiplicity of *nomoi* or conventions in the various cities, as well as through consideration of what follows from such distinctions as the difference between hearsay and what we see with our own eyes. In the former case, central to the idea of nature is the *nomos/physis* dichotomy. In the latter case, nature is associated with that which an individual can vouch for independently of commonly held and repeated opinions.[26] "Nature" so understood, now has more in common with homogeneity than heterogeneity. The Socratic approach to "nature," which seeks the heterogeneity of the various tribes, seems to be a consciously adopted form of moderation in the face of the initial, more radical search for "nature" qua one.

Be that as it may, the first complication we confront is that Strauss also links terms like pre-philosophic or pre-theoretical experience with "natural." Much of Strauss's later work is devoted to trying to recover this pre-philosophic, "natural" awareness. I would argue that this undertaking is a decidedly postmodern maneuver that takes off from a specific modification of the German Phenomenological tradition—especially as it is articulated by Heidegger.[27] The very task is decidedly un-Greek. This Phenomenological task of unpacking leads to a "recovery" of *an* idea of "nature" that is different than the concept of nature Strauss asserts the Greek philosophers discovered precisely *in opposition* to pre-theoretical awareness which Socrates then moderated. In some ways, the Phenomenological unpacking ends up closer to the Socratic understanding.

If the concept "nature" has a fluid, historical element, as would seem to be indicated, why should the initial Greek manifestation, or its Socratic modification/moderation, be taken as the definitive manifestation? More to the point, I would maintain Strauss is ultimately grafting different notions of "nature" side by side. As I will argue in a moment, Strauss got the initial impetus for this idea from Nietzsche.

Using the Bible as his exemplar, Strauss asserts that in the pre-theoretical horizon man is not meant to be a knowing, wondering or contemplative being. It is "natural" to live a simple life in compliance with the law.[28] Straussian Platonists also understand that there is everywhere and always an arena of law, opinion and custom.[29] That too is "natural." The detachment from this pre-theoretical everydayness that is intrinsic to philosophy is thereby "unnatural" in that it rests on a detachment and alienation from primary, pre-philosophic attachments. These "natural" bonds formed the necessary background against which philosophy launched its initial pursuit of wisdom, i.e., the discovery of the philosophic concept "nature." But we can immediately turn the last point around yet again by observing that the wonder-driven pursuit of wisdom, to the extent that it is driven by the powerful inclination of a distinctive or unique kind of being, is also "natural."

Obviously there is an extraordinary fluidity to the term "nature" in Strauss's thought that is similar to the fluidity in *Beyond Good and Evil*. My suggestion is that Strauss eventually follows his Nietzsche in seeing a variant of "nature" in pre-history, another historical variant initiated by the Greeks, modified in the Socratic method, and yet another that is possible in the future. All three coexist in the metaphor Athens.[30] Athens, as it comes from the hand of Strauss, is a hybrid constructed of elements taken most notably from Plato, Xenophon, Aristotle, Nietzsche, and Heidegger.

Strauss's discussion of pre-theoretical awareness parallels Heidegger's discussion of "everydayness." For Heidegger, everyday perception is pre-theoretical and shaped by a distinctive "World." That pre-theoretical revelation of reality is always prior to any theoretical perception or philosophic detachment. Theoretical detachment is, therefore, always derivative and if not unnatural, at least "inauthentic." What Strauss does is give this abstract Heideggerian account of everydayness substantive manifestation by passing it through various Greek writers. For example, Strauss not only adds the flesh and blood of distinctive kinds of individuals with competing ends taken from the Platonic dialogues, but he also articulates Heidegger's "World" by importing a large element of what Aristotle meant by "regimes." When Strauss is done, everydayness is determined by the substantive ends that distinctive tribes of individuals pursue which in turn are shaped by the shared view of the good of a particular group that shares a specific regime. To reduce the matter to a formula, Strauss politicizes Heidegger's abstract Phenomenological accounts of "everydayness" and "World." Strauss is also at pains to remind us that we are always confronted with competing regimes with different constellations of ends and different views of the ultimate good. This is what forms the very sinew of the political—contrary to Schmitt, for example, who sees political differences grounded in the generic "dangerousness" of man or the formal need for the we/they dichotomy.

Strauss not only gives sinew and ligature to Heidegger's account, he turns the issue of everydayness against Heidegger. Here, he borrows an element from the Socratic turn. Again, in interrogating everyday experience we always find that the world comes forth as a multiplicity of tribes or "whats." But eventually, even in the Socratic variant of the interrogation of everydayness, one is led to speculate on the origin or "cause" of the multiplicity of things. The Socratic response to this "natural" inclination is, according to Strauss, to make the tribe or class to which things belong the cause of the thing. The answer to the question "what is" a certain thing points toward its essential nature which it shares with the other members of its tribe. The "what" of the various things defines their Being—they *are* this what. Pre-Socratic thought, already driven toward pursuing a concept of "nature" as cause, tried to think the cause directly and in abstraction from determinate beings—i.e., qua Fire, Water, Air, One, Number, etc. Like the pre-Socratics, Heidegger tried to think Being in abstraction from determinate beings.[31]

But Strauss does not stop here. He complicates matters by admitting that the thinking of the "real," non-Socratic Socrates went beyond working out the articulation of the multiplicity of things, the ensemble of "whats." The real Socrates did not stop with the easygoing conclusion that the tribes of the various things are their causes. Real philosophy always attempts to grasp the Whole and to think the origin of the Whole qua One. For Strauss this means that philosophy is always led in the direction of the question *quid sit deus*. But Strauss is almost completely silent regarding the noetic foundation of the seemingly necessary speculations toward which he alleges that "real" philosophy always moves. Strauss is just as silent in this regard as is Nietzsche about the life of the real thinkers who stand behind the "philosophers of the future." Hence it remains unclear whether for Strauss there is any continuity between philosophy in its Socratic manifestation and in its more comprehensive "speculative" (for want of a better designation) mode.

It would appear, however, that both a Socratic thinker and what we are tentatively calling a speculative thinker converge on one conclusion. It is ultimately impossible to have total, apodictic knowledge about the Whole. For both, at the core of Being resides a mystery. Hence philosophy, no matter how construed, is not and never can culminate in a system of knowledge; it culminates in a "way of life" pursued by human beings of a very distinctive kind. This is precisely Nietzsche's conclusion.

We can offer one further expansion regarding what we are calling speculative thought, which is part of what Strauss means by Athens. Eventually thought is driven away from reflecting primarily on "external" reality and toward an interrogation of the nature of the inquirer. To again reduce the matter to a formula, mind or soul comes to take precedence over "nature." According to Strauss, this happened at Athens. It goes without saying that a thinker like Hegel would concur that mature thought becomes reflexive; he would not accept that this occurred until long after Athens—the turn to reflexivity being prepared by Christianity through its deepening of self-consciousness. This may or may not give added credence to the idea that what Strauss meant by Athens was a hybrid of Greek and late Modern (a.k.a. German) elements. However we deal with the historical question, high reflexivity is central to what Strauss means by Athens.

With the turn toward reflexivity, regardless of when it originated, the philosophic enterprise itself comes to take center stage. Henceforth the philosopher scrutinizes not only what he does in thinking, but also reflects on the very possibility of his enterprise and why it is of any value. Philosophy, born of a questioning and wondering instinct, to some extent rises above that instinct on the wings of its reflexivity, a reflexivity that is precisely what Revelation rules out of court before the fact. Reflexively interrogating itself, thinking points toward articulating the ground of the very possibility of thinking. This almost inevitably leads away from everyday experience.

What we have said to this point has to be made consistent with Strauss's central argument that what happened in Athens at the dawn of philosophy was the simultaneous turn to *political* philosophy. Political philosophy as Strauss uses the term is precisely what follows from reflexivity. Strauss argues that the turn to political philosophy was primarily undertaken for prudent or defensive reasons—and thereby involved a newfound concern for political rhetoric—rather than because of any unavoidable epistemic dependence of thought on everyday experience—as the Socratic method seems to imply. This concern presupposes that philosophy had already become reflexive enough to see itself with self-conscious clarity as in principle in rebellion against the city and the various conceptions of justice of the various cities. Political philosophy is a fully self-conscious brand of philosophy. In a parallel fashion, Nietzsche depicted past, prejudiced philosophy as an initially instinctive activity which rises to reflexive clarity about itself, its presuppositions, and its needs only with the free-spirited philosophers of the present. For Nietzsche, there are many historical manifestations of philosophy. They occupy rungs on a ladder leading to a fully self-conscious philosophy. Both Strauss and Nietzsche point toward the need for a full, self-conscious brand of philosophy. Each sees it as culminating in a distinctive way of life outside and beyond everyday experience.

Strauss is never clear about just how dependent thought ultimately is on pre-theoretical awareness. From Heidegger we get a clearer answer regarding the relation between philosophy and everydayness. Everydayness is simply determinative. Every form of theoretical detachment takes off from the world revealed to us in our collective doing and making. For Strauss, it appears that philosophy can stand far enough outside its world to plot alternate paths into the future. In this, Strauss seems closer to his Nietzsche than to Heidegger. Heidegger denied to philosophy this level of self-consciousness. Whether philosophy can ever completely emancipate itself from everyday experience and primary associations, and hence how much purchase it can get on modifying the future, remains an open question. At present, all I want to suggest, for proving the matter is beyond the scope of the present undertaking, is that what Strauss means by Athens is a synthesis of elements drawn from the Greeks and the Germans. The Germans set the task; the Greeks supply the substance and the moderation.

VI

Returning to Strauss's essay on *Beyond Good and Evil*, we have dealt with the prominence Strauss gives to religion, the need for a transition to a uniquely constituted future, and the various gradations of "philosophy." We must now thematically attend to what Strauss designates the "problem of nature." I have already suggested the complicated, if not conflicting, ways Strauss uses the term "nature." Again, in the last analysis I believe Strauss follows Nietzsche in significant ways.

Strauss asserts that for Nietzsche "nature" is something to be hoped for in the future. While it can be argued, as the moderns did, that we find the natural in the beginnings of human history, it is primarily at the end of history, or in the post-historical world, that Strauss's Nietzsche hoped to encounter the natural. Strauss twice repeats the observation that nature is a problem for Nietzsche but that he cannot do without it. The same appears to be true for Strauss. The Greek philosophers carved out and polished a concept of nature, linking it with the universal and unchanging. The moderns eventually made nature problematic by unleashing a new natural science and a new political science that had as their end, from the beginning, the eradication of unchanging nature and thereby of natural limits. We now see that those sciences themselves are without assignable limits at a time when nature dissolves as even a foil. Both Nietzsche and Strauss try to respond to this problem.

Nietzsche's response was to will the eternal recurrence which has as its end the "reintegration of man into nature." Despite the term "reintegration," Strauss makes much of Nietzsche's claim that man has never yet been natural. For Nietzsche, Strauss asserts, even in the pre-theoretical period prior to the origin of philosophy, man was not natural. Paradoxical as it might initially seem, the reason for this assertion is that at that time man had no end that differentiated him from the beasts. Furthermore, until the day after tomorrow, it will not be possible for mankind to affirm all that is and has been. We have feared, despised and revengefully attempted to transcend temporal reality from the beginning. Never yet has there been a self-conscious, affirmative, yes-saying to this world. That possibility still awaits us in the future as our end. Pursuing that end or telos is what will make us "natural" for the first time.

While Nietzsche asserts that mankind has never yet been natural, he does admit that at one time we were "instinctive," and for him that is at least a very close cousin of the natural. Nevertheless, following Aristotle, Nietzsche puts the primary locus of the natural in the end or telos and not in our beginnings or the simple, mechanical or efficient causality we share with the beasts. But the matter is more complicated. The Aristotelian ends are built into the constitution of the various things. The Nietzschean end is not pregiven and has nothing about it of necessity, whether telic or efficient. Its coming to be depends on a unique prior history that leads up to the intervention of Nietzsche.

Nietzsche seems to praise the instinctive. He says that late-modern humanity has ceased to be instinctive, becoming "de-natured" and timid. In response, he seems to praise the high, unselfconscious instinctiveness of the Caesars and Alcibiadeses of the world. This praise goes so far as to praise even their cruelty, the opposite of our present, de-natured timidity and compassion. By this argument, the unreflexive assertiveness of a few distinct individuals is closely akin to the "natural." The benefit to life of their assertiveness and even cruelty, for the two are unavoidably linked, is that they can become the basis of a long-term compulsion against the "natural," utilitarian impulse to immediate gratification and pleasure. We share that with the beasts. This long-term compulsion impresses a form or "nature" upon mankind. Conventional behavior eventually congeals as "nature"—*nomos* becomes *physis*. All form-giving, and this includes especially morality, is dependent upon this kind of tyranny against "nature" which forms our "nature." But we moderns have fled this form-giving tyranny and are "de-natured." We must be "reintegrated into nature."

What Strauss stresses is that for Nietzsche, "nature" is ultimately something to pursue that we can actualize in the future, not by going back to some manifestation of instinctiveness from the past. To get to that future, we must rise above the unreflexive Caesars and Alcibiadeses of the past to the philosophers of the future. They are allegedly the most comprehensive beings in whose existence all of Being is affirmed. They have as their goal the overall development of mankind. Using the old *nomos/physis* distinction, Nietzsche plots a path to a new conception of "nature," to be found in the future, where *nomos* and *physis* in their traditional usages merge. If this merger is possible, the initial showing of "nature" as the other of convention should not be taken as the last word.

Strauss makes a point of observing that the chapter title "Toward a Natural History of Morals" is the only chapter title that explicitly refers to nature.[32] It is in this chapter that Nietzsche makes much of morality being based on a tyranny *against* "nature." In the discussion of philosophy and religion in the prior chapters, both had been posited by Nietzsche as powerful "instincts." The philosophers of the future will be less instinctive than their traditional predecessors, but also less reflexive than the free spirits. From all of this Strauss concludes that "the subjugation of nature depends on men with a certain nature." They will become the future basis of law, and long-term compulsion. Everything aims at the justification of *these* philosophers. They are the linchpins of the project to bring unbounded affirmation and with it the return of a sense of the noble and the related faith in rank and hierarchy. There is a striking resemblance between this outcome and where Strauss arrives in his discussion of Classical Natural Right.

Strauss's "Natural Right" position must be differentiated from his discussion of the "Natural Law" tradition, which in many ways represents a betrayal of its ancestor. Unlike the Natural Law tradition, Natural Right does not culminate in a specific universal morality or a best regime valid everywhere and always. The Natural Right position is far more flexible because the focus is primarily on the existence of a hierarchy of "natural" types of human beings with the philosopher at the peak. Moral and political matters must be adjusted to ever changing circumstances in light of the need to maintain that natural hierarchy. On this, Nietzsche and Strauss are in almost perfect agreement.[33] Beyond that, Natural Right also stands for the same things Strauss means by Platonism. Politics, religion, and morality are natural dimensions of life, as is genuine philosophy. Philosophy is the highest and most self-sufficient life, but laws are still needed. Hence lawgivers are needed. Philosophy itself cannot give those laws; hence it must justify those who must. Strauss's Nietzsche stands for all of these things.

When Strauss is finished interpreting Nietzsche, Nietzsche stands for a future that is "natural," in that there will be a long ladder of rank and hierarchy, at a peak of which stands the philosophers of the future. They are the justification of all of existence because on a rung just above them, invisible from the base, are the true Nietzschean philosophers. One may say of Nietzsche's ladder that it is a conventional construction, in the traditional sense, except for the one rung at the top that is "natural." Without the peak, the rest of the ladder would have no meaning whatsoever; it would be a ladder to Nothing.

Moralities and regimes are "conventional," albeit the need for them is "natural." They must be judged in light of the extent to which the highest of human possibilities remains possible. To that end, an attempt may need to be made to argue that there is continuity between morality, law, religion and philosophy. But the continuity is questionable. The only way we can take our bearings regarding the Whole is to judge it in light of its highest manifestation—highest because most comprehensive and reflexive. Perhaps that possibility can only truly come to pass for the first time in the future.[34] That would make the future "natural" for the first time.

All of past history would be a movement toward that possibility. The accidental past would be redeemed and have meaning only if this new naturalness came to pass. There was a close cousin of nature in the beginning—instinct—and there is nature in the future as an end to pursue. There is, therefore, something resembling eternal return.

To make a very long story short, as we must bring ours to a close, what Strauss presents as the Classical Natural Right position was quickly swamped by the rigidities of the Natural Law tradition. That Natural Law tradition reached its first peak in Aquinas. The rigidities of his teaching were reproduced in a reaction against it in the modern Natural Law teaching of Hobbes. The reaction to the modern Natural Law tradition led through a series of wave-like intensifications to the birth and expansion of the historical consciousness which both Strauss and his Nietzsche oppose by attempting a move forward into a novel future. In Strauss's case, the move includes a loving reinterpretation of both Jerusalem and Athens. With that reinterpretation comes the return of the Natural Right tradition.

VII

Beyond the call to wonder, to questioning and searching, seen as a manifestation of the highest "way of life," what kind of concrete "project" has Strauss bequeathed?[35] Taken in panoramic perspective Strauss appears to have purposely left us with the untranscendability of various tensions: Philosophy and the City, Athens and Jerusalem, Ancients and Moderns, and more than a few others that are less prominently displayed. Strauss has concluded that life is best served by the ongoing, healthy interplay of irresolvable tensions. Much as life and truth come into opposition for Nietzsche, they do for Strauss as well. What is good for life is not the final truth for philosophy which concludes among other things that its own activity is the most comprehensive. Philosophy is a mysterious part of the natural whole. Like every other natural species or tribe, this one always runs the risk of becoming extinct. It is impossible to predict, as any environmentalist will testify, how the natural whole is affected by the elimination of one of its parts. But if, as both Strauss and his Nietzsche thought, philosophy is nature's highest and most comprehensive part because through it mind comes reflexively into the whole, its loss could be devastating. Strauss seems to have concluded that if the present momentum of the increasingly global West is not reversed, the future might not continue to be conducive to philosophy. Nietzsche's *willing* of the eternal recurrence implies the same thing.

Strauss's late text on Nietzsche signals predictions regarding what is to come. Forthcoming in that vision is a diminution of the tension between philosophy and the city. Because of the success of modern philosophy, we can predict the possible abolition of the political, especially if modern science were to eradicate the natural diversity that stands as its ground. That still hangs in the balance. To preserve its own distinctive form of diversity, philosophy must speak up on behalf of diversity per se. To continue to defend itself *against* the city as it did in its first manifestation would leave philosophy aiming its cannons in the wrong direction. The political should be defended. Likewise, to continue to rail against philosophy being diminished if it even appeared to be the handmaiden to theology, as was reasonable in the middle ages, would represent a misallocation of resources in the world that is coming. Philosophy must defend Jerusalem or give way to ambiguous new gods. It should be kept in mind that the defender is clearly higher than the defended.

Defending philosophy primarily against either theology or the city has become an antiquarian undertaking. Contrary to either of those antiquarian undertakings, Strauss posits unavoidable tensions between Philosophy and the Political and between Philosophy and Revelation at a time when all the parties are in danger of extinction. I have tried to suggest that both Strauss's Athens and his Jerusalem represent amalgams of Ancient and Modern elements. It is not surprising therefore that there have been such diverse interpretations of his work. I maintain that most of those diverse interpretations are consistent with the tensions Strauss wants to put in place.[36] I believe that Strauss thought he needed a variety of different positions to be adopted—i.e., taken seriously—if he was to modify the features of the future he saw coming.[37] It was imperative that there be believers, lawgivers, patriots, thinkers of all colors and sizes, and on and on. The existence of this diversity is the presupposition of both Strauss's Natural Right position, and the project of his Nietzsche.

While Strauss thought that it was necessary to hold on to rationalism in the age of the collapse of modern rationalism, it was also necessary that there be laws. To the extent that, contrary to modern philosophy, philosophy is transformed into a mysterious *way of life* rather than a public *system of knowledge*—and Nietzsche is at the forefront of this undertaking—future philosophers in principle will not be lawgivers in any but the most general and detached way. Strauss understood as well as Heidegger that a global, technological civilization was coming wherein we would be possessed of immense power with no assignable limits to its exercise. He does not appear to have believed that philosophy can ultimately assign those limits any more than did Heidegger. That leaves in its wake a concrete political and moral problem. There is a need for laws and lawgivers. But there is no need to quit serviceable ones that already exist. They can be lovingly modified.

The solution to the impending postmodern problem, as Strauss saw it, seems to presuppose the need for the existence of different individuals able to pursue different ends—i.e., different visions of the good life.[38] That in turn would bring with it serious debate about the most important things. Therein the political would remain a feature of the future world, no matter how local or global the venue of the debate. For Strauss, the political implies a serious conflict over the nature of the good which given the mystery at the core of Being can never yield apodictic answers. The debate can be eternal, albeit all publicly adopted answers are doomed to being replaced eventually. There need not be armed camps and war. But there will be some degree of conflict and confrontation. That is intrinsic to both our "nature" and the nature of the Whole. While the interplay of diversity could easily be quite unpredictable, Strauss was unwilling to let matters eventuate in the amorphous possibilities he attributed to both Nietzsche and Heidegger. He wanted to link future possibilities to past traditions. Far more than the late modern authors from whom he draws, Strauss wanted a more or less predictable future. In the end, the belief in the possibility of predictability seems to rest on the presupposition of an unchanging nature. But Strauss was always reticent to simply assert that theoretical possibility. Therein lies the problem of nature in Strauss's thought which I believe remains unresolved.

Be that as it may, there is no mystery why, in the aftermath of Nazi inhumanity, and throughout the Cold War threat of universal tyranny, Strauss could be a perfectly unproblematic defender of Washington. Openness to debate about the good was precluded by both. Acceptance of natural human diversity, no matter how defined, was openly opposed. Washington still allowed openness to a more "natural" form of politics. To the extent that openness remains, Strauss would continue to defend Washington. But there is a problem here for Strauss. Moscow, Berlin and Washington all rested on the efforts of modern philosophy which for Strauss moved with wave-like necessity from its more modest beginnings to its destructive end. To reject modern rationalism would seem to carry with it the conclusion that all of the political and moral dispensations descending from it must be rejected as well.

But Strauss asserted that it was an affront to common sense not to see the clear superiority of Washington to either Moscow or Berlin. This was true whether we looked at the matter from the rarefied perspective of philosophy, or the more straightforward common sense articulation of reality shared by millions of individuals in everyday life. The problem for Strauss is that this move seems to give greater priority to everyday, common-sense experience—and the *practical reason* that emanates from it—over theoretical or speculative reason no matter how we articulate it, than Strauss ever succeeds in successfully defending. I know of nowhere in his corpus where Strauss defends anything like the priority of practical reason this understanding requires. We are back to the troubling question of where the philosopher stands who puts in place all the tensions he presumes are beneficial to life. Is it not practical wisdom rather than theoretical or speculative reasoning that tells him what is necessary? By the same token, I see no statement of Strauss's anywhere that points out the noetic foundation of a truly autonomous speculative philosophy even though in the last analysis I think he follows Nietzsche in positing a certain detached solitude for future philosophy. Perhaps there is some middle ground here, but Strauss remains silent regarding what it is. Maybe in line with what Klein indicated, Strauss did try to live in two worlds, if not precisely the two Klein had in mind. But the relation of those two worlds—the everyday and the speculative—remains obscure. As a result, the ultimate ground of Strauss's defense of Washington remains unclear.

That said, let us assert the following: For Strauss, Washington stood for a form of practice that was far more natural than the available alternatives. And this is true despite the fact that its *Constitution* is descended from the modern theoretical principles that aimed at routing nature. Beyond that, Strauss's Washington is open to and indeed already linked with Jerusalem. Strauss repeatedly quoted Nietzsche's observation that it was impossible to have Biblical morality without the Biblical God. But for Strauss there is no need to construct some synthesis of Caesar with the soul of Christ to retain that link. The link to the Biblical tradition is already imbedded in the practice of Washington. What was needed was to defend the dignity of the life of the believer. One does not have to create a new belief or wait for new gods with no assurance that either would be forthcoming. Finally, Washington, at its best, offers an environment where modern constructivism does not so virulently unleash itself that the natural articulation of reality with its everyday understanding and primary attachments gets routed, despite its being a child of the Enlightenment. Washington is potentially more immune to the excesses of modernity than any of the other modern alternatives yet seen. But without some new, future, postmodern end to pursue, it may not remain immune forever.

That said, in the aftermath of the Cold War, with no sign of a revitalized Nazism on the horizon, Strauss's relation to Washington would have changed. In this new environment, Strauss would be free to criticize elements in the moral and political life of Washington. American political life is becoming less and less natural—and moral discourse is becoming increasingly abstract, consider for example, Rawls—and the vitality of concern for things like honor, morality and the holy are precarious. And Strauss would surely criticize the creeping uniformity of late-modern civilization. Indeed, it would be the moral and cultural underpinnings of late-modern civilization that Strauss would have criticized more than Washington's concrete parchment regime or laws. But he would probably oppose the transfer of more and more issues that were strictly political into administrative and bureaucratic venues. And he would no doubt wish a reversal of contemporary trends in theology, hoping to see Jerusalem interpreted more in the direction of resoluteness and fortitude than what he would see as an easygoing, democratizing latitudinarianism.

But I think it is inappropriate to drive Strauss very hard in the direction of specific policy issues because he would have shied away from allowing political philosophy to become confused with political ideology, no matter how dignified the ideology or the regime it supported. For Strauss there could never be a perfect regime or contradiction-free society, hence political philosophy had to remain an open-ended undertaking. In the last analysis, Strauss was a partisan of philosophy rather than of any specific regime.

To the extent that the American regime remains open to diverse natural possibilities, our past Western tradition *and* the need for change, it would in Strauss's eyes remain worthy of a serious philosophical defense. But to do so, Washington would have to remain open to *both* continuity and change. Depending on that

openness, Washington would remain either a threat or a shelter for future humanity, a prison or a haven.

NOTES

1. See *On Tyranny: Including the Strauss-Kojève Correspondence*, ed. Victor Gourevitch and
Michael S. Roth (New York: Free Press, 1991). See also my "The End of History or a Portal
to the Future: Does Anything Lie Beyond Late Modernity?" in *Francis Fukuyama and His
Critics*, ed. Timothy Burns (Lanham, Md.: Rowman & Littlefield, 1994).

2. *Spinoza's Critique of Religion* (SCR) (New York: Schocken Books, 1965), p. 25.

3. "Correspondence of Karl Löwith and Leo Strauss," trans. George Elliot Tucker,
Independent Journal of Philosophy 5/6, 1988, pp. 177–92. We should also note that Strauss says
something similar regarding Heidegger. He claimed that nothing so massively affected him
"in the years in which [my] mind took [its] lasting direction as the thought of Heidegger."
He also says of Heidegger that he is the only "great thinker" of the twentieth century. "An
Unspoken Prologue," *Interpretation*, Vol. 7/3 (September 1978), pg. 2. See *The Rebirth of
Classical Political Rationalism* (RCPR), (Chicago: University of Chicago Press, 1989), pg. 29.
See also *What Is Political Philosophy?* (WPP), (Chicago: University of Chicago Press, 1988),
pg. 246. We will return to the issue of Heidegger below, although on this occasion, reflec-
tion on Nietzsche's influence will take the lead.

4. *Independent Journal*, p. 183.

5. Shadia Drury has attributed such a position to Strauss. See *The Political Ideas of Leo
Strauss* (New York: St. Martin's Press, 1988). While this argument has became a staple for the
New York Times whenever it mentions Strauss's name, as well as in the essays of individuals
like the liberal polemicist Stephen Holmes, I agree with Robert Pippin regarding the abject
superficiality of this position. See Robert Pippin, *Idealism as Modernism* (New York: Cambridge
University Press, 1997), p. 212. "The idea of Strauss's 'philosopher' as Nietzschean 'superman,'
'creating values,' is an absurd overstatement and misses a very central issue in Strauss's account,
the problem of nature, nowhere explored with any sensitivity in Drury's book." I will argue
below that Pippin is quite correct in seeing the "Problem of Nature" as a, if not the, central
issue linking Nietzsche and Strauss.

6. Laurence Lampert is one of the first to see this in his subtle account in *Leo Strauss and
Nietzsche* (Chicago: University of Chicago Press, 1996). While Lampert sees some of the elements Strauss and Nietzsche share, he ultimately takes Strauss to task for not following what
he (Lampert) sees as the logic of where Nietzscheanism leads. In effect, he accuses Strauss of
a certain cowardice that eventuates in a conservatism that refuses to speak the truth in public. Lampert's Nietzsche, on the other hand, intended a general "enlightenment" and emancipation from myth. Humanity was to resolutely stare into the abyss en masse. It seems to me
that Lampert may have missed the real thrust of *Nietzsche's* project. To a certain extent, he
seems to understand Strauss better than Nietzsche.

7. Indeed, as Lampert notes, Nietzsche's presence is massive in the early work *Philosophy
and Law* (PL). It can be seen prominently as well in the early work on Spinoza and in later
works such as *Natural Right and History* (NRH) (Chicago: University of Chicago Press, 1950),
especially pp. 9–80.

8. The essay is included as one of the central chapters in Strauss's last book, *Studies in*

Platonic Political Philosophy (SPPP) (Chicago: University of Chicago Press, 1983), pp. 174–191. That Strauss designated the essays in this volume "Platonic" is a key to what Platonism meant for him.

9. In comparing *Beyond Good and Evil* and *Zarathustra* Strauss says that *Beyond Good and Evil* had always seemed to him to be Nietzsche's most "beautiful" work. He notes that Nietzsche thought that *Zarathustra* was his most "profound" work. Strauss observes that profound and beautiful are two different things. He seems to have purposely avoided using Nietzsche's most profound work as his vehicle. In short, Strauss purposely chose not to deal with Nietzsche's most philosophic text.

10. See "Heideggerian Existentialism," in RCPR, p. 43.

11. See especially in this regard PL and the "Introduction" in *Persecution and the Art of Writing* (PAW) (Glencoe, Ill.: The Free Press, 1952).

12. Indeed, Strauss points out that one of the most significant differences between the Jewish and Christian traditions is that the one is legalistic and the other arrives at a more or less apolitical set of tenets of faith. For what it is worth, authors who took on scholarly significance for Strauss like Machiavelli and Nietzsche had argued that Christianity undermined the political. Be that as it may, Strauss is clear that the ultimate outcome of modernity, whether as secularized Christianity or not, is a threat to abolish the political. Hebrew Revelation in Strauss's rendition does not.

13. Strauss even cites Deuteronomy 4:6 in support (SCR, p. 30).

14. Yet Strauss could still make a more visceral argument that it is "honorable" to love one's own—i.e., to affirm the lot in life into which one is unavoidably thrown. One must keep in mind the status of honor in Strauss's thought. See Leo Strauss, "Why We Remain Jews," in *Leo Strauss: Political Philosopher and Jewish Thinker*, ed. Walter Nigorski and Kenneth L. Deutsch (Lanham, Md: Rowman & Littlefield, 1994).

15. See "Progress or Return," in RCPR, p. 264.

16. RCPR, p. 44.

17. We should keep in mind the assertion that Strauss explicitly made that the concern with past and future intrinsic to modern thought, and especially late-modern thought, comes at the expense of the primacy of the eternal. "Progress or Return," in RCPR, p. 239. It represents a more or less complete substitution of the temporal for the eternal. Strauss, like his Nietzsche, was concerned with the past and future and the possibility of a transition that could link them with some degree of continuity.

18. SCR, p. 29.

19. The moderns tried to eliminate the mysterious by replacing the visible world with a hypothetical one constructed by the mind. In that effort, Strauss argued, it remained precisely as hypothetical as orthodoxy and every bit as much based on faith. And the world theoretically and practically constructed by man could never be totally successful which would be the only argument in its favor. As we will see shortly, from Heidegger Strauss learned a powerful critique of that constructivism and a way back to the visible world, and thereby back to "nature." That opening informed his vision of Athens.

20. SCR, p. 31.

21. I deal with this at greater length in my *Nietzsche, Heidegger and the Transition to Postmodernity* (Chicago: University of Chicago Press, 1996), pp. 135–171.

22. Strauss also seems to point to the present as a privileged moment. See *The City and Man* (CM) (Chicago: Rand McNally, 1964), p. 9. "[T]he crisis of our time may have the accidental advantage of enabling us to understand in an untraditional or fresh manner what was

hitherto understood only in a traditional or derivative manner. This may apply especially to classical political philosophy. . . ."

23. For Nietzsche that meant, at least initially, the "great politics" hegemonized by a united Europe that would usher in global rule for the first time.

24. Strauss clearly never accepted that the doctrine of the ideas was central to Platonism, or even that Plato had any specific metaphysical doctrine.

25. Prior to the discovery of the philosophic concept nature—already approached by the Sophists—"pre-philosophic" awareness focused on the "custom" or "way" of the various individual things. In this fashion, the custom or way of a dog was equated with that of trees, Persians, athletes and so on. As is true of his depiction of the pre-Socratics, Strauss asserts that there is no philosophic concept like "nature" in the Bible. The Bible also discusses "custom" or "way," not "nature." In this regard, the Bible is "pre-philosophic" or "pre-theoretical." This is a conclusion that even some of those who consider themselves Straussians are wont to reject. See Hadley Arkes, "Athens and Jerusalem: The Legacy of Leo Strauss," in *Leo Strauss and Judaism*, ed. David Novak (Lanham, Md.: Rowman & Littlefield, 1996), pp. 1–23.

26. NRH, pp. 81–120.

27. Husserl had argued that there was pre-theoretical awareness. All scientific knowledge was derivative from this "primary" knowledge of the world. But Husserl ultimately linked that awareness to an openness to pure essences grasped by a decidedly modern, abstract, theoretical ego. Heidegger deflected Husserl's insight in the direction of the "everydayness" of sensibly perceived, publicly shared reality. See "Philosophy as Rigorous Science and Political Philosophy" in SPPP, pp. 29–37, and "An Introduction to Heideggerian Existentialism" in RCPR, pp. 27–46. Strauss follows Heidegger in that he wants to lodge the pre-theoretical in a publicly shared reality.

28. Following Heidegger, Strauss also argued that pre-theoretical experience is not only political and moral, but always contains an element of the holy. This is what Strauss borrowed most significantly and then modified most creatively, Heidegger's understanding that the everyday articulation of things unavoidably contains an element of the holy—e.g., the "Fourfold." Strauss deflects this notion in the direction of his discussion of Revelation. Straus and Heidegger both see the pre-philosophic life-world as a world of nations (hence politics), morality and faith. But Strauss is always far more substantive in articulating what this means.

29. Straussian Platonists further know that while the philosophic pursuit of wisdom may be instrumental in changing the everyday content of opinion, it will never lead to the overcoming of opinion and its replacement by universal wisdom.

30. In between the Greek beginning and the future we have Christianity and Modernity, both of which attempted a journey *away* from "nature."

31. Heidegger argued for the need to get directly to the issue of Being without passing through the determinate particularity of any distinct things. He felt that any doctrine that focused on beings led inevitably to the mastery and domination of beings intrinsic to modern technology. Strauss's unstated response to Heidegger is that one must always ask the question, "What is this thing?" For Strauss, one cannot, or at least should not, try to get to the Being of a thing except by proceeding through discrete beings. Or to cast the matter in a Heideggerian light, one cannot get to Being in abstraction from beings.

32. Strauss then, seemingly non-sequitously, wonders out loud if nature could be the theme of the entire second half of the book.

33. An unavoidable question remains: Upon what foundation does the person making the practical adjustments called for by this understanding of Natural Right stand?

34. Strauss did assert that no one had *ever* spoken more magnificently about what a philosopher was than Nietzsche. And Nietzsche's discussion of philosophy, in Strauss's eyes, leads up to the philosophers of the future.

35. We might note that to say that philosophy is primarily a "way of life" presents a metaphor that hardly basks in the light of full clarity.

36. Needless to say, a few of the prominent interpretations are based on the inability to understand either Strauss or the sources he attempts to hold in tension.

37. It is not necessary that Strauss saw how all the parts would fit into a whole all at once. That clarity may have come over time.

38. The diversity toward which Strauss points was not the now fashionable group diversity associated with the mantra of race, class, gender and ethnicity. Strauss pointed toward the diversity of genuinely different types of individual who pursue different ends.

9

Strauss's Generalized Agnosticism and American Liberalism

Aryeh Botwinick

llan Bloom speaks for a large group of Strauss's disciples when he says that "The Framers held that the rational conviction of the truth of the principle of natural right was essential for fighting the American Revolution, for establishing a constitution, and for preserving it."[1] I believe that at best this reading represents only one way of connecting Strauss with the American Founding and the liberalism that has been nurtured and practiced by our political regime. Without having to probe very far below the surface of Strauss's writings, one can come up with a different image of the values and principles he cherishes—and an altered understanding of the reasons as to why he cherished them. I would also suggest that it is possible to read the Framers (and most acutely Madison in Federalist Number Ten) as reflecting this transformed reading of American liberalism—so that interpreting Strauss in a certain way offers us a hermeneutical key for reconceptualizing the theoretical stakes in the American Founding.

In what follows, I would like to make a case for reading Strauss as a mitigated skeptic who embraces liberalism precisely for its affinities with mitigated skepticism. I will then attempt to show how Federalist Number Ten can be read to reinforce an analogous linkage between liberalism and skepticism.

I

I will present a sampling from Strauss's writings of his grappling with skepticism, and of his rejection of extreme skepticism in favor of versions of mitigated skepticism. With regard to social science, Strauss says that it "is always a kind of self-knowledge. Social science, being the pursuit of human knowledge of human things, includes as its foundation the human knowledge of what constitutes humanity, or rather, of what makes man complete or whole, so that he is truly human."[2] The continuity of the "stuff" linking the investigator to what he is investigating inhibits the emergence of a completely neutral, objective social science. Several factors are at work here. One is because the subject matter of social science is man, human bias is too pervasive and deep-rooted to facilitate a completely neutral and disinterested study of human and social phenomena. Another factor minimizing the "objectivity" of social science is almost the antithesis of the first. In social science we would not want a thoroughly unbiased account of a particular issue because the human and social entities and interactions that social scientists study—and the personality of the observer—are so completely suffused with overlays of human interpretive reconstructions that a totally neutral study would distort and deface the very phenomena it sought to comprehend. The idea of scientific neutrality seems to be hopelessly out of place within the sphere of social science. Thirdly, the metaphysical continuity between the investigator and what is being investigated is suggestive of the possibility that the identities of both might be transformed as a result of the investigation at hand, thus defeating the possibility of a neutral study. The upshot of all three factors is a skeptical attack on the idea of social science, but Strauss ends up roundly endorsing certain forms of social inquiry and investigation. He says that

> to treat social science in a humanistic spirit means to return from the abstractions or constructs of scientistic social science to social reality, to look at social phenomena primarily in the perspective of the citizen and the statesman, and then in the perspective of the citizen of the world, in the twofold meaning of "world": the whole human race and the all-embracing whole.[3]

For the external perspective of the scientistically motivated observer Strauss would substitute the internal perspective of the citizen or statesman who builds on the commonalities subsisting between himself and his subject matter to formulate an agenda of interesting questions and to come up with a series of answers that are deliberately qualified as to time, place, and historical location. What such a suitably redefined social inquirer comes up with will also be subject to doubt and reinterpretation, but nevertheless Strauss finds it immensely more acceptable than the global aspirations of the external observer. The knowledge base and claims of such an internally situated observer are mitigated in contrast to the claims put forward by the scientistically motivated observer and consequently the skeptical counterarguments that one can address to the internal observer are correspondingly deflated and reduced.

Strauss's critique of relativism can be succinctly stated: It fails to meet the test of reflexivity.

> I fear that the field within which relativists can practice sympathetic understanding is restricted to the community of relativists who understand each other with great sympathy because they are united by identically the same fundamental commitment, or rather by identically the same rational insight into the truth of relativism. What claims to be the final triumph over provincialism reveals itself as the most amazing manifestation of provincialism.[4]

Instead of relativism turning out to be a true universalism, Strauss unmasks it as one additional variety of provincialism. The relativist that Strauss criticizes is relativistic about everything except the truth of relativism. To be consistently relativistic, however, requires one to be equally relativistic about the truth of relativism. Extreme relativism is in a certain way self-refuting—in the way that extreme skepticism is self-refuting. Only modified versions of both can withstand philosophical criticism—can meet the test of reflexivity.

In his critique of Isaiah Berlin's classic, "Two Concepts of Liberty," the nub of the issue for Strauss is reflexivity. "Liberalism, as Berlin understands it, cannot live without an absolute basis and cannot live with an absolute basis."[5] According to Strauss, the paradox from which Berlin's presentation of liberalism cannot extricate itself is that liberalism must be committed to the truth of relativism at the same time that it is relativistic about truth.

With regard to Nietzsche, Strauss identifies a central issue of reflexivity:

> I have in mind his interpretation of human creativity as a special form of the universal will to power, and the question that this interpretation entails, namely, whether he did not thus again try to find a sufficient theoretical basis for a transhistorical teaching or message. I have in mind, in other words, his hesitation as to whether the doctrine of the will to power is his subjective project, to be superseded by other such projects in the future, or whether it is the final truth.[6]

Nietzsche's concept of the will to power confronts a daunting paradox of self-referentialism. If Nietzsche intends that all human exertions—including intellectual exertions—be regarded as manifestations of a will to power, then what is to exempt Nietzsche's own formulation of the theory of the will to power from being subsumed under the category of "Expression of a Will to Power"? If, on the other hand, Nietzsche wants to privilege his theory of the will to power from falling under the rubric of "Will to Power," on what basis can he consistently do so? The paradox surrounding Nietzsche's work is directly evocative of the self-referential paradox concerning skepticism. If one is being consistently skeptical, is one not compelled to doubt the truth of skepticism as well?

In his diagnosis of existentialism, Strauss points to the vexing consequences of reflexivity. "Existentialism admits the truth of relativism, but it realizes that relativism, so far from being a solution or even a relief, is deadly. Existentialism is the reaction of serious men to their own relativism."[7] Since to be consistently relativistic requires one to be relativistic about one's own relativism, the relativist is not even able to deduce an ethic of simple toleration from his own moral principle. In a frenzied recognition that relativism cannot even sanction its own putative self-realization, the relativist invokes "commitment" as his touchstone for the organization of the moral life. But "commitment" from Strauss's perspective becomes an involuted testament to the intractability of "reflexivity" as an issue bedeviling moral deliberation and action.

With regard to Heidegger, a variation of the paradox surrounding reflexivity emerges into full prominence:

The analytics of *Existenz* had culminated in the assertion that the highest form of knowledge is finite knowledge of finiteness; yet how can finiteness be seen as finiteness if it is not seen in the light of infinity? Or in other words, it was said that we cannot know the whole; but does this not necessarily presuppose awareness of the whole?[8]

Heidegger's critique of our ability to know the whole—his pursuit of a theory of a "finite knowledge of finiteness"—both has to allude to knowledge of the whole in order to adduce a content for itself and has to concede intellectual space to what it rejects in order that the theory that it affirms might have explanatory power. If all that we ever have is "finite knowledge of finiteness," then this theory constitutes a gigantic tautology. In order for a "finite knowledge of finiteness" to retain its *explanatory* force and for invocations of this concept to constitute more than tautologies, the metaphysical approaches that a "finite knowledge of finiteness" rejects must somehow continue to exist even after Heidegger has affirmed that all we ever have access to is a "finite knowledge of finiteness." The explanatory force of a "finite knowledge of finiteness" is parasitic upon the continued existence of contrasting metaphysical understandings concerning the possibility of our achieving a knowledge of the whole. Issues of reflexivity thus come to undermine Heidegger's stress on a "finite knowledge of finiteness."

Strauss invokes the issue of reflexivity in his critique of historicism—in his discussion of its destructive impact upon natural right:

> There cannot be natural right if human thought is not capable of acquiring genuine, universally valid, final knowledge within a limited sphere or genuine knowledge of specific subjects. Historicism cannot deny this possibility. For its own contention implies the admission of this possibility. By asserting that all human thought, or at least all relevant human thought, is historical, historicism admits that human thought is capable of acquiring a most important insight that is universally valid and that will in no way be affected by any future surprises. The historicist thesis is not an isolated assertion: it is inseparable from a view of the essential structure of human life. This view has the same trans-historical character or pretension as any natural right doctrine.[9]

Historicism inconsistently asserts that all the products of human culture have to be construed historically—except the historicist thesis itself which provides us with a trans-historical key for understanding human culture.

What are some of the logically and metaphysically specific features of a mitigated skepticism that enable Strauss to surmount the difficulties he diagnoses in other arguments? I will begin by trying to show how the version of mitigated skepticism that I am calling a generalized agnosticism enables Strauss to surmount an issue of consistency present in his essay on "The Mutual Influence of Theology and Philosophy." In that essay, Strauss observes that "Generally stated, I would say that all alleged refutations of revelation presuppose unbelief in revelation, and all alleged refutations of philosophy presuppose already faith in revelation. There seems to be no ground common to both, and therefore superior to both."[10] The problem inherent in this formulation is how could Strauss pronounce upon the mutual incommensurability of philosophy and revelation when according to his mapping of the theoretical terrain these two approaches are mutually exhaustive. According to this premise, Strauss would have to stand either in the domain of philosophy or in the domain of revelation. From what higher perspective therefore is he licensed to pronounce upon their mutual incommensurability?

A significant incidental benefit of a generalized agnosticism is that it does not foreclose the nature of the logic that most accurately reflects the structure of reality. It enables us to conceive suspending the law of the excluded middle and thereby circumventing the contradiction present in Strauss's account of the relationship between philosophy and revelation. The contradiction is present only if the law of the excluded middle is presumed to hold. In that case our alternatives are restricted to A and not-A (philosophy and revelation). But if from the perspective of a generalized agnosticism we can project the suspension of the law of the excluded middle (and invoke multivalued logics that map that suspension), then our alternatives are increased beyond A and not-A and the inconsistency is resolved. Under such a logical dispensation, we are able to circumvent violation of the law of contradiction because our alternatives are increased beyond A and not-A—and we can invoke the dichotomy between reason and revelation without either affirming or denying its predication upon exceeding this dichotomy.

Strauss almost openly embraces a generalized agnosticism in his essay on "Relativism" when he asks: "Can there be eternal principles on the basis of empiricism, of the experience of men up to now? Does not the experience of the future have the same right to respect as the experiences of the past and the present?"[11] A consistent skepticism requires one to be open to the possibility that the future will totally not resemble the past. If we are properly skeptical of our skepticism, we have to entertain the possibility that what we have ruled out on the basis of our critical canons will actually happen. What we thought we knew, we might not have known. At the same time what we consigned to the alien and the exotic and even the unintelligible might come to pass.

An agnostic is committed to the permanence of questions and to the transitoriness and insubstantiality of answers. Strauss's generalized agnosticism is thus reflected in *Natural Right and History*[12] when, in opposition to historicism, he speaks about certain enduring questions:

> Far from legitimizing the historicist inference, history seems rather to prove that all human thought and certainly all philosophical thought, is concerned with the same fundamental themes or the same fundamental problems, and therefore that there exists an unchanging framework which persists in all changes of human knowledge of both facts and principles.[13]

Strauss's advocacy of a non-scientistic, internalistic, interpretive social science discussed above also encounters a problem concerning circularity which can be most satisfactorily accommodated by a generalized agnosticism. Strauss's internalism—his arguing that we "look at social phenomena primarily in the perspective of the citizen and the statesman"[14]—cannot be defended on internalist grounds. The communities and traditions of citizens and statesmen cannot be justified in the name of "community" and "tradition" without these terms becoming circular concepts. Strauss, however, implicitly affirms circularity in the primacy that he assigns to tradition and community in his internalist social science.

A generalized agnosticism enables Strauss to legitimize a recourse to circularity. A generalized agnosticism conjures up an indefinite openness toward the future, since even skepticism cannot be embraced with certainty. This has the effect of willy-nilly transforming all of our arguments into circular ones. Circularity can be viewed as proceeding on the premises of the incompleteness, and, therefore, also the at least partially unknown character, of objective reality. Since reality is incomplete and therefore also partially unknown, circularity—building the salient point(s) of one's conclusion into one's premise(s)—constitutes an artful philosophical strategy for producing a symmetrically designed piece of argument that will provisionally fill in our objective-knowledge gap. If there is no firm external check against a premise or an argument as a whole (as there is not, according to a generalized agnosticism), then circularity becomes a fact of (logical) life. In a generalized agnostic universe, circular argument yields a thought construct that serves as a surrogate for a reality that is not otherwise conceptually containable or referrable. The circular argument confers durability and weight upon its components when reality provides none.

Strauss's conceptualization of Socrates' innovation as consisting in "the discovery of noetic heterogeneity"[15] also gives rise to a problem of reflexivity. The issue of reflexivity which Strauss himself identifies in Heidegger—that Heidegger cannot theorize a "finite knowledge of finiteness" without simultaneously invoking an awareness of the whole (a position which he rejects)—can also be raised in relation to Strauss's presentation of Socrates' position. Socrates' "noetic heterogeneity" has to concede intellectual space to what it rejects in order that the theory that it affirms might have explanatory force. If "noetic heterogeneity" is definitive of reality, then the theory constitutes a gigantic tautology. In order for "noetic heterogeneity" to retain its explanatory force and for invocations of this theory to constitute more than tautologies, the metaphysical approaches that "noetic heterogeneity" rejects must somehow continue to exist even after Socrates affirms (in Strauss's version) that the world is characterized by "noetic heterogeneity." The explanatory force of "noetic heterogeneity" is parasitic upon the continued existence of contrasting metaphysical understandings which articulate a more homogeneous and unified vision of reality.

Here, again, a generalized agnosticism inviting cultivation of multivalued logics enables Strauss to render his construal of Socrates' position coherent. From a multivalued logical perspective, Strauss is able to avoid violation of the law of contradiction conjured up by his simultaneous attribution to Socrates of an affirmation and denial of "noetic heterogeneity" because his alternatives are increased beyond A and not-A. He can thus invoke the doctrine of "noetic heterogeneity" without either affirming or denying its predication upon the simultaneous logical existence of a doctrine of noetic homogeneity.

In the light of our discussion so far it will also be possible to provide a new gloss upon Strauss's famous doctrine of "esoteric teaching."[16] From the perspective that I have been advancing in this chapter, "esoteric teaching" is not only a politically and ethically motivated concept, but is also responsive to important epistemological and metaphysical requirements. In the latter senses it bears strong affinities with Michael Polanyi's notion of "tacit knowledge."[17]

Given the dilemmas concerning reflexivity that we have been considering throughout this paper, a paradigm of knowledge which emphasizes how the full extent and import of one's teaching is not fully formulated seems especially attractive. "Tacit knowledge" and "esoteric teaching" help to dissolve reflexivity as a source of anxiety in philosophy because they place this problematic in a context where our models of knowledge are statements that are more "knowing" than anything they directly state or justify. The inability to unravel the presuppositions and implications of some of our statements to render them more fully coherent with the explicit statements themselves which the dilemmas concerning reflexivity call attention to have now through the medium of "esoteric teaching" been accommodated to a model of discourse in which not everything is—or can be—stated. Instead of the dilemmas surrounding reflexivity constituting an aberration, they have now been reconceptualized as defining a significant norm of discourse.

II

The role of "method" in Madison's argument in Federalist Number Ten can be linked with Strauss's notion of "esoteric teaching" and its affinities with "tacit knowledge" that we have just discussed. The nature of the problem that Madison proposes to solve in Federalist Number Ten is posed in the idiom of classical political philosophy. "The instability, injustice, and confusion introduced into the public councils," Madison writes, "have, in truth, been the mortal diseases under which popular governments have everywhere perished, as they continue to be the favorite and fruitful topics from which the adversaries to libery derive their most specious declamations."[18] Madison thus defines his problem by invoking a cyclical conception of political time. Democratic regimes have always been doomed to political instability by the factious predominance of their public councils, which causes the political pendulum to swing in a completely opposite direction and leads to the establishment of tyranny as the only means for restoring political order.

As the solution to the problem of staving off indefinitely the destabilizing forces of cyclical political time, Madison resorts to a method that he believes has been overlooked by previous political writers and and practitioners, and for which, as Thomas Pangle emphasizes,[19] he is heavily indebted to Montesquieu. The method consists in the forms of institutional manipulation that enable a designer of states to convert a direct democracy into a republican regime, emphasizing the strategic decision-making role played by political representatives and the prospect of a mutual restraining and cancellation process emerging to blunt the force of factious incursions against the public good that a large society characterized by political representation affords.

When viewed phenomenologically, "method" might be described as a means of being able to discover in the homely materials of one's problem a clue to its solution. Without having to import entities from outside the framework of one's problem, one is able to fashion a solution. There is a more radical phenomenological approach that one can take to the idea of method. According to my first account, a solution to one's problem is only implicitly present in the entities going to compose the problem. The precise configuration of the solution still has to be teased out of the initial materials by the imaginative investigator or theorist. According to a second approach that I am presenting now, "method" simply refers to the way(s) a problem is institutionalized so that it can be preserved in its original form as a problem without requiring or provoking solution. From this perspective, the very institutionalization of a problem involves a distancing and containment process that staves off the need for a solution indefinitely. The problem gets played out by being reenacted continually and never needs to be solved in a more overt, official sense. From the current vantage point, to speak of a solution in a context where emphasis is being placed on the search for and application of "right method" is methodologically redundant.

Madison's problem in Federalist Number Ten is twofold: epistemological and practical. Epistemologically, no group tendering claims in the political arena can demonstrate the superior wisdom or justness of its claims in contrast to those of its adversaries and competitors. Madison adopts a Hobbesian and Augustinian view concerning the tainted and limited character of reason:

> As long as the reason of man continues fallible, and he is at liberty to exercise it, different opinions will be formed. As long as the connection subsists between his reason and his self-love, his opinions and his passions will have a reciprocal influence on each other; and the former will be objects to which the latter will attach themselves.[20]

Madison confronts the dual problem of not being able to adjudicate rationally between the competing claims of different groups and of not being able to contain the power conflicts that result when rational resolution of an absolutist sort has been ruled out. What he proposes to do at this point can be conceptualized simply by saying that he institutionalizes the conflict. He encases it in a more remote setting than that of its original enactment, spearheaded by surrogate advocates, called representatives, in lieu of the original combatants who pressed their claims initially. The transfer of locale and substitution of personnel (the distancing occurring on both levels) allows the conflict to continue without its becoming destructive of either the persons or interests of the original competitors or the institutional structures formed to house and contain their conflicts. From this second phenomenological perspective, the number and diversity of the original combatants are to be seen as features of the original conflict situation itself, which is simply transferred to an institutionalized setting and is not an innovation conjured up from the initial materials defining the nature of the problem.

Madison's approach reduces itself to postulating the idea of balance as the appropriate resolution to both his epistemological and power perplexities.

> The influence of factious leaders may kindle a flame within their particular States but will be unable to spread a general conflagration through the other States. A religious sect may degenerate into a political faction in a part of the Confederacy; but the variety of sects dispersed over the entire face of it must secure the national councils against any danger from that source. A rage for paper money, for an abolition of debts, for an equal division of property, or for any other improper or wicked project, will be less apt to pervade the whole body of the Union than a particular member of it, in the same proportion as such a malady is more likely to taint a particular county or district than an entire State.[21]

What contains religious and political factions is simply their having to confront within a unified institutional setting countervailing factions of an equally insistent sort, which ensures that the residue of deliberation and policy that results from their interaction will more closely approximate to the public interest than any faction's special advocacy taken by itself would. In short, it is the balance struck between opposing forces in an institutionalized setting that serves as the surrogate for Madison for both epistemological certainty and preponderance of power enjoyed by any would-be combatant. In a knowledge and power vacuum, "balance" assigns rewards and distributes penalties. The idea of balance becomes a shorthand way of expressing the primacy of the institutional structure in the achievement of an interim peace.

The idea of method in my second sense as an institutionalization of a problem betrays strong continuity with the notions of "esoteric teaching" and tacit knowledge. The connection between the idea of method in my second sense as an institutionalization of a problem and the concept of tacit knowledge is that "method" represents a solution to a major epistemological dilemma encapsulated in the doctrine of tacit knowledge. By postulating only explicit dimensions to knowledge, one cannot account for how the formulation and transmission of knowledge takes place. Problems of interpretation, translation, and judgment suggest that on a sheerly explicit level we are bereft of a satisfactory theory concerning how our statements "work." The theory of tacit knowledge calls attention to the way in which any statement that we make appears poised on the brink of being overwhelmed by a boundless range of problems that prevents the statement from getting off the ground at all. The restraining protocols summarized by the notion of tacit knowledge that inhibit an inquirer from thoroughly rationalizing the bases of his knowledge claims are transmuted by the idea of method in my second sense into a procedure for stabilizing the identity and boundaries of a statement(in Madison's case, the statement of the problem of factions) through externalizing the statement by continual reenactment. Also, Madison's recourse to method renders the statement's philosophical intractability innocuous—the very source of its pragmatically ordained and achieved solution. It is only because the statement has no philosophical resolution in a narrow substantive sense that it can be resolved in a broader "methodical" sense. The political arrangements of the modern age, characterized by the presence of large institutional structures, can thus be seen from this perspective as a response to certain key dilemmas of skepticism.

III

Strauss's politics is forged in the image of the epistemological concerns that we have been considering throughout this essay. The political implications of a generalized agnosticism are to continually try to dissociate what appear as the positive value commitments of liberalism from its negatively formulated, methodologically inspired, process-oriented precepts. Thus, Strauss aims for what he has called a "rational liberalism"[22] which is to say a liberalism that is completely institutionally self-aware of the limitations of reason. Strauss is critical of the secularist value overlay of modern liberalism. It engenders a false sense of certainty which is inimical to the broader value commitment to openness of liberalism. Strauss is critical of behavioral political science—as well as of modern liberalism generally—because they rest "on a dogmatic atheism which presents itself as merely methodological or hypothetical."[23] He says that "just as our opponents refuse respect to unreasoned belief, we, on our part, with at least equal right must refuse respect to unreasoned unbelief."[24] Strauss therefore advocates a liberalism that is open to the regenerative powers of religion.

   Because of his epistemological commitments, Strauss is equally opposed to the rarefied technical vocabularies in which modern liberal politics is both conducted and criticized by governmental bureaucrats, social scientists, as well as by humanists. He would like to see the public life and discourse of liberal democracies characterized by the triumph of common sense over philosophy in a technical sense—the triumph of the generalized vocabularies of everyday life over the specialized vocabularies of philosophy and the natural and social sciences. He praises the classical political philosopher for not abandoning "his fundamental orientation, which is the orientation inherent in political life."[25] "Classical political philosophy," Strauss says, "was essentially 'practical.'" Its primary concern "was not the description, or understanding, of political life, but its right guidance."[26] A primary motivating factor in the mistrust of technical vocabularies and the affirmation of everyday, common sense vocabularies is that the former both claim to achieve— and betoken independently of their official pronouncements—premature closure, whereas common sense vocabularies maintain a fluidity and an openness to experience which suggests that reality—or individual sectors of it—have not yet been fully grasped or defined. The mistrust of technical vocabularies and the promotion of common sense talk also harbors a tremendous democratic potential in theoretically extending the promise of democratic life to encompass more and more strata of the population.

The pace of social change in a liberal democracy has to be modulated to accommodate to the ideal of democracy as "an aristocracy which has broadened into a universal aristocracy."[27] Elsewhere Strauss says that "only choice, in contradistinction to mere desire, makes something a man's value."[28] In order to facilitate the emergence of a democratic mass capable of making wise and informed choices—and not merely being swayed by momentary impulses and desires—time and public nurturance are required. Public policy has to be assessed at least in part in terms of its likelihood to evoke thoughtful responses from citizens and to enrich public discourse, and not just in terms of its promotion of some sort of felicific calculus.

Strauss's affirmation of liberal democracy is partially based upon his awareness that a life bounded by the category of tradition has become increasingly inaccessible in the modern age. "We have lost," he says, "all simply authoritative traditions in which we could trust, the *nomos* which gave us authoritative guidance, because our immediate teachers and teachers' teachers believed in the possibility of a simply rational society. Each of us here is compelled to find his bearings by his own powers, however defective they may be."[29] The acids of an extreme rationalism have corroded the viability of tradition so that tradition cannot be artificially rehabilitated in the modern world. The kind of politics that is compatible with our social and psychological condition which debars us from deliberately re-forming traditions is the mutually restraining individualism of a liberal democratic society. This, according to Strauss, becomes the only viable political surrogate for tradition.

The case for democracy in Strauss rests upon the skeptical limitations of philosophical reason. The case for liberalism in Strauss rests upon the implications of reflexivity. Skepticism itself cannot be fully trusted. Liberal brakes on democratic rule are therefore required to ensure that not even a democratic reading of the common good is translated into public policy in its entirety. Ultimately, for Strauss, politics—like knowledge and understanding—represents movement toward a continually receding shore.

In the end, Strauss's "rational liberalism" becomes its own theodicy. "All evils," he says, "are in a sense necessary if there is to be understanding. It enables us to accept all evils which befall us and which may well break our hearts in the spirit of good citizens of the city of God. By becoming aware of the dignity of the mind, we realize the true ground of the dignity of man and therewith the goodness of the world, whether we understand it as created or as uncreated, which is the home of man because it is the home of the human mind."[30] Since we can never proceed beyond understanding toward a serene expectation of its realization or toward a secure practical translation of our insights—and since we are also bidden by Strauss not to become bewitched by large-scale programs of social and economic melioration which always embody an imperfect and imprecise reason—in the end all we are left with are the consolations of the understanding.

The most enduring image that emerges from Strauss's writings is that of all of Western intellectual experience forming a seamless web—an eternal now—a series of completely reversible menus of speculation and action—where it is just as intelligible to move from religion as a way of life to philosophy as a way of life as it is to move from philosophy to religion. The project of modernity of fashioning out of the resources of the self a set of guidelines for thought and action is forever taking place—and is forever renewed.

NOTES

1. Allan Bloom, ed., *Confronting the Constitution* (Washington, D.C.: AEI Press, 1990), 2.
2. Leo Strauss, *The Rebirth of Classical Political Rationalism*, selected and introduced by Thomas L. Pangle (Chicago: University of Chicago Press, 1989), 6.
3. Ibid., 8.
4. Ibid., 12.
5. Ibid., 16.
6. Ibid., 26.
7. Ibid., 36.
8. Ibid., 38.
9. Leo Strauss, *An Introduction to Political Philosophy*, ed. Hilail Gildin (Detroit, Mich.: Wayne State University Press, 1989), 114.
10. Leo Strauss, "The Mutual Influence of Theology and Philosophy," *Independent Journal of Philosophy/Unabhaengige Zeitschrift für Philosophie* 3 (1979):117.
11. Strauss, *Rationalism*, 16. Fred Dallmayr in a recent essay also reads Strauss in a generalized agnostic light—where a sustained openness to an indefinite future becomes the prevailing note: "With respect to the battle of ancients and moderns, agonistic difference implies that both ancient and modern philosophy allow a process of mutual questioning and contestation, while simultaneously preserving the integrity of their respective positions. This means that ancient philosophy must permit itself to be contested by modern philosophical thought, particularly by the modern accent on freedom and autonomous agency; surely ancient modes of social stratification and patriarchal governance cannot avoid being placed under pressure by more democratic ideas of self-governance of our age. This pressure, in my view, concurs quite well with Strauss's repeated admission that the point is not simply to abscond nostalgically into the past but to recapture somehow the memory of the past—for the present and the future. Conversely, modern philosophy must likewise undergo the trial

of contestation by facing up to the teachings of classical philosophy (and perhaps of non-Western traditions of thought as well). In this respect, the classical notion of "virtue" seen as a corollary of human embeddedness—and as a counterpoint to atomistic self-reliance—surely deserves close attention in our time of widespread anomie." (Fred Dallmayr, "Leo Strauss Peregrinus," *Social Research,* Vol. 61, No. 4 (Winter 1994), 896–97).

12. Leo Strauss, *Natural Right and History* (Chicago: University of Chicago Press, 1953).

13. Cited in Strauss, *Introduction,* 113–14.

14. Strauss, *Rationalism,* 8.

15. Ibid., 142.

16. Leo Strauss, *Persecution and the Art of Writing* (Glencoe, Ill.: Free Press, 1952); Strauss, *Rationalism,* 63–71.

17. Michael Polanyi, *Personal Knowledge: Towards a Post-Critical Philosophy* (Chicago: University of Chicago Press, 1958); *The Tacit Dimension* (Garden City, N.Y.: Doubleday Anchor Books, 1967).

18. Alexander Hamilton, James Madison, and John Jay, *The Federalist Papers,* ed. Clinton Rossiter (New York: New American Library, 1961), 77.

19. Thomas L. Pangle, "The Philosophic Understanding of Human Nature Informing the Constitution," in Bloom, *Confronting the Constitution,* 9–76.

20. Hamilton, Madison, and Jay, *Federalist Papers,* 78.

21. Ibid., 84.

22. Strauss, *Rationalism,* 29.

23. Strauss, *Introduction,* 148.

24. Ibid.

25. Strauss, *Rationalism,* 51.

26. Ibid., 57.

27. Strauss, *Introduction,* 313.

28. Ibid., 152.

29. Ibid., 318.

30. Ibid., 319.

10

Locating Leo Strauss in the Liberal-Communitarian Debate

Ronald J. Terchek

$\mathcal{L}$eo Strauss has been a significant participant in some of the most important debates in contemporary political theory. His presence is obvious in the quarrel between the ancients and moderns and in debates about philosophy and politics. However, he has been largely missing in the heated and sometimes acrimonious debate during the past quarter century in the United States that has pitted liberals and communitarians against one another. This essay seeks to place Strauss in this debate.

Ignited by John Rawls' theory of justice,[1] liberals, whether agreeing with his basic argument or offering a replacement for it, defend the proposition that the integrity or rights of individuals ought to be our first concern and ought not to be depreciated in favor of other goods. Whether they turn to their own canon, as Rawls does with Kant, Nozick with Locke, or Hayek with Adam Smith, or whether they leave canonical texts behind, liberals make the individual the center of their concern. Sometimes, their commitment is expressed in the language of rights; sometimes discussion revolves around the dignity and worth of each individual; sometimes it emphasizes equal regard and respect for each person. Whatever their specific gammer, liberals assume not only the essential equality of persons but also sufficient rational capacities for each person to determine what is best for that person. Working with these premises, contemporary liberals ask for "neutral" institutional practices that assure equal treatment for everyone.

Communitarians recoil at these constructions. It is not that they want to jettison liberty or freedom; rather they seek to make room for other goods that they see ignored or discounted in liberalism, and they respond to what they discover to be defective in contemporary liberal society. Michael Sandel finds liberal agents are unencumbered, Alasdair MacIntyre holds they are emotive, and John Pocock sees them as civically lethargic.[2] However much communitarians specify different problems, they find that contemporary society is a loose arrangement of self-regarding individuals interested in satisfying their own interests or desires and, most alarming for these critics, assigned responsibility for defining the good for themselves. The reason, communitarians argue, is that modern liberal society has no moral core except to privilege individuals. With no recognized center which can convince, each individual fills the void with personal preferences about what is good, true, and appropriate. In such a society, on the communitarian gloss, we encounter relativism and loneliness. Communitarians want other goods to stand at the center of their project because they believe that liberty can only be achieved in a solid community.

For his part, Strauss detects much that is deeply disturbing in modern society, and his arguments frequently parallel communitarian ones.[3] He finds "no reminder of duty and exalted destiny" today but a "sham universality." This is a time when "the danger of universal philistinism and creeping conformism" threatens to overwhelm everything.[4] In modern society, bereft of any settled moral standard, Strauss holds that each person is given leave to decide how to apply that power. This reflects "the uneasiness which today is felt but not faced," that is, relativism.[5] Because many of the defects that Strauss observes in contemporary America have been noticed by many communitarians as well, his unique contribution to the debate will not be found in his critiques of the insistent privileging of rights over duties, the secularism of the age, or the depreciation of a liberal education.[6] His arguments about the nature of the crisis and how to think about responding to it is what makes Strauss a unique contributor to the debate but an unlikely partisan of any particular position.[7]

A NOTE ON NATURAL RIGHT

One of the distinguishing features of Strauss's writings centers on classical "natural right." On his account, natural right enables us to think about the good, to ask hard questions about justice, and to recognize nature is the center, not the abstracted individual or the ideal community. "Natural" must be distinguished from "what is human, all too human. A human being is said to be natural if he is guided by nature rather than by convention, or by inherited opinion, or by tradition, to say nothing of mere whims."[8]

For Strauss, there is a difference between the good and the pleasant. Today, we are said to emphasize the latter which is "connected with the satisfaction of wants" and, given our relativism, we do not distinguish among different wants. This is a mistake for Strauss who holds that the variety of wants is "not a bundle of urges; there is a natural order of the wants."[9] Some are biologically necessary, but some are higher, and Strauss seeks to keep the wants in a natural or "hierarchic order" which supplies "the basis for natural right as the classics understood it." A life stuck on necessity or the pleasures of the "brute" is defective and the life devoted to the highest human potentialities is "well-ordered or healthy." For Strauss, this means that "The life according to nature is the life of human excellence or virtue, the life of a 'a high-class person,' and not the life of pleasure as pleasure."[10]

Strauss contrasts his understanding of classical natural right with modern natural right, and the latter is found not only to be lacking but dangerous. Its menacing character comes with its historicity and relativism (and therefore its opposition to permanent principles of morality); its reliance on science and the ways science can be applied (and therefore its opposition to contemplation and dialectics); its bid for certainty, particularly political certainty (and therefore its blindness to the inherent tensions Strauss sees between philosophy and the conventional); and its search for perfectionism (rather than to struggle against such efforts).

THE COMPLICITY OF SCIENCE

Strauss's view of science highlights how far he sees the modern age departing from classical natural right. He finds that modern science is offered as a replacement for classical natural right, promising "that it would reveal to us the true character of the universe and the truth about man."[11] However, it fails to keep its pledge. One reason Strauss wants to pay attention to science is that he sees it as pretentious, making claims it cannot deliver. In shattering classical natural right, Strauss sees science creating a void which leaves the modern world rudderless.

> It goes without saying that a science which does not allow of value judgments has no longer any possibility of speaking of progress except in the humanely irrelevant sense of scientific progress: the concept of progress has been replaced by the concept of change. . . . Furthermore, science . . . admits that it is based on fundamental hypotheses which will always remain hypotheses. The whole structure of science does not rest on evident necessities.[12]

Strauss finds that science and technology have fractured the classical telos which had given purpose, coherence, and direction to the world.[13] Today, the scientific emphasis on the empirical and its predilection of methods of verification signal what is considered to be important and true. Experimentation and mathematical processes displace the dialectic as the way of approaching the truth. However, Strauss finds these scientific methods are incomplete, ignoring the central features of the human condition. For this reason, he argues that "Man's humanity is threatened with extinction by technology."[14] One reason is that science has increased the power available to human beings, but modern science "is absolutely incapable of telling men how to use that power."[15] As Strauss understands matters, "The fundamental dilemma, in whose grip we are, is caused by the victory of modern natural science. An adequate solution to the problem of natural right cannot be found before this basic problem has been solved."[16]

Strauss sees science disrupting the natural order. Having plucked bits and pieces from the cosmos to examine and explain, scientists do not know how to return the material they have analyzed to the natural order which is now fragmented and disconnected.[17] For many, however, this presents no problem because science is said to enable us to master the bits and pieces of the cosmos.[18] Strauss wants to challenge this confidence, insisting that "mastery leads, if its ultimate consequences are drawn, to the ultimate degradation of man. Only by becoming aware of what is beyond human mastery can we have hope."[19] He is also concerned about the lack of control modern men and women have over their science. As he sees it, the

> essential difference between our view and the classical view consists then, not in a difference regarding moral principle. . . . The difference between the classics and us with regard to democracy consists exclusively in a different estimate of the virtues of technology.[20]

On this account, when we abolish the "moral and political control" of technology, we invite "disaster or the dehumanization of man."[21] For all of its problems, Strauss notices that there are positive elements to modern science. For example, it provides more people with more leisure (something available to only a few in the classical world) that he sees necessary for a liberal education. "An economy of plenty," he reasons, removes the restrictiveness that accompanies economies "of scarcity." Unlike some who can see only the benefits of increased productivity, Strauss recognizes a dark side which cannot be tamed in the modern world.[22]

The prominence Strauss gives to science distinguishes his critique of the crisis from communitarians who do not contend with how the modern world is organized by science nor ask whether science has undermined the goods and practices that communitarians value. In making science part of his critique of modernity, Strauss means to challenge answers that he finds simplistic or utopian. For him, efforts to revive a "tradition" that does not pay attention to a world that has been reconstituted by science is an effort bound to fail and is often dangerous.

ORDINARY MEN AND WOMEN

For many, what is ordinary about ordinary persons is they care about themselves and their attachments; they love their spouse, parents and children, attend to their property and livelihoods, and are loyal to their friends and community. In their ordinariness, they practice not the great but the small virtues which, together with their attachments and the conventions of their society, give them purpose and direction. Indeed, these are the things that most ordinary men and women live for (and sometimes fight and even die for).

The lives of ordinary men and women are marked by both pleasures and pains as well as by their ideas of right and wrong. Their reality is not only grounded in their attachments and experiences but also in the standards of their society. The ordinariness of life, as I read Strauss, acts as a force of gravity which continually draws ordinary persons back to the earth.[23] As such, Strauss's ordinary persons do not see what the philosopher as philosopher sees.[24] They are said to be attached to what is perishable while the philosopher is dedicated to the eternal.[25] For this reason, the knowledge of ordinary persons and the knowledge of the philosopher are radically different. The philosopher "alone knows what a healthy or well-ordered soul is. . . . The good order of the soul is philosophizing."[26] Summarizing Xenophon with approval, Strauss writes,

> Chiefly concerned with eternal beings, or the "ideas" and hence also with the "idea" of man, [the philosopher] is as unconcerned as possible with individual and perishable human beings and hence also with his own "individuality," or body, as well as with the sum total of all individual human beings and their "historical" procession. He knows as little as possible about the way to the market place to say nothing of the market place itself, and he almost as little knows whether his neighbor is a human being or some other animal.[27]

The ordinary men and women whom Strauss surveys live in a cave, away from the bright sun. There, they take pleasure in the ordinary things of life and look for purpose, something found in the shadows they see in the cave. As Strauss sees them, ordinary persons are not inherently mean-spirited but they can be. This can occur if their world of illusions, their life in the cave, is threatened by the philosopher who tells them that the things they want most as ordinary people are ephemeral and that they have been staring at the shadows of real happiness. They do not want to be told real happiness means forsaking their illusions about family, children, property, possessions, security, and conventional purpose. Not surprisingly, the revelations of the philosopher are unwelcome. Rather than treated as a liberator, the philosopher is condemned, like Socrates. For this reason, Strauss finds "The conflict between the philosopher and the city [dominated by ordinary men and women] is inevitable."[28] Strauss finds no solution to the conflict in part because the philosopher and ordinary persons are radically different.

> The philosopher is immune to the most common and the most powerful dissolvent of man's natural attachment to man, the desire to have more than one has already and in particular to have more than others have; for he has the greatest self-sufficiency which is humanly possible. . . . Since he fully realizes the limits set to all human action and all human planning (for what has come into being must perish again), he does not expect salvation or satisfaction from the establishment of the simply best social order. . . . He will try to help his fellow man by mitigating, as far as in him lies, the evils which are inseparable from the human condition.[29]

Strauss's philosophers are said to be able to do this because they are not burdened by interests as ordinary men and women are, that is, as contemporary voters are.

Rather than being directed by their attachments, Strauss's philosophers are disinterested participants, guided by their search for the eternal.[30] This reading of the detached philosopher, of course, is resisted in modern philosophy; beginning with Hobbes, the modern temper assumes the universality of interests and argues that individual attachments cannot ever be completely discarded by anyone. Moreover, Strauss's distinction between philosophers and ordinary persons finds no comfortable home in the modern world, dedicated as it is to the principle of equality. For his part, Strauss wants to keep the distinction between the philosopher and ordinary persons because, if it is lost, he fears that all that remains is the mundane and we stand powerless to resist the merely pleasurable.

CANONICAL ANTECEDENTS

Many communitarians have drawn materials from the cannon, both to argue against the individualism and hedonism that they see in liberalism as well as to offer alternative frameworks and practices of the good community. Some, such as MacIntyre, look to Aristotle, Augustine, and Aquinas; others turn to Rousseau, and still others find Machiavelli offers the strongest argument on behalf of civic virtue and duty.[31]

Although communitarians often disagree with one another in their commentaries on Aristotle, Machiavelli, and Rousseau, most communitarian glosses of canonical texts share an important outlook. These commentaries generally assume that a fit, however loose, can be tailored between canonical constructions of the good community and the capacities of ordinary men and women today. In this way, canonical texts are said to supply reliable and applicable guides for today. Such guides are said not only to inform us about the causes of the crisis but also to provide the materials to build a community where a sense of civic duty is robust and the incoherence and relativism of modern society is overcome.

Strauss will have none of this. It is not just that he offers a radically different reading of canonical texts; much more importantly, his reading reflects his own distinct understanding of philosophy and politics, particularly his resistance to claims that assume there is a neat solution to the problems which ail us today. Ambiguity and paradox, not fixity and stability, are the mark of politics for Strauss. It is helpful to consider briefly Strauss's own readings of some of the canonical texts used by various communitarians in order to locate his larger argument. To do this, it is necessary to say a few words about why Strauss believes the ancient philosophers contribute something that later philosophers do not. As Strauss understands it,

> Classical political philosophy is non-traditional, because it belongs to the fertile moment when all political traditions were shaken, and there was not yet in existence a tradition of political philosophy. In all later epochs, the philosophers' study of political things was mediated by a tradition of political philosophy which acted like a screen between the philosopher and political things, regardless of whether

the individual philosopher cherished or rejected that tradition. From this it follows that the classical philosophers see the political things with a freshness and directness which have never been equalled.[32]

Strauss's classical philosophers are of the city, not apart from it; "they did not look at political things from the outside, as spectators of political life." As such, they can challenge the "narrowness of the lawyer, the brutality of the technician, the vagaries of the visionary, and the baseness of the opportunist." Classical philosophy, on this account, "is free from all fanaticism because it knows that evil cannot be eradicated and therefore that one's expectations from politics must be moderate."[33]

The distinction Strauss draws between classical philosophy and the modern political philosophers favored by various communitarians can be seen in his treatment of Machiavelli and Rousseau. Unlike readings that understand Machiavelli as a champion of civic republicanism, Strauss finds him to be "an evil man."[34] For Strauss, Machiavelli founds his republic on fratricide; for communitarians who look at his founding, Numa is the real founder of Machiavelli's Rome.[35] More importantly for Strauss, Machiavelli is "the first of a long series of modern thinkers who hoped" to establish a new politics "by means of enlightenment."[36] On his account, Machiavelli introduces the modern presumption that reason can tame politics and refashion the human condition to make the illusive utopia into a reality.[37]

It turns out that the communitarian reading of Rousseau will not satisfy Strauss in providing an alternative to the dangers of modernity in spite of Rousseau's return "to the world of virtue and the city." Rousseau's problem is that, in offering his general will, he "tries to guarantee the actualization of the ideal, or . . . to get rid of that which essentially transcends every possible human reality."[38]

One reason Strauss would find canonical communitarianism to be inadequate to mount an effective challenge to the crisis is tied to his view of the intractable conflict between political philosophers and ordinary men and women. A more robust reading of Aristotle, an emphasis on Rousseau's positive arguments, or a kinder and gentler version of Machiavelli are insufficient for Strauss. For him, it is necessary to retain the distinction between the perishable and eternal and notice that many communitarians make tradition into another form of convention, with all of its disabilities.

Strauss would also find that many communitarians seem to make convention, something which they often call tradition, the standard of the good. For him, however, there is no way to eliminate the conflict between the conventional and the good. Strauss's position stands in sharp contrast to the way many communitarians approach the relationship between (an idealized) convention and the good regime. Pocock, for one, offers us patriotic citizens who sacrifice for the republic and Sandel gives us an encumbered person who freely accepts duties and responsibilities. The primary issue for Strauss is about neither sacrifice nor duty; it is about the good and an understanding how it is in tension with convention.

One reason Strauss would find communitarian thinking faulty, if not danger-ous, stems from his views of virtue. From his perspective, both liberals and com-munitarians have made virtue small.[39] None really reaches for the intellectual virtues but is interested in what ordinary people can deliver. Strauss, for one, does not mean to deprecate keeping promises or contracts or obeying the law, but he steadily refuses to make these the stuff of the highest virtues. What he finds abhorrent in modern readings is a relativism that accepts every claim to virtue as being as worthy as any other claim; what is missing in these accounts for Strauss is a discussion of a hier-archy of virtues which places the intellectual virtues at the apex.

STRAUSS AND NIETZSCHE

One of the features of the liberal-communitarian debate that Strauss would find perplexing is its general silence about Nietzsche. Although MacIntyre takes up Nietzsche, it is to condemn him and then ask his readers to choose Aristotle over Nietzsche. MacIntyre's Nietzsche does not expose the empty core of modernity, reveal that its proudest trophies (such as science and the modern state) are sterile, or show the ominous future of modernity leads to the relativism and nihilism of the last man. Strauss's Nietzsche, on the other hand, assaults modernity in order to arrest the slide to nihilism but takes a wrong turn in looking to the overman rather than in reviving classical natural right as the solution. As Strauss understands mat-ters, Nietzsche takes on a "great political responsibility" by exposing the reigning ideologies of the day as shams but, providing no direction, "he could not show his readers a way toward political responsibility. He left them no choice except that between irresponsible indifference to politics and irresponsible political options."[40]

For Strauss, the post-Nietzschean era cannot be healed either by imposing modernist solutions or by pretending that the old order can be reconstructed. The debris of the late modern world cannot be used to give coherence and purpose. What is necessary, for Strauss, is to accept two kinds of limits in thinking about pol-itics. One, reflecting his reading of natural right, concerns the continuing struggle between philosophy and the ordinary, the eternal and perishable, and nature and convention. The other has to do with the inability of moderns to talk about a telos or cosmological standard that flourished in the ancient world. What has been rent by modern science and philosophy cannot be made whole in the modern world, something Nietzsche knows but, apparently, most communitarians do not.

STRAUSS AND AMERICA

According to Strauss, the core of liberal democracy is revealed by Spinoza, "the first philosopher who was both a liberal and a democrat" and who "founded liberal democracy, a specifically modern regime."⁴¹ Rejecting classical natural right, Strauss's Spinoza frees the passions to roam in new places with new appetites. As Strauss sees it, liberalism invites individuals to give reign to their desires, elevates the mundane to the center, spawns relativism, depends on an undirected and unmediated science to provide more and more satisfactions, and promotes secularism.

Given his attack on modernity, his criticisms about various aspects of American society, and his critique of Spinoza, one might expect Strauss to find the United States laboring under the dark legacy of modernity. And in many ways he does. He asks, for example, about the "dangers threatening democracy, not only from without but from within as well. Is there no problem of democracy, of industrial mass democracy?"⁴² And his answer is yes. However, Strauss sees himself as a friendly, helpful critic who seeks to preserve what he takes to be best in the American regime rather than reject it because it does not measure up to an ideal that flourished over two thousand years ago. Because he recognizes the post-Nietzschean complications of restoring a fractured cosmos, he cannot be the kind of conservative who takes everything in the current arrangement as a good.

Why should Strauss be attracted to a regime which sponsors individualism, promotes materialism, disdains duties, and frequently equates the good with pleasure? The answer comes in the ways Strauss understands and reacts to the political consequences of modernity. One way has to do with how its rationalism, relativism, and utopianism can lead to moral catastrophe, something he finds in the emergence of Nazism and Soviet communism. The other has to do with how other modern regimes can approach a second best or acceptable polity even if it cannot embody what Strauss takes to be the best. For him, the tensions between politics and philosophy and the conflict between pleasure and truth are unavoidable in any good regime; indeed one of the marks of the thoroughly corrupt regime for Strauss is that these tensions have been obliterated. Such a regime has room neither for philosophers nor the truth. With this in mind, he argues that it is both possible and necessary to judge among regimes in order to avoid the decadent and promote the second best, something that is prudent and decent.⁴³

One practice that particularly concerns Strauss in modern, liberal society is the way it values education. Unlike moderns, Strauss's classical thinkers are preoccupied with the formation of a moral character that aims at virtue. Today, much education is a matter of "instruction and training." More disturbing to Strauss is the proclivity of modern education to teach people to get along, to be good members of the group. As such, "Democracy has not yet found a defense against the creeping conformism and the ever-increasing invasion of privacy which it fosters."⁴⁴ Strauss expects that a liberal education guards against these dangers by speaking to those who can approach perfection. As he understands matters, "Not all men are equally equipped by nature for progress toward perfection, or not all 'natures' are 'good natures.'"⁴⁵ To sort out differences in capacity in the modern world, he wants to see a robust equality of opportunity in place, but it is his own unique version. For him,

A society is just if its living principle is "equality of opportunity," i.e., if every human being belonging to it has the opportunity, corresponding to his capacities, of deserving well of the whole and receiving the proper reward for his deserts. . . . In a just society, the social hierarchy will correspond strictly to the hierarchy of merit and of merit alone.[46]

How this will happen in practice, however, is something that is unclear. Strauss does not make the usual construction of equality of opportunity as played out in competitive markets his expression of equality of opportunity; rather he offers a form of meritocracy, one which is difficult to specify in practice.

PLACING STRAUSS IN THE CONTEMPORARY DEBATE

Strauss's opposition to liberalism is part of his critique of modernity and his defense of political philosophy, but for all his affinities with many communitarians, he proves to be ill-fitted to participate in their debate with liberalism. He would find that most communitarians carry too heavy a debt to modernity; moveover, when communitarians reach to the classical tradition Strauss finds that they leave its essential core behind. For this reason, what Strauss says of Carl Schmitt can be applied to most communitarians: "His critique of liberalism occurs in the horizon of liberalism: his unliberal tendency is restrained by the still unvanquished 'systematics of liberal thought.' The critique introduced by Schmitt against liberalism can therefore be completed only if one succeeds in gaining a horizon beyond liberalism."[47]

Strauss would find many communitarians still mired in liberal thought, struggle though they may against what they take to be its worst manifestations. Why would Strauss find this to be the case? One answer, and the easy one, is that so many communitarians rely on modern thought to critique liberalism. For Strauss, liberalism is one manifestation of modernity, embodying many of its generic flaws. To save contemporary society with Machiavelli or Rousseau makes no sense to Strauss who sees both drinking from the same well as liberals. All deny classical natural right and accept a kind of relativism.

The second reason Strauss would fault much of the communitarian gloss is that he finds it misunderstands political philosophy. He would take strong exception to communitarian efforts to drag liberal agents from the "unnatural" cave to the bright sunlight. For all of its problems, the "natural" cave has salutary characteristics compared with the "unnatural cave (into which we have fallen, less through the tradition than through the tradition of the polemic against the tradition)."[48] For Strauss, any exit worth taking from the "unnatural" cave leads to the "natural" cave. Communitarians, like their liberal targets, on this reading, decline to see the limits of their thoughts and aspirations. Each fails to see the constraints inherent in the human condition. In their own ways, each imbibes the heady elixir of rationalism and science that defines modernity, and neither can shake the habit.

What, then, does Strauss have to say about our present discontents? What advice does he give to philosophers as political philosophers? It comes as the answer to his question, "In what then does philosophic politics consist? In satisfying the city that the philosophers are not atheists, that they do not desecrate everything sacred to the city, that they reverence what the city reverences, that they are not subversives, in short, that they are not irresponsible adventurers but good citizens and even the best of citizens."[49] Strauss's recommendation is directed at preserving "what the city reverences." Given that he does not reverence everything that liberal democracies reverence, what are we to make of this? The answer, I think, is that Strauss wants philosophers to act moderately and prudently, to work at the margins, and to be decent as well as encourage decency. One expression of this is to resist the temptation to think abstractly, what he takes to be one of the great errors of modernity because it moves away from the natural. Moreover, in attempting to apply its abstractions to the real world, modern theory makes the mistake of converting the real world into an abstraction.[50] Modern political philosophers are said to do this when they take apart a once coherent, integrated telos to study and understand its pieces. In doing so, the modern temper fractures and fragments what was once joined together. Both modern philosophy and science generate knowledge about parts, not the whole. In making use of this knowledge, the parts have changed, not merely in the sense that we know more about them but, for Strauss, in the more important sense that they have lost the relatedness they enjoyed in the classical telos. Strauss has continually insisted that no "real" solution can reflect perfectionism and efforts to find one are dangerous, whatever their source. In the context of the contemporary debate in political theory, Strauss finds that this applies to liberal as well as communitarian solutions.

NOTES

1. See John Rawls, *A Theory of Justice* (Cambridge: Harvard University Press, 1971) and *Political Liberalism* (New York: Columbia University Press, 1993). For alternative liberal views, see Bruce Ackerman, *Social Justice and the Liberal State* (New Haven: Yale University Press, 1980) and Ronald Dworkin, *Taking Rights Seriously* (Cambridge: Harvard University Press, 1978).

2. Michael Sandel, *Liberalism and the Limits of Justice* (New York: Cambridge University Press, 1982); Alasdair MacIntyre, *After Virtue* (Notre Dame: Notre Dame University Press, 1981) and J. G. A. Pocock, *The Machiavellian Moment* (Princeton: Princeton University Press, 1975). The best-known contribution by a Straussian to this literature comes from Allan Bloom, *The Closing of the American Mind* (New York: Simon and Schuster, 1987).

3. "If we look . . . at what is peculiar to our age or characteristic of our age, we see hardly more than the interplay of mass taste with high-grade but strictly speaking unprincipled efficiency" (*Liberalism Ancient and Modern* [New York: Basic Books, 1968], 23).

4. Leo Strauss, *The Rebirth of Classical Political Rationalism* (Chicago: University of Chicago Press, 1989), 31.

5. *Rebirth of Classical Political Rationalism*, 35–36.

6. Nor does he offer a unique lament in criticizing public officials who pander to instrumentally driven voters. As Strauss sees matters, "The political man is characterized by the concern with being loved by all human beings regardless of their quality" (*On Tyranny* [New York: Free Press, 1963], 212).

7. See John Gunnell on the idea of crisis in political theory (*Between Philosophy and Politics* [Amherst: University of Massachusetts Press, 1986]).

8. *What is Political Philosophy?* (Westport, Colo.: Greenwood Press, 1973), 28.

9. Leo Strauss, *Natural Right and History* (Chicago: University of Chicago Press, 1953), 126.

10. *Natural Right and History*, 127.

11. *Rebirth of Classical Political Rationalism*, 32.

12. *Rebirth of Classical Political Rationalism*, 33.

13. Some of Strauss's critics misrepresent his position when they argue that his telos provides us with concrete answers. For his part, Strauss holds that the telos serves as a standard and through a philosophical, that is dialectical, inquiry we can understand how those standards might be approached in our own unique setting.

14. *Rebirth of Classical Political Rationalism*, 42.

15. *Rebirth of Classical Political Rationalism*, 32.

16. *Natural Right and History*, 8.

17. According to Strauss, "Philosophy strives for knowledge of the whole. The whole is the totality of the parts" (*What is Political Philosophy?* 39).

18. I discuss the relationship of science and the cosmos in *Gandhi: Struggling for Autonomy* (Lanham, Md.: Rowman & Littlefield, 1998), ch. 4.

19. *Rebirth of Classical Political Rationalism*, 43.

20. *What is Political Philosophy?* 37.

21. *What is Political Philosophy?* 37.

22. In *Liberalism Ancient and Modern*, Strauss holds that the ideals of classical natural right are often corrupted in practice in the ancient world, and the reason is often because of scarcity. He argues that the "demand of justice that there should be a reasonable correspondence between the social hierarchy and the natural hierarchy" is corrupted by ancient oligarchs who pretend they were not only necessary but also naturally the best. "With the increasing abundance it became increasingly possible to see and to admit the element of hypocrisy which had entered into the traditional notion of aristocracy." In economies of plenty, it becomes possible "to abolish many injustices or at least many things which had become injustices" because we no longer accept the idea that social inequalities reflect natural ones. He goes on to argue that in many ways, we can work with several equality premises in an economy of plenty, such as equality of opportunity and basic political equality (*Liberalism Ancient and Modern*, 21).

23. For a different view than Strauss's of ordinary persons, see Ronald Terchek, *Republican Paradoxes and Liberal Anxieties* (Lanham, Md.: Rowman & Littlefield, 1997), 236–239.

24. One of the differences Strauss sees between the philosopher and ordinary persons is that the "attachment" of the former "to his friends is deeper than his attachment to other human beings, even to his nearest and dearest [that is his family]" (*On Tyranny*, 214).

25. "The philosopher's attempt to grasp the eternal order is necessarily an ascent from the perishable things" (*On Tyranny*, 215).

26. *On Tyranny*, 215. Strauss's ordinary persons seek comprehensive answers and do not know what Strauss's philosophers know, namely that knowledge is destined to be incom-

plete and the knowledge we possess stands alongside of our ignorance. As Strauss puts it, "Knowledge of ignorance is not ignorance. It is knowledge of the elusive character of the truth, of the whole" (*What is Political Philosophy?*, 38).

27. *On Tyranny*, 212.

28. *On Tyranny*, 219. Strauss holds that "Every society regards a specific human type . . . as authoritative. When the authoritative type is the common man, everything has to justify itself before the tribunal of the common man" (*Natural Right and History*, 137).

29. *On Tyranny*, 214.

30. "While trying to transcend humanity (for wisdom is divine) or while trying to make it his sole business to die and to be dead to all human things, the philosopher cannot help living as a human being who as such cannot be dead to human concerns, although his soul will not be in these concerns. The philosopher cannot devote his life to his own work if other people do not take care of the needs of his body" (*On Tyranny*, 213).

31. On Aristotle, see MacIntyre, *After Virtue*; on Rousseau, see William Sullivan, *Reconstructing Political Philosophy* (Berkeley: University of California Press, 1982); on Machiavelli, see Pocock, *Moment*.

32. *What is Political Philosophy?* 28.

33. *What is Political Philosophy?* 29.

34. Leo Strauss, *Thoughts on Machiavelli* (Glencoe, Ill.: Free Press, 1958), 9. For Pocock, Machiavelli teaches republican citizens about subordinating self-interest in favor of the general good and warns about the danger of corruption, whether it appears in government or society. As Strauss sees it, Machiavellian "virtue is nothing but civic virtue, patriotism or devotion of collective selfishness" (*What is Political Philosophy?* 42).

35. *Thoughts on Machiavelli*, 13.

36. *What is Political Philosophy?* 46.

37. Pocock, for one, finds that Machiavelli is preoccupied by fortune and decay and finds that any Machiavellian republican settlement is fragile.

38. *What is Political Philosophy?* 51.

39. "For Plato, what Aristotle calls moral virtue, is a kind of halfway house between political or vulgar virtue which is in the service of bodily well being (of self preservation or peace) and genuine virtue which, to say the least, animates only the philosophers as philosophers" (*City and Man* [Chicago: Rand McNally, 1964], 27).

40. *What is Political Philosophy?* 55.

41. Leo Strauss, *Spinoza's Critique of Religion* (New York: Schocken Books, 1965), 16.

42. *The Rebirth of Classical Political Rationalism*, 31.

43. Strauss also finds the American political regime embodies important elements of classical natural right. He holds "liberal democracy . . . derives powerful support from a way of thinking which cannot be called modern at all; the premodern thought of our western tradition" (*What is Political Philosophy?* 98).

44. *What is Political Philosophy?* 38. Strauss goes on to argue that democracy can resist this if it is ready to "return to the classic's notions of education: a kind of education which can never be thought of as mass-education, but only as higher and highest education of those who are by nature fit for it" (38).

45. *Natural Right and History*, 134–135.

46. *Natural Right and History*, 148. In market economies, merit is determined by the market; Strauss wants to deny its applicability. However, his conception of merit troubles those who have something different in mind than philosophizing abilities as well as those who

want distributions to be attentive to a variety of needs that are unattended by conventional conceptions of merit.

47. Heinrich Meier, *Carl Schmitt and Leo Strauss,* translated by J. Harvey Lomas (Chicago: University of Chicago Press, 1995), 119.

48. Leo Strauss, *Philosophy and Law* (New York: Jewish Publication Society, 1987), 112.

49. *On Tyranny*, 220.

50. *On Tyranny*, 220.

Part Three

The First Generation

· *11* ·

In re George Anastaplo

John A. Murley

Just because you can do it doesn't mean it can be done.
—*Sara Prince Anastaplo, to her husband*

I

George Anastaplo, who was born in St. Louis in 1925, has long been distinguished among the first generation as perhaps the most "liberal Straussian." Not that he is conventionally liberal, as may be seen in the puzzlement Studs Terkel exhibited when interviewing him.[1] Nevertheless, over a fifty-year career Anastaplo has recorded serious reservations about the Cold War policies of the United States, including our involvement in Vietnam.[2] And independent of how much punishment he thought the dictator Saddam Hussein personally deserved, Anastaplo was critical of the Persian Gulf War. He considers that war poorly advised, in part the result of the personal anger of a provoked President who was willing to manipulate the United Nations and American public opinion, and "virtually force upon the Congress a fait accompli." He remains quite dubious about our overwhelming support of a war that inflicted enormous casualties on a subject people "unable to defend themselves at all from our devastating sea, air, and ground attacks."[3] But Anastaplo can be "hawkish" when needed. He supported in word and in deed the Second World War as well as the initial United Nations response in 1950 to the invasion of South Korea. He is also on record as favoring a much tougher response during the Iran Hostage Crisis than was exhibited by the United States, whereas elsewhere in the Middle East he leans toward a "greater Israel" policy.

In domestic politics Anastaplo opposed McCarthyism and its harmful contemporary manifestations. He supports well-thought-out and carefully monitored affirmative-action measures as well as governmental aid to inner-city parochial schools. He also favors much more stringent gun regulations and has questioned

159

the usefulness of capital punishment in our circumstances. He has urged support for various public welfare/public works programs, directed at "the long depression" that continues to hold in its grip large numbers in our inner cities. On the other hand, he has over the years been easier on the shortcomings of former President Nixon than have liberals, and harder on the shortcomings of President Reagan during the Iran-arms/Contra-aid affair than have conservatives.[4] As for President Clinton, although Anastaplo has observed certain "Lincolnesque" characteristics in him, he believes that Clinton's resignation was called for after his August 1998 "confession." In addition, he is dubious about the surprise missile attacks ordered by Clinton in August 1998 upon Afghanistan and the Sudan as well as about the December 1998 bombardment of Iraq, though less dubious about the NATO disciplining of Serbia.[5]

One reason Anastaplo may appear to be one of the most liberal Straussians is because he has been the most politically active of the first generation. This is not meant in the sense of holding political office, or of participating as a political consultant, or of serving as a member of an administration in Washington or in Illinois—for there have been other Straussians much more involved than he has been in those ways. Rather, he has been a public "player," as may be recognized in his decade-long bar admission litigation, in his service as director of research for the Illinois Governor's Commission on Personal Privacy (1974–1976), in his outspoken exposure of and engagement with the Greek Colonels between 1967 and 1974, and even in his defense of other tourists during his family's 1960 camping trip in the Soviet Union.

C. Herman Pritchett, past President of the American Political Science Association and former Chairman of the Political Science Department at the University of Chicago, nicely summed up Anastaplo's public opposition to bullies and dictators:

> On April 24, 1961, the Supreme Court of the United States, by a vote of five to four, affirmed the action of the Illinois Supreme Court which, by a vote of four to three, had upheld the decision of the Committee on Character and Fitness of the Illinois bar which, by a vote of eleven to six, had decided that George Anastaplo was unfit for admission to the Illinois bar. This was not Anastaplo's only such experience with power structures. In 1960 he was expelled from Soviet Russia for protesting harassment of another American, and in 1970 from the Greece of the Colonels. As W. C. Fields might have said, any man who is kicked out of Russia, Greece and the Illinois bar can't be all bad.[6]

Leo Strauss, evidently after reading Anastaplo's 1961 *Petition for Rehearing* to the United States Supreme Court, wrote this short letter to him of June 22, 1961: "This is only to pay you my respects for your brave and just action. If the American Bench and Bar have any sense of shame they must come on their knees to apologize to you." We can be reminded by this letter that just as George Anastaplo is not a conventional liberal, so Leo Strauss was not a conventional conservative. Another perspective on Anastaplo's liberalism was offered by the unconventional conservative thinker Willmoore Kendall who, commenting on Anastaplo's remarkable bar admission case, described Anastaplo as "himself the author of perhaps the only 'apology' of our time that demands a place in any anthology of American Oratory. . . ."[7]

Most recently, Anastaplo has felt obliged again to be a public "player," this time in opposing that form of McCarthyism of the Left, which is contemporary "political correctness." Responding to accusations of racial heresies in his law school courses, he has produced what amounts to a manual showing how vulnerable academics of goodwill might respond in their own circumstances to situations that, however politically sensitive, are destructive of responsible political and academic discourse if not countered with a restrained vigor.[8]

II

Anastaplo's work habits and level of energy remain astounding. Laurence Berns reports that one of the most striking things about him, first noticed when they were together in the College of the University of Chicago in 1947, was that "he did and does, quite naturally without any apparent strain, the work of about three men." In more than forty years of teaching at Dominican University (formerly Rosary College), Loyola University of Chicago School of Law, and elsewhere, he has never missed a class because of illness or accident. Over those forty years, Anastaplo has also conducted at least two seminars each quarter (the equivalent of a second full-time teaching post) in the Basic Program of Liberal Education for Adults at the University of Chicago.

Anastaplo's running afoul of the Illinois Bar (beginning in 1950), reinforced perhaps by his reluctance to leave permanently his native Midwest, made unlikely a post in graduate departments of political science. Even so, for two years he flew six times a semester to the University of Dallas to offer three-day marathon graduate seminars that met for ten to twelve hours a day. And for a decade he convened "The Irregular Seminar on Political Philosophy" for graduate students (mostly in political science) at the University of Chicago. Participants in that seminar consider it to be one of the best experiences of their graduate school years.[9] If all this were not sufficient for "about three men," Anastaplo continues to attend, as he has for more than a quarter of a century, the weekly Thursday afternoon Physics Colloquium at the University of Chicago, ministering to an interest in physics that is derived from his demonstrated talent in mathematics.[10] And for some years now, weather and daylight permitting, Anastaplo bikes the ten miles each way for his classes at Loyola University of Chicago School of Law. Anastaplo's energy is evidently in part attributable to a sound physical constitution and moderate habits.[11]

Anastaplo did not allow his ordeal with the Illinois Bar Inquisitors to define him. Representing himself in his bar admission litigation, he made the arguments he thought appropriate, and when the United States Supreme Court finally ruled against him in 1961, he walked away from the practice of law.[12] Denied a career at the Bar and circumscribed in his academic career, he recognizes that his somewhat accidental bar admission difficulties may have had a profoundly liberating effect, permitting and encouraging him "to explore as teacher (and hence as student), without any sustained concern for ordinary academic achievement, only the books written over the centuries by the most thoughtful men."[13]

Among the first generation of Straussians, Anastaplo may have the widest range of subjects upon which he has published well-documented books and articles.[14] Those subjects include ancient philosophical and literary texts, legal and constitutional issues, modern philosophical and literary texts, contemporary political issues, Biblical texts, non-Western thought, and modern scientific issues posed by the work of Subrahmanyan Chandrasekhar, the cosmology of Stephen Hawking, and the physics of Aristotle. Reflecting the Renaissance-man diversity of Anastaplo's scholarship is the recently published collection, "The Scholarship of George Anastaplo." In that Symposium John Alvis discerns ten rules of literary criticism that Anastaplo observes in his study of ancient and modern literature; Larry Arnhart discusses the status of nature and natural right in Anastaplo's examination of non-Western texts; Laurence Berns focuses on Anastaplo's classicism, offering a spirited criticism of Anastaplo's spirited critique of American foreign policy; Christopher Colmo investigates Anastaplo's treatment of freedom, nature, and community; Stephen Vanderslice discusses Anastaplo's essays on religion, in relation to the good man, the good citizen, and the good society; and I review various facets of Anastaplo's constitutionalism.[15]

To date Anastaplo has published ten books, and hundreds of articles, including nearly a dozen book-length law review collections, identified as "Explorations," a genre he developed.[16] Considerable care is devoted by him to whatever he writes, no matter where it is to appear. Mindful of Carl Van Doren's observation to a meddlesome publisher "I write, you print," Anastaplo prefers having his texts and his annotations published as he has written them rather than having them revised for publication in prestigious journals. Thus he is able, in his deservedly renowned notes, to range far and wide, calling forth ancient, modern, and contemporary "friends" as guides to support the moral, intellectual and political life of a free people. He freely cites his own work, cross-referencing for the interested reader the text now at hand to what he has offered elsewhere. As he has observed: "I have not written the things I have, with the care I have, only to have them 'lost' in diverse journals."[17]

III

Vital to Anastaplo's study of American constitutionalism is his opinion that the Constitution of 1787 is a well-crafted text that requires and rewards careful reading. Richard H. Cox (another of the "first generation" of Straussians) has observed that Anastaplo's commentaries on the Constitution and on its Amendments "treat the Constitution as a coherent whole whose parts throw light upon each other and thus require careful, sustained study."[18] A proper reading of the Constitution, Anastaplo maintains, depends on the recognition that

> there is a sense to the whole of the Constitution, that the document can be thought about, part by part as well as in terms of the relations among the parts. This thinking about the Constitution—the very insistence that it can be thought about—is critical. . . .[19]

> No one mind could control completely what went into the Constitution. But it is only when one mind takes a subject and molds it that there is even the opportunity for the kind of unity which sees chance eliminated and every part fitted into the whole. . . . The quest for a unified interpretation is complicated by the fact that a constitution, unlike a play or a philosophical work, must be immediately applied to practical problems. Thus theoretical formulations, which permit the philosophical writer to seek a unity on the highest level, may not be useful for this purpose. Was the mistake of the early American politicians to assume there had to be such consistency? But what alternative is there in expounding a constitution? Indeed, what alternative is there other than repeated recourse to the fundamental principles and issues which provide guidance for the resolution of the conflicts in allegiances implicit in practical affairs?[20]

Careful reading by him of well-constructed texts reflects the influence of Leo Strauss. Anastaplo first looked in on classes of Leo Strauss while he was still in law school. After his bar admission controversy, he was able to audit Strauss's courses regularly for more than a decade. One can see, in the arguments about the Declaration of Independence and the right to revolution that Anastaplo made at age 25 to the Character and Fitness Committee of the Illinois Bar, that he had (independent of Strauss) developed a strong interest in natural right and its meaning for American Constitutionalism. One can also see that he was well on his way to developing his understanding of and admiration for his fellow Midwesterner, Abraham Lincoln. From Strauss, Anastaplo received guidance as to the important issues raised by Anglo-American and modern political thought, with special emphasis upon the work of Hobbes and Locke, and behind them Machiavelli. Anastaplo also learned from Strauss that a proper grasp of these and like thinkers depends upon an appreciation of the ancient political and moral principles, both classical and biblical, of which these thinkers were very much aware. His studies with Strauss permitted him to refine and deepen his early inclinations and to come to grips with modernity and the desperate struggles of our time, reinforcing in the process his long-standing respect for the virtue of prudence. (The influence of Leo Strauss was evident by the time Anastaplo prepared, in 1961, his *Petition for Rehearing*, the last document he filed in the United States Supreme Court. Passages from that document are quoted at the end of this chapter.)

Anastaplo also has long drawn upon and been the most persistent academic defender of the constitutional views of William Winslow Crosskey, another of his teachers at the University of Chicago. The influence of these two teachers, Strauss and Crosskey, is found in his report that "[Mr. Crosskey] tried to read the Constitution itself with the care and seriousness with which Mr. Strauss approached the greatest works in political philosophy."[21] To the way of reading illuminated by Strauss, Anastaplo joins Crosskey's constitutional jurisprudence.

The common ground shared by Crosskey and Anastaplo is found in Crosskey's insistence that

> The Constitution of the United States . . . is internally consistent in a remark-
> able degree, an extraordinarily fine example of eighteenth-century legal crafts-
> manship, and a great credit to Gouverneur Morris and James Wilson whose work
> it chiefly is. . . . The scheme of the Constitution is simple and flexible: general
> national power, subject only to a few simple limitations, with the state powers,
> in the main, continuing for any desired local legislation. So, if the Constitution
> were allowed to operate as the instrument was drawn, the American people
> could, through Congress, deal with any subject they wished, on a simple, straight-
> forward, nation-wide basis; and all other subjects, they could, in general, leave to
> the states to handle as the states might desire.[22]

Anastaplo agrees with Crosskey that the Constitution created a government of ple-nary powers, with the Congress possessing all the national legislative power, espe-cially the authority to oversee "all gainful activity of the United States." Anastaplo reads the authority of Congress to regulate commercial activity "among the several States" to include, but not to be limited to, trade moving between the states. Thus he has long doubted that the traditional judicial distinction between "interstate" and "intrastate" commerce ever had any foundation in the Constitution, indepen-dent of whatever use it may have in political debate. Further the Constitution gives to Congress the power to enact legislation "necessary and proper" for all the objects of government, including those recognized in the Preamble to the Constitution.[23] He finds instructive the insistence of the Framers of the Confederate Constitution of 1861 upon removing all "general welfare" language from the Confederate Constitution.[24] Thus Herman Beltz, reviewing Anastaplo's *The Amendments to the Constitution: A Commentary*, observed:

> Although Anastaplo is a professor of law, his writing on the Constitution is decid-
> edly nonlegalistic. Adopting the perspective of the political scientist, he analyzes
> constitutional developments not only in relation to their social and cultural con-
> text, but also in the light of moral and political philosophy. I do not imply that
> Anastaplo gives anything less than the most thoughtful and scrupulous attention
> to the constitutional text. Indeed, his concern for the words of the Constitution
> and the ideas and principles to which they refer, gives his commentaries their
> distinctive character as philosophically informed, humanistic treatises.[25]

The Preamble has usually been regarded as a rhetorical flourish that adds nothing to the enumerated powers found in the Constitution. Anastaplo, as did Crosskey, reads the Constitution by the light of the comprehensive ends found in the Preamble.[26] For Anastaplo, the Preamble explains why "We the People" "ordained and established" the Constitution, a constitution which provides the republican form required to meet the ends of a national government.[27] The Preamble serves furthermore as the link between the Declaration of Independence and the Constitution. Thus, the "one People" of the Declaration becomes "We the People" of the Preamble. "We the People," having exercised the inalienable right of revolution recognized in the Declaration of Independence, then exercised an inalienable right to institute a new government through the Constitution.

It is from this perspective that Anastaplo joins the supreme authority of the people in a regime "dedicated to the proposition that all men are created equal" to the constitutional supremacy of the legislature. On Anastaplo's reading of the Constitution, "Congress is to have the decisive, or authoritative, voice as to what the controlling measures of the United States are to be," with both the President and the Supreme Court properly subordinate to it. Congress is given all the law-making power granted by the Constitution while "the Executive and the Judicial branches are dependent upon, and bound by, the laws Congress chooses to make."[28]

IV

Anastaplo, consistent with his emphasis upon the supremacy of the legislature, maintains that too much is now made of Presidents and presidential authority. For more than seventy years there has been considerable support by Democrats and Republicans, liberals and conservatives alike, for an aggrandizement of the Presidency at the expense of Congress. This, together with the "growing reliance upon public opinion polls and referenda," suggests for Anastaplo "the danger that we are moving from a republican regime grounded in representative legislatures to a plebiscitary democracy in which much is made of Presidents . . . who cannot fail to disappoint the expectations of those who depend upon them, both at home and abroad."[29]

The expectation that Presidents can solve all problems has bred both public discontent and constitutional risk, raising for Anastaplo serious questions about the modern Presidency. Can any President deliver all he is tempted to promise? How are we to discuss and deal with the issues that confront us as a people? Should "We the People" look to a single citizen to solve our problems? Do such expectations reflect a smothering of the American genius for republican government? "Is there not something demeaning to a republican people to make what we now do of our Presidents and of their families and other intimates? Among the consequences of our unbecoming obsequiousness, . . . [of the way we now kowtow to the President,] which the mass media 'naturally' exploit, is that we are diverted both from serious politics and from a proper reading of the Constitution."[30]

Anastaplo has long been critical of the mass media's effect on our self-discipline, on our politics, and on the modern Presidency.[31] The effect of the media on Presidents and presidential elections has often reduced political discourse to little more than images designed to manipulate the electorate and to reduce complex issues to sound bites and bumper-sticker slogans. "[M]odern Presidential politics play much better on television. The President is easy to dramatize; the Congress tends to be boring. All the Congress does is talk (or deliberate); the President acts (with little or no show of deliberation required). That which can be readily presented by television in an 'interesting' way affects what we are now apt to consider government to be."[32]

The disparity in appearances between Congress and the President, reinforced by television, "does not settle the question of where the ultimate power lies." For Anastaplo, the critical question centers on how far the powers of the President go and what the President is able to do. "It is important," Anastaplo argues, "to insist that the President is very much confined by the Constitution." Most troublesome for him is the increasing "emancipation of Presidents from Congressional guidance and sound political assessments," an emancipation that is apparent in the errors surrounding Vietnam, Watergate, the Iran-arms/Contra-aid affair, and the presidential maneuvering that foreclosed any real Congressional deliberation leading to the Persian Gulf War. It is this "presumptuousness of Presidents," who have become "regal and extra-constitutional in character," that leads Anastaplo to question the movement toward a plebiscitary-based Presidency that is in danger of becoming an "incipient Caesarism."[33]

V

Both too much and not enough, Anastaplo argues, is made of the "Judicial Power of the United States." Too much has been made of judicial review, with the Supreme Court tending for more than a century to turn itself into "a superlegislature," entitled and obliged to review the laws passed by Congress. It remains an open question for Anastaplo whether the Court in *Marbury v. Madison* was "wrong, or at least not clearly right," when it asserted that the First Congress had overreached its Constitutional authority in Section 13 of the Judiciary Act of 1789. Doubt that judicial review of acts of Congress was intended, Anastaplo argues, should be raised by the fact "that the slightest acquaintance with the British Constitution . . . [or] Blackstone's Commentaries would have reminded the Framers that the Legislature is by nature supreme, not any court, nor the executive alone, whatever its part in the legislative process may be and thus the Framers would have known that if something other than legislative supremacy had been intended, it should have been provided for unequivocally by the Constitution."[34] The somewhat similar presidential veto power was fully discussed and spelled out in detail, as was the authority of the Congress to override such a veto. Although Federalist No. 78 may seem to argue for judicial review, there is no indication at all in the Constitution that judicial review of acts of Congress was intended.

Related to Anastaplo's argument about the undue emphasis now placed on judicial review is his contention that not enough emphasis is placed on a full realization of the Court's proper role in developing a general common law. He argues that fully to understand the Constitution one must recognize the degree to which it takes for granted and relies upon the common law. Some cases posing common law issues were understood by the First Congress to be part of the Supreme Court's jurisdiction over "all cases in law and equity arising under this Constitution." The question addressed in *Swift v. Tyson* (1842), in a diversity-of-citizenship dispute involving negotiable instruments, was whether the United States Supreme Court had to take its lead from a state judicial system in settling the common law for commercial-law issues raised by the case.[35] The question arose because Section 34 of the Judiciary Act of 1789, enacted by the First Congress, provides, "The laws of the several states, except where the Constitution, treaties, or statutes shall otherwise provide or require, shall be regarded as rules of decision in trials at common law in the Courts of the United States, in cases where they apply."

Anastaplo argues, as did Crosskey, that Section 34 did not have to be made any more explicit than it is because it was generally understood that, when faced with conflicting common-law precedents in diversity cases, the Courts of the United States (which we know as the federal courts) would make their own independent determination of what the applicable law was. This, he argues, was the intended approach. Both Anastaplo and Crosskey acknowledge that the election of Thomas Jefferson and the ascendant Anti-Federalists and later "states' rights" positions supported the view that common-law cases should be authoritatively decided by state courts and should not be subject to any Supreme Court oversight. By 1938 the "states rights" view of "a juridical system with many bodies (the states) but no head had triumphed."[36]

Anastaplo traces depreciation of the Supreme Court's role in common-law cases back, at least in part, to the Southern insistence on a narrow interpretation of the commerce power of Congress in order to make it more likely that the General Government would not interfere with how the Southern States dealt with slavery. The formal end of the Supreme Court's independent role in common-law cases came when the Court in *Erie Railroad Co. v. Tompkins* abandoned *Swift v. Tyson* by asserting that there is no "federal common law" in the United States, thus renouncing any role for itself in expounding an authoritative reading of a national (or truly common) common law.[37] Since *Erie* the Court has assumed a subordinate position, attempting to address in the typical diversity cases only two less important questions: (1) Which state's common law is controlling here? (2) What does that state's common law have to say about the issue in question?[38]

For Anastaplo, *Swift* and *Erie* depend upon divergent positions on fundamental issues in constitutional law and politics, including the question of the nature of law, the relationship between unwritten law (including the common law) and positive law, the role of the Supreme Court in jurisprudence, the relationship between Congress and the Court, the relation between national and state courts, and even the extent of the Congressional power to regulate commerce. The Court in *Erie*, by rejecting the existence of a federal common law, also tacitly rejected the understanding of the Framers, evident in *Swift*, that there are enduring standards of right and wrong which judges discover and apply to the cases that come before them. Anastaplo argues, in the mode of *Swift*, that the Court's role in expounding the Common Law

> is not a historical question or even a question about the original intention of the Framers. Rather, it is a question about the very nature of law and how justice is to be arrived at by courts working on their own, somewhat independently of legislatures. It is a question about the way that reason and nature may be looked to in establishing justice, something that common-law courts have always been thought of as most adept in doing. . . .
>
> The common law is a way of applying, case-by-case, the enduring standards of the community, and in such a way as to bring the community along, even as reforms are being made. It is salutary to emphasize here that common-law judges discover the law; they do not simply make it. Reason looks to nature (instead of will looking to desire) in declaring the rule that is to be followed.[39]

Erie proclaimed, in effect, that all law, written or unwritten, is positive law. Anastaplo argues that contemporary jurisprudence has looked to law "not as the product of reasoning with a view to justice, but rather as merely the exercise of sovereign power, and the States could be looked to as sufficient repositories of such power."[40]

Law, whether unwritten or in statutes or in judicial decisions, is now widely regarded as simply the expression of the power and will of the sovereign, at least by the more sophisticated judges and their counterparts in the academy. Even so, Anastaplo notices that the Supreme Court, using the Fourteenth Amendment and the doctrine of incorporation, has, in recognizing "a second bill of rights" applicable to the states, acted in a way "that may be somewhat similar to what English common-law courts did in the seventeenth and eighteenth centuries in building up the great body of common law privileges and immunities." This has allowed the General Government to protect the citizens of this country "against state infringements of traditional (if not even natural) rights."[41] We are thus reminded by Anastaplo, that this development is an example of what courts can do as expositors of the principles of a regime.

VI

We return now to the constitutional authority of Congress. Anastaplo offers, in *The Constitution of 1787*, a persuasive reading of the structure and substance of Article I.[42] It is widely believed that the Constitution is an instrument of enumerated powers, powers which are found mostly in Section 8 of Article I. Anastaplo suggests that there is in the Constitution even more power, particularly economic power, taken for granted to achieve the great ends of government expressed in the Preamble than that provided for "either expressly or by implication" in the bare enumeration in Section 8. He notices that the common-defense power has always been regarded as very broad, even though it is given no greater emphasis in that section than the general-welfare power. Thus he finds little constitutional basis for interpretations which have assumed that much more can be done by Congress for the common defense than for the general welfare when the explicit constitutional authority for both seems to be similar in scope.[43]

One explanation for this discrepancy Anastaplo suggests is found in the cramped interpretation of the power of Congress under the Commerce Clause that became critical, as we have noticed, to the South's attempt to protect its interest in slavery.[44] Three Southern States in the Constitutional Convention had demanded a twenty-year moratorium upon Congressional power to prohibit the international slave trade if they were to ratify the Constitution. In support of his broad reading of the Commerce Clause, Anastaplo asks,

> Does not this [1808-slave-trade] guarantee implicitly recognize that without it the Congress would have been able, at once, to forbid Americans to engage in the international slave trade? A further question: If so, what would have permitted Congress to do this? The answer: The Commerce Clause with its grant of power to Congress to "regulate Commerce with foreign Nations." This leads to still another question: What does the grant of power to Congress to "regulate Commerce ... among the several States" permit Congress to do about the slave trade moving between the States of the Union, to say nothing of slavery's influence and effects upon the commercial life of the Country as a whole. Does not the twenty-year international slave-trade guarantee tacitly recognize a quite broad commerce power in the Congress of the United States, and perhaps also a broad general-welfare power?[45]

Anastaplo identifies seventeen sets of congressional powers in Section 8 of Article I, sets of powers that he divides into seven categories: financial, commercial, monetary, intellectual, judicial, defensive, and managerial. He believes that five of the seven categories are, to some degree, overlapping, reflecting a variety of opinions about the pre-Constitution character and usage of those powers. He suggests that some of the listings were meant to assure for Congress powers that had previously been thought by some to be either judicial or executive in nature and, in some instances, powers that had been previously exercised only by the states.

The power to borrow and coin money had been thought by some to be part of the domestic authority of the English Crown; the power to declare war and to raise armies had been thought by some to be part of the Crown's military authority; and the great power to regulate commerce had been thought by some to be part of the states' authority. All now are explicitly (but not necessarily exclusively) given to the national legislature, probably in part "to suppress executive [as well as state?] pretensions."[46]

Thus the provision of Article I for "[a]ll legislative powers herein granted," Anastaplo contends, is not limited by the enumeration in its Section 8 nor later by the Bill of Rights, but only by such prohibitions as those found in Section 9 of Article I. Section 8 reflects the attempt of the country as a whole to permit self-government, restoring "to the national legislature the plenary powers over matters of obvious national concern, such as taxation, commerce, peace, and war, that had been imprudently denied under the Articles of Confederation." Anastaplo argues that the powers provided for by the Constitution were intended to be, from the beginning, far more extensive than they are yet recognized to be in principle, however broad they may now be in practice.[47]

One intention of listing congressional powers, as has been indicated, was to clarify the location of each of those powers within the national government rather than to spell out an exhaustive enumeration of congressional power. This caution, Anastaplo notices, has had "a perverse effect"—it may even be "a cosmic joke": the intention of Section 8 "to fill out and confirm the authority of Congress and to avoid controversy might have had the unanticipated result of making the powers enumerated here virtually the only generally recognized powers of Congress."[48]

The necessities of the twentieth century, Anastaplo acknowledges, have promoted the expansion of specific powers found in Section 8 and secured for Congress almost the full range of intended powers required to deal with the social and economic interests of the American people. But that full recognition, he contends, "has come about in such a way as to obscure the order and symmetry," and ultimately the authority, of the Constitution.[49] The commerce power has proved decisive in determining the scope of the General Government as well as serving the cause of justice and civil rights all over the country. It is now generally acknowledged that Congress may regulate as much of the economy of the United States as it deems necessary for the general welfare, including, for example, the regulation of commerce so as to discourage segregation.[50] But, as Anastaplo observes, this latter development (which is sufficiently, perhaps better, authorized by Section 5 of the Fourteenth Amendment) has occurred in such a way that it can seem to many citizens that the Constitution has had either to be circumvented or "to grow" in order to serve contemporary needs.

From Anastaplo's reading of the Commerce Clause and of the rest of Article I, Section 8, it is evident that his constitutional perspective is neither one of "a living Constitution" nor one of "original intent," as conventionally understood. He suggests that both are partially correct. Proponents of original intent are correct in that "we do want reliable guidance from our constitutional instruments; while proponents of a living constitution are correct in that we do want to be able to take care of pressing and ever-changing needs." But he contends that both are also incorrect in that "a living or growing Constitution need not be resorted to if it should be recognized what the true original intent of the Framers of the Constitution was, an intent to invest Congress with broad powers to regulate both the economy of the Country and its interests in the world at large. Those originally broad powers have been enhanced by such constitutional amendments as the Fourteenth, which permit the General Government to supervise many activities in the States, particularly those concerned with race relations and with the administration of justice."[51]

VII

Related to Anastaplo's reading of the Constitution of 1787 is his reading of the Bill of Rights and the other amendments to the Constitution. It is perhaps an overstatement to suggest that Anastaplo thinks that none of the amendments with the exception of the Thirteenth Amendment have been required. But he does maintain that none of the amendments thus far has touched the core of the Constitution or reduced the authority of the Government of the United States. Thus, the Framers of the Constitution did not intend to threaten the liberties and rights, or the privileges and immunities, of citizens. He argues that it is highly unlikely that the First Congress, led by several members who had been in the Constitutional Convention, would have proposed the Bill of Rights if they had believed it undermined what had been done two years before. The Bill of Rights "makes explicit, or confirms, what had been taken for granted or at least had been aimed at from the outset. Even the Civil War amendments—the Thirteenth, Fourteenth and Fifteenth Amendments —are consistent with, if not called for by, the American Constitutional spirit."[52]

The 1791 amendments were largely declarative of rights, privileges, and immunities long recognized in the Anglo-American Common Law tradition out of which American constitutionalism developed. In *The Constitutionalist*, his mammoth treatise on the First Amendment, Anastaplo summed up in 1971 his understanding of the speech and press clause:

> The First Amendment to the Constitution prohibits Congress, in its law-making capacity, from cutting down in any way or for any reason freedom of speech and of the press. The extent of this freedom is to be measured not merely by the common law treatises and cases available on December 15, 1791—the date of the ratification of the First Amendment—but also by the general understanding and practice of the people of the United States who insisted upon, had written for them, and ratified (through their State Legislatures) the First Amendment. An important indication of the extent of this freedom is to be seen in the teachings of the Declaration of Independence and in the events leading up to the Revolution.

Although the prohibition in the First Amendment is absolute—we see here a restraint upon Congress that is unqualified, among restraints that *are* qualified— the absolute prohibition does not relate to all forms of expression but only to that which the terms, "freedom of speech, or of the press" were then taken to encompass, political speech, speech having to do with the duties and concerns of self-governing citizens. Thus, for example, this constitutional provision is not primarily or directly concerned with what we now call artistic expression or with the problems of obscenity. Rather, the First Amendment acknowledges that the sovereign citizen has the right freely to discuss the public business, a privilege theretofore claimed only for members of legislative bodies.[53]

The provision for amendments, Anastaplo recognizes, reinforces the idea that "We the People" are and remain a self-governing people. Despite conservative "original intent" understandings that seek to limit the Ninth Amendment and to expand the Tenth Amendment, both amendments remind us that the rights of the people and the powers provided for in the Constitution remain in the control of the people. The Ninth Amendment acknowledges that there are rights of the people neither dependent on government nor expressly set forth in the Constitution or in the Bill of Rights. The Tenth Amendment says in effect that the Constitution means what it says about the division of power between the National Government and the governments of the states.[54] What that division of power is, it is argued, is determined by other parts of the Constitution, not by the Tenth Amendment.

Throughout his study of the Constitution, Anastaplo indicates where and how he draws upon the constitutional history of Crosskey. Even so, he transcends his law school teacher's constitutional history in that he reads the Constitution even more carefully than did Crosskey. Both of them emphasize the common-law context of the Constitution. But Anastaplo makes much more than did Crosskey of natural right and hence of the Common Law's foundation in nature and reason. On Anastaplo's reading, the great task of the Constitution was to establish the framework of government within which the self-evident truths of the Declaration of Independence would be applied and preserved. Anastaplo undergirds Crosskey's constitutional history and legal positivism with an understanding of nature and political philosophy as the basis for understanding those documents.[55] In this he is very much a student of Leo Strauss.[56]

VIII

Politics and morality cannot be separated in any political community. But a democratic republic, more than any other, depends on the character of its citizens. Anastaplo continually places before the reader both the virtue of prudence—which is concerned with what is right by nature and is possible in the circumstances—and the best regime. His constitutionalism always includes, in one way or another, an

examination of the habits and assumptions concerning the moral and political standards that form the character of the people presupposed by the Constitution.
Laurence Berns noticed this when he wrote to Anastaplo: "You are spelling out the
virtues, the discipline, the qualities of character and behavior not usually thought
about or expressed—though vaguely felt—that went into the making of the
Constitution and that are required to make it work as it was intended to work."[57]
    How to maintain and reinforce the virtues required for republican self-gov-
ernment has been recognized by some as the "Achilles' heel" of American constitutionalism. One scholar referred to the question, "How shall 'we the people' be
kept virtuous?" as "the missing section of *The Federalist*."[58] The first answer to this
question was that the formation and care of the moral and intellectual character of
citizens were left as the responsibility of the states. But slavery, segregation, and large-
scale violations of the rights of citizens in the administration of criminal justice,
have long compromised that claim.
    Pervading Anastaplo's writings on the United States is an insistence that decent
self-government ultimately depends on the character of the people. As early as his
first major essay (for the Leo Strauss *Festschrift*) "Human Being and Citizen: A
Beginning to the Study of Plato's Apology of Socrates" (1964) and his first essay on
the Declaration of Independence (1965), Anastaplo adopted for himself George
Washington's observation in 1789: "There is no truth more thoroughly established
than that there exists, in the economy and course of nature, an indissoluble union
between virtue and happiness, between duty and advantage, between the genuine
maxims of an honest and magnanimous policy, and the solid rewards of public prosperity and felicity; since we ought to be no less persuaded that the propitious smiles
of heaven can never be expected on a nation that disregards the eternal rules of
order and right which heaven itself has ordained."[59] Even the best of constitutions,
Anastaplo reminds us, is insufficient if the people do not maintain the spirit, the discipline, and the moderation, that is, the habits, necessary to make proper use of "the
great guarantees enshrined in the Constitution of 1787 and its Bill of Rights."
Republican government, even under a well-crafted Constitution cannot be
expected to prosper when a people's character and habits are no longer sound. It is
the duty of the government to promote such soundness. The American people, he
maintains, are truly self-governing and truly free "only when they know what they
are doing," which includes possessing a self-awareness grounded in the recognition
that competence, moderation, self-restraint and civility are necessary to decent and
sustained self-government.[60]
    Anastaplo closed in 1971 the text of *The Constitutionalist* with this reaffirma-
tion of American constitutionalism:

> American republicanism remains not only "the world's best hope" but also the
> noblest testimony that men have today of their faith in one another—in, that is,
> the ability of man to use his reason properly to secure for himself and his pos-
> terity the good things of this life. Timid men should be reassured that our repub-

lican experiment not only has worked, but has worked much better than eighteenth-century republicans had any right to hope for: it may well be the best which our political circumstances, nature, and traditional opinions will admit. The republican of our day, however subject to continual re-examination his salutary opinions should be, is entitled to conclude, "We must not be afraid to be free."[61]

This reaffirmation was also voiced on the occasion of the Bicentennial of the Constitution, with Anastaplo adding his toast: "On to three hundred!"[62]

IX

Anastaplo's high regard for American Constitutionalism is, however, not without qualification.[63] Our political circumstances and our traditional opinions have, he recognizes, undergone significant changes during the second half of the twentieth century. Though critical of some contemporary practices and policies, he nevertheless shuns prophecies of doom. Instead he seems to have kept before himself, as he keeps before his readers, "the old saying" of Leo Strauss "that wisdom cannot be separated from moderation" and the understanding "that wisdom requires unhesitating loyalty to a decent constitution and even to the cause of constitutionalism."[64]

From this perspective, Anastaplo reminds us that a well-established constitutionalism with its built-in sense of restraint may provide the best access for us to enduring standards of good government. Depending on the people's soundness of character, the very language of constitutionalism, such as equal protection, and due process can become the language of prudence and justice.[65] How one regards the Constitution as well as the status of revelation and other manifestations of the divine can affect, among other things, the soundness of the family as the fundamental source of the moral instruction of a people. As our customs and manners become ever more diverse it must be our constitutional principles that unite and help define "We the People."

However modern American republicanism may have been at its foundation, it shares with classical republicanism the understanding that the human capacity for reason allows for discernment of universal principles of moral and political right. Anastaplo draws upon that discernment to clarify the sources of American republicanism and to protect the supports of that republicanism from those aspects of contemporary life that threaten them. His constitutionalism may thus be understood to correct both a pessimistic critique that exaggerates the shortcomings of the American regime and an indiscriminate defense that insufficiently recognizes what is faulty about that regime.

Anastaplo has acknowledged in *The Constitutionalist*, as well as in his later writing, that his work has at its core a tension inevitable "for anyone who tries to live with both the *Apology of Socrates* and the Declaration of Independence—for anyone, that is, who finds himself drawn to two public declarations which are, despite their superficial compatibility, radically divergent in their presuppositions and implications. Thus, an attempt is made herein to see American constitutional law and political thought from the perspective of our ancient teachers."[66] A full account of the tension between the *Apology of Socrates* and the Declaration of Independence would also be a full account of the tension between ancient political philosophy and modern social thought. Anastaplo neither disparages modern constitutionalism because it is not classical constitutionalism nor subordinates practical political teachings to philosophy's metaphysical interests. We have recognized that although he keeps the focus of the best regime before his readers, he does not allow the best regime in speech to become the enemy of a good regime in practice. If the best regime is rare except in speech, an actual good regime requires considerable care by the most talented among us.[67]

The tension in Anastaplo's constitutionalism exists because he is a partisan both of philosophy and of liberal democracy. That is, he is a partisan of both the Spirit of 399 B.C. and the Spirit of 1776 A.D. In practice this means that he is a partisan of liberty under the rule of law in a regime which is rooted in consent of the governed. This he considers the best available alternative to the rule of philosophy in our time. The *Apology of Socrates* is arguably the finest public speech to an ancient democracy, as Lincoln's Gettysburg Address is the finest public speech to a modern democracy. In his *Apology*, Socrates invokes a way of life derived from moral and political standards rooted in reason's grasp of human nature. American republican constitutionalism may have received at Gettysburg its authoritative interpretation when Abraham Lincoln looked back to 1776 and the Declaration of Independence as the beginning of "a new nation conceived in Liberty, and dedicated to the proposition that all men are created equal." Lincoln reaffirmed for the American people, North and South, the Declaration's self-evident truths derived from nature's standard as the "sheet anchor of American republicanism." In the *Apology*, one can see the attractions of antiquity in the embodiment there of reason and virtue. In the Gettysburg Address one can see the attractions of modernity with its devotion to freedom, equality, and widespread personal fulfillment.

Anastaplo's constitutionalism is located where the stream of the ancient understanding of virtue and the stream of the modern principles of natural right intersect. It is the Declaration of Independence that marks the intersection of those streams: "[T]he Declaration of Independence reflects an awareness among the American people of that which is by nature right. . . . Old-fashioned notions about that which is by nature right, influenced it seems by a sense of morality reaffirmed and refined by long-established religious influences, helped shape the Declaration of Independence in ways that Plato and Aristotle can perhaps help us notice."[68]

From a different beginning leading to a different end, modern constitutionalism can, much like classical constitutionalism, look to reason to secure the advantageous and the just. One part of the modern rebellion against classical political philosophy had at or near its center the recognition that however noble classical political philosophy was, classical political practice was often wretched for all but a very few citizens. Modern political philosophy has substantially advanced the conquest of nature by modern science in order to secure the "relief of man's estate." The considerable enlargement in material abundance, reinforced by widespread protection of private property, has contributed to the enhancement of citizenship for the benefit of the many and, it is hoped, for the security of all.

X

The beneficial effect that ancient political philosophy can have on modern political practice is represented, at its best, by American constitutionalism. And American political practice is grounded in the Declaration of Independence and the Constitution. Anastaplo seeks to recall the perspective of classical republicanism, where possible, in support of modern political practice. This means, in effect, fusing respect for excellence in all its forms with both the demands for equality and the consent of the governed. Anastaplo offered in *The Constitutionalist* an observation on the character of the American people that continues to inform his study of American constitutionalism:

> Is it not evident that the only practical access to nobility for this people remains its dedication to freedom and to the manliness, disciplined self-confidence, humanity, pride, and even justice which can be said to be implied by that freedom? A vigorous defense of freedom seems to me the only cause which can have an enduring appeal for our young, especially when its defense is coupled, as it can be, with integrity of character. Those who dilute our ancient faith in freedom threaten the principal support of our regime. The swelling crusade for the justice of equality can have permanent worth only if our freedom, with its implications of excellence, can be preserved.[69]

Abraham Lincoln insisted that the self-evident truth that "all men are created equal" was "the father of all moral principle" among us. Anastaplo acknowledges the contribution of a dedication to equality to the pursuit of justice and the protection of rights since the Declaration of Independence and the Civil War. But over the natural principle of equality he elevates the no less natural principle of freedom as the other mainstay of the American regime. To the degree one values equality, Anastaplo insists, to that degree at least one must protect freedom.[70]

Modern freedom depends upon the concept of self-legislation and is ultimately justified by that capacity of a people to govern itself which makes effective freedom possible. It is our equality as self-governing citizens that is precious, not an equality under the despotism either of tyrannical government or of personal self-indulgence.[71] Even so, it can sometimes be a short step (especially in a democracy) from the equality of all men to the equality of the opinions and desires of all men, no matter how pernicious those opinions and desires may be. An emphasis upon equality, Anastaplo warns, can lead to a numbing mediocrity, to a radical individualism, and to a demand for private rights amounting to a despotism of the individual "self" over the interests of the community, or the common good.

Leo Strauss recognized a half century ago that the nation dedicated to the modern natural-right teaching of the Declaration of Independence had become, "no doubt partly as a consequence of this dedication, the most powerful and prosperous of the nations of the earth." But, he added, "Does this nation in its maturity still cherish the faith in which it was conceived and raised? Does it still hold those 'truths to be self-evident'?"[72] The succeeding decades have given us little reason to deny the importance of these and like questions. Truths, to say nothing of self-evident truths regarding the ends of political life, seem everyday less evident, if not irrelevant to contemporary political life.

The classical discovery of natural standards ascertainable by reason permitted an appreciation of prudence or practical wisdom. What the best constitutional form is for any particular people depends in large part, we have noticed, on the character of that people and the moral, political, and social conditions of their time. These are the materials that the prudent statesman must take into account and work with. Recognition of the limits imposed by time and place are critical to prudence. A prudent statesmanship depending on circumstances sometimes requires making the best of a bad situation. But it is, Anastaplo maintains, only an awareness of the best that permits sensible determinations of what is possible and what must be settled for in any set of circumstances.[73] He contends that the foundation for a justified hopefulness rests on a well-crafted Constitution appropriate to our democratic opinions, nature, and circumstances which takes for granted a comprehensive system of justice. It rests also on a citizenry that recognizes and respects the enduring standards of public morality and discipline that the Constitution embodies.[74]

Anastaplo's constitutionalism does appear to be intimately related to his Classicism. The promise that modernity held out for all mankind is expressed by the Declaration's dedication to "Life, Liberty, and the Pursuit of Happiness." Modern liberal constitutional government exists to secure and protect the personal rights of all, thereby protecting the private pursuit of individual happiness. As Leo Strauss wrote: "The quarrel between the ancients and the moderns concerns eventually and perhaps even from the beginning, the status of 'individuality.'"[75]

I have, in the opening section of this chapter, quoted the letter written by Leo Strauss to George Anastaplo after receiving the June 1961 *Petition for Rehearing* filed by him in the United States Supreme Court. It is fitting to conclude my account of this somewhat unusual Straussian by reprinting here the opening and closing paragraphs of that 1961 *Petition for Rehearing*, passages in which (it can be said) Leo Strauss must have recognized his influence:

Introduction

> And let us not be weary in well
> doing: for in due season we
> shall reap, if we faint not.
> —*Galatians*, vi, 9.

It is highly probable that upon disposition of this *Petition for Rehearing*, petitioner will have practiced all the law he is ever going to. That is, he recognizes that this petition cannot reasonably be expected to affect a decision of this Court reached after long deliberation. Nevertheless, petitioner is obliged, if only to complete his effort, not to let pass unnoticed the errors in the Opinion of this Court.

Since no one would profit from a mere repetition of arguments developed in earlier briefs, this petition is directed primarily to a discussion of the novel problems raised by the Opinion of this Court. Petitioner will then have discharged the obligation to the profession and to the community that he assumed when this Court permitted him to appear as counsel *pro se*. That is, he will not only have stated his legal position but will also have recorded, among the papers he has filed in this Court, an adequate answer to the arguments that have been marshaled against him.

It must also be recorded that this entire controversy is itself but an image of a much more fundamental one which bears on the problem of the education and character of the citizen as well as of the lawyer. We must try to take seriously again the concern and conditions for virtue, nobility and the life most fitting for man.

Petitioner, exercising the prerogative of one retiring from a profession, would advise the new lawyer that he learn well not only the tools of his craft but also the texts that have come to us from the ancient world. It is in those texts that one may find the best models, both in word and in deed, for the conduct of oneself in public as well as in private affairs. It is there that the better natures are most likely to be exposed to the accents and majesty of human excellence.

★ ★ ★ ★ ★ ★ ★

Conclusion

We have suggested that the exclusion order should be reversed, with instructions to the Illinois bar authorities on remand that they reconsider the record already made in this case without giving any adverse effect to petitioner's allegedly "subversive" views on the right of revolution and the Declaration of Independence. This modification would seem to be consistent with the position actually taken by this Court in its Opinion.

Reasons have also been advanced for a reversal and remand that would be even more respectful of the record and of natural justice, a remand with the ruling that petitioner has clearly established his character and fitness for the practice of law. That is, we suggest that the record in this case has still to be given its due.

It is only by an ungenerous disregard of the record as it developed, of the kind of challenges petitioner alone faced and of the manner in which he met them, that the action of the Illinois authorities has been upheld. The record—both before the committee and on appeal—that record of testimony and briefs remains as a guide to reforms that are needed in the education and character of the American bar.

Petitioner is satisfied he has acted as one ought. He is further satisfied that his actions will continue to serve the best interests of the bar and of the country. The generous sentiments of the dissenting opinions elicited by his cause in Chicago, in Springfield, and in Washington keep alive hopes for the success of efforts to make the institutions and laws of our people a reflection of decency and perhaps even of nobility.

Petitioner leaves in the hands of the profession—lawyers, law teachers and judges alike—the career he might have had. He trusts he will be forgiven if he retains for himself only the immortal lines of another exile (*Inferno*, xv, 121-124), "Then he turned back, and seemed like one of those who run for the green cloth at Verona through the open fields; and of them seemed he who triumphs, not he who loses."[76]

NOTES

1. Interviews by Studs Terkel in *Law and Philosophy: The Practice of Theory: Essays in Honor of George Anastaplo*, eds. John A. Murley, William T. Braithwaite and Robert L. Stone (Athens: Ohio University Press, 1992), II, pp. 504–38. I wish to thank Laurence Berns for his many helpful suggestions drawn upon throughout this essay.

2. George Anastaplo, *Human Being and Citizen: Essays on Virtue, Freedom and the Common Good* (Chicago: Swallow Press, 1975), pp. 151–54; Anastaplo, *The American Moralist: On Law, Ethics and Government* (Athens: Ohio University Press, 1992), pp. xvi–xix, 108–21, 199–214, 225–95, Anastaplo, "'McCarthyism,' the Cold War, and Their Aftermath," 43 *South Dakota Law Review* 103–71 (1998). See also Anastaplo, "The Rosenberg Case and the Perils of Indignation," *Chicago Lawyer*, June 1979 (reprinted in Anastaplo, "On Trial: Explorations," 22 *Loyola University of Chicago Law Journal* 994–1009 [1991]).

3. "Overwhelming Power and a Sense of Proportion," in George Anastaplo, "On Freedom: Explorations," 17 *Oklahoma City University Law Review* 613, 618, 620, 589–630 (1992); Anastaplo, "U.S. turned its back on freedom in Iraq," *Chicago Sun-Times*, December 29, 1998, p. 22. See the exchange between Laurence Berns and Anastaplo in "The Scholarship of George Anastaplo—A Symposium," 26 *The Political Science Reviewer* 250, 90–113, 248–57 (1997). See also John A. Murley, "Our Character is Our Fate: The Constitutionalism of George Anastaplo," ibid., pp. 36–37, which I draw upon throughout this essay.

4. Anastaplo, *The Amendments to the Constitution: A Commentary* (Baltimore: Johns Hopkins University Press, 1995), pp. 88–89; *The American Moralist*, pp. 108–21, 319–26, 367–74, 422–30; *Human Being and Citizen*, pp. 160–74. See also Anastaplo, "Penalty of Death Read in New Light," *Chicago Daily Law Bulletin,* April 25, 1998, pp. 23, 35. (This essay is appended to the "Crisis and Continuity" article cited in note 5, below.)

5. See George Anastaplo, "What Do We Really Want to Learn About the President?" *Public Interest Law Reporter,* April 1998, pp. 2–7; "Crisis and Continuity in the Clinton Presidency," *Public Interest Law Reporter,* July 1998, pp. 1–7. See also Anastaplo, "Spiro Agnew's Example," *New York Times*, September 11, 1998, p. A26; Anastaplo, "Unseemly Characters," *Chicago Sun-Times*, September 13, 1998, p. 38A. See as well Anastaplo, "Bugs in the System," *Chicago Sun-Times*, September 23, 1998, p. 50.

6. See "What's Really Wrong With George Anastaplo?" in Anastaplo, *Human Being and Citizen*, p. 105. See, on how a citizen of a republic may speak to tyrants, "Dissent in Athens," in ibid., pp. 3–7. Anastaplo's steady stream of Letters to the Editor suggests how a citizen should speak to his fellow citizens on issues of the day. This he call his "busybody mode." See, e.g., Anastaplo, "Sports may benefit from NBA lockout," *Chicago Tribune*, December 3, 1998, sec.1, p.28 ("5-foot putts" should be "4-foot putts"); note 5, above, note 58, below. Anastaplo's activities as a citizen prompted a committee of his former students to nominate him annually for the Nobel Peace Prize between 1980 and 1992. The first letter to the Nobel Peace Prize Committee putting his name in nomination was by Malcolm P. Sharp, one of Anastaplo's teachers at the University of Chicago Law School. See note 21, below.

7. Leo Strauss to George Anastaplo, June 22, 1961 (photocopy in possession of the author). See George Anastaplo, *The Artist as Thinker: From Shakespeare to Joyce* (Athens: Ohio University Press, 1983), p. 474, n. 282. What Leo Strauss thought notwithstanding, perhaps because they have long thought his bar admission case "imprudent" or, perhaps more so, because they believe Anastaplo made too much of Strauss's Jewishness in his "On Leo Strauss: A Yahrzeit Remembrance" (reprinted in Anastaplo, ibid. pp. 250–72), or more recently perhaps because of Anastaplo's older-brother-like criticism of Allan Bloom's *The Closing of the American Mind*, in *Essays on the Closing of the American Mind*, ed. Robert L. Stone (Chicago: Chicago Review Press, 1989), pp. 225–34, 267–84, there appears to be, however, quiet, determined reservations concerning George Anastaplo among some of his fellow Straussians. See Anastaplo, "Leo Strauss and Judaism," *The Great Ideas Today* (Chicago: Encyclopaedia Britannica, 1998), his review of Kenneth Hart Green's *Jewish Philosophy and the Crisis of Modernity*. See also George Anastaplo, "Law & Literature and the Bible: Explorations," *Oklahoma City University Law Review* 23, appendix B (1999). See as well Willmoore Kendall, Book Review, *The American Political Science Review* 61 (September 1967), 783; *Law and Philosophy*, I, ix–xii; Anastaplo, "Notes toward an 'Apologia pro vita sua,'" *Interpretation* 10 (January 1982), pp. 333–34. For the bar admission controversy, see *In re Anastaplo*, 121 N.E. 2d 826 (Ill. 1954); 163 N.E. 2d 429 (Ill. 1959); 163 N.E. 2d 928 (Ill. 1960); 366 U.S. 82 (1961). See also George Anastaplo, *The Constitutionalist: Notes on the First Amendment* (Dallas: Southern Methodist University Press, 1971), pp. 331–418; "What is still Wrong with George Anastaplo? A Sequel to 366 U.S. 82 (1961)," *DePaul Law Review* 35 (1986), pp. 583–86; "A Letter to the President of the Chicago Council of Lawyers," Chicago, Illinois, October 18, 1995 (reprinted in "'McCarthyism,' The Cold War, and Their Aftermath," pp. 125–27.) See as well "Subversion Then and Now," in Anastaplo, "Freedom of Speech and the First Amendment: Explorations," *Texas Tech Law Review* 21 (1990), pp. 1941, 2041f. See for comments on (including tributes to) Allan Bloom, Anastaplo, "'McCarthyism,' the Cold War, and Their Aftermath," pp. 156–63, 165–66, 169–70.

8. George Anastaplo, "'Racism,' Political Correctness, and Constitutional Law: A Law School Case Study," 42 *South Dakota Law Review* 108–64 (1997). See Anastaplo, *Campus Hate-Speech Codes, Natural Right, and Twentieth Century Atrocities* (Lewiston, N.Y.: Edwin Mellen Press, 1999). Twenty-five years ago, Anastaplo was the first, and perhaps remains the only, political scientist to publish a systematic argument for the abolition of broadcast television. Although he recognized his proposal had no chance of adoption, he entitled it "Self-Government And The Mass Media: A Practical Man's Guide." See *The Mass Media and Modern Democracy*, ed. Harry M. Clor (Chicago: Rand McNally Co. 1974) (reprinted without notes in Anastaplo, *The American Moralist*, pp. 245–316).

9. Anastaplo's four semester-long courses at the University of Dallas were on Plato, Aristotle, Machiavelli, and Hobbes. One former student of Anastaplo, commenting about his own law school experience, writes of Anastaplo's classes in jurisprudence and constitutional law at Loyola University of Chicago School of Law as the place "where [he] learned about law while earning a J.D. from the University of Chicago." See Robert L. Stone, "Commerce and Community in the Constitution of The United States," in *Law and Philosophy*, II, 771. See George Anastaplo, "Law & Politics," 25 *Political Science Reviewer* 127–50 (1996). See also Anastaplo, "The Bar Exam and a Proper Legal Education," *Chicago Daily Law Bulletin*, November 6, 1998, pp. 20–21; "Bar Examination Put Under Microscope." ibid., November 26, 1998, p. 5. Another perspective on Anastaplo was offered in "A Sketch," prepared by William Spielberger, a Chicago attorney (May 19, 1997):

> A number of years ago, while still a student at the Loyola University School of Law, I was walking with a classmate down North State Street on a cold, foggy morning. A block or so ahead of us we saw a man in a raincoat and stocking-cap waiting to cross the street at a red light. Because of the fog and the distance, we could not determine whether the man was old or young, rich or poor. Then we saw him retrieve a copy of the Chicago Sun-Times from a waste-basket and read it during the couple of minutes before the light turned green. As we approached, my companion exclaimed, "Oh my gosh, it's Professor Anastaplo! Isn't it awful that he is acting like a bum!" I responded that from my point of view, he was acting in a manner which is not at all unusual for him. Even in the briefest or most unpleasant of situations, he manages to find something of interest and instructive to reflect upon. By doing so, he also manages to instruct his students in an interesting way.

Another former student, Professor Stephen Vanederslice of Louisana State University offered this observation:

> In Plato's *Hippias Major* Socrates considers *to kalon*—the fine, the beautiful, the noble. When Hippias imagines that "the fine" must always be something obviously magnificent, Socrates asks what would be more "fine" to use with a smooth, finely-fired (and fragile) pot full of hot soup, a stirring spoon of gold or one of figwood. Hippias must acknowledge that the unpretentious wooden spoon is better because it is somehow more suitable to the fragile pot of hot soup than is the more splendid golden one. "The fine" is thus the fitting, which is also in some way the best.
>   The reader of the *Hippias* naturally calls to mind further instances of *to kalon*, such as actions which can also be fine or noble if they are exactly what is fitting for a particular situation. Thus we might consider a famous action of Socrates to be noble or fine. He refused to follow the orders of the murderous Thirty Tyrants to go arrest a just man, Leon, and bring him from Salamis to be executed. As the wooden spoon

was fitting for the fragile pot of hot soup, so was Socrates' principled resistance a fitting response to the Thirty.

Even as the example of the figwood spoon and the pot retains its simple charm, the example of Socrates' response to the Thirty remains humanly compelling to this day. Indeed, a good human example may be forever, not of course in that it goes unforgotten, but inasmuch as it does stand for all time. Whoever does hear of it, soon or late, recognizes it, is drawn to it, and is affected by it as an instance of the noble, the fine, and the beautiful.

Just yesterday, shortly after a panel of the American Association of Law Schools meeting in New Orleans, I had occasion to introduce one of the panelists, a quite distinguished law professor from the Yale Law School, to my old teacher, George Anastaplo. As soon as the Yale panelist heard Anastaplo's name, he said, "Oh. I'm honored to meet you. You are one of my heroes." I was bold enough to ask the Yale man, "Why is that? Why is he one of your heroes?" He answered, "Because he is a man of consistent principle, and someone who has been willing to take positions which have cost him some 'inconvenience.'"

The "inconvenience," of course, has been the denial to Anastaplo by the Illinois Supreme Court of career in the practice of law. Anastaplo had ranked first in his law class at the University of Chicago, but in a fateful decision (in 1950), he resisted, on principle, the Committee on Fitness's muscular questions implying that there is no right to revolution under the American regime, a right (and a duty) explicitly permitted and in extreme cases commanded by the plain language of the Declaration of Independence. At bottom, one should note, this right of revolution acknowledges the human being's capacity for reason, the citizen's ability to reflect, deliberate, and choose according to principle and prudence the regime most likely to lead to his well-being and happiness, and hence the good.

Anastaplo's position in defense of the right of revolution was not very popular in the 1950's, and it is not necessary, in fact, for the good citizen to go around looking for ways to be provocative. When it became clear, however, what Anastaplo was being required to assent to, he could not but take his position in defense of the principles of the Declaration. He did not think it right to abandon sound principles because of the national passions of the moment. His position was rejected when he took his case to the Supreme Court, but his position has since been generally vindicated.

It was Anastaplo's adherence to "consistent principle" in his defense of the Declaration, in the face of "inconvenience"—and then his brilliant, exemplary subsequent life—which impressed itself so on the very successful Yale law professor. This made George Anastaplo a "hero," and this, in turn, made it an "honor" to meet him.

Even after years, it seems, a good example, a human action which is fine, is like a gem: brilliant, diamond-like—in a way, perhaps, indestructible—standing forever. A good human action stands as an enduring reminder of what human beings are capable of; makes us true believers; helps us keep faith in the high possibility when much seems to fail us, to suffer compromise and adulteration. It is gratifying to catch the glint of such consistent principle in action or, as it was for the Yale man, to meet the "heroic," to meet a man in whom a particle of the divine truly resides, which particle, and the fine, noble, and beautiful action it inspires, gives off a glint which endures, I think, forever.

Another former student, also a professor, could notice that Anastaplo, who earned his B.A. in the College of the University of Chicago, graduated first in his class at the University of Chicago Law School, and earned a Ph.D. from the University of Chicago, has, despite his prodigious published scholarship and his sterling reputation as a classroom teacher (including forty years teaching in the Basic Program of Liberal Education for Adults at the University of Chicago), never been offered a regular faculty position at the University. See "The Scholarship of George Anastaplo—A Symposium," pp. 16–17. This silliness by the University of Chicago was carried beyond the absurd when "no one could be found" to teach the Human Being and Citizen course at the University of Chicago in 1983. See Robert L. Stone, "Reader suggests a HBC teacher," *Chicago Maroon*, April 15, 1983, p.7. The University of Chicago's shunning of one of its distinguished sons has been in effect for nearly fifty years, continuing one of the most ignoble responses in academia to McCarthyism. See Anastaplo, " 'McCarthyism,' the Cold War, and Their Aftermath," pp. 115–27. But the University of Chicago's loss has been the gain of the Loyola University of Chicago School of Law. See Anastaplo, "Law & Politics," pp. 129, 141, n. 7. Instrumental in Anastaplo's Loyola appointment were Professor William T. Braithwaite and Dean Charles W. Murdock, of the Loyola School of Law. Also useful were letters in support of that appointment by Professors Gerald Gunther, Stanley N. Katz, Charles E. Rice, and A. J. Thomas Jr. and by Judge Abner J. Mikva. (Copies of the letters supplied to the Loyola School of Law Faculty are in possession of the author.) See also Anastaplo, "What a Difference a Dean Makes," *National Law Journal,* September 12, 1983, p. 12.

10. Anastaplo's mathematical ability is apparent to readers of pages 806–8 in *The Constitutionalist*. See Anastaplo, review of Joe Sachs's translation of Aristotle's Physics, *Interpretation*, Spring 1999. See also "Notes toward an 'Apologia pro vita sua,'" p. 339. An introduction to Anastaplo's ongoing relationship with the University of Chicago since his Bar Admission Case can be found in Anastaplo, "'McCarthyism,' the Cold War, and Their Aftermath," pp. 105–28. See as well Anastaplo, "What is still Wrong with George Anastaplo?" pp. 551–647; Anastaplo, "The University of Chicago," *Academic Questions*, Spring 1998, pp. 74–77.

11. See the discussion by Andrew Patner, Larry Arnhart, Laurence Berns, Christopher Colmo, Stephen Vanderslice and John A. Murley in the WBEZ Transcript, "George Anastaplo, Human Being and Citizen," in "The Scholarship of George Anastaplo—A Symposium," pp. 7–9, 16. Anastaplo's responses to potentially incapacitating afflictions have reflected his insistence that the body should be in the service of the soul, rather than the other way around. See also John Alvis, "Thinker as Thinker: A Remedy For Literary Criticism Today," ibid., p. 24.

12. See "Farewell Letter to the Illinois Supreme Court, 1961," reprinted in Anastaplo, *The Constitutionalist*, pp. 406–07. See also "A Letter to the President of the Chicago Council of Lawyers," Chicago, Illinois, October 18, 1995 (cited in note 7, above). See as well the text at note 76, below. For an eye-witness account of Anastaplo's Oral Argument before the Supreme Court, see Laurence Berns, "Letter Regarding the Oral Argument in 1960 Before the U. S. Supreme Court, 1961," in Anastaplo, *The Constitutionalist*, pp. 362–65. See also Laurence Berns's "Foreword," to *Law and Philosophy*, I, xiii–xvi.

13. Anastaplo, *The Constitutionalist*, p. xi. See, regarding Anastaplo's first regular academic appointment, "On Freedom: Explorations," pp. 699–700. See also Anastaplo, "What is Still Wrong With George Anastaplo?" pp. 552, 601–8, 645–47. During the Second World War, Anastaplo enlisted in the Army Air Corps at seventeen, obtained his wings and commission at nineteen, and flew thereafter as a navigator in the Pacific, Europe, North and Central

Africa, and the Middle East. After his sometimes harrowing experiences in the Air Corps, the frowns of the bar-admission authorities, as well as of educational institutions and colleagues, were unlikely to have any intimidating effect.

14. In this respect, the Platonic Plutarch can be said to be his model. Anastaplo often urges his readers not to read his notes until they have first read the text itself. His notes have been described as gothic, as a treasure trove, as a guide to liberal education, and, by Laurence Berns in his review of *The Constitutionalist*, as "a little university, a second University of Chicago. . . ." (*Dallas Morning News*, November 28, 1971, p. 6H (reprinted in Anastaplo, "Notes toward an 'Apologia pro vita sua,'" pp. 322–23). It has been noticed that Anastaplo has raised annotation to an art form. My own more modest notes, echoing his, are an attempt to blaze a trail for those whose introduction to Anastaplo will be this essay.

15. "The Scholarship of George Anastaplo—A Symposium," pp. 1–248. The diversity of Anastaplo's work may be seen in the organization by its editors of *Law and Philosophy*, the two-volume Festschrift in his honor. Additional biographical information occasioned by celebration of his fiftieth birthday can be found in "Summing Up: Body and Soul," in *The American Moralist*, pp. 582–91, and by celebrations of his sixty-fifth and seventieth birthdays, in "The Oklahoma Lectures: Lessons for the Student of Law," 20 *Oklahoma City University Law Review* 153–79 (1995). See also George Anastaplo, "Thursday Afternoons," in S. *Chandrasekhar: The Man Behind the Legend*, ed. Kameshwar C. Wali (London: Imperial College Press, 1997), pp. 122–29, and "On the Chandra Observatory," *Chicago Sun-Times*, January 29, 1999. See as well George Anastaplo, "Samplings," 27 *The Political Science Reviewer* 345–78 (1998). (See www. cygneis.com/anastaplo)

16. In addition to the books already cited, George Anastaplo is the author of *The Constitution of 1787: A Commentary* (Baltimore: Johns Hopkins University Press, 1989); *The Thinker as Artist: From Homer to Plato & Aristotle* (Athens: Ohio University Press, 1997); and *Abraham Lincoln: A Constitutional Biography* (Lanham, Md.: Rowman & Littlefield, 1999). *The Constitution of 1787* was first developed in a series of lectures celebrating the bicentennial of the United States Constitution in the College of Liberal Arts at the Rochester Institute of Technology during the 1985–86 academic year.

Anastaplo's series of book-length law-review "Explorations" include:

i. "Human Nature and the First Amendment," 40 *University of Pittsburgh Law Review* 661–778 (1979).

ii. "What is Still Wrong with George Anastaplo? A Sequel to 366 US. 82 (1961)," 35 *DePaul Law Review* 551–647 (1986).

iii. "The United States Constitution of 1787: A Commentary," 18 *Loyola University of Chicago Law Journal* 15–249 (1986).

iv. "Church and State: Explorations," 19 *Loyola University of Chicago Law Journal* 61–193 (1987).

v. "Slavery and the Constitution: Explorations," 19 *Texas Tech Law Review* 677–786 (1989).

vi. "Freedom of Speech and the First Amendment: Explorations," 21 *Texas Tech Law Review* 1941–2086 (1990).

vii. "The Constitution at Two Hundred: Explorations," 22 *Texas Tech Law Review* 967–1112 (1991).

viii. "On Trial: Explorations," 22 *Loyola University of Chicago Law Journal* 765–1118 (1991).

ix. "On Freedom: Explorations," 17 *Oklahoma City University Law Review* 465–726 (1992).

x. "The Amendments to the Constitution of the United States: A Commentary," 23 *Loyola University of Chicago Law Journal* 631–865 (1992).

xi. "Rome, Piety and Law: Explorations," 39 *Loyola of New Orleans Law Review* 1–149 (1993).

xii. "Lessons for the Student of Law: The Oklahoma Lectures," 20 *Oklahoma City University Law Review* 17–218 (1995).

xiii. "Law & Literature and the Bible: Explorations," 23 *Oklahoma City University Law Review* 515 (1999).

xiv. "Law & Literature and Shakespeare: Explorations" (in course of preparation).

Included in Anastaplo's series on non-Western thought are "An Introduction to Confucian Thought" (1984); "An Introduction to Hindu Thought: The Bhagavad Gita" (1985); "An Introduction to Mesopotamian Thought: The Gilgamesh Epic" (1986); "An Introduction to Islamic Thought: The Koran" (1989); "An Introduction to Buddhist Thought" (1992); "An Introduction to North American Indian Thought" (1993); "On the Use, Neglect, and Abuse of Veils: The Parliaments of the World's Religions, 1893, 1993" (1994); "An Introduction to 'Ancient' African Thought" (1995). All of these articles have been published in *The Great Ideas Today* and are to be collected in a volume by Rowman & Littlefield. See also his article, "On Beginnings," in *The Great Ideas Today*, which includes discussions of Hesiod's Theogony, of the Bible, and of Stephen Hawking's *A Brief History of Time*. Much more than is offered here can be found in "George Anastaplo: Autobiographical Bibliography," in *Law and Philosophy*, vol. II, pp. 1073–1145.

If one takes 1983 (with its "Notes toward an 'Apologia pro vita sua'") as the midpoint of Anastaplo's publications, one can look back to "Human Being and Citizen: A Beginning to the Study of Plato's Apology of Socrates," in *Ancients and Moderns: Essays in the Traditions of Political Philosophy in Honor of Leo Strauss*, ed. Joseph Cropsey (New York: Basic Books, 1964; reprinted in *Human Being and Citizen*) and to "The Declaration of Independence," 9 *St. Louis University Law Journal* 390 (1965) (to be reprinted in *Abraham Lincoln: A Constitutional Biography*), as critical beginnings. One can then look forward to the works anticipated in "Notes toward an 'Apologia pro vita sua,'" pp. 341–43, now mostly published, and see a perspective and a direction that are remarkably consistent. One may thus discern a program of publication thought through well in advance.

Had Thomas I. Emerson (of the Yale Law School) not recommended against its publication by the University of Chicago Press, it is likely that *The Constitutionalist* (1971) would have been published (albeit with far fewer notes) about the same time as Anastaplo's essays on the *Apology of Socrates* (1964) and "The Declaration of Independence" (1965). The direction of his thought would then have been apparent early in his publications.

17. Anastaplo, "Notes toward an 'Apologia pro vita sua,'" pp. 342, 341–43, 338. See also Anastaplo, "Don Quixote and the Constitution," in *The Supreme Court and American Constitutionalism*, eds. Bradford P. Wilson and Ken Masugi (Lanham, Md.: Rowman & Littlefield Publishers, Inc., 1998), p. 93. See as well Anastaplo, "American Constitutionalism and the Virtue of Prudence: Philadelphia, Paris, Washington, Gettysburg," in *Abraham Lincoln, The Gettysburg Address and American Constitutionalism*, ed. Leo Paul S. de Alvarez (Dallas: University of Dallas Press, 1976), pp. 78, 128–29. See as well Anastaplo, "Samplings," pp. 450–54. For a hint regarding the prominence of the number 17 in Anastaplo's work, as well as the benefit of "principles stated clearly and forthrightly," see Leo Paul S. de Alvarez, "An Introduction of George Anastaplo" (Constitution Day, September 17, 1995, The University of Dallas).

18. *Four Pillars of Constitutionalism: The Organic Laws of the United States,* Introduction by Richard H. Cox (Amherst, New York: Prometheus Books, 1998), pp. 69–70.

19. Anastaplo, *The Constitution* of 1787, p. 61. See Anastaplo, "How to Read the Constitution of the United States," 17 *Loyola University of Chicago Law Journal* 1 (1985).

20. Anastaplo, *The Constitutionalist,* p. 29.

21. Testimony to Crosskey's thoroughness is found in Anastaplo's 1971 observation: "Whenever I have tracked down an obscure publication on constitutional law or history in the University of Chicago Library, the most recent and often the only name on the card (many years before) has usually been Crosskey's." *The Constitutionalist,* p. 568. See also Anastaplo, "Mr. Crosskey, the American Constitution, and the Natures of Things," 15 *Loyola University of Chicago Law Journal* 245 n.143, 227 n.57 (1984); "Crosskey's Constitutional Blockbuster and the Limits of History," *Modern Age,* Spring 1983, pp. 365–70. See as well, Malcolm P. Sharp, "Crosskey, Anastaplo and Meiklejohn on the United States Constitution," 20 *University of Chicago Law School Record* 51 (1973).

Anastaplo acknowledges in his writings various educational influences: his Carterville (Illinois) Community High School teachers, Elbert Fulkerson, Fred Lingle, and Georgia Lingle; his University of Chicago College teachers, Henry Rago, Donald Meiklejohn, Henry Finch, John Hawthorne, and Richard Weaver; his University of Chicago Law School teachers, Edward H. Levi, Walter Blum, Bernard Meltzer, William Winslow Crosskey, Malcolm Sharp, Harry Kalven, and Wilbur Katz; his Committee on Social Thought teachers at the University of Chicago, David Grene, Yves Simon, Edward Shils, Friedrich A. von Hayek, Peter H. von Blanckenhagen, and Otto von Simson; and from the general community, Robert Maynard Hutchins, Hugo Black, Alexander Meiklejon, Jacob Klein, Mortimer Adler, and John Van Doren. See Anastaplo, "Samplings," pp. 349–62; Anastaplo, "'McCarthyism,' The Cold War, and Their Aftermath," pp. 167–71; "Lessons for the Student of Law: The Oklahoma Lectures," pp. 133–52. See also Anastaplo, "Malcolm P. Sharp and the Spirit '76," *Law Alumni Journal,* The University of Chicago Law School, Summer 1975, pp. 18–24; Anastaplo, "A Little Touch of Harry," 43 *University of Chicago Law Review* 43 (1975), p. 26. See as well note 6, above.

22. William W. Crosskey, *Politics and the Constitution in the History of the United States* (Chicago: University of Chicago Press, 1953). See Anastaplo, *The Constitution of 1787,* p. ix.

23. See Anastaplo, *The Constitution of 1787,* pp. xviii, 52–58, 311 n.37.

24. See Anastaplo, *The Amendments to the Constitution,* pp. 125–34.

25. See Herman Beltz, review of *The Amendments to the Constitution,* in 40 *American Journal of Legal History* 395–97 (1996).

26. Anastaplo, *The Amendments to the Constitution,* pp. 125–34. See also Anastaplo, "Constitutionalism and Prudence," p. 80.

27. Anastaplo, *The Constitution of 1787,* pp. 13–14, 51.

28. Ibid., pp. 32–33, 117.

29. Anastaplo, *The Amendments to the Constitution,* p. 227. See also Willmoore Kendall, "The Two Majorities," in *Willmoore Kendall Contra Mundum,* ed. Nellie D. Kendall (Lanham, Md.: University Press of America, 1994), pp. 202–27.

30. Anastaplo, *The Constitution of 1787,* pp. 122–23.

31. "The Pentagon Papers and the Abolition of Television," in Anastaplo, *The American Moralist,* pp. 245–274. See also Anastaplo, *The Constitution of 1787,* p. 39; *The Amendments to the Constitution,* p. 237.

32. Anastaplo, *The Amendments to the Constitution,* p. 214 (emphasis added).

33. See Anastaplo, *The American Moralist*, pp. xvii–xviii; *The Constitution of 1787*, pp. 79, 109–110, 32–33, 317–19. See as well his arguments for retention of most of the Electoral College system, pp. 100–105, 272–73, 314, n. 66; *The Amendments to the Constitution*, pp. 215–16, 445, 250–51. See also Anastaplo, "Did Anyone 'In Charge' Know What He Was Doing," in *A Weekend with the Great War*, ed. Steven Weingartner (Chicago: White Mane Publishing Co. 1997), pp. 3–18 (to be included in the expanded 1999 edition of *Campus Hate-Speech Codes, Natural Right, and Twentieth Century Atrocities*). See as well Anastaplo, "On Freedom: Explorations," pp. 604–30.

34. Anastaplo, *The Constitution of 1787*, pp. 143–44.

35. Ibid., pp. 134–35. See William T. Braithwaite, "The Common Law and the Judicial Power: An Introduction to Swift-Erie and the Problem of Transcendental versus Positive Law," in *Law and Philosophy*, II, 774–818.

36. See Braithwaite, "The Common Law and the Judicial Power," pp. 786–88, 774, 814 n.4.

37. Ibid., p. 804.

38. See Anastaplo, *The Constitution of 1787*, pp. 128–33.

39. Ibid., pp. 132, 138. An article by Anastaplo on what the Erie doctrine can teach us about the nature of law is to be published in the *Brandeis Law Journal* in 1999.

40. Anastaplo, *The Constitution of 1787*, pp. 129–32, 136–38, 319–20. This is a Thrasymachean view of things.

41. Anastaplo, *The Amendments to the Constitution*, p. 170; *The Constitution of 1787*, p. 69. See also Anastaplo, "The Supreme Court Is Indeed a Court," in *Is the Supreme Court the Guardian of the Constitution?* ed. Robert A. Licht (Washington, D.C.: The AEI Press, 1993), pp. 22–33.

42. A critical concern of this essay is with George Anastaplo's study of the Constitution of the United States. His studies in religion and the Bible, philosophy, literature, and non-Western texts can illuminate for us his work on the Constitution. Though it is impossible to sum up his scholarship in a note, perhaps a tentative step may be taken by noticing the reliance in Anastaplo's non-constitutional work upon the idea of nature, upon prudence and natural right, and upon their bearing on legal, moral and political judgments. From his earliest major essay, "Human Being and Citizen: A Beginning to the Study of Plato's Apology of Socrates," through his series of introductory essays on non-Western traditions of thought, he has looked again and again to the ancient and modern teachers of the Founders and thereafter of the citizens of the American regime. The idea of nature as reflecting an established and ascertainable order to the universe seems to have first come to light in Greek thought. The understanding of the good and the bad, the just and the unjust in modern as well as in ancient natural-right thinking, is enhanced by the discovery of nature. What is best for any people is determined in part by circumstance and by their character and limitations. The prudent statesman is guided both by an awareness of nature and by an awareness of the conditions in which he must work. But, as Anastaplo has reminded us, "It is one thing to figure out what natural right calls for in any situation. It is, unfortunately, quite another thing to be able to share one's conclusions effectively with one's less thoughtful or more passionate fellows." Anastaplo, "On Trial," p. 1033. See also Arnhart, "George Anastaplo on Non-Western Thought," in "The Scholarship of George Anastaplo—A Symposium," pp. 215–20. Throughout his non-constitutional work Anastaplo has shown that the Bible, literature, and other manifestations of the divine can be helpful in recognizing the natural and moral principles that the Constitution depends upon: "for even the snow on the boughs can evoke the image of cherries in bloom." Anastaplo, "Samplings," p. 369.

43. Anastaplo, *The Amendments to the Constitution*, pp. 51, 65, 310. See Crosskey, *Politics and the Constitution*, pp. 363–78.

44. Throughout his works on the Constitution, Anastaplo addresses the issues and implications related to the existence, the defense, and the abolition of slavery, with special attention paid to the Declaration of Independence, to the attractions and pitfalls of equality, and to Abraham Lincoln. See Anastaplo, "The Declaration of Independence," p. 390. See also Murley, "Our Character is Our Fate," pp. 61–63. See, for Anastaplo's single most extensive published treatment of slavery thus far, "Slavery and the Constitution: Explorations," pp. 677–786. Worthy of extended discussion by itself is his study of the Emancipation Proclamation of 1862–1863. This is chapter 11 in *The Amendments to the Constitution*. (It is included in his *Abraham Lincoln* book.) His close reading of the Emancipation Proclamation has given us new insight into the Proclamation, reflecting the heights a truly superior President, acting as Commander-in-Chief, may attain. In a message, dated August 25, 1995, and titled "A Tribute to George Anastaplo," Harry V. Jaffa wrote:

With the publication of his Commentary on the Amendments Anastaplo has complemented and completed his Commentary on the Constitution of 1787. This is a major event in the history of the Constitution itself. George's commentaries, unlike any others, belong to a tradition very different from that of legal commentaries, as usually understood. They have more in common with Leo Strauss's *The Argument and the Action of Plato's "Laws"* than with any other contemporary work. As Strauss approached the Torah of reason with the reverence of the Torah of revelation, Anastaplo has brought a lifelong devotion to the American Constitution to his task.

Since it will be some time before I can have assimilated his magisterial work, I mention here only one of its features. The chapter on the Thirteenth Amendment is preceded by one on the Emancipation Proclamation. This is absolutely necessary, although George is perhaps the only one who would have recognized that fact. After nearly a half century of constant reading and re-reading of Lincoln, and about Lincoln, I can say categorically that this chapter is the finest scholarly writing on Lincoln's words that I know. My feeling is that George must have sat at Lincoln's elbow as he composed the Proclamation of September 22, 1862, and discussed it with him, paragraph by paragraph. As proof of the possibility that one can understand a great writer as he understood himself, it is the definitive refutation of historicism.

This generous tribute to Anastaplo was prepared by Jaffa for a panel, "The Scholarship of George Anastaplo," sponsored by The Claremont Institute for the Study of Statesmanship and Political Philosophy, at the Annual Meeting of the American Political Science Association, Chicago, Illinois, August 31, 1995. Thereafter it was included in "George Anastaplo, Human Being and Citizen," for "The Scholarship of George Anastaplo—A Symposium," pp. 12–13.

This is the most recent public installment of a forty-year dialogue between Jaffa and Anastaplo. Nearly two decades ago, Anastaplo described Harry Jaffa as "the most instructive political scientist writing in this country today." See Anastaplo, *The Artist as Thinker*, pp. 476–81. See also Anastaplo, *Human Being and Citizen*, pp. 61–73; "American Constitutionalism and the Virtue of Prudence," p.165; "On the Historic Significance of Abraham Lincoln's 'House Divided' Speech: For Harry V. Jaffa, Seventy-five and Still Counting," prepared for The Lincoln-Douglas Debates Symposium (Ottawa, Illinois, August

28, 1993) (published in Anastaplo, *Abraham Lincoln: A Constitutional Biography*). See as well the exchanges in Harry V. Jaffa, *Original Intent and the Framers of the Constitution: A Disputed Question* (Washington, D.C.: Regnery Gateway, 1994) (with Bruce Ledewitz, Robert L. Stone, and George Anastaplo). Both Anastaplo and Jaffa published "A Conversation with Harry V. Jaffa at Rosary College" (River Forest Illinois, December 4, 1980). See Harry V. Jaffa, *American Conservatism and the American Founding* (Durham, N.C.: Carolina Academic Press, 1984), pp. 48–75; Anastaplo, *The Artist as Thinker*, pp. 476–81. A thoughtful introduction to the relationship between the work of George Anastaplo and that of Harry V. Jaffa is found in Laurence Berns's essay, "Aristotle and the Moderns: On Freedom and Equality," in *The Crisis of Liberal Democracy: A Straussian Perspective*, eds. Kenneth L. Deutsch and Walter Soffer (Albany, N.Y.: State University of New York Press, 1987), pp. 148–66. See as well, Anastaplo, "Don Quixote and the Constitution," p. 94, n. 3.

45. Anastaplo, *The Constitution of 1787*, p. 64.

46. See ibid., pp. 54–57, and at p. 280 the chart of the powers of Congress found in Article I, section 8. See also Crosskey, *Politics and the Constitution*, pp. 409–508. See as well Anastaplo, *The Constitution of 1787*, pp. 128–33, for his discussion of the "burdens on interstate commerce" doctrine.

47. See Anastaplo, *The Constitution of 1787*, pp. 56–66.

48. Anastaplo, "Mr. Crosskey, the American Constitution, and the Natures of Things," pp. 197, 232 n. 87. See also Anastaplo, *The Constitution of 1787*, p. 57.

49. See Anastaplo, *The Amendments to the Constitution*, p. 235; *The Constitution of 1787*, p. 57.

50. See ibid. See also Anastaplo, "'Racism,' Political Correctness, and Constitutional Law: A Law School Case Study," pp. 108–64.

51. Anastaplo, "Samplings," p. 374.

52. See Anastaplo, *The Constitution of 1787*, pp. 11, 24, 60–67, 228; *The Amendments to the Constitution*, pp. 34–41, 102–106, 168, 187, 229–36, 389–93. See also Anastaplo, "The Making of the Bill of Rights, 1791," in *The Great Ideas Today*, pp. 318–75. See as well Anastaplo, "To Amend Means to Improve," *Congressional Record*, vol. 141, March 3, 1995 (inserted in the Record by his law school classmate, Congresswoman Patsy T. Mink). (During Anastaplo's decade-long encounter with the Greek Colonels, a number of his articles about Greece were inserted in the *Congressional Record* by another of his law school classmates, Congressman Abner J. Mikva.)

53. Anastaplo, *The Constitutionalist*, pp. 14–15. See Anastaplo, "Freedom of Speech and the First Amendment: Explorations," pp. 1941–2086. See also Anastaplo, "Censorship," in *Encyclopaedia Britannica* (15th ed.). For extended discussions of "church and state issues," see Anastaplo, "The Religion Clauses of the First Amendment," 11 *Memphis State University Law Review* 151 (1981); "Church and State: Explorations," pp. 61–194. See as well Stephen Vanderslice, "George Anastaplo on Religion," 26 *Political Science Reviewer* 114–54 (1997); note 16 (item xiii) above.

54. See Anastaplo, *The Constitutionalist*, pp. 159, 644; *The Constitution of 1787*, pp. 21–24, 52, 310; *The Amendments to the Constitution*, pp. 92–102.

55. See Crosskey, *Politics and the Constitution*, pp. 557–58; Anastaplo, "Mr. Crosskey, the American Constitution, and the Natures of Things," pp. 208–09, 252–53. See also Anastaplo, "Teaching, Nature, and the Moral Virtues," in *The Great Ideas Today*, pp. 2–45. See as well Anastaplo, "Natural Law or Natural Right?" 38 *Loyola of New Orleans Law Review* 915 (1993).

56. A listing of George Anastaplo's writings on Leo Strauss can be found in note 1 in Anastaplo's contribution to this volume.

57. Anastaplo, *The Constitution of 1787*, p. xvii. See also Anastaplo, "Constitutionalism and Prudence," pp. 93, 106.

58. *Willmoore Kendall Contra Mundum*, pp. 399–402. In this context it is worthy of note that Anastaplo's constitutionalism depends less on the "intentions of *The Federalist*" or on "the intentions of the Framers"—that is, less on what this or that Framer said here or there— than on what they did: the Declaration of Independence and the Constitution. It can also be said that Anastaplo looks less to the Framers and more to the teachers of the Framers. See Anastaplo, "The Founders of Our Founders: Jerusalem, Athens, and the American Constitution," in Jaffa, *Original Intent and The Framers of The Constitution*, pp. 181–97, Anastaplo, "Lessons of ancients still applicable today," *Chicago Sun-Times*, January 15, 1999, p. 38. See also Anastaplo, "The Constitution at Two Hundred," pp. 1036–42, 1053–62; Murley, "Our Character is Our Fate," pp. 58–60, 81. See as well Anastaplo, "Lessons for the Student of Law," pp. 44–45.

59. Anastaplo, "The Declaration of Independence," p. 390.

60. See Anastaplo, *The Constitution of 1787*, pp. 164, 31, 38; *The Amendments to the Constitution*, pp. 32, 20, 236–37.

61. Anastaplo, *The Constitutionalist*, p. 285. "We must not be afraid to be free" is the concluding sentence of Justice Hugo L. Black's dissenting opinion in *In re Anastaplo*, 366 U. S. 82, 116 (1961). Justice Black prefaced his conclusion by observing, "Too many men are being driven to become government fearing . . . because government is being permitted to strike out at those who are fearless enough to think as they please and say what they think." Justice Black asked that this portion of his opinion be read from at his funeral service in 1971. See Memorial Addresses and Other Tributes . . . Hugo LaFayette Black, 92d Cong., 1st Sess., House Document No. 92–236 (Government Printing Office, 1972), pp. 64–65; Roger K. Newman, *Hugo Black: A Biography* (New York: Pantheon Books, 1994), pp. 502–7, 699. See also Anastaplo, "Mr. Justice Black, His Generous Common Sense, and the Bar Admission Cases," 9 *Southwestern University Law Review* 977 (1977). Justice William Brennan is reported to have said that Justice Black's dissenting opinion "immortalized George Anastaplo." See Newman, *Hugo Black: A Biography*, p. 507. See also George Anastaplo, "Justice Brennan, Due Process, and the Freedom of Speech: A Celebration of *Speiser v. Randall*," *John Marshall Law Review* 20 (1986), p. 7. Justice Black's "We must not be afraid to be free" statement was featured in an exhibit of American and Russian "dissidents" (including a portrait of George Anastaplo), which toured the Soviet Union before the dissolution of the communist regime. (This exhibit was organized by Harrison Sheppard, a San Francisco lawyer.) Anastaplo is preparing for publication his decade-long correspondence with Justice Black. See 405 U.S. xxvii–xxviii (1972). See as well, note 76, below.

62. Anastaplo, "The Constitution at Two Hundred: Explorations," 22 *Texas Tech Law Review* 1097, 1109.

63. "A salutary patriotism occasionally obliges us, at the risk of seeming naive, to overlook the limitations and problems of the American Republic while we sing its praises." Anastaplo, *The Constitutionalist*, p. 283. Patriotism is also exhibited in the dedication to *The American Moralist*:

To
THE SACRED MEMORY
of
SEVEN VERY YOUNG MEN
we grew up with in Carterville, Illinois
and who went off to war with us a half-century ago
but
WHO NEVER RETURNED

64. Leo Strauss, "Liberal Education and Responsibility," in *Liberalism Ancient and Modern* (New York: Basic Books, 1968), p. 24.

65. See Anastaplo, *The Amendments to the Constitution*, p. 145.

66. *The Constitutionalist*, p. 420. See Anastaplo, *The Amendments to the Constitution*, pp. 101, 107, 123. See also Anastaplo, "Constitutionalism and Prudence," p. 125; "A Beginning to the Study of Plato's Apology of Socrates," p. 12; "On Freedom: Explorations," p. 465.

67. See Anastaplo, "On Freedom: Explorations," pp. 666–85.

68. Anastaplo, *The Amendments to the Constitution*, p. 124. See, on the significance of the declining importance of Plato and Aristotle for American constitutionalism, "Education in the New Republic," ibid., pp. 107–24. Harry V. Jaffa has many times said that Anastaplo was the first to notice that the Declaration of Independence refers to God as legislator, then as judge, and then as executor of the law. See Anastaplo, "The Declaration of Independence," pp. 404–5; *The Constitution of 1787*, p. 21.

69. Anastaplo, *The Constitutionalist*, pp. 284–85.

70. See George Anastaplo, review of Harry V. Jaffa, "Equality & Liberty," in *Human Being and Citizen*, pp. 61–73. For further discussion of this position see Anastaplo's 1997 and 1998 *South Dakota Law Review* collections, "'Racism,' Political Correctness, and Constitutional Law: A Law School Case Study," and "'McCarthyism,' The Cold War, and Their Aftermath." (These two collections are being prepared by Anastaplo for publication in one volume, *What Can a Man Do? On "McCarthyism," "Racism," and "Political Correctness."*) Liberty and Equality are examined in Anastaplo, *Liberty, Equality & Modern Constitutionalism: A Sourcebook* (to be published in 1999, in two volumes, by the Focus Publishing Company).

71. See Laurence Berns, "Aristotle and the Moderns on Freedom and Equality," p. 153.

72. Leo Strauss, *Natural Right and History* (Chicago: University of Chicago Press, 1953), p. 1.

73. Anastaplo, *The Constitutionalist*, pp. 144–65. See also Anastaplo, "We the People, The Rulers and the Ruled," *The Great Ideas Today*, p. 64.

74. Anastaplo, *The Constitution of 1787*, pp. 8–9.

75. Strauss, *Natural Right and History*, p. 323.

76. Anastaplo, *The Constitutionalist*, pp. 381–82, 399–400. See, on the end implicit in the notion of a beginning, Anastaplo, "On Beginnings," p.140. See also Irving Dilliard, ed., *One Man's Stand For Freedom: Mr. Justice Black and the Bill of Rights* (New York: Alfred A. Knopf, 1963), pp. 413–15. See as well note 61, above.

· *12* ·

Walter Berns: The Constitution and American Liberal Democracy[1]

Gary D. Glenn

WHAT DOES BERNS' STUDY OF THE CONSTITUTION HAVE TO DO WITH LEO STRAUSS?

To my knowledge, Berns never explicitly discusses why he studied American political thought or constitutional law, rather than following Strauss in studying history of political philosophy. His books seldom cite or mention Strauss.[2] Only one of them even contains, among the usual acknowledgments of intellectual debt, an expression of gratitude which follows in its entirety. "To . . . the late Leo Strauss, I owe more than I am willing to express here."[3] "Willing" suggests he was able but chose not to. Why?

Berns may once have explained this silence about Strauss in the context of commenting on its absence in another of Strauss' prominent students. "Other Strauss students are extremely reticent about invoking his [Strauss'] name, and for a very good reason. Strauss did not found a cult or a movement, and one does him honor by *not* speaking of him too much, lest the pupil's failings appear to be those of the teacher."[4] Berns describes this reticence as "moderation."

In this same place, Berns understands "moderation" as requiring a particularly sharp disjunction between political philosophizing and ruling. Socrates, he says, "lived quietly with his fellow Athenians while hardly letting them know he philosophized, and he certainly never tried to be their king. He was concerned with preserving philosophy, not aggrandizing." To restore and preserve Socratic philosophizing was arguably Strauss' main goal. If Berns shared that goal, he chose another way of pursuing it, namely as a scholar and defender of the Constitution.

Berns' emphasis on moderation may be a clue to Strauss' influence on both his vocation of constitutional study and his manner of pursuing it. For Strauss taught "[T]hat wisdom requires unhesitating loyalty to a decent constitution and even to the cause of constitutionalism" is a contemporary inference from "the old saying that wisdom cannot be separated from moderation."[5]

It may shock contemporaries to describe Berns as moderate since moderation is today commonly understood to so depreciate spiritedness that one does not take a decided part. But both Berns' constitutional scholarship and his regular forays into political controversy, are characteristically spirited, decided, and combative. He hits hard and he takes sides. Moreover, moderation today sometimes means to stand in an unprincipled middle between principled extremes. But he is not moderate in that way either. No one would say Berns lacks principles.

In *what* way then is Berns' constitutional understanding moderate? It is almost certainly not in relation to the poles or extremes of contemporary politics, i.e. liberalism and conservatism, for Berns' moderation usually puts him in the company of conservatives. However both early and late in his career he has dissociated his thought from conservatism. Moreover, what he does among conservatives is try to orient them to the Constitution which suggests that what he defends is not primarily conservatism but the Constitution.

In *Freedom* (1957) he had explicitly dissociated himself from both "libertarian ideas" and "the so-called conservative movement" which embodied those ideas. "The [then] contemporary political theory of conservatism may be characterized by the fact that it concludes its inquiry at the point where, historically, political philosophy began."[6] But even in 1957, conservatism had non-libertarian Burkean ideas. Berns also rejected this conservatism.

> What the traditionalists have done, and what Burke did before them, is to confuse the separate (but related) realms of theory and practice . . . it is . . . an error for the traditionalists to suggest that theory follow practice, or that our history provides all the political guidance our practice needs. In the place of the criteria for the judgment of political right and wrong provided by political philosophy, these writers have substituted the criteria provided by ancestors, or in the case of the sophisticated, provided by History.

That the conservatism of 1957 "accepts and defends the institutions and values of the contemporary West" (quoting Clinton Rossiter) "can only be the result of chance . . . the conservative by definition, wants to preserve traditional principles, i.e. our principles" because they are ours not because they are good or true.[7] This may be what he meant by conservatism stopping where political philosophy begins.[8] At any rate, again in 1997 he publicly broke with the conservatives at *First Things*.[9]

Presumably, a conservatism which defended traditional principles only insofar as they could be defended as good or true on the basis of political philosophy would be the only conservatism with which Berns' moderation would be fully at home today. Perhaps the neoconservatism of the American Enterprise Institute with which he is associated is such. But he has never retracted his emphatic 1957 rejection of "the conservative movement." Nor, in principle, does there seem to be any reason why he could not be in the liberal camp today if there were a liberalism free of the "ideologist error . . . that practice conform to theory," i.e., which was open to moderation as Berns following Strauss understands it.[10] Perhaps at least some sectors of today's conservatism, defective as conservatism as such may be, are open to that moderation in a way today's liberalism is not.

Strauss himself studied the history of political philosophy, not the Constitution, and most Constitutional scholars pay little attention to the history of political philosophy. However, Strauss gave reasons, explicitly learned from the history of political philosophy, why loyalty to a decent constitution is important. Those reasons presumably illuminate Berns' constitutional understanding.

Strauss understood moderation in relation to "the twin dangers of visionary expectations from politics and unmanly contempt for politics."[11] If Berns' moderation is Straussian moderation, it tries to take its fundamental bearings from (as distinguished from making its tactical alliances with) alternatives which are permanent because they belong to the human situation as such, or at least to the regime, not from current (i.e., "running and heedless") political extremes or alternatives (i.e., passing fashions or fads). To take one's bearings from changing political configurations which history somehow throws up from time to time (such as contemporary liberalism and conservatism) would be a species of what Strauss called "historicism," the form in which philosophic nihilism which breeds political extremism, presents itself in our time. To speak to contemporary matters, in light of permanent (natural) or more permanent (regime) understandings, is perhaps necessary and even socially responsible. To take one's fundamental bearings from contemporary matters is not. Strauss regarded such historicism as the greatest alternative, and threat, to political philosophy at least in our time and perhaps in principle.[12]

BERNS' LIBERAL CONSTITUTION

Berns' constitutional scholarship typically aims to moderate the visionary liberalism which has dominated the Supreme Court, and hence constitutional law, during most of his lifetime. For example, the essays collected in *Defense* (1984) defend the Constitution against that liberalism's desire to circumvent or abuse it in order to achieve its ideas of the good, and to which the Constitution is opposed: world government, pacifism, pornography and obscenity, sexual and racial equality of conditions not merely equality of natural and constitutional rights, direct popular election of the President because of contempt for the moderating effects of constitutional federalism, and legal recognition of the priority of religiously grounded claims over positive law.[13] In the academic world whose horizons extend from liberal to left, these positions appear conservative. However, his break with *First Things* (below pp. 199-200) shows that he attempts to moderate conservatives as well.

Strauss taught that moderation "requires unhesitating loyalty to a decent constitution and even to the cause of constitutionalism."[14] Such loyalty fairly characterizes Berns' scholarship but needs to be carefully understood for he unflinchingly acknowledges the Constitution's complicity regarding slavery.[15] His loyalty is man-ifested respecting this matter, which most casts doubt on the Constitution's decency, partly by arguing that this complicity was unavoidable and partly by stressing that the Constitution opened previously closed doors to slavery's disapprobation and eventual extinction. Thus, he shows that almost no one at the Constitutional Convention defended slavery as good or just; that the odiousness of the word "slav-ery" prevented its use in the Constitution so that not one word of the Constitution needed to be changed when it became practicable to do away with slavery; that the Constitution (in contrast to the *Articles*) provided Congress power to ultimately extinguish slavery; and that the post-Convention rise and triumph of the Southern reading of the Constitution, especially the commerce clause and the "migration or importation" clause of Article I, Section 9, constituted a rejection of "the originally intended meaning."[16] Thus the original Constitution, while compromising with indecency as a lesser evil than having no union, achieved such decency as was pos-sible in the circumstances and laid the groundwork for thitherto impossible polit-ical progress on this matter. It was not the original Constitution but rather "men of the stature of Jefferson and Madison . . . [who subsequently] joined in a more or less deliberate campaign to distort the original meaning of the Constitution . . . on behalf of slavery." To say nothing of Chief Justice Roger Taney.[17] Thus does he defend the Constitution against the charge that it is racist but still acknowledges its fateful compromise with racism.

The Constitution to which Berns is loyal "is—clearly and overwhelmingly—liberal" (i.e., the liberalism of modern political philosophers)[18] and its decency is that of the *Declaration of Independence*.[19] Hence its decency is liberal decency under-stood as limited to securing natural rights and emphatically not concerned with citizen virtue beyond obeying the laws which secure those rights.[20] In denying gov-ernment its traditional right to more fully form citizen virtue "the Framers of the Constitution deprived Americans of much if not all, of a traditional conservative agenda." Hence, "[t]he only appropriate agenda for today conservatives is to defend the liberal constitution—if necessary, to defend it from the liberals."[21]

Berns' loyalty to the Constitution has led him to defend the liberalism it embodies against today's liberals who are less interested in following the liberal Constitution than in having the judiciary "give it meaning" in order to use its authority to mandate policies which are either not mandated, or contrary to, it.[22] But Berns is distinguished from others who take seriously the Constitution's orig-inal meaning, especially conservatives like Robert Bork, in that he understands it in light of the history of political philosophy. That orientation he took from Strauss though it is not clear that the relation of the Constitution to the history of politi-cal philosophy, as Berns understands it, is necessarily Strauss'.[23]

Berns' understanding of the Constitution's liberalism is decisively informed by what he learned from Strauss about what modern political philosophers tried to do to, with and about revealed religion. Strauss' argues the moderns sought to undermine revealed religion's credibility by denying the possibility of miracles, by

Biblical criticism and by denying that God had revealed himself to man.[24] "[T]he modern tradition was originated by Machiavelli and perfected by such men as Hobbes and Adam Smith. It came into being through a conscious break with the strict moral demands made by both the Bible and classical philosophy."[25] Berns continues, in the direction pointed by Strauss, that the primary liberal means to effectuate this break is commerce which "was intended by Locke, Smith, and some others, to be—a substitute for religion or, more precisely, a substitute for Hobbes's substitute for revealed religion" by shifting people's attention from salvation in the next world to prosperity in this. The Constitution's fostering of "arts, manufactures and commerce . . . might have been written by Adam Smith."[26]

The Constitution's liberal substitute of commerce for religion, and its subordination of religion, is a theme Berns returns to again and again in succeeding books.[27] It is perhaps the most important consequence of his understanding the Constitution in light of the history of political philosophy. Hobbes' leviathan was the original modern substitute for "ineffectual" and "old fashioned morality." Modern liberal commerce is not only a more politically effective moral teaching than the "useless" preaching of old fashioned religious morality; but preaching religion is dangerous to political peace and freedom "[f]or every Good Samaritan produced by preaching there was a score of religious zealots . . . eager to do unto others what they understood God wanted done unto them, but disagreeing as to what God wanted done."[28] Modernity and thus the Constitution establish liberal separation of church and state.[29]

Berns goes beyond anything Strauss says (or as far as I can see means) in saying that the Constitution embodies modernity's anti-religious intention. Berns' vigorous explication of modern philosophers' separation of church and state and commercial way of life, seems to defend and commend both. Both presuppose Hobbes' doctrine of the state of nature. Strauss however says "Hobbes' doctrine of the state of nature . . . should be abandoned [because it] construct[s] human society by starting from the untrue assumption that man as man is thinkable as a being that lacks awareness of sacred restraints. . . ."[30] It seems that either Berns disagrees with Strauss, or the Constitution embodies an erroneous fundamental idea.

However, that may be, Berns grants that liberal modernity needs the self-restraint which religion can help provide. Evidently commerce is not enough. But liberal governments may not do much directly to foster such restraint.[31] Still, Berns stands against the mainstream[32] of constitutional scholars in finding that the Constitution permits state funding of religious institutions, especially schools, on a non-preferential basis.[33] Fundamentally, however, liberal governments teach at least "religious toleration" which "probably does depend on a way of life from which weakened belief follows as a consequence." That way of life is not "open and official declaration of unbelief" but rather commerce. Thus does the American Constitution follow Hamilton who follows Locke and Smith.[34]

This discussion makes clear another important difference between Berns' constitutional understanding and those originalisms less informed by the history of political philosophy. Berns grants that "the majority of the people who had anything to do with" the presence in the Constitution of the prohibition of religious tests and the first amendment religion clauses, these clauses meant only separation of church and the national state, not of church and state as such. "[T]he people and the politicians at the state level were not then disposed to join in some Lockean statement of unbelief, however disguised." But the commercial way of life "leads men, perhaps imperceptibly, away from those [religious] issues characteristic of life in a preconstitutional age." More than that, a political consequence of belief in Jesus' authority is "the impossibility of constitutional government as we know it."[35] Thus the original constitutional tension between liberalism and revealed religion would, and apparently should, gradually be resolved, via a commercial way of life, in favor of liberalism.

Berns does not quite say this is inevitable but his writing leans in that direction and seems to imply that it should be chosen. At least, I do not find him arguing that the original tension should be maintained. He argues for subordination not tension.[36] And, unlike Tocqueville whom he sometimes cites favorably concerning religion, Berns does not acknowledge the "duty of lawgivers . . . to raise up the souls of their fellow citizens and turn their attention toward heaven." However, he does cite Tocqueville that religion is "the most precious heritage of aristocratic times"[37] which leads him to criticize the Courts' extending the establishment clause from neutrality among religions to neutrality between religion and irreligion.[38] He makes a strong argument that the Constitution as originally meant permits liberal governments to foster religion in a non-discriminatory way and prefer religion over irreligion.[39] But he says the Constitution follows modern political philosophers who found religion mostly a political problem partly because "religious passions are the most difficult to harness." Tame religion, which accepts its subordinate status, is compatible with constitutional government. Serious religion is not.[40]

The difference, as it emerges here, between Berns' constitutional understanding and that of the originalists like Bork or Rehnquist is something like this. What "the majority" of the founders understood particular clauses to aim at is less these clauses' constitutional meaning than what the most philosophically insightful founders (primarily Jefferson and Madison) understood the Constitution as a whole to aim at. If there is a tension between these, one should not deny the majority's understanding but neither should one reasonably expect it to indefinitely prevail against the general constitutional tendency. The Constitution *is* more fundamentally what its general tendency is that what its authors meant by specific provisions.

Perhaps nothing is more unusual (almost unique) among contemporary constitutional scholars, than Berns' intransigent defense of law-abidingness. He appears to regard the danger of lawlessness as the most fundamental threat to our Constitution and to the political and social democracy to which it gives form. "The Constitution is above all a formal document."[41] But there is a dangerous tension between the liberal form and the democratic substance. Democratic people "do not readily understand the importance of forms." Yet democracies need forms more than other regimes because forms are "a barrier between the strong and the weak, the government and the governed."[42] The Constitution both gives form to the government and protects the governed from the government. "Constitutionalism . . . is government limited mainly by its forms."[43] And the form which citizens and government encounter on a daily basis is not separation of powers, judicial review, or executive veto but law itself. Hence, the absolute importance of law-abidingness which is the common ground for his constitutional objection to serious religion, to judicially created rights, and to the dominant jurisprudence in the most prestigious law schools. These teachings all justify or encourage lawlessness and thus tend to bring back the state of nature.[44]

His constitutional objection to serious religion is that it leads men to disobey positive law by legitimizing "appeal from the sovereign or the law to a body of religious doctrine or to 'conscience.'" But this appeal unjustly "claim[s] a moral superiority, in flat defiance of the proposition that all men are created equal." It claims "that . . . private judgment is superior to the public judgment, . . . [which is] the private judgment of a majority that, in a democracy, are transformed into law."[45] "[A]ccording to liberalism, one renders unto Caesar whatever Caesar demands and to God whatever Caesar permits."[46] But serious religion, by placing duties to God or conscience above law (exemplified for Berns by the Amish, the Catholic "peace Bishops," and conscientious objectors) creates the continuing danger of bringing back the state of nature.[47]

This objection that serious religion leads to lawlessness sufficiently explains his criticism of, and public break with, the *First Things* symposium in which mostly religious conservatives questioned whether it was time to begin withdrawing allegiance from the "American regime."[48] The grounds for this questioning was that "the judicial usurpation of democracy" had proceeded so far, and in such a direction, that decent people might have to begin to think about giving allegiance to moral law over the constitutionally illegitimate judicial oligarchy that has usurped government by the people.

Berns explicitly agrees that the courts "have indeed usurped power that the Constitution assigns to other agencies of the government, or to the states." That is, the Court has acted unconstitutionally and thus illegitimately. They have done so by disrespecting the most fundamental constitutional form, namely "constitutionality—which is to say, the distinction between what is politically desired and constitutionally permitted."[49]

But he does not go so far as to say this usurpation makes the regime of doubtful legitimacy.[50] Perhaps he regards "the regime" as something more fundamental and lasting than the contemporary judicial usurpation which the symposiasts call "the American regime"[51] and perhaps the regime in Berns' sense is endangered by the symposiasts' undermining of allegiance to what they call the regime. This is suggested by his rejection of the symposium's "angry and morally indignant discourse" as precisely the sort of "zealous opinions" which the Constitution "excluded or at least inhibited." By resorting to such indignation, Berns suggests, the symposium gives support to the view that a right to break the law has become preferable to the present judicial usurpation. Berns disagrees. He appears to believe the Constitution correct in presuming the danger of zeal, anger and moral indignation to be greater than the problem of judicial usurpation. Indeed, such usurpation is objectionable partly because it gives rise to the moral indignation of those like the symposiasts.[52] But it is better to assuage their constitutionally justified anger by persevering in the struggle to return the Court to its constitutionally legitimate place rather than risk returning our country to the state of nature. And the better way to that better end is to persevere in trying to convince the thoughtful, by reasoned argument, that the judges have acted unconstitutionally, instead of trying to convince the morally indignant to withdraw their allegiance from the political order.[53]

Berns managed to get along with the mostly seriously religious conservatives at *First Things* until he was past 70. Strauss once remarked that Socrates' ability to live peaceably with Athens until he was 70 showed a greater harmony between that regime and philosophy than would be suggested by Socrates' apparent favoring of Sparta. Something similar might be said of the relation of Berns' liberal constitutionalism and the religious conservatives.[54] In particular, it is not clear that Berns' objections to the political effects of serious religion involves an hostility to or disbelief in serious religion. Warning "the devout Jew, Christian or Moslem" that they cannot accept certain crucial aspects of liberal constitutionalism could as well emerge from a concern to alert such people to the danger to their souls from such constitutionalism.[55]

CONCLUSION

In general, Berns regards the Constitution as wholly modern. It is Hobbesian in commanding an absolute duty to obey the law, Lockean in securing natural rights through separation of powers and liberty of conscience, Hobbesian and Lockean in subordinating religion to the state, and Lockean and Smithian in promoting commerce as a way of life.

Still, he once acknowledges that "more than modern natural right and law went into the founding of the United States." While the founders' principles "forbade the use of the laws directly to generate virtuous habits . . . they understood the need to preserve such habits and they did not regard it as improper for the laws to support the private institutions (for example churches) in which they were generated . . ." Similarly, the founders would have agreed with Tocqueville that "the family may have no place in liberal theory, or the theory of modern natural rights [citing Locke], but it was indispensable to the perpetuation of the liberal state."[56] Hence, liberal governments are constitutionally able to support families for the same reason they are permitted to support Churches.

Berns thus appears sympathetic to liberal government's efforts to preserve both the family and such virtue as already exists in the people. To that end, he wrote an entire book trying to reopen the question of censorship's constitutionality.[57] Moreover, these "non modern natural right elements" are largely[58] holdovers from pre-modern morality. And, if regimes as classically understood either founder on such incoherencies or else their dominant tendency overcomes the residual antithetical remnants of the old order, then liberal governments' efforts to preserve the premodern elements—especially religion and the family—would appear in principle to be either futile or else to undermine the liberal Constitution. But, if so, why wouldn't someone loyal to that Constitution seek to preserve rather than resolve the tension between its modern and premodern elements?

Since Berns resolves them, his loyalty to the Constitution seems limited by his attachment to the truth about it. That is, he loudly defends the liberal Constitution against especially (but not only) liberals who oppose or are indifferent to parts of it. But he also quietly points to the deficiencies of the political philosophy it embodies, lest these unknowingly insinuate themselves into the souls of the attentive and thoughtful who might otherwise be simply loyal to it. This might be a contemporary way of living "quietly" among one's fellow citizens while hardly letting them know one philosophizes. Naked defense of the Constitution might be the best disguise for moderately teaching its fundamental and enduring defects.

NOTES

1. Originally presented on a panel "Leo Strauss and the Study of the American Regime" at the 1997 meeting of the American Political Science Association.

2. Berns has published five books on the Constitution and constitutional law. *Freedom, Virtue, and the First Amendment* (Regnery, 1957), hereafter cited as *Freedom*; *The First Amendment and the Future of American Democracy* (Chicago: Gateway, 1976, 1985), hereafter cited as *Future*; *In Defense of Liberal Democracy* (Chicago: Gateway, 1984), hereafter cited as *Defense*; and *Taking the Constitution Seriously* (Lanham, MD: Madison Books, 1987, 1992), hereafter cited as *Taking*. In addition *For Capital Punishment: Crime and the Morality of the Death Penalty* (Lanham, MD: University Press of America, 1991) partly takes its bearings from the Constitution. Berns himself would insist that the focus of his work is not constitutional law but the Constitution. His major work on political philosophy proper is the chapter on John Milton in Leo Strauss and Joseph Cropsey eds., *History of Political Philosophy*.

3. *Future* (1985), p. ix.

4. Walter Berns, "A Reply to Harry Jaffa," *National Review*, January 22, 1982, pp. 44, 45. 1959), p. 23. This reticence is so marked that at least once he quotes Strauss without attribution. "Or, in the words of someone else, the fact that it is difficult to decide which of two mountains whose peaks are hidden by clouds is higher than another, is no reason why we cannot decide that a mountain is higher than a molehill." *Freedom* (1965), p. 225. The Strauss quote is in "What is Political Philosophy?" in *What is Political Philosophy? And Other Studies* (Glencoe, IL: The Free Press, 1959), p. 23.

5. Leo Strauss, "Liberal Education and Responsibility" in *Liberalism Ancient and Modern* (New York: Basic Books, 1968), p. 24. Leo Strauss, "Restatement on Xenophon's *Hiero*" in *On Tyranny* (Glencoe, IL: The Free Press, 1963), p. 197.

6. *Freedom* (1957), p. ix.

7. *Freedom* (1957), pp. 17–18.

8. Cf. *Taking* (1987), pp. 240–41 where he objects to Burke (without identifying him) because many of the substantive institutions he had defended (primogeniture, entail, titles of nobility, a social class structure, and an established church) are prohibited by the Constitution.

9. See below pp. 199–200.

10. *Virtue*, p. 18.

11. "Liberal Education and Responsibility," p. 24.

12. Leo Strauss, *Natural Right and History* (Chicago: University of Chicago Press, 1953), Introduction, pp. 5, 18. Ch. 1. "What Is Political Philosophy," pp. 26–27.

13. *For Capital Punishment* (1991) is an extended elaboration of Chapter 9 of *Defense*.

14. "Liberal Education and Responsibility," p. 24.

15. "Complicity" is my word which I hope captures Berns' view. For his understanding of slavery and the Constitution see *Defense*, Part IV, pp. 199–298; *Taking*, pp. 40–63, 144–46, 238–39.

16. *Defense* (1984), pp. 223, 214.

17. Ibid., pp. 224–25. "At his worst, however, Jefferson was no match for Chief Justice Taney and his majority colleagues in the *Dred Scott* case." *Taking*, p. 46.

18. *Freedom* (1957), p. ix.

19. While this theme occurs throughout his writings, he describes *Taking* (1987) in particular as "an explanation of the Constitution by reference to the Declaration of Independence," p. 11. See especially his review of Garry Wills', *Inventing America*, ibid., pp. 242–51.

20. Ibid., pp. 11–12.

21. *Taking* (1992), p. 241.

22. See the discussion in *Taking* (1987) on judicial creation of rights, pp. 206–7, on anticipating ratification of the Equal Rights Amendment, pp. 229–31, and on the judicial revision of the Constitution generally and of capital punishment in particular, pp. 232–41.

23. Cf. Strauss' reasons why "liberal or constitutional democracy comes closer to what the classics demanded than any alternative that is viable in our age." Victor Gourevitch and Michael S. Roth eds., Leo Strauss, "Restatement on Xenophon's *Hiero*" in *On Tyranny* (New York: The Free Press, 1991), p. 194.

24. *Spinoza's Critique of Religion* (New York: Schocken, 1965), esp. Ch.1. *Thoughts on Machiavelli* (Seattle: University of Washington Press, 1958, 1969), Ch. IV. "The Mutual Influence of Theology and Philosophy," *Independent Journal of Philosophy* (1979), p. 115ff. (Originally published 1954 in Hebrew). *Taking* (1992), pp. 157–58 and note 13.

25. Strauss, "Restatement," p. 192

26. *Taking* (1992), pp. 180, 173, 170. I know of no place where Berns defends the liberal Constitution against the critique common to classical and Christian morality, namely, that a life of commerce fosters vice and that "[f]ighting one vice with another is the most dangerous strategy there is. You know what happens to kingdoms that use alien mercenaries." C. S. Lewis, *The Pilgrim's Regress* (Grand Rapids: Eerdmann's, 1958), p. 184.

27. *Defense* (1984), Part V, esp. Ch. 18, 20, & 21. *Future* (1985), Ch. 1 & 2. *Taking* (1987), Ch. 4.

28. More precisely, separation of church and state derives not from religious toleration but from "an altogether different principle," namely, a natural right of everyone not to be governed in matters of religion provided they "demean themselves as good citizens" (quoting Washington). Berns argues that asserting such a natural right is "to deny revelation." *Taking,* pp. 164–67.

29. To my knowledge, Berns does not confront other meanings of constitutional separation of church and state than that which subordinates religion to the state. Roger Williams' "wall of separation between the garden of the church and the wilderness of the world," whose metaphor Jefferson plays upon in his letter to the Danbury Baptists (thereby seeming to suggest to these constituents that the Constitution embodied Baptist political theology, if one can speak of Baptist political theology), was for the sake of the independence, not subordination, of the church from the state. And John Courtney Murray thought the First Amendment religion clauses "articles of peace," a merely practical way for different churches and religions to get along peaceably without any commitment to subordination. *We Hold These Truths: Catholic Reflections on the American Proposition* (New York: Sheed & Ward, 1960), pp. 56–63.

30. Strauss, "Restatement," p. 192.

31. *Defense* (1984), pp. 59–60.

32. Strauss encouraged students to have the courage to stand against the mainstream of current democracy in defense of democracy. "Democracy has not yet found a defense against the creeping conformism . . . it fosters." "What Is Political Philosophy," p. 38.

33. *Future* (1985), pp. 60–79 esp. 71.

34. *Taking,* pp. 180, 173ff.

35. Ibid., pp. 167, 180, 157.

36. Already in *Natural Right and History* (1953), p. 75, Strauss argued that from the point of view of both philosophy and theology, unassisted reason and revelation were mutually irrefutable. Hence to prefer reason over revelation was dogmatic, that is, unreasonable. He further maintained that the tension between reason and revelation was the energizing principle of the West. The gist of Berns' constitutional understanding seems to reject this in favor of a Hobbesian, typically modern resolution of the tension in favor of reason over revelation.

37. *Taking* (1987), pp. 222. J. P. Mayer ed., George Lawrence trans., *Democracy in America* (New York: Harper and Row, 1969), pp. 543, 544.

38. *Future* (1985), p. 70.

39. *Future* (1985), pp. 55–79.

40. Although Jefferson provides the link between Locke's teaching of religious toleration/liberty of conscience and the Constitution (*Taking,* pp. 158–64), Berns implies that Jefferson and Madison were wrong in not understanding the necessity for the triumph of an industrial and commercial way of life (p. 146). Apparently, their concern for slavery and agriculture moderated their project for undermining serious religious faith. That is, a kind of moderation can be achieved by what Joseph Cropsey once called "the temperate equilibrium of error." That is, a kind of moderation can issue from incoherence as well as from political philosophy. "Liberalism and Conservatism" in Robert A. Goldwin ed., *Left, Right, and Center* (Chicago: Rand McNally, 1965), p. 59.

41. *Taking* (1987), p. 188.

42. Ibid., p. 182, quoting Tocqueville approvingly.

43. Ibid., pp. 184–85.

44. *Taking*, pp. 188, 182, 184–85. "Locke emphasizes law and, in effect, the sovereignty of law instead of the sovereignty of a Hobbesian Leviathan, because in his view there is safety in law, and there is (or can be) safety in the process by which law is made." Ibid., p. 187.

45. *Future* (1985), p. 50. This is identical grounds for his objecting to the modern understanding of judicial review in which justices, in the name of the Constitution, make private judgments about what the Constitution should mean. *Defense* (1984), p. 41.

46. Ibid., p. 44

47. Thus the essays denying a constitutional right of exemption from otherwise constitutionally valid laws (conscientious objection, compulsory schools attendance, etc.). See *Future*, esp. pp. 45–50, and *Defense*, Ch. 18, 20 & 21. Berns seems not to object to such exemptions "when the law as a matter of grace" grants them. *Future*, p. 44. But if the people can consent to such exemptions as a matter of grace, why can they not embody that grace in the Constitution? Perhaps this question is answered by the fact that they have not done so. Indeed, in 1789 Madison unsuccessfully proposed such an amendment to the First Congress. Perhaps Berns' objection, then, is that the Court has transformed these exemptions from matters of grace into constitutional rights.

48. The symposium was published in *First Things*, November 1996. Berns announced his disagreement and resignation from the editorial advisory board in the January 1997 issue. For his explanation of his break see *Commentary* February 1997, pp. 19–21. The Symposium and the serious responses to it are published in Richard John Neuhaus ed., *The End of Democracy?: The Judicial Usurpation of Politics* (Dallas: Spence Publishing Co., 1997). Neuhaus comments on Berns' resignation on pp. 192–94.

49. *Taking* (1987), p. 12.

50. I believe Berns would also disagree with the symposiasts that the usurpations of the Court make the *regime* illegitimate. If anything it is the Court, not the regime, which is illegitimate.

51. This would be consistent with Strauss' classical view that the regime is not the law and hence not the written constitution but "the underlying arrangement of human beings" in "regard to control of communal affairs." *Natural Right and History* (Chicago: University of Chicago Press, 1953), p. 136. Cf. Berns. "[O]ur rights may have their foundation in nature or in a duly enacted statute, but for their security they depend ultimately on the support not only of public official[s] but of public opinion." That's regime. *Taking* (1987), p. 227.

52. However, the Constitution's "republican (or limited) government . . . depended on confining the business of government to issues that did not give rise to zeal, anger, or moral indignation." Berns acknowledges that the Court's failure to do that provoked the symposiasts' "angry and morally indignant discourse." *Commentary*, February 1997, p. 21.

53. Ibid., pp. 19–21.

54. See Leo Strauss, "Restatement on Xenophon's *Hiero*," p. 205.

55. *Taking* (1992), pp. 162ff.

56. *Defense* (1984), pp. 59–60.

57. But censorship is useful only to preserve, not to instill, restraint. See generally *Freedom* (1957), esp. pp. 238ff. "The complete absence of all forms of censorship . . . is theoretically untenable and practically infeasible," p. 251.

58. Not entirely. There is a place for a very attenuated Lockean family (*Second Treatise*, Ch. 6). But the marriage is not permanent, parents' duties to the children have no self-interested ground (thus on Lockean grounds casting doubt on how well child rearing duties will be performed) and children's duties to the parents depends on how big the estate is.

· 13 ·

Allan Bloom: Strauss, Socrates, and Liberal Education

Walter Nicgorski

$\mathcal{W}$ithout doubt the most widely known and most controversial student of Leo Strauss has been Allan Bloom. Bloom might not have earned those titles simply on the basis of his translations of and commentaries on Plato's *Republic* and Rousseau's *Émile*. Bloom, however, holds those titles beyond contest because of his provocative and long-running best seller, *The Closing of the American Mind*.[1] Leo Strauss is not acknowledged as its source or inspiration in *The Closing*; in fact, he is mentioned but once and in a quite incidental way in Bloom's nearly 400-page book.[2] That much of *The Closing* appears as a late 1980s cultural critique and concerns the possibility of liberal education in the contemporary university seems to provide more reason for distancing Bloom at his moment of greatest public impact from his avowed teacher Leo Strauss. Strauss, after all, had died nearly a generation before *The Closing* appeared, and his interests might seem otherwise focused. What direct writing he did on liberal education and the university was done well before, at the very start of the 1960s.[3] Furthermore there is record of a break between Strauss and Bloom and even some speculation that there was a philosophical disagreement of a fundamental nature. Yet Strauss has been taken by some (and by most of those who are aware of Strauss's teaching and Bloom's past at the University of Chicago) to be the dominant and a pervasive influence on Bloom's thinking and specifically on *The Closing*.

An inquiry into Strauss's influence through Allan Bloom on higher education in America requires then attention to the nature of the tie between Strauss and Bloom. Since higher education for both of them is primarily education toward or in philosophy, to examine that tie is to explore the common ground and possible differences in their thinking as it appears in their writings. Such an exploration could not, of course, be responsibly confined to *The Closing* and Strauss's writings directly on education, yet a comprehensive comparison of Bloom and Strauss would draw one beyond the limits set for this essay. The apparent impact of Allan Bloom through *The Closing* provides an occasion and a use-

205

ful focal point through which to ask what is and what might be Leo Strauss's legacy to American higher education.

THE STRAUSS-BLOOM CONNECTION

Although throughout Bloom's published work one finds a pattern of rare citation of Leo Strauss and thus a consistency with *The Closing*'s singular mention of Strauss, Bloom's debt to Strauss is evident. This could not be missed by a reasonably attentive reader whose efforts had extended no further than to the books of widest public impact by each, Strauss's *Natural Right and History* and Bloom's *The Closing*.[4] Most notable and most significant is that the thematic of Bloom's book, a closing of the American mind—a closing especially evident in the nation's leading universities—around the dogma of relativism regarding the good and the true, seems a reflection of Strauss's analysis of the crisis (the rejection of natural right) that stirred his inquiry into natural right and history. In the introduction to his book by that title, Strauss explains how natural right is abandoned in favor of unlimited tolerance and that this abandonment leads to nihilism and necessarily to the acceptance of intolerance "as a value equal in dignity to tolerance."[5] As Strauss unfolds this argument, one can see in his very language how profoundly this book forged in the 1940s reveals an understanding of the patterns of thought and events that so exercised Bloom in the 1980s. Strauss writes of "generous liberals" holding that "unlimited tolerance is in accordance with reason" because of "our inability to acquire any genuine knowledge of what is intrinsically good or right." In this view, Strauss finds a

> particular interpretation of natural right according to which the one thing needful is respect for diversity or individuality. But there is a tension between the respect for diversity or individuality and the recognition of natural right. When liberals became impatient of the absolute limits to diversity or individuality that are imposed even by the most liberal version of natural right, they had to make a choice between natural right and the uninhibited cultivation of individuality. They chose the latter. Once this step was taken, tolerance appeared as one value or ideal among many, and not intrinsically superior to its opposite.

Within this framework of a modern slide from a genial liberal tolerance to a dogmatic, now even sometimes politically correct, intolerance, Bloom's *Closing* incorporates other themes either launched or given influential form in Strauss's *Natural Right*. Thus Bloom sees the social contract tradition undermined by a tendency to uncritical openness and draws attention anew to how a Germanic tradition in thought contributes to the destruction of a decent liberalism in the West. Bloom also considers the roles of Rousseau and Nietzsche in raising an understandable protest against the shallowness of modernity, a protest that takes forms which contribute to the slide to the nihilism of post-modernity, and points to Nietzsche and

Max Weber as formative figures for contemporary intellectual life. And then too in the vein of Strauss, Bloom sees the suicide of modern science insofar as it comes to embrace cultural relativism, and he finds events such as the initial Russian competitive success in space exploration bringing to greater public attention the important question of "why science?"[6] Even this limited recalling of the congruence of important aspects of the argument of *The Closing* with Strauss's thought gives credence to observations like those of Harry Jaffa who finds that "Strauss's words and Strauss's thoughts echo and re-echo" throughout the book.[7] George Anastaplo, like Jaffa well-prepared to comment by close and long study with and of Strauss, hears in *The Closing* "dozens, if not hundreds, of echoes" of Strauss's work.[8] William Galston, brought by his teacher Bloom to read Strauss, later finds the "same difficulties" with Bloom's *Closing* that he had with Strauss's argument in *Natural Right*.[9]

Others less favorably disposed to Strauss or Bloom have focused on the latter as a spokesman for the former or, at least, for the tradition or school allegedly founded by Strauss, and this despite Bloom's reticence and self-limitation to a single incidental mention of Strauss in his book of public impact. One hostile reviewer of Bloom is able to credit him with using "arcane Straussian concepts to produce a popular work of cultural criticism."[10] In a similar vein, Robert Bellah appreciates that Bloom has "condescended" from the usual Straussian preoccupation with textual commentary to provide a "lively, bitter" and "stimulating" Straussian picture "of our current social, cultural, and intellectual condition."[11] And Richard Rorty trumpets his response to Bloom's book as a manifestation of the Straussian version of "that old time philosophy."[12]

Not only then is Bloom's tie to Strauss broadly evident, but it also seems that it is self-confessed in ways more significant than conventional acknowledgments and a plethora of citations to Strauss's writings could ever be. Given only the congruency of themes noted above, Bloom would have had to have been thoroughly and hence implausibly naive to think he could hide his debt to Strauss. Yet, he chose in the case of *The Closing* with its broader intended audience, not only to forego formal citations of Strauss, the consistent general practice throughout his scholarly career, but also not to put his dependence on Strauss front and center in the way it appears at various times both before and after the publication of *The Closing*. Rather than seeing this as a lapse in scholarly responsibility, that choice may be plausibly explained as a rhetorical strategy for conveying the thought of Leo Strauss while not bringing "Strauss's name to public attention";[13] such a strategy might be motivated by the desire to advance those ideas free from the encumbrance of the controversies over Strauss and Straussianism already well heated in the academic world for more than a generation before *The Closing* appeared; it might also, or alternatively, have been motivated by the desire to protect Strauss's name from the contentious battles of the frontlines of "culture" criticism and the politics of the contemporary university.[14] Strauss generally eschewed those frontlines; as Bloom strode there he seems to have preferred to bear responsibility himself for the way he used the Straussian heritage in those battles.

This second explanation of a rhetorical strategy bears a close relationship to what Werner Dannhauser, Bloom's friend from graduate school days to death, suggests as the reasons for Bloom's mentioning Strauss but once and incidentally in the book. Dannhauser points to Bloom's "modesty and a wish to stand on his own two feet amidst controversy."[15] Modesty may seem uncharacteristically Bloomian and also an unlikely attribute to link with the desire to stand on one's own, yet such hesitations might give way when one understands such modesty as rooted in a sense of living the philosophical life with an attendant awareness both of philosophy's inherent limits and of deep debt for having been led to that life. So seems to be the case with Allan Bloom, for here is a philosophical modesty that some even find too self-denying;[16] it is a modesty paradoxically entangled with the pride of finding a superior way of life, the true way of happiness, and it is an unqualified and genuine modesty bred of respect and debt to his teacher and guide into this philosophical life, Leo Strauss. Thus Bloom's relationship to Strauss is too profound and significant for ordinary credits and citations; Bloom is deeply indebted and at the same time protective of the name and thought of Strauss as he appropriates the philosophical legacy of Strauss to the events of his day.[17]

Bloom can be found understanding himself in just such a relationship to Strauss. The evidence for this claim is found in the substantial oral consensus on how Bloom spoke of his debt to Strauss in private, in the dedication ("To Leo Strauss Our Teacher") of Bloom's first book done with Harry Jaffa,[18] and in a full appreciation of Bloom's memorial essay on Strauss and then the fact and the manner of his reprinting it in 1990.[19] The significance of the last of these evidentiary points warrants elaboration here. Bloom chose to republish the memorial essay in *Giants and Dwarfs*, a collection prepared in the years immediately following the appearance of *The Closing* and while the controversy it provoked was still at high tide; one strain in the concerns raised by the book, as we have seen, was the absence of his acknowledgment of Strauss's influence. Bloom placed the essay on Strauss first among three selections in a section entitled "Teachers." The Strauss essay running to more than twenty pages is twice as long as that on Raymond Aron which follows and more than three times the length of the final piece on a teacher, that on Alexandre Kojève. The significance of this piece for the present inquiry is not, however, so much persuasively found in such superficial considerations as in what Bloom actually says about Strauss in the essay and in the preface to the 1990 collection. In the four-page preface, Strauss is mentioned only once (Socrates, seven times); the acknowledgment of Strauss is, however, of some moment.

> These essays are a partial record of a life which began with Freud and ended with Plato in a search for self-understanding. The decisive moment of that life was the encounter with Leo Strauss. I was nineteen years old, and at first everything he taught was the absolute Other for me, an Other which, if it was true, seemed to deny my special individuality. But I finally learned from that great man that self-actualization depended on seeing what the human possibilities are and that they

live in flesh and blood in old books. Since then the path to self-knowledge has been for me the interpretation of the books which teach about the philosophic way of life and which tend to be discrete mixtures of philosophy and poetry.[20]

This direct testimony of Strauss's critical part in turning Bloom to the philosophic way of life thus introduces and justifies his including in the collection the '74 memorial essay where he spoke of Strauss more directly, more fully and more unqualifiedly as a philosopher than ever in his published work. Bloom likely reveals here some of what attracted him to Strauss and perhaps even is measuring himself against this significant presence in his life. In the early lines of the memorial essay, Bloom points to the body of Strauss's works as where Strauss himself located his enduring essence. Strauss "was dedicated to intransigent seriousness as opposed to popularization." His was "a life in which the only real events were thoughts." Accordingly, his was a life given essentially to "the solitary, continuous, meticulous study of the questions he believed most important. His conversation was the result or the continuation of this activity." "Neither daunted nor corroded by neglect or hostility," Leo Strauss was, concludes Bloom, "a philosopher." And then Bloom quickly adds, that Strauss would never have said this of himself,

> for he was too modest and he had too much reverence for the rare human type and the way of life represented by that title to arrogate it to himself, especially in an age when its use has been so cheapened. My assertion is particularly paradoxical, inasmuch as Strauss appears emphatically to be only a scholar . . . . But appearances can be deceiving, particularly when our prejudices are in part responsible for them. A survey of Strauss's entire body of work will reveal that it constitutes a unified and continuous, ever deepening investigation into the meaning and possibility of philosophy. It is the product of a philosophic life. . . .[21]

Surely at the time of republishing the memorial essay, if not earlier, Bloom must have recognized that perhaps disposition and clearly circumstances had given his life a somewhat different character from that of Strauss. One need not draw the conclusion that Bloom was either a conscious "popularizer" and/or such a devotee of a range of pleasures to the effect that he could not but be less than intransigently serious about the philosophic life.[22] It does seem clear, however, that events intruded, or Bloom, contrary to the tendency of Strauss, let them intrude between the period of his student days and frequent contact with Strauss in the '50s and Bloom's writing of *The Closing*. Taking up a regular academic appointment in 1963, Bloom's love of wisdom and books had to survive if not thrive within the channels and challenges of a conventional university setting. Finding curricular space and appropriate structure for what seemed right and dealing with a university ambience that was ever more deeply troubled as America moved through the '60s and into the '70s seemed to provide many events and some of moment which brought Bloom to write about higher education well before he stirred the nation with *The Closing*.[23] That Bloom would have met events with resources of thought and inspiration derived from Strauss's formative influence upon him and that he may well have seen it a duty to bring that thought to bear on events without implicating Strauss in his every application and especially in his most contentious forays are hardly unreasonable suppositions. Bloom as teacher, as his friend Dannhauser noted, did not give rise to Bloomians; he did not even try that. Rather, and this might fairly be said of his teaching in the widest sense of that term, he pointed his students and readers to Strauss whose legacy, Dannhauser added, he did more than anyone to secure.[24] It can also be fairly said that with Strauss he pointed to peaks of human achievement. Strauss had written of liberal education that it "reminds those members of a mass democracy who have ears to hear, of human greatness."[25] The young scholar Nasser Behnegar upon recalling this passage has justly observed that "Allan Bloom, following Strauss in his own way, used his prodigious natural talents to render this noble but intrinsically pleasant service to American democracy."[26]

THE FOCUS ON EDUCATION

Bloom's self-confessed focus on education, even to the point of defining his own inquiry and scholarship around the widely regarded two greatest educational treatises of the West, Plato's *Republic* and Rousseau's *Émile*,[27] may seem to distance him from Strauss, for Strauss's direct writings on education are putatively minor among his works and little noticed. In making education a focus, however, Bloom could well be seen among Strauss's students as having taken a course to which Strauss most directly pointed. This conclusion gains credibility once one has more fully appreciated that Strauss is most often found teaching and writing about "education" without elevating that term to prominence and that Bloom's concerns are deeply with the philosophic life even as he teaches and writes about education.

In an unusually self-reflective statement, Strauss writes,

> I own that education is in a sense the subject matter of my teaching and my research. But I am almost solely concerned with the goal or end of education at its best or highest—of the education of the perfect prince as it were—and very little with its conditions and its how.[28]

Strauss adds that "the most important conditions . . . are the qualities of the educator and of the human being who is to be educated." That Strauss's central interest was educating to philosophy provides some explanation of his scant attention to the usual struggles for control and honor in the academic world. As Bloom says of him, "He was active in no organization, served in no position of authority, and had no ambitions other than to understand and help others who might also be able to do so."[29] Given the nature of the educational goal that chiefly concerned him, Strauss had very modest expectations for support beyond a relative few. But Strauss was not given to civic irresponsibility or to the incapacity to calculate the danger of the absence of effort on behalf of philosophy.

Strauss appears to go after bigger game than what was often at stake in the ordinary academic struggles; these were the large and formative currents of thought such as historicism and positivism that shaped or deeply affected the universities and often through them modern life. In those opening chapters of *Natural Right and History* and later in his essays on "Social Science and Humanism" and "Relativism" which were published at essentially the same time (1956 and 1961 respectively)[30] as his direct lectures on education,[31] Strauss can be seen engaged in weakening or removing the obstacles to the possibility or renewal of philosophy. It is in this sense, as Behnegar has astutely observed, that "Strauss's political activity, to the extent one can speak of such a thing, was primarily realized in education: his most passionate polemics were directed against trends or tendencies in the academy."[32] And it is in this respect that Bloom is clearly Strauss's most direct student and the one who has, chiefly through the impact of *The Closing*, significantly extended Strauss's critical concerns about higher education into the contemporary debate over it. In 1997 ten years after *The Closing* appeared and had its dramatic success in sales, the most prominent press organ for American higher education described it as "a classic . . . not in the sense of great literature—but in the sense that it focused lasting attention on academe in a way that has not been done since."[33] Even its critics, continued this report, credit Bloom with making the character of higher education "a matter of public debate" before a "wide audience."

LIBERAL EDUCATION: NATURE, MEANS, AND CONDITIONS

Beneath the "passionate polemics"—in fact that which gives rise to them in Strauss and Bloom—is the basis, in what Strauss taught and Bloom extended, for an enduring legacy with respect to education. Bloom like Strauss understands liberal education as experience of greatness, emphatically inclusive of the beautiful.[34] Such experience assumes exposure, chiefly to books marked by such greatness, but the experience is usually had only with the prod of the caring and questioning teacher. Questioning is the appropriate mode for the student to engage greatness, and the teacher is midwife to that experience and its fruit. "Particularly the teacher dedicated to liberal education" writes Bloom in the opening pages of *The Closing*, "must constantly try to look toward the goal of human completeness and back at the natures of his students here and now, ever seeking to understand the former and to assess the capacities of the latter to approach it."[35] Bloom, gingerly to be sure, adds that such a teacher is "guided by the awareness, or the divination, that there is a human nature, and that assisting its fulfillment is his task. . . . Moreover there is no real teacher who in practice does not believe in the existence of the soul, ..."[36]

The central question in liberal education continues to stem from the Delphic injunction to "know thyself." Bloom thought it was an injunction in each of us who are truly alive. This "serious business" of self-knowledge seems to be the core quest that opens to a variety of questions.[37] And these are the great questions that higher educational institutions should maintain "front and center" and that "must be faced if one is to live a serious life."[38] Those questions are enumerated in *The Closing* as concerning "reason-revelation, freedom-necessity, democracy-aristocracy, good-evil, body-soul, self-other, city-man, eternity-time, being-nothing."[39] Since these include the fundamental or the highest and deepest philosophical questions, a reader sees that for Bloom like Strauss liberal education is on a trajectory to philosophy; at the least it provides an experience latent with potential to awaken the philosophical life. If Bloom seems to move to the heights or depths more quickly and manifestly than is the case in Strauss, Bloom cannot, however, be said to be unaware that only a few will sufficiently awaken to pursue the philosophical life, for one must suppose that Bloom enjoins the teacher to be ever "assessing the capacities" for a reason.

Just as Bloom by and large represents Strauss's position on the nature and goal of liberal education, so like Strauss he guardedly endorses "the good old Great Books approach" as "the only serious solution" to the problem of providing liberal education in the troubled context of the modern university.[40] Bloom clearly did not mean to support every ship flying the Great Books colors, for in *The Closing* he reports that he is well aware of and agrees with "the objections to the Great Books cult." He then enumerates so many such objections and so cavalierly (ending his enumeration with "and so forth") that a reader might well be led back to an earlier writing where his endorsement of this mode of education concludes in a way that reveals what was likely his greatest fear about a Great Books approach. "Thus," he writes, "liberal education consists largely in the painstaking study of these [great] books. The study requires long and arduous training, for these books are not immediately accessible to us."[41] This plea in 1974 was for "most careful attention" to these books "because they are expressions of teachers such as we are not likely to encounter in person, because in them we find the arguments for what we take for granted without reflection, and because they are the sources for forgotten alternatives." Bloom either did not intend at that point to make such a course of study sound so forbidding to undergraduates (wanting perhaps to caution against a facile popularization of Great Books education) or he came by the time of his writing *The Closing* to more openness to an undergraduate experience with these books, an experience that necessarily would have entailed a first reading of many of them. In *The Closing* he observes the high level of student satisfaction when the Great Books are at the center of their curriculum: they "feel they are doing something that is independent and fulfilling, getting something from the university that they cannot get elsewhere."[42] In endorsing the Great Books approach as the best option around, Bloom measures it against his expectations that liberal education should draw students to the permanent questions and foster the "love of truth and passion to live a good life."[43]

At its best, according to Bloom, the university would support liberal education not only by keeping the fundamental questions "front and center" but also by preserving "the treasury of great deeds, great men and great thoughts" and by encouraging "the noninstrumental use of reason."[44] Bloom, however, almost seems to despair that the modern universities he knew were up to the job. He has no doubt that the universities, their leadership and faculties, and the broader society rather than the students are primarily responsible for the obstacles to liberal education. With some exaggeration, to be sure, Bloom at one point regards the "theoretical life" as all but extinct in the universities; at another time, he writes that "almost all that is institutional stands in the way of the study of books" and that it was "almost impossible" to actualize the education he proposed.[45]

It never seems, however, to have been total despair, for Bloom kept reaching out to persuade and exhort to his way. In the 1990 Preface to *Giants and Dwarfs*, he muses that "because the educational scene in the United States is now bleak does not mean that this will always and everywhere be so."[46] In the end, he seems to have settled essentially where Leo Strauss was with respect to significant educational reform within the universities, that is, he held to exceedingly modest expectations. "The book on education" for Bloom, Plato's *Republic*, is seen by him as an assist in reaching a "moderation" of expectations and a certain "resignation" with respect to these matters.[47]

What hope Bloom had for the philosophical life and American democracy is paradoxically tied to the universities that so disappointed him. Bloom observes in praise of Raymond Aron, "he knew that the university is the central institution in democratic society," and Bloom explores that truth about the modern university in *The Closing*.[48] He notes that the natural rights teaching "established the framework and atmosphere for the modern university" and there was accordingly "a special kinship between the liberal university and liberal democracy."[49] Whatever incipient difficulties for human excellence might lay within the premises of this modern partnership, there was very much to be said—and it was decisive in the light of the attacks on the university during and since the 60s—for the joint commitment to freedom and reason with the university's special charge as a center of reason. "The most important function of the university in an age of reason," writes Bloom, "is to protect reason from itself, by being a model of true openness."[50] He would have that openness allow, if it could not nourish, Socratic inquiry and Socratic rationalism, thus making place for non-instrumental reason. Independent of this or that reform, or critique of, or frustration with, the university, Bloom's overall objective took its bearings from Strauss's return to Socrates which Bloom wholly appreciated and personally embraced.[51]

Though Strauss's return was for him the result of a personal search, of his thinking through the crisis of modern natural right, and was not, in its origin or first vintage, a mere educational reform, it can be called "a return" not primarily as an individual circling back or reversion by Strauss but chiefly as an attempted act of leadership within the philosophical tradition of the West. Strauss clearly knew there were educational implications in and educational obstacles to the renewal he sought. To the degree consistent with his call to and disposition for an essentially private life, Strauss would have approved what he clearly inspired in Bloom, namely all prudent efforts (genuine openness being their precondition) toward a Socratic recentering of the university.

The matter of Strauss's legacy via Bloom with respect to education cannot, however, be left there, for the story here told can give rise to at least two misunderstandings. It might, for one, incline us to measure this aspect of Strauss's legacy by looking for evidence of university reform such as curricular change, new mission statements, etc. Strauss, however, sought above all to educate individual persons while arguing his case for the renewal of a certain kind of inquiry. Those persons, such as Allan Bloom, educated others in the same spirit. It is in such individuals whether directly or indirectly, by personal teaching or by writings, that Strauss's legacy has made its mark and has been genuinely remarkable to foe as well as friend. There is, of course, no guarantee that such a Socratic renewal will prevail or even broadly survive in the academy or in the philosophical tradition. Furthermore, such a renewal, given the nature of Socratic practice, would never be simply captured or entirely at ease in any institutional form.

The core of Strauss's legacy might also be misunderstood by taking a too constricted view of the return to Socrates and thus seeing it essentially as the commonly discussed "Socratic method" in teaching. What Socrates held up to Strauss, and to Bloom through Strauss, was a way of life, a deeply serious and focused life that sought such truth as humans most needed by questioning the opinions that were serving at best more or less adequately to direct their lives. It was this questioning that arose in the ordinary horizon of life that pointed to and thus possibly led to the most fundamental queries about the human condition and thus provided a framework for understanding liberal education. Within this framework and hence out of the Socratic renewal that is the legacy of Strauss arises the question of the nature and certainty of Socratic wisdom, or the nature of Socratic skepticism. In seeking to be life-directive, the Socratic way also must encounter the divine and in the world of the Book that means the claims of Revelation. On these matters Bloom has been seen, perhaps only because his rhetoric sometimes invites it, to be both more skeptical than Strauss and less impressed with the strength of the claims of Revelation. Whether and to what extent this is a correct view requires the inquiry of another day and context. This much is clear: approaches to these fundamental matters divide those most receptive to Strauss's legacy. That there be continuing attention to those concerns, marked by philosophical acumen, care and civility, would itself constitute a triumph of that legacy.

NOTES

1. *The Republic of Plato* (New York: Basic Books, 1968, 1991); *Émile; or On Education* (New York: Basic Books, 1979; London: Penguin Classics, 1991); *The Closing of the American Mind:*

How Higher Education Has Failed Democracy and Impoverished the Souls of Today's Students (New York: Simon and Schuster, 1987).

2. This mention (*Closing*, 167), with no specific citation of a text of Strauss, occurs when Bloom is discussing the Lockeanism of Americans with its emphasis on "well-being" and the "reasonableness" of balancing their passions and recognizing the rights of others. Bloom then writes, "As Leo Strauss put it, the moderns 'built on low but solid ground.'" As George Anastaplo and others have noted, this is really a quotation by Strauss from Winston Churchill. "In re Allan Bloom: A Respectful Dissent," in *Essays on* The Closing of the American Mind, ed. Robert L. Stone (Chicago: Chicago Review Press, 1989), 278, n. 12. Stone's quite comprehensive collection of reactions to and reviews of *The Closing* has proved very useful in examining the response to the book; nearly all the selections Stone reproduced initially appeared elsewhere. For an assessment of certain significant reviews of *The Closing*, see Charles E. Butterworth, "On Misunderstanding Allan Bloom: The Response to *The Closing of the American Mind*," *Academic Questions* 2 (Fall, 1989), 56–80.

3. Strauss's two such direct writings were based on addresses given in 1959 and 1960 in the context of The Basic Program of Liberal Education for Adults at the University of Chicago. The first "What is Liberal Education?" was reprinted from an official University of Chicago publication in *Education for Public Responsibility*, ed. C. Scott Fletcher (New York: Norton, 1961), 43–51. The second, "Liberal Education and Responsibility," appears to have been initially published in *Education: The Challenge Ahead*, ed. C. Scott Fletcher (New York: Norton, 1962), 49–70. The text of both addresses was reprinted after editing as the first two essays in Strauss's *Liberalism Ancient and Modern* (New York: Basic Books, 1968). Strauss also prepared a single essay from substantial portions of the two earlier addresses and published it under the title "Liberal Education and Mass Democracy" in *Higher Education and Modern Democracy*, ed. Robert A. Goldwin (Chicago: Rand McNally, 1967), 73–96. A commentary on and interpretation of these writings is found in Walter Nicgorski, "Leo Strauss and Liberal Education," *Interpretation* 13 (May, 1985), 233–50.

4. This is not to suggest that the immediate public impact of these books was comparable. George Anastaplo (Stone, 267) has no doubt properly estimated "that more copies of *Closing* have been sold than of all the books published by Mr. Strauss and his other students combined." It is, of course, another question as to which might have the deepest and thus most enduring impact on universities and public life; in this respect, Bloom's book and overall work can be seen as in the service of the thought evident in Strauss's *Natural Right and History* (Chicago: University of Chicago Press, 1953).

5. Strauss, *Natural Right*, 5.

6. *The Closing*, 27ff., 314; 144ff., 323; 206ff., 298ff.; 194 ff; 49–50, 204.

7. Harry V. Jaffa, "Humanizing Certitudes and Impoverishing Doubts: A Critique of *The Closing of the American Mind*," in Stone, 138.

8. Anastaplo, 268.

9. William A. Galston, "Socratic Reason and Lockean Rights: The Place of the University in a Liberal Democracy," in Stone, 122.

10. Paul Gottfried, "A Half-Open Mind," in Stone, 13.

11. Robert N. Bellah, "Academic Fundamentalism," in Stone, 91–93. Similarly, Shadia Drury finds that "those who came closest to understanding" *The Closing* were "those who recognized the book as a jazzy version of the work of Leo Strauss." Not meaning to undermine Bloom with this comment, she adds "it is no mean feat to jazz up the ideas of Leo Strauss." *Alexandre Kojève* (New York: St. Martin's Press, 1994), 161, 252 n. 3. In a subsequent book, flawed in other respects by serious misunderstandings of the writings of both Strauss

and Bloom, she views *The Closing* as a "popularization" of Strauss's ideas. *Leo Strauss and the American Right* (New York: St. Martin's Press, 1997), 6, 15, 111.

12. Richard Rorty, "Straussianism, Democracy, and Allan Bloom I: That Old Time Philosophy," in Stone, 94–103.

13. This phrase and the idea of viewing Bloom's reticence as a rhetorical strategy comes from Will Morrisey's "How Bloom Did It: Rhetoric and Principle in *The Closing of the American Mind*," in Stone, 51–60, 59. Each of us elaborates the rhetorical strategy in somewhat different but not necessarily mutually exclusive ways. Jaffa and Anastaplo view Bloom's silence as, at the least, a lapse in scholarly responsibility, though Anastaplo concedes that Bloom never hesitated in private conversations and public interviews to acknowledge Strauss as an important source of his thinking and at one point speculates that Bloom, like Alcibiades vis-à-vis Socrates, kept Strauss out of sight. Stone, 138–39, 150; 268, 278 n. 12, 272.

14. Just how successful Bloom was in distancing Strauss from any kind of responsibility for *The Closing* is indicated by an examination of *Beyond Cheering and Bashing: New Perspectives on The Closing of the American Mind*, eds. William K. Buckley & James Seaton (Bowling Green, Ohio: Bowling Green State University Popular Press, 1992). This collection of eighteen essays is occasioned by Bloom's *Closing* and the general concern with and reexamination of higher education which it stimulated. Nearly all the essays are on or take off from Bloom's book; nearly all are unfriendly to Bloom's perspectives, and nearly all are by scholars and teachers of literature. Only one of the contributors mentions Strauss, noting an earlier acknowledgment by Bloom that Strauss was his teacher. Thus outside of political science/political philosophy circles or those associated in some way with the University of Chicago, the Bloom/Strauss relationship is generally unknown or not regarded as notable. The single contributor who mentions Strauss would have reason to know of the Strauss/Bloom connection for he had been an undergraduate student of Bloom's who took "the two best classes of his undergraduate career" during Bloom's "banner years" at Cornell. Kenneth Alan Hovey, "The Great Books vs. America: Reassessing *The Closing of the American Mind*," 90–91.

15. "Allan Bloom and the Critics," in Stone, 89.

16. For a sampling of those who find Bloom's approach to philosophy not rising above "longing" and to truth, see John Podhoretz, "An Open Letter to Allan Bloom," Eva Brann, "The Spirit Lives in the Sticks," and Pamela Proietti, "American Feminists versus Allan Bloom," in Stone, 67, 186, 217–18.

17. Gary Glenn, in preparing his piece for this volume, drew my attention to an observation of Walter Berns where Berns was likely writing with Bloom among others in mind when in 1982 in his public dispute with Harry Jaffa he observed, "Other Strauss students are extremely reticent about invoking his name and for good reason. Strauss did not found a cult or a movement, and one does him honor by *not* speaking of him too much, lest the pupil's failings appear to be those of the teacher." "A Reply to Harry Jaffa," *National Review* (January 22, 1982), 44.

18. *Shakespeare's Politics* (New York: Basic Books, Inc., 1964). In the same year and at this early point in the public manifestation of his scholarship, Bloom published an interpretive essay on Jonathan Swift's *Gulliver's Travels* in a festschrift for Strauss (*Essays on the Tradition of Political Philosophy in Honor of Leo Strauss*, ed. Joseph Cropsey [New York: Basic Books, 1964]). That essay, "Giants and Dwarfs: An Outline of *Gulliver's Travels*," was republished as the title essay in the 1990 collection of Bloom's essays from which I quote in what follows. Not surprisingly given the time and occasion, Bloom here confesses a great debt to Strauss though not citing any specific texts of Strauss. One might see in what he writes a specification of at

least certain important ways in which Leo Strauss was his teacher. Introducing Swift's treatment of the Quarrel between the Ancients and Moderns, Bloom writes, "In our time, only Leo Strauss has provided us with the scholarship and the philosophic insight necessary to a proper confrontation of ancients and moderns, and hence his works are the prolegomena to a recovery of Swift's teaching." Bloom then highlights contributions of Strauss to a contemporary capacity to appreciate Swift's teaching and concludes with the observation that "*Gulliver's Travels* is in both substance and form a model of the problems which we have been taught to recognize as our own by Leo Strauss. It is fitting that this essay be designed to do him honor; its content is beyond acknowledgment indebted to his learning." *Giants and Dwarfs: Essays 1960–1990* [hereafter cited as *G & D*] (New York: Simon and Schuster, 1990), 37–38. Four years later in 1968, Bloom published his translation of and interpretive essay on *The Republic of Plato*. Strauss is cited only once in the extensive footnotes; however, in the "Preface" (p. xx) Bloom observes, "The interpretive essay relies heavily on Leo Strauss' authoritative discussion of the *Republic* in *The City and Man* (Chicago: Rand McNally, 1964)." In 1968, 1970 and 1972, Bloom as a general editor of a series for Cornell University Press wrote brief forewords to Strauss's works on Xenophon. In each case, his praise of Strauss and assessment of his significance goes beyond customary comments of editors of series; most notable is his sentence in the 1972 book, *Xenophon's Socrates:* "As is always the case with Professor Strauss's books, this one is difficult to access; but to those who wish to understand the texts and the phenomena to which they refer, his works are a permanent possession."

19. The essay ("Leo Strauss: September 20, 1899–October 18, 1973") originally appeared in *Political Theory* in November 1974. It is later included in the 1990 collection of Bloom's essays *G & D*, 235–55.

20. "Preface," *G & D*, 11–12. In the same year in which Bloom published these words, he extensively and profoundly acknowledged a debt to Strauss in the two concluding paragraphs to an "Introduction" he wrote as editor of the collection entitled *Confronting the Constitution* (Washington, D.C.: The AEI Press, 1990), 5–6. Though, as in other instances, the volume contains scant scholarly citations of Strauss—and none in Bloom's included essay on Rousseau—in the "Introduction" Bloom observes that nearly all the contributors to the volume are "students of, or students of students of, Leo Strauss. This great man reinterested us in America by teaching us how to read our country's political texts and demonstrating how wise they are."

21. "Leo Strauss," *G & D*, 235–36, 239.

22. Kojève, writing Strauss in April 1961 from Paris, describes Bloom as appearing less serious than Stanley Rosen. In the same paragraph he indicates that he sees Bloom rarely, at least partly because Bloom is busy on his translation of *The Republic*. This stay in France by Bloom appears to have followed, if not been caused by, the "serious break" between Bloom and Strauss "around 1960" which Dannhauser reports. Bloom had been studying with Kojève in Paris, by his own report, as early as 1953, and that is backdrop for appreciating how close the Strauss/Bloom relationship was in the period before the "break," for in 1956 Strauss wrote Kojève lamenting their loss of contact and naming Bloom as their present link. Bloom, continued Strauss to Kojève, "reminds me on proper occasions of our considerable disagreements as well as our more fundamental agreement." "The Strauss-Kojève Correspondence" in Leo Strauss, *On Tyranny*, eds. Victor Gourevitch and Michael Roth (New York: The Free Press, 1991), 305, 263–64; Werner Dannhauser, "Allan Bloom: A Reminiscence," in *Political Philosophy and the Human Soul*, eds. Michael Palmer and Thomas L. Pangle (Lanham, Maryland: Rowman & Littlefield, 1995), 5.

218   Walter Nicgorski

Some have speculated that the break grew from Strauss's disapproval of Bloom's indulgences and less than ascetic way of life. As one who had only two casual introductions to Allan Bloom and heard him lecture twice and, on the other hand, had much exposure and interaction with Leo Strauss in personal meetings and seminars (1961–66), I hesitate to traverse far into comparative analysis of dispositions and characters and prefer to rely essentially on what has been written by and about each. Clearly Bloom bares his soul more; his work has more confessional moments; his loves are open while Strauss is more guarded and impersonal. One cannot help but notice Bloom's greater emphasis on the erotic dimension of learning and philosophy; one senses a great appreciation for the simple liberation and exhilaration of learning and philosophy. At the same time Bloom's interests seem to run as much to literature and music as to philosophy. In *The Closing* (133), Bloom insists that students need to be "lovers" to be educated and (79) looks in them for "a passionate relationship" to art and thought. Perhaps Bloom signals his own disposition and consequent need when later in the same work (237) he praises Plato for both enchanting and disenchanting eros and notes that we need both. Writing of his distaste for participation in educational reform movements and obviously having the highest pleasures in mind, Bloom rejects for himself delayed "gratification now for the sake of unsure futures." A few years later he is found praising Strauss for the sober wisdom that brought Bloom himself and others to a new appreciation for the American political tradition. "Western Civilization" in *G & D*, 19; *Confronting . . .* , 6.

For claims that Bloom's interpretation of Plato is not that of Strauss in important respects and suggestions that Bloom's disposition and way of life may be entailed in these differences, see Gregory Bruce Smith, "Leo Strauss and the Straussians: An Anti-democratic Cult?" *PS* (June, 1997), 189 n. 13; Laurence Lampert, *Leo Strauss and Nietzsche* (Chicago: University of Chicago Press, 1996), 159 n. 23.

23. The most widely known of these writings were "The Crisis of Liberal Education" which initially appeared along with an essay of Strauss (see note 3 above) in *Higher Education and Modern Democracy*, 121–39, and has been reprinted in *G & D*, "The Democratization of the University" which initially appeared in 1971 in *How Democratic Is America?*, ed. Robert A. Goldwin (Chicago: Rand McNally, 1971), 109–36, and also has been reprinted in *G & D*, and "The Failure of the University," *Daedalus* 103/04 (1974), 58–66.

24. Dannhauser, "Allan Bloom: A Reminiscence," 5.

25. "What is Liberal Education?" in *Liberalism Ancient. . .* , 5.

26. Nasser Behnegar, "The Liberal Politics of Leo Strauss," in Palmer and Pangle, 265.

27. In *The Closing* (381), Bloom writes of *The Republic* as "*the* book on education" for himself "because it really explains to me what I experience as a man and a teacher, . . ." In his "Preface to the Second Edition" of *The Republic of Plato* (p. x), he writes of the *Émile* as the "greatest modern book on education." Also see his "Introduction" to *Émile, or On Education* (3–4), Michael Zuckert, "Two Cheers (At Least) for Allan Bloom," in Stone, 74; Dannhauser, "Allan Bloom: A Reminiscence," 2. Very early among his publications, Bloom is found singling out Plato and Rousseau as "poet-philosophers" most instructive for considering "the real problem of art." "Introduction" to Jean-Jacques Rousseau, *Politics and the Arts: Letter to M. D'Alembert On The Theatre* (Ithaca, New York: Cornell University Press, 1960), xxxiv. More on them as "philosopher-poets" is found in the *Émile* "Introduction" (21–22). Much later Bloom remarks that half of his last and posthumously published book is "a confrontation between the two greatest philosophical teachings about eros." *Love and Friendship* (New York: Simon and Schuster, 1993), 35. On Bloom's view of Rousseau's kinship to Plato, see *The Closing*, 169–70, 177; "Rousseau: The Turning Point," in *G & D*, 231–32.

28. "Liberal Education and Responsibility" in *Liberalism Ancient* . . . , 9. A fuller commentary on this passage is found in "Introduction," *Leo Strauss: Political Philosopher and Jewish Thinker* eds. Kenneth L. Deutsch & Walter Nicgorski (Lanham, Maryland: Rowman & Littlefield, 1994), 24–25.

29. "Leo Strauss," *G & D*, 236.

30. Essays reprinted in *The Rebirth of Classical Political Rationalism*, ed. Thomas L. Pangle (Chicago: University of Chicago Press, 1989).

31. Above, n. 3.

32. Behnegar, 251–52.

33. Courtney Leatherman, "10 Years After Bloom's Jeremiad, Scholars Weigh Its Significance," *The Chronicle of Higher Education*, 17 January 1997, A14–15.

34. *The Closing*, 288; "Preface," *G & D*, 9.

35. *The Closing*, 19.

36. *The Closing*, 20.

37. *The Closing*, 20–21, 343; "Western Civ" in *G & D*, 19–20.

38. *The Closing*, 252, 227–28.

39. *The Closing*, 227.

40. *The Closing*, 344. Also, with respect to the study of politics, see "The Study of Texts," in *G & D*, 297, 314. *The Closing* and Bloom's endorsement there and elsewhere of the Great Books approach stirred and contributed significantly to the "canon" debate that was particularly intense in the late 1980s and early 1990s. Bloom discussed his adversaries in this debate in "Western Civ," in *G & D*, especially 24–25.

41. "The Failure of the University," 60. On another occasion, still some years before *The Closing*, Bloom wrote, "He who has read one book well is in a position to read any book, while he for whom books are easy currency is rendered incapable of living fully with one." "The Study of Texts," in *G & D*, 309.

42. *The Closing*, 344.

43. *The Closing*, 343–45.

44. *The Closing*, 252, 249.

45. "The Failure of the University," 59; "The Study of Texts," in *G & D*, 314.

46. "Preface," in *G & D*, 9.

47. *The Closing*, 380–81; also, *G & D*, 346 and "Western Civ," in *G & D*, 19–20.

48. "Raymond Aron: The Last of the Liberals," in *G & D*, 265; *The Closing*, especially 251 ff.

49. *The Closing*, 288.

50. *The Closing*, 253.

51. "Leo Strauss," *G & D*, 240, 250 and "Preface"; *The Closing*, 267–68, 272–73, 310–12; *Love and Friendship*, 431–32.

· *14* ·

Joseph Cropsey: Modernity and the American Regime

Christopher A. Colmo

$\mathcal{J}$oseph Cropsey's inquiry into the American regime emphasizes the problematic locus of sovereignty within the regime. Where do we look for the American regime? Do we look to the rhetorical expression of our ideals in the Declaration of Independence and the Constitution? Or do the aspirations articulated in these authoritative documents—our "parchment regime"—depart so far from the reality of our lives as to belie the true character of those for whom they claim to speak? Surveying both the authoritative documents and life as it is lived in these United States, Cropsey sees "life, liberty, and the pursuit of happiness" embodied in the parchment regime, while family and property are the dominant elements of our lived experience. But far from being a disjunction, the legal regime and the lived regime cohere together in the thought of "proto-modernity, the classic modernity of Hobbes and Locke."[1]

Much in the regime of our country can be seen to have its roots in the liberalism of Thomas Hobbes, yet our regime does not embody Hobbes's notion of sovereignty. Hobbes's intention was to establish or restore political sovereignty, and therewith the rule of reason, in the face of the competing claims of revealed religion. In pursuit of this goal he advocated neither separation of powers nor separation of church and state.[2] His construction did, however, include a self-limitation of the sovereign in the name of political freedom. In Hobbes, the self-limitation of the sovereign can be seen to strengthen the sovereign's authority. In the United States, this self-limitation can be seen to undercut the very sovereignty Hobbes sought to create. The self-restriction of our official or Constitutional regime leaves unregulated or ungoverned an "extended regime" of religion, art, science, and private thought, along with its expression in the public domain, all of which "hover over and penetrate our way of life and help fix us in a mode of existence."[3] The phrase "extended regime" might, with equal justice, be applied to the authority of the Church in the form that Hobbes confronted it. Hobbes's concern, at the incep-

221

tion of modernity, and Cropsey's philosophic reflection on politics at the close of
the twentieth century are joined by the problem of sovereignty when the latter is
confronted by the competing claims of an "extended regime." Finding the roots of
liberalism in Hobbes, Cropsey finds there also a standard by which to judge of the
sovereignty of the American regime.

Hobbes's rehabilitation of sovereignty takes the form of a two-pronged
attack against the tradition he inherited, one line directed against Aristotle and
the other against the scriptural element of the tradition. Both critiques indict
the tradition for placing the responsibility for judgments of good and evil in the
hands of private men. "Hobbes's reaction against the scriptural element of the
tradition pervades his work, and is fundamental." Hobbes's reaction against
Aristotle, however, "if not less earnestly intended, yet loses some of its point upon
examination."[4]

Indeed, Hobbes's attempt to place sovereignty clearly in the hands of the
political authorities seems in significant ways to be a return to elements of the
polis that Aristotle endorsed by calling them natural. Hobbes argued for the clear
subordination of religious authority to secular authority or, in Cropsey's words,
for the "redintegration of 'church' and 'state.'" In order to restore the primacy of
civil over ecclesiastical authority, Hobbes of necessity argued for the hegemony
of natural reason.

> [T]he hegemony of natural reason is the theoretical condition for the hegemony
> of the civil sovereign. To this extent it is legitimate to be reminded of antiquity
> by the opening of modernity.[5]

When the clergy must speak on matters of faith, which are beyond reason, they do
so, nevertheless, as representatives of the sovereign and with a view to securing peace
and preservation, which are the sovereign's legitimate goals. Should a dispute arise,
as seems inevitable, as to what is spiritual and what temporal, the deciding voice is
stipulated by Hobbes in *De Cive*.

> But it is reason's inquisition, and pertains to *temporal right* to define what is spir-
> itual, and what temporal.[6]

Religion is a public, not a private, matter, and the voice of the civil sovereign is
the deciding voice. In opting for the hegemony of reason and the redintegration
of church and state in a civil society that bears some resemblance to the *polis*, the
modern Enlightenment looks like a recurrence to the profane Enlightenment of
antiquity.[7]

Of course, Hobbes does not see the unity of the commonwealth as natural in
the way that Aristotle does. Hobbes's construction is based on a description of the
state of nature from which follows the rational desideratum of the social contract
(a clear case of an ought derived from an is). For Hobbes, nature is without thought
or purpose. Cropsey draws to our attention the striking theological expression given

in *Leviathan* to Hobbes's non-teleological view of nature through the dictum "God has no Ends."[8] Cropsey manages to formulate this well-known situation in terms that are, nevertheless, arresting. Hobbes represents

> the proto-modern teaching that nature, far from abhorring a vacuum, is or approaches one. In important respects, nature is a moral void and rather an opportunity for the mind of man than a preceptor to it.[9]

Moral relativism is the political implication of Hobbes's state of nature. Changing his metaphor from void to flux, Cropsey does not flinch from drawing out the relevance of these reflections to the American regime. "[T]he principle incarnated unchangingly in the Constitution is a principle of moral flux."[10]

Hobbes's sovereign comes to light as an artificial mechanism for the imposition of conventional stability upon the flux of nature. In Freudian terms, one might say that the superego is the indispensable invention of the ego seeking refuge in civil society from the rampaging ids of self and others.[11] The absolute sovereign is the executor of absolute conventionality arising from both the necessity and the opportunity created by the moral indifference of nature. Hobbes builds, on a foundation of relativism, a structure of sovereignty limited by constitutional guarantees and conducive to personal freedom.[12]

In keeping with the thought that "politics originates nothing," Cropsey marshals the evidence for treating Hobbes as the source of the main conventions of modern liberalism.[13] It is my intention, not to recapitulate that evidence in detail, but to give only so much as to indicate the meaning of each of its elements. Hobbes's relativism follows from his well-known assertions to the effect that good and evil are merely names "that signify appetites and aversions," the diversity of which among different men is not susceptible to ordering or ranking. With respect to constitutional guarantees, Cropsey points to Hobbes's insistence upon such fundamentals of liberalism as the right against self-incrimination, the presumption of innocence before the law, the rule against unusual punishment, and the denial of legality to prohibitions enacted *ex post facto*. Finally, the sphere of personal freedom, thus also of contract and economic activity generally, extends to all that the sovereign does not expressly forbid.[14]

Hobbes sees his defense of convention as a departure from Aristotle's too-great confidence in nature. Cropsey is not ultimately persuaded by Hobbes's tendency to regard pagan antiquity as "trusting nature to civilize man."[15] The Enlightenment represented by Hobbes lacked that trust, but for Cropsey's purposes it is not enough to describe modernity alone as the Enlightenment. He recognizes both a Socratic Enlightenment and a modern Enlightenment.

> By an Enlightenment I mean a radical ingathering, scrutiny, revision and reorganization of the moral and intellectual patrimony, with the specific intention of bringing mankind closer to a life dominated by the truth of man's positive relation to reason.[16]

Man's positive relation to reason does not culminate in simple trust in nature. To Cropsey, "Socrates appears as a man of the middle," one "who provided the most moderate and at the same time the most elevating resolution of the question, How is man situated in the Whole."[17] But Socrates' moderation does not equate with the political passivity of man with respect to nature; rather, he makes "vast concessions to the indispensability of political contrivances, institutions that not only do not flow from nature but violate it."[18]

The nature of nature requires that moderation be blended with spiritedness, both on the level of philosophy and of politics.[19] Philosophy is not wisdom. Something remains unknown, and the natural human fear of the unknown can only be balanced by courage. Cropsey raises the question, "Is not courage the characteristic philosophic virtue, and spiritedness the indispensable philosophic temper, considering that something about our future, on earth and wherever else, is and must necessarily be dark?"[20] He answers his own question many pages later.

> This prepares us to learn from the *Apology* that the philosophic life has as its end a wisdom desired above all other good things, pursued in full acceptance that the quest must remain unconsummated and that therefore the necessary condition of the best life is a certain highheartedness, the spiritedness of patience, the *thumos* that encompasses courage and comports with the submissiveness or acceptance fostered on the political plane by the complete statesman.[21]

Spiritedness is a necessary part, or at any rate a "condition," of the way of life to which knowledge of one's own ignorance is essential.

Philosophy and politics exist on "disparate planes,"[22] but that spiritedness is a necessary element of the political is at least as obvious as its admixture in the philosophic. Cropsey's account of Plato's *Statesman* contains the following summary.

> As the portrait of the human condition has taken shape, it shows us abandoned by the god, implanted in an inhospitable nature, left to our own resources, and now discovering that we ourselves, as rulers and as ruled, are an obstacle to our happy preservation.[23]

This portrait of the human condition derives from a dialogue in which the dominant interlocutor is not Socrates but the Eleatic Stranger. Plato never speaks in his own name. Cropsey removes the ambiguity this creates, if not from the dialogue then at any rate from his account of the dialogue, when he adds, "Plato begins with a view of a state of nature rife with danger and hostility, and argues to an unrivaled monarch with authority over the orthodoxy of the subjects."[24] Hobbes might object to this interpretation of Plato primarily on the grounds that it very much diminishes the originality of Hobbes himself. Nor would Hobbes find much to argue with in the content of the common ground Cropsey elsewhere implies between Socrates and Protagoras.

It would be supreme folly to conclude that if a transcendental basis for virtue has not been certified by the universe, a valid immanent one is unavailable. If living and commodious living and the pursuit of wisdom in peace depend on the flourishing of cities, why disparage as merely conventional the orders and rules that nourish the polities?[25]

Cropsey does not see the necessity of what is currently called "foundationalism" to a healthy political life, nor does he find this necessity in Plato. How then are we to distinguish between Plato and Hobbes?

Let us put the question in a more manageable form. How are we to distinguish the spiritedness of the ancients in opposition to indifferent or malign nature from the spirited modern opposition to the same thing? Cropsey gives at least one answer to this question in a passage that describes without naming what the ancients understood by magnanimity and what Aristotle understood as one of the peaks of the moral virtues.[26] The paragraph deserves to be quoted in its entirety.

The spirited desire of man for self-dependence, or emancipation from nature, reaches beyond calculation in the interest of self-preservation. It carries him up to a morality higher than the social virtues, to morality which is the noble simulation of independence by the dependent, of considerate indifference to the things loved and the things hated, the things desired and feared. It is an expression of man's natural preference for being, i.e. being himself, and his natural aversion to non-being; and it takes the form of a uniquely human resistance against everything natural or non-human that man shares with the rest of the whole. Moral virtue thus presents itself as a fortifying of human nature, a prideful assertion against the external natural order.[27]

The morality of the ancients can be distinguished from that of the moderns by the greater role assigned to magnanimity by the former, a virtue the moderns saw as sustaining a dangerous element of vanity on a foundation of poetry.[28]

Speaking of Socrates, Cropsey says that he was "distinguished . . . from his modern successors by his having kept man's nobility always in sight as his star and compass."[29] Does nobility here refer to man's moral nobility, encompassing magnanimity, or to the nobility of philosophy? Far from being simply the same, these two seem to exist in tension as rival forms of human freedom, a tension not unrelated to the tension between philosophy and poetry. Is it possible to banish the highheartedness of magnanimity from political life without at the same time banishing the highheartedness that is the condition for philosophy? It is an open question, though not among the moderns, who allow the deeds of the magnanimous man and the speeches concerning the philosopher-king to atrophy simultaneously.

Whether or not they remain joined of necessity, the nobility of classical political philosophy was not separated from the thought that philosophy is the best way of life. As Cropsey notes, the highheartedness of philosophy is inseparably connected to the philosopher's knowledge of his own ignorance. The political problem arising from the Socratic view of philosophy as the best way of life stems directly from the ineradicable element of doubt or skepticism involved in that way of life and the ineradicable element of closure or "ethnocentrism" involved in political life.[30] Every political community is a particular political community. A skeptical sovereign might be an unsteady sovereign, instilling doubt and uncertainty, not peace and prosperity, in his unhappy subjects. The problem is exacerbated if the skeptical sovereign is a democratic sovereign subject to the influence of demagogues.[31] A solution might be found if political wisdom could be made to replace philosophic ambiguity. In contrast to the intellectual modesty of the Socratic Enlightenment, Cropsey speaks of the "ideological characteristic of modern thought," by which he means "the wish to establish political life directly upon the whole truth about the whole," a wish he sees as "nearly kin to the aspirations of the Enlightenment."[32] Cropsey ascribes this wish to Hobbes, but he makes it quite plain that Hobbes did not, and knew that he did not, possess the whole truth about the whole. Nor did Hobbes think that he could narrow the gulf between philosopher and non-philosopher by causing the truth that he did know to become the cultural property of all.[33] The same can be said for Descartes and other figures of the Enlightenment.[34] Hobbes's "wish" was motivated by his urgent need to compete with a revelation that did in fact claim to have the whole truth about the whole. His solution was to restore secular sovereignty on a foundation of secular science, whose apparent claim to wisdom far exceeded that of philosophy proper.[35] Hobbes's pervasive and "fundamental" conflict with human claims to supernatural wisdom leads him to exaggerate the encouragement Aristotle gives to private judgments of right and wrong.[36] The same conflict also leads Hobbes publicly to exaggerate, in open contrast with philosophic antiquity, his own claim to wisdom.

The "ideological character" of modern thought is also at issue when Cropsey describes Descartes' project "to achieve certainty of knowledge for the good of man." After reminding us that certainty does not differ from the removal of doubt, Cropsey goes on to say:

> The modern Enlightenment can claim to have found the method for removing doubt about the natural whole by redrawing its boundaries to exclude the dubitable; but it did not, nor does it think it did, thereby render the whole of our universal setting exhaustible by science: modernity repeats in its own mode the wisdom of Socrates, which was to know that he did not know.[37]

To put it somewhat differently, from Cropsey's point of view, proto-modernity is still philosophy.[38]

At one point, Cropsey suggests that we might measure the distance between Hobbes and the ancients by reflecting on how far the former is from agreeing with the ancient thought that "to be is to be intelligible."[39] For the moderns, not the intelligibility of being but the ambiguity of nature offers the opportunity for the mind of man to create something that resembles being.

The firm structure made by man can rest only upon the flux, if not void, with which nature provides us as the human opportunity, the occasion that enables men to achieve greatness.[40]

The flux of nature is an opportunity in that it allows for the rational redirection of the efforts of most men towards goals that are best for them because most in keeping with their capacities. Absolute sovereignty in the political realm requires the separation of politics from the Socratic philosophy that understood itself as contemplative to the extent that it understood the world in the fullest sense as being beyond man's power to change or even to completely understand. Is this separation made possible by a new understanding of nature in which nothing is beyond man's power, or is it made possible merely by redefining the political so as to exclude what cannot be mastered? Cropsey suggests the latter.

The self-limiting character of Hobbes's absolute sovereign might be interpreted as illustrating this point. Sovereignty as Hobbes presents it has its roots in man's natural liberty, but Hobbes is ever mindful that the prudent sovereign benefits from the appearance of freedom on the part of his subjects. In Hobbes's *Dialogue between a Philosopher and a Student of the Common Laws of England*, the Philosopher says that it concerns kings "in their own interest to make such Laws as the people can endure, and may keep them without impatience, and live in strength and courage to defend their King and Countrey, against their potent neighbours."[41] The paradoxical demand that the king rule in the interest of his subjects is here replaced by the more manageable problem of showing the king his own true interests. The problem is solved by redefining it.

The scope of personal freedom is enlarged and the legitimate function of the sovereign circumscribed by the way in which Hobbes grounds both in natural liberty. "[S]ince the construction is strictly limited in its aim to the natural or primary end of preservation, it may not legitimately prescribe obligations that reach to edification or beyond."[42] In an essay that brings Hobbes to bear directly on the theme of "the United States as regime," Cropsey succinctly expresses the source of the restrictions on sovereignty that give rise to constitutional guarantees and personal freedoms.

> Inseparable from [Hobbes's formulations of natural rights and the state of nature] is Hobbes' reservation to men of the right to preserve life, and their natural freedom to seek the means thereto, as well as the large measure of private discretion that belongs to men as they deliberate on the ends of their actions and seek their satisfaction, if not their contentment, in life.[43]

While the acts of the prudent sovereign will appear as much as possible to be for the good of his subjects, that good is not merely the common good; it contains a large element of private happiness dependent upon the secure acquisition of property.

Sovereignty for Hobbes has its roots in natural liberty. The character of modern political liberty can be seen in the difference between Aristotle and Hobbes over the legitimate basis and scope of privacy or individualism. In defense of personal freedom, Hobbes achieves "a perfect reversal of the ancient political formula that the citizen is free to do only what the law expressly permits."[44] For Hobbes, the citizen—any citizen—is free in all things in which the sovereign has promulgated no rule. For Aristotle, the legitimate claim of the individual against the city, his sovereign, was rooted in philosophy understood as the possibility of knowledge that transcends the horizon of any one political community. Philosophy itself was thought to be well beyond the plausible aspirations of the ordinary citizen. By contrast, the individualism of proto-modernity is rooted not in the rare qualities of mind and heart that would allow a man to transcend the city but in the universal inability to transcend our own bodies and our concern with our own preservation. Men are "created equal" by modernity itself, which has decided to exclude from political consideration the only fact that would render men unequal in a way relevant to ruling and being ruled.[45] Hobbes restores sovereignty through an appeal to natural reason, but in a way that rejects reason as a ground for discriminating among men. In Cropsey's formulation, "reason is the best, but the life of reason is not the best life."[46]

Cropsey is confident that proto-modernity is original, at least in this: "it was possessed by a spasm of optimism for the fate of man for which there is no profane precedent."[47] This "spasm of optimism" led to "the political liberation that is one of the jewels in the crown of modernity."[48] Whatever the nature of this liberation, it does not consist in the truths of philosophy becoming the cultural property of the vast majority of men. In Cropsey's account, the Enlightenment takes shape as a deliberate, i.e., self-conscious, project for the separation of the multitude of men from the highest aspirations of man simply. The absolute sovereignty and absolute certainty that belong to the modern political project do not contaminate the philosophic purity of proto-modernity. Politically, however, the Enlightenment is a project to disseminate modernity's horizon as if it were the whole truth about the whole. Confined within its own political horizon, modernity lacks the element of skepticism that would allow it "to consider all possible answers to all possible questions." In other words, the ideological character of modern political philosophy leads ultimately, if not inevitably, to the politicization of thought itself and, hence, to "the death of philosophy."[49] Whether such a project originated in a manic high (Cropsey's "spasm of optimism") or a depressive low is an open question. Cropsey nowhere comments on Rousseau's observation that there is no enslavement so complete as that which preserves the forms of freedom.[50] In comparison with classical political philosophy, liberalism obviously accentuates the forms of freedom. Whether it is, in substance, a project for political liberation or for domestic captivity might ultimately depend on the truth or falsity of Rousseau's judgment and its applicability to the political order he helped to create. Plato might have regarded such a project as unnecessary in one sense and unnatural in another. As to the first point, every city is a cave of some sort, with little need for the philosopher to actively contribute to the narrowing of its horizon.

Concerning the second point, what is in a way unnatural about the liberal horizon is its stultifying aspect. Cropsey notes "the absence of any exaltation, vivacity, or high-heartedness," the lack of which he sees as one of the continuing sources of modernity's dissatisfaction with itself.[51] Adam Smith, for example, certainly falls within the mainstream of classical liberalism, but his works are not without expressions of concern for the enervating effects of division of labor upon the laborers who must also be citizens. In Cropsey's view, however, Smith overestimates the extent to which the narrowness and pettiness of economic life under the capitalist dispensation deprive men of their spiritedness.

> The institutionalization of acquisitiveness does seem to have fostered a self-assertiveness, aggressiveness, or simple egotism that comports particularly well with egalitarianism, and that might be called the variety of spiritedness peculiar to liberal society.[52]

From the classical point of view, judged, that is, by the standard of magnanimity, the spiritedness of the acquisitive democrat is at fault not so much for its selfishness as for its smallness, lack of dignity, or failure of true self-respect. But from the modern point of view, the more pressing problem for liberal society, precisely because it is compatible with simple egotism, is the question how spiritedness is to be reconciled with sociality.

When Cropsey reflects on "the spirited wells of modernity,"[53] his gaze falls not only on the hardening or toughening that Machiavelli tried to instill in men or on Hobbes's defense of sovereign political authority, but also, and in a crucial way, on Rousseau's portrait of Emile. Emile is educated so as to combine in one human being a self-dependent hardihood or virility and a sociality based on compassion sustained within the monogamous family. Division of labor is replaced by the versatility to which Emile is educated. Here, then, is a solution to the problem of combining spiritedness and sociality within liberal society. To the question "Is it possible?" Cropsey answers with a reservation: "This scheme would come to ruin among passionate men." Whether the scheme is desirable probably depends on whether one thinks that self-dependence in the form manifested by Emile has not made too many concessions to the petty and the narrow, which were Adam Smith's original concern.[54]

The problem of freedom as described by Hobbes is not limited to the bourgeois hedonism it promotes. "The whole truth about the whole" upon which Hobbes and others built is, of course, the truth of modern science. On this view, man is part of the mechanism of nature. As we have seen, the situation of man within nature devoid of reason or purpose creates the opportunity for the human conquest of nature. But the project for the conquest of nature, which includes man within it, "came to be seen as problematic for the hope of man's himself remaining unmastered by nature." Man's situation within nature reveals itself as "a state of servitude that is excruciating, demoralizing, and at last intolerable." Neither Spinoza "nor

230 Christopher A. Colmo

Rousseau, Kant or Hegel contemplated renouncing the natural science of Newton or Bacon."[55] The result as Cropsey sees it is that each modern thinker has reacted to the problem of human freedom within the scope of the horizon that is itself the source of the problem. The tendency, exemplified by Marx, has been to provide for ever greater freedom on the basis of an ever greater conquest of nature.

> Satiety through technology will be the Paradise Regained in which man will eat of the fruit of the tree of science, expel want, and dwell in the house of concord forever, in the brotherhood of man without the fatherhood of God.[56]

The modern response to the discontents of modernity has been to radicalize its own goal on the assumption "that the cure for a disorder is an intensified application of the cause that brought it on."[57]

We have seen above that for Cropsey, Socrates was "a man of the middle." This was so because the Socratic Enlightenment consisted in moderating much that was extreme or one-sided in pre-Socratic thought.

> Socratism appears as a turning point in Greek and thus in all thought, as the cautious deradicalization of its extremes of spiritualism, cultism, and metaphysical dogmatism, accomplished through a careful sifting of the best resources available.[58]

The Socratic Enlightenment is an "Enlightenment of prudent expectations."[59] This view of the Socratic Enlightenment exposes an important contrast with the modern Enlightenment.

> There is reason to think that the history of philosophy in the modern age has been a record of the radicalization or intensification of the primary conceptions, a course opposite to that which came to a climactic point with the philosophizing of Socrates.[60]

If Cropsey finds many of the harsh truths of modernity to have impinged forcefully upon the thought of antiquity,[61] and if the purity of the ancient philosophic quest is yet visible to him in those moderns who lower their standards in pursuit of a more stable political order, there remains, nevertheless, as in the passage above, a clearly articulable difference between ancients and moderns.

The consequence for the American regime of the self-intensification of modernity is "that the concrete liberalism of our time does not see itself as bound to a doctrine of irresistible sovereignty."[62] The self-limitation of the liberal regime combined with the natural impetus of each individual to exercise his liberty to the fullest undercuts the very sovereignty which, according to Hobbes, makes possible the union of liberty with safety and prosperity. The drive for ever greater political freedom for the individual—necessarily at the expense of the scope of sovereignty— accelerates the natural impetus just mentioned. In a thought with obvious consequences for the American regime, Cropsey raises the question whether a regime that so limits its sovereignty as to endanger its own existence deserves to be called a regime. Is not an "unambiguous animus to persist in existence" a "minimum ingredient of the goodness of anything"?[63] Political morality must not be so construed as to render sovereignty impossible.

As a consequence of the self-limitation of our regime "in the name of freedom," little scope is given to the regulation of religion, art, music, thought, and science. This observation has fertile implications for Cropsey's view that much that shapes or controls our way of life is placed beyond the reach of the formal structures of sovereignty. In this way, the self-criticism and self-dissatisfaction of modernity, some vulgar but some belonging to the highest philosophic thought, becomes part of our "extended regime." This "extended regime" is rendered "ungovernable" for our regime in the narrow sense.[64] The "extended regime," or, as we more often say, the open society, threatens sovereignty. But the ideology of the open society creates, as we have seen, merely a new type of closed society. Where then is the threat to sovereignty? Do the two parts of Cropsey's argument contradict each other? Or does Cropsey mean to say that modernity has the worst of two worlds? It is a closed society because every society is a closed society; it is deprived of the benefit most societies derive from their closed horizon because its belief in its own openness deprives it of the self-knowledge that would allow it to clearly affirm its own principle. Blind to its own horizon, it is blind to the principle of its own preservation.[65]

The fact that we have an extended regime, "alien to the regime but unrepressed by the regime," impelled by self-dissatisfaction to unremitting criticism of the regime, is sufficient to make the United States both "the microcosm of modernity" and "an arena in which modernity is working itself out."[66] That it is working itself out through the intensification of the disorders to which it is prone is not a hopeful prospect. One might take some comfort from "a national decision to adhere to moderate proto-modernity," but the utility of this policy will depend upon the existence of a sovereign steadfast in its execution.[67]

NOTES

1. "Introduction: The United States as Regime and the Sources of the American Way of Life" in Joseph Cropsey, *Political Philosophy and the Issues of Politics* (Chicago: University of Chicago Press, 1977), 5. See the review by Timothy Fuller in *American Political Science Review* (1979) 73: 846–47, as well as Gregory Bruce Smith, "On Cropsey's World: Joseph Cropsey and the Tradition of Political Philosophy," *Review of Politics* (Spring 1998).

2. On separation of powers, see the interesting formula attributed to Cropsey in Murray Dry, "The Separation of Powers and Representative Government," *The Political Science Reviewer* (Fall 1973) 3:44.

3. Cropsey, *Issues*, 2; see also Joseph Cropsey, "The End of History in the Open-ended Age? The Life Expectancy of Self-evident Truth" in A. M. Melzer, J. Weinberger, M. R.

Zinman, eds., *History and the Idea of Progress* (Ithaca and London: Cornell University Press, 1995), 105.

4. "Hobbes and the Transition to Modernity" in Cropsey, *Issues*, 291–314, at 307 (first published in Joseph Cropsey, ed., *Ancients and Moderns: Essays on the Tradition of Political Philosophy in Honor of Leo Strauss* [New York: Basic Books, 1964]), as well as Joseph Cropsey, "On Ancients and Moderns," *Interpretation* (1990) 18/1: 31–51, at 47–8. A German version of this essay appears as "Ueber die Alten und die Modernen" in Heinrich Meier, ed., *Zur Diagnose der Moderne* (Munich and Zurich: Piper, 1990).

5. Cropsey, *Issues*, 295.

6. Quoted in Cropsey, *Issues*, 308.

7. Cropsey, *Issues*, 295 and 308: cf. Aristotle, *Nicomachean Ethics* 1145a11–12.

8. Cropsey, *Issues*, 297.

9. "Modernization: United States Policy and the Meaning of Modernity" in Cropsey, *Issues*, 167.

10. Cropsey, *Issues*, 171.

11. Cf. Joseph Cropsey, "Radicalism" in *Issues*, 140–54, at 147–48.

12. Cropsey, "Liberalism, Nature and Convention," *The Independent Journal of Philosophy* (1983) 4: 21–7, at 21, and Joseph Cropsey, "Liberalism, Self-Abnegation and Self-Assertion" in Timothy Fuller, ed., *The Prospects of Liberalism* (Colorado Springs: Colorado College Studies, No. 20, 1984), 32–41.

13. Cropsey, *Issues*, 15. See also Joseph Cropsey, "Political Life and a Natural Order" in *Issues*, 221–30, at 229: "The deepest current of action is the production of the ground of human life by human thought."

14. Cropsey, "Liberalism, Nature and Convention," 21.

15. Cropsey, "Ancients and Moderns," 48.

16. Cropsey, "Ancients and Moderns," 45.

17. Cropsey, "Ancients and Moderns," 40, 45. See also Joseph Cropsey, "The Whole as Setting for Man: On Plato's *Timaeus*," *Interpretation* (1990) 17/2: 165–91.

18. Cropsey, "Ancients and Moderns," 37, and "Political Life and a Natural Order" in Cropsey, *Issues*, 226–27.

19. Spiritedness is the theme of a *Festschrift* in honor of Joseph Cropsey. See Catherine H. Zuckert, ed., *Understanding the Political Spirit* (New Haven and London: Yale University Press, 1988).

20. Joseph Cropsey, *Plato's World: Man's Place in the Cosmos* (Chicago: University of Chicago Press, 1995), 26. Cropsey's other writings on Plato include "Plato's *Phaedrus* and Plato's *Socrates*" in *Issues*, 231–51, and "On Pleasure and the Human Good: Plato's *Philebus*," *Interpretation* (Winter 1988–89) 16/2: 167–92.

21. Cropsey, *Plato's World*, 150. Cf. Leo Strauss, *The City and Man* (Chicago: Rand McNally, 1964), 110–11: ". . . while there is a philosophic eros, there is no philosophic indignation, desire for victory, or anger. (Consider [*Republic*] 536b8–c7)." If this is the full range of spiritedness, then Strauss does not allow of a philosophic spiritedness. Cropsey does. If we take Socrates' deeds as being more telling than his words, then the passage cited by Strauss tells in Cropsey's favor. Does the "endurance" of *Republic* 390d point to a kind of philosophic spiritedness?

22. Cropsey, *Plato's World*, 150.

23. Cropsey, *Plato's World*, 134.

24. Cropsey, *Plato's World*, 143–44.

25. Cropsey, *Plato's World*, 25.

26. For explicit reference to magnanimity, see Joseph Cropsey, "Toward Reflection on Property and the Family" in *Issues*, 207–17, at 216.

27. Joseph Cropsey, "Political Life and a Natural Order" in *Issues*, 221–30, at 226.

28. Or what "could be called a sham." Cropsey, *Issues*, 226.

29. Cropsey, "Ancients and Moderns," 45.

30. Cropsey, "Ancients and Moderns," 42, 45, and *Issues*, 170, where Cropsey speaks of "rational 'ethnocentrism'."

31. Consider Joseph Cropsey, "On Situation Ethics," *Perspective* (Winter 1967) 3/1: 8–10 (Gambier, Ohio: Kenyon College), especially toward the end.

32. Cropsey, *Issues*, 312.

33. Cropsey, *Issues*, 304.

34. Cropsey, "Ancients and Moderns," 49, and Joseph Cropsey, "Religion, the Constitution, and the Enlightenment" in Timothy Fuller, ed., *Understanding the United States Constitution, 1787–1987* (Colorado Springs: Colorado College Studies, No. 24, 1988), 25–35, at 33.

35. Cropsey, *Issues*, 312–13; see C. Colmo, "Reason and Revelation in the Thought of Leo Strauss," *Interpretation* (Fall 1990) 18/1: 152–3.

36. See note 4 above.

37. Cropsey, "Ancients and Moderns," 49. Recognition of the "wisdom of Socrates" is evident in Cropsey's skepticism concerning the alleged end of history. History in the fullest sense cannot end until all of the questions of philosophy have been answered, but this "whole truth about the whole" is not available to us. Cropsey, "The End of History," 101. On the relation between "Platonic Enlightenment" and the end of history, see Cropsey, *Plato's World*, 144.

38. Cropsey, "Ancients and Moderns," 31.

39. Cropsey, *Issues*, 302. This thought needs to be interpreted in a way compatible with the very large role that *pi*, "the symbol of the irrational in the universe," plays in Cropsey's interpretation of Plato. See *Plato's World*, 25. Things irrational or incommensurable are, nevertheless, "doubtless subject to ranking and comparison." *Plato's World*, 111.

40. Cropsey, *Issues*, 171.

41. Thomas Hobbes, *A Dialogue between a Philosopher and a Student of the Common Laws of England*, ed., with an "Introduction," by Joseph Cropsey (Chicago: University of Chicago Press, 1971), 166; also, 47.

42. Cropsey, "Liberalism, Nature and Convention," 22.

43. Cropsey, *Issues*, 6.

44. Cropsey, "Liberalism, Nature and Convention," 21.

45. Cropsey, *Issues*, 303–4.

46. Cropsey, *Issues*, 302. See also, Joseph Cropsey, "On the Mutual Compatibility of Democracy and Marxian Socialism," *Social Philosophy and Policy* (Spring 1986) 3/2: 4–18.

47. Cropsey, "Ancients and Moderns," 49.

48. Cropsey, "Ancients and Moderns," 51.

49. Cropsey, *Issues*, 168.

50. Rousseau, *Emile*, tr. A. Bloom (New York: Basic Books, 1979), 120.

51. Cropsey, *Issues*, 8.

52. Cropsey, *Issues*, 212–13. Cropsey's writings on Adam Smith include "'Capitalist' Liberalism" and "The Invisible Hand: Moral and Political Considerations" in *Issues*, 53–75 and 76–89; *Polity and Economy: An Interpretation of the Principles of Adam Smith* (The Hague:

234 Christopher A. Colmo

Martinus Nijhoff, 1957); "Smith, Adam" in *Encyclopedia Americana* (1994), 25: 53–4; and "Wealth of Nations, The" in *Encyclopedia Americana*, 28: 526–27.

53. Cropsey, *Issues*, 15.

54. Cropsey, *Issues*, 213–17, as well as Joseph Cropsey, "The Human Vision of Rousseau: Reflections on *Emile*" in *Issues*, 315–29.

55. Cropsey, "Liberalism, Nature and Convention," 23–4. On the relation between political philosophy and natural science, see the crucial distinctions drawn in Joseph Cropsey, "Reply to Rothman," *American Political Science Review* (June 1962) 56/2: 353–59, at 358.

56. "Conservatism and Liberalism" in Cropsey, *Issues*, 128.

57. Cropsey, *Issues*, 166; see also *Issues*, 153. Cf. Dewey's dictum, ". . . the cure for the ailments of democracy is more democracy," quoted in Leo Strauss and Joseph Cropsey, eds., *History of Political Philosophy*, 3rd ed. (Chicago: University of Chicago Press, 1987), 867. For a brief comment on Dewey, see Joseph Cropsey, "Commentary on 'Revolutions and Copernican Revolutions'" in N. H. Steneck, ed., *Science and Society* (Ann Arbor: University of Michigan Press, 1975), 103–7.

58. Joseph Cropsey, "The Dramatic End of Plato's Socrates," *Interpretation* (1987) 14/2: 155–75, at 174.

59. Cropsey, *Plato's World*, 159.

60. Joseph Cropsey, "The Dramatic End of Plato's Socrates," 174–75. Cropsey concludes his essay with the observation that the decline of society has been compatible with theoretical Enlightenment in both its ancient and modern forms, a discovery that can be cheering only to those "singularly devoted to truth."

61. For example, Joseph Cropsey, "Justice and Friendship in the *Nicomachean Ethics*" in *Issues*, 252–73, at 258.

62. Cropsey, "Liberalism, Nature and Convention," 22.

63. "Political Morality and Liberalism" in Cropsey, *Issues*, 131–39, at 139. See also Cropsey, "The End of History," 115.

64. Cropsey, *Issues*, 2–3, 12; "The End of History," 105–7.

65. Joseph Cropsey, "Activity, Philosophy and the Open Society" in George W. Carey, ed., *Order, Freedom, and the Polity* (Boston: University Press of America, 1986), 149–60. Cf. Cropsey, "Strauss, Leo" in David Sills, ed., *International Encyclopedia of the Social Sciences (Biographical Supplement)* (New York: Free Press, 1979), vol. 18, 746–50, at 747. Of Strauss, Cropsey writes,

> Generally thought of as a political conservative, he feared for a liberalism that he saw as threatened with confusion by its own theory at a time when its survival demanded a capacity to call good and bad by their names and to act accordingly with conviction.

66. Cropsey, *Issues*, 7, 13.

67. Cropsey, *Issues*, 166.

· *15* ·

Refinding the Founding: Martin Diamond, Leo Strauss, and the American Regime

Michael P. Zuckert

$\mathcal{M}$artin Diamond was one of the first students of Leo Strauss to turn in a sustained and fruitful way to the study of the American regime. By any standard, Diamond's body of work must also be judged among the most significant produced on America by any of Strauss's students: He contributed in a signal way to the reorientation of the study of the American founding that began in the 1960s, and his work on *The Federalist* as a text and the founders' theories on federalism and democracy are major accomplishments. Probably none of Strauss's students has had such a widespread influence as Diamond did. As Charles Kesler said, Diamond's well-known interpretation of *Federalist* 10 has "over the course of the past few decades come to prevail in most sections of the academy, and has molded several generations of students who have gone on to employ it, as citizens and as scholars, in the making and analysis of American public policy."[1] That judgment, strong as it is, was recently endorsed by both parties to a heated debate in the journals over the merits of Diamond's reading of *The Federalist*, and was vindicated by the claims for Diamond's work made by such well-known public intellectuals as George Will, Jeane Kirkpatrick, and William Bennett.[2] The former Drug Czar, for example, attested that "Martin Diamond explained the thinking of the founders to a generation of students. Part of that generation—myself included—took these lessons into government." Senator Patrick Moynihan went even further: "Martin Diamond almost single-handedly established the relevance of the thought and doings of the Founding Fathers for his generation."[3]

Diamond accomplished so much in a remarkably brief time—his first and perhaps most influential essay, "Democracy and *The Federalist*," appeared in 1959 and he died, all untimely, a scant eighteen years later. Moreover, he never wrote a book, but instead published a series of essays that together make up but one book-sized statement; in addition, he co-authored a textbook on American politics. In the case of the latter, Diamond's contribution was sufficiently significant that it has been

235

reprinted separately and remains in print more than thirty years after the text initially appeared—a most unusual fate for a segment of a textbook.

Despite the brevity of his career and the relative paucity of his writings Diamond had the impact he did in part because of the intensely focused character of his work. Unlike many other of the "first generation" students of Strauss, Diamond had almost only one topic—the founding, in particular *The Federalist*, and even more in particular, the Madisonian contribution to both. He wrote about his subject in a catholic and wide-ranging way, but for the most part he stuck with his topic.

Despite the brevity and the focus, Diamond's career shows three fairly distinct phases, marked by some relatively important shifts of view. Starting with his 1959 essay and running through the publication of his textbook in 1966, Diamond published a series of essays laying out the main themes of his study of the founding.[4] For several years thereafter he wrote little and when he returned to print he strayed from his chosen specialty for the one and only time in his professional career. Between 1970 and 1971 he wrote a series of essays focusing not on the substance of the American political order, but on the nature of political studies and political education.[5] In 1973 he returned to the substantive matters that had occupied him earlier and in a series of important essays restated, modified, and deepened his earlier positions.[6] A sign of the rapid recognition Diamond's work was receiving is the fact that many of the essays of this period are lectures or statements for symposia where Diamond had in effect been assigned a topic by an event coordinator or editor or, in one case, by a congressional committee.

Although my focus here is not on "Diamond's development," it is worth a moment to reflect on Diamond's three periods. Although his work has remarkable power to stand out from the time at which he produced it, nevertheless, in retrospect, one can discern some clear historical connections. The hiatus in his substantive work coincides with the eruption onto the American scene of the protests of the late 1960s, of the New Left, and of the ever weirder circuses of political theories that o'ertopped one another year after year. These protests and new theories challenged both the American order and Diamond's understanding thereof, and it is tempting to view his hiatus years as devoted to thinking through the new situation. His first new writings after the hiatus—on the nature of political studies and education—show the signs of an effort to become more self-conscious about what he had been doing in his previous studies, and about what political scientists ought to be doing. His first new substantive essay, a 1973 piece on "The Utopian Grounds for Pessimism and the Reasonable Grounds for Optimism" addresses explicitly the utopian hopes for the future and the immoderate criticisms of the present launched by the New Left. Then, in the writings of his third period he also shifted emphasis a fair amount, in part at least in response to the challenges posed by the extreme egalitarianism and negativity toward America by the New Left. For example, where he had earlier been unfriendly to federalism, he warmed to it substantially in the 1970s; where he had been ambivalent about "the new science of politics" he found at the heart of *The Federalist* he became a much more wholehearted supporter.

Diamond's thought evolved, then, in part in response to political events and the challenge of new modes of political thought. Even more significantly, however, Diamond was engaged in a great grappling with the thought of Leo Strauss himself. We may understand his three periods as stages in his coming to terms with Strauss; Strauss posed to Diamond, as he did to others of his students, some difficult, even harsh, puzzles and dilemmas, which Diamond worked through in a manner that proved quite different from that taken by other first generation students of Strauss. In Diamond's first period he took three central things from Strauss: 1) his subject matter—the American regime, and especially the American founding; 2) his methodology—the focus on the political thought of the founding generation; and 3) his particular approach to that material—via the notion of "the new science of politics," a form of Strauss's important distinction between ancient and modern political philosophy.

His second, or more methodological phase, is the period when Diamond tracked Strauss's work most closely, recapitulating many of his teacher's views on matters like the inseparability of facts and values, and the necessity for political education of a certain sort in modern mass democracies.

Diamond's third period is in some ways the most interesting of the three, however, for here he struggled most strenuously with the problem of reconciling his two loves—Leo Strauss and James Madison. They needed reconciling because Diamond saw Madison (and the Americans more broadly) as practitioners of "the new science of politics," i.e., of modern political philosophy, which, according to Strauss, was not only inferior to ancient political philosophy, but was also unable to withstand the pummeling of later versions of modern philosophy, degenerating ultimately into relativism, nihilism, and perhaps worst of all, modern social science. Although Strauss always expressed admiration and respect for America, nonetheless Diamond's firm identification of America with modernity posed an intense problem all the way down to his Straussian roots. In his third period, Diamond worked out a kind of reconciliation, partly with the aid of Alexis de Tocqueville, between Strauss and Madison, and also between himself and America's modernity. Here was where Diamond parted company from many other students of Strauss, who responded to the Straussian dilemmas in quite different ways.

DIAMOND AND STRAUSS: AGAINST THE STRAUSSIANS

Martin Diamond was one of the first students of Leo Strauss to turn in a sustained and fruitful way to the study of the American regime. Other students of Strauss had, for the most part, focused their attention on the heady subjects of political philosophy, following on and joining in Strauss's own enterprise of recapturing and reinterpreting the tradition. Neither Strauss himself nor most of his early students spent time on the non-canonic materials to which Diamond turned. (There were some who did precede Diamond down that path—Harry Jaffa and Walter Berns particularly come to mind.) In the circles around Strauss, in fact, there appeared to be an implicit prestige hierarchy, a pecking order of worthy topics for study. Strauss was himself so persuasive in his attempt to restore the dignity of classical political philosophy that the study of the ancients appeared to his students to be the most worthy pursuit. Other political philosophy, suitably gradated, stood lower in rank, but still much higher than practical politics or the work of non-philosophers, like the American founders.

Partly because of his own background in socialist politics, where the line between theory and practice was less marked, partly because of the trail-blazing examples of Jaffa's studies of Lincoln, Diamond concluded that this focus of political studies solely on the historical tradition of political philosophy was quite misguided and untrue to the classical political science Strauss himself was attempting to restore. That is, Diamond appealed to the principles of Strauss's political science in order to overcome a prejudice among the Straussians against the study of supposedly lesser lights like James Madison and Thomas Jefferson. Diamond went so far in his attempt to reorient Strauss-inspired political studies as to conclude that "at the beginning, if not at the center of the liberal [arts] study of politics, for this time and place, must be the respectful, supportive, and ultimately philosophical consideration of the great writings and principles and history of the American polity."[7] "Such a study," Diamond mused, is especially valuable for "the young student who becomes fascinated by antiquity."[8] The study he commends is self-consciously meant as an antidote to an effect Diamond discerned in those particularly smitten by Strauss.

Nonetheless, Diamond saw his turn to American sources as mandated by Strauss's own political science. Two lines of thought at or near the core of Strauss's recovered Socratism pushed Diamond in this direction. He took seriously Strauss's emphasis on *political* philosophy, that is, on the discovery that philosophic inquiry always occurs as a politically situated activity. As Strauss put it, political philosophy is philosophy that recognizes or takes seriously the *problem* of philosophy and the city. The political community is not and can never be philosophical; philosophy by its nature is at least potentially in conflict with the city. Political philosophy is philosophy that deports itself both prudently and justly in the face of that conflict or potential conflict. Both necessity (the vulnerability and dependence of philosophy on the city) and justice (the duty to return good for good, or at least to do no harm) require that philosophy self-consciously accommodate itself to the city.[9] Diamond spoke of this "accommodation" as a kind of "coming to terms" with the polity. "The way to come to respectable terms . . . is to give the decent polity and its constitutive opinions a central and respected place in the teaching of political things." At the least, philosophical inquiry and the education built on or leading to it give due honor and respect to the "constitutive opinions" of the community, in the case of America, to "the founding documents of this political order, the Declaration of Independence and the Constitution."[10] At the most, the political philosopher serves as a kind of support, perhaps even advocate for the reigning order, always assuming, that is, that it is not a "truly abominable" order.[11]

This kind of accommodation is not merely a matter of prudence and justice, however. "To come to such terms is also in principle the dialectically sound way to begin the educational ascent."[12] Diamond obviously means to evoke Socrates' account of the ascent from the cave. Strauss taught that the beginning point for political philosophic inquiry is neither the Cartesian *cogito* nor the modern social scientist's equivalent, raw behavior. Political inquiry begins with opinion and attempts to ascend to the truth to which the opinion points, or which it confusedly contains, for political opinion contains "a rational intimation of what is really just."[13] The model is Socrates, who began by examining the opinions of his fellow Athenians. Diamond was famous for a quip to the effect that certain of his contemporaries who misunderstand the Socratic method do the same—study politics via an examination of the opinions of the Athenians. To follow Socrates and Strauss today requires not beginning with the Athenians, but with the opinions of the Americans, and subjecting them to Socratic scrutiny. One must begin with what is one's own, with what is naturally familiar, and move toward the philosophic universal from there. That led Diamond to his conclusion about the centrality of the study of American materials for us, and to a deep reservation against the unspoken (sometimes spoken) snobbism of the Straussians.[14]

DIAMOND AND STRAUSS: AGAINST THE PROGRESSIVES

Just as Strauss pointed Diamond toward his subject matter, so he pointed him toward his approach to that subject matter. Diamond was not, of course, the first to study the founding, and the field he discovered when he turned to it was, he would have said, poorly cultivated. By the mid-fifties the study of the founding had securely belonged to historians of the progressive persuasion, Charles Beard and his heirs, for roughly half a century. "Beard's influence was immense and . . . his argument came to be treated as having settled the fundamental question."[15] Beard's was "the conventional academic wisdom on the subject."[16]

Diamond objected frequently and strenuously to the chief substantive conclusions of the Beardians—that the Constitution was an aristocratic or oligarchic reaction against the democratic forces and ideas that made the revolution, that the Constitution was the product of the personal and class interests of the wealthy, designed to protect their own property from troublesome democratic majorities. Indeed, it would not be too much of an exaggeration to say that Diamond's corpus was devoted above all to placing a negative sign to all that the Progressives said: the Constitution was not anti-democratic but was in fact more clearly and definitively democratic than the Declaration of Independence itself.[17]

Diamond also objected to the method of the Progressive historians, the explanation of events in terms of interests alone. Beard, for example, had "dug out of neglected archives information on the *personal* economic holdings and interests of the convention delegates," and "argued that they deliberately designed an unde-mocratic Constitution to protect themselves and their class."[18] In orienting them-selves around interest, the Progressive historians shared much with the political scientists, especially the pluralists of Diamond's day, who took interest as their chief category of analysis, and even with those political scientists who made power cen-tral to their approach to politics. Contrary to what some have said of Diamond, he rejected this focus of the pluralists and the progressives: Diamond shared a thought or two with the pluralists, but on the whole he was as much an opponent of theirs as he was of Beard himself. Diamond imbibed from Strauss the idea that political inquiry must in method be philosophical or dialectical. For Diamond the commit-ment to a philosophical mode of political science had two dimensions, both of which spoke decisively against the Progressivist-pluralist methodology. "Politics is constituted," Diamond insisted, "by the rivalry of human opinions regarding justice and the common good." The proper orientation of political study, then, is, as we have already noted, toward these opinions. Any methodology that reduces these opinions to mere expressions ("epiphenomena") of "underlying interests and pas-sions" severely distorts the phenomena of politics: it is "profoundly to degrade both the political and the science that studies it."[19] Merely as a matter of description, interest is not an adequate orienting concept, for while interests are real enough and even "profoundly influence political opinion" they "cannot by themselves deter-mine opinion."[20] An interest can lead a person "to favor or oppose a policy because it will or will not put money into his pocket," but, Diamond insists, "that does not end the matter." The mere fact that interests must always be ferreted out (as with Beard, "unmasked") tells us something decisively important: "the man or the group or the politician has to make arguments; they have to support the result they desire with an opinion that makes sense to others and, for that matter, usually to them-selves as well."[21] Interests do not go out in public naked; indeed, they clothe them-selves in arguments about justice and the common good, but, Diamond asks, "what is it in the argument that makes *sense* and hence persuades?" Diamond's answer: "I can conceive of no other explanation for the . . . content of opinion, than a per-ception, a rational intimation, of what really is just."[22] One wonders whether a philosophically minded pluralist might not have an alternate answer to Diamond's question, but his observation is quite unexceptionable—the chief facts about poli-tics are not naked interests. A non-question-begging political science begins with the phenomena as they actually appear, and not with an a priori reductionist analy-sis of the phenomena. Thus Diamond's method in approaching the founding was entirely different from that of Beard (or Robert Dahl)—he focused on the opin-ions as most revealing.

The philosophical or dialectical or Socratic approach to politics is necessar-ily also evaluative. The opinions that are the chief focus of study are themselves decisively evaluative, and the claim-in-chief they raise is about the political good. To take them seriously is to take seriously the claims about the good and the just that they raise. Diamond follows Strauss, therefore, in challenging the fact-value distinction and all forms of positivism that interfere with, or decree impossible this central task of political science. Diamond goes so far, indeed, as to suggest that the Progressive historians turned to interest precisely because they were such "value-free" social scientists. "The modern relativistic or positivist themes, implicitly employed by most commentators on the Founding Fathers, deny the possibility of such true knowledge [of political good and its contrary] and therefore deny that the founding Fathers *could* have been actuated by knowledge of the good rather than by passion or interest."[23] It must be said, however, that no matter how much this may describe the political analysis of some it is hardly a persuasive account of the turn by Beard and his fellows to an analysis in terms of interest—surely Beard was untouched by any aspiration toward *wertfreiheit*. However that may be, it should be apparent how much Diamond's method of political study owes to Strauss. As he said in one of his two significant methodological statements, "Leo Strauss . . . is the source of what I have said here to a greater extent than I can acknowledge."[24]

DIAMOND AND STRAUSS: THE NEW SCIENCE OF POLITICS

Diamond's work on the founding was so important not only because he was one of those who helped cure us of the maladies of misunderstanding imposed by the Progressive historians—an honor he shares with many others who helped break the spell of Beard—but even more because he opened up a truer, a theoretically more interesting and finally a more usable version of the founding. In this he shares honors also with fellow Strauss students like Harry Jaffa and Herbert Storing, and historians like Bernard Bailyn, Gordon Wood, and Lance Banning. Although not all of Diamond's conclusions have held up under subsequent scrutiny, yet on the whole his approach remains remarkably persuasive, far more so, for example, than the one that came into vogue as "the republican synthesis."[25]

Diamond laid out three chief themes in his construal of the thought and deeds of the founders in his very first published pieces: the true place of democracy (or, in their language, republican or popular government) in the thought and deeds of the founders; the true character of federalism in the American constitutional order; and finally, the commitment to the new "science of politics" that firmly linked Diamond's interpretation of the founding with Strauss's political philosophy. These were not three random themes, for, as Diamond saw it, the central themes of the founding as expressed in its most important text were just these. "*The Federalist* teaches a new and true republicanism which involves crucially a new view of the problem of union." Both novelties, in turn, rest on the new "science of politics."[26]

A brief sketch like this can never do justice to the richness and the nuance of Diamond's teaching on these three matters. At risk of presenting a caricature, let me give a few sentences on each of his three main themes. The reader can readily refer to Diamond's own expositions for fuller statements.

(1) *Democracy*: contrary to the claims of Beard and latter day quasi-Beardians like Dahl, Richard Hofstadter, James MacGregor Burns and Gordon Wood, the founders were not anti-democrats. They were just the opposite—wholly committed to democracy (or republicanism, that is, representative democracy). As partisans of democracy they were not so foolish as to blind themselves to those defects of democracy that history and theory had revealed. Intelligent partisans attempt to ensure the survival of their favored orders by recognizing and attempting to guard against the weaknesses most likely to endanger them. Such was the perspective of Madison et al. Democracy suffered from well-known deficiencies—a tendency to incompetent government because it involved government by the inexpert, and to oppression by majority factions, productive in turn of turbulence. Nonetheless, the founders neither turned their backs on democracy, nor attempted to fix it by recourse to non-democratic expedients (or supplements) as had been the standard pattern in past practice and theory.[27] Rather, in a formula Diamond burned into our brains by his emphasis on it, they sought "a republican remedy for the diseases most incident to republic government." Or, they sought "a wholly popular" solution to the problems of popular government. That the writings of the framers are rife with declamation against the evils of republican government, Diamond demonstrated, measured not their disgust but the depth of their commitment to it. "They were not founding any other kind of government; they were establishing a democratic form, and it was the dangers peculiar to it against which all their efforts had to be bent."[28]

(2) *Federalism*: Diamond's view of federalism in the constitution was quite idiosyncratic, perhaps the most novel of the many novel things he had to say. Rather than seeing it as the glory of American constitutionalism as many (especially conservatives) did, or as yet one more checking and stalemating device of a structure meant to thwart majority rule, as many liberals did, Diamond in his early work saw it as an unstable compromise, with no intrinsic principle or goodness of its own.[29] Diamond's thinking about federalism took two points of departure, the Madisonian theory of the extended republic, to be discussed below, and the puzzling (in light of our presuppositions on the subject) characterization of the American union in *The Federalist* as "in strictness neither a national nor a federal Constitution, but a composition of both."[30] Diamond made sense of this description when he discovered that according to eighteenth century usage, "federal" and "confederal" were exact synonyms, and not the names of two different sorts of unions. That we have transferred the name "federal" to the kind of union established in the Constitution, a union characterized by "a division of supremacy . . . between member states and a central government," has led us to believe that this is a genuinely third sort of entity, between a national and a confederal system. Diamond denied that, or at least insisted that the framers understood it quite differently: "We now regard as a unique principle what they regarded as a mere compound."[31]

Diamond's rediscovery of the original meaning of federalism had three important implications. He was, first, enabled to appreciate federalism in a much more nuanced way than usual; he was able, for example, to understand very clearly the point of Madison's complex investigation of the federal and national elements in the Constitution in *Federalist* 39.[32] He was also able to recapture the real point of the commitment by some to genuine federalism (or confederalism) in the "small republic federalism" defined by Montesquieu. He was able, in other words, to penetrate behind the legalism and obsession with sovereignty that arose after the founding to appreciate the political significance of the struggle over the nature of the union. He saw very clearly that the ultimate issue actually was republicanism—the partisans of federalism thought republicanism could thrive only in a small place, the partisans of nationalism, Madison at their head, believed the reverse.[33]

Third, and perhaps most important, Diamond came to see federalism as a grafting onto a constitutional scheme essentially national in character some features of a federal sort. Thus his insistence on seeing it as a "mere compound"; it is a compound with a definite tilt in the direction of one of its constituents. In his early work at least Diamond was convinced the "compound" had no coherence or power to persist: *The Federalist*, Diamond concludes, "sees conflict between the national and federal principles in the composition created by the Constitution and, when read carefully, shows the reason why the national principle may be expected and may be hoped to predominate."[34] Federalism, according to Diamond, is not one of the great achievements of the Federalists. The leading lights of their party in fact sought a national system and had to settle for the compound that emerged from the convention. But the compound leans distinctly in the national direction, and over time could be expected to evolve in that direction, as did indeed occur.

The founders, or at least those most worthy of our respect, were both more democratic and more nationalist in Diamond's version than they had traditionally appeared to be. Diamond's founders are, in other words, far more like us, like post–New Deal America, than earlier scholars had made them out to be. As Diamond quite explicitly says in his first and perhaps most programmatic statement, his reading "makes the founders available to us."[35] In finding a "usable past" Diamond again reveals the marks of Strauss's influence, for the latter had broken with all notions of progressivism or historicism which seemed to foreclose the past from being "available" for us. Of course the past that Strauss meant to make available was not the same past that Diamond made available. That was an issue Diamond had continually to face, one that apparently troubled him a good deal until, late in his life, he achieved a solution that seems to have satisfied him.

(3) *The New Science of Politics:* The framers' problem-in-chief, Diamond discovered, was to develop a "wholly popular" solution for the ills to which popular governments are prone. The possibility of the solution was opened up for them by their adherence to and further development of the new "science of politics," that is, modern political philosophy as initiated by Machiavelli and Hobbes. That political science as Diamond presents it consists of both a general approach to politics

and a series of specific institutions, structures, and practices. At the more specific level Diamond identifies three institutions of particular importance to the framers: representation, the separation of powers, and the extended republic. Representation, the product of monarchies, turns out to hold great promise for republics, for it allows popular regimes to avoid some of the worst problems direct democracies faced in the past.[36] Not only does it allow much larger, and therefore much stronger republics, but it allows a certain distance between the people and their governors while maintaining popular contact. This allows room for the injection of competence and expertise, virtue and wisdom in the rulers beyond what the populace in itself might offer.[37]

The separation of powers builds on representation and adds yet further dimensions of competence through the development of division of labor in governance. It increases the safety of the community by introducing checks and balances, "auxiliary precautions" to the safeguards contained in the electoral system.[38] From Diamond's point of view, however, the simply decisive device was the extended republic, for while representation and the separation of powers can temper the majority they do not of themselves protect against the ultimate evil of democracy—majority faction, or majority tyranny. The extended republic can offer hope just here where the other devices lose their efficacy. As Diamond reiterated throughout his works, the extended sphere, or, as he translated it, the large commercial republic, saved popular governments from majority tyranny by the effect it had on the kind of majorities that could form within it. As Diamond said, quoting Madison in *Federalist* 51: "In such a republic popular majorities will still rule, but now 'among the great variety of interests, parties, and sects which it embraces, a coalition of a majority of the whole society could seldom take place on any other principle than those of justice and the general good.'"[39] The extended republic, that is, the conduct of politics in the largest feasible arena, supplies the ultimate answer to the problem of republicanism and thus points decisively, Diamond believed, away from the older federalism (and even the modern hybrid) toward a simply national arrangement. "Madison's solution to the problem of faction . . . takes its bearing not from the federal but from the unitary [national] mode of government."[40] This insight, in turn, undergirds Diamond's way of treating federalism (at least in his early writings) and shows clearly how the "new science of politics" lies beneath Diamond's rendition of both the republicanism and federalism themes.

With regard to the "new science" in general Diamond always emphasized how "deeply indebted" he was "to the late Professor Leo Strauss, whose instructive account of the 'battle of the books,' ancient and modern, has done so much to restore to our understanding the meaning of the modern enterprise." "The American Founding," Diamond always insisted, must be understood "in the context of . . . this new science of politics."[41] Diamond saw the Americans' adherence to the new science of politics as an integral part of the modern break with earlier theory and practice. He followed Strauss in understanding modernity as a "lowering of the aims and expectations of politics" in favor of the greater likelihood of achieving the end in view, even if the end lacked the elevation or dignity of the ends sought earlier. The new science took its bearings not "from the highest possibilities of human nature," but rather took an "aggressively more 'realistic'" idea of human nature. The new science would take man as he actually *is*, would accept as primary in his nature the self-interestedness and passion displayed by all men everywhere and precisely on that basis would work out decent political solutions.[42]

Diamond found tracks of this modern realism all through *The Federalist*. For example, in *Federalist* 43 "the great principle of self-preservation" is pronounced the basis for the objects and aims of "all political institutions." Diamond takes this to be "perhaps the most explicitly fundamental utterance of *The Federalist*."[43] He finds the founders to have revised their notion of the means to successful politics in the modern direction along with their revision of the ends. Instead of relying on a strenuous moral education aimed at "bringing toward completeness or perfection the relative few who were actually capable of fulfilling their humanness," the American founders followed the modern political philosophers in building on the far more universal and reliable passions and interests of humanity. "Employing the 'new science of politics,' Madison had discovered in 'interest' its latent possibility."[44] Diamond summed up the general character of the Americans' "new science of politics" in a quip by Strauss: "From the point of view of modern thought, [Strauss] says, 'what you need is not so much formation of character and moral appeal as the right kind of institutions, institutions with teeth in them.' The Americans followed [the moderns] in their reliance on institutions, and not the ancients regarding the necessity of character formation."[45] That is to say, the most pervasive presence of "the new science of politics" in the American regime is not this or that particular institution, but the thorough reliance on institutions as such, institutions of a sort which, as Diamond put it once, "smacked much of 'private vice public good.'"[46] As Diamond emphasized, Madison rejected a reliance on "moral or religious motives."[47]

DIAMOND AND STRAUSS: ON THE WORTH OF THE AMERICAN REGIME

With his analysis of the character of modern political philosophy Strauss provided Diamond with the thread that he used to find his way through the American founding. But Strauss also left Diamond with a problem of great difficulty: According to Strauss, the turn to modernity had been ill-advised. Diamond's response to the challenge posed by Strauss evolved over time, as is visible in the differences between the most important statement of his first period and the most important statement of his last period. In his 1959 essay "Democracy and *The Federalist*" Diamond emphasizes the adherence to the new "lower" science of politics: "Other political theories had ranked highly, as objects of government, the nurturing of a particular religion, education, military courage, civic spiritedness, moderation, individual excellence in the virtues, etc. On all of these *The Federalist* is either silent, or has in mind only pallid versions of the original, or even seems to speak with contempt."[48] Perhaps because of his own background in socialist politics Diamond is very impressed early and late with the way in which Madison's version of "the new science" represents "a beforehand answer to Marx."[49] "Madison's solution to his problem worked astonishingly well. The danger he wished to avert has been averted and largely for the reasons he gave." Yet Diamond hardly pauses to revel in Madison's successes; he may have succeeded in solving the problem of majority tyranny (and class warfare), but "it is possible to question now whether he did not take too narrow a view of what the dangers were . . . We may yet wonder whether he failed to contemplate other equally grave problems of democracy."[50] Although Diamond does not specify what these other "grave problems" are, we can note here strong echoes of Strauss's own reservations about the modern democratic venture. Diamond also wonders "whether his remedy for the one disease had not had some unfortunate collateral consequences."[51] Diamond appears to have in mind here "the reliance on ceaseless striving after immediate interest," a striving which, as Tocqueville pointed out, robs society of "that calm . . . which is necessary for the deeper combinations of the intellect."[52] Again, the tracks of Strauss's concerns with the very highest human possibility, the pursuit of philosophy, are very visible here. Diamond, in a word, joins Strauss in decrying the lowering of sights, the loss of moral dignity that is the price for social peace in the modern order. The founders' "liberalism and republicanism are not the means by which men may ascend to a nobler life; rather they are simply instrumentalities which solve Hobbesean problems in a more moderate manner."[53]

Diamond concludes by pondering the merits of the Madisonian solution even as a means to its own political ends. In this he echoes closely the then recently published study of Lincoln by his then friend Jaffa. The founders, he thinks, made "a powerful distinction . . . between the qualities necessary for founders and the qualities necessary for the men who came after." The founders require great virtues— dedication to the public good and immense political wisdom—but those who come after them, they seem to think, can get by with much less—that self-interest on which Madison so heavily relies, and a "veneration" for the system within which they act. "The reason of the founders constructs the system within which the passions of the men who come after may be relied on."[54] Diamond, however, does not believe this is sufficient provision for the "perpetuation" of the regime. "Does not the intensity and kind of our modern problems seem to require of us a greater degree of reflection and public-spiritedness than the founders thought sufficient for the men who came after them?"[55] Diamond thus seems headed in the same direction as Jaffa in *The Crisis of the House Divided*—toward the notion that great and good as the American founders may have been, there is a need to transcend or supplement them in the direction of the ancients, a transcendence Jaffa found in Lincoln. Around this same time Diamond gave a talk on Lincoln in which he endorsed a modest version of the Jaffa thesis.[56] In any case, Diamond in the late

1950s and early 1960s endorses the view that America, because modern, falls short of the politically best. That is, he recognizes a real tension between his two loves—James Madison's regime is found wanting according to the standards of Leo Strauss's political philosophy.

During his third and last period, during the mid-1970s, Diamond comes to a quite different mode of relating Strauss and Madison. He retains his loyalty to both and finds a deeper harmony between them than before. The most important statement of his final position is the essay "Ethics and Politics: The American Way," his most comprehensive statement. The explicit theme of the essay is the relation between the American regime and Aristotelian (read, Straussian, in the context) political science. Diamond draws what has become by 1977 his very familiar contrast between the high aspirations articulated in the classical teaching on politics and the much less rigorous, less noble, less elevated goals of the modernist Americans. The American regime, he concedes, "does indeed have roots in the new political science of Hobbes."[57] Does that mean, he wonders, that "America [is] little more than a clever social arrangement." Does America satisfy the requirements of a genuine political community according to Aristotle/Strauss, that is, does it produce an *ethos*, a form of character marked by "virtues or excellences"?[58] In its modest aspirations, low demands, eschewal of virtue, dependence on self-interest, etc., etc., does the American regime in fact fall short of the good?

In this last phase, Diamond gives a much more favorable account of America. His argument has two main elements. First, he emphasizes in a way he did not earlier the modern critique of the classical political science. In the 1959 essay he had noticed, almost in passing, that Madison had "deprecated . . . the efficacy" of the kind of "moral and religious motives" on which the ancients had relied.[59] In his later writings, however, beginning with the 1976 essay on "The American Idea of Equality," he dwells at length on the modern critique of the pre-modern orientation. "But that strenuous and demanding ancient political art, the moderns charged, had been ineffective and excessive—that is, 'utopian.' Despite two millennia of such elevated teachings, man's estate had still not been relieved; greed and vainglory ruled under the guise of virtue or piety."[60] The moderns do not merely raise such accusations against the ancients, but, according to Diamond, they do so "with some justification," for "ancient and medieval political practice had not vindicated the high aims and claims of pre-modern thought."[61] So the first part of Diamond's new position is an endorsement of the modern reservations against the ancient political science.

Second, just as he announced pre-modern theory a failure in practice, so he insisted that modern theory was a success. "From the point of view of the generality of mankind, the new policy delivered on its promises. In comparison with the pre-modern achievement, it raised to unprecedented heights the benefits, the freedom, and the dignity enjoyed by the great many."[62] Diamond still conceded that there were costs to modern success—"the solid but low foundation of American political life." But Diamond refuses to leave matters there. "While the American founders turned away from the classic enterprise regarding virtue, they did not thereby abandon the pursuit of virtue or excellence in all other possible ways. In fact, the American political order rises respectably high enough above the vulgar level of mere self-interest in the direction of virtue."[63]

The details of Diamond's argument are not necessary in this context as much as is his general point: the American regime is not a regime in the full Aristotelian sense, but, he concludes, it "manifestly qualifies as an authentically political community or regime" in that it "molds its citizens into a particular human character on the pattern of . . . some particular idea of what is 'advantageous and just.'"[64] The character thus formed is not just a character, i.e., something with a shape of some sort, but a mode of excellence or virtue. America differs from Aristotle's regime, however, in that character (virtue) formation here does not occur via the laws directly, but in the private sphere, in the sphere of liberty. The liberal regime, the regime dedicated to liberty and thus the regime that self-consciously turns away from the comprehensive public moral formation of classical theory, nonetheless does engage in moral formation of its own in its own way. Although the "bourgeois virtues" may be of lower status than those sought by pre-moderns, they are nonetheless real and more securely produced than the more "utopian" higher virtues. Diamond, in other words, no longer quite accepts the formula that modernity involves a severe lowering or decline. He even recurs to the theme, which, from a Straussian point of view had seemed most damning in 1959: "One should also note gratefully that the American political order, with its heterogeneous and fluctuating majorities and with its principle of liberty, supplies a not inhospitable home to the love of learning."[65] For Diamond, then, modernity does not necessarily represent a "lowering of the sights," or at least not very much of one. And what it loses in elevation of aim it gains back in elevation of attainment. Diamond reconciles Madison and Strauss, therefore, by arguing that Madison's regime could achieve the ends, in its own way, that Strauss had taught were most important. Diamond became an unequivocal supporter of modern liberal democracy, but his defense always bore the marks of his teacher, and could never be confused with the kind of loose relativism and toleration characteristic of pluralists like Dahl or ironists like Richard Rorty.

NOTES

1. Charles Kesler, "*Federalist* 10 and American Republicanism," in Charles Kesler, ed., *Saving the Revolution* (New York: The Free Press, 1987), 16.

2. Alan Gibson, "The Commercial Republic and the Pluralist Critique of Marxism: An Analysis of Martin Diamond's Interpretation of *Federalist* 10," *Polity* 25, no. 4 (Summer 1993), 498–499; Jeffrey Leigh Sedgwick, "Martin Diamond's Interpretation of *Federalist* 10: A Response to Alan Gibson," *Polity* 25, no. 4 (Summer 1993), 529.

3. Dustjacket of William Schambra, ed., *As Far as Republican Principles Will Admit: Essays by Martin Diamond* (Washington, D.C.: The AEI Press, 1992).

4. I include the following essays in Diamond's first period (all reprinted in *As Far as Republican Principles Will Admit*): "Democracy and *The Federalist*: A Reconsideration of the Framers' Intent" (1959); "Lincoln's Greatness" (1960); "What the Framers Meant by Federalism" (1961); "*The Federalist's* View of Federalism" (1961); "*The Federalist*" (1963); "Conservatives, Liberals and the Constitution" (1965).

5. I include the following essays in Diamond's Second Period (all reprinted in *As Far as Republican Principles Will Admit*): "The Problem of Reading in an Age of Mass Democracy" (1970); "On the Study of Politics in a Liberal Education" (1971); "The Dependence of Fact Upon 'Value'" (1972).

6. I include the following essays in Diamond's final period (all reprinted in *As Far as Republican Principles Will Admit*): "The Utopian Grounds for Pessimism and the Reasonable Grounds for Optimism" (1973); "The Ends of Federalism" (1973); "The Revolution of Sober Expectations" (1973); "The Declaration and the Constitution: Liberty, Democracy, and the Founders" (1975); "The Forgotten Doctine of Enumerated Powers" (1976); "The American Idea of Equality: The View from the Founding" (1976); "*The Federalist* on Federalism: Neither a National nor a Federal Constitution" (1977); "The Electoral College and the American Idea of Democracy" (1977); "Teaching about Politics as a Vocation" (1977); "Ethics and Politics: The American Way" (1977); "The Separation of Powers and the Mixed Regime" (1978).

7. "On the Study of Politics," in *As Far as Republican Principles*, 281.

8. Ibid., 280.

9. Ibid., 276–77; "Teaching About Politics," in *As Far as Republican Principles*, 286–92.

10. "Teaching about Politics," 305.

11. Ibid., 304.

12. Ibid., 305.

13. "Dependence of Fact Upon 'Value'," in *As Far as Republican Principles*, 317.

14. "Teaching about Politics," 305–306.

15. "The Declaration and the Constitution," in *As Far as Republican Principles*, 228.

16. "The American Idea of Equality," in *As Far as Republican Principles*, 242.

17. It was this side of Diamond's work that ultimately led to the gargantuan attack on him by his former friend and fellow student of Strauss, Harry V. Jaffa. Diamond could never resist the *bon mot* or the elegant formula, and he was often led to overstate his own position for the sake of countering the Progressives. Where Beard saw a democratic Declaration and an anti-democratic (pro-liberty) Constitution, Diamond insisted on a non-democratic (pro-liberty) Declaration and a democratic Constitution. For the sake of symmetry he went so far as to claim the Declaration supplies "no guidance" whatever on the question of form of government. In the context of his work, it is clear this is part of his polemic against Beard et al., but it is surely an overstatement. Jaffa was right to call him on this, but it must be said that Jaffa's reading of Diamond's work is wooden to the point of petrification and marked by a complete lack of interpretive generosity ("Revolution of Sober Expectations," 211, 214–15; Jaffa, *How to Think About the American Revolution*).

18. *The Founding of the Democratic Republic* (Itasca, Ill.: Peacock, 1981) (original date, 1966), 47–48.

19. "Dependence of Fact upon 'Value,'" 311.

20. Ibid., 316.

21. Ibid.

22. Ibid., 317.

23. "Democracy and *The Federalist*," 22–23.

24. "Teaching about Politics," 308; see also, "Facts and Values," 389, n. 4.

25. This is a more controversial claim than the bald assertion of it can support, but it would take me too far afield to explore the issues here. For some recent discussions, see Thomas Pangle, *The Spirit of Modern Republicanism* (Chicago: University of Chicago Press, 1988); and Paul Rahe, *Republics Ancient and Modern* (Chapel Hill: University of North Carolina Press, 1992).

26. "*The Federalist*," 41, 47, 57.

27. Ibid., 47–48.

28. "The Declaration and the Constitution," 236; "Democracy and *The Federalist*," 22.

29. "Conservatives, Liberals, and the Constitution," in *As Far as Republican Principles*, 76–77. Federalism was perhaps the clearest issue on which Diamond modified his thinking in his third period. In a series of restatements on the topic Diamond defended the decentralization federalism made possible along Tocquevillian lines. He even gave a spirited defense of the constitutional scheme of enumerated powers. How well this sits with his early and late enthusiasm for the extended republic is a question worth pondering.

30. "*The Federalist*," 39.

31. "What the Framers Meant by Federalism," in *As Far as Republican Principles*, 94, 95.

32. "*The Federalist's* View of Federalism," in *As Far as Republican Principles*, 120–23.

33. Ibid., 102–105; "*The Federalist*," 41–42; "The Ends of Federalism," in *As Far as Republican Principles*, 148–49.

34. "*The Federalist's* View of Federalism," 133.

35. "Democracy and *The Federalist*," 27.

36. "*The Federalist*," 45.

37. *Founding of the Democratic Republic*, 79–80.

38. Ibid., 85–90.

39. "*The Federalist*," 56; see also, *Founding of the Democratic Republic*, 78; "Ethics and Politics," in *As Far as Republican Principles*, 351–52.

40. "*The Federalist's* View of Federalism," 142–43.

41. "The American Idea of Equality," in *As Far as Republican Principles*, 248; see also "Separation of Powers," in *As Far as Republican Principles*, 62; "The Declaration and the Constitution," 232, 386, n. 9.

42. "The American Idea of Equality," 248–49.

43. "*The Federalist*," 28.

44. "Ethics and Politics," 352; see also "The Declaration and the Constitution," 238.

45. "The Declaration and the Constitution," 386.

46. "Ethics and Politics," 353; see also "The Declaration and the Constitution," 238.

47. "*The Federalist*," 54.

48. "Democracy and *The Federalist*," 31.

49. Ibid., 32.

50. Ibid., 34.

51. Ibid.

52. Ibid., 34–35.

53. Ibid., 29.

54. Ibid., 35.

55. Ibid., 36.

56. "Lincoln's Greatness," in *As Far as Republican Principles*, 258–62.

57. "Ethics and Politics," 358.

58. Ibid., 359.

59. Ibid.; see also "Democracy and *The Federalist*," 34.

60. "The American Idea of Equality," 248; see also "Ethics and Politics," 344; "Separation of Powers," 62–63.

61. "Ethics and Politics," 355.

62. Ibid.

63. Ibid., 359.

64. Ibid., 364.

65. Ibid., 363.

· *16* ·

Paul Eidelberg: The Mixed Regime
and the American Regime

Will Morrisey

"Straussian" scholars often stand accused of ill-disguised elitism. Paul Eidelberg disguises nothing, providing a candidly "aristocratic" account of the American regime and of politics generally. Yet Eidelberg is not really a Straussian.

He is unquestionably a Strauss-influenced scholar. Having attended Strauss's graduate courses at the University of Chicago, where he received his advanced degrees, Eidelberg never fails to pay his respects to his teacher. But he does not hesitate to disagree with Strauss and Strauss's students on the character of the American regime and on the enterprise of political philosophy. He positions himself against Martin Diamond's "democratic" interpretation of the regime, and he opposes the tendency of many Straussians to trace the regime's principles to the political philosophy of John Locke. In the latter stance, he resembles Harry V. Jaffa. However, whereas Jaffa gives a richer account of the explicit theoretical underpinnings of the regime—as an exegete of the Declaration of Independence, he is nearly unrivaled in the twentieth century—Eidelberg concentrates first on the regime's structural dimensions and then moves to a consideration of the statesmanship of the Founders. He first comes to sight as an "institutionalist" political scientist, never wholly satisfied with the political *philosophy* that originated in ancient Greece. His turn, in mid-career, to an emphasis on Judaic studies and Israeli politics, puts him forthrightly on the side of "Jerusalem," not "Athens."

In America, Eidelberg is best known for contending that the American Founders intended to establish not a democracy but a mixed regime, a regime that would provide natural aristocrats, like the Founders themselves, with a strong voice in public councils. He differs from "institutional" political scientists in his emphasis on statesmanship, the application of principles to action. The Founders "constitute a class of their own, a class of politicians," a class of men animated by the "aristocratic" passion for honor and fame.[1] How do such men *deliberate?* To consider the deliberations of statesmen is to transcend both the reductionism of materialists like Charles Beard and the conventionalism of institutionalists.

Pointing to the Founders' adherence to the doctrine of popular sovereignty and to the lack of a stable, European-style class system that might be directly expressed in political institutions, Diamond classifies the American regime as a democratic republic. The regime is "undemocratic" only in the sense that it features strong safeguards against "direct" and "participatory" democracy. Representation, separation, balance of powers, and federalism merely mitigate democracy, protect it against demagogues and mobs, make it decent.

Eidelberg replies that mitigations of democracy by definition must be non-democratic. They may or may not be antidemocratic. For example, although the United States Senate as originally designed appears democratic in contrast to the English House of Lords, in contrast to the Council of Athens in Aristotle's day it looks quite oligarchic (P: 22). Without a careful analysis of exactly how the Founders modulated popular sovereignty, no easy classification of their regime is possible. Eidelberg proceeds inductively, deriving the ends of the regime primarily from its structure, the institutions the Founders designed.

He begins with the House of Representatives, intended to be the "grand depository of the democratic principle" in the national government (P: 53). The short terms of House members make rapid turnover possible. James Madison's celebrated "pluralism," however, made feasible by the extension of the sphere of one government over a large population, is precisely a divide-and-rule strategy intended to restrain the democracy in order to make the democratic principle operate in a responsible manner in the government. The device of representation allows the national government really to govern, not merely to reflect, mass opinion. Madison's republic is unmixed in that it makes no formal, institutional recognition of separate classes. Instead, Madison envisions "a *de facto distribution of power* comparable to that which existed in mixed regimes of the classical variety" (P: 73).

The Senate is in one sense a clearly oligarchic institution, affording each state equal representation regardless of population. This was more than a mere compromise between large states and small, inasmuch as (for example) New York voted for equal representation, whereas smaller South Carolina voted against it. As for its class composition, the Senate's "oligarchism" is mitigated by the members' election by state legislatures, "whose composition [was] only partly aristocratic" (P: 84) and was, in some cases, quite democratic.

Further, in Alexander Hamilton's opinion, the relative lack of artificial class distinctions in America does not prevent natural distinctions between the few and the many. Such natural classes are not stable—two geniuses may bring forth a brood of dunces—but the natural aristocrats who will arise must be given scope for their abilities. In practice, "superior acquirements" will be afforded by wealth, in the form of superior education (Hamilton, quoted in P: 120). The vices of the rich—avarice, ambition—on balance favor the prosperity of the country, and partake less of moral depravity, than the vices of the poor. The rich also have a particular interest in defending the rights of property, rights that citizens of all classes need, but that the poor are too ready shortsightedly to sacrifice. The more the rich are threatened by the poor, the more the rich will make extra-legal arrangements to protect themselves. Rich *and* poor must have a place—hence the need for a mixed regime, "a true political union" (P: 135). Such a union would provide institutional support not for the sake of "capitalism" but for *politically* determined *national* purposes.

Madison emphasizes natural aristocracy more than wealth but does not diverge fundamentally from Hamilton with respect to the function of the Senate. Senators should be "men noted for wisdom and virtue," aristocrats, who will check and balance the more democratic House (P: 146). Operationally, popular sovereignty will be limited in the sense, as Madison famously writes, that the reason of the people, not their passion, will be made to prevail. Property rights originate in human faculties; government's "first object," though not its only object, is to protect those faculties and thereby protect property rights, among the other natural rights. American republicanism "imposes certain limits on the principle of equality" (P: 154). Justice is not some simple, across-the-board equality, but "a mixture of democratic justice and oligarchic-aristocratic justice: (P: 155), of natural equality—that each *person* enjoy equal protection under the laws—and protection of natural inequalities—that each person, in enjoying equal protection, be allowed to excel, sustain himself, or fail, and to rule or to defer.

The Senate will take particular interest in the rule of law because the Senators' long terms of office will help to ensure continuity in law, in accordance with the Aristotelian and Madisonian teaching that too much reform is bad for any regime. Stable laws engender reverence—a popular passion, admittedly, but a counterweight to the destabilizing popular passions of envy and resentment. Reverence fosters deference, a habit democracy by itself lacks, self destructively. The rule of law makes community possible, giving *reason* the *authority* it otherwise would have only "in theory."

"[T]he secret of Madison's rhetoric lies simply in this: it seeks to promote aristocratic ends under a facade of democratic arguments" (P: 162). Madison differs from Hamilton in his willingness to let the Senate remain co-equal with the House. Hamilton wanted the Senate to take the legislative initiative, with the House merely checking the oligarch-aristocrats when they overreach. "Hamilton wanted *the political*"—meaning, finally, the aristocratic, the "thumotic," those souls preoccupied with *ruling*—to be the ruling principle of the whole. "He wanted the government to govern" (P: 164). He "loved liberty, but liberty with grandeur of purpose" (P: 165). Madison, by contrast, wanted "the soul of the American citizen" itself to be "in tension," pulled between aristocratic and democratic ends. He wanted this tension reflected in the American national legislature.

The president will preserve the balance between the two legislative branches, owing his election to neither the few nor the many. The electoral college as originally designed kept the presidential appointment insulated from popular voting. A national, popular election is "a most dangerous means of providing public education" (P: 189), as it makes the presidency a prize for demagogues and spoilsmen. The electoral college also insulated the appointment from corruption by the rich, who would have great difficulty buying votes in conventions held in each of the states, rather than in one place, where things could be more easily "managed." Thus the electoral college enabled the president to be "monarchic" in the Aristotelian sense: sufficiently independent to rule reasonably. The electoral college made possible a jointure between wisdom and power.

The unitary executive can unite reason and spiritedness, prudence and the passion for fame, in a manner that makes him responsible to public opinion, the deliberate sense of the community. Armed with independence sufficient to resist the rush of political passions, the president can give "the enlightened and respectable members of the community time to exert their influence on society at large" (P: 197), to moderate and elevate public discourse when some great issue is at stake. The president even has the independence needed gently to reprove the people, "expos[ing] error and vice" (P: 201). No president, under this system, need practice a politics of compassion, pretending to feel the very pains and sorrows of the people. An American president can safely "endure without resentment the resentment of others," and "pursue noble ends though they be unpopular" (P: 201). Magnanimity, not compassion, will characterize the greatest presidents.

Eidelberg sees the danger of carrying this "aristocratic" or "thumotic" motif too far. Government must have limits. Because, in this model, the people cannot readily supply those limits—as they can in Thomas Jefferson's model—there must be a feature of the government itself that sets limits. Limited government means government that "restricts the legislative (but not only the legislative) power by fixed or permanent laws" (P: 203); constitutional laws. Against Jefferson, Eidelberg argues that the Supreme Court is the only branch of government that can serve as the arbiter on questions of constitutionality.

Eidelberg admits that the only real restraint on the Court is the prudence of its members and that the intended scope of judicial review "does not admit of being clearly ascertained" (P: 214). Jeffersonian popular sovereignty cannot solve this problem in principle. Popular sovereignty is not coterminous with the principles of *natural* justice, which bind men "not in virtue of having been willed but in virtue of their universal (or general) validity," their authority over men as men. Nor can popular sovereignty justly overturn what Eidelberg classifies as the "civilizational" components of the Constitution—checks and balances, division of powers. These components would fail if applied in a barbaric society, but they are both needed and workable in a civilized one. Eidelberg goes so far as to claim that the Tenth Amendment implies that the powers *delegated* to the federal government by the people are thereby *divested*; they are irreclaimable sovereign powers (P: 317, n. 36). This means that Jefferson's favored means of the expression of popular sovereignty, the authority of the states' governments, has been *permanently* curtailed with respect to the *exercise* of "civilizational" and natural rights with respect to the operations of the national government. Eidelberg even more emphatically rejects Jefferson's claim that all three branches of government must engage in constitutional interpretation and review. This "political monstrosity" would quickly reduce to an appeal to popular sovereignty (P: 236). At best, Jefferson's approach would allow the legislative branch to predominate, making the regime more purely Lockean than originally intended.

Does the Constitution then mean whatever the Supreme Court justices say it means? Eidelberg denies this. The Constitution, he argues, is hardly an amorphous statement. Judges cannot flagrantly contradict the Constitution—maintain, for example, that it means "tyranny is good." They should not legislate. They should provide exegesis and application of the intentions of the Founders and of the authors of the constitutional amendments, in accordance with their oath to uphold the Constitution. The Court must exercise prudence, "the wisdom of present decision," guided by philosophy—particularly by civilizational and natural justice—mediated by law (P: 224). Only a prudent and law-abiding Court can reinforce the noble prejudice among the people in favor of the Constitution and its defenders. Without that prejudice, the people will be prey to the endless flux of egalitarianism/relativism, the synthesis of opinion and mere passion.

Because "the Supreme Court is without material power," it is "safe to entrust it with the function of judicial review" (P: 237). But this safety is only immediate. Long term, the Court's every decision has the potential effectively to modify the Founders' intentions, that is, to corrupt them. Eidelberg responds in two ways to this danger. First, he observes that an openly capricious, "activist" Court would undermine its own authority. "[I]f the judicial interpretation of the Constitution were simply to reflect the changing opinions of popular majorities, the Supreme Court might as well be a temporary body chosen by the people or by the people's representatives" (P: 241).

Second, he actually endorses "creative interpretation" of the Constitution, cautioning that this requires "judgment of a most wise and subtle kind" (P: 245, 246). But this also requires a more extensive civic education than the Founders provided, if not a more extensive civic education than the Founders wanted. Eidelberg does not mean that such an education would sufficiently improve the citizens at large, transform them into vigilant Jeffersonian yeomen. If "government is to control itself" and "*not* be controlled by the governed"—as the un-Jeffersonian Eidelberg would have it (P: 258)—then the "aristocratic" dimension of the Founders' mixed regime must be rehabilitated and strengthened, first and foremost among the natural aristocrats.

A Discourse on Statesmanship addresses this need to ensure that enlightened statesmen be at the helm more often than they have been in the recent past.[2] The book's "primary purpose" is to foster a "comprehensive political science" that synthesizes Aristotelian structuralism with Whiteheadian natural science—that is, with a biology that has assimilated Nietzschean thought (D: 145–146). Eidelberg focuses on statesmanship as "the coordination of political theory and political practice" (D: 3); he intends his new political science to be architectonic/constructive as well as descriptive/analytical. The deconstructive and constructive tasks of the statesman involve "bring[ing] certain interests into the foreground while retreating others into the background" (D: 10). By "modify[ing] the moral and intellectual horizon of his audience, the statesman contributes to the constitution of the character of the people" (D: 11). To avoid mere assertion of the will or *arbitrary* creativity, Eidelberg has recourse to the criterion of comprehensiveness, including the good of the whole.

Unfortunately, Eidelberg argues, statesmanship has gone unappreciated by contemporary political scientists "Left" and "Right." Marxists, with their materialist reductionism, make statesmanship seem ineffectual, "epiphenomenal." Straussians, with their exaltation of political philosophers at the expense of political men, make statesmanship seem petty. To redeem statesmanship from such critics, Eidelberg adopts and adapts Aristotle's quadrimodal political science, with its discussion of the best regime in theory, the best in practice, the best in a given set of circumstances, and the best means of changing or of preserving a regime. Eidelberg associates Aristotle's political science with Aristotle's natural science, specifically, the theory of quadrimodal causation (teleological, formal, material, and efficient, respectively). The statesman prudently employs these regime criteria, thereby participating in the larger natural order they reflect, and does so in terms consistent with that order. In so doing, Madison-like, he "enlarges the role of reason and virtue in public life" (D: 53).

This framework enables Eidelberg to enunciate a critique of what has been called "postmodernism"—and to do so in advance of that phenomenon's popularization in the United States (D: ch. 2, especially p. 67). The yoking of Nietzsche and egalitarianism makes no sense. Autonomy requires a self. Yet postmodernists typically want to dissolve the self—while still insisting on individual autonomy or the self-defined "identity" of a social group. The radical democracy of "postmodernism" remains within the Hobbesian horizon, wherein reason is subordinated to the passions. Reason is therefore prey to the Hobbesianism political settlement, which is nothing like the democracy favored by many "postmodernists." That is, "postmodernism" only gives the wheel of modernity another spin.

Acting very much like the scholarly equivalent of his statesman, Eidelberg brings certain interests into the foreground while retreating others to the background in order to effect a synthesis of ancient and modern political science and to employ this synthesis in redeeming the American regime from critics reductionist and high-toned, alike. He brings out the aristocratic peroration of the Declaration, in which the Founders pledge to each other their lives, fortunes, and sacred honor. Honor, an aristocratic motif, links the ancient political philosophers with the moderns via the thought of Francis Bacon, Eidelberg claims (D: 94–95). The highest form of honor, the permanent honor the Founders called fame, can only be won by attachment to the public good. Although in no way contradicting the natural or species equality asserted in the Declaration's preamble, this natural inequality, founded upon the inequality of human faculties among individuals, and upon the inequalities of external property often resulting therefrom, forms a reasonable foundation for deference, reverence for law, education in accordance with the rule of reason, and the greatness of individuals and the nation governed by such individuals.

In institutional terms, what the Founders call "democratic" is not especially democratic at all, in light of Aristotelian criteria. Further as the *Philosophy* argues, the Constitution sets strict limits on democracy, even as defined by the Founders. Although Straussians contend that the Founders' new science of politics rests on the low but solid ground of self-interested passion, Eidelberg denies that the Founders were bourgeois/utilitarian types. *Their* Locke was not anti-Christian, and they upheld a "classical sense of honor" among their fellowmen, whom they held to be naturally social (D: 116).

The formal requirement of government by election rather than by lot—particularly by elections that refine raw popular votes—makes possible a logothumotic politics, a politics of reason and honor—rather than a Machiavellian, thumoerotic politics—a politics of passion (D: 132). The modest compensation of elected representatives also tended to dilute the ambition of the indigent for public office, appealing rather to gentlemen.

In terms of function, Aristotle identifies three ruling elements of any government structure: the deliberative assembly, the magisterial offices, and the law courts. Eidelberg regards these functions to be roughly correspondent to the Founders' legislative, executive, and judicial branches. He synthesizes the deliberative function of "ancient" assemblies with the legislative emphasis of the "moderns" through his above-mentioned epistemology of comprehensiveness and disciplined "creativity" or architectonics, whereby the statesman of greatness of soul as it were incorporates the public good into himself—making it part of "his own," and thus something that will be defended by a thumotic man. For the Founders, George Washington was such a man, although Eidelberg mentions the examples of Hamilton and Madison more frequently.[3] The magistracy or executive is also a deliberative office, but deliberation for its occupant centers on commands and enforcement. As for the judiciary, officeholders there exercise reason forensically, determining not so much what is expedient or what is harmful, but what is just.

Materially, Aristotle does not argue that a mixed regime requires clearly defined classes, "each represented in insitutions constituted by *wholly* different political principles" (D: 196). A middle-class population with many and diverse kinds of property will serve quite well, as Madison sees. Such diversified property will not admit the simple classifications that the traditional mixed regime accommodated. But the new mixed regime is no less a mixed regime for that, only a more complex and subtly designed one.

With respect to the regime's final cause, Eidelberg affirms, with Aristotle, that "monarchy"—the political symbol of the rule of reason—is the best regime in theory. The Founders "monarchize" most conspicuously with the office of the president. Significantly, three of the first four American presidents supported a national university; the other founded a state university; all supported the cultivation of the arts and sciences in order to establish a more perfect, i.e., a more rational union, the political equivalent of the statesman's own greatness, comprehensiveness, of soul. Patriotism, or love of one's own country, seeks the perfection of the beloved, while prudently recognizing that the best can be the enemy of the good if the unachievable best is misused to denigrate an achievable good. In this sense, patriotism would animate a national university where future statesmen would be educated.

The statesman's "politics of magnanimity" (D: ch. 7, passim) rescues the principle of self-interest from contumely not merely by enlightening but by strengthening, enlarging, and articulating the self. Although caring more for the enlightenment of the many than did Aristotle, Madison and the other Founders cared no less for the enlightenment and the enlargement of the few. True self-interest is happiness, requiring "every necessary moral ingredient" (D: 247). "Contrary to the Straussian school, the founders never conceived of 'institutional substitutes for virtue'" (D: 251)—only institutional guards against vice. In Aristotle as in Madison, the political man seeks honor, the esteem of his peers, not "for itself" but for "the confirmation of his own virtue or excellence, namely, practical wisdom" (D: 259). Moreover, wisely "promoting the public good is the articulation of his self" (D: 260). The statesman is neither selfish nor unselfish in the conventional sense, but comprehensive. Fame extends honor beyond the living to new generations.

The soul of the magnanimous statesman—Hamilton is Eidelberg's preferred example—synthesizes the desiring, "erotic" virtues of the "ancients" with the sense of obligation demanded in the Bible. "This sense of obligation"—"which tempers [the statesman's] love of fame"—"is not truly integral to classical political philosophy—I mean to the *philosophical* strata of classical wisdom," which, while disinterested, cannot be described as altruistic (D: 263). Magnanimity or soul-comprehensiveness differs from Aristotelian-philosophic soul-completeness by being subject to change. There is always, for the human soul, a more perfect union, never a fully perfected one.

Eidelberg's magnanimous man is primarily a node of patterned and patterning energy, secondarily a perceiver of "external" reality. The classical philosopher, though by no means a passive observer—he understands that philosophy itself is an "interest," in need of political defense—nonetheless lives in accordance with the opposite priority. To Eidelberg, by contrast, "the problem of the philosopher is to comprehend the whole by incorporating into himself and *bringing* into unity the disjoined and partial perspectives of men" (D: 315 [emphasis added]). Eidelberg's statesman "rescues from mutual obstructiveness the diverse purposes and pursuits of men and thus facilitates their coordination and mutual intensification. But the richer unity he thereby brings into existence bears the impress of his own individuality" (D: 270). Reason as he uses it is both analytic and synthetic, deconstructive and constructive/architectonic. Unlike "modern" historicist reason, it is *also* noetic— the criteria for prudential judgment "are not simply imposed upon, or reducible to, the data" (D: 272). Noesis operates *through* an *individual*. So that such noesis is not prejudiced, crabbed, narrowly partial, or partisan, the soul of that individual must be large and well-articulated, comprehensive. The data perceived by the soul are "not susceptible to an infinitude of relationships" (D: 272, n. 30). This makes noetic perception and reasoning about perceptions possible. As for the passions, they are hierarchical in character, sometimes intensifying this noetic *and* deconstructive/constructive statesmanly reason, sometimes interfering with it. They are to be treated accordingly (D: 273). A political community founded upon such principles, well understood by statesmen, will achieve excellences surpassing those of any ancient polls and any existing modern state.

Woodrow Wilson took America on an entirely different course. With the constitutional amendments instituting the income tax, the direct election of Senators, and women's suffrage, Progressives prepared the grounds for the political ascendancy of the New Deal regime. "Jefferson's so-called 'Revolution of 1800' was nothing in comparison with the *second founding* envisioned by Wilson; and more than Jefferson, Wilson was a disciplined and constructive thinker with whom, among American statesmen, one can only compare men of the caliber of Madison and Hamilton" (D: 281–282).

Wilson rhetorically sought the elevation of "the *average man*," an elevation requiring the subordination of the oligarchs who had dominated the country since the 1870s. Elected government officials should depend upon the people: hence such Progressivist devices as initiative, referendum, and recall. "Government was no longer to protect the few from the many, so much as to protect the many from the few" (D: 291). Not Madisonian divide-and-rule but concentration of popular power would characterize Wilsonian democracy as reconstructed by Wilsonian political science. The president as party leader is a majoritarian instrument—although, as with all models emphasizing leadership rather than statesmanship, there is always some suspicion as to who is leading whom.

Wilsonian political science diverges from Wilsonian rhetoric as much as it diverges from the political science of the Founders. Wilson prefers the British constitution, whereby any law enacted by the legislature is automatically constitutional; the state, not the people, is sovereign. The additional feature of a (supposedly) nonpartisan, neutral civil service—in addition to a standing, professional, national military force—operating under the assumption that "technical men are more likely to be honest than party men" (D: 298), completes the apparatus of European statism. Political technicism forms one part of Wilson's "German historicism" (D: 301). Wilsonian scientific technique and efficiency replace Hamiltonian prudence and energy.

To make his democratic rhetoric effective and to establish the rule of his neo-Hegelian political science, Wilson seeks to dissolve two popular prejudices: that the old is good (the practical basis of reverence for the Constitution) and that wealth has a reasonably close relation to merit and hard work (the practical basis for esteem for commerce). The theoretical basis of both republicanism and commerce is natural right; Wilson does not popularize an attack on it, although, as a historicist, he quietly discards it. In place of reverence for the old and esteem for the presumed merit of the wealthy, Wilson magnifies resentment and appeals to compassion. The late David Broyles, Eidelberg's most careful reader, observes that Wilson's politics of compassion redirects the thumotic passions.[4] The newly authoritative thumocratic passions of envy and compassion are, above all, sustainable—difficult for any future statesman to counteract. Egalitarianism can be used to buttress a largely unelected state apparatus "fronted" by skilled rhetoricians. The mixed regime of the Founders becomes, on the rhetorical level at least, a democracy. "[C]ompassion and intelligence are to join in the task of alleviating the human condition by equalizing all conditions" (D: 347). A historicist, organicist, progressivism replaces the "Newtonian" balance of the Founders' regime. Whiggish distrust of political power gives way to "German" leadership, with the president apparently on history's leading edge. This is "nothing less than Caesarism, but of the profoundest kind" (D: 358)—a quasi-Nietzschean amalgamation or "gnostic union" of Caesar and Christ (D: 358). It may be a Caesarism more rhetorical than real, depending upon how effectively the "leader" can subordinate the supposedly neutral state bureaucracy.

Eidelberg's two shorter studies—*On the Silence of the Declaration of Independence* and *Beyond Détente*—reaffirm the teachings of the *Philosophy* and the *Discourse*.[5] His later writings in the field of Judaic studies, complemented by a rich array of policy analyses and polemics on Israeli politics, in many respects form a logical extension of his "American" writings. His emphasis, in the latter, on the rule of law and the need for scope for the thumotic aspect of the human soul comport well with Judaism, as does his insistence—contra the Straussians—that reason and revelation do not contradict one another (D: ch. 7, passim).[6] His insistence on the centrality of Jewish law reflects his sense that biology alone—even the philosophically informed biology of a Hans Jonas—does not provide a sufficient counterweight to German historicism, particularly in its Nietzschean and Heideggerian forms.

Eidelberg's scholarship on the American regime has considerable relevance to several outstanding issues much debated by American political scientists now. In the late 1960s and early- to mid-1970s, his frankly "aristocratic" tone could not have been more untimely. Diamond's "democratic" interpretation of the American regime surely had more appeal. But such questions as whether the regime is democratic, mixed, or oligarchic, and whether John Locke's philosophy must be regarded as its theoretical foundation, remain very much with us. Eidelberg's arguments on these matters remain stimulating. His argument on Wilson's project has been seminal, at least among Strauss-influenced scholars. Perhaps more urgently, as mentioned previously, Eidelberg refutes the attempt to historicize American political science along German lines and refutes, more or less in advance, the various attempts to employ "German" epistemological motifs for democratic purposes. His own Nietzsche-influenced, but not Nietzsche-dominated epistemology is at once more compatible with the "aristocratic" character of Nietzsche's thought, sensitive to the political implications of epistemology, and less vulnerable than Nietzsche is to tyrannical misuse. The "postmodernists"—who fail to understand the radically undemocratic character of their own epistemological presuppositions—might find an effective remedy in the consideration of what Eidelberg was writing a quarter of a century ago. If "Straussians" are to be classified among "postmodernists" in some very broad sense of that term,[7] they will find in Eidelberg no correction with respect to the matter of democracy and tyranny, which they scarcely need, but perhaps an intelligent dialogic partner in addressing the perennial question of "Jerusalem and Athens."

NOTES

1. Paul Eidelberg, *The Philosophy of the American Constitution: A Reinterpretation of the Intentions of the Founding Fathers* (New York: Free Press, 1968), p. 17. Hereafter referred to as "P" along with page references in the text.

2. Paul Eidelberg, *A Discourse on Statesmanship: The Design and Transformation of the American Polity* (Urbana: University of Illinois Press, 1974.) Hereafter referred to as "D" in references in text.

3. A good example of this phenomenon in recent times is Charles de Gaulle, who explicitly identified himself with an "idealized" or ennobled image of France. For an excellent recent account, see Daniel J. Mahoney, *De Gaulle: Statesmanship, Grandeur, and Modern Democracy* (Westport, Conn.: Praeger, 1996).

4. David Broyles, "American Politics: The Statesman's View," *Political Science Reviewer* 12, (Fall 1982), pp. 129–165.

5. See Paul Eidelberg, *On the Silence of the Declaration of Independence* (Amherst: University of Massachusetts Press, 1976), and *Beyond Détente: Toward an American Foreign Policy* (La Salle: Sherwood Sugden, 1977). The "silence" of the Declaration of Independence is its aristocratic conception of human nature, discussed previously.

6. See Paul Eidelberg, *Jerusalem vs. Athens: In Quest of a General Theory of Existence* (Lanham, Md.: University Press of America, 1983), and *Judaic Man: Toward a Reconstruction of Western Civilization* (Middletown, N.J.: The Caslon Company, 1996).

7. See Catherine Zuckert, *Postmodern Platos: Nietzsche, Heidegger, Gadamer, Strauss, Derrida* (Chicago: The University of Chicago Press, 1996).

· 17 ·

A New Birth of Freedom:
Harry V. Jaffa and the Study of America

Charles R. Kesler

$\mathscr{H}$arry V. Jaffa is the Straussian political scientist about whom his long-time friend William F. Buckley, Jr., wrote memorably, "If you think Harry Jaffa is hard to argue with, try agreeing with him." This *bon mot*, the opening sentence of Buckley's warm Foreword to Jaffa's 1984 volume, *American Conservatism and the American Founding*, played off the evident assumption that it was "nearly impossible" to agree with this scholar whose passionate devotion to the integrity of the American political tradition had led him into renowned, often acerbic, disputes with his closest philosophical and political friends, including many fellow students of Leo Strauss who are profiled in this book—Martin Diamond and Walter Berns, most notably. Yet Buckley's Foreword, a perceptive defense and explanation of Jaffa's ways, demonstrated that it *is* possible to agree with him and have him agree with you, temporarily, at least!

As exasperating as his arguments may be, however, one has to admit that it is almost impossible not to learn from them. His first book, *Thomism and Aristotelianism*, was an interpretation of Thomas Aquinas's *Commentary on the Nicomachean Ethics* in which Jaffa set out to disentangle pagan from Christian ethics. His purpose was to determine whether Aristotle's investigations of moral phenomena in all their richness might cure the self-impoverishment of modern social science—its presumptions that reason could neither confirm nor deny the truth of any moral claim, and hence that science ought to be "value-free." The challenge was to meet modern social science on its own ground—reason alone, unassisted by divine revelation of any sort—and to show that Aristotle's observations were more empirical, more faithful to the facts of moral and political life than the so-called scientific accounts. Precisely in order to meet this challenge, Aquinas's appeal to reason "informed by faith" (*fide informata*) had to be radically distinguished from Aristotle's reliance on natural reason alone. The positivism and relativism of modern social science were deeply rooted in modern philosophy—in the revolt against Aristotelian science that began in the 16th and 17th centuries. Jaffa's *Thomism and*

Aristotelianism thus contributed to the re-opening of an old question: whether Aristotle's *Ethics* might not be the true ethics.[1]

Jaffa's first book did not purport to answer this question directly, though it did provide its own penetrating interpretation of the *Nicomachean Ethics*. Instead, *Thomism and Aristotelianism* was a kind of propaedeutic, liberating Aristotle from Scholastic theology and not incidentally justifying the right of the Straussians rather than the Neo-Thomists to speak on behalf of the Philosopher. With the way cleared to move from Thomism back to Aristotelianism, a real test of the latter's adequacy as a guide to understanding moral and political affairs was possible. This demonstration of classical political science's vitality, indeed of its indispensability for the understanding of modern politics, was a chief object of Jaffa's second book, *Crisis of the House Divided: An Interpretation of the Issues in the Lincoln-Douglas Debates*.[2]

Unlike his fellow students of Strauss, who commenced their study of America with the Founding, Jaffa began his scholarship on America *in medias res*, with the great crisis over slavery that precipitated the Civil War. His consideration of the issues raised by Abraham Lincoln and Stephen Douglas required Jaffa to turn back to the Constitution and especially to the Declaration of Independence, of course, but he appealed to the Founding in order to illuminate the 1858 debates, not vice versa. His focus was the statesmanship of Lincoln and Douglas, not the political thought of the Founding per se. In pursuing this goal, he brought to the analysis of America several different themes of Strauss's scholarly project—the distinction between ancients and moderns, the interpretation of John Locke and his followers as decisively modern, the importance of statesmanship, the reciprocating dignity of reason and revelation, and even, to some extent, the significance of prophecy as a political format for philosophy.

The horizon of Jaffa's interpretation of America was thus much broader than that of his contemporaries, though in *Crisis* his view of the Founding was very similar to theirs. For almost all of them, the Founding was fundamentally Lockean, and as they had learned from Strauss, Locke was fundamentally Hobbesian. In the beginning was Strauss's chapter on John Locke in *Natural Right and History*, as it were; that, together with Strauss's thematic essays on the history of political philosophy (especially "What is Political Philosophy?") had taught his students that the significance of Locke lay not so much in his overt political teaching but in his philosophical underpinnings.[3] In *Natural Right and History*, the Locke of popular sovereignty, natural rights constitutionalism, and the right of revolution took a back seat to the Locke of private property and the state of nature. According to Strauss, Locke's account of property showed most clearly the true character of his state of nature doctrine—namely, that nature is a hostile, amoral, penurious condition from which man has to flee if he is to acquire knowledge, power, and comfortable security. Furthermore, Strauss showed that Locke's support for the liberation of acquisitiveness led to his solicitude for private property and for the bourgeois society dedicated to "the joyless quest for joy." In seeking primarily to understand the origins and character of modern natural rights, Strauss thus emphasized the similarities between Hobbes's and Locke's understanding of nature and society, not the conspicuous differences between their political teachings.

Strauss's students applied this view of Locke, in effect, to the study of America. In different ways, each started from the notion that the Founders had created a nation and a Constitution dedicated to the "solid but low" principles of Lockean liberalism. Martin Diamond's interpretation of *The Federalist* was perhaps the clearest and most influential statement of this case.[4] Yet given the more or less inevitable declension that Strauss had discerned in modern thought, his students knew that Hobbesian-Lockean liberalism was, in the long run at least, more low than solid. In the course of their careers, each of the Straussians struggled with this implication, and many discovered elements in the Founding that called for a higher or at least more complicated view of America. In some of his later essays, for example, Diamond supplemented *The Federalist*'s account of American institutions with Alexis de Tocqueville's, in order to show that federalism and decentralized administration provided room for a certain republican virtue in our politics. Walter Berns wrote extensively on such pre-liberal or higher liberal components of the Founding as the censorship of obscenity and pornography, tough libel laws, and nonpreferential assistance to religion. Herbert J. Storing limned the high statesmanship displayed in the Founding's great deliberative moments—at the Federal Convention, and again in the debates between the Federalists and Anti-Federalists (in whom he found at least a few lingering elements of pre-modern republicanism). Paul Eidelberg found in the same materials the makings of a new version of the ancient idea of the mixed regime, which he argued, controversially, had been the Founders' goal all along.[5]

Jaffa's first, and second, thoughts about America were different from any of these. In *Crisis of the House Divided*, he made one of his themes the distinction between the Founders' liberalism, which he agreed was basically Lockean (understood as Strauss had understood him), and Lincoln's higher and more comprehensive view of politics.[6] In Jaffa's account, the Founding was "modern" in the sense that it took its bearings by the egalitarian and "egotistic" view of natural rights, i.e., the Hobbesian-Lockean view. But the character of Abraham Lincoln was that of a proud or great-souled man, fiercely conscious of his own superlative virtue. Lincoln was an "ancient" or more precisely a classical exemplar of statesmanship, a magnanimous man whose character and activity became intelligible on the basis of Aristotle's *Ethics*, not on the basis of *Leviathan* or the *Second Treatise*.[7] Jaffa's America was not entirely "modern" then, for it contained within it and indeed its survival as a free society depended on the virtues of a great-souled statesman. Nor was Jaffa's America exclusively "modern" in the sense that Lincoln was an anachronism or a throwback to an earlier time—the startling appearance of a species previously thought extinct, as though America were the Jurassic Park of classical statesmanship. However modern were the principles of the American Founding, and Jaffa emphasized their Lockean provenance, *Crisis of the House Divided* was Jaffa's demonstration of the thesis that nature was the ground of politics, that nature had not been eclipsed by history, and that the distinctions of nature, including virtues and vices, remained permanently relevant to the understanding of political life.

Through his interpretation of Lincoln's statesmanship, that is, he showed the permanent relevance of classical natural right even to the politics of the United States. Jaffa's focus on statesmanship throughout his writings was not a form of sentimental hero worship but rather an application of classical political science, which insisted that the low be seen in the light of the high, rather than the high in light of the low. The latter viewpoint distorted the noble words and deeds that politics at its best could display. By contrast, the highminded viewpoint did not prevent the base elements of politics from revealing themselves in their fullness.[8] For example, Lincoln's magnanimity, his consciousness of his own excellence, was inseparable from his reasons for opposing slavery and defending the Union and the Constitution. Jaffa's interpretation of Lincoln's Lyceum Address built to the conclusion that the goodness of democracy itself depended on Lincoln's correctness in affirming that his own excellence and the proposition "that all men are created equal" were compatible, indeed, that each somehow implied the other. But how could magnanimity keep house with democracy?

It is easy to see how democracy might stand in need of magnanimity. American republicanism, Jaffa averred, is based on the equality of all men, but it depends in fact on founders and political saviors who were, to say the least, uncommon men. Other types of regimes depend on great men, too, of course, and aristocratic regimes reward them by elevating such men to the ruling class. Mixing nature with convention, these regimes then typically treat great virtues and talents as if they were heritable, and the natural aristocracy elides into a hereditary or artificial aristocracy. Republicanism stops short of rewarding such men by recognizing in them a right to rule, though often and especially in dire situations it will happily elect them to (temporary) office. In a strange way, however, American republicanism is more aristocratic than professed aristocratic regimes, inasmuch as it insists on recognizing and rewarding merit in non-hereditary ways. That is, it prefers its aristocracy straight, not mixed. It tries through elections to capture the talents and virtues of the natural aristocracy without letting it become an artificial one, though (under republican theory) even natural aristocrats' rule must be consented to by the people in order to be legitimate. All that is clear, and it explains why great men might occasionally by tapped, for utility's sake, by popular government. But it does not explain why *they* should choose *it*—why great souls should identify with the form and substance of popular government. After all, his people's neediness hardly mattered to Coriolanus.

Lincoln was an even more perfect example of the magnanimous man than Coriolanus, however, and Jaffa argued that it was this, paradoxically, that allowed Lincoln to embrace the cause of popular government. In *Crisis*, Jaffa developed the point through a comparison between Lincoln's position in the Lyceum Address and the argument of Callicles in Plato's *Gorgias*. Like Callicles, Lincoln admits that there are men who belong to "the family of the lion, or the tribe of the eagle" whose "genius for and will to domination," in Jaffa's words, "makes them virtually a species apart" from ordinary men. The natural superiority of these geniuses leads them to disdain the rule of law among equal citizens, for men like Alexander, Caesar, and Napoleon (Lincoln's examples) are radically unequal: they are a law unto themselves. That these great men were also destroyers of republican regimes is therefore not surprising. For "if their superiority is real," Jaffa commented, "as Lincoln no less than Callicles appears to affirm, then morality must in fact consist in whatever vindicates their superiority," however infamous that may appear to republicans and others deluded by "what is commonly called morality."[9]

What is it, however, that actually vindicates the superiority of such unequal men? By exploring this question, Jaffa threw new light on the sense in which Lincoln and the classics affirmed "a political role transcending that of Caesar and opposed to Caesar." Callicles had argued that the natural ruler's lust for domination would make him despise a regime of equal rights. "But the Calliclean thesis is not pushed far enough by its advocates," responded Jaffa. For the Caesar who one minute contemns the opinions of the weak (including their opinion of justice) in the next moment is seeking "the adulation of these selfsame weaklings." In other words, Callicles assumes "a qualitative similarity in the superior and inferior men, believing that the superior have the same pleasures as the inferior and differ only in their ability to gratify themselves." The "immortal" fame that stems from political success may be the highest good from the popular point of view, but it is not in fact the highest good; and in the best men, the appetite for political fame is therefore subordinated to the passion for genuine human excellence. The desire for this higher good makes the best men moderate or self-controlled in all their other appetites, which to inferior men is a wonderful phenomenon, for while the self-control of an Olympic athlete in respect of the pleasures of ordinary life is understandable, the moderation of a man who could (but refuses to) rule as a tyrant and thus gratify at whim his every appetite—achieving immorality and immortality all at once!—is wondrous. The one who can act as if there were a good beyond political fame must therefore be more than a man. This man of godlike virtue, as Aristotle described him, who can look down on fame itself, is "the antithesis to the Caesarian destroyer of republics." He is "the savior of republics."[10]

In the best case, a political savior's actions will succeed, which combined with the mysteriousness (from the popular viewpoint) of his motives may well win for him an even greater political glory than Caesar's. But "the actual achievement of such glory is incidental or accidental," because "the true statesman in the highest sense" aims not at fame but at virtue. "He alone can save his country who can forgo the honors of his countrymen," Jaffa explained. "Like Aristotle's great-souled man . . . he alone is worthy of the highest honor who holds honor itself in contempt, who prefers even to the voice of his countrymen the approving voice heard only by himself, 'Well done, thy good and faithful servant.'"[11] This is a striking formulation of the virtue of magnanimity, combining Aristotle's account with a quotation from the biblical parable of the talents, a part of Jesus's discourse with his disciples on the mount of Olives. In the New Testament, these words are spoken by a master, back at his estate after a long trip, who praises the servants to whom much was given, from whom much was expected, and by whom much had been accomplished.[12] Jaffa converted the master's praise of his servant into the magnanimous man's praise of himself, in keeping, one might say, with Aristotle's own discussion of magnanimity as the proud self-consciousness of moral excellence. In *Thomism and Aristotelianism*, Jaffa had described the magnanimous man as "the highest *nonphilosophic* human type" who desires to achieve a divine good insofar as he understands the divine to be a moral agent. That is, even as the gods are held to be great benefactors of men, so the magnanimous man desires to be a great benefactor.[13]

Yet to be a "good and faithful servant" is not quite the same thing as the magnanimous man's pride and pleasure in knowing that, compared to himself, "nothing is great." Strictly speaking, the magnanimous man does not conceive of himself as a servant to anyone or anything, not even virtue, which for him is inseparable from the actions and contemplation of his own greatness; like the gods, he is a benefactor, not a servant. To be sure, it is possible to understand the great-souled man's supreme moral virtue as being in the service of a higher virtue, what Aristotle would call intellectual virtue; but this would be to violate the horizon of the high-minded man's own self-understanding. "To explain to him that morality is good because it is a means to an end that is better than morality," argued Jaffa, "would be destructive of the motive that makes him concentrate all his energies in supreme actions of moral virtue, in which he thinks that he will attain a supreme good."[14] This does not mean that the magnanimous man may not "at the same time be something more than magnanimous," and Jaffa explicitly left open the possibility that the philosopher may also be magnanimous—though assuredly then his motives for great actions would not be the same as those of a non-philosophic magnanimous man.[15]

Still, by ascribing to Lincoln and to Aristotle the notion that the highminded man may consider himself a "good and faithful servant," Jaffa stressed a pious side of the great-souled statesman that is not apparent in Aristotle's *Ethics*. This sort of piety or sense of duty has Platonic roots but is more obviously Christian.[16] In his study of Lincoln in *Crisis*, Jaffa put together again, at least partly, the threads of classical political philosophy and Christianity that he had taken pains to disentangle in his first book. Jaffa suggested, gently, that Lincoln's understanding of himself transcended that of a magnanimous man. Whether this transcendence was in the direction of the love of God or the love of the Good or both is a difficult question, which Jaffa did not explicitly answer. Certainly, the Biblical God is a god of particular providence and of moral actions, and so is a source of duties and a kind of model for statesmanship as well as salvation. Platonic political philosophy had blended with Biblical religion in many striking forms, however, throughout the history of Judaism, Islam, and Christianity. Perhaps the most relevant to the case at hand was the tradition, arising from Alfarabi and Maimonides, of understanding prophecy as the supreme form of rational or philosophic legislation. Although

Strauss had written extensively on it, Jaffa did not appeal to this tradition in *Crisis*, even though he called attention to Lincoln's prophetic role in summoning the American people back to their "ancient faith." At any rate, in seeking to be a good shepherd to his flock, Lincoln looked explicitly to the Biblical tradition and invoked or alluded to God in explaining his own statesmanship and the Union's cause.[17] And Jaffa, in interpreting Lincoln, placed particular emphasis on his efforts to weave together revelation and reason in defense of American republicanism.

Tracing the many implicit connections in Lincoln's thought between political salvation and the salvation of individual souls, Jaffa argued that the Lyceum Address confirmed that "the qualifications of a savior . . . require a temptation in the wilderness." Even the savior "of the political soul of a free nation" must know "all the attractions of becoming the destroyer before he can become the savior." Jaffa showed persuasively that Lincoln disclosed those attractions to the attentive listener or reader of the Lyceum Address, but that Lincoln revealed at the same time his utter rejection and "triumph" over them.[18] Insofar as Lincoln was a magnanimous man, there was no room in his character for such a temptation, which would imply the presence of bad or excessive desires that would have to be conquered by reason. The high-minded man, according to Aristotle, is truly moderate in his desires.[19] The role of the political savior seems then to require a more Christian view of virtue, in which what Aristotle would call continence—the triumph over temptation—would be nobler than the achievement of moral good without temptation. Or at the least, Lincoln's role as a political savior required acknowledgment of temptation, whether or not he had actually experienced it.[20]

Jaffa's emphasis on the political savior took off from Lincoln's sense of the dangers presented by a Caesar-figure. Elaborating on Lincoln's quiet suggestions, Jaffa cast Lincoln as the figure who could save the republic from Caesarism. In painting this dramatic confrontation, Jaffa was guided less by Aristotle than by Shakespeare, one of Jaffa's—and Lincoln's—favorite authors, whose profound combination of classical rationalism and Christianity provided another matrix against which to view the drama of Lincoln's life and statesmanship.[21] The epigraphs of *Crisis* are Shakespearean: a passage from *Measure for Measure* on the problem of magnanimity, as it were, and a passage from *Macbeth*, relevant to the injustice of slavery. "O, it is excellent to have a giant's strength," announces the former, "but it is tyrannous to use it like a giant." The giant's strength is not given for him alone, in other words, but also for the common good; or to put it in Christian context, strength is not given for the sake of the strong but for service to God, which means, in this world, for the sake of the weak, too. In Lincoln's character, Jaffa argued, both "the giant's strength" and an incredible moderation and justice in the use of it reached their consummation. He quoted with approval Clinton Rossiter's famous eulogy: "Lincoln is the supreme myth, the richest symbol in the American experience. He is, as someone has remarked neither irreverently nor sacrilegiously, the martyred Christ of democracy's passion play." To which Jaffa added: "Many things in Lincoln's life, like the accident of his death, may have been fortuitous—or providential—but the myth that came to life with his passing was neither." It was, instead, Lincoln's own Shakespearean achievement, "the finely wrought consummation, of philosophic insight and a poetic gift."[22]

Lincoln was more than a magnanimous man, then, but Jaffa emphasized his magnanimity in order to illustrate, in the clearest terms possible, the continuing relevance of classical political philosophy to modern social science and to the understanding of American politics. By discovering a strikingly "ancient" trait in the midst of a modern political crisis, Jaffa also demonstrated *ad oculos* that the history of politics was not determined utterly by the history of political philosophy. Politics was a human activity with natural roots; nature did not change, and the nature of politics did not change, though of course changing political ideas and circumstances had enormously affected the manifestation, in mid-19th century America, of man's political capacity.

Nonetheless, Jaffa did not conceal the fact that Lincoln's enterprise involved a reinterpretation of the political principles of the American Founding. In fact, he advertised the novelty of Lincoln's interpretation and lauded it as a major feature of his greatness. Lincoln saw that the Founders' political understanding was "incomplete," according to Jaffa, because it had neglected the high for the sake of the low or, rather, because it had tried to understand the high in light of the low. Jaffa centered his discussion of this issue, as had Lincoln, on the meaning of the equality clause of the Declaration of Independence. Jaffa addressed the issue first in the context of the Lyceum Address, and again and more extensively in his interpretation of the Lincoln-Douglas debates.

In the first case, Jaffa argued that the "irreducible meaning" of the Declaration was that "the government of man by man, unlike the government of beasts by man, is not founded in any natural difference between rulers and ruled." Moreover, he associated Lincoln's view with Jefferson's on this "irreducible" contention: "As Jefferson was fond of saying, and Lincoln sometimes echoed, some men are not born with saddles on their backs to be ridden and others with spurs to ride them." This argument became a staple of Jaffa's subsequent discussions of the Declaration.[23]

But Jaffa then raised an objection, posed by Lincoln in the Lyceum Address, to this equality: if some men belong to "the family of the lion, or the tribe of the eagle" and are by nature so superior as to be virtually a species apart, then would not their submission to their inferiors be "a violation of natural right"? Jaffa answered that the savior or preserver of republics, having undergone his temptation in the wilderness, had "no desire for those things with respect to which the law lays constraints" on the "grasping passions" of ordinary men. For such a man "to claim superior rights would be absurd because such a claim would imply an appetite for those political goods" for which he has no desire. "All men *are* created equal," Jaffa wrote, "because those who are really superior are in the decisive sense above humanity." Here, then, the argument is *not* that "the government of man by man . . . is not founded in any natural difference between rulers and ruled," but rather that the natural differences are so great as to approximate the difference between god and man. The godlike political savior does not press his advantages, however, thus exhibiting the gentleness that in juxtaposition with his strength makes him so wondrous. Human equality remains "the decisive *political* truth," Jaffa concluded, "because those who might with justice deny it have no motive to deny it, while those who do deny it can only do so because of an unjust motive."[24]

Extreme human inequality and fundamental human equality were both true. This result may itself seem either too good to be true—a "*political* truth" is hardly the whole truth—or too true to be good, insofar as it appears to sideline all human virtue that fell short of the godlike. But Jaffa's point was that it was impossible to do justice to human equality and to human inequality at the same time in politics. On the one hand, the godlike man was not a god, after all, but only godlike, and hence had both to know his limitations and to acknowledge what was due him simply by virtue of his humanity.[25] On the other hand, it was natural to the superior man *not* to demand recognition of his superiority from those who might marvel at it but could never understand it. His "mastery" consisted not in exploiting other men but in "confirming and enhancing his fellow citizens' capacity for self-improvement" and chastening "any backsliding from the convictions that entitle them to be considered rational men."[26]

Jaffa tried further to moderate these tensions between equality and inequality in his second, extended discussion of the Declaration in *Crisis*, where the context was not magnanimity and political salvation but the debate over Amerian slavery and American freedom. Lincoln proved, by his reinterpretation of the Founders' precepts, that the equality of man was a higher principle than it might seem, that a more high-minded view of human equality was possible and desirable, according to Jaffa. To begin with, however, the Founders "read the Declaration as an expression of the sentiments of Locke's *Second Treatise of Civil Government*, wherein many of them had read, almost from childhood" that all men are naturally in a pre-civil state of nature, a state of perfect freedom and equality, though also of insecurity. This state of nature was the primeval basis of human or natural rights, rights based on the indefeasible passion of self-preservation. The right to life thus sprang from the passion for life, or rather from the passionate aversion to death, especially violent death. Given the "egotistical" quality of these rights, all duties in the state of nature were merely conditional. From "the strictly Lockean standpoint," no man was "under an obligation to respect any other man's unalienable rights until that other man is necessary to the security of his own rights." Equality was therefore a fact of human nature, an inconvenient and problematic fact because it led to a natural condition of insecurity verging on a *bellum omnium contra omnes*. The insecurity could be overcome—the right to life could be secured—only by leaving the state of nature for civil society. For the Founders, civil society was constituted by a movement away from nature, away from a highly undesirable condition under natural law and towards one in which minimal conditions of human welfare may be secured by positive law.[27]

By contrast, the idea of a pre-political state of nature "plays no significant role" in Lincoln's thought. For him, "all men are created equal" did not imply a condition from which men had a right to escape, but a condition "*toward* which men have a *duty* ever to strive." In the "predominantly Lockean interpretation" of the Declaration, civil society was constituted by the movement away "from the condition in which the equality of all men is actual"; but in Lincoln's "subtle reinterpretation," civil society is constituted by "the movement *toward* a condition in which the equality of men is actual." The natural state of man, in short, was not pre-political but political—a good civil society, in which the equality of man was secured, to the extent possible, by wise laws. In the full sense, however, equality remained a "standard maxim for free society," as Lincoln called it, a lofty goal for both public and private life, which could only be approximated and therefore would engender a "striving for justice" that "must be an ever-present requirement of the human and political condition."[28]

Lincoln "transforms and transcends" the original meaning of "all men are created equal," treating the proposition "as a transcendental goal and not as the immanent and effective basis of actual political right." But he does not destroy the original meaning: "Lincoln's morality then extends the full length of Jefferson's, but it also goes further," Jaffa wrote. Jaffa's case rested on Lincoln's reinterpretation of human rights. Whereas Jefferson had taught Americans to claim and assert their natural rights, Lincoln instructed his countrymen to *respect* "what they had asserted." To be sure, Jefferson had warned his fellow citizens of the divine wrath that might befall them for the injustice of slavery. But "the Lockean root of Jefferson's conviction— the deepest root of Jefferson's generation—regarded this precept as pre-eminently a requirement of enlightened self-interest," according to Jaffa. Whereas Jefferson, influenced by Locke, saw "all commands to respect the rights of others as fundamentally hypothetical imperatives"—i.e., "*if* you do not wish to be a slave, then refrain from being a master"—Lincoln saw them as "categorical" imperatives as well. "As I would not be a *slave*, so I would not be a *master*," he said famously. This implied that all men by nature have "an equal right to justice," not as an inference from their passions, but as a dictate of distributive justice or proportional equality— an acknowledgment by right reason of their status as rational animals, as *men*. Because all men have such a right to justice, they also have "a duty to do justice, wholly irrespective of calculations as to self-interest."[29]

The Kantian language was a bit misleading, because in this celebration of Lincoln's statesmanship Jaffa certainly did not mean to exclude prudence from the moral horizon. On strict Kantian terms, of course, prudence has no moral significance because the rules of morality brook no exceptions: "categorical" morality means that the circumstances and probable consequences of moral and political action do not matter. For the statesman, however, such prudential considerations are essential to wise moral and political action. What Jaffa meant to say, and did say at other points in his surrounding discussion, was that while man's duties were not derivative from his rights or self-interest, what his duties were in any particular circumstance would have to be decided with a view to justice and the common good. The fundamental point for Lincoln was that man's rights and duties were correlative: each arose from man's status as an imperfect rational animal, as a being whose place was in between God and the beasts. The law of man's nature reflected his place in nature, and his rights were under the authority of that law: e.g., no human being had a right to treat another like a dog, nor to rule like a god over his fellows. To this extent, Lincoln resubordinated natural rights to natural law. But this was natural law with equality as its leading edge and major precept—a new formulation not found in Aquinas, for instance, nor even in Jefferson, at least as described by Jaffa in *Crisis*.

In the course of his debates with Douglas, Lincoln showed what it meant to subordinate or incorporate natural rights under a natural law standard. He denounced as an absurdity Douglas's celebrated "don't care" policy—his value-neutral attitude toward the spread of slavery, which he thought a local question that should be decided by popular sovereignty in each territory. Douglas's prescription was absurd, Lincoln argued, because slavery was wrong and the "don't care" policy "tolerated the notion that there was such a thing as a right to do wrong." Here, then, natural rights bumped up against natural law. For the Lockean doctrine of an unalienable right to liberty, commented Jaffa, meant "that no one can consistently appeal to *my* sense of right to give up *my* liberty, but it does not mean that a man who enslaves another violates the enslaver's sense of *what is right*." In other words Lincoln "confounds the meaning of *a right*, meaning an indefeasible desire or passion, with *what is right*, meaning an objective state or condition in which justice is done." Lincoln never rejected or attacked natural rights in the Lockean sense, but he realized that "right conceived as subjective passion does *not* forbid us to do what is objectively wrong; it only directs us to do whatever we deem necessary for *our* lives and *our* liberty." And so he tried to find a foundation for rights in objective reason, in "an objective condition" discernible by reason, rather than in subjective passion.[30]

Lincoln's "reconstruction" of the Founders' meaning provided a higher and more consistent ground on which to be pro-freedom and anti-slavery than the egotistical or Lockean view of rights, whose objections to slavery were always in some sense conditional. Moreover, by condemning the enslavement of men who were by nature capable of freedom, Lincoln made effective for the first time in human history Aristotle's own distinction between natural and unnatural slavery, according to Jaffa.[31] But Lincoln's "creative interpretation" led also to a higher view of America. America was no longer based on a minimal social contract providing for mutual defense and prosperity, but was a regime or political community—in something like the classical sense—dedicated to, and constituted by, an opinion of justice.[32] Jefferson thought in terms of justice, too, but Jaffa maintained that for Jefferson the political association was more about preventing injustice than achieving justice; hence politics was essentially a necessary evil. Hence, too, "Jefferson was always more concerned to remind the people of their rights than of their duties. He emphasized what they should demand of their government rather than what they must demand of themselves."[33] For Lincoln, however, "the freedom of a free people resides above all in that consciousness of freedom which is also a consciousness of self-imposed restraints." But what was true of a free, and great, people was also true of "the highest ambition of the loftiest souls," whose ambition culminated not in domination but in the highest service they could render to others—namely, the perpetuation of the rule of law in democratic government.[34]

Since the publication of Crisis of the House Divided, Jaffa's principal research interest has been the American Founding. As the result of almost four decades inquiry, he has deepened and sharpened his understanding of that event and its principles. His second thoughts will be summed up in A New Birth of Freedom, the long-promised sequel to Crisis of the House Divided. Jaffa has completed the massive manuscript for the first volume of this now two-volume work, and plans to publish the first volume as soon as practicable. In this new book, which will follow Lincoln into the early years of his presidency, Jaffa admits that in Crisis he had failed to understand Lincoln completely because (to adapt Strauss's words on a similar occasion) he had read Lincoln too literally, by not reading him literally enough. That is, Jaffa writes that he had been wrong in arguing that Lincoln's understanding of natural rights transformed and transcended that of the Founders. Jaffa had thought that Lincoln's "Aristotelianizing," i.e., his high-minded view of human rights, was original, whereas Lincoln had been right all along in disclaiming originality and tracing his view of justice to the Founding and particularly to the Declaration of Independence.[35]

Jaffa came to this realization partly as a result of a re-examination of the Founders' arguments for religious freedom. In Crisis he had regarded the Founders' arguments for the separation of church and state as a pure emanation of Enlightenment rationalism. Even in so pious a document as George Washington's Farewell Address, Jaffa detected only "the mingling, like oil and water, of the rationalism and religion of the eighteenth century." There was "no trace of reverence in Washington's discussion of the need for reverence," nor in The Federalist's similar pleadings, nor in Jefferson's; for all of them, "the sacred is treated as a necessity of the profane." In Lincoln, however, "the profane is transformed into the sacred," and the Civil War, as interpreted by him, fused religious passion and secular rationalism into the canon of America's "political religion."[36] In re-thinking the Founders' views on religious liberty, however, Jaffa discovered in them a profound meditation on, and response to, the changes that Christianity over many centuries had wrought in politics; and in this context, even the most Enlightened of the Founders' arguments glowed with a reasonableness and a true charity that bespoke a genuine love of man's highest ends.

To explore Jaffa's new view of religious freedom as the solution to a problem immanent in Western Civilization is beyond the scope of this chapter; but some brief comments, at least, would not be out of order. The starting point of his re-evaluation was probably the natural theology of the Declaration, which he increasingly featured in his accounts. Although natural reason may not be able to prove that God exists, it can prove that a divine nature would carry to perfection those incomplete perfections discoverable in man ("reason, justice, mercy") without the corresponding imperfections. At the Declaration's core as understood by the Founders, Jaffa thus emphasized, was an ontological doctrine of man's place in an intelligible universe, which reason and Revelation agreed in conceiving of as crowned by a perfect Being—the cause and end of the universe's intelligibility. Accordingly, both natural and revealed morality rested on the premise that man is neither beast nor God.[37] What had once been the Declaration's "irreducible meaning," a kind of least common denominator among interpretations of the document, now became for Jaffa its heart and soul; and the differences between Lincoln's and the Founders' understanding of human equality began to be elided or to seem less significant. This objective and even commonsensical account of man's place in a rationally structured universe—especially in contrast to the historicist and nihilistic arguments of later philosophers and their votaries—suggested more and more to Jaffa that the Founders were not far from Lincoln's view of human rights as something high-minded or God-given: that natural rights were expressions not of a base but of a noble and lawful freedom.[38]

From Lincoln's point of view, of course, it was he who was following the Founders on this question. Jaffa has come to the conclusion that Lincoln was right about that. Lincoln *had* learned from the Declaration of Independence that human rights were the dispensations of a just God or of an intelligible nature. But the Founders had come to this conclusion as part of their general confrontation with the problem of political authority in Christendom. Before the advent of universal monotheism, Jaffa points out (following Fustel de Coulanges's enduring analysis), each city had its own sheltering deities and the city's laws and its founding were in various ways the work of these gods. The ancient city's laws were, as far as its citizens were concerned, a species of divine law, an assumption that was shattered, however, by the rise of Christianity. The One God did not play favorites with earthly cities. His was a heavenly city. The various cities of men were then left to find a new reason why their citizens should obey them. Christianity's severing of the classical relation between God (or gods) and the Law led to a millenium-and-a-half of *stasis* in the West, of conflicts between Pope and Emperor, Emperor and Pope, culminating in the wars of the Reformation. Seeking to escape the holocausts of the Old World, the American Founders found in the doctrine "all men are created equal" a solution to the hitherto insoluble problem of civil war within Christendom, reasons Jaffa. The doctrine announced that God's authority was manifest not in kings, popes, or parliaments, but in the people, whose rule was for the first time to be understood as the collective expression of individual rights, imbued in each individual by the Creator. So in popular government based on the social contract, divine authority was finally reunited with the rule of law.[39]

But the doctrine of rights *limited* even as it authorized popular sovereignty. The purpose of government was limited to the securing of men's rights, including above all the right of conscience, which was the individual and political liberty that resulted from men's duty to worship their Creator in the manner they thought most agreeable to Him. Liberty of conscience was protected even against the people themselves—a guarantee made explicit, for the first time in human history, in many of the state constitutions, in the prohibition of religious tests for office in the U.S. Constitution, and in the First Amendment. Purer, non-persecuting forms of Christianity could now thrive. The civil war in the Christian West had been waged partly over the definition of true religion, which meant over the true definition of theological and intellectual virtue; this warfare had been destructive of religious faith, moral virtue, and political decency, not to mention of the civic friendship that was practically a precondition of the more intimate friendships in which intellectual virtue could be pursued. Under these circumstances, the self-assertion of virtue had actually become inimical to political decency and moderation. For this reason, the Founders did not make their revolutionary political reforms in the name of virtue itself, much less in the name of true religion, but in the name of human liberty. As a consequence of excluding direct claims to rule based on superior virtue, however, the Founders opened a new avenue for moral virtue to reassert itself as a qualification for election to office and as an informal criterion of citizenship and statesmanship. With church separated from state—with the theological virtues prescinded from political rule, and vice versa—magnanimity was again free to show itself for what it was. George Washington became possible, as it were; and Abraham Lincoln, too.[40]

What becomes of Lincoln's greatness in Jaffa's new estimation? Lincoln was, Jaffa writes, less original but more profound than he had originally thought. Lincoln distilled the political thought of the Founding to its purest, most concentrated form, and expressed it with supreme eloquence. By defining the issues of the Civil War, that "people's contest," in terms of the people's fidelity to their "ancient faith," he effectively joined with the Founders in order to defend the Law against those who had abandoned it in order to worship the golden calf of slavery. In *Crisis*, Jaffa had seen the Civil War as the greatest (and characteristic) drama of American politics, pitting equal natural rights against majoritarianism in a "modern" dispute that could be reconciled only by Lincoln's magnanimous statesmanship. In *A New Birth of Freedom*, however, Jaffa depicts the Civil War as a world-historical drama in which Lincoln personifies the classical prudence and high-toned natural rights teaching of the Founders, in opposition to the Confederacy, whose most sophisticated apologists base their defense of it, and of slavery, on some of the most willful, historicist, and collectivist elements of modern political philosophy. For Jaffa, the "new birth of freedom" signifies more now than the nation's rebaptism in its Aristotelianized "political religion." While definitely including the nation's re-dedication to the principles of the Revolution, Lincoln's "new birth of freedom" means also America's baptism of fire, so to speak, as the model regime and exemplary empire of the modern world—as the best regime neither of the ancients nor the Church but of the civilization formed by the confluence of faith and reason. Jaffa calls the United States or, more precisely, its principles—for he is describing a regime in speech, as articulated by Lincoln and the Founders—nothing less than "the best regime of Western civilization."[41]

Finally, a few words on Jaffa as a controversialist and avowed conservative. Like Strauss, Jaffa seldom wrote a theoretical work without adverting to the practical situation or crisis to which it might be related. The maladies of modern social science that Jaffa set out to cure or ameliorate in *Thomism and Aristotelianism*, for example, were not merely theoretical ills; they were intimately bound up with "present-day political problems," he wrote, meaning both the external confrontation with Communism and the internal weakness or demoralization of the Free World. In *Crisis*, he indicated that the issues of the Lincoln-Douglas debates lived on in the current struggles over civil rights (and over the Cold War), and that the academic dispute over the interpretation of the 1858 debates was itself a kind of continuation of those debates. Unlike Strauss, Jaffa forthrightly calls himself a conservative, and he has made the Founding and Lincoln central to his conservatism. Since he regards the current academic and political debate over the meaning of the Civil War and the Founding as a kind of continuation of those great contests, he has freely adopted a polemical style in his many essays on contemporary politics, and especially in his many critiques of modern American conservatism.[42] But he is interested in conservatism mainly because he thinks it is the best means by which "the best regime of Western civilization" may be perpetuated.

In *How to Think About the American Revolution* (1978), *American Conservatism and the American Founding* (1984), and *Original Intent and the Framers of the Constitution: A Disputed Question* (1994),[43] Jaffa exposed, somewhat acerbically, the far-reaching alienation of modern conservatives—paleo, neo, originalist, libertarian, Straussian, traditionalist, populist, "doughfaced" Northern, and Southern—from their own political tradition. The American political tradition, he insisted, had as its central idea the Lincolnian, and Jeffersonian, understanding of human equality. This equality of natural rights was not the enemy or even the opposite of freedom, but freedom's foundation or counterpart, inasmuch as men deserved to be free because they were equally human beings. Jaffa labors to reconstruct American conservatism along Lincolnian lines, and he disagrees with many of his friends' preference for Tocquevillian, Burkean, or Hayekian conservatism because he denies that any of these schools quite does justice to America. For that very reason, he deems the alternatives insufficiently attentive to the challenging demands of Aristotle's approach to natural and political right, which Jaffa has, for more than four decades, sought to apply to, or to elicit from, America. Martin Diamond put it nicely once, that in the beginning political philosophy consisted of the Socratic critique of the opinions of the Athenians, and that for a long time it consisted of the study of the Socratic critique of the opinions of the Athenians. But Harry V. Jaffa has shown, said Diamond, that political philosophy may consist also of the Socratic critique of the opinions of the Americans.

NOTES

1. Harry V. Jaffa, *Thomism and Aristotelianism: A Study of the Commentary by Thomas Aquinas on the Nicomachean Ethics* (Westport, Conn.: Greenwood Press, 1979; orig. ed., 1952), p. 14.

2. Harry V. Jaffa, *Crisis of the House Divided: An Interpretation of the Issues in the Lincoln-Douglas Debates* (Chicago: University of Chicago Press, 1982; orig. ed., 1959), pp. 1–3, 10–14.

3. Leo Strauss, *Natural Right and History* (Chicago: University of Chicago Press, 1953), pp. 202–251; Strauss, *What is Political Philosophy? and Other Studies* (Westport, Conn.: Greenwood Press, 1973; orig. ed., 1959), pp. 9–55, esp. pp. 49–51. Cf. *Ibid.*, pp. 302–305.

4. See, for example, Martin Diamond, "The Federalist," in Leo Strauss and Joseph Cropsey, eds., *History of Political Philosophy*, 2nd edition (Chicago: Rand McNally, 1972; orig. ed., 1963), pp. 631–651. "Other political theories had ranked highly, as objects of government, the nurturing of a particular religion, education, military courage, civic-spiritedness, moderation, individual excellence in the virtues, etc. On all of these *The Federalist* is either silent, or has in mind only pallid versions of the originals, or even seems to speak with contempt." Diamond, "Democracy and *The Federalist*: A Reconsideration of the Framers' Intent," in William A. Schambra, ed., *As Far As Republican Principles Will Admit: Essays by Martin Diamond* (Washington, D.C.: American Enterprise Institute, 1992), pp. 17–36, at 31.

5. See, for example, William Schambra, ed., *As Far as Republican Principles Will Admit*, chs. 7–8, 21; Walter Berns, *Freedom, Virtue, and the First Amendment* (Westport, Conn.: Greenwood Press, 1969; orig. ed., 1957); Herbert J. Storing, *What the Anti-Federalists Were FOR* (Chicago: University of Chicago Press, 1981); Paul Eidelberg, *The Philosophy of the American Constitution* (New York: The Free Press, 1968).

6. On Strauss's "authoritative exposition of Hobbesian and Lockean natural-right doctrine," see Jaffa, *Crisis of the House Divided*, p. 425n21.

7. *Crisis*, pp. 216–219, 325–327.

8. Cf. Leo Strauss, *Liberalism Ancient and Modern* (New York: Basic Books, 1968), p. 207.

9. *Crisis*, pp. 211–214.

10. *Crisis*, pp. 212–217.

11. *Crisis*, p. 218.

12. See Matthew 25:21, "His lord said unto him, Well done, thou good and faithful servant: thou hast been faithful over a few things, I will make thee ruler over many things: enter thou into the joy of thy lord." Cf. Matthew 25:23, 26–30.

13. *Thomism and Aristotelianism*, pp. 116, 120–123, 138–140. In *Nicomachean Ethics*, Book X, Aristotle makes clear that the gods cannot have moral qualities because the divine good, as such, is contemplation, and the gods must be thought of as being perfectly self-sufficient. *Nicomachean Ethics* 1178b7–22. Cf. also *Metaphysics* 1074b15–35, and Jaffa, *Thomism and Aristotelianism*, p. 212n5.

14. *Thomism and Aristotelianism*, p. 140; Aristotle, *Nicomachean Ethics*, 1124b10–18, 1124b30–1125a4, 1125a15.

15. *Thomism and Aristotelianism*, p. 141. For a different view, see Rene Antoine Gauthier and Jean Yves Jolif, eds., *L'Ethique a Nicomaque: Introduction, Traduction, et Commentaire*, 2nd ed. (Louvain: Publications Universitaires, 1970), vol. 2, part 1, pp. 272–273, 278–279, 283–284, 290–291, 293–296. And cf. *Crisis*, pp. 260–261.

16. In his 1972 Introduction, Jaffa remarked that *Crisis*, like the Lincoln-Douglas debates themselves, was a form of the Thomistic disputed question, which was itself a form of the Socratic dialogue. *Crisis*, pp. 8–9.

17. *Crisis*, pp. 218–219 and pp. 415–416n15. Consider also pp. 220 and 226.

18. *Crisis*, pp. 220–222.

19. Aristotle, *Nicomachean Ethics*, 1124a1–4, 14–21, 1146a10–17. Cf. *Crisis*, pp. 354–355.

20. On Lincoln's view of the inescapable limits of political salvation, see *Crisis*, ch. 10, "The Teaching Concerning Political Moderation," *passim*.

21. "For Brutus—at least Shakespeare's Brutus—although a man of purest intentions, was a guileless bungler. It was Cassius who possessed the wisdom of the serpent, who would have murdered Anthony instead of allowing him to speak at Caesar's funeral. The man who would be a match for Caesar must somehow combine the virtues *and* political capacity of which Aristotle speaks; he must somehow unite, in his single person, the goodness of Brutus and the wiliness of Cassius." *Crisis*, p. 215. Jaffa notes that "this interpretation of *Julius Caesar* was suggested to me by Prof. Leo Strauss." *Crisis*, p. 415n14.

22. *Crisis*, pp. 15, 215–216, 232, 261, 264. Cf. Jaffa, *American Conservatism and the American Founding* (Durham: Carolina Academic Press, 1984), p. 68.

23. *Crisis*, p. 211. Cf., e.g., Jaffa, *Equality and Liberty* (Oxford: Oxford University Press, 1965), pp. 137–138; *The Conditions of Freedom* (Baltimore: Johns Hopkins, 1975), pp. 150–153; *How to Think About the American Revolution* (Durham: Carolina Academic Press, 1978), pp. 40–42; *American Conservatism and the American Founding*, pp. 40–41.

24. *Crisis*, pp. 210–213, 217, 222.

25. Thus Jaffa quoted Lincoln's remarks on July 10, 1858: "It is said in one of the admonitions of the Lord, 'As your Father in Heaven is perfect, be ye also perfect.' The Savior, I suppose, did not expect that any human creature could be as perfect as the Father in Heaven; but he said, 'As your Father in Heaven is perfect, be ye also perfect.' He set that up as a standard, and he who did most towards reaching that standard, attained the highest degree of moral perfection. So I say in relation to the principle that all men are created equal, let it be as nearly reached as we can." *Crisis*, pp. 316–317.

26. *Crisis*, p. 341.

27. *Crisis*, pp. 314–328.

28. *Crisis*, pp. 318–321.

29. *Crisis*, pp. 225, 318–327.

30. *Crisis*, pp. 328–329.

31. *Crisis*, pp. 342–346.

32. Jaffa deployed this interpretation of America as, in principle, a kind of regime in his later dispute with Martin Diamond, which concerned Diamond's contention that the Declaration provided "no guidance" as to the best form of government that Americans should adopt. See Jaffa, *How to Think About the American Revolution*, pp. 75–140. In this book, Jaffa contended that the views of Lincoln and the Founders on republicanism as the best kind of regime were virtually identical. But cf. his earlier remarks, in the context of the Supreme Court's "one man, one vote" decisions, in *The Conditions of Freedom*, pp. 158–159.

33. *Crisis*, pp. 322, 328.

34. *Crisis*, p. 306.

35. On this point, cf. *Crisis*, pp. 318 and 328.

36. *Crisis*, pp. 237–245.

37. See, for example, *The Conditions of Freedom*, pp. 152–156.

282   Charles R. Kesler

38. Cf. *Crisis*, p. 211, and *How to Think About the American Revolution*, pp. 41–43, 104–111, 131–135.

39. See Jaffa, "Equality, Liberty, Wisdom, Morality, and Consent in the Idea of Political Freedom," *Interpretation* (January 1987), vol. 15, no. 1, pp. 24–28; and Jaffa, *The American Founding as the Best Regime: The Bonding of Civil and Religious Liberty* (Claremont: The Claremont Institute, 1990), 26pp.

40. *Ibid.*

41. *The American Founding as the Best Regime, passim.*

42. Cf. *American Conservatism and the American Founding*, pp. 135–138. "I have, I think, sufficiently proved that the academic debate about the American political tradition is for the most part little more than a concealed (or unconscious) form of the political debate. Conducting my argument by political, rather than academic speech, is part of my attempt to restore to this debate both its seriousness and its vitality." In so doing, Jaffa understands himself to be demonstrating "both the possibility and the necessity of natural right becoming political right." *Ibid.*, pp. 135, 138.

43. Jaffa, *Original Intent and the Framers of the Constitution: A Disputed Question* (Washington, D.C.: Regnery Gateway, 1994).

· *18* ·

Back to the Future:
Ralph Lerner's Political Thought

Miriam Galston

𝑅alph Lerner's life work is, on its face, preoccupied with the past. Quite apart from his numerous studies of the political thought of the founding period in America, he has also studied, written, and taught extensively about medieval Islamic and Jewish philosophers.[1] Yet anything more than a casual reading of his writings reveals that Lerner does not worship the past for its own sake, just as any amount of time in his company reveals a modern man—practical, sensible, humorous, energetic, curious about the details of the here and now, and relentlessly forward looking. This essay focuses on the ways in which Lerner's exploration of the founding period has relevance for today's problems and tomorrow's solutions.

One of the most intensely discussed themes among contemporary moral, political, and legal thinkers is the possibility of and the conditions for self-governance and autonomy.[2] Although the thought of many eighteenth and early nineteenth-century American political thinkers is often associated with elitism on the part of the ruling classes and indifference, if not disdain, for the independence of ordinary citizens,[3] Lerner's investigation of revolutionary America reveals that the Founders were preoccupied with our modern concerns with self-governance and autonomy in a variety of important ways.

First and foremost, one of the centerpieces of Lerner's critique of much current historical scholarship is that it presumes that ideology, rather than ideas, motivated the major players during the revolutionary period.[4] The "new historians," as Lerner calls them, do not take the Founders' statements, ideas, and arguments at face value—that is, as products of their considered and analytical reflection on their times, practices, and culture. Rather, they see them as the psychologically or sociologically inevitable manifestations of their times, practices, and culture. The new historians concede that the Founders' ideas were part of their attempts to make sense of the world in which they lived, a world of upheavals and lacking adequate customs or precedents to deal with the issues of the day. For the new historians, however, this effort was ideologically constrained: the reasoning of the revolutionaries, like that of people in general, could not distance itself sufficiently from the contemporary situation to achieve independence of mind and thoughtful deliberation.[5]

In contrast, a theme of all of Lerner's works, and the explicit theme of *The Thinking Revolutionary* and *Revolutions Revisited*, is the ability of some people, some of the time, to attain just such independence. He defends this position, first, by producing evidence, concrete cases, of the writings of individual Founders that exhibit a concern with the integrity of ideas as well as with their utility. His examples are drawn largely from the thought and actions of such figures as Benjamin Franklin, Thomas Jefferson, Benjamin Rush, and John Quincy Adams. The new historians have, of course, focused much attention on these individuals, among others, and have found in them support for their ideological assessment of the Founders' limitations. Lerner's innovation is to recognize that the past, precisely because of its distance from our time and modes of thinking, may represent a distinctive, even foreign, way of looking at the world. In assuming a fundamental kinship between their way of thinking and ours, we run the risk of injecting into the past the brand of ideological determinism that is prevalent in our times but may have been foreign to theirs.[6] As a result, because of our contemporary doubts about people's ability to transcend their cultural horizons, we tend to understate the level of the Founders' deliberateness and their expectations for the practical effects of their ideas. In short, for Lerner, the Founders' intellectual limitations should be one of the objects of a proper historical inquiry rather than its operational premise.[7]

One of Lerner's conclusions is that the Founders were in fact deeply respectful of tradition. At the same time, they recognized the uniqueness of their situation and saw themselves as overthrowing much of the old regime and contributing to an experiment in enlightened self-governance.[8] Ultimately it was this conviction that motivated their reflection on the status quo and their deliberateness in selective borrowing from the past and innovating with an eye toward the future.[9] "Among the most thoughtful in each generation one finds a measured regard for their respective past along with a professed commitment to surpass it."[10] This commitment often expressed itself in the hope that future generations would be able to enjoy the fruits of the revolution and its liberating innovations to a greater degree than could their predecessors.[11] Like succeeding generations, but for different reasons, the Founders recognized the past as both admirable and limiting.[12]

Lerner also concludes that the Founders were keenly aware of the need to temper the dictates of theory with the exigencies of political reality.[13] He emphasizes that the American Enlightenment, in contrast to the French Enlightenment, had different objectives and different approaches to realizing them. The American Enlightenment was a product of practical experience and observation, not just "pure theorizing." The difference, in a word, was between Voltaire and Jefferson, or between political philosophy and political science.[14] As a consequence, Lerner notes wryly, the American approach may have at times displayed "an appalling lack of theoretical clarity and coherence." Yet, by the same token, it avoided some of the European Enlightenment's "delusions."[15]

Perhaps it was the Americans' practical orientation that led them, as believers in the long-term integrity of the political process, to accept practices, including the treatment of persons of color, that they found morally objectionable. Lerner is no apologist when he recounts the details: not only does he acknowledge that Jefferson's modest proposal to free slaves in Virginia would have taken an interminably long time to achieve its goal,[16] but he narrates with meticulous detail the mistreatment of persons of color by thoughtful revolutionaries and others.[17] Lerner contrasts the slavery of the classical world, which "was limited to the body," with Tocqueville's damning characterization of American slavery as "altogether singular and singularly cruel" because it enslaved both the body and the soul.[18] And he notes candidly the final irony, that the whites' treatment of the blacks increased the servile nature of the whites themselves and made them less, not more, fit for self-governance.[19]

In short, Lerner does not exaggerate the revolutionaries' talents or achievements. Although his defense of their thoughtfulness and their belief in the importance of ideas may be dismissed by some as romanticizing the Founders' vision, in fact his conclusions are balanced, even understated. Some of the revolutionaries were deliberate and thoughtful, others were not.[20] Those who were, combined the insights of political philosophy with the wisdom of practical experience. They were hopeful and sober both.[21] They were reasonable in the deep sense of being committed to the power of ideas, aware of the importance of grounding the new in the old, and cognizant of the power of political pressures.

For Lerner, not only were the Founders capable of overcoming the ideological determinism posited by the new historians in that they reached a certain critical distance from the assumptions and opinions of their times. Lerner's Founders believed in the ability of *citizens* to live reasoned lives and thus to attain a significant measure of autonomy and self-improvement. Moreover, they considered it "axiomatic" that educating citizens to live such a life was a necessary, if not sufficient, condition of establishing and maintaining a republican form of government.[22]

Detailing the Founders' differing approaches to educating the citizenry is one of Lerner's central purposes. In this regard, Lerner elaborates Benjamin Franklin's hope to inspire the public to master its passions, especially its passion for material acquisitions, and to instil greater self-reliance in ordinary citizens by encouraging them to be less slavish to authorities.[23] Implicit in Franklin's approach is the conviction that lasting self-government cannot be achieved unless individuals internalize certain beliefs and related behaviors through habituation and the resulting transformation of their character. Jefferson's belief in the capacity of individuals for self-governance expressed itself in such things as his efforts to revise and improve the laws of Virginia, to establish a genuine university there centering on a secular rather than a divine curriculum, and to construct a library of national stature.[24] For Lerner, all of Jefferson's proposals reveal his deep belief in the possibility of freeing human minds from antiquated strictures and his judgment that legislation can play an important role in creating the conditions of liberation.[25] Further, according to Lerner, the practice of the United States Supreme Court Justices, while riding circuit, to exhort juries through political charges should itself be seen as an illustration of the Justices' belief in the educability of those who heard their sermons and the significance of taking part in their education.[26] Ultimately the justices' efforts to teach "people how to be good republicans" reflected their conviction that free government depends upon more than the wisdom and protection of constitutional rights characteristic of the judiciary's institutional role. Rather, Lerner's thesis is that for the members of the judiciary themselves, as for Abraham Lincoln decades later, "in this and like communities, public sentiment is everything."[27]

Contrary to the conventional understanding, Lerner observes that the Founders' approach to the protection of private property was part of their rejection of the "hierachical world" of "settled privilege" favored in Europe. They linked property rights to human rights as well as to economic growth; economic inequality to equality of opportunity; and the emphatic guaranty of inalienable rights to "an active, querulous citizenry, quick to be jealous [of established power], mistrustful of officialdom, and quick to act on their misgivings."[28] Thus, in Lerner's view the protection of these rights was the soil that would nourish citizens' capacity for self-governance and freedom.

The preceding aspects of Lerner's political analysis[29] thus contrast sharply with the familiar story that the Founders hoped to inject stability in the embryonic union exclusively by harnessing and building upon individuals' self-interest coupled with the enlarged sphere of the emerging commercial republic, presumably because they were pessimistic about the degree to which the population at large was fit to govern itself. The narrative that emerges from Lerner's historical research challenges this understanding as unidimensional and substitutes for it one that emphasizes both the aspirations as well as the fears of the Founders. They were realists who understood well the baser instincts of the populace. In this regard they attempted to erect a series of institutional structures that would curb the body politic's worst excesses. The Founders were far from being cynics, however. A democratic republic could not long survive shored up by external checks and external circumstances alone.[30] Moreover, they believed in the possibility as well as the desirability of citizen virtue, and spent no small part of their energies on cultivating the conditions most conducive to its emergence and maintenance.[31]

In the process, the Founders believed that they were breaking with the rigid elitism and encrusted hierarchichal structures of the past.[32] Benjamin Franklin, for example, saw the threat to politics from vanity, which led him to attack "pretension in high places and low, [and] aristocratic or pseudoaristocratic presumptuousness."[33] Thomas Jefferson identified as one of his three most significant legacies his proposal for ensuring religious liberty in opinions and practices so that people would be free to follow "the evidence proposed to their minds."[34] The spirit of republican egalitarianism can also be seen in Jefferson's proposals relating to inheritance laws, such as his proposal to eliminate decedents' abilities to restrict the alienation of their property so as to perpetuate "patrician dynasties" and the bill he introduced to end the discrimination in favor of male heirs.[35]

Lerner is the first to admit the ambiguity of the evidence and, thus, presumably, the tentativeness of his conclusions. He notes that at times the Founders stressed the importance of statesmenship and civic minded leaders leading the nation; at times the importance of maximizing citizen virtue and adopting educational measures designed to tap into the potential for such virtue wherever it may exist; and at times the importance of institutional structures, both because of their role in educating citizens and leaders alike to the opportunities for public spirited service and as an insurance policy against the predictable departures from the idealized roles just sketched. For Lerner, taken together, these differences of emphasis thus represent the deliberate, thoughtful insights of a group of exceptional leaders aware of the liberating possibilities for self-government present in the newly emergent republican form of government as well as the variety of destructive excesses to which such freedom was prone.[36] In other words, the differences in emphasis on the part of individual revolutionary leaders, as well as the variations within the thought of individual Founders at different times,[37] may reflect their insights into the psychological, social, and political complexities of the new nation rather than a lack of deliberateness or decisiveness about the most effective direction for realizing its republican potential.

It is thus not surprising that Lerner elaborates in many places the Founders' misgivings about the role of virtue as the cement holding the republican building blocks together. Publius, Lerner notes, "knew that while 'the people commonly *intend* the PUBLIC GOOD,' they do not always '*reason right* about the *means* of promoting it.'"[38] The first Justices similarly assumed that the state of mind prevalent among citizens was the principle of self-interest, and that it was this inclination that they aimed to counteract in their efforts to educate citizens to civic virtue.[39] Lerner gives a thoughtful and disturbing account of the commercial republicans, namely, those Founders who hoped that the moderate passions of citizens of a commercial republic would serve as a safeguard against the ambitions of budding despots, aristocrats, and clerical enthusiasts alike.[40]

And yet, as the American revolution became increasingly distant, the revolution itself became a quasi-mythical moment in Americans' common past to be reckoned with. The Founders were able to defend their departures from the past relatively openly because of the revolutionary atmosphere at the end of the eighteenth century, even as their innovations were constrained by the pull of tradition in the form of people's existing habits and practices. The Founders' successors, in contrast, were faced with a more complex challenge. As the republic developed and the population and its circumstances changed, there was a need for the laws and practices of the country to evolve accordingly.

At the same time, the Founders' successors, faced with these changes and the developments culminating in the Civil War, recognized two general truths. First, it was critical for the republic to remain true to the "principles of the regime," which encompassed a love of reason as well as a love of liberty.[41] As Lerner puts it, figures such as Abraham Lincoln and John Quincy Adams were committed to "binding a diverse public in a diverse land to a singular and ennobling ideal," so that the "principles of American revolutionary constitutionalism" would continue to influence the moral and intellectual improvement of mankind.[42]

Second, it was critical for the leaders to make clear and for the population at large to understand that the political changes occurring were merely a reworking of features of the original revolutionary design. Thus, to some extent, the Founders' successors were forced to disguise their creative responses to changed circumstances by casting them as continuations of the original founding event and its canonical, hence relatively uncontroversial, interpretations.[43] Their need to conceal the degree to which nineteenth century practices had to diverge from their eighteenth century counterparts was not inconsistent with their belief in certain permanent principles inherent in a democratic republic since unchanging principles may generate radically different applications depending upon the circumstances surrounding the application. In short, the crises of the nineteenth century tested the ability of the body politic to absorb new truths without losing faith in the integrity of many old truths or of truth as such.[44]

Lerner's political thought thus can be divided into two types of reflections. On the one hand there are his reflections on foundings, especially revolutionary foundings, and in particular, the American revolutionary founding. These involve how to uproot a large part of people's habits, feelings, and ways of thinking, while at the same time retaining enough continuity with the past to make use of its accumulated wisdom and to inject familiarity into what is fundamentally a new endeavor. On the other, there are Lerner's reflections on what he calls "kalam," the explanation and defense, not only of the regime thus instituted, but of its successive incarnations that are threatened, among other reasons, by people's instinctive hostility to innovation.[45]

Lerner appears to distinguish the kalam of the revolutionary Founders from that of their successors. Both involve a certain amount of rhetoric, understood loosely as the art of making arguments that appeal to an audience's experiences, beliefs, interests, and ideals. In other words, both involve an appeal to the past as part and parcel of setting a new course for the future. Yet the reader gets the impression that the challenge of the Founders' successors may well have been more complex than that of the Founders because of the greater complexity of social and economic conditions that they faced coupled with the need to keep the faith with the Founders' legacy.

This leads, willy nilly, to the question of Lerner's own kalam. In one place he notes the importance of watching the "feet as well as the mouth of a politician, a political thinker, and an interpreter of a political thinker."[46] Surely Lerner is both a political thinker and the interpretor of political thinkers. This forces us to wonder how he expects his interpretation of the American founding to influence our understanding of the legitimacy of the present regime and the prospects for this nation as we move into the next century; for, one suspects that Lerner's writings, like those of Tocqueville, belong "not only to that large class of histories that have something to tell but also to that smaller class of works that have something to teach."[47] It also forces the reader to ask whether, or to what extent, he has emulated the Founders' successors by emphasizing the restorative aspect of his historical researches and understated their reconstructive aspect.

It is beyond the scope of the present analysis to resolve these issues. As a prelude to an inquiry into Lerner's kalam, however, certain observations seem appropriate. Many of Lerner's writings take the form of history laced with political theory. In his capacity as a historian, therefore, he must balance historical criteria with the practical and political concerns uppermost in the mind of a political theorist. For example, Lerner's agenda likely includes the goal of explaining and defending the Founders' wisdom, motives, prescriptions, and actions in terms intelligible to and persuasive for contemporary audiences. As a student of the past with an eye on the future, he is preoccupied with the prospects in America for self-governance—rational freedom, and not just autonomy or license—against the backdrop of contemporary suspicions of the rule of law and distrust of authority. These attitudes are arguably the long-term consequences of the Founders' own efforts to reeducate their contemporaries. In any event, Lerner's essays seem animated by the twin desires to sharpen readers' appreciation of the function of reason in political life and to sensitize them to the perils of an excessive love of freedom for its own sake. These are truths that the Founders' and their successors sought, in their various ways, to communicate. The task of their successors in our times is to convey these truths in a fashion that will help bridge the gap between the strengths of our unique past and our prospects for an enlightened future.

NOTES

1. Because of the strict page limits imposed upon the contributors to this volume, this essay focuses on Lerner's *The Thinking Revolutionary*, *Revolutions Revisited* and "Facing Up to the Founding." See the select bibliography at the end of this essay.

2. See the writings of Amy Gutman, a political theorist, and Frank Michelman, a legal theorist.

3. These attitudes are sometimes inferred from the Founders' efforts to protect private property. For Lerner's discussion and criticism of this inference, see "Facing Up to the Founding," pp. 251–53.

4. In *The Thinking Revolutionary*, pp. 4–6, Lerner analyzes the "ideological" historical approach of Gordon Wood, Bernard Bailyn, J.G.A. Pocock and others. See also his discussion in "The Constitution of the Thinking Revolutionary."

5. These issues are discussed in the Prologue to *The Thinking Revolutionary*, "The Constitution of the Thinking Revolutionary," and *Revolutions Revisited*, pp. 13–14.

6. See especially *The Thinking Revolutionary*, pp. 31–32.

7. See below, p. 285, for an instance in which Lerner identifies the failings of certain Founders, including those he considers thinking revolutionaries.

8. See especially "Facing Up to the Founding," pp. 254–55, 258–59, and *The Thinking Revolutionary*, p. xiv (the Founders combined a "rare blend of boldness and caution").

9. See "Facing Up to the Founding," p. 250 (they didn't start from scratch, but used what "had proved serviceable").

10. *Revolutions Revisited*, p. xiii, see *id.*, pp. 37, 40, 41, 54.

11. *Revolutions Revisited*, pp. 46–47 (in the words of John Adams, "I must study Politicks and War that my sons may have liberty to study Mathematicks and Philosophy. My sons ought to study Matematicks and Philosophy, Geography, natural History, Naval Architecture, navigation, Commerce and Agriculture, in order to give their children a right to study Painting, Poetry, Musick, Architecture, Statuary, Tapestry and Porcelaine." 3 *Adams Family Correspondence* 342 (1963–73).

12. *Revolutions Revisited*, pp. 49–51.

13. See *The Thinking Revolutionary*, pp. 12, 63. See also *id.*, p. 61 (Jefferson recognized the gap between "grand-sounding principles" and their implementation in practice; and he was aware that "confusing right and capacity might be fatal.").

14. *Revolutions Revisited*, pp. 36–37.

15. *Revolutions Revisited*, pp. 37–38.

16. *The Thinking Revolutionary*, pp. 66–69.

17. *The Thinking Revolutionary*, Chapters 4–5. Lerner notes that the moral sentiments and ideas of some of the Founders—such as Jefferson, Knox, and George Washington—were different from those who simply thought the Indians were lazy or inferior to whites. Yet he also recognizes that the policies of the former were as doomed to failure as those of the latter because they presupposed "the remolding of Indian character after a white image." *Id.*, pp. 164–171.

18. *The Thinking Revolutionary*, pp. 188–89.

19. See *The Thinking Revolutionary*, pp. 191.

20. *The Thinking Revolutionary*, pp. 30–31. See also Lerner's comparison of the manner in which Chief Justice John Jay attempted to influence and educate people in their jury charges while riding circuit and that of Justice Samuel Chase. *Id.*, pp. 98–114. In particular, Lerner notes that Chase's impatience and immoderation led him to exhort his audiences "[s]tarting not from where his audience was, but from where (in his judgment) they ought to be," as a result of which he missed the opportunity to be an effective educator.

21. *Revolutions Revisited*, p. 54. See, for example, *The Thinking Revolutionary*, p. 63 (describing the legislative project of Jefferson and his fellow revisors as "[w]ishing to soar, but obliged as sober legislators always to touch Virginia soil").

22. *The Thinking Revolutionary*, p. 91, and the citations in the paragraphs that follow.

23. This is detailed in Chapter 1 of *The Thinking Revolutionary* and Chapter 1 of Part I of *Revolutions Revisited*. Lerner notes his own doubts about the long-term viability of Franklin's approach, especially his hope of assuring individuals' self-control by linking it to their desire for respectability. *Revolutions Revisited*, pp. 16–18. Lerner also observes that Franklin's approach to educating the citizenry, if successful, would trade the stability of a decent society for the grander opportunities possible in a society motivated by higher aspirations. *Id.*, p. 34, see also p. 12.

24. This is described in Chapter 2 of *The Thinking Revolutionary*, which outlines Jefferson's attempt to induce the Virginia Assembly to review and revise "the entire legacy that had up to then shaped life and institutions in the colony and the commonwealth".

25. Although Jefferson believed that laws could establish institutions (such as a secular or humanistic-oriented university) and practices (freedom of religion) to liberate the human mind, he also believed that it was not the province of the civil government to shape the opinions of its citizens. Rather, he had faith that the free flow of opinion and argument would ultimately lead to the triumph of the truth. See *id.*, p. 87. See also *Revolutions Revisited*, pp. 43–44.

26. This aspect of American history is elaborated in Chapter 3 of *The Thinking Revolutionary*. See also his discussion of John Adams' views on education. *Id.*, pp. 22–29. Lerner observes that after the practice of political charges while riding circuit had been abandoned, the Justices of the Supreme Court continued the education of citizens through their often unanimous opinions during the tenure of Chief Justice Marshall, and the rationales underlying their decisions can be seen as serving the same function today. *Id.*, pp. 135–36.

27. *The Thinking Revolutionary*, p. 134. For the approaches of other Founders toward educating the citizenry, see *Revolutions Revisited*, pp. 44–46.

28. See "Facing Up to the Founding," pp. 253–55.

29. See the preceding three paragraphs.

30. See *Revolutions Revisited*, p. 38 (arguing that for the Founders, political institutions and social arrangements would be "an extension of the people's education" because securing a democratic republic cannot be "produced magically from above").

31. See, for example, *The Thinking Revolutionary*, p. 27 (John Adams); *id.*, p. 117 (quoting James Madison to the effect that institutions alone cannot sustain republican government in the absence of citizen virtue). Lerner notes that all of the Founders believed that the civic virtue required by a commercial republic such as America was easier to attain and likely to be more stable than classical civic virtue. *Id.*, pp. 195–96.

32. Lerner discusses the Founders' ideas that aimed at greater egalitarianism or democratization of the American republic, yet he also addresses their continuing elitism in many areas. See, for example, *The Thinking Revolutionary*, pp. 115ff., in which Lerner examines whether the members of the judiciary were seen by the Founders as by and large superior to the citizens in general and, thus, more capable than the latter to serve as custodians of the regime's values.

33. *The Thinking Revolutionary*, p. 48; *Revolutions Revisited*, p. xii–xiii.

34. *The Thinking Revolutionary*, pp. 86–87. See, however, *id.*, note 46 (suggesting that Jefferson intended to support religious belief as such).

35. *The Thinking Revolutionary*, p. 72. Jefferson's proposal to make college available at public expense had greater democratization as its objective as well, although the assistance was available only to those who were deemed qualified rather than being available to the public generally. See *id.* pp. 79–80. Lerner also notes that Jefferson's egalitarianism nonetheless contemplated, even "promoted," natural inequalities as part and parcel of "a regime of republican equals." *Id.*, p. 63. The natural inequality that Jefferson supported, however, was one of talent and merit, not accidents of birth. *Id.*, p. 81.

36. See, for example, Lerner's assessment of Jefferson's sense of the "legislator's long view": "With apparent hopeless circularity, the problem seemed to demand simultaneously that society be made worthy of free men and that individuals be made fit for free society." *The Thinking Revolutionary*, pp. 88–90. See also *id.*, pp. 121–22, 129 (Publius recognized that both the leaders and the citizens need more than self-interest for the republic to endure, but also worried that the requisite degree of virtue would not be forthcoming).

37. See, for example, Lerner's account of Madison's views on citizen virtue. *The Thinking Revolutionary*, pp. 116–18.
38. *The Thinking Revolutionary*, p. 129.
39. *The Thinking Revolutionary*, p. 135.
40. *The Thinking Revolutionary*, Chapter 6.
41. See *Revolutions Revisited*, p. 51; see also *id.*, p. 65 (referring to "the founding opinions fundamental to the perpetuation of the regime").
42. *Revolutions Revisited*, pp. 52–53.
43. See *Revolutions Revisited*, pp. 62, 64–66.
44. See *Revolutions Revisited*, p. 62 (Although "'Necessity' may dictate change," "wise legislators" will avoid appearing to overrule the founding fathers.), p. 66 (making the same point whenever a statesman seeks "to settle his public's mind about some distressing issue of the day").
45. This is discussed in Chapter 4 of *Revolutions Revisited*. Lerner notes in this regard that kalam, or the defense of a regime, may itself be innovative, and not merely protective of the exisiting order. *Id.*, p. 62.
46. Review of Zuckert's book, p. 148.
47. *Revolutions Revisited*, p. 122.

SELECT BIBLIOGRAPHY

Lerner, Ralph. *Revolutions Revisited: Two Faces of the Politics of Enlightenment.* Chapel Hill, N.C., 1994.
———. "Facing Up to Founding." In *To Form a More Perfect Union: The Critical Ideas of the Constitution*, eds. Herman Belz, Ronald Hoffman, and Peter J. Albert, 250–71. Charlottesville, Va., 1992. A shortened version of this article appears as chapter 3 of *Revolutions Revisited*.
———. *The Thinking Revolutionary: Principle and Practice in the New Republic.* Ithaca, N.Y., 1987.

Roger Masters: Natural Right and Biology

Larry Arnhart

*A*s compared with other students of Leo Strauss who became prominent political scientists, the intellectual career of Roger Masters seems strange. As a graduate student at the University of Chicago, Masters wrote his dissertation on Jean-Jacques Rousseau under Strauss's supervision. He then established his scholarly reputation in the 1960s through his writings on Rousseau's political philosophy. At that point, it appeared that Masters would follow the same path taken by many of Strauss's students who have devoted their lives to writing meticulous commentaries on the classic texts of political philosophy. But after publishing his book on Rousseau in 1968, Masters began to write about evolutionary biology. For example, he suggested that Rousseau's account of man in the original state of nature should be compared with recent studies of orangutans as evolutionary ancestors of human beings; and he argued that Aristotle's claim that human beings are by nature political animals was confirmed by recent sociobiological theories of human evolution and animal sociality.[1] Most recently, he has explained Machiavelli's concept of political leadership as rooted in a natural tendency to dominance hierarchies that human beings share with other primates.[2] The history of political philosophy is largely a debate about human nature.[3] And Masters believes that debate can be clarified, if not even resolved, by appealing to Darwinian theories of human nature. To many of Strauss's students, such ideas seem ridiculously perverse. Yet a few Straussians have been persuaded by Masters that this turn to Darwinian biology is essential for solving what Strauss called "the problem of natural right."

In the Introduction to *Natural Right and History*, Strauss claimed that the most serious problem for the ancient Greek idea of natural right is that it seems to have been refuted by modern natural science.[4] Natural right in its classic form requires a teleological view of nature, because reason can discern what is by nature good for human beings only if they have a natural end. Strauss thought Aristotle had the clearest view of this dependence of natural right on natural teleology. Modern natural science, however, seems to deny natural teleology by explaining natural phenomena as determined by mechanical causes that act without ends or purposes. This creates a dilemma. If the science of man is to be part of a nonteleological science of nature, then human action must be explained by reduction to physical impulses, which seems inadequate to explain human ends. The only alternative appears to be "a fundamental, typically modern, dualism of a nonteleological natural science and a teleological science of man," but this rejects the comprehensive naturalism of the premodern exponents of natural right such as Aristotle and Thomas Aquinas. Neither reductionism nor dualism is fully satisfactory. Strauss concluded: "The fundamental dilemma, in whose grip we are, is caused by the victory of modern natural science. An adequate solution to the problem of natural right cannot be found before this basic problem has been solved."

"Needless to say," Strauss then added, "the present lectures cannot deal with this problem," because the lectures published as *Natural Right and History* are "limited to that aspect of the problem of natural right which can be clarified within the confines of the social sciences." A few years later, in a letter to Alexandre Kojeve, Strauss observed that "the difference between Plato and Aristotle is that Aristotle believes that biology, as a mediation between knowledge of the inanimate and knowledge of man, is available." To Masters this suggests that if Strauss had attempted to resolve the problem for natural right created by the apparent refutation of natural teleology by modern natural science, he would have had to consider Aristotle's biology in the light of modern Darwinian biology.[5] To decide whether natural right is truly natural so as to be comprehensible through a science of nature, we must look to biology as the science that mediates between the natural sciences of the nonhuman universe and the social sciences of human conduct. In turning to biology, therefore, Masters has shown how the Straussian project for reviving the ancient idea of natural right might be supported by a modern biological theory of human nature.

In his first book, *The Political Philosophy of Rousseau*, Masters studied Rousseau's attempt to return to a classic understanding of human nature, as an alternative to modern hedonism, while accepting modern natural science. Masters concluded that although Rousseau failed, his failure illuminated Strauss's insight into the fundamental problem of modern thought: despite the evident progress of modern natural science, there seems to be no scientific account for the ends of human life that escapes reductionistic materialism, and yet a metaphysical dualism that separates the science of nature and the science of man seems untenable.[6] While modern civilization rests upon the power of modern natural science and its technical products, modern science seems unable to judge the ends or purposes to which its fruits are directed.

In later writings—such as *The Nature of Politics* and *Beyond Relativism*—Masters tries to resolve this dilemma by proposing a revival of ancient Greek naturalism through a biological science of human nature that is neither reductionistic nor dualistic.[7] His biological naturalism is not reductionistic, he argues, because it recognizes the irreducible causal complexity in the levels of organization displayed by living things (from genes to organisms to social groups to ecosystems). And yet his natu-ralism is not dualistic, because although human beings are unique in their linguis-tic and intellectual capacities, these capacities are understood as emergent products of living nature.

The major objections to such a biological naturalism arise from four dichotomies: mechanism versus teleology, facts versus values, determinism versus freedom, and nature versus nurture. The mechanistic causality of natural science cannot explain the purposefulness of human action. The scientific study of natural facts gives us no guidance for moral values. The determinism of scientific laws denies human freedom. And scientific explanations of natural instincts cannot account for human culture as a product of social learning. Masters rejects these four objections as resting on false dichotomies. In defense of Masters, I will elaborate his reasoning in response to these four objections.[8]

NATURAL TELEOLOGY

Against the false dichotomy of mechanism versus teleology, Masters contends that modern science recognizes formal and final causes as well as material and efficient causes.[9] "Chaos theory" in modern mathematics and physics suggests that form or being can be prior to matter or becoming. And although Darwinian biology does not support a cosmic teleology of supernatural design, it does support an imma-nent teleology of functional adaptation. While the history of evolution by natural selection depends on events that are not purposeful, it produces living beings whose behavior is purposeful. As was the case for Aristotle, modern science finds natural purposefulness not in the inanimate phenomena of physics but in the living beings of biology.

To appeal to nature as a source of moral norms implies a teleological con-ception of nature as having ends, goals, or purposes. When Aristotle claims that man is by nature the most political animal, he implicitly invokes a natural teleology: polit-ical life is natural for man because it is the end or goal (*telos*) of his development, and "nature is an end."[10] Any notion of natural right depends on such a teleologi-cal conception of nature.

While Aristotle sometimes speaks of nature as acting like an artisan, he intends this to be taken metaphorically rather than literally. While believing that art imi-tates nature, he never infers from this that nature's activity requires the conscious, intentional action of some supernatural or cosmic agent. The final cause of a nat-ural object exists in the object itself. Nature works not like a shipbuilder building a ship, Aristotle explains, but like a doctor doctoring himself.[11]

Darwin's biology does not deny—rather, it reaffirms—the immanent teleol-ogy displayed in the striving of each living being to fulfill its specific ends.[12] Darwin agrees with Aristotle that organic beings are self-maintaining wholes. The hackneyed examples of organic self-development are still valid: acorns still grow into oak trees and puppies into dogs. Reproduction, growth, feeding, healing, courtship, parental care for the young—these and many other activities of organisms are goal-directed.

As Masters explains it, this idea of natural teleology as accepted by both Aristotle and Darwin does not require any belief in a Divine Creator as the source of nature's purposefulness. Aristotle and Darwin can explain the teleological order in the animal world as a purely natural process that does not presuppose any biblical faith in an omnipotent and providential God as the origin of nature's ends. This leads Masters to suggest that the real controversy surrounding teleology in the modern world is what Strauss called the conflict between Athens and Jerusalem, Reason and Revelation.[13] Darwinian biology would support a return to Aristotelian natural right as founded on a purely natural teleology comprehensible to natural reason. But this would provide no comfort for those who believe that moral order requires religious faith in a God who enforces that order.

In fact, some of the neoconservative intellectuals influenced by Strauss—such as Irving Kristol—seem to reject Darwinism because they fear that it subverts the religious beliefs that support the moral life of common people. In explaining the great influence of Strauss on his thinking about religion and politics, Kristol observes that Strauss "was an intellectual aristocrat who thought that the truth could make *some* minds free, but he was convinced that there was an inherent conflict between philosophic truth and the political order, and that the popularization and vulgarization of these truths might import unease, turmoil, and the release of popular passions hitherto held in check by tradition and religion."[14] So when Kristol criticizes Darwinian biology and claims that "the religious fundamentalists are not far off the mark when they asssert that evolution, as generally taught, has an unwarranted anti-religious edge to it," this leads some observers to infer that Straussian neoconservatives like Kristol attack Darwinism as a threat to religion, not because they are sincere religious believers themselves, but because they think religious belief is a "noble lie" that is necessary for those common people who could not live moral lives if they faced the philosophic truth of atheism.[15]

Masters follows Strauss in affirming the tension between reason and faith, Athens and Jerusalem, in which neither can refute the claims of the other.[16] If natural right is truly natural, then it belongs to the realm of natural experience known to natural reason without any need for a religious faith that would transcend nature. That is why Strauss criticized Thomas Aquinas for implying that "natural law" might require supernatural support. Strauss wondered "whether the natural law as Thomas Aquinas understands it is natural law strictly speaking, i.e., a law knowable to the unassisted human mind, to the human mind which is not illumined by divine revelation."[17] Following Strauss's lead, Masters argues that the idea of natural right rests on a natural teleology that can be known by natural reason without divine revelation, and one expression of natural reason is the natural science of Darwinian biology. Classical natural right does not require a Biblical view of the universe as created by God. In contrast to Kristol, therefore, Masters insists that as long as Darwinian science sustains the teleological basis of natural right, there is no reason to fear Darwinism as a threat to the moral health of society.

NATURAL MORALITY

Against the dichotomy of facts versus values, Masters argues that the natural facts about human needs and desires can guide our judgments about moral values.[18] Just as the facts of health shape medical practice, the facts of human nature shape moral practice generally. And although David Hume is commonly thought to be the leading proponent of the fact-value dichotomy, Masters believes that Hume's reliance on the natural moral sentiments or the "moral sense" manifests an ethical naturalism similar to Aristotle's.[19] Like Hume, Masters appeals to "moral feeling" as the natural basis for morality; and like Darwin, Masters sees this natural moral sense as part of human biology.[20] In a manner that resembles the argument of James Q. Wilson in *The Moral Sense*, Masters explains the moral inclinations of human beings—such as parental care and other forms of social bonding—as rooted in the human brain as a product of natural selection.[21]

Masters argues that the natural moral sense arises from the combination of moral emotions such as anger, guilt, and shame and moral judgments in applying social rules to particular cases.[22] The moral emotion of anger, for example, has been recognized by Aristotle, Adam Smith, and other political philosophers as a powerful motivation for punishing those who violate our sense of justice.[23] Masters suggests that this and similar emotions have been shaped by natural selection in evolutionary history to enforce reciprocity in human social life. So when Straussians like Walter Berns defend capital punishment as an expression of the natural moral passion of anger, they are appealing to a principle of natural right rooted in human biology.[24]

Other moral emotions such as love and sympathy enforce affiliative bonding such as the tie between parents and children. Parental care of children is a biologically natural desire that Strauss recognizes as a manifestation of natural right. In Plato's *Republic*, Socrates proposes that in the just city the male and female rulers should rule equally and communally, which would require abolishing the family. If nursing and parenting children were done communally, then women would be free to do almost everything men do. Some scholars, like Natalie Harris Bluestone, believe that Plato's Socrates stated all the basic arguments for complete sexual equality that would later be developed by feminists.[25] Strauss insists, however, that the city in the *Republic* is against nature. "The just city is against nature because the equality of the sexes and absolute communism are against nature."[26] Furthermore, he contends, Plato intended that careful readers would see that his just city is impossible because it is unnatural, and therefore the *Republic* is actually an implicit critique of utopian idealism. Bluestone points out, however, against Strauss's reading of Plato, that Plato's Socrates declares his proposals to be "according to nature."[27] She believes Socrates is right about this: since men and women are by nature identical in everything except their reproductive organs, any sexual differences in the social division of labor—such as women handling most of the child-care—must be conventional rather than natural and therefore open to change. Unlike Bluestone, who denies that there is any biological basis for psychic differences between men and women, Strauss agrees with his student Allan Bloom in affirming "the natural teleology of sex" as rooted in human biology. "Biology forces women to take maternity leaves. Law can enjoin men to take paternity leaves, but it cannot make them have the desired sentiments."[28]

Yet even as Bloom seems to endorse the idea of natural teleology as rooted in human biology, he also suggests that such natural teleology is only an illusion, even if a noble illusion. "I mean by teleology," Bloom writes, "nothing but the evident, everyday observation and sense of purposiveness, which may be only illusory, but which ordinarily guides human life, the kind everyone sees in the reproductive process."[29] The qualifying phrase—"which may be only illusory"—allows him to simultaneously deny and affirm the truth of natural teleology, which creates a strangely ambiguous position that one can find among many of Strauss's students. Straussians like Bloom often seem to adopt a Kantian dualism that separates non-human nature and human culture, which would deny Aristotelian natural right. But sometimes they seem to support a revival of Aristotelian natural right as rooted in a science of human nature—the stance that has been most vigorously defended by Masters.[30] In developing this latter position, Masters must reject the Kantian antithesis between nature and freedom.

NATURAL FREEDOM

Against the dichotomy of natural determinism versus human freedom, Masters argues that knowledge of the biological causes of human behavior promotes human freedom rightly understood.[31] He rejects the Kantian conception of freedom as completely autonomous human choice or "free will" belonging to a "noumenal" realm that is inaccessible to sense experience. If freedom is more properly understood as the capacity for deliberate choice, then knowledge of human biology can often increase our freedom. For example, understanding the causes of dyslexia makes it easier to find ways to overcome this disability. Similarly, if we know that some people have a biological propensity to alcoholism, violent aggression, or any other disruptive behavior, such knowledge increases their responsibility to control their bad propensities through medical treatment or proper habituation.

Kant's primary argument for a radical separation of the natural *is* and the moral *ought*, which would render natural right indefensible, was that such a separation was a necessary condition for the freedom of the will that must be assumed in all moral judgment.[32] For morality to be possible, moral agents must be able to transcend nature through "free will." The human experience of the moral *ought*, Kant insists, shows us "man as belonging to two worlds."[33] This is what Strauss identifies as "a fundamental, typically modern, dualism of a nonteleological natural science and a teleological science of man." Those who accept Kant's dualism must conclude that biology and the natural sciences in general have nothing to contribute to our understanding of morality, because morality is an utterly autonomous realm that transcends nature.

One possible reason for why Strauss found such dualism unsatisfactory is that it was one of the fundamental themes in Martin Heidegger's philosophic endorsement of Nazism. Arguing against "biologism," which treats human beings as rational animals rooted in the natural world, Heidegger believed that National Socialism would vindicate the spiritual freedom of the German people as "world-building" historical beings who transcend their natural animality. This dichotomy between the freedom of human history and the determinism of animal nature supported Heidegger's historicist nihilism as unconstrained by natural right.[34]

In contrast to this Kantian notion of human freedom as freedom *from* nature, Masters and other proponents of natural right would argue that our moral experience requires a notion of human freedom as freedom *within* nature. For Aristotle, Hume, and Darwin, the uniqueness of human beings as moral agents requires not a "free will" that transcends nature but a natural capacity to deliberate about one's desires.

NATURAL NURTURE

Against the dichotomy of nature versus nurture, Masters argues that human behavior emerges from a complex interaction between instinct and learning, the innate and the acquired, genes and environment.[35] He illustrates the interplay of nature and culture in political behavior through his studies of how the facial displays of leaders affect audiences. There is a natural human repertoire of facial displays shared with nonhuman primates—signifying anger/threat, fear/evasion, and happiness/reassurance—that is effective in any human culture, although there are also subtle variations that reflect cultural differences. Despite the importance of cultural learning for human beings, there is no radical separation between human culture and animal instinct, because other animals have some capacity for individual and cultural learning, and even the most impressive manifestations of human learning (such as language) depend on inherited instincts of the brain that have been formed by natural selection. As is true for other animals, human beings are born with natural propensities that are shaped by learning to reflect the variable conditions of the social and physical environment. Nature must be nurtured.

Masters believes that his biological naturalism allows us to judge political regimes by standards of natural right without falling into either dogmatism or relativism.[36] His naturalistic criteria of justice are not dogmatic because they vary according to the physical and social conditions of any particular regime. And yet his criteria are not relativistic because they show that some regimes are closer than others to the central tendencies of the natural behavioral repertoire shaped by human evolution. For most of evolutionary history, human beings have lived in hunter-gatherer bands and other small groups, and although every modern nation-state is far from that ancient way of life, constitutional democracies more closely approximate the freedom and equality of hunting-gathering groups than do totalitarian or autocratic states. The failure of Soviet Marxism as a massive social experiment in environmental determinism suggests that human nature is not infinitely malleable. It also suggests that democratic capitalism is more compatible with human nature as shaped by evolutionary history than any of the modern alternatives.[37]

Aristotelian natural right, Masters emphasizes, is neither dogmatic nor relativistic because it affirms the necessary interaction of nature and nurture, and thus it rejects the Sophistic view that nature and nurture are antithetical. Modern behavioral ecology supports this interactionist stance: like all social animals with complex nervous systems, human beings are naturally adapted for learning flexible responses to the changing physical and social environments in which they find themselves.[38] Human ethics is part of human ecology, because human communities develop those standards of right and wrong conduct that seem to satisfy human desires within the ecological conditions of each community. Prudence is required, therefore, in judging how best to satisfy the natural propensities of human beings in particular circumstances. Aristotle was correct in declaring that "although there is something that is right by nature, all is variable."[39]

For example, it is natural for most human beings to have strong desires for sexual coupling and parental care that are best satisfied by the institution of marriage. For that reason, marriage is found in all human societies.[40] We should expect great variability in marital practices, however, in response to the variable physical and social conditions of human life. And yet we should expect to see recurrent patterns that reflect the natural propensities of human beings. Monogamy will be more common than polygyny, because the latter will be disrupted by the sexual jealousy of the co-wives. Polyandry will be extremely rare because of the intense sexual jealousy of husbands sharing a wife. And any attempt to abolish the family completely and establish a community of wives and children will fail in the long run because it is "contrary to nature."

CONCLUSION

In his effort to root the idea of natural right in modern natural science, and thus solve what Strauss believed was the fundamental problem of natural right, Masters challenges the dichotomies that have traditionally separated the humanistic study of ethics from the scientific study of nature. There is no absolute gap between mechanism and teleology if a full explanation of living beings requires accounting for formal and final causes as well as material and efficient causes. There is no absolute gap between *is* and *ought* if human morality is founded on a natural moral sense. There is no absolute gap between nature and freedom if human freedom expresses a natural human capacity for deliberate choice. And there is no absolute gap between nature and nurture if habituation and learning fulfill the natural propensities of human beings. If Masters is right in these claims, then the science of the human good is part of the science of human nature.

Although I find the arguments of Masters largely persuasive, I suspect that many readers will disagree. As Strauss indicated, most contemporary scholars have responded to the apparent refutation of ancient naturalism by modern natural science in one of two ways—reductionism or dualism. The reductionists will agree with Masters that moral feelings are governed by the emotional control centers of the brain, but they will conclude from this that belief in the objectivity of morality is only a useful illusion. The dualists, including many of the students of Strauss, will insist that human biology is irrelevant to human ethics and politics, because human beings as rational beings differ in kind and not just in degree from all other animals, and for that reason Darwin's evolutionary account of human morality and intellect is wrong. Yet for those of us who regard both of these opposing positions as inadequate, the alternative offered by Masters in his attempt to solve the problem of natural right is one of the most exciting intellectual projects of our time.

NOTES

1. See Roger Masters, "Politics as a Biological Phenomenon," *Social Science Information* 14 (1975): 7–63; and Masters, "Jean-Jacques is Alive and Well: Rousseau and Contemporary Sociobiology," *Daedalus* (Summer 1978): 93–105.

2. See Roger Masters, *Machiavelli, Leonardo, and the Science of Power* (Notre Dame, IN: University of Notre Dame Press, 1996).

3. See Larry Arnhart, *Political Questions: Political Philosophy from Plato to Rawls*, 2nd ed. (Prospect Heights, IL: Waveland Press, 1993).

4. Leo Strauss, *Natural Right and History* (Chicago: University of Chicago Press, 1953), 7–8. Masters has offered his reading of this passage in two papers—"Classical Political Philosophy and Contemporary Biology," a paper presented at the 1978 meetings of the Conference for the Study of Political Thought in Chicago, and "Evolutionary Biology and Natural Right," in Kenneth L. Deutsch and Walter Soffer, eds., *The Crisis of Liberal Democracy: A Straussian Perspective* (Albany: State University of New York Press, 1987), 48–67.

5. The remark to Kojeve appears in a letter that has been published in the revised edition of Leo Strauss's *On Tyranny*, edited by Victor Gourevitch and Michael S. Roth (New York: The Free Press, 1991), 279. Masters quotes this passage in his *Machiavelli, Leonardo, and the Science of Power*, 207.

6. See Roger Masters, *The Political Philosophy of Rousseau* (Princeton, NJ: Princeton University Press, 1968), 66–89, 106–18, 418–20, 428–30.

7. See Masters, *The Nature of Politics* (New Haven: Yale University Press, 1989), and Masters, *Beyond Relativism: Science and Human Values* (Hanover, NH: University Press of New England, 1993).

8. My points are more fully developed in *Darwinian Natural Right: The Biological Ethics of Human Nature* (Albany: State University of New York Press, 1998).

9. Masters, *Nature*, 143–46, 241, 247–48; Masters, *Relativism*, 17, 36–41, 126–29, 136–38, 149–52, 201–3, 223–24.

10. Aristotle, *Politics,* 1252b28–1253a19.

11. Arisotle, *Physics,* 199b30–32.

12. For the argument that Darwinian biology supports teleology, see two papers by James G. Lennox—"Teleology," in Evelyn Fox Keller and Elisabeth A. Lloyd, eds., *Keywords in Evolutionary Biology* (Cambridge: Harvard University Press, 1992), 324–33; and "Darwin *Was* a Teleologist," *Biology and Philosophy* 8 (1993): 409–21.

13. See Masters, "Evolutionary Biology," 57, 59–60, 62–63.

14. Irving Kristol, *Neoconservatism: The Autobiography of an Idea* (New York: The Free Press, 1995), 8.

15. For the attack on Darwinism, see Irving Kristol, "Room for Darwin and the Bible," *The New York Times*, September 30, 1986. For the argument that this shows the influence of Strauss, see Ronald Bailey, "Origin of the Specious," *Reason* 29 (July 1997): 22–28.

16. Masters, *Relativism*, 6–7, 152–53.

17. Strauss, *Natural Right and History*, 163.

18. Masters, *Nature*, xiv–xv, 21–22, 179–86, 226–27, 231–33, 239–41; Masters, *Relativism*, vii–viii, 4–11, 33–34, 42–45, 106–34, 145–55.

19. Masters, *Relativism*, 115–16, 124, 130, 220.

20. Masters, *Nature*, 246; Masters, *Relativism*, 9, 64, 111, 130–31, 155, 211, 215–16.

21. See James Q. Wilson, *The Moral Sense* (New York: The Free Press, 1993).

22. See Roger Masters, "Naturalistic Approaches to Justice in Political Philosophy and the Life Sciences," in Roger Masters and Margaret Gruter, eds., *The Sense of Justice: Biological Foundations of Law* (Newbury Park, CA: Sage Publications, 1992), 67–92.

23. See Larry Arnhart, *Aristotle on Political Reasoning: A Commentary on the "Rhetoric"* (DeKalb: Northern Illinois University, 1981), 114–34; Adam Smith, *The Theory of Moral Sentiments* (Indianapolis, IN: Liberty Press, 1982), 67–71, 86–91.

24. See Walter Berns, *For Capital Punishment: Crime and the Morality of the Death Penalty* (New York: Basic Books, 1979).

25. See Natalie Harris Bluestone, *Women and the Ideal Society: Plato's "Republic" and the Modern Myths of Gender* (Amherst: University of Massachusetts Press, 1987).

26. Leo Strauss, *The City and Man* (Chicago: University of Chicago Press, 1977), 127.

27. See Plato, *Republic* 456b–c.

28. Allan Bloom, *The Closing of the American Mind* (New York: Simon and Schuster, 1987), 110, 130–31.

29. Bloom, *Closing*, 110.

30. See Bloom's *Closing*, 110–16, 126, 130, 166, 181, 300–301, 307, 357–58. Leon Kass would be another example of someone influenced by Strauss who vacillates between Aristotelian naturalism rooted in human biology and Kantian historicism rooted in human transcendence of biology through culture. See Kass, *Towards a More Natural Science* (New York:

er 17 (November 1991): 14–26; Kass, *The Hungry Soul* (New York: Free Press, 1994), 208–15; and Kass, "The Permanent Limitations of Biology," an unpublished paper.

31. Masters, *Nature*, 235–38; Masters, *Relativism*, 111–12, 130–31.

32. See Immanuel Kant, *Critique of Pure Reason*, translated by Norman Kemp Smith (New York: St. Martin's Press, 1965), 409–15, 464–79.

33. Immanuel Kant, *Critique of Practical Reason*, trans. Lewis White Beck (Indianapolis, IN: Bobbs-Merrill, 1956), 90.

34. See Martin Heidegger, *Being and Time*, trans. John Macquarrie and Edward Robinson (New York: Harper and Row, 1962), 71–75; Heidegger, "Political Texts," in Richard Wolin, ed., *The Heidegger Controversy: A Critical Reader* (Cambridge: MIT Press, 1993), 54, 59, 62, 64, 68; Heidegger, "Letter on Humanism," in *Basic Writings*, ed. David Farrell Krell (San Francisco: HarperCollins, 1993), 226–230, 245, 254; James F. Ward, *Heidegger's Political Thinking* (Amherst: University of Massachusetts Press, 1995), 68–81; and Anne Harrington, *Reenchanted Science: Holism in German Culture from Wilhelm II to Hitler* (Princeton, NJ: Princeton University Press, 1996).

35. Masters, *Nature*, 17, 29, 33–36, 71, 130–36; Masters, *Relativism*, 7–9, 24–26, 68–69, 74, 87, 116, 119–22, 138–43, 145–55.

36. Masters, *Nature*, xiv, 186, 223–33, 245; Masters, *Relativism*, 55, 94, 118–19, 135, 198–200.

37. The idea that democratic capitalism conforms to human nature as shaped by evolutionary history has been argued by Alexandra Maryanski and Jonathan Turner in *The Social Cage: Human Nature and the Evolution of Society* (Stanford, CA: Stanford University Press, 1992).

38. Masters, *Relativism*, 124–29; Masters, *Machiavelli*, 94–99.

39. Aristotle, *Nicomachean Ethics*, 1134b29–30.

40. See Donald Brown, *Human Universals* (Philadelphia: Temple University Press, 1991); Carol Ember and Melvin Ember, *Anthropology*, 7th edition (Englewood Cliffs, NJ: Prentice Hall, 1993); and William Stephens, *The Family in Cross-Cultural Perspective* (New York: Holt, Rinehart and Winston, 1963).

· 20 ·

Herbert Storing: The American Founding and the American Regime

Murray Dry*

I. HERBERT J. STORING: TEACHER OF TEACHERS[1]

Herbert J. Storing (1928–1977) taught in the Department of Political Science at the University of Chicago from 1956 to 1977. At that time, Storing's teacher, Leo Strauss, also taught in the Department.[2] After Joseph Cropsey joined the Department in 1958, he and Storing became good friends and shared a suite of offices. From 1958 until 1967 Chicago's political science graduate students had the good fortune to be able to study with three outstanding teachers: Strauss and Cropsey taught political philosophy while Storing taught courses in American constitutional law and public administration. Storing taught these subjects from a perspective informed by political philosophy.[3] At the same time, he treated American politics as worthy of study, respect, and support on its own terms. In fulfilling this task, Storing prepared at least as many teachers who did not identify themselves with Strauss as those who did.[4]

Graduate students at Chicago in the 1960s did no practice teaching, nor did they receive any special instruction in teaching. Perhaps it was assumed that teaching can only be learned through the activity itself, and that that should not commence until one knows something. On the other hand, perhaps one can learn about teaching as a student. Students of Herbert Storing, by following the example of their teacher, learned how to teach at the same time that they learned about the American political regime.

As a classroom teacher, Storing pursued reasoned argument on the most important topics in American constitutionalism with rigor and clarity. He provided a full syllabus which contained an outline of the topics of the course as well as reading assignments. He combined clear lectures on the assigned material with ample opportunity for questions and comments from students. Storing's presentations involved careful expositions of writings, and he often contrasted two different approaches to a given problem of government. At some points he would indicate why he preferred one argument to another. Students asked questions, made comments, and, on occasion, expressed a disagreement with Storing's interpretations or judgments. These exchanges were an important part of the education Storing provided his students. Students were both respected as serious participants in the inquiry and they were obliged to follow and develop the argument fully. In this way, Storing's students were preparing themselves to become teachers who would also take their material and their students seriously. To support the notion that his students were partners in study and to encourage a respect for that activity, Storing employed the formal address with his students, e.g., Mr. or Miss or Mrs., and he referred to himself, on his syllabi, as Mr. Storing.[5] Finally, he read his students' work with diligence and provided them with a constructive assessment of their work. Often written work does not allow for the same sort of questioning which can occur in a classroom situation. Storing's own writing, however, reflects the dialectical character of his teaching; he asks good questions and he considers the important objections to his argument.

In this essay, I describe Storing's achievement as a teacher of political science and connect that achievement to the influence of Leo Strauss on the study of the American regime. This task may be self-evident since Storing acknowledged himself to be a Straussian, taught courses in two fields in American politics which can be subsumed under the term American constitutionalism, and, moreover, taught many of the same graduate students who studied with Strauss. However, to the best of my knowledge, Storing did not refer to Strauss in his classes, perhaps because he did not want students to think that American politics was a mere extension or application of political philosophy. Storing was so clearly his own man in his classroom teaching and in his scholarship, that no one ever thought of him as the executor of someone else's design. Storing did provide a road map for tracing Strauss' influence on his own work. Shortly after Strauss' death in 1973, Storing wrote an essay, entitled "The Achievement of Leo Strauss."[6] Considering Strauss' achievement as a *political scientist*, Storing wrote: "Strauss addressed himself to three prime characteristics of [contemporary] political science: its distinction between facts and values; its attempt to dissolve political things into their pre-political elements; and its blind assumption that the world of liberal democracy is the world as it is and ought to be."[7]

On the first point, Storing explained that Strauss denied that value questions were outside the realm of rational discourse at the same time that he acknowledged the importance of facts. Since common sense knowledge, "which is always 'valuing' knowledge . . . , provides the only access to the world of politics we have," it must be our starting point. This leads to Storing's second point, that in opposition to the approach to politics which reduces it to economics, sociology, or psychology, Strauss revived "the view of politics as architectonic, as forming the human materials, including the sub-political lives and motivations, to its ends. . . . He showed the formative importance of times of founding and crisis, the very times typically ignored by political scientists."

Storing's third observation is that Strauss identified a critical paradox in the work of American "value free" political scientists: having reduced politics to the subrational sphere of preferences with no rational foundation, they nonetheless reflect the view that "liberal democracy is both natural and good." Since the political scientist cannot argue the case on the merits, he therefore "nails his liberal democratic preferences to the mast" and proceeds "on to the scientific work with a clean conscience," without "any serious examination of the case against liberal democracy." Strauss, Storing writes, "made his students confront the enemies of liberal democracy," both ancient and modern. If such an approach did not lead to unqualified admiration of liberal democracy, it did allow students to appreciate the rational defense that could be made for a regime that combined consent with the securing of individual rights. Taken together, this meant that "Strauss' constructive project was to recover sight of the ends of political life for a profession that had blinded itself to such considerations." By exploring the writings of modern political philosophers, as well as the writings of ancient political philosophers, Strauss invited "a fresh and serious examination of the American Declaration of Independence, not as a reflection of the times but as the truth." Furthermore, "he turned to the great men and the great books of political philosophy as teachers, not sociological resources."[8]

I will use this account of Strauss' achievement as a political scientist[9] as the standard to connect Storing's achievement as a teacher and scholar of the American regime to Strauss' influence.[10] I will examine Storing's work in three areas: (A) the American Founding; (B) the Civil War and the Refounding, or Race and the Regime; and (C) the American Presidency and Bureaucracy. I intend to show how Storing's work in each of these areas reflects his agreement with Strauss on the inadequacy of the Weberian "fact-value" distinction,[11] the importance of treating politics on its own terms, and the need for a comprehensive perspective on liberal democracy.

II. THE AMERICAN FOUNDING

The first two areas reflect Storing's interest in critical periods in American political and constitutional history. In his approach to these critical periods, Storing took seriously the speeches as well as the deeds of those who were responsible for governing. He took American politics seriously, after the fashion of Strauss' revival of the importance of the citizen's perspective on government.[12] To judge a Jefferson, a Madison, a Hamilton, a Lincoln or a Frederick Douglass from the strictest intellectual standard did not require the assumption that these thoughtful practitioners were all knowing about politics. But taking their arguments seriously does put the student in a position to learn from these thinker-statesmen, and not to assume, without argument, that politics is governed exclusively by necessity and chance and never by deliberation and choice. Only by taking seriously the arguments that are offered, and demonstrating their flaws or limitations, can one conclude with confidence either that the thought is defective or incomplete. And the more one studies first rate political thought, as Storing did, the easier it is to distinguish between it and run of the mill opinions.

Storing provides a very good example of this in his introduction to *What the Anti-Federalists Were For*.[13] He claims that the Constitution of the United States was "distinctive, even unique, in the extent to which it was the product of deliberation." That deliberation involved a dialogue, in which the Anti-Federalist critics played an important part. In addition, while the Constitution settled many questions, concerning "a lasting structure of rules and principles," Storing maintains that "the political life of the community continues to be a dialogue," in which the Anti-Federalist concerns still play an important part. Citing the work of prominent American historians, such as Merrill Jensen, Gordon Wood and Bernard Bailyn, Storing distinguishes his approach from theirs; where they focus on social forces and treat thought as "ideology," as reflective of the fundamental forces, Storing looks to the arguments of both sides of the debate over the Constitution, in order to understand the issues as the participants did.[14] In describing how he will present the Anti-Federalist thought, which means how he will make coherent the diverse expressions of many individuals, Storing writes: "We are looking not so much for what is common as for what is fundamental." Just as Storing focuses on Madison on the Federalist side because he "sees farther or better,"[15] so Storing focuses on the more thoughtful Anti-Federalists, such as "Brutus," "Federal Farmer," and "Maryland Farmer." And while Storing agrees in part with Cecelia Kenyon, whose well-known essay on the Anti-Federalists called them "Men of Little Faith,"[16] he thinks that by taking their arguments seriously one can understand what their concerns were and recognize their merit, even if, on balance, one judges, as Storing did, that the Federalists had the stronger argument.[17] To sketch out the argument we need to start with the framing of the Constitution in the Federal Convention.

A. The Federal Convention

Storing interpreted the framers' deliberations leading up to the "Great Compromise" in a manner which did justice to principled differences as well as practical accommodations. The framers agreed on the most fundamental principles, such as the protection of individual rights in some form of republican government; but they disagreed on others, such as the structure and character of republican government. Storing focuses on "the *question* of principle, the *answer* in practice, and the way great politicians move from one to the other."[18] That question concerned the relationship between the union and the states: which one was natural and primary and which one was artificial and secondary? Under the Articles of Confederation, the states were primary; under the nationalist Virginia Plan, proposed at the outset of the Federal Convention, the union was primary. Storing points out that the deep-est ground of this argument is reflected in two speeches on the nature of the Declaration of Independence. In support of the states, Luther Martin (of Maryland) argued that they declared their independence of one another as well as Great Britain, and hence remained the sovereign parties of any compact. In support of a strong national government, James Wilson (of Pennsylvania) argued that the United States declared their independence collectively, and hence the union was primary, the states secondary. This issue could not be resolved on legal principles alone, nor did it lend itself to unqualified compromise; it required a choice of one principle (national)[19] over another (federal), a choice grounded in reasoned argument.

The "Great Compromise," the first major achievement of the Convention, gave the small states equal representation in the Senate but on the basis of the Virginia Plan. It was a partial victory for the nationalists, and, Storing says, all they could win without risking irretrievable loss in ratification. The two sides "found the grounds of compromise," Storing writes, "in their common desire 'to form a more perfect union,' though their ideas of a perfect union differed."[20] To help us under-stand the ingredients of such a political achievement, Storing reminds us of the moderating effects that were conducive to its success: of Hamilton's Plan for a "high mounted" government, which gave the Virginia Plan the middle ground between the Hamilton Plan and the New Jersey Plan; of Franklin's appeals to God, to prayer, and to the Revolution, which cooled tempers at a critical moment; of William Johnson's very matter of fact statement of the grounds for the compromise which subsequently resulted; of Abraham Baldwin's crucial change of vote, against his con-viction and his state's interest, to avert stalemate; and, of course, of the contribution of the presiding officer, George Washington, who spoke only once (and then in the spirit of conciliating those who had doubts about the adequacy of representation) but whose very presence reminded all of the importance of union.[21]

The creation of the presidency was the second major achievement of the Convention. That critical office was constructed in full knowledge of the opinion, cogently stated by George Mason, that republican government is incompatible with a strong unitary executive, that it relies instead on "the love, the affection, the attachment of the citizens to their laws, to their freedom, and to their country."[22] Storing agreed with Hamilton's equally cogent response, that the enlightened friends of republican government who held Mason's opinion had better hope that they were wrong, since "energy in the executive is a leading character in the def-inition of good government."[23] Storing argues, moreover, that the presidency is the keystone to the constitutional system of checks and balances. The problem was "how to inform some parts of a government that was *basically* popular with a spirit that would not be *simply* popular," and to prevent the checks and balances from reaching a perfect equilibrium in which no action was possible. "The Founders' response to both of these difficulties," Storing wrote, "culminates in the Presidency, an institution that, far more than federalism, represents the Founders' achievement and their challenge."[24]

B. The Ratification Debate

Storing argues that the Anti-Federalists lost the debate over the Constitution not merely because they were "less skillful politicians, but because they had the weaker argument."[25] On the other hand, their reservations against the new form of republican government draw our attention to a vulnerable feature of American government: its fundamental reliance on interest, with no explicit provision for cultivating and sustaining public spiritedness and virtue.

The Anti-Federal arguments about the primacy of the states in a truly federal system rested on the conviction that the liberty which was characteristic of republican government could only be preserved with a small homogeneous population residing in a small territory. Storing identifies three basic components of this "small republic" argument:

> Only a small republic can enjoy a voluntary attachment of the people to the government and a voluntary obedience. Only a small republic can secure a genuine responsibility of the government to the people. Only a small republic can form the kind of citizens who will maintain republican government.[26]

The first point is that a people's confidence in their government comes from their knowing the governors; this induces the sensible and virtuous part of the community to declare in favor of the laws, and to support them without an expensive military force. The second point is that responsibility follows from a "full and equal representation," which means representatives "should be a true picture of the people; possess the knowledge of their circumstances and their wants; sympathize in all their distresses, and be disposed to seek their true interests."[27] Conceding that the elective principle itself will produce a refinement in government, Anti-Federalist Melancton Smith (New York) argues that the more numerous state legislatures satisfy this requirement to a greater degree than the federal legislature can, and that they contain enough of the middling class for satisfactory representation.[28] On the third point, the Anti-Federalists argue that "government operates upon the spirit of the people"[29] as well as vice versa and that this mutual dependence is ignored in the Constitution. A republican citizenry must be free, independent, and homogeneous. This discussion of the proper character traits of a republican citizen frequently emphasized religion. Storing quotes one illustrative example from Mercy Warren's *History of the American Revolution*: referring to the Europeans, whom she fears the Americans will follow, Warren writes:

> Bent on gratification, at the expense of every moral tie, they have broken down the barriers of religion, and the spirit of infidelity is nourished at the fount; thence the poisonous streams run through every grade that constitutes the mass of nations.[30]

Notwithstanding that statement, Storing argues that "the Anti-Federalist position was not so much that government ought to foster religion as that the consolidating Constitution threatened the healthy religious situation as it then existed."[31]

Even conceding the merits of the small republic position, was it compatible with union? The Massachusetts Anti-Federalist "Agrippa" proposed that commerce could supply the bond of union rather than coercive government. The problem here, as Storing points out, is that a voluntary recognition of mutual dependence was precisely what characterized the inadequate Articles of Confederation. This attempt to reconcile the small republic position with union produced an interesting shift in the Anti-Federal treatment of federalism. Their original position was that the states are the soul of a confederacy. The Federalists, on the other hand, who were unabashed nationalists in the Federal Convention, shifted to the view that the Constitution was a mixture, partly federal partly national. Then the Anti-Federalists shifted, calling true federalism what they had previously called a mixture, or partial consolidation. The mixture that was now called true federalism involved, for the Anti-Federalists, a division of power and responsibility whereby the states had sufficient means to insure their status. The Federalists claimed this was true of the Constitution. "The road is broad enough," Storing quotes Oliver Ellsworth: "but if two men will jostle each other, the fault is not the road." Speaking on behalf of the Anti-Federalists, Storing replies: "But the very breadth of the road, the lack of restriction on the powers of the general government, and its independence of the states, seemed to the Anti-Federalists to make jostling inevitable with the states likely to find themselves in the ditch."[32] The Anti-Federalists proposed a strict delineation of state and federal powers, combined with a limited federal tax power over imports, supplemented by requisitions from the states. Storing comments: "[I]t should be considered whether this arrangement, which would have been widely accepted among the Anti-Federalists, would not have been the mode of revenue raising most consistent with the 'new federalism,' and what its rejection implies for the new 'federal' system."[33]

In his account of the Federalist reply to the small republic argument, Storing contrasts the Anti-Federalist concern over too strong a government with the Federalist concern about the evils of majority faction. While they did not emphasize this concern, the Anti-Federalists shared it. Both sides supported the majority principle and yet both knew that some applications of that principle infringe on individual rights. The Anti-Federalists "were inclined to think . . . that harm is more often done by the tyranny of the rulers than by the licentiousness of the people." Moreover, for the Anti-Federalists, the threat of licentiousness was met in the same way as the threat of tyranny: "By the alert public spiritedness of the small, homogeneous, self-governing community."[34] On the other hand, the Federalists relied on effective administration and effective representation to meet the threat of licentiousness.[35] As Storing summarized the Federalist reply, the Anti-Federalists "saw civil society as a teacher, as a molder of character, rather than as a regulator of conduct,"[36] as the Federalists saw it. As for the Anti-Federalist attempt to reconcile the small republic view with union, Storing earlier introduced Hamilton's forceful argument, that if a rational alternative is not firmly embraced, "the absurdity must continually stare us in the face of confiding to a government, the direction of the most essential national interests, without daring to trust it with the authorities which are indispensable to their proper and efficient management."[37]

When Massachusetts ratified the Constitution with the understanding that amendments would be taken up immediately, the Anti-Federalist attempt to gain support for conditional ratification, which would have required a second convention, failed, and the Constitution was well on its way to ratification.[38] Since the Bill of Rights as passed secured the Constitution and closed off Anti-Federal opposition, Storing finds the common view that the Federalists gave us the Constitution and the Anti-Federalists gave us the Bill of Rights, inaccurate.[39]

In a sense, the bill of rights is the Anti-Federalist legacy to us. For the Anti-Federalists, the foundation of good government requires "expressly reserving to the people such of their essential natural rights, as are not necessary to be parted with."[40] To the Federalists this seemed to be putting the cart before the horse. As Storing puts it on their behalf, "however necessary a reservation of rights may be, how can the foundation of government be laid in reservations against that very government?" For the Federalists the Constitution *is* a bill of rights.[41] But the Anti-Federalists were able to point to the extensive governmental powers and to the possibility of majority tyranny. Why not, they said, include a bill of rights for safety? What did they have to lose? Storing responds again for the Federalists: "Loose and easy talk about rights was likely to distract attention from the difficult but fundamental business of forming a government capable of doing the things that have to be done to protect rights."[42] The Anti-Federalists were less concerned about this danger since they did not regard the need for government as "the bedrock of the free republic."[43] The Anti-Federalists emphasized bills of rights to restrict governmental power but also to help form a republican character in the people. To make this point Storing quotes the "Federal Farmer": "If a nation means its systems, religious or political, shall have duration, it ought to recognize the leading principles of them in the front page of every family book."[44]

Storing concludes that the Anti-Federalists had the weaker argument because they never successfully met Hamilton's challenge, from Federalist #23, to cease attempting to reconcile contradictions and firmly embrace a rational alternative. They wanted the small republic but they also wanted union, and the latter required the great and complex republican government of the Constitution. Storing concludes that the constitutional system, "designed so that . . . the ordinary operations of government would call for little more than the reliable inclination of men to follow their own interests, ... has been remarkably, if not gloriously, successful."[45] But, if the Federalists supplied the foundation, "the Anti-Federalist reservations echo through American history; and it is in the dialogue, not merely in the Federalist victory, that the country's principles are to be discovered."[46]

The Anti-Federalist reservations against the Constitution were based on the need for republican virtue. Since the Federalists acknowledged this need, the Anti-

Federalists could argue, Storing writes, that the Constitution "is distinguished, not by emancipation from this old dependence but by a lack of much attention to the question of how that necessary republican virtue can be maintained." The Federalists took for granted "a certain kind of public-spirited leadership" and "the republican genius of the people." Storing wonders whether this is a reasonable assumption. "Can a legal system for the regulation of private passions to the end that those passions may be more fully gratified serve as the foundation of civic virtue?"[47] Storing's answer is "No."

> The Anti-Federalists saw, although sometimes only dimly, the insufficiency of a community of mere interest. They saw that the American polity had to be a moral community if it was to be anything, and they saw that the seat of that community must be the hearts of the people.[48]

Storing completed his account of the Bill of Rights in an essay entitled "The Constitution and the Bill of Rights," which he wrote in 1975, shortly after completing his essay on the Anti-Federalists. In it, he shows how Madison steered amendments through the House of Representatives which broadened support for the Constitution without surrendering any power to the states, as the Anti-Federalists wanted.

Storing's own position on a Bill of Rights, on the basis of his last treatment of the subject, is mixed. On the one hand, he sides with the Federalists in questioning whether a constant emphasis on natural rights, including the right of revolution and popular sovereignty, fosters either popular support for government or responsible government. Even if the principles are true, they can endanger government. Storing thinks this is why Madison shied away from the "standard setting, maxim describing teaching function of bills of rights that the Anti-Federalists thought so important."[49] On the other hand, in his conclusion Storing refers to the Bill of Rights, especially the First Amendment, "as a statement in legal form of the great end of free government, to secure the private sphere, and the great means for preserving such a government, to foster an alert and enlightened citizenry."[50] Even so, Storing's final word is that it is in the Constitution's "design of government with powers to act and a structure arranged to make it act wisely and responsibly . . . not in its preamble or epilogue [the Bill of Rights], that the security of American civil and political liberty lies."[51]

III. THE CIVIL WAR AND THE REFOUNDING, OR RACE AND THE REGIME

As a follow-up to his course on the American Founding, Storing taught a course on the Constitution and the Civil War. In some versions this course began by examining the Federal Convention's treatment of slavery and then moved on to consider the major Supreme Court decisions on slavery, the Lincoln-Douglas debates, the speeches of President Lincoln, and the Court's major Reconstruction decisions. For Storing, the existence of slavery, and its tacit recognition in the Constitution, was on the one hand the "flaw" in American government, whose principles declared the natural right of each human being to liberty.[52] On the other hand, it was difficult to imagine what more the framers could have done in 1787 without jeopardizing the Union. And since there was no explicit reference to slavery in the Constitution, Storing pointed out how former slave and former abolitionist Frederick Douglass was able to argue that the Constitution was a freedom document.[53] In his treatment of the constitutional crisis that led to the Civil War, Storing highlighted Abraham Lincoln's understanding of the principles of American government and his ability to communicate them to his fellow citizens as well as Lincoln's prudent actions as President. While Storing did not write a great deal about Lincoln,[54] his essay on Frederick Douglass[55] demonstrates how Douglass came to appreciate and later celebrate Lincoln's statesmanship. And toward the end of his talk on "Liberal Education and the Common Man," in 1975, Storing described Lincoln's achievement as he quoted part of Douglass' speech on Lincoln and indicated that Lincoln was also Booker T. Washington's model.[56] To Storing, Lincoln succeeded in completing and in some ways in correcting the American Founding.[57] That is, Storing saw Lincoln as interpreting the principles of free government to include a morality that goes beyond expediency, as well as consent of the governed and the Hamiltonian principle of "energy in the executive."[58] Lincoln's position on slavery was that the Missouri Compromise should be restored as slavery was morally wrong, but that the framers' need to acknowledge the institution's existence, since they could not eliminate it, meant that the federal government did not have the power to abolish it in the states where it existed.[59] And President Lincoln's position on secession was that it was "sugar-coated" rebellion: it fell between the two stools of revolutionary action, which was justified only by the serious violation of constitutional rights, and ordinary political action, which allowed a constitutional majority to govern, as long as it did not violate constitutional rights.

Storing's interest in Reconstruction led him to study the political thought of prominent Black American political leaders. He wrote essays on Frederick Douglass[60] and Booker T. Washington and compiled an edition of African-American political thought, entitled, *What Country Have I? Political Writings of Black Americans.* The first part of the title came from a question Frederick Douglass asked while he was an abolitionist. In his introduction, Storing used Douglass' question to explain his interest in the political thought of Black Americans. Aware that Douglass came to affirm America as his country, Storing wrote that "the question does not thereby lose its potency."

> This question is the glass through which the black American sees "his" country. It is a glass that can distort. Anger, frustration, hopelessness, confusion, excessive inwardness often result from the black's situation; and they can lead to blindness and an utter incapacity to see the country in anything like its true shape. But the

glass of the black's peculiar situation can also provide a clean, sharp view of America, exposing its innermost and fundamental principles and tendencies, which are largely ignored or vaguely seen through half-closed eye [sic] by the majority of white Americans, whose circumstances do not compel them really to look at their country and to wonder about it. This does not mean that the black is necessarily revolutionary—most blacks are not; but it does mean that he takes seriously the possibility of revolution, or rejection, or separation. He thus shares the perspective of the serious revolutionary. He appeals, at least in thought, from the imperfect world of convention and tradition . . . to the world of nature and truth. In important respects, then, black Americans are like a revolutionary or, more interestingly perhaps, a founding generation. That is, they are in the difficult but potentially glorious position of not being able to take for granted given political arrangements and values, of having seriously to canvass alternatives, to think through their implications, and to make a deliberate choice.

To understand the American polity, one could hardly do better than to study, along with the work and thought of the Founders, the best writings of the blacks who are at once its friends, enemies, citizens, and aliens.[61]

Storing thus takes politics seriously by taking both thought and action seriously. This accounts for his interest in both Lincoln's statesmanship and Frederick Douglass' understanding of that statesmanship. It also accounts for his appreciation of the Black-American's taking revolution seriously as an option. At the same time, if one concludes that the regime is fundamentally just, even for blacks, and most African-American political leaders did, that has implications for political action. That is why Storing criticized Martin Luther King, Jr.'s doctrine of civil disobedience: an across the board claim that one can disobey a law one regards as unjust, as long as one does so openly with a willingness to accept the penalty, threatens habitual law abidingness, and thus runs the risk of undermining the necessary conditions for a regime which supports robust freedom. The approach confuses the subject's perspective with the citizen's.[62] Storing used Frederick Douglass' shift from abolitionism to support for Lincoln to make the point that the reformer's dictum that "the purity of the cause is the success of the cause," was subordinate to the morality of doing as much good as possible. This point went together with Storing's pointing out that Douglass' reaction to the Supreme Court's *Dred Scott* decision was fundamentally different from his reaction to the Court's decisions in the *Civil Rights Cases;* whereas the former decision "thrust the Negro out of any participation in the American political community," by denying that he could ever become a citizen, the latter, which struck down a federal law aimed at prohibiting segregation in privately owned places of public accommodation, "although wounding the Negro in the house of his friends, did not threaten to turn him out of that house, as *Dred Scott* had."[63]

Storing's treatment of the principles of American government reflected the appreciation of a friend who knew its strengths as well as its weaknesses. In this respect Storing followed Strauss (and de Tocqueville). One prominent example concerned the Federalists' conviction that the offices of government had to be constructed so that ambition and avarice would be turned to public benefit. "Enlightened statesmen will not always be at the helm."[64] Another example came from Lincoln's speech, in 1838, to the Young Men's Lyceum, "On the Perpetuation of Our Political Institutions."[65] What starts out as unqualified praise for the Founders for establishing free political institutions turns into a subtle criticism of those principles, in so far as they rely on enlightened self-interest, or at least an acknowledgment that foundings are never complete. That is because Lincoln understood the problem of ambition as inherent in the human condition, that "towering genius disdains a beaten path," and will have fame by hook or by crook.[66] For this reason, the principles of modern self-government, which give great weight to security and comfort, may not always suffice to maintain political liberty.

Storing's most dramatic demonstration of the limits of individual rights and consent appears in his essay "The Founders and Slavery."[67] As much as he admired Lincoln for his understanding of the principles of American government, his rhetorically effective means of presenting his position, and his decisive deeds, Storing showed how the position of the southern slave states might be derived from those very same principles. After acquitting the Founders of the charge that they betrayed their principles in the matter of slavery in the land of freedom (the argument here draws on Lincoln's distinction between setting a standard and attaining it fully), Storing proceeds to argue that the very principle of individual liberty "contains within itself an uncomfortably large opening toward slavery."[68] As shocking as this statement appears, its elaboration simply reveals the close connection between rights and self-interest, which leads us back to the Anti-Federalist reservations. Storing's elaboration clearly reflects his study of modern political philosophy with Strauss.[69]

> Thus the slave owner may resolve that it is necessary to keep his slaves in bondage for the compelling reason that if they were free they would kill him; but he may also decide, on the same basic principle, that he must keep them enslaved in order to protect his plantation, his children's patrimony, his flexibility of action, on which his preservation ultimately depend; and from that he may conclude that he is entitled to keep his slaves in bondage if he finds it convenient to do so. All of this presumes of course that he can keep his slaves in bondage. Nor does it in any way deny the right of the slave to resist his enslavement and to act the part of the master if he can. This whole chain of reasoning is a chilling clarification of the essential war that seems always to exist, at bottom, between man and man.[70]

Slavery is admittedly an extreme case, but the general problem concerns the likely disjunction between wisdom and commitment to the common good on the one hand and political power on the other hand. Storing liked to point to the outstanding qualities, moral and intellectual, of a Lincoln or a Douglass as models by which to judge those in positions of authority, at the same time he reminded us that "American society is robust enough to take a good deal of mauling."[71]

IV. THE PRESIDENCY AND THE BUREAUCRACY

This discussion of the task of statesmanship, or political leadership, leads to the third area of Storing's work, on the Presidency and the Bureaucracy.

Shortly before his death, at the age of forty-nine, Storing accepted an appointment at the University of Virginia, as Director of the Study of the Presidency at the White Center for Public Affairs and as the Robert Kent Gooch Professor of Government and Foreign Affairs. With his work on the Anti-Federalists behind him, Storing planned to shift his teaching and research focus to the Presidency and to public administration in modern American government.

As Storing viewed the founding as a dialogue of continuing importance for American politics, so his teaching and writing about the presidency emphasized what had been settled as well as what had changed. Storing demonstrated how our current questions continue to reflect founding themes. Let us start with the office and its powers. The office is unitary and its occupant possesses "the executive power," as well as a qualified veto over legislation. In his introduction to the 1969 reissuing of Charles Thach's book, *The Creation of the Presidency, 1775–1789*, Storing calls the work "so useful and so sound as to be indispensable."[72] But Storing also suggests that Thach was too willing to take a strong republican executive for granted. Storing begins and ends his introduction with Hamilton's account of the presidency in the *Federalist*. On the other hand, what Thach took for granted, Arthur Schlesinger did not. But what Schlesinger, writing in 1973 amidst the debate over war powers, the impoundment of funds, and Watergate, unflinchingly characterizes as a Presidency which "has gotten out of control and badly needs new definition and restraint,"[73] Storing characterizes as the inherent tension between republican responsibility and executive energy. Drawing on the *Federalist*, the emergency powers cases, and Lincoln's defense of his suspension of the privilege of *habeas corpus* in 1861, Storing argues for a flexible view of the constitutional boundaries between Congress and the President. This is another way of allowing an expansive interpretation of "the executive power" and "the commander in chief" power, at the same time that Congress is free to contest any presidential action. The problem concerns necessity and its relation to the Constitution, America's fundamental law. The other practical alternative, which Justice Jackson[74] and Schlesinger advocated, is to acknowledge an "emergency prerogative." Storing, following the *Federalist*, argues against such a position.

> On the one hand, the resort from the Constitution to prerogative tends to undermine the Constitution. But, on the other hand, constitutional barriers will not be able to resist real necessity. So the conclusion the founders drew was that the Constitution must lie with the grain of nature; it must 'constitutionalize' prerogative, so far as any law can do that.[75]

This discussion of the office of the presidency led to a discussion of presidential powers. Another aspect of the office, apart from its number, is its mode of election, known as the "electoral college" system. This indirectly popular mode of election served the purpose, in Storing's view, of insulating the president from direct popular pressure, and thus allowing him some independence at the same time that it provided republican legitimacy. Between the presidencies of Jefferson and Jackson, first the mode of election and then the character of the presidency became more democratic, that is, more popularly controlled. Storing had occasion to note the significance of each change and to connect it to founding principle.

In 1977, Storing testified in defense of the electoral college before the Subcommittee on the Constitution of the Senate Judiciary Committee.[76] Senator Birch Bayh, chairman of the Subcommittee, advocated a direct popular election; his special concern was the likelihood, which last occurred in 1888, of a candidate's receiving a majority of the electoral votes, and winning the election, but finishing second in the popular vote. More than anything else Storing's testimony, written and oral, reveals his aversion to what he called "simplistic democracy" and his interest in what he called "outputs" as well as "inputs," which meant the effect of a given electoral scheme on the quality of persons chosen and the operation of government. Storing maintained that while the mode of electing the president did not work as the framers intended, it nonetheless "achieves to a remarkable extent the ends the framers wanted to achieve."[77] Storing referred to the element of popular participation, political stability, a place for politically active individuals, a place for the states, independence of the president, and the character and intelligence of the presidents elected. He identified the two party system as a major source of these benefits and suggested that a direct popular vote would weaken those parties.

That is because the "winner take all" rule, which the large states have an incentive to employ under the current system, and which thereby forces all states to employ, discourages third party efforts and encourages compromise within the two major parties. In addition, since he rejected the simplistic view of democracy, which equates legitimacy with responsiveness to popular wishes, Storing did not think that the election of a president whose popular vote total was less than his opponent would create a constitutional crisis.[78]

The other change, effected by President Jackson, was to identify the president as a direct representative of the people as much as members of Congress. Jackson was the first president to use both the executive veto and the removal power for political purposes; he also assumed leadership of the Democratic party.[79] Storing, who taught this material regularly in his course on the American Presidency, wrote about the conflict between Jackson and the Whigs this way:

> When Andrew Jackson defended his removal of subordinates even contrary to congressional legislation, he presented a view of administration as well as a view of democracy. Administration was seen as residing crucially in the president, with the administration serving as his eyes and hands. The Whig view, on the other hand, rested not only on a different (more pluralistic) view of American politics,

but also on a different view of administration. The Whigs saw public administration not as a closed hierarchy leading to the top but as pools of official discretion, loosely connected but largely independent. Jackson and the Whigs were primarily concerned with what today we would call the issue of responsibility—Jackson to the president; the Whigs to the law. But the implicit views of public administration are especially interesting here, and the Whig view in particular since it is the one that seems always to lose. This view emphasizes the importance of the exercise of experienced, informed, responsible discretion as the heart of administration. Sound discretion, not obedience to higher command, is the essence of good administration, though both, of course, are always involved. Administrative structures should be built to provide the right conditions for this informed good judgment—independent regulatory commissions are a case in point.[80]

Thus Storing, noting the democratization of government under the Constitution, approved of independent regulatory commissions as a means of retaining the benefits of sound discretion in administration, along with presidential control of the executive branch.

This discussion of the presidency leads to a discussion of the bureaucracy in American government. Storing notes in several places that the dominant view of public administration is that of scientific management. That means that public administration is considered as a subset of administration simply and the focus is on rules for efficiency. This view of administration goes together with a populist view of politics; together they form a view of government which sharply divides everything into the expression of the popular will on the one hand (politics), and the implementation of that will on the other (administration). We have already seen how Storing criticized both formulations, in light of a more complex, and hence more comprehensive, understanding of liberal democracy and the American polity. Some brief illustrations of his position follow.

In his 1977 essay on statesmanship,[81] Storing, drawing on the work of Herbert Simon, identifies "two critical principles of the current understanding of practical reason, or rational decision-making:" "the notion of the 'one best method' and the assumption that all practical reasoning is essentially economic reasoning." On the first point, Storing maintains that any attempt to get the "one best way" leads to an unending and hence irrational process of information seeking, because the information at a decision-maker's disposal is always incomplete. Rather than to say, as Simon does, that "these conditions limit rationality," Storing contends that "one of the most important elements of practical reason—or 'rational' decision-making— is precisely how well or poorly such limits are grappled with." Storing points out that Simon acknowledges the impossibility of "maximizing," which he then replaces with "satisficing." This refers to settling for an approximation of "maximizing," which Storing finds commonsensical. While "for Simon it is a necessary falling short of reason," Storing thinks "we 'satisfice' because we have the wits to know that we cannot maximize and that we would be insane to try to do so." On the second point, Storing acknowledges the contribution of the economic approach to practical reason (this approach reduces everything to the instrumental value of "utility"), but he contends that such an account of practical reason is incomplete, because it cannot tell us about the requirements of an adequate defense or how to secure the legitimate rights of minorities.[82]

Storing's critique of a simplistic, or "populist," view of democracy and his critique of the scientific understanding of practical reason are both present in his account of the way to think about the bureaucracy in American government. Storing argued that Leonard White, whose administrative histories of the first hundred years of the American republic he admired, was moving away from an emphasis on the process of administration, and toward a view of administration that identified it with the distinctive character of government. Likewise, in his essay entitled, "Political Parties and the Bureaucracy," Storing criticizes the civil service reform movement for taking too strict a stance against politics, i.e., the spoils system. "Although the reformers often described their movement as a return to the original principles of the American republic, they paid too little heed to the Founders' warning that a government fit for angels is not fit for men."[83]

Storing argues that both the spoils system and the reformers shared the view that the civil service "should be responsive to the will or 'values' of the people," with the difference that one does it by a thorough mixture and the other does it by a thorough separation. Storing argues that the civil service should have "a political agency in its own right," in order to be able to act as a thoughtful, experienced partner for the politically elected officials. He argues moreover, that the Hoover Commission's proposal for a senior civil service envisioned such a partnership, after the British model, and he cites examples of its success. While the framers did not "anticipate the full significance of the administrative state," Storing does find "a close harmony between the original intention of the system of checks and balances and the political role of the modern civil service."[84] That is, the civil service must act as a partner to the political branches of government, and it must follow the laws (Congress) as it assists the political appointees in the executive branch in the administration of government.

Finally, in his *Plan for Studying the Presidency*, a version of which was submitted to President Ford, Storing proposes a Presidential Commission along the lines of FDR's Committee on Administrative Management, which report led to the establishment of the Office of the White House in 1939. Storing praised the Committee for setting an agenda "for *thinking about* the executive and modern American government." He criticized the Committee for playing down the "political side of 'executive management,'" and for emphasizing the role of "chief executive and administrator." Storing's three main proposals concerned how one understands the powers of government, how one understands administration of government, and how one understands the relation between the presidency and Congress in light of "the tension between the president's role as 'chief administrator' and his role as a participant in checks and balances."

Each of these points reflects the ways in which Storing understood American government as a complex arrangement of offices which were constructed to satisfy the different objectives of consent of the governed and of an energetic administration of government.

V. CONCLUSION

Herbert Storing took from his study with Leo Strauss an awareness of the limitations of the positivistic approach to politics and an appreciation of the need to take seriously the arguments that were made for political action, as well as the action itself. In addition, his focus on the American founding and the founding principles of American government was informed by Strauss' appreciation of the strengths and his cautions about the weaknesses of liberal democracy. From the perspective of political philosophy, this form of government's chief strengths lie in its stability and its capacity to provide for security and prosperity. Because the popular element is the strongest, the mistakes it makes, as Alexis de Tocqueville noted, tend to be retrievable. In his classroom teaching as well as his writing, Storing taught that the Founders' understanding of government included an appreciation of the strengths and weaknesses of the principles of free government and that their achievement, the American Constitution, reflected that understanding, by providing for popular participation and checks and balances, including an independent and energetic executive and an independent judiciary.

Storing's work, his writings and his teaching, reflected his twofold view that the Constitution "established a lasting structure of rules and principles," and that "the political life of the community continues to be a dialogue."[85] As he developed that dialogue, Storing showed not only how the Anti-Federalists as well as the Federalists played an important part in it, but also how Lincoln did, how Black American political thinkers such as Douglass, Washington, DuBois, King and Malcolm X did, and how those responsible for the development of the modern administrative state did.

Storing knew that some scholars did not appreciate the understanding and the work of the Founders as he did. For some critics, the Founders' views were either not sufficiently democratic or not sufficiently scientific. For the historian John Hope Franklin, their views reflected racial prejudice and "set the stage for every succeeding generation of Americans to apologize, compromise, and temporize on those principles of liberty that were supposed to be the very foundation of our system of government and way of life."[86] Responding on behalf of "one of the thoughtful Founders,"[87] Storing thinks the Founder would acknowledge the remarkable progress but still wonder whether it has been shown that the races can live together. Regarding the temporizing, Storing asks, on behalf of the Founder, "what more could have been done?" Noting that "prejudice . . . is inherent in political life," Storing writes: "To criticize a Jefferson or a Lincoln for yielding to, even sharing in, white prejudice is equivalent to demanding either that he get out of politics alto-gether—and leave it to the merely prejudiced—or that he become a despot."[88] While Storing's Founder notes that the tolerance which extreme heterogeneity requires leads to the "superficiality of social bonds and community values," he is also intrigued by W.E.B. Dubois' creative account of how diverse nationalities can be American citizens, with common political ideals and language, at the same time that they also identify by racial and (we would add today) ethnic groups.[89] "Reflecting on thoughts like these," Storing's Founder "might concede that the huge problem of racial heterogeneity, which his generation saw but could not mas-ter, may show the way to deal with another problem, which they did not see clearly, the political and moral defects of mere individualism."[90] Thus Storing shows us the wide range of human types that make up a democratic society such as ours. He shows us the importance and the limits of politics, especially a democratic politics which gives free rein to the peaceful passions.[91] At the same time, he directs us to the best possible understanding of those principles, so that American government can be as strong and secure as possible. Reminding us in many different contexts that our government is constructed so that freedom is secured without reliance on "enlightened statesmen," Storing nonetheless highlights America's best examples of political leadership, for students to understand and for practitioners to understand and to imitate as well as they can.

NOTES

* I would like to thank Joseph Cropsey, Paul Carrese, and Damjan de Krnjevic-Miskovic for their thoughtful comments on earlier drafts of this essay.
1. When he left the University of Chicago in 1977, Storing's students honored him at a gathering in which he was celebrated as a "teacher of teachers." I was one of his graduate students from 1962 to 1968, and one of my students, Frank Kruesi, was present at the farewell ceremony, as a student of Storing's.
2. As a graduate student, Storing also studied with C. Herman Pritchett (constitutional law) and Leonard White (public administration). This information came from Joseph Cropsey and Robert Scigliano.
3. When he first started teaching at Chicago, Storing taught standard constitutional law courses. My colleague Paul Nelson took a two quarter sequence in constitutional law from Storing during the fall and winter quarters, 1958–1959. By the 1960s, Storing had devel-oped special courses in the Founding, the Constitution and the Civil War, and the Presidency.
4. During my six years as a graduate student at Chicago, I took six courses with Storing, wrote my dissertation under his direction, and served as a research assistant for him in con-nection with his work on the writings of the Anti-Federalists. Later I assisted in the final edi-torial work on *The Complete Anti-Federalist* (Chicago: University of Chicago Press, 1981) after Storing's sudden and untimely death in 1977. I also studied with Strauss and Cropsey.
5. I have learned from Joseph Cropsey that the practice of addressing faculty members as Mr. or Mrs. or Miss, rather than Dr. or Professor, was introduced by the administration of the University (from a letter, dated April 22, 1998).

6. The essay appeared in the *National Review*, vol. 25, December 7, 1973. It was reprinted in *Toward a More Perfect Union: Writings of Herbert J. Storing*, ed. by Joseph M. Bessette, (Washington, D. C.: AEI Press, 1995) hereinafter cited as *Writings*. This excellent 469 page collection contains much of Storing's work, including hitherto out of print essays and some previously unpublished material.

7. *Writings*, p.445.

8. *Ibid*, pp. 445–447. Strauss referred to the Declaration of Independence in the introduction to his *Natural Right and History* (Chicago: University of Chicago, 1953) p. 1. And in his introduction to *Thoughts on Machiavelli* (Glencoe, IL.: Free Press, 1958), Strauss writes that "to the extent that the American reality is inseparable from the American aspiration, one cannot understand Americanism without understanding Machiavellianism[,] which is its opposite," p. 14.

9. Storing did not claim to be exhaustive in his account of Strauss's work. He did not mention Strauss' work on two important themes or conflicts: poetry versus philosophy, and reason versus revelation. Each of these, however, transcends political science as a profession, which is to say political science in the narrow sense.

10. Another important source for the link between Strauss and Storing is their collaboration in *Essays in the Scientific Study of Politics* (New York: Holt Rinehart and Winston, Inc., 1962).

Storing edited the volume and wrote a lengthy critique of Herbert Simon's work (pp. 63–150), as well as a brief preface (pp. v–vii). Other chapters were written by Walter Berns, Leo Weinstein, and Robert Horwitz. Strauss wrote the Epilogue, which has since become famous for its "no holds barred" approach to value free political science (pp. 307–327). It also contains ample evidence to support Storing's three part characterization of Strauss's political science.

11. See Max Weber, "Science as a Vocation," in *From Max Weber: Essays in Sociology*, ed. by H. H. Gerth and C. Wright Mills, (New York: Oxford University Press, 1946), pp. 129–156, esp. 145–146; and see Strauss's critique in *Natural Right and History* (Chicago: University of Chicago Press, 1953), chapter two.

12. In his introduction to *The City and Man*, Strauss contrasts the scientific with the prescientific understanding of political things. The latter view, which is also called the "common sense view of political things," is the understanding of "political things as they are understood by the citizen or statesman." Strauss goes on to write that Aristotle's *Politics* "contains the original form of political science: that form in which political science is nothing other than the fully conscious form of the common sense understanding of political things." Leo Strauss, *The City and Man*, (Chicago: Rand McNally, 1964), pp. 11–12.

13. Herbert J. Storing, ed., *The Complete Anti-Federalist* (Chicago: University of Chicago, 1981), seven volumes. Volume one contained his essay, which was also published separately in paperback at the same time. The full title is *What the Anti-Federalist Were For! The Political Thought of the Anti-Federalists*.

14. *What the Anti-Federalists Were For*, pp. 3–4.

15. *Ibid.*, p. 6.

16. Cecelia Kenyon, "Men of Little Faith: The Anti-Federalists and the Nature of Representative Government," *William and Mary Quarterly*, Jan 1955; also "Introduction," in *The Anti-Federalists* (Indianapolis: Bobbs Merrill, 1966).

17. Storing, *What the Anti-Federalists Were For*, p. 71.

18. "The Constitutional Convention: Toward a More Perfect Union," first published in Morton J. Frisch and Richard J. Stevens, eds., *American Political Thought: The Philosophic*

Dimension of American Statesmanship, second edition F.E. Peacock Publishers, 1983) p. 55; also in *Writings*, p. 22.

19. Supporters of this principle called themselves "nationalists." The term "nationalist," as used in the Federal Convention, referred to a supporter of a strong central government; it had nothing to do with ethnic identification, as it often does today.

20. *Writings*, p. 36.

21. *Ibid*, pp. 25–34, 20.

22. Storing quoted this in his introduction to a new edition of Charles Thach's *The Creation of the Presidency* (Baltimore: Johns Hopkins University Press, 1969), pp. ix–x. See also *Writings*, p. 374. The quotation comes from Mason's notes of his June 4 speech in the Federal Convention; see Max Farrand, ed., *The Records of the Federal Convention* (New Haven: Yale University Press, 1937), vol. I, p. 112.

23. This comes from the first paragraph of *Federalist* #70.

24. "The Problem of Big Government," p. 81 in *A Nation of States; Essays on the American Federal System*, ed. by Robert A. Goldwin (Chicago: Rand McNally, 1961), p. 81; also in *Writings*, p. 301.

25. *What the Anti-Federalists Were For*, p. 71. In addition to Storing's *The Complete Anti-Federalist*, for a more extensive account of the lesser known federalist writers, see Storing's "The 'Other' Federalist Papers: A Preliminary Sketch," in the bicentennial edition of *The Political Science Reviewer* VI, pp. 215–47; this is also in *Writings*, pp. 77–107.

26. *Ibid.*, p. 16.

27. *Ibid.*, p. 17. Storing is quoting Melancton Smith, from his arguments in the New York Ratification Convention. Smith and "Federal Farmer" made the strongest Anti-Federalist arguments on representation.

28. Another component of the responsibility argument involved the political significance of jury trials, which some Anti-Federalists regarded as even more important than representation to prevent "those usurpations which silently undermine the spirit of liberty." This is from the Maryland Farmer; see *The Complete Anti-Federalist*, [Maryland] Farmer, IV, 5.1.65. Storing quotes this in *What the Anti-Federalists Were For*, p. 19.

29. *Ibid.* This is also from Smith.

30. *What the Anti-Federalists Were For*, p. 22.

31. *Ibid.*, p. 23.

32. *Ibid.*, p. 34. Ellsworth, a member of the Federal Convention from Connecticut, was also a member of Connecticut's Ratification Convention. Storing quotes from a speech he made on 7 January 1788; see Jonathan Elliot, ed., *The Debates in the Several State Conventions on the adoption of the Federal Constitution as recommended by the General Convention in Philadelphia in 1787* (Philadelphia: J. P. Lippincott Company, 1891), vol. II, p. 195.

33. *Ibid.*, p. 36.

34. *Ibid.*, p. 40.

35. *Ibid.*, pp. 42–43. Storing refers to Hamilton's statement in *Federalist* #27 that the people's affections will be won over by superior administration, which he expects from the federal government, and Madison's statement, in *Federalist* #63, to the effect that Americans improved on ancient uses of representation by succeeding in excluding the people "in their collective capacity" from any share in government.

36. *Ibid.*, p. 47.

37. *Ibid.*, p. 29, quoting from *Federalist* #23.

38. See Robert Allen Rutland, *The Ordeal of the Constitution: The Anti-Federalists and the*

Ratification Struggle of 1787–1788 (Boston: Northeastern University Press, 1966); Michael Allen Gillespie and Michael Lienesch, eds., *Ratifying the Constitution*, (Lawrence, Kansas: University of Kansas Press, 1989); Murray Dry, "The Debate Over Ratification of the Constitution," in *The Blackwell Encyclopedia of the American Revolution*, edited by Jack P. Greene and J.R. Pole (Cambridge, MA: Blackwell, 1991), pp. 471–486.

39. See *What the Anti-Federalists Were For*," pp. 64–70. See also Storing's essay, "The Constitution and the Bill of Rights," in M. Judd Harmon, ed., *Essays on the Constitution of the United States* (Port Washington, N.Y. : Kennikat Press, 1978), pp. 32–48. It is reprinted in *Writings*, pp. 108–128, and will be discussed further below.

40. *What the Anti-Federalists Were* For, p. 66. Storing is quoting "Brutus" here.

41. See *Federalist* #84.

42. *Writings*, p. 69.

43. *Ibid.*, p. 69.

44. *Ibid.*, p. 70. See *Complete Anti-Federalist*, Federal Farmer XVI, 2.8.196

45. *Ibid.*, p. 72.

46. *Ibid.*, p. 72.

47. *Ibid.*, p. 73.

48. *Ibid.*, p. 76. At the same time, Storing, who approached his study wondering whether the Anti-Federalists agreed fundamentally with the Federalists, concluded that they did. Responding, in a footnote, to Gordon Wood's view that the Anti-Federalists were self-sacrificing "traditional" republicans, Storing wrote that "the Anti-Federalists are liberals—reluctant and traditional indeed—in the decisive sense that they see the end of government as the security of individual liberty, not the promotion of virtue or the fostering of some organic common good." See *ibid.*, note 7, p. 83. Storing's point about the Anti-Federalists' thought and his disagreement with Wood both reflect Strauss' account of the difference between ancient and modern political philosophy. See infra, note 67, for citations to Strauss' writings.

49. "The Constitution and the Bill of Rights," in *Writings*, p. 125.

50. *Ibid.*, p. 128.

51. *Ibid.* Storing's point is the Federalist one, that the Constitution secures liberty for the American people through the structure of government it establishes, along with its ample powers. Today, we tend to identify the Bill of Rights with judicial review. Elsewhere in this essay, Storing speculated on how constitutional law might have been different if no Bill of Rights had been added. See p. 118.

52. Readers today are wont to interpret the Declaration of Independence's statement that "all men are created equal" as referring to white males, since blacks were enslaved and women in general did not have the vote. This is not how the Founders understood it, for reasons that Lincoln explained best: first, the reference is to natural rights, not to political rights or other equality claims that might be made; second, no one claimed that this statement of aspiration was, or could be, fully realized at the time. See Lincoln's Speech on Dred Scott, at Springfield, Illinois, June 26, 1857, in *Lincoln: Selected Speeches and Writings*, texts selected and notes by Don E. Fehrenbacher (New York: Vintage/Library of America, 1992), pp. 120–121.

53. See Storing, "The Case Against Civil Disobedience," first published in *On Civil Disobedience*, ed. by Robert A. Goldwin (Chicago: Rand McNally, 1969), p. 108; in *Writings*, p. 248. In his *What Country Have I? Political Writings of Black Americans*, Storing includes Douglass' "Fourth of July Oration of 1852; in it Douglass wrote, "[I]nterpreted as it ought to be interpreted, the Constitution is a GLORIOUS LIBERTY DOCUMENT." (New York: St. Martin's Press, 1970), p. 37.

54. Storing assigned Harry Jaffa's book, *Crisis of the House Divided: An Interpretation of the Issues in the Lincoln-Douglas Debates* (Garden City, New York: Doubleday & Company Inc., 1959) in his course on the Civil War and the Constitution.

55. "The School of Slavery: A Reconsideration of Booker T. Washington," in Robert A. Goldwin, ed., *100 Years of Emancipation* (Chicago: Rand McNally, 1963), pp. 47–79; also in *Writings*.

56. *Writings*, pp. 438–439.

57. Storing's final examination in *The Constitution and Civil War* course, Winter 1966, contained the following question: "Describe as fully as you can the character of Lincoln's 'completion' or 'correction' of the American Founding."

58. From *Federalist* #70.

59. The Emancipation Proclamation does not contradict this position, since, as an emergency war power, the Proclamation extended only to states which were in rebellion.

60. "Frederick Douglass," in Morton J. Frisch and Richard G. Stevens, eds., *American Political Thought: The Philosophic Dimension of American Statesmanship*, second ed. (ND: F.E. Peacock, 1983), pp. 215–236; also in *Writings*, pp. 151–175.

61. *What Country Have I? Political Writings of Black Americans*, Storing's Introduction, pp. 2–3; also in *Writings*, pp. 206–207.

62. Storing's argument against civil disobedience as a principled doctrine resembles Lincoln's argument against secession in this respect: each doctrine falls between revolutionary and conventional political action and, as a result, fails to satisfy the requirements of consent of the government and individual rights. I believe that Storing developed his argument against civil disobedience from his study of Lincoln's argument against secession. See Storing, "The Case Against Civil Disobedience," in *Writings*, pp. 236–258.

63. Storing, "The Case Against Civil Disobedience," in *op. cit.*, p. 113; also in *Writings*, pp. 252–53.

64. Madison wrote this in *Federalist* #10. While the immediate context is the extended sphere, the same consideration applied to his argument on checks and balances in *Federalist* #47 and #51.

65. See *Lincoln: Selected Speeches and Writings*, pp. 13–21.

66. *Writings*, p. 19.

67. This essay first appeared, under that title, in the Bicentennial issue of the St. John's College publication, *The College*, in July 1976, pp. 17–25. It was then republished in *The Moral Foundations of the American Republic*, ed. by Robert H. Horwitz (Charlottesville University Press of Virginia, 1977) under the title "Slavery and the Moral Foundations of the American Republic," pp. 214–233. It also appears under the revised title in *Writings*, pp. 131–150.

68. *Writings*, pp. 142–143.

69. The most obvious sources are Strauss's accounts of modern political philosophy, especially his accounts of Hobbes and Locke. See *What is Political Philosophy? And Other Studies* (Chicago: University of Chicago, 1959), chapter one, esp. pp. 40–50; and *Natural Right and History* (Chicago: University of Chicago, 1953), chapter five.

70. *Ibid.*, pp. 143–144.

71. "The Case Against Civil Disobedience," in *Writings*, p. 258.

72. In *ibid*, p. 370.

73. Arthur M. Schlesinger, *The Imperial Presidency* (Boston: Houghton Mifflin Company, 1973), Forward, p. x; quoted by Storing in "The Presidency and the Constitution," a talk delivered at Beloit College, March 1974, in *Writings*, p. 379.

74. This is a reference to Justice Jackson's approach to the problem of emergency powers in war time in the case of *Korematsu v. United States*, 323 U.S. 214 (1944).

75. See "The Presidency and the Constitution," in *Writings*, p. 381. Storing quotes from *Federalist* #25.

76. This testimony was originally published in *The Electoral College and Direct Election: Supplement, Hearings before the Subcommittee on the Constitution, of the Committee of the Judiciary, United States Senate, 95th Congress, 1st session,* July, August 1977, pp. 129–149. Storing's written testimony is in *Writings*, pp. 395–402. Martin Diamond also testified before the Subcommittee. He also opposed a direct popular election of the president, and he submitted the pamphlet he had written in support of the Electoral College. See the above cited *Hearings*, pp. 149–185, for his testimony, followed by his pamphlet. A comparison of Storing's testimony with Diamond's reveals a substantial agreement among these two men, who were good friends, along with a difference in style. Diamond plays the role of the advocate (and he does it very well, I believe), whereas Storing is, as always, the teacher.

77. *Writings*, p. 397.

78. *Writings*, p. 401.

79. President Jackson vetoed the bill to renew the national bank in 1832 and then he used his removal power to control the government's policy regarding the immediate transfer of funds from the national bank to state banks, some three years before the expiration of the national bank's charter. See Leonard White's *The Jacksonians: A Study in Administrative History 1829–1861* (New York: Free Press, 1954), chapter 2. As a related, follow up development to the democratization of the presidency, Jeffrey Tulis, who acknowledges his debt to his teacher ("Whatever merit this book displays as a theoretical work derives from the wisdom of my teacher, Herbert J. Storing"), wrote about the development of "popular or mass rhetoric . . . [as] a principal tool of presidential governance." See Jeffrey K. Tulis, *The Rhetorical Presidency* (Princeton, New Jersey: Princeton University Press, 1987), pp. ix, 4.

80. "American Statesmanship: Old and New," originally published in Robert A. Goldwin, ed., *Bureaucrats, Policy Analysts, Statesmen: Who Leads?* (Washington. D.C.: AEI Press, 1980); also in *Writings*, p. 425.

81. "American Statesmanship: Old and New," first published, in an incomplete form, as Storing died before finishing it, in *Bureaucrats, Policy Analysts, Statesmen: Who Leads?* ed. by Robert A. Goldwin (Washington, D.C.: AEI Press, 1980); it also appears in *Writings*, pp. 403–428.

82. *Writings*, pp. 422–424. I have limited myself to Storing's brief account of Simon. For his full account, see Storing's essay on Simon in the *Essays on the Scientific Study of Politics*, supra. note 9.

83. *Ibid.*, p. 312.

84. *Ibid.*, p. 320.

85. *What the Anti-Federalists Were* For, p. 3.

86. *Ibid.*, p. 147. This, and the remaining references, come from Storing's "The Founders and Slavery," also published under the title "Slavery and the American Republic." see above note 67. Storing quotes Franklin from his essay, "The Moral Legacy of the Founding Fathers," published in the *University of Chicago Magazine*, Summer 1975, p. 13.

87. Storing does not name the Founder. While one must think of Madison, "the Founder" is, of course, Storing himself, drawing on his study of the Founders and his study of political philosophy, with Leo Strauss as his teacher.

88. *Ibid.*, p. 148.

89. DuBois' "The Conservation of the Races" appears in Storing, *What Country Have I?*, pp. 76–88; see especially p. 82.

90. *Ibid.*, p. 149.

91. See Strauss, *What is Political Philosophy?*, supra note 67, p. 49, for his discussion of acquisitiveness in Locke, and Montesquieu.

Part Four

American Political Institutions

· 21 ·

Congress and Straussian Constitutionalism

John A. Murley

> Congress is where "We the People of the United States" are con-
> fronted by themselves, but in a more elevated form.
>
> *George Anastaplo[1]*

Leo Strauss wrote of the strengths and weaknesses of liberal democracy, but little about the specifics of American government and nothing explicitly about the Congress of the United States.[2] Though he spent much of his time cultivating his own garden, he repeatedly endorsed both "the old saying that wisdom cannot be separated from moderation" and the understanding "that wisdom requires unhesitating loyalty to a decent constitution and even to the cause of constitutionalism."[3] He recognized the dignity of American constitutionalism and kindled in his students a profound interest in the philosophical and constitutional foundations of the American regime. It is typical of Straussian constitutional scholars that they take the Constitution seriously even as they concentrate on the Founding and the Civil War and the Cold War. In this essay, I draw upon various scholars who have been influenced by Leo Strauss or by Leo Strauss's students.

Some Straussian scholars, in taking the Constitution seriously have depended considerably upon *The Federalist*. Thomas Jefferson identified *The Federalist* as "the best commentary on the principles of government, which ever was written."[4] The quality of *The Federalist* alone would be sufficient to make it particularly attractive for Straussian scholars. (The Strauss-Cropsey *History of Political Philosophy* contains a chapter on *The Federalist*.) It is in *The Federalist* that one can notice significant treatment of conflicting ancient and modern approaches: the fame and glory of the few and the liberty and self-preservation of the many. These contrasting approaches reflect the distinctions Leo Strauss drew between ancient and modern political thought. In these approaches one can see as well his understanding that American constitutionalism draws support from political principles that are not simply modern.

331

I. THE FEDERALIST PAPERS AND
SEPARATION OF POWERS

So successful has *The Federalist* interpretation of the design and intention of the Constitution been that it is sometimes difficult to distinguish between the Constitution itself and *The Federalist* interpretation of it. The immediate purpose of *The Federalist* was to gain ratification for the proposed Constitution in the State of New York. It can be wondered whether the views of Publius can be assumed to be representative of the Federal Convention. For example, Alexander Hamilton's speech of June 18th may have effectively dampened his influence in the Constitutional Convention. Willmoore Kendall was perhaps the first to coin the term "The Federalist Constitution"—that is, the understanding of the Constitution one has upon reading *The Federalist*. It is "The Federalist Constitution," he observed, that is characterized by separation of more or less equal powers, by judicial review, by ambition countering ambition, and by "energy in the Executive." While "the Philadelphia Constitution"—that is, the Constitution as it came from the Convention—is characterized not by three coordinate and equal branches, not by judicial review, and not by "energy in the executive." Rather the "Philadelphia Constitution" is characterized by the supremacy of the legislature, a Congress that was "hardly less 'powerful' than the Parliament of Great Britain."[5]

This should not be surprising. The Declaration of Independence said that "the History of the present King of Great Britain is a History of repeated Injuries and Usurpation, all having in direct Object the Establishing of an absolute Tyranny over these States." A decade later the Constitution, exhibiting the American people's continuing concern with executive power, hedges in executive authority even as it expanded legislative authority.[6] Yet *The Federalist* can be read as emphasizing the need for the monarchic elements of secrecy, dispatch, and "energy in the executive" even as it soft-peddled new changes in the understanding of Federalism and Union. Unlike *The Federalist*, the Constitution is silent about separation of powers, executive prerogative, and judicial review.

The allocation of governmental authority in the legislative, executive, and judicial articles does encourage the opinion that separation of powers is the most distinctive feature of the Constitution. This is reflected in the common understanding of separation of powers shared by those who favored and by those who opposed the Constitution. That understanding may be seen by Madison's paraphrase, in Federalist No. 47, of the well-known warning of Montesquieu: "the accumulation of all powers legislative, executive and judiciary in the same hands, whether of one, a few or many, and whether hereditary, self appointed, or elective, may justly be pronounced the very definition of tyranny."[7] Separation of powers is also described in Federalist No. 51 as the great "auxiliary precaution," that is, the great aid of the principle of representation in the prevention of tyranny, either of the majority or of the government.[8]

Another feature of Straussian scholarship, derived at least in part from *The Federalist*, is the idea that limited constitutional government is not the same as weak government. Straussian constitutional scholars, while not always in agreement, have tended to look to the Presidency and to the Supreme Court rather than to the Congress for the authoritative principles of the American republic. The Supreme Court is seen as the "republican schoolmaster" providing the ongoing education and constitutional morality required for an effective rule of law. The Presidency is seen as the office capable of attracting persons with the highest political ambitions, including that love of power and that pursuit of glory thought necessary to provide the unity, energy, and dispatch required of leadership for a competent modern democratic government.[9]

Martin Diamond, in challenging the Progressive historians' view that the Constitution was an anti-democratic document supporting an economic elite, spelled out how *The Federalist* accommodated the multiplicity of interests that would make possible the conditions for a decent and stable democratic-republic. For Diamond the separation of powers was part of that improved science of politics which provided for elements of energy and competence in a manner fully compatible with a wholly popular government.[10] Diamond recognized that an effective separation of powers depended, at least in the United States, upon a society formed not only by the principle of representation but also by the extended commercial life that would encompass a diversity of economic interests based on private property.

Paul Eidelberg disagreed with Diamond's democratic interpretation. He, too, drew upon *The Federalist*, finding in the separation of powers the means by which the Framers provided for a Mixed Regime. The Framers, according to Eidelberg, limited popular sovereignty to the House of Representatives. The smaller Senate, with its longer terms, was designed to provide the aristocratic/oligarchic check upon the democratic House. The President, shielded somewhat by the Electoral College from the demands made by popular election, would supply the monarchical motivation of fame and glory, the motivation of the "noblest minds," to pursue grand (however unpopular) policies, serving thereby as a check upon the Congress. Eidelberg also argued that judicial review, whatever the original intentions of the Framers, is an aristocratic and necessary protection for the rule of law.[11]

More recently Harvey C. Mansfield has combined and expanded upon both Diamond and Eidelberg. He has, from the perspective of modern democratic "necessity," drawn the issue even more sharply: separation of powers is the means for the constitutionalism of democratic modernity "to appeal to virtue." He looks to *The Federalist* understanding that separation of powers—most particularly the executive's quest for honor and glory—is the means by which modern popular government secures for itself energy, deliberation, and competency while, at the same time, "compell[ing] Americans to abandon the supremacy of the legislature."[12] Mansfield thus endorses, in effect, the notion that The Federalist Constitution was meant to replace the Philadelphia Constitution.

Was separation of powers a means of introducing non-democratic elements into the constitutional order? Was it the means of reining in Congress while emancipating the Presidency? While all agreed, during the framing and ratification of the Constitution, that separation of powers was a good thing, did both the Framers of the Constitution and the Anti-Federalists have one view of separation of powers while the authors of *The Federalist*, though sharing perhaps that view, had another understanding of separation of powers?

Publius was correct in his observation that "enlightened statesmen will not always be at the helm," however mistaken he may have been in his prediction "that the office of president will seldom fall to the lot of any man, who is not in an eminent degree endowed with the requisite qualifications and who are not pre-eminent for ability and virtue."[13] Every President is not a Washington or a Lincoln. The Presidency has had accidental occupants, and perhaps even more often has been demeaned by self-aggrandizement and crude Machiavellian maneuvering. The decline of the party system and the increasingly plebiscitary hue of the presidency should caution against an undue emphasis on the Presidency at the expense of the Congress. However well the Supreme Court has served as "republican schoolmaster," it is also appropriate to recall that during the constitutional crises related to slavery and to civil rights legislation in the nineteenth century and in the constitutional crises related to the Great Depression in the twentieth century, the Congress was superior in judgment to the Supreme Court.[14] Moreover, the Supreme Court has, for nearly a century, often depended upon a jurisprudence of legal positivism about which Straussians tend to be critical.

Leo Strauss made two observations that can be said to point to Congress and away from the President and the Court. For Machiavelli, the origin of the Roman Republic was a fratricide. On the other hand, Strauss points out that "the United States may be said to be the only country in the World which was founded in explicit opposition to Machiavellian principles."[15] The evidence for Strauss's observation is found in *Natural Right and History* where he recognizes: "The nation dedicated to the proposition 'We hold these truths to be self-evident, that all men are created equal, that they are endowed by their Creator with certain unalienable Rights, that among these are Life, Liberty, and the pursuit of happiness' has now become, no doubt partly as a consequence of this dedication, the most powerful and prosperous of the nations of the earth."[16] The moral principles of natural right articulated in the Declaration of Independence, the first of the Organic Laws of the United States, reflect an explicit opposition to "Machiavellian principles." It is the Declaration's principles, drawn from Revelation and from natural right, that make compelling the political principles of the Constitution.[17]

Harry V. Jaffa, who has looked primarily to the character of Abraham Lincoln, and to Lincoln's understanding of the Declaration of Independence, to explain America, reminds us that the supremacy of Congress is the direct result of the doctrine of unalienable rights and natural equality of all men taught by the Declaration of Independence.[18] In a government based on consent of the governed, competent majority rule compatible with minority rights is the goal of democratic decision-making. It is the natural equality of man that is the foundation upon which rest the consent of the governed, individual rights, and constitutional rule by the majority. The Southern attempt at secession challenged this understanding.

George Anastaplo, in his unique commentaries on the text of the Constitution, has emphasized the supremacy of the legislature, concluding that "the supreme authority of the people in a regime 'dedicated to the proposition that all men are created equal' is recognized in repeated indications by the Constitution that the legislature is ultimately the controlling branch of government." Anastaplo (drawing upon the work of William Winslow Crosskey) has made a persuasive case that the powers of government listed in Article I, Section 8, the "enumerated powers," are listed not simply to limit Congress, but in part to make sure that powers once claimed by the executive or by courts or even by the states would be clearly recognized as belonging to Congress.[19]

The Constitution created a government of extensive powers. Most of those powers were entrusted to the Congress. Article I is the longest article by far, nearly one half of the Constitution of 1787. The powers and limitations provided for in the legislative article affect everything else found in the Constitution of the United States. The Constitution makes it clear that "in republican government the legislative authority, necessarily, predominates."[20] Presidents and Justices of the Supreme Court may be impeached by Congress but members of Congress as such may not be similarly disciplined by the Executive or the Court. The Supreme Court is established by the Constitution but Congress has the authority to shape the Court by providing for its size and for regulating most of its important activities. The Presidents' provisional veto can be overridden as can be, in effect, the Court's exercise of judicial review. And neither the President nor the Court is given a role in the amending process.[21]

The Framers of the Constitution were partisans of representative democracy and majority rule; they were not simple populists. An independent executive executing the laws enacted by the Congress and an independent judiciary which insures that the legislature is not exempt from the laws it makes were critical to the Framers' constitutional design for a stable, just and competent government. The Constitution provides for a division of governmental labor. The assumption behind such a division of labor, Herbert J. Storing noticed, is "that all governments perform certain kinds of functions, which are best performed in distinctive ways and by distinctive kinds of bodies."[22] The boundaries called for by the separation of powers have developed over two hundred years largely as a result of the day-to-day exercise of authority by Congress, the President, and the Courts. For example, it has been recognized (at least up to the Second World War) that deliberation by a representative legislature is safer and better suited for changing the status of the country from peace to war, whereas executive authority exercised by a single person is better suited to commanding the armed forces necessary to fight a war. Similarly, it has been recognized that although foreign affairs in general are negotiated better by a single representative, they are rendered safer if some legislative body must approve the treaty that has been negotiated. In addition, domestic legislation can be expected to be less parochial if the executive, who often may have a larger view, is fortified by a conditional veto. In these ways separation of powers works toward stability and efficiency even as it serves as a barrier to governmental oppression.

Representation, law-making, and deliberation all require "a detailed knowledge of the diverse interests, opinions and passions of the people. Many representatives, frequently elected, can perform this function better than one individual."[23] Unlike the British Parliament, Congress is the powerful legislative body it is because its authority is in principle independent of Executive leadership. Separation of powers in the Constitutional scheme works within Congress somewhat as it does in the relations between Congress and the President. The Constitution gives the power of the purse to Congress and especially to the House of Representatives, the chamber closest because of its mode of election to the people. This was done, James Madison recognized, because Congress's authority over the nation's purse "may in fact be regarded as the most complete and effectual weapon with which any constitution can arm the immediate representatives of the people, for obtaining a redress of every grievance, and for carrying into effect every just and salutary measure."[24]

The fact that the executive and the judiciary contribute to effective and decent government does not nullify the dominance of Congress in the Constitutional design; nor does it subtract from the republican principle of dependence upon the people through representation.[25] The Constitution does not depend principally upon the separation of powers or the President's veto or the Court's exercise of judicial review to check Congress. The primary check on Congress is supplied by popular elections, with supplementary checks supplied by the requirement that all legislative and amendment proposals be approved by both houses of Congress. The agreement of both the House and the Senate, but not that of President or of the Court, is required for these proposals to be approved. There is, on the other hand, nothing in the Constitution which prevents one chamber of Congress from refusing to go along with proposed legislation or amendments emanating from the other chamber.[26]

II. REPRESENTATION

The primary protection against both governmental tyranny and majority oppression, as well as the means for effective and efficient government, is found in the quality of representation in Congress that the continental democratic republic would make more probable. In the decade between the Declaration of Independence and the Constitutional Convention it became apparent that the smaller and homogenous state legislatures could be as oppressive and foolish as the Articles of

Confederation Congress was inefficient. The great object of the Convention of 1787 was to achieve for the Union a stable, decent and democratic government. It was apparent by 1787 that even the smallest states were already too large for that "direct" or "pure" democracy in which all citizens could assemble to conduct the affairs of the community. The democratic traditions of the people required a scheme of representation. Any proposed government, it was recognized, had to be "strictly republican" and "wholly popular." Thus Publius could acknowledge that the fundamental remedy provided by the Constitution was "a government in which the scheme of representation takes place, opens a different prospect, and promises the cure for which we are seeking." It was in recognition of population, democratic traditions, and geography that *The Federalist* speaks of representation resulting "in the total exclusion of the people in their collective capacity" from the government but not "in the total exclusion of the representatives of the people" from the administration of government.[27]

Representation then was necessary and, though a threat sometimes to stability, representation was also an opportunity.[28] For the Framers of the Constitution representation was the major means for reconciling the requirement of consent of the governed with the requirement of political wisdom.[29] A representative Congress would provide the arena for the workings of decent democratic–republican government.[30] The republican principle demands rule by the majority, but decent republican government depends upon deliberative rule. The extended commercial republic made possible by the modern principle of representation would provide that society of diverse interests necessary to blunt and moderate the interests and ambition, the injustice and foolishness endemic to the "majority faction" already evident in the thirteen states. James Madison, writing to Thomas Jefferson, lamented his inability at the Constitutional Convention to persuade a majority of the Convention to give to Congress a veto over state legislation.

> A constitutional negative on the laws of the States seems . . . necessary to secure individuals agst. encroachments on their rights. The mutability of the laws of the States is found to be a serious evil. The injustice of them has been so frequent and so flagrant as to alarm the most steadfast friends of republicanism. . . . A reform therefore which does not make provision for private rights, must be materially defective.[31]

A similar sentiment can be found throughout *The Federalist*. The legislatures that Madison feared were the faction-dominated legislatures of the states. A national bicameral Congress, large enough to be representative and small enough to be deliberative, would provide an institution favorable enough to disciplined discourse to blunt the injustice and shortsightedness that often characterized the legislatures of the state governments. The Constitution thus seeks to remedy the kinds of defects seen in the relatively homogenous state legislatures, not to circumscribe the authority of the Congress.

In opening his defense of the proposed Constitution, Publius gave voice to what was widely recognized: that "it seems to have been reserved to the people of this country to decide the question whether or not good government could be established through reflection and choice."[32] This suggests that one characteristic of this democratic people was their ability to discern in some of their numbers the best in themselves. Implicit in this claim was the idea that the larger the body from which to choose, the better would likely be the choice of the people. Willmoore Kendall was echoing this sentiment of Publius when he described Congressional elections as the choosing of the most "virtuous," that is, those "whose merit may recommend [them] to . . . the esteem and confidence" of their fellow citizens.[33] This is not, however, the Burkean notion of an aristocratic uninstructed trustee representative. What is being represented is the voice of the community, organized in a variety of capacities, each directed toward the safety and happiness of the community. When we elect a representative we are electing someone to act for ourselves in place of ourselves. We elect representatives not simply because we cannot all be in Washington ourselves but also because we think that those elected, because of time, knowledge, and interest, will be able to act at least as competently as we ourselves can act, especially when tempered by the competency, interest, and arguments of their fellow representatives. We believe therefore that both our individual interests and the common good of the community, in the long term as well as in the short, will be more adequately served by our representatives than they would be served by ourselves directly.[34]

Even during a time such as ours of relatively weak political parties, Representatives and Senators are still elected as Republicans or Democrats. They seek election to the Congress with at least some known minimal legislative policy preferences corresponding in general to the broad views of their party. Party allegiance, however weakened, remains one of the indicators of policies that serve to recommend present and potential members of Congress to the "esteem and confidence" of the electorate. In this manner Representation holds out the promise of aligning consent of the governed both with the views of the governed and with practical wisdom. The virtue of representation is, then, the virtue of prudence, the practical wisdom to decide what is the best that can be done here and now in the circumstances we find ourselves.

The application of principles to policy requires knowing what are the best ends to be obtained. But no less so, in most if not in all circumstances, prudence may amount to the equitable and skilled regulation of opposite, diverse and often rival interests. Thus it was underscored that in the Congress "the public voice, pronounced by the representatives of the people, will be more consonant to the public good than if pronounced by the people themselves, convened for that purpose."[35] It is in the Congress where the reason of the people is brought to bear upon the passions of the people. And it is in the Congress where the views of "We the People" are to be refined and enlarged into the "deliberative sense of the community."[36] Understood in this manner, both necessity and principle combine to remove many sources of conflict between popular rule and representation. In short, representation offers a substitute for the direct popular rule of the people without ignoring the opinion or the authority of the people.

Vital to a democratic republic is ruling and being ruled in turn. In a democratic republic those who make the laws live under those laws. Modern representation is not intended to be a perfect reflection of each and every subset of "We the People." Any principle of selection, including free democratic elections, will prevent that. Ancient democratic elections sometimes combined universal suffrage with selection by lottery. Modern democratic elections add to universal suffrage the aristocratic element of merit. Every election asks the voters to choose who is the best candidate.[37] In this manner modern democratic elections certainly can produce representatives who are an enhanced reflection of those represented. But we should not expect routinely to find in Congress men and women of a higher order than the people who elect them. The strength of the representatives lies not in their superior virtue, but in their skills (however developed and recognized) in achieving the public policy required for the ends of safety and happiness.

In a liberal democracy public policy and public opinion must go hand in hand. Abraham Lincoln, who again and again linked the moral principles of the Declaration of Independence to the political principles of the Constitution, observed, "In this and like communities, public sentiment is everything. With public sentiment nothing can fail; without it nothing can succeed."[38] The irreducible core of republican government is found in the forming, as well as in the following, of public opinion by deliberation in a representative assembly. Representation is the means for making more likely that "We the People" at our best will be the public voice. It is a misreading both of the Declaration of Independence and of the Constitution to suppose that because the Framers feared the rule of the faction-dominated state legislatures, they also feared rule by the majority in Congress. Certainly, the design of the Constitution does not suggest that the Framers sought a remedy for the problems of democracy in the monarchic or aristocratic elements associated with the executive of the court.

III. DELIBERATION

It is the Congress that talks, deliberates and decides, reflecting thereby the role of practical wisdom in governmental affairs.[39] But many accounts, both scholarly and journalistic, suggest that deliberation in both chambers of Congress has declined dramatically since the 1960s. Members of Congress are widely portrayed as the captives of special interests willing to sacrifice the common good in pursuit of the funds vital to securing reelection. Neither principles of representation nor principles of deliberation, but logrolling, compromise, bargaining and side deals, are believed to be decisive in the Congress.[40] For too many citizens Will Roger's cynical witticism, that "Congress is the best money can buy," has never seemed more accurate.[41] Deprecation of Congress is so widespread that during the presidential campaign of 1996, Lamar Alexander, a presidential candidate, could suggest, without a trace of humor or fear of correction, that the Congress be sent home after six months so as to limit the harm they do.

The case for decent self-government rests not with the Executive, nor with the Court, but with the representative Legislature. No one denies that Congress must be, as well as that it must appear to be, more responsible.[42] Fundamental to this essay is the opinion that self-government may not survive if the feeling becomes widespread either that the people are unworthy or that their representatives are incapable of conducting themselves sensibly. May we not wonder whether scholarly and journalistic indignation towards the Congress is justified? For instance, most people when asked, respond that their Representative or Senator is hardworking and energetic, a faithful representative and a good legislator. It is too many of the other Members of Congress who are the problem.[43]

Both scholarly and popular dissatisfaction with the President or the Supreme Court is nearly always connected with a particular President or a particular opinion of the Court or a particular Justice, but not with the Presidency or the Court itself. It is otherwise with Congress: "Congress bashing is a venerable part of American political discourse."[44] The apparently moribund term-limits movement as well as the short-lived line-item veto and the "ratification" of the 27th Amendment are only the most recent forms of Congress-bashing.[45] Journalists and academics, it seems, are teaching the general body of citizens to identify the partisan maneuvering of the political parties or the foolish antics of this or that member as defects of the Congress. This perspective is enhanced by journalists and scholars who shy away from, if they do not disdain, that interplay of congressional and electoral politics, public policy, and special interests which characterizes the robust democratic politics of the United States. Congress is expected to transform often fractious public opinion into acceptable public policy, without public disagreement or dissent, without bargaining or compromise, and without appearing to be enthusiastic Democrats or enthusiastic Republicans.

The tendency to focus on the wheeling and dealing of democratic politics in a large and diverse republic has been encouraged by television. Simply put, modern presidential politics "plays" much better on television than does Congressional politics.[46] A century of war and economic dislocation has helped create for the Presidency a dramatic if not imperial aura never intended by the Framers. Television routinely portrays the President as possessing information, insight and hence prerogatives not available to the Congress. He is shown offering leadership and taking charge in the name of the people. Presidential elections, the President, his family and friends are now the most pervasive feature of American politics and government. George Anastaplo has asked, "Is there not something demeaning to a republican people to make what we now do of our Presidents and of their families and other intimates? . . . Among the consequences of our unbecoming obsequiousness, which the mass media 'naturally' exploit, is that we are diverted both from serious politics and from a proper reading of the Constitution."[47]

Even as television enhances and dramatizes the presidency, it portrays Congress as a vacillating and confused multitude, unable to do much itself but skilled at crippling presidential initiatives and programs. In the early 1960s one Congressional observer noticed that at least since the early years of this century it is nearly routine for the American people to send to Washington a Congress and a President at odds with respect to their agenda, perspectives, and goals. Divided government, with one or both houses of Congress controlled by one party and with the presidency controlled by the other party, has been the rule in the latter half of the twentieth century. The issues change, the parties switch sides, as do Presidents and Congresses. What remains constant is the tension between the President and the Congress and their respective supporters. This tension results, at least in part, from the tendency in some quarters to identify the position of the President with "high principle" in politics. Consequently, as Willmoore Kendall argued, the task of politics and of intellectuals is somehow to "educate" the Congress and, beyond the Congress, the electorate to acceptance of the President's programs. Almost by definition, gridlock is understood to result from Congress's unwillingness to accept, as the concrete manifestation of "high principle," the political and legislative agenda of the President.[48]

Does Congress still "refine and enlarge the public views" into "the cool and deliberative sense of the community"? It has long been something of an insiders' joke to observe the dismay of tourists in Washington as they watch the often distracted activities on the floor of the House and Senate. Woodrow Wilson faulted Congress for not being a more parliamentary body, seriously and openly debating the issues of the day and enacting national legislation on the basis of clear ideological choices. But even Wilson recognized that the serious work of deliberation and law-making in the Congress is carried out mainly in Committees and Sub-Committees.

Recent sober Congressional scholarship, combining sound theory with a sensible evaluation of important legislative case studies, has taken a more favorable view of the Congress. Joseph M. Bessette has called into question the easy assumptions and explanations that often portray Congress simply as an institution of side-deals, logrolling, and bargaining, a place ruled by mere self-interest in pursuit of reelection. His analysis of important legislation and important Legislators in both Houses recognizes that there is some truth to these charges. But he also shows that partisan party politics and self-interest cannot alone account for the outcome of the most important legislation. As with so many other areas of contemporary life, it may well be that institutional constraints on self-interest in Congress have declined since the 1960s. Still, Bessette shows that a considerable high-minded devotion to the common good remains the goal of a significant number of members of Congress. Deliberation, particularly by those in the Committee and Subcommittee leadership positions, continues to play a more important role in the legislative process than is generally acknowledged. No doubt Congress may not deliberate in all cases as thoroughly as it ought, but Congress deliberates much more than is usually believed.[49]

Congressional deliberation is defined by Bessette as "reasoning on the merits of public policy" for "some public good—some good external to the decision makers themselves."[50] As Bessette demonstrates, deliberation on the merits of proposed legislation is not necessarily at odds with the self-interest of individual Members or with their efforts to maximize benefits to their constituents in order to improve their prospects for reelection. Legislators, even in the pursuit of the narrowest self-interest concerned only with reelection, must deliberate on what truly benefits their constituents or the interest groups they support. The most homogenous legislative district will include a variety of conflicting opinions about what benefits the district. Often on major issues in domestic policy, and in foreign affairs as well, there is not a clear division of opinion to guide legislators. The variety of opinion that is to be expected in a diverse country requires legislators to exercise a substantial degree of independent judgment. Members of Congress are forced to seek information and to determine the best course of action.

Congress is a complex organization made up of independently elected members who have to take into account other complex organizations including political parties and "caucuses" guided by sectional or economic interests or ideological views of government. The Committees and Subcommittees of Congress form an intricate system that requires significant amounts of deliberation. Bessette highlights Congressional deliberation in diverse contexts and forums. For instance, one aspect of deliberation rarely noticed, he reminds us, begins at the earliest decision stage in the legislative process, when members of both Houses, their staff, representatives of concerned interest groups, and executive branch staff come together, in both formal and informal settings, to begin discussions about sponsoring proposed legislation. Even at this early stage choices are made and positions are taken, if only tentatively, which need to be defended on some basis other than mere self-interest.

Bessette reminds us that essential to the deliberative process, from beginning sponsorship to the successful vote on the floor, is the gathering of information, a task for which Congress is well suited. Five hundred and thirty-five legislators from different parts of the country are supported by thousands of staff members. Each Committee and Subcommittee has the support of professional staff, as do the Congressional Budget Office and the Congressional Research Service. The significant increase of professional staff in the contemporary era has allowed Congress to keep pace with the expertise found in the executive branch and to provide Congress an independent source of information with which to judge proposed legislation and to oversee the vast bureaucracy.[51] Lobbyist for special interests, as they attempt to persuade Committee and Subcommittee members of the merits or defects of proposed legislation, offer a significant means by which members of both Houses can become knowledgeable about important legislation.

Congress is a complex institution because modern legislation in a vast and diverse commercial republic is complex. No member of Congress can expect to have personal expertise in more than a small part of the legislative agenda that Congress deals with each year. Committees and Subcommittee augmented by the variety of caucuses dealing with economic, party and regional issues, are the places where considerable information and legislative expertise are acquired and where substantive deliberation goes on. As Bessette observes:

> Although newly elected members may carry with them into the legislature policy preferences on some subjects, they will face many issues there for the first time. It is unlikely that their prior experience will have exposed them to the range and breadth of issues they will be forced to confront in Congress, especially in the areas of foreign and military policy, which have no direct corollary in state and local government or in the private sector. Moreover, even veteran members of Congress are forced to address new issues as they move to new committees or as the legislative agenda changes over time.
>
> Thus, the members of Congress are often required to make decisions in areas where they do not have settled views. Unless the representative or senator simply defers to others on these new issues, he or she must become sufficiently informed to make reasoned decisions in committee or on the floor.[52]

Information, while necessary, is not sufficient for good or successful legislation. The prospects of success for major proposed legislation lays in the building of majority coalitions. At each stage of the legislative process, from the first informal setting to a successful vote on the floor of each chamber, ever-larger coalitions of majorities comprising very different interest in Congress are required.[53] It is well recognized as befits a Congress of independent representatives, that power is widely dispersed in both Houses with many points at which proposed legislation can be modified, derailed or defeated. Most bills die in committee.

Facts, and reasoned arguments required to explain the facts, must be offered to persuade legislators who may have different even conflicting views and interests. Such reasoned argument need not always, or even most of the time, appeal to a simple homogenous common good or to one or more overarching national interests. Most often the reasoned appeal is to principles of equity and justice on behalf of a part of the whole. The practical effect, however partisan, slow, expensive or sloppy it may be, comes near to Publius's observation and hope in *The Federalist*, that representation in the extended republic will make it more likely that "a coalition of a majority of the whole society could seldom take place on any other principles than those of justice and the general good" that arise out of the "permanent and aggregate interests" of the parts.[54]

Tactics of compromises, side deals, and bargaining over the division of government "pork" are not incompatible with considerable deliberation. There are certainly higher and lower grades of pork. Besides, "pork" may be, at least in part, in the eye of the beholder. As one astute observer has remarked, pork also can be "the necessary glue that holds political coalitions together."[55] Aid to depressed maritime industries in Maine necessary to stabilize employment there may have the appearance of pork in Nebraska. Similarly price supports for farmers in Iowa may seem less than compelling to residents of New York City. Opposing pork in principle means thinking that outside observers always know what is better for the state or district than do its representatives in Congress. Or, put another way, is the common good or the public interest best served only by thinking about what is good for the country from a national perspective? The Constitution assumes that majority coalitions will be formed between "opposite and rival interests." It is these opposite and rival interests, including the bargaining, compromise, and side deals over pork, that help serve as sentinels against "unjust combinations of a majority of the whole." In this manner the pursuit of pork can make it more likely that members of Congress will be able to provide a voice for those they represent.

IV. A MORE RESPONSIBLE CONGRESS

Popular and scholarly disdain with Congress suggests a misunderstanding of what it is that Congress is designed to do and how Congress is to do it. To be sure, journalists and scholars alike are devoted to democracy in theory, but often do not wish to be confronted by the rough and tumble of the democratic process. Contrast an older and more realistic view of democratic legislative practice:

> The regulation of these various and interfering interests forms the principal task of modern Legislation, and involves the spirit of party and faction in the necessary and ordinary operations of government.

> . . . what are many of the most important acts of legislation, but so many judicial determinations, not indeed concerning the rights of single persons, but concerning the rights of large bodies of citizens; and what are the different classes of legislators, but advocates and parties to the causes which they determine?[56]

The common good is not simply the sum total of the parts. Neither is it something apart, and recognizably distinct, from the good of the parts that make up the whole. Should we not wonder how it is that one person can claim, or can be expected to represent, the common good of a nation as large and as diverse as is the United States? In Federalist No. 2, Publius observed that "Providence has been pleased to give to this one connected country, to one united people, a people descended from the same ancestors, speaking the same language, professing the same religion, attached to the same principles of government, very similar in their manners and customs."[57] That people and that country no longer exist. In some Congressional districts, scores of languages are spoken and nearly as many religions are practiced. Our manners and customs are becoming ever more diverse. Nor is the United States any longer one connected country, but extends from Maine to Maui, from Key West to the Aleutians. We do remain one people to the extent that we remain dedicated to the principles of republican government.[58] Just as no legislative body can act with the dispatch of a single executive, so no single person can be expected to represent the diversity or to possess the flexibility to deliberate about the vast number of legitimate interests that make up the common good of democratic politics as well as Congress.

We have noticed that among those influenced by Leo Strauss there have been differences of emphasis about where the authoritative principles of American government reside. Even so, the perspective common to those influenced by him is that the United States is superior to any viable alternative.[59] However parochial and irresponsible Congress may sometimes be, the remedy for republican government is not an undue dependence on a monolithic Presidency. The republican remedy is a more disciplined and responsible Congress demanded by a more disciplined and responsible people.

One example would be ending the repeated recourse to threats of filibustering in the United States Senate. The recourse to what is called a "supermajority" is now required or threatened to be required for routine legislation. Both the Framers of the Constitution and members of the First Congress restricted the use of such supermajorities to the few instances identified in the Constitution. It is a "perverse use of party discipline" to require supermajorities to resolve issues in either house of Congress. One scholar has suggested that "the current Senate rule that keeps a bare majority from ending debate, even after a reasonable time for discussion of the relevant issues, is probably unconstitutional."[60] A second example is the extraordinary amounts of money now necessary for election campaigns and too often spent for miserable negative television sound bites. This is a particularly corrosive element of contemporary politics which cannot help but harm our republican institutions.[61]

Both the restoration of responsible majority rule in the Senate and of responsible political campaigns depends upon an informed public opinion. Changes in theories of constitutionalism or in the structure of the Constitution cannot counteract for long, if at all, the long-term effects of undisciplined character and undisciplined politics. In short, "We the People" have to revive and insist upon, a reliable standard both of electoral politics and of constitutionalism in this country. A proper respect for the political philosophy resurrected by Leo Strauss should contribute to the general education needed for "We the People" to play our part in sustaining Republican government.

NOTES

1. George Anastaplo, *The Amendments to the Constitution: A Commentary* (Baltimore: Johns Hopkins University Press, 1995), p. 185.

2. See Kenneth L. Deutsch and Walter Soffer, eds., *The Crisis of Liberal Democracy* (Albany, N.Y.: State University of New York Press, 1987), p. 1.

346   John A. Murley

3. Leo Strauss, "Liberal Education and Responsibility" in *Liberalism Ancient and Modern* (New York: Basic Books, 1968), p. 24.

4. Thomas Jefferson Letter to James Madison (November 18, 1878), in *The Life and Selected Writings of Thomas Jefferson*, eds. Adrienne Koch and William Peden (New York: Modern Library, Random House, 1944), p. 452.

5. Willmoore Kendall, "How to Read 'The Federalist'" (with George W. Carey) in *Willmoore Kendall Contra Mundum*, Nellie D. Kendall, ed. (Lanham, Md.: University Press of America, 1994), pp. 411–13. Willmoore Kendall was an established political theorist with a national reputation when Leo Strauss began to publish his work in the United States. In what must be regarded as a unique occurrence in the discipline of American political science, Kendall, in a series of book reviews and essays devoted to Strauss and his early students, indicated his increasing attraction to, and the importance of, the work of this new group of political theorists, as different from the old political scientists, he said, "as chalk from cheese." See Willmoore Kendall, *The Conservative Affirmation* (Chicago: Henry Regnery Company, 1963), pp. 202–3, 249–52, 257–60. See also Willmoore Kendall, review *Ancients and Moderns: Essays on the Tradition of Political Philosophy*, ed. Joseph Cropsey, 61 *American Political Science Review* (September 1967), pp. 783–84. See as well Willmoore Kendall, "John Locke Revisited," in *Willmoore Kendall Contra Mundum*, pp. 418–56. On both the limitations and the usefulness of *The Federalist*, see George Anastaplo, *The Constitution of 1787: A Commentary* (Baltimore: Johns Hopkins University Press, 1989), pp. 225–26; Anastaplo "The Constitution at Two Hundred: Explorations," *Texas Tech Law Review* 22 (1991), pp. 1053, 1036–37; Anastaplo, "Notes toward an 'Apologia pro vita sua,'" *Interpretation* 10, no. 1 (1982), p. 331. See as well John A. Murley, "Our Character is Our Fate: The Constitutionalism of George Anastaplo," *Political Science Reviewer* 26 (1997), pp. 56–57.

6. For a different interpretation of the Declaration's indictment against George III, see Joseph M. Bessette and Gary J. Schmitt, "Executive Power and the American Founding," in *Separation of Powers and Good Government*, Bradford P. Wilson & Peter W. Schramm, eds. (Lanham, Md.: Rowman & Littlefield Publishers, 1994), p. 52.

7. See James Madison, Alexander Hamilton, and John Jay, *The Federalist*, ed. Jacob E. Cooke (Middletown, Conn.: Wesleyan University Press, 1961), No. 47. p. 324. All references are to this edition.

8. For a wide-ranging discussion of *The Federalist* including the ends of separation of powers, see the essays in *Saving the Revolution: The Federalist Papers and the American Founding*, Charles R. Kesler, ed. (New York: Free Press, 1987.) See also the essays in *Separation of Powers and Good Government*. See as well *Separation of Powers—Does It Still Work?* Robert A. Goldwin and Art Kaufman, eds. (Washington, D.C.: American Enterprise Institute for Public Policy Research, 1986).

9. See David F. Epstein, *The Political Theory of The Federalist* (Chicago: University of Chicago Press, 1984), pp. 184–85.

10. See Martin Diamond, *As Far as Republican Principles Will Admit*, William A. Schambra, ed. (Washington, D.C. : The AEI Press, 1992), pp. 47–49. Martin Diamond identified the Founders in large part, with Publius/James Madison. More recently the tendency of Straussian scholars has been to identify the Founders with Publius/Alexander Hamilton. For example, see James W. Ceaser, "Doctrines of Presidential-Congressional Relations," in *Separation of Powers and Good Government*, pp. 92, 94, 97, 101.

11. See Paul Eidelberg, *The Philosophy of the American Constitution* (New York: Free Press, 1968), pp. 3, 19–28, 55–67, 197–99, 203–11.

12. Harvey C. Mansfield Jr., *America's Constitutional Soul* (Baltimore, Md.: Johns Hopkins University Press, 1991), pp. 140, 148.

13. *The Federalist* No.10 (p. 60) and No. 68 (p. 460).

14. See Anastaplo, *The Constitution of 1787: A Commentary*, pp. 142–43.

15. Leo Strauss, *Thoughts on Machiavelli* (Glencoe, Ill.: Free Press, 1958), p. 13.

16. Leo Strauss, *Natural Right and History* (Chicago: University of Chicago Press, 1953), p. 1. See also Harry V. Jaffa, *Original Intent and the Framers of the Constitution: A Disputed Question* (Washington, D.C., Regnery Gateway, 1994) (with Bruce Ledewitz, Robert L. Stone, and George Anastaplo), p. 23.

17. See *Four Pillars of Constitutionalism: The Organic Laws of the United States*, Introduction by Richard H. Cox (Amherst, N.Y.: Prometheus Books 1998).

18. See Harry V. Jaffa, "Defenders of the Constitution: Calhoun versus Madison, A Bicentennial Cerebration" (Constitutionalism In America: The Bicentennial Project of the University of Dallas), p. 5.

19. See Anastaplo, *The Constitution of 1787*, pp. 32, 26–73. See also Anastaplo, "The Constitution at Two Hundred: Explorations." See as well Anastaplo, "Mr. Crosskey, the American Constitution, and the Natures of Things" 15 *Loyola University of Chicago Law Journal* 184 (1984), Anastaplo, "Lessons for the Student of Law: The Oklahoma Lectures," 20 *Oklahoma City University Law Review* 19 (1995), Anastaplo, "We the People: The Rulers and the Ruled," *The Great Ideas Today* (Chicago: Encyclopaedia Britannica, Inc. 1987) 52–72, and Anastaplo, " Robert's Rules of Order and the Conduct of Deliberative Assemblies in the United States," *The Great Ideas Today* (Chicago: Encyclopaedia Britannica, Inc. 1996) 232–57.

20. *The Federalist*, No. 51 (p. 350). For a different perspective on Congress, see *The Presidency in the Constitutional Order*, Joseph M. Bessette and Jeffrey Tulis, eds. (Baton Rouge: Louisiana University Press, 1981). See also Gary J. Schmitt, "Jefferson and Executive Power: Revisionism and the Revolution of 1800," *Publius, The Journal of Federalism*, No. 17 (Spring 1987).

21. See Anastaplo, *The Constitution of 1787*, pp. 111, 181. This is not to deny that at any given time the President may exercise considerable political influence.

22. Herbert J. Storing, *What the Anti-Federalists Were For* (Chicago: University of Chicago Press, 1981), p. 60.

23. William F. Connelly Jr., "Congress: Representation and Deliberation" in *The American Experiment: Essays on the Theory and Practice of Liberty*, Peter Augustine Lawler and Robert Martin Schaefer, eds. (Lanham, Md.: Rowman & Littlefield Publishers, Inc., 1994), p. 175.

24. *The Federalist* No. 58 (p. 394).

25. For a different view, see William Kristol, "The Problem of the Separation of Powers: Federalist 47–51," in *Saving The Revolution*, pp. 100–130.

26. See Anastaplo, *The Constitution of 1787*, pp. 32–36, 40, 46, 179–91. Compare the dominance of the House of Commons in the British Parliament. If the House of Commons insists on having its way it will eventually have it.

27. *The Federalist*, No.10 (p. 62), No. 63 (p. 428). For different views, see the suggestion by Walter Berns that representation was a means of keeping the people out of government. "Does the Constitution 'Secure These Rights'?" in *How Democratic Is the Constitution?*, pp. 65–66; Bradford P. Wilson, "Separation of Powers And Judicial Review," in *Separation of Powers and Good Government*, p. 69. See also David F. Epstein, *The Political Theory of The Federalist*, pp. 81–107; Paul Eidelberg, *The Philosophy of the American Constitution*, pp. 225–27, 317 n.37. See as well *The Federalist* No. 63. (p. 428).

28. See Storing, *What the Anti-Federalists Were For*, p. 43.

29. See Strauss, *Natural Right and History*, p. 141.

30. See Diamond, *As Far as Republican Principles Will Admit.*This was summed up by Martin Diamond's felicitous phrase, "decent even though democratic," ibid., p. 220.

31. Quoted in Robert A. Goldwin, *From Parchment to Power* (Washington, D.C.:The AEI Press, 1997), p. 59.

32. *The Federalist*, No. 1 (p. 3).

33.Willmoore Kendall, "The Two Majorities," in *Willmoore Kendall Contra Mundum*, p. 216, n. 29.

34. See Joseph M. Bessette, *The Mild Voice of Reason* (Chicago: University of Chicago Press, 1994), pp. 2, 45; Harry V. Jaffa, *The Conditions of Freedom* (Baltimore: Johns Hopkins University Press, 1975), p. 159. See also George Anastaplo, "A Return To Bristol With Edmund Burke," in "Lectures for the Student of Law," 20 *Oklahoma City University Law Review* 69–85 (1995).

35. *The Federalist*, No. 10 (p. 62).

36. Ibid., No. 63 (p. 425), No. 71 (p. 482).

37. See Laurence Berns, "Our Political Situation: Good Government, Self-government, and American Democracy," *The Great Ideas Today* (Chicago: Encyclopaedia Britannica, Inc. 1997), p. 83.

38. *Collected Works of Abraham Lincoln*, Roy P. Basler, ed. (New Brunswick: Rutgers University Press, 1953), III, 27.

39. Anastaplo, *The Constitution of 1787*, p. 42.

40. See Bessette, *The Mild Voice of Reason*, pp. 55–66.

41. See L. Peter Schultz, "Congress and the Separation of Powers Today: Practice in Search of a Theory" in *Separation of Powers and Good Government*, p. 185; William F. Connelly Jr., "Congress Representation and Deliberation," p. 171.

42. For useful critiques of many contemporary Congressional practices: see John Alvis, "Willmoore Kendall and the Demise of Congressional Deliberation," *The Intercollegiate Review* (Spring 1987), pp. 57–66; Gordon S. Jones and John A. Marini, eds., *The Imperial Congress: Crisis in the Separation of Powers* (New York: Pharos Books 1988); L. Gordon Crovitz & Jeremy A. Rabkin, eds., *The Fettered Presidency: Legal Constraints on the Executive Branch* (Washington, D. C.: American Enterprise Institute 1989); Edward J. Erler, *The American Polity: Essays on the Theory and Practice of Constitutional Government* (New York: Crane Russak, 1991).

43. See Richard F. Fenno Jr., "If, as Ralph Nader Says, Congress is 'The Broken Branch,' How Come We Love Our Congressman So Much?" in Norman J. Ornstein, ed., *Congress in Change: Evolution and Reform* (New York: Praeger, 1993). See also John R. Hibbing and Elizabeth Theiss-Morse, *Congress as Public Enemy* (Cambridge: Cambridge University Press, 1995), p. 43.

44. L. Peter Schultz, "Congress and the Separation of Powers Today," in *Separation of Powers and Good Government*.

45. At the end of its June 1998 term, the Supreme Court, in *Clinton v. City of New York* declared, by a vote of 6–3, the Line Item Veto Act unconstitutional. Justice Anthony M. Kennedy, concurring with Justice John Paul Stevens's opinion for the Court, reminded all citizens, "Abdication of responsibility is not part of the constitutional design. Failure of political will does not justify unconstitutional remedies." Justice Kennedy also said that the primary end of separation of powers is liberty, not energy, economy, or efficiency. The line-item veto "compromises the political liberty of our citizens." "Liberty is always at stake when one or more of the branches seek to transgess the separation of powers . . ."

46. See Anastaplo, *The Amendments to the Constitution*, p. 214. See also George Anastaplo

"The Pentagon Papers and the Abolition of Television," in *The American Moralist* (Athens, Ohio: Ohio University Press, 1992), pp. 245–74. It should be recognized that Anastaplo's proposal to abolish television was not offered with an expectation that it would be adopted, but rather to dramatize a diagnosis.

47. Anastaplo, *The Constitution of 1787*, pp. 122–23.

48. Kendall, "The Two Majorities," pp. 202, 226–27.

49. See Bessette, *The Mild Voice of Reason*, pp. 67–149.

50. Ibid., pp. 77–149.

51. The importance of individual members of Congress as compared to the British Parliament can be seen when one compares the resources and staff support provided a member of Congress with the resources provided to the typical member of Parliament. A member of Parliament may receive "a desk, a filing cabinet, and a telephone, but not always in the same place." James Q. Wilson and John J. Dilulio Jr., *American Government*, seventh ed. (New York: Houghton Mifflin Co., 1998), p. 302.

52. Ibid. pp. 54–55.

53. See ibid. pp. 46–51. (Italics omitted.)

54. See *The Federalist*, No. 51 (p. 353), No. 10 (p. 57). For the trail-blazing analysis of the relationship between the extended republic and multiplicity of interests in *The Federalist*, see Diamond, *As Far as Republican Principles Will Admit*.

55. James Q. Wilson, "Democracy Needs Pork To Survive," *Wall Street Journal*, August 14, 1997, p. 16.

56. *The Federalist*, No. 10 (p. 59).

57. Ibid., No. 2 (p. 9).

58. See John A. Rohr, "The Legitimacy of the Administrative State," in *Constitutionalism In Perspective*, ed. Sarah Baumgartner Thurow (Lanham, Md.: University Press of America 1988), III, 96; William F. Connelly Jr., "Congress: Representation and Deliberation" p. 176.

59. See Leo Strauss, *What is Political Philosophy?* (New York: Free Press, 1959), p.113.

60. George Anastaplo, "The Spirit of the Law," *Chicago Sun-Times*, November 11, 1998, p. 18. See also Anastaplo, "Robert's Rules of Order and the Conduct of Deliberative Assemblies in the United States."

61. Everyone knows what is corrupting our political process: huge campaign expenditures that force conscientious legislators to spend far too much of their time in the dispiriting activity of raising money, far too much reliance on public opinion polls and talk about the "horse race," attack campaigning and journalism, the decline of political civility, "the demoralizing happenstance found in the primary system we now have," rampant demagoguery, and so on. See Berns, "Our Political Situation: Good Government, Self-government, and American Democracy," p. 92. The fundamental political issue of our time has been well framed:

> The significance of the natural is again and again considered, and sometimes denied, in these readings. This bears upon the question of what the best way to live is, which depends in part upon what the permanent nature of the human being is. This may be seen in a problem, implicit in many of these readings, which is particularly important in a commercial republic: the problem of the use and abuse of the desire for gain. It is intriguing to notice how often the problem of avarice crops up in one setting after another, especially when (as could be deen in the history of the great Roman republic) the threat of foreign danger recedes. The problem of avarice, or the status of "natural liberty" and hence of acquisitiveness, is critical to the question of the best way to

live, and hence of the best way to order a community. (Virtually the last word in Plato *Apology* is directed to this problem.) An understandable concern for a reliable prosperity, supported by the stern discipline of the the Market and stimulated by the ever-changing temptations of Globalization, can neglect the legitimate concerns of the community both for the character of its citizens and for the stability of social ralations. Here as elsewhere the proper role of religion, and of religious liberty, in the governance of the community can be debated.

From the General Introduction of the two-volume *Liberty, Equality and the Modern Constitutionalism: A Source Book*, ed. George Anastaplo (Newburyport, Mass.: Focus, 1999). For a different perspective, see the essay by Thomas G. West, "The Decline of Free Speech in Twentieth-Century America: The View from the Founding," in *Liberty Under Law: American Constitutionalism Yesterday, Today, and Tomorrow*, Kenneth L. Grasso and Cecilia Rodriguez Castillo, eds. (Lanham, Md.: University Press of America, 1997).

22

Executive Power and the Presidency

Robert Eden

> Imagine that all the greatest scientists down to about the end of
> the eighteenth century—the Archimedes, the Newtons, the
> Galileos, and the Descartes—are gathered in some part of the
> lower world, and a messenger from earth brings a dynamo for
> them to examine at their leisure. They are told that this appara-
> tus is used by the living to produce movement, light, or heat.
> They look at it, they set it going. Next, they take it to pieces, and
> inspect and measure each part. In short, they do all they can . . . .
> But they know nothing about the electric current, they know
> nothing about induction, they know only about mechanical
> transformation. "What are all those coiled wires for?" they ask.
> They are forced to recognize their incompetence. So, all knowl-
> edge and all human genius, united in the face of this mysteri-
> ous object, fail to discover its secret, fail to guess the new fact
> established by Volta, and other facts discovered by Ampère,
> Faraday, et al. . . .
>
> —Paul Valéry[1]

Valéry reminds us that the electric dynamo rests upon a science of electricity, lacking which we would be stymied by this inscrutable device. Here "the light by which
we are guided" is the history of science, duly attentive to works of theory and discovery.[2] Somewhat analogously, the history of political philosophy is our guide in
the book on which I shall comment, Harvey C. Mansfield's *Taming the Prince*.
Mansfield shows that a history duly attentive to political philosophy can shed comparable light on executive things. Like the power-generating dynamo, the "executive" is an artifact of the modern scientific revolution, which Mansfield explores in
its wider but less familiar political implications. Executive power has a peculiarly
theory-laden history because it entered history by way of a novel philosophical
teaching.[3] Far from being coeval with political life, it is a recent, history-shaping

invention. The creature of Machiavelli's doctrine, and the cutting edge of his revolutionary politics, "the executive" comes to light in Mansfield's inquiry as the most important of those modern "inventions of prudence" to which Madison alluded in *Federalist* #51. The historian can no more comprehend execution without its theory than he could decode Valéry's dynamo without electrical science.

Since we do not generally regard our executive, the American presidency, as an office generated by philosophic initiative or embodying a theory, this thesis is evidently at odds with received opinion. Mansfield's thesis will appear especially outlandish to readers influenced by Leo Strauss, for Strauss took pains to discourage his students from thinking of the presidency in this way.[4] Strauss sought to recover the citizen's perspective, the way things appeared to men immersed in social or political life before what Max Weber called "the disenchantment of the world by science"; or as Strauss preferred to put it, prior to the discovery of nature with the emergence of science or philosophy. Strangely enough, he taught that a principal task of political science today was to recapture the look of political things from this pre-philosophic angle—how social life comes to light for citizens unequipped with the lenses of philosophy and as yet unaffected by the profound changes that its meddling has wrought in social life.[5] Strauss's insistence on the primacy of the citizen's perspective was not embraced by all his students in every field, to be sure. But it was certainly taken to heart by those who studied the presidency. One distinctively Straussian contribution to presidential studies, over the last few decades, has been the effort to elevate the reasoning of presidents to a novel ascendancy in (or over) American political thought, and thereby to exhibit the presidency as the product in large measure of their thoughtful statesmanship.[6] Mansfield's restatement of the effectual truth of Machiavelli's executive teaching is bound to strike many of Strauss's students as a reversal of his principle of emphasis: Strauss clearly displayed Machiavelli's ferocious assault on the naive civilian viewpoint in order to repel that attack; whereas Mansfield appears to reinforce and further Machiavelli's challenge to the citizen's perspective.[7]

An index of that reversal might be the remarkable contrast between Mansfield's Preface and Strauss's Introduction to *Thoughts on Machiavelli*. "The United States," Strauss observed, "may be said to be the only country in the world which was founded in explicit opposition to Machiavellian principles."[8] If Strauss's initial theme was the distance between Machiavelli and the American Founding, Mansfield's is their convergence, in the creation of the executive. Far from opposing Machiavelli, Mansfield suggests, the Framers adopted a strong, Machiavellian executive.[9] In their Constitution, "the devices of Machiavelli are made available to the office first held by George Washington."[10] Mansfield invites us to study this marriage, whereas Strauss began with the divorce: "At least to the extent that the American reality is inseparable from the American aspiration, one cannot understand Americanism without understanding Machiavellianism, which is its opposite."[11] Rejecting this point of departure, Mansfield conveys the strong first impression that the Founders' debt to Machiavelli is most evident in the primary institution through which their regime presents itself to the world and to its own citizens: a president "elected to administer the executive government of the United States."[12]

This impression is reinforced by the opening of Mansfield's account of the American Founding, in his final chapter. Although "the executive seems sovereign in the realm where practice is not subject to theory" (248). Mansfield contends that this appearance is misleading. For "it was precisely in regard to the executive that the Constitution was most in need of the theorizing of political science, and most indebted to it" (250). Thus in Mansfield's culminating chapter the presidency initially comes to light as a creature of modern theory. Speaking of the adoption of the Constitution, Mansfield writes, "Now *the* theory has a formal embodiment in an office; it becomes *a* theory in practice, identified with what each president makes of it" (248).

But by this point in the book the attentive reader is bound to ask: Which theory? For Mansfield has developed four modern theories of execution and executive power in chapters on Machiavelli, Hobbes, Locke, and Montesquieu. Although cognate, they are very different. Perplexity on this score is intensified when Mansfield highlights the features of *The Federalist*'s presidency that diverge from all four of the modern teachings on executive power that he has thus far explicated in Parts II (The Discovery of Executive Power) and III (The Constitutional Executive). In the course of Chapter 10, Mansfield effectively demonstrates that none of the four is "formally embodied" in the presidential office. Accordingly, this chapter on *The Federalist* is intended "to show what new doctrine they [the American Founders] produced" (248). As Mansfield unfolds the striking originality of *The Federalist* (and of the Constitution it expounds), he shows that "the formal embodiment" of the theory entailed a profound rethinking. Taken in conjunction with *The Federalist*'s meditation on that "embodiment," the American Founders' moment in the history of the executive proves to be a theoretical event of considerable stature in its own right, amounting to a complete reassessment of the modern doctrine of executive power. A formal embodiment that yields a new doctrine entails more than a mere actualization; it is a theoretical reformulation. Indeed, if Mansfield did not repeatedly insist on the executive character of the presidency, one might wonder whether *The Federalist*'s "new doctrine" was a theory of executive power at all; or conclude (to adopt one of Mansfield's fine distinctions), that the American president was a "practical executive not understood as executive" (and hence not bound to consider himself as executive) (73).

Before the theory of modern executive power could be formally embodied in an office of the American Constitution, it had to pass through a lengthy deliberation, in the Constitutional Convention. Reflecting on what these deliberations accomplished (and guiding their sequel in the Ratification debate), *The Federalist* articulated a new teaching on the executive. Mansfield argues that these deliberations simultaneously transformed the received understandings of republicanism and of the executive power; by qualitatively modifying two hitherto unreconciled traditions, it made their union possible. Neither the resulting constitutionalized republicanism nor the republicanized executive is intelligible without the other; Mansfield's chapter shows *The Federalist* devoting equal attention to reformulating them together.

In the course of this deliberately republican Founding, according to Mansfield, the executive which these modern theorists had invented and refined was separated from their doctrines. While the purposes to which they had subordinated it were not entirely stripped away, even these purposes were given a new twist by the new *Federalist* doctrine. Thus as early as *Federalist* #17, the characteristic modern preoccupation with an effective executive receives a novel turn. "Contrary to Machiavelli, the people will be impressed more by steady administration than by sensational examples"(251). Mansfield does not say the people will be unimpressed by sensational examples, nor that steady administration precludes them; but whereas the Machiavellian "effectual truth" by which government is judged necessarily requires and excuses criminal deeds of execution, the republicanized executive of *The Federalist's* doctrine does not (251; cf.124–125, 131–134, 142).

Moreover (and despite the emphasis on consent in The Declaration of Independence), Mansfield notes that for Publius,

> contrary to Hobbes, Locke, and the republicans, the people's consent to obey is not effective enough. They must like their government, rather than merely obey it, if it is to be effective. And they will like it more for its good administration than because it is derived from their consent. Publius elevates the modern demand for results to a requirement of good performance.... The stage is set for a new kind of responsibility in executives—constitutional and republican. (251)

Even Publius's greatest reliance upon the received doctrine of executive power entails innovation. As Mansfield has argued, "the creation of executive power was made possible, indeed it was created, by a recognition—new to republican theory and contrary to previous republican theorists—of the power of necessity." (252) But when *The Federalist* teaches this recognition of necessity to republicans hitherto reluctant to acknowledge necessities, that recognition changes in character. Seen "from the battlefront of human recalcitrance"(49), where citizens stubbornly insist on making their own choices, it loses its scientific neutrality and its capacity to neutralize republican political life. Necessity comes to light in *The Federalist* as the potential ally or enemy of republican choice. Mansfield had shown earlier that the "Machiavellian moment," far from being an endorsement of republican choice, was a reorientation of politics toward the dreadful origins of organized social life, where necessity silences choice.

Its thrust was "to make all men aware of the necessity of tyranny, and therefore to throw very cold water on the ardent hopes they have cherished for any notion of justice that would oppose necessity"(182). By contrast, "Publius recognizes necessity, but does not draw the Machiavellian conclusion. As we shall see, this recognition does not become an excuse for doing ill, but an incentive for doing better than what is merely necessary" (252).

The Federalist's most important doctrinal borrowing is from Locke. It initially appears to be without modification; because it requires inspection, we quote Mansfield's analysis at length:

> It is characteristic of the American Constitution, by contrast to the republican tradition, to constitutionalize necessities in the manner of Locke. Those necessities limiting our choice, which we would like to wish away, are brought into the Constitution so that the people, through their government, can choose how to deal with them after having anticipated the necessity for doing so. That is how reflection enables choice to contend with "accident and force," which cannot in fact be removed from human affairs. (255)

> But the Constitution constitutionalizes the necessities of republican experience—and in no respect more obviously than in the executive. In its "energy" or quickness, the executive deals more than any other branch with the accidents and force that may thwart or disturb republican choice. By dealing with such necessities, the executive actually represents them in the Constitution. The provision for a strong executive thus reflects a realistic recognition by the people, in ratifying the Constitution and electing a President, that emergencies will arise that may confound their choices. (256)

Yet precisely here the Constitution (and *The Federalist's* teaching) add a dimension that was absent from Locke: "Republican choice is improved by the same forms in the Constitution that represent, or constitutionalize, necessities" (257). The term "forms" is chosen advisedly. As Mansfield has explained, Machiavellian skepticism about forms makes it difficult for those whose political science is confined by modern horizons to appreciate the full potentiality of the formalities of liberty; notwithstanding Locke's great concern for liberty, his constitutionalism is vexed by this difficulty.[13] But serious citizens need not accept this harness, and Mansfield highlights the reasons Publius gave for slipping out of it.

Judging from Mansfield's earlier chapters, the reader would not have expected that the modern executive power could be employed for the purpose of improving republican choice; Mansfield has consistently stressed Machiavelli's contrary intention.[14] Yet Mansfield finds that nothing prevents Machiavelli's devices from being re-appropriated against his intent and turned to republican purposes that Locke had not contemplated.

> But it is especially in the executive that republican choice acquires new capability. For the executive not only makes decisions in emergencies, as one ingredient of "energy," but also, as another ingredient, supplies the consistency in administration that makes possible "extensive and arduous enterprises" (Federalist 72). Such enterprises are familiar to us today as the long-term programs of legislation and administration—the New Deal, the Reagan Revolution—which always have their origin in the executive branch. Precisely the branch that most

recognizes the limits to human choice arising from emergencies, also best extends human choice in the capability to set a general direction for policy now and in the future. An able executive will improve upon the occasions of his decision. He will make his quick reactions consistent with his general program, so that his quickness is not merely willful but somehow adheres to his lasting intent. (257)

Locke, by contrast, "leaves no place in the constitution for the executive's program, a combination of law and discretion in which the choice of legislation is guided by a long-term choice of policy" (259). Thus *The Federalist* undertook a task foreign to the modern political philosophers who introduced and refined the executive power, according to Mansfield.

. . . . in teaching republicans to bow to the necessities represented especially in the need for executive power, *The Federalist* also shows republicans how to choose better, because more lastingly, while not departing from the republican principle that all government should be derived from the people. Thus it teaches republicans to be better republicans. (257)

Although Mansfield insists upon the contribution of modern executive power to the presidency and its character as an executive office, his account suggests that *The Federalist's* presidency was also released from the biases or constraints of modern theory in the course of this deliberately republican Founding. Publius's new doctrine proves to be substantially new, at odds not only with the Machiavellian doctrine whose discovery Mansfield had taken such pains to trace, but also with the liberal constitutionalist doctrines of Locke and Montesquieu.[15] The American presidency expounded by *The Federalist* relies significantly, yet very selectively, upon the modern tradition of executive power. Although the devices of executive action refined by Machiavelli (and toned down by the philosophic founders of modern liberalism) may be in a measure available to American presidents, Mansfield argues that the republican and constitutional character of the presidency defines the measure.

. . . . we know what to expect from our government and from ourselves through the powers and duties defined in the Constitution. When all branches or even all citizens have a prerogative power, no one has a responsibility because no one has a definite responsibility. Loss of constitutional definition leads to loss of responsibility. The Constitution must define neither too little nor too much. But it is in defining executive power, the power that most resists definition, that the problem lies. For a constitutional people, nothing is more difficult, nor more necessary, than to define what executive power is. (291)

Mansfield had observed that under Locke's executive and legislative division, "Men cannot take their bearings from their humanity alone but must proceed with their attention divided between desire and necessity" (211). The adoption of Locke's model constitution would therefore entail a heavy sacrifice. "Loss of a sense of responsibility for a whole"—for a constitutional whole that comprises both desire and necessity or that takes its bearings from our humanity—is the price, Mansfield warns, of Locke's rejecting the possibility of Aristotle's "kingship over all" (211). In Mansfield's judgment, however, the Constitution retains that possibility. His account of the new doctrine propounded by Publius culminates in this astonishing conclusion:

> As a formal possibility, Aristotle's kingship of virtue remains in the Constitution. Nothing in it prevents the emergence of such a king, except for the same practical problems that stand in the way elsewhere. The Constitution adopts that which precludes kingship in order to create a republican executive rather than a king; nevertheless, constitutional powers broad enough to meet necessities may also be strong enough to satisfy virtue. The Machiavellian principle of anticipating necessity by the use of virtue may be interpreted in the interest of virtue. Just as the people may elect rather than rule, so those with outstanding virtue may run for election and act within constitutional restraints instead of ruling. In a rare case such a person may rule through the constraints, that is, may succeed in using them to serve his virtue. (275)

This represents a remarkable reversal. Mansfield had demonstrated in Chapters 6–9 that under all the modern doctrines of executive power prior to the American Founding, the executive was never held within the orbit of the law or under the control of virtue. Here, near the end of Chapter 10, he concludes that the new doctrine brought forth by the Constitution and *The Federalist* yields a responsible republican executive which is outside neither the law nor the rule of virtue; but it seems that he has done so by making the executive a placeholder for Aristotleian kingship. Mansfield pithily summarizes the peripetia of Chapter 10 thus: "The Constitution formalized the ambivalence of virtue—republican or super-republican—in the ambivalence of executive power, weak or strong" (275). This jujitsu summation is evidently designed to stagger the reader and provoke a thorough reassessment of the book's argument.

Parts II and III seem to run contrary to Aristotelian common sense and to mimic the moderns while explaining their attempt to reconstruct political life through audacious theoretical projects. But in appropriating modern political science, which mixes theory and practice and dissolves or supersedes common sense, Mansfield is guided by Aristotle. These two parts, despite their careful tracing out of Machiavelli's executive thought and its impact on liberal constitutionalism, reflect Mansfield's effort to separate what the moderns meld together in their endeavor to unite knowledge and power. Their work thus becomes available to both philosophers and citizens in a new light.

On the one hand, their projects required them to disguise or efface the politically significant contemplative life. Mansfield shows that Machiavelli, Hobbes, Locke, and Montesquieu lived that life nearly to the hilt; and so the chapters Mansfield devotes to them develops the bios theoretikos as a standard for the most serious minds.[16] This articulation is, one might argue, Mansfield's "critical political science," which serves to "mock the impossible desires" which the moderns systematically flattered.[17] Mansfield makes perspicuous the two ways of life, of the philosopher and of the citizen or statesman, which the moderns confounded.

On the other hand, by showing how Publius interprets such devices as the executive, Mansfield discloses a constructive possibility. All the political artifices forged by the founders of liberalism may be rediscovered and made freshly available as "modern inventions of prudence" or as means to be employed by Mansfield's working political science, which is modelled on Aristotle's.

Part I on the pre-history of the executive therefore occupies two distinct positions, or fulfills two different functions, in Mansfield's teaching. Initially it serves as a background against which Machiavelli's revolutionary discovery of the executive can appear in its true magnitudes. Later, Mansfield's reader may begin to gather in the combinatorial side of his working or constructive political science.[18] The modern regimes in which the Machiavellian executive is embedded are, as Mansfield demonstrates, well-conceived projects to defeat common sense and confound those who view politics from the citizen's perspective. In these regimes, constructive reform is made doubly difficult by a doctrinal reinforcement of human recalcitrance: modern political philosophy teaches that rule as such is unjust.[19] Presidential scholars may learn from Mansfield's study how to address this peculiarly modern resistance to constructive reform. Understood in this light, these latter parts (II and III) adumbrate a practical political science framed for our circumstances.

Some may consider that in interpreting Machiavelli, Mansfield has gone too far in appreciating "the cunning and violence that prudence needs to have at its command whether in the worst or in the best cause." (111) His inquiry seems to run contrary to a tendency in Straussian presidential studies, as I have indicated. Have "the fundamental considerations that kept Aristotle from uncovering executive power" (74) led Mansfield to uncover it further, now that it has become the universal and primary mode of governance? However that may be, by taking Machiavelli's challenge to its limit, Mansfield has enabled us to appreciate fully, and perhaps for the first time, how the Constitution and *The Federalist* repelled Machiavelli's assault on responsible citizenship.

Scholars unaffected by Strauss will also be jarred by Mansfield's thesis, but for very different reasons. They may well conclude that Mansfield's radicalism undermines American constitutional morality, by indicting its foundational ideas and especially its unexamined democratic assumptions. *Taming the Prince* is refreshingly candid on this score. Certainly Mansfield would not have undertaken this effort if he thought it were possible to rescue modern liberal constitutionalism by drawing more deeply upon its proper resources or merely by returning to its roots. Mansfield's study is a remorseless demonstration that, from its earliest beginnings in Locke and Montesquieu, liberal constitutionalism never categorically repudiated Machiavelli's politics. It was instead a subtly accommodating effort to preserve his acquisitive principle and his prince in a tamer form.[20] The pride of modern liberalism is a kinder, gentler self-aggrandizement.

Mansfield shows, moreover, that when Locke and Montesquieu tame the prince they do so largely by befuddling our standards of deliberation and judgment, so that one might as well call their efforts a Machiavellian taming of public morality: qua executive, the executive of the liberal constitutionalists is never within the orbit of the law or under the control of virtue (106). The question Mansfield's study poses is whether the executive, which he shows to be at the root of liberal constitutionalism, ever was or can ever be a healthy root of constitutional self-government. *Taming the Prince* thus challenges what liberalism teaches about constitutional morality. Mansfield argues that Locke and Montesquieu adopted the opposition between form and reality, or between constitutional form and political reality, which Machiavelli discovered and exploited.[21] Only in a political community ruled by the dogma that constitutional forms are unbridgeably divided from the real goods or powers men seek through politics is the field fully open for the Machiavellian prince and for the Machiavellian art of combining formal or constitutional weakness with informal or unlawful strength.[22] Such ambivalence is the essence of the executive, Mansfield demonstrates; and its foundation or precondition in public opinion is a moral prejudice against rule.[23] Locke's morality, which Mansfield contends is "our morality," makes us at once loathe to take responsibility for ruling others and eager to punish those who do.[24] When we tame the prince by enhancing the fundamental opinions that rule out any alternative, what we are taming is not primarily the executive. For—to say nothing of necessity!—whenever lawful routine threatens to entrap and imperil us, whenever its mills grind out injustice, we have no remedy but to unleash or untame executive action. Like Nature, we may throw it out with a pitchfork, but inexorably it comes back. By Mansfield's account, our Lockean morality depraves the part of the soul that can only be perfected when we assume political responsibility for our selves. This (according to Mansfield, following Aristotle) includes the responsibility for ruling others along with ourselves.[25]

At first glance Mansfield's inquiry appears quite tangential to presidential studies and remote from the issues that excite public attention today. His study goes no further than 1789, before the presidency (as Americans have known it for more than two hundred years) began. The actions of American presidents fall outside his purview, as well as their thoughts on executive power. But presidential studies as Mansfield frames it is primarily a deliberation about a profoundly troubling and disputable office. As a conversation among serious citizens, its center of gravity is philosophic without being historical or academic: it continues the original debate which the Constitutional Convention initiated over the place of monarchy and Machiavellian tyranny in our fundamentally popular form of government.[26] However, what is most controversial will neither be acknowledged in the public conversation nor discussed, if presidents and presidential scholars censor their wisdom.[27] Mansfield reminds us of this practical dimension of presidential studies by taking the floor to advance the debate. In this respect, *Taming the Prince* is one of the more remarkable interventions by a good mind into American public life. It bears comparison with Hamilton's much-maligned speech during the 1787

Convention—an initiative that staggered the delegates but succeeded in advancing their deliberations swiftly (and in the event, irrevocably) toward the inherently strong presidential office the Constitution established.[28]

NOTES

1. Paul Valéry, "The Outlook for Intelligence" in *Valéry, History and Politics* (Princeton, N.J.: Princeton University Press, 1970): 133.

2. Tocqueville, *Democracy in America*, Vol.2, Bk.1, ch.10.

3. Harvey C. Mansfield, Jr., *Taming the Prince: The Ambivalence of Modern Executive Power* (New York: Free Press, 1989): xv–xviii, 5–13, 19–20, 121ff. All page numbers in parentheses in the text are to this edition, as are page numbers in the footnotes below, unless otherwise indicated.

4. Leo Strauss, *Liberalism Ancient and Modern* (New York: Basic Books, 1968): 206–215. Wilson C. McWilliams argues that Strauss's emphasis led his students to neglect "more purely theoretical American thinkers—Emerson, for example, who might have been expected to be of special interest, given his links to Nietzsche." See "Strauss and the Dignity of American Political Thought," *The Review of Politics*, Vol.60 #2 (Spring, 1998): 231–246.

5. Leo Strauss, *What is Political Philosophy, and other Studies* (Chicago: University of Chicago Press, 1959): 78–81; *Natural Right and History* (Chicago: University of Chicago Press, 1953): 78–80, 81–119, 120–122; Leo Strauss, *On Tyranny: Revised and Expanded Edition Including the Strauss-Kojeve Correspondence*, ed. Victor Gourevitch and Michael S. Roth (New York: The Free Press, 1991): 26–28, 184–186, 207.

6. Morton J. Frisch and Richard A. Stevens, *American Political Thought: The Philosophical Dimension of American Statesmanship* (New York: Scribners, 1971): 5, 23–50, 125–144, 191–236; Harry V. Jaffa, *The Crisis of the House Divided: An Interpretation of the Lincoln-Douglas Debates* (Seattle: University of Washington Press, 1973); Charles R. Kesler, "Woodrow Wilson and the Statesmanship of Progress," in *Silver*, op.cit., pp. 103–127; Jeffrey K. Tulis, *The Rhetorical Presidency* (Princeton, N.J.: Princeton University Press, 1987); James W. Ceaser, *Presidential Selection: Theory and Development* (Princeton: Princeton University Press, 1979); Sidney M. Milkis, *The President and the Parties: The Transformation of the American Party System Since the New Deal* (Oxford: Oxford University Press, 1993).

7. Leo Strauss, *What is Political Philosophy, and other Studies* . 40–43, 46–47; Strauss, *The City and Man* (Chicago: Rand McNally, 1964): 11–12.

8. Leo Strauss, *Thoughts on Machiavelli* (Seattle: University of Washington Press, 1958): 13.

9. Mansfield, ibid., xvi–xvii, xxii.

10. Ibid., xix.

11. Strauss, *Thoughts on Machiavelli*, 14.

12. George Washington, "Farewell Address," para.1, reprinted in Patrick J. Garrity and Matthew Spalding, *A Sacred Union of Citizens: George Washington's Farewell Address and the American Character* (Lanham, Md.: Rowman & Littlefield, 1996): 175.

13. Pp. 186–190, 198, 203–204, 209–211.

14. Pp. 70, 81, 89, 91, 95, 115–116, 128–129.

15. Pp. 259–260, 293–294.

16. Pp. 148, 167, 178, 214–215, 292–293.

17. Pp. 45–46,108, 115–118, 147–148, 174, 178, 198, 211, 214–215.

18. Compare 46–47, 51–53.

19. Pp. xxiii, 16–20, 50–51, 89,91,95,104,116, 127–129, 148; see also Robert Eden, "The Ambivalent Executive in the Political Philosophy of Hobbes," *The International Hobbes Association Newsletter* (July 1990).

20. Pp. 127, 129, 151, 175, 196, 287–290.

21. Pp. 13–16, 28–33, 71, 127–129, 139, 288–290.

22. Pp. xvi, 1–4, 13–20, 28–33, 71, 137–139, 148–149, 153, 171–174, 286.

23. P.153; see Eden, "The Ambivalent Executive."

24. Pp. 208, 211, and the passages in the next note.

25. Pp. xxiii, 18–19, 29–30, 39–40, 42–43, 70, 208–209, 270–271, 291–294.

26. See xv–xvi, xxiii, 18–19, and 278: "In the American Constitution the office of the executive permits and encourages a continuing dispute about the nature of executive power."

27. Pp. 165, 167, 176–178, 294–297. "If the executive and the people for whom he acts are capable of acting responsibly, we need a political science capable of discerning responsibility. Such a political science is essentially Aristotelian, as opposed to the Machiavellian political science that invented the modern executive," 291.

28. See "Speech in the Convention on a Plan of Government, June 18, 1787," in Morton J. Frisch, ed., *Selected Writings and Speeches of Alexander Hamilton* (Washington,D.C.: American Enterprise Institute, 1985): 90–116.

23

The Supreme Court: Republican Schoolmaster

Ralph A. Rossum

ℛalph Lerner has described the United States Supreme Court as a "republican schoolmaster," intended by the framers of the American Constitution to be "an educator, molder, and guardian of the manners, morals, and beliefs that sustain republican government."[1] Straussian scholarship on the Supreme Court has been largely built on this understanding. As Walter F. Berns has noted, through the cases it decides, the Court offers "authoritative definitions of what is permissible in the name of liberty and what is impermissible"; in so doing, it has "a profound effect on our opinions, our habits, our tastes, and ultimately, therefore, on the future of republican government in the United States."[2] Straussian constitutional scholars identify and examine the Court's teaching on the principles of the American constitutional order to determine whether and how well the Court has discharged this "awesome responsibility"[3] assigned to it by the framers. They treat the justices as teachers from whom they can gain instruction on the principles, problems, and prospects of the American democratic republic.[4]

Straussian constitutional scholarship ranges over many topics and pursues many different approaches and questions.[5] Nonetheless, it can be characterized by three distinctive features: It takes seriously and as worthy of careful study 1.) the opinions of the Court itself, 2.) the political and legal thought of its most prominent justices, and 3.) the Constitution and what it originally meant (as opposed to what it means to the contemporary Supreme Court).

The first distinctive feature of Straussian constitutional scholarship is that it takes the Supreme Court seriously, treating its opinions as the source of serious instruction on the American constitutional order and therefore as worthy of serious study and consideration. While it finds most opinions wanting, it insists that it is only by beginning with the assumption that an opinion may actually teach the reader some important lesson that the rare exceptions will be identified and their value derived. In this respect, Straussian constitutional scholarship differs from most other scholarship on the Court, which tends to view the Court as solely a political institution; the justices as simply reflecting their ideological, demographic, educational, and professional predilections; and their opinions as either unimportant—because merely epiphenomenal—or as interesting only because they reveal how coalitions are built or agenda are advanced.

Straussian constitutional scholars are open to the possibility that the Court can be a teacher from whom they can learn about the American regime; they begin, at least, with that assumption. Therefore, they engage in a careful reading of what the justices have actually written to gain instruction on the ends of republican government and their relation to such principles as freedom, property, equality, representative government, and fairness. John A. Rohr, for example, argues that an attentive citizenry can be taught how to understand, appreciate, and apply what he calls "regime values" (i.e., the ends that the American political system is designed to secure) through a careful study of U.S. Supreme Court opinions.[6] Rohr is especially interested in concurring and dissenting opinions, as they offer the reader "the opportunity to follow a public debate in a highly structured and formal context." This public debate, he observes, "necessarily points to higher questions on the nature of the common good."

Straussian constitutional scholars consider a Court opinion as a text to study, not as a datum to process. Thus, *American Constitutional Law*, a constitutional law casebook edited by two Straussians, begins by declaring that "[c]ases should be examined not merely to foster an appreciation of what court majorities have thought of particular issues at certain points in time . . . , but also to gain a deeper and fuller understanding of the principles that lie at the very heart of the American constitutional system."[7] To that end, it gives lengthier excerpts from fewer cases and more extensive passages from concurring and dissenting opinions than other casebooks, thereby allowing the reader to enter fully into the argument before the Court; it also gives priority to those (often older) cases where the constitutional principles at issue are most fully elaborated (rather than most recently considered).

Court opinions are, of course, written by individual justices, and a second distinctive characteristic of Straussian constitutional scholarship is that it takes seriously the political and legal thought of its most prominent justices. Their studies of John Marshall, Joseph Story, Roger Taney, Oliver Wendell Holmes, George Sutherland, and Felix Frankfurter are illustrative. Central to these studies has been what these justices have taught about natural rights.

Thus, Robert K. Faulkner, both in his magisterial book on John Marshall[8] and elsewhere, argues that the "Great Chief Justice" understood that the "purpose" of the Constitution was to "attend to the basic needs and thus the natural rights of men: protecting the lives, the liberties, the property, of as many people as possible."[9] That purpose was "the guiding star of Marshall's constitutional interpretation."[10] Faulkner approaches Marshall as a teacher and explores what "his thought reveals" concerning the "political philosophy at the core of American jurisprudence." What he finds is a jurisprudence based on the principles of classical liberalism that is capable of protecting "interested" and "acquisitive" individualism but that "fails to encourage high and unusual aspirations."[11]

Peter Schotten finds a similar natural-rights jurisprudence in the writings of Joseph Story.[12] He shows how Story's strong belief in the principles of the Declaration of Independence led him to favor a strong national government ("a strong and enduring Union comprised a necessary condition for the protection of important natural rights"[13]) and to oppose fervently slavery and the slave trade. Schotten concisely summarizes Story's jurisprudence by concluding that it was "based on the writings of Publius and the political philosophy of Locke, his desire to promote an enduring veneration for the Constitution so interpreted, his efforts to place all American law within this legal context, his conviction that the Constitution's final authority must be avoided if at all possible, and his judgment that its primary and most obvious meaning must never be compromised."[14]

Hadley Arkes's impressive new book on Justice Sutherland is subtitled: "Restoring a Jurisprudence of Natural Rights."[15] Arkes uses the opinions of this much-maligned member of the "Four Horsemen" to provide a primer on the limits of governmental power.[16] He faults contemporary conservative jurists, the political heirs to Sutherland's opposition to the New Deal (e.g., Chief Justice William Rehnquist[17]), for rejecting the natural-rights principles of Sutherland's jurisprudence and for embracing instead the principles of legal positivism, and he criticizes contemporary liberal jurists (e.g., the late Justice William Brennan) for likewise rejecting the premises of natural-rights jurisprudence even as they ground their decisions in an appeal to its logic. Arkes argues that Sutherland's defense of natural rights not only provides the basis on which to re-establish logical coherence for contemporary judicial conservatism but also exposes the fundamental inconsistencies that lie at the heart of contemporary judicial liberalism.[18]

Not all the justices who have attracted the scholarly attention of Straussians have embraced a natural-rights jurisprudence. Roger Taney, for example, is presented by Kenneth M. Holland as "the first legal positivist to serve as Chief Justice."[19] Holland traces Taney's emphasis on manmade or positive law to his enthusiasm for Jacksonian democracy and its belief in the wisdom of the people, and to his "severe distaste" for the abolitionists' natural-rights attack on slavery. Holland also explores the profound consequences of Taney's legal positivism. It led him, Holland argues, to deny the claims of vested rights, to argue that convention and not nature is the source of all political rights, and to reject the doctrine of inherent crimes. It "rendered him incapable of making judgments as to what was the core and what was the periphery of the Constitution," and it therefore led him "to the mistaken assessment that Negro citizenship on a national scale was a greater threat to the quality of popular government than the perpetuation of slavery."[20] It led him to become a supporter of southern secession even though he was still sitting on the High Bench; in so doing, it led to his being "hooted down the pages of history."[21]

The embrace of legal-positivist premises has not always led to condemnation; in the twentieth century, it has more commonly led to popular adulation, as in the cases of Oliver Wendell Holmes and Felix Frankfurter. Nonetheless, Walter F. Berns argues that, as a consequence of Holmes's legal positivism, "no man who ever sat on the Supreme Court was less inclined and so poorly equipped . . . to teach . . . what a people needs to know in order to govern itself well."[22] Holmes's legal positivism led him to embrace judicial restraint, but not because of a well-developed understanding of the judicial role but because, as Berns points out, "he was simply of the opinion that what others regarded as constitutional questions were in fact merely political questions to be decided with finality in the political process." For Holmes, "the majority, or the stronger, were to rule and would receive no instruction from him concerning the manner of their rule because, in this area, the Constitution did not care."[23]

Likewise, Richard G. Stevens faults Frankfurter for his legal positivism, attributing to it his easy acceptance of the notion of a living constitution. As Stevens points out, a living constitution can evolve (or devolve) in many ways; absent a natural-rights benchmark, there is no way to judge the transformation. A cancer, after all, "is a living thing." Stevens observes that it is a "small step" from embracing new rights in the name of a living constitution to rejecting old rights on the ground that while they might have been constitutionally protected yesterday, they are not today.[24] Legal positivism tied to the notion of a living constitution can easily lead to "judicial willfulness"; however, it can also lead to judicial "abandonment of the Constitution as a limitation on government." Stevens criticizes Frankfurter's legal positivism for teaching that the Constitution is a "neutral document" not aimed by its founders at justice, and he rejects Frankfurter's particular doctrine of judicial restraint, based on that legal positivism, for teaching that "nothing is just but as we will it so."[25]

A third distinctive feature of Straussian constitutional scholarship is that it is committed to "taking the Constitution seriously." In fact, two Straussians have published books with that exact title.[26] Most constitutional scholars pay little or no attention to the Constitution itself; they quote approvingly Charles Evans Hughes's famous words that "the Constitution is what the Court says it is" and approach the Constitution almost exclusively through what the Court has said about it in its most recent opinions.[27] They treat the Constitution as an empty vessel, devoid of meaning, until content is poured into it by the Court. Straussians, by contrast, insist that the Constitution has independent meaning and therefore must be kept central to the study of constitutional law.[28] While they certainly turn to Court opinions for instruction on what the Constitution means, they distinguish the Constitution from its judicial gloss. And in seeking to understand the Constitution on its own terms, they generally follow Joseph Story's sage advice in his *Commentaries on the Constitution of the United States:*

> [T]he Constitution is to be expounded in its plain, obvious, and common sense, unless the context furnishes some ground to control, qualify, or enlarge it. Constitutions are not designed for metaphysical or logical subtleties, for niceties

of expression, for critical propriety, for elaborate shades of meaning, or for the exercise of philosophical acuteness, or judicial research. They are instruments of a practical nature, founded on the common business of human life, adopted to common wants, designed for common use, and fitted for common understandings. The people make them, the people adopt them; the people must be supposed to read them, with the help of common sense; and cannot be presumed to admit in them any recondite meaning or any extraordinary gloss.[29]

This aptly summarizes George Anastaplo's approach in *The Constitution of 1787: A Commentary*.[30] Proceeding "section by section" and reflecting on its provisions as an ordinary citizen would, Anastaplo concludes that the Constitution tends toward legislative supremacy. He also concludes that judicial review is highly suspect; noting the "complete silence in the Constitution about judicial review," he wonders "if it is likely ... that judicial review was indeed anticipated, when nothing was said about it, considering the care with which [for example] executive review is provided for."[31]

Taking the Constitution seriously (or, as Story put it, expounding the Constitution in its "common sense") means paying attention not only to its text but also to its context—to what those who drafted and ratified it intended for it to accomplish. It means identifying, through a careful study of documentary evidence, the ends of the Constitution and the means for their achievement.[32] Francis Canavan has described this means-ends approach[33] well:

> When deciding whether an exercise ... of any power of government exceeds constitutional limits, the Court cannot draw a conclusion from the letter of the Constitution as though it were deriving a theorem in geometry. It must decide what the letter of the document means in the light of history, precedent, and other relevant considerations; what ends it was designed to achieve or evils to avert; how they are to be reconciled and combined with other constitutional ends, and how the attainment of these ends is affected by the facts of the case.[34]

Straussian constitutional scholars are originalists;[35] they seek to identify and preserve the Constitution's original meaning,[36] convinced that, in the words of James Madison, "[i]f the sense in which the Constitution was accepted and ratified by the Nation ... be not the guide in expounding it, there can be no security for a consistent and stable [government] more than for a faithful exercise of its powers."[37] They have sought the original meaning of such basic constitutional features as separation of powers[38] and federalism;[39] not surprisingly, they have also sought the founding generation's original understanding of the judicial article itself.[40]

The bulk of their attention, however, has been directed toward the original meaning of the Bill of Rights and the Fourteenth Amendment. Herbert J. Storing's and Robert A. Goldwin's work on the First Congress's adoption of the Bill of Rights is especially instructive. Storing argues that Madison "took a narrow view of the meaning of a bill of rights ... with the aim of preserving not only the constitutional scheme [from the prospect of a second constitutional convention] but also the vigor and capacity of government [from the prospect of disabling structural amendments]."[41] Goldwin elaborates on this theme in a splendid book whose title is its thesis: *From Parchment to Power: How James Madison Used the Bill of Rights to Save the Constitution*.[42] Storing and Goldwin both observe that Madison sought to have his amendments incorporated into the body of the Constitution itself on the grounds that "it will certainly be more simple, when the amendments are interwoven into those parts to which they naturally belong."[43] However, Madison's Federalist colleagues, who unenthusiastically joined his efforts to adopt a Bill of Rights even though they saw no need for one, refused to accommodate him on this matter. They agreed with George Clymer that the amendments should be placed at the tail of the Constitution so that the Constitution "would remain a monument to those who made it; by a comparison, the world would discover the perfection of the original, and the superfluity of the amendments."[44] Of course, in the twentieth century, the Bill-of-Rights tail has come to wag the Constitutional dog; contemporary constitutional law now regards the original Constitution as a "superfluity (when not an actual threat) to the protection of rights, and ascribes "perfection" to the Bill of Rights—or more accurately, to activist judges interpreting (or better still, non-interpreting) its provisions.[45] Storing reflects on "what our constitutional law would be like today if there had been no Bill of Rights."

> Its focus would presumably be to a far greater extent than it is today on the powers of government. We might expect a more searching examination by the Supreme Court of whether federal legislation that seems to conflict with cherished individual liberties is indeed "necessary and proper" to the exercise of granted powers. We might expect a fuller articulation than we usually receive of whether ... "the end" aimed at by given legislation "is legitimate." Might this not foster a healthy concern with the problems of *governing*, a healthy sense of responsible self-government?[46]

The absence of a Bill of Rights might have obliged the Court to teach more about the limits of governmental power; its passage, however, has allowed the Court to teach other lessons concerning the meaning of its particular provisions. Straussian constitutional scholars have compared the Court's current understanding of these provisions with their original meaning. In books and articles alike, they have addressed the original meaning of such Bill of Rights provisions as the free speech and press clauses,[47] the religion clauses,[48] the due process clauses of the Fifth and Fourteenth Amendments,[49] the criminal procedural provisions of Amendments Four through Eight,[50] the Ninth and Tenth Amendments,[51] and the putative "right to privacy."[52] They have also explored the relationship of the Bill of Rights to the Fourteenth Amendment (i.e., the incorporation doctrine[53]) as well as the original meaning of the Fourteenth Amendment's citizenship[54] and equal protection clauses[55] and its grant of enforcement powers to Congress under Section 5.[56]

Straussian constitutional scholars find that the typically narrow, original meaning of these provisions contrasts strikingly with the expansive, contemporary interpretations given them by the High Bench. Exploring the deleterious consequences that flow from these interpretations, they charge the Court with rendering opinions that "steadily erod[e] the conditions of civil liberty, to the point where it is appropriate to wonder about the future of liberal democracy in the United States."[57] Thus, for example, they criticize the Court's practice of construing the Constitution on the basis of "the evolving standards of decency that mark the progress of a maturing society,"[58] describing it as a means for transferring power from the popular branches to an "imperial judiciary."[59] Likewise, they condemn the Court's emphasis on group (as opposed to individual) rights in its opinions on racial discrimination, charging that it makes majority and minority interests more fixed and monolithic; renders "factious combinations"—with their attendant "instability, injustice, and confusion"—all the more likely; and therefore compromises the "republican remedy for the diseases most incident to republican government" as spelled out in *Federalist* No. 10.[60] And, they object to the Court's arrogant teaching in *Cooper v. Aaron* (1958) that its interpretations of the Constitution are as much "the supreme Law of the Land" as the Constitution itself.[61]

Most of all, however, they have attacked the Court's understanding of the First Amendment. Straussian constitutional scholars have paid as much attention as they have to "free speech and the place of religion in civil society" for "they concern the essentials of how we order our lives together."[62] Since the First Amendment "states the fundamental requirements of republican government in America,"[63] they regard it as the "first task of constitutional scholarship" to recover "the original meaning"[64] of its famous words: "Congress shall make no law respecting an establishment of religion, or prohibiting the free exercise thereof; or abridging the freedom of speech, or of the press; or the right of the people peaceably to assemble and to petition the Government for a redress of grievances."

They begin by considering the ordering of its provisions. Rejecting the operating premise of most constitutional scholars that the First Amendment is a "jumble of chaotic parts that could have been put together in any order whatsoever," they argue that it has an "internal coherence" that explains why "it begins with religious and then goes on to political considerations."[65] David Lowenthal makes this argument most explicitly. He insists that "the First Amendment is not difficult to interpret. It was not intended to change the body of the Constitution but to stipulate expressly certain limitations on the national government in the name of republican government." He notes that its "two main parts, one religious, the other political," parallel the approach that John Locke took in his writings; Locke first settled the religious question in favor of religious liberty in his *Letter of Toleration*, and then subsequently concentrated in his *Second Treatise of Government* on the role of government in a civil society with little reference to religion, since at that point he assumed it to be a simply private affair. Lowenthal argues that the framers of the First Amendment adopted Locke's approach, recognizing that they "could deal with civil or political questions only after the religious question is removed from contention. This explains why the amendment begins by preventing a national religious establishment (while also keeping Congress from interfering with state establishments), and protects the private practice of all religions." That accomplished, Lowenthal continues, the First Amendment "turns its attention to the means whereby the new national government can be kept responsive to the people. The freedom of speech and press is linked with the right to assemble peaceably and petition the government because all are necessary, together, for sustaining the public and open criticism essential to republican government."[66]

Beginning with the religion clauses, Straussian constitutional scholars argue that a careful consideration of their words makes it clear that Congress is prohibited from making laws concerning an establishment of religion (i.e., Congress "can neither provide for religious establishments of its own nor interfere with any State religious establishments then existing or later to be developed"[67]) and is barred from preventing the free exercise of religion (i.e., it cannot disallow or forbid various religious groups from practicing their religions as they see fit).[68] An establishment of religion means preferring one religion over others and giving it alone official status, special privileges, or financial support (i.e., Congress is not prohibited from providing aid to religion on a nondiscriminatory basis).[69] And religion itself means "worshipping a being or beings higher than man, and in association with others" (i.e., free exercise of religion is different from "free exercise of thought or moral endeavor.").[70]

They support their understanding of the religion clauses by focusing especially on the First Congress's use of the words "respecting" and "*an* establishment." Thus, Michael J. Malbin argues that the framers of the First Amendment used the word "respecting" because of the "dual purpose" it could serve: It not only prohibited laws respecting (i.e., "tending toward") a national establishment of religion but also prohibited laws respecting (i.e., "with respect to") existing or future state establishments.[71] Likewise, he argues that the authors of the First Amendment used the words "*an* establishment" to ensure the legality of nondiscriminatory religion aid.

> Had the framers prohibited "*the* establishment of religion," which would have emphasized the generic word "religion," there might have been some reason for thinking they wanted to prohibit all official preferences of religion over irreligion. But by choosing "an establishment" over "the establishment," they were showing that they wanted to prohibit only those official activities that tended to promote the interests of one or another particular sect.[72]

Given the framers' original understanding of the First Amendment, it is not surprising that these scholars are quick to attack the Supreme Court's complete misconstruction of the establishment clause in the seminal case of *Everson* v. *Board of Education*[73] and of the free exercise clause in such cases as *Wisconsin* v. *Yoder*,[74] *United States* v. *Seeger*,[75] and *Welsh* v. *United States*.[76] They attack *Everson* for two primary reasons: First, Justice Black's majority opinion ignored altogether the debates in the First Congress; it relied instead on Jefferson's metaphor in his letter to the Danbury

Baptist Association of a "wall of separation between church and state"[77] to hold that the establishment clause not only bars nondiscriminatory aid to religion but also forbids the government from fostering religious belief "in order to achieve a secular end."[78] Second, it incorporated the establishment clause through the Fourteenth Amendment to apply to the states, provoking the unanswerable question of how the establishment clause, intended by its framers to prevent the federal government from tampering with state establishments of religion, can possibly be construed to mandate precisely such tampering.[79]

They attack *Yoder, Seeger,* and *Welsh* as particularly egregious examples of the key defects of the Court's free-exercise jurisprudence. Walter Berns has described *Yoder,* which held that a member of the Old Order Amish religion could disobey Wisconsin's valid law requiring parents to cause their children to attend school until the age of 16, as "a palpable and unprecedented misconstruction of the Constitution, palpable because in this one respect it can be said that Old Order Amish is now an established religion of the United States (insofar as they alone are exempt from the operation of this law), and unprecedented because this was the first time the Court had held that one's religious convictions entitle one to an exemption from a valid criminal statute."[80] They criticize the Court in *Seeger* for expanding religious belief to include non-religious belief—it held that any "sincere and meaningful" belief "occup[ying] in the life of its possessor a place parallel to that filled by the orthodox belief in God" was religion. And, they attack the Court in *Welsh* for going to "even more absurd lengths"[81] and holding that any beliefs "about right and wrong" are religious if they are "held with the strength of traditional religious convictions."[82] They typically conclude their consideration of the religion clauses by observing that the Court's understanding of establishment and free exercise is so hopelessly confused that it feels compelled, under the establishment clause, to subordinate religious beliefs to such an extent that they cannot be encouraged even on a nonpreferential basis, while simultaneously feeling obliged, under the free exercise clause, to exalt religious belief (including non-religious or irreligious belief) to such an extent that the believer is free to disobey an otherwise valid law.[83]

Their criticisms of the Court's construction of the second part of the First Amendment, prohibiting the abridgement of the freedoms of speech and press or the rights to assembly and petition, are no less pointed. They see these two freedoms and two rights (hereafter referred to simply as free speech) as "necessary instruments and safeguards of republican government"—as "the means by which the people are able to communicate with each other and with the government about public affairs."[84] As a consequence, they argue that the First Amendment should not be construed to shield political movements that seek the overthrow of republican government[85] or to protect vulgar or obscene expression that undermines the moral dispositions of the people. However, they charge, that this is precisely the construction that the justices on the Supreme Court have given it. They attribute the Court's failure in this regard to the fact that John Marshall never had the occasion to write a definitive statement on the meaning and purpose of free speech in a republican government; Marshall, after all, was "a man firmly attached to republican principles and with a demonstrated and unequaled capacity to expound and defend them."[86] Instead, the United States had to wait until the early twentieth century for such a statement, and, when it finally came, it was from the pen of Justice Holmes, whose understanding of free speech was so impoverished and whose commitment to republican government was so attenuated that he could write in his dissent in *Gitlow* v. *New York*: "If in the long run the beliefs expressed in proletarian dictatorship are destined to be accepted by the dominant forces of the community, the only meaning of free speech is that they should be given their chance and have their way."[87]

Straussian constitutional scholars argue that free speech was protected by the framers of the First Amendment to facilitate "the promotion of thought and deliberation about matters of public interest—to the end that this shall be an enlightened republic."[88] And, as Francis Canavan has argued: "[E]nd or purpose is a limiting principle, regulating and restricting the uses or means to those which in some way contribute to the end. If a freedom is guaranteed for the sake of a certain end, those uses of the freedom which make no contribution to that end, or are positive hindrances to its achievement, are abuses of the freedom and cease to enjoy the protection of the guarantees . . . ."[89] The Court, however, has ignored this principle and, over time, has come to regard the First Amendment as protecting not only political speech but all speech (regardless of content)—and further still, not only all speech but in fact all expressive activity (from flag burning to nude dancing) communicating any message, rational or otherwise; as the Court held in *Cohen* v. *California*, it protects "not only ideas capable or relatively precise, detached explication but otherwise inexpressible emotions as well."[90] Instead of viewing free speech as a means to the end of republican government, the Court has come to view freedom of expression as an end in itself, which it will protect even if it undermines the moral character and decency of the citizenry needed to sustain self-government. Arguing that there is a connection between self-rule and self-restraint, Straussian constitutional scholars criticize the Court for protecting, and thereby legitimizing, unrestrained self-expression at the expense of self-rule. After all, the Supreme Court as a republican schoolmaster educates "most forcefully by what it allows and does not allow to appear in public."[91] Most urge the Court to return to the original meaning of the First Amendment and to restrict the ambit of its protection solely to political speech; they note that if the Court were to do so, it would not leave non-political speech wholly unprotected. As George Anastaplo argues, non-political speech would still be protected by the due process clauses of the Fifth and Fourteenth Amendments which protect our rights to liberty, property, and privacy—rights "more individualistic and less civic-minded (or public spirited) in their primary orientation than are the speech and press clauses of the First Amendment."[92]

Straussian constitutional scholars also criticize the Court for incorporating free speech to apply to the states. They point out that the framers of the First Amendment were willing to restrict Congress's control over free speech only because the states, under their police powers to protect public safety and public morals, were left free to do so.[93] The states served the purpose of a safety valve, allowing restrictions on the federal government to remain secure. Incorporation, however, has rendered inoperative this safety valve, and, by doing so, has reduced the Court to an "engineer" who, by trying "to protect too much" has succeeded in "protecting nothing adequately. If, as the courts often say, the Fourteenth Amendment extends fully against the states all the restraints on the government of the United States imposed by the First Amendment, there may be here an instance of 'engineers' who, forgetting the nature of government and of men, tried to protect too much and perhaps sacrificed that which had once been securely protected."[94]

Incorporation not only leads to the potential that political speech will receive less protection at the federal level than the framers of the First Amendment anticipated, it also imposes a "heavy," "dangerous," and "needless burden" on the federal judiciary. To cite one example, prior to incorporation, the states were free to regulate obscenity, vulgarity, and other non-protected expressive conduct, subject only to the limits of their own state constitutions as interpreted by their state courts; since incorporation, however, the federal courts and especially the Supreme Court have been forced to grapple with these issues. In the process, the Supreme Court has disgraced itself with such relativistic drivel as "one man's vulgarity is another's lyric."[95] Additionally, it has demonstrated itself incapable of resolving the complex questions it has arrogated to itself; for example, on the issue of pornography, it remains mired in the same definitional confusion that prompted Justice Stewart to confess in *Jacobellis* v. *Ohio*[96] in 1963 that while he "could never succeed in intelligibly" defining it, "I know it when I see it." Finally, and far worse than merely embarrassing itself, the Court has placed the country itself at risk; by finding it not only "politically uninteresting"[97] but also constitutionally irrelevant how the people in a republican government choose to entertain themselves, it has helped to undermine decent behavior, which, as David Lowenthal observes, is not "the spontaneous product of primordially free individuals" but rather is "the socially inherited product of reason and experience working through centuries to bring our raw natural appetites under control."[98]

While Straussian constitutional scholars agree among themselves that the First Amendment protects only political speech and that it was wrongly incorporated to apply to the states, they differ among themselves over the level of protection that political speech should receive. At one end of the continuum is George Anastaplo, who argues that the First Amendment absolutely protects political speech and provides for "completely unfettered (even 'subversive' if not 'treasonous') public discourse of the public business."[99] At the other end is David Lowenthal, who advances what he calls the "clear danger" rule but which is more commonly called the "bad tendency" rule; it holds that "both Congress and the state legislatures have the constitutional power to make it a crime to advocate, promote, prepare, or incite to the commission of a crime."[100] In the middle is Francis Canavan, who argues for a sophisticated "balancing" rule in which "a scale of kinds of utterances that are protected in varying degrees by freedom of speech and press" is weighed against "a scale of public interests that justify, in proportion to their importance, limitations on that freedom."[101] Also in the middle is Walter Berns, who applauds the "clear and present danger" rule for reducing the possibilities that Congress and the state legislatures will abuse their powers yet who also admires the "bad tendency" rule for "never losing sight of the connection between freedom of speech and republican government"; in the end, he prefers the exercise of judicial prudence to the application of court-made rules, announcing that "there can be no formulaic substitute for sound judgment."[102]

As is readily apparent, Straussian constitutional scholars have roundly criticized the Court for its arrogant and willful refusal to render decisions in conformity with the original meaning of the Constitution, and for its failure to discharge its responsibilities as a "republican schoolmaster." They have done more, however, than merely criticize and condemn. Taking the Constitution seriously has led them to explore means of restraining the Court and correcting the constitutional damage that it has wrought. Several means of curbing the Court have been identified. In *The Supreme Court and Constitutional Democracy*, John Agresto discusses at length various of these means, including the amendment process, impeachment, denial of jurisdiction, and Court-packing. He finds them, however, to be "too heavy or too blunt a set of instruments to use against the Court," and therefore he ultimately advocates the rather modest remedy of congressional re-enactment of the "rejected statute in a revised form or on a different constitutional base."[103] Gary L. McDowell favors stronger medicine; he urges Congress to use its powers to organize and oversee the judicial judiciary to revise the rules of civil procedure on such matters as standing, class action, joinder, declaratory judgments, and equitable relief.[104] Others go further still and argue that Congress should use its plenary power under Article III, §2, to restrict the Court's appellate jurisdiction and thereby deny it the opportunity to rule on certain constitutional questions; they note that Hamilton described this remedy in *Federalist* No. 80 as the appropriate means to "obviate or remove" any "inconveniences" arising from the Court's exercise of its powers.[105]

This essay began by describing the Supreme Court as a "republican schoolmaster" whose responsibility it is to "transfer to the minds of the citizens the modes of thought lying behind legal language and the notions of right fundamental to the regime."[106] Straussian scholars have demonstrated, however, that the contemporary Court has failed abysmally in this respect; they find, to their regret, that what the Court teaches today more often undermines than sustains republican government. Through its opinions, the Court teaches that the "mode of thought lying behind legal language" is oblivious to, if not contemptuous of, the original meaning of the Constitution and that the "notions of right fundamental to the regime" are not the natural-rights principles that underlie the original Constitution but the historicist and legal-positivistic premises of the justices themselves. If the Court continues to teach these lessons, it is unlikely that Straussian constitutional scholarship will continue to be characterized by the three distinctive features discussed above. Straussian constitutional scholars will doubtless find it impossible to continue to take seriously the Court and its justices, given what they are doing to the Constitution.

NOTES

1. Ralph Lerner, "The Supreme Court as Republican Schoolmaster," in *1967 Supreme Court Review* (Chicago: University of Chicago Press, 1967), pp. 127–128.

2. Walter F. Berns, *The First Amendment and the Future of American Democracy* (New York: Basic Books, 1976), p. ix.

3. *Ib.*

4. Some go even further and argue that the justices can and should be "statesmen." See Harry M. Clor, "Judicial Statesmanship and Constitutional Interpretation," *South Texas Law Journal,* Vol. 26, no. 3 (Fall 1985), pp. 397–433, and Gary J. Jacobsohn, *Pragmatism, Statesmanship, and the Supreme Court* (Ithaca, NY: Cornell University Press, 1977).

5. See Richard G. Stevens, "The Prospects for Constitutional Law," *The Political Science Reviewer,* Vol. XXVI (1997), pp. 238–330.

6. John A. Rohr, in *Ethics for Bureaucrats: An Essay on Law and Values* (New York: Marcel Dekker, Inc., 1978), p. 70.

7. Ralph A. Rossum and G. Alan Tarr (eds.), *American Constitutional Law*. 2 volumes (5th Ed.; New York: St. Martin's/ WORTH, 1999), Vol. I, p. viii.

8. Robert K. Faulkner, *The Jurisprudence of John Marshall* (Princeton: Princeton University Press, 1968).

9. Robert K. Faulkner, "John Marshall," in Morton J. Frisch and Richard G. Stevens (eds.), *American Political Thought* (2d ed.; Itasca, IL: Peacock Publishers, 1983), p. 91.

10. Faulkner, *The Jurisprudence of John Marshall*, p. xiii.

11. Faulkner, "John Marshall," pp. 90, 228, 19, and 33. For other Straussian treatments of Marshall, see Morton Frisch, "John Marshall's Philosophy of Constitutional Republicanism," *Review of Politics*, XX (January 1958); Christopher Wolfe, *The Rise of Modern Judicial Activism: From Constitutional Interpretation to Judge-Made Law* (Rev. ed.; Lanham, MD: Rowman & Littlefield, 1994), pp. 39–72, and Michael P. Zuckert, "Epistemology and Hermeneutics in the Constitutional Jurisprudence of John Marshall," in Thomas C. Shevory (ed.), *John Marshall's Achievement: Law, Politics, and Constitutional Interpretations* (New York: Greenwood Press, 1989).

12. Peter Schotten, "Joseph Story," in Morton J. Frisch and Richard G. Stevens (eds.), *American Political Thought* (2d ed.; Itasca, IL: Peacock Publishers, 1983), pp. 117–141.

13. *Ib.*, p. 122.

14. *Ib.*, pp. 122, 135.

15. Hadley Arkes, *The Return of George Sutherland: Restoring a Jurisprudence of Natural Rights* (Princeton, NJ: Princeton University Press, 1994).

16. Most of Sutherland's attention focused on the federal government, but in *Home Building & Loan Association* v. *Blaisdell* (1934), Sutherland voted against the power of a state to impose a mortgage moratorium during the Great Depression. Arkes defends Sutherland's argument that this moratorium violated the Contract Clause against Chief Justice Hughes's majority

opinion and also against fellow Straussian Gary Jacobson's criticisms of Sutherland in *Pragmatism, Statesmanship, and the Supreme Court.*

17. Arkes mentions Rehnquist's "The Notion of a Living Constitution," *Texas Law Review*, Vol. 54 (1976), p. 693.

18. See John C. Eastman and Harry V. Jaffa, "Understanding Justice Sutherland as He Understood Himself," *University of Chicago Law Review*, Vol. 63 (Summer 1996), pp. 1147–1374.

19. Kenneth M. Holland, "Roger Taney," in Morton J. Frisch and Richard G. Stevens (eds.), *American Political Thought*, pp. 169–194, 170.

20. *Ib.*, p. 193.

21. Charles Sumner, *Congressional Globe*, 38 Cong., 2 Sess., 1012 (February 23, 1865). Quoted in Holland, p. 185.

22. Walter F. Berns, "Oliver Wendell Holmes, Jr.," in Morton J. Frisch and Richard G. Stevens (eds.), *American Political Thought*, pp. 295–318, 298.

23. *Ib.*, p. 308. See also Walter F. Berns, "*Buck* v. *Bell*: Due Process of Law?" *Western Political Quarterly*, Vol. 6 (December 1953), pp. 762–765, and Robert Faulkner's comparison of Marshall natural rights teaching to Holmes's legal positivism in *The Jurisprudence of John Marshall*, Appendix I: Justice Holmes and Chief Justice Marshall," pp. 227–268.

24. Richard G. Stevens, "Felix Frankfurter," in Morton J. Frisch and Richard G. Stevens (eds.), *American Political Thought*, pp. 337–360, 347. See also Richard G. Stevens, *Frankfurter and Due Process* (Lanham, MD: University Press of America, 1987).

25. Stevens, "Felix Frankfurter," pp. 356, 360. See also Gary Jacobson's similar conclusions in *Pragmatism, Statesmanship, and the Supreme Court*, pp. 158–160.

26. Gary L. McDowell (ed.), *Taking the Constitution Seriously: Essays on the Constitution and Constitutional Law* (Dubuque, Iowa: Kendall/Hunt, 1981), and Walter F. Berns, *Taking the Constitution Seriously* (New York: Simon and Schuster, 1987).

27. For a critique of Hughes's statement, see Rossum and Tarr, *American Constitutional Law*, Vol. 1, pp. 1–3.

28. See L. Peter Schultz and Gary L. McDowell, "Herbert Storing and the Study of Constitutional Law," *Politics in Perspective*, Vol. 13, no. 1 (Fall 1985), p. 54.

29. Joseph Story, *Commentaries on the Constitution of the United States*, Vol. 1 (Boston: Hilliard, Gray and Company, 1833), pp. 436–437. Not all Straussians follow Story's rules of interpretation. See Sotirios A. Barber, *On What the Constitution Means* (Baltimore: Johns Hopkins University Press, 1984), and *The Constitution of Judicial Power* (Baltimore: Johns Hopkins University Press, 1993), whose approach is more "aspirational" and who regards constitutional law as "an independent moral voice in American politics."

30. George Anastaplo, *The Constitution of 1787: A Commentary* (Baltimore: Johns Hopkins University Press, 1989). See also John A. Murley, "Our Character as our Fate: The Constitutionalism of George Anastaplo," *Political Science Reviewer*, Vol. XXVI (1997), pp. 36–89.

31. Anastaplo, *The Constitution of 1787: A Commentary*, pp. 47–48. "[The Supreme Court] has been kept from its full realization as a court, and as a national teacher of what law is, by its diversion into that career as a superlegislature which easily follows from making much of a general power of judicial review." *Ib.*, p. 135. Most Straussians readily embrace judicial review; however, see Christopher Wolfe, *The Rise of Modern Judicial Review*, who rejects all but what he calls the "traditional form" of judicial review, and Matthew J. Franck, *Against the Imperial Judiciary: The Supreme Court vs. the Sovereignty of the People* (Lawrence, KS: University Press of Kansas, 1996), who rejects the claim that "the Supreme Court more than the other branches of government holds the paramount and final position in determining the mean-

ing of the Constitution," p. 3. See also Ralph A. Rossum, "The Least Dangerous Branch?" in Peter Augustine Lawler and Robert Martin Schaefer (eds.), *The American Experiment: Essays on the Theory and Practice of Liberty* (Lanham, MD: Rowman & Littlefield, 1994), pp. 241–258, whose views on this matter are quite similar to Anastaplo's.

32. Straussian constitutional scholars have distinguished themselves by publishing those Founding-era documents essential for understanding the ends and means of the Constitution. Herbert J. Storing's *The Complete Anti-Federalist*, 7 Vols. (Chicago: University of Chicago Press, 1981), with its painstaking research, meticulous editing and annotations, and seminal essay explaining what "The Anti-Federalists Were For," comes immediately to mind; so, too, does Ralph Lerner's masterful contribution to Philip B. Kurland and Ralph Lerner (eds.), *The Founders' Constitution*, 5 Vols. (Chicago: University of Chicago Press, 1987).

33. Rossum and Tarr consistently employ this "means–ends" approach in their casebook, *American Constitutional Law*. See also Rossum, "A Means-Ends Approach to the Study of the Constitution and Constitutional Law," *Politics in Perspective*, Vol. 13, no. 1 (Fall 1985), pp. 36–48.

34. Francis Canavan, "Freedom of Speech and Press: For What Purpose," *American Journal of Jurisprudence*, Vol. 16 (1971), reprinted in McDowell, *Taking the Constitution Seriously: Essays on the Constitution and Constitutional Law*, p. 321.

35. They would embrace the approach described by Sir William Blackstone: "The fairest and most rational method to interpret the will of the legislator is by exploring his intentions at the time when the law was made, by signs the most natural and probable. And these signs are either the words, the context, the subject matter, the effects and consequences, or the spirit and reason of the law." Blackstone, *Commentaries on the Laws of England*, 4 vols. (London, 1765–69), Vol. I, p. 59. By contrast, most contemporary constitutional scholars reject originalism and would endorse instead the words of the political scientist, Martin Shapiro: "As with all other constitutional provisions, it is not the founders' intentions but our intentions that count. It is, I think, a universally accepted truism that the glory of our Constitution is that it is a generally worded, and thus highly flexible, document that allows—indeed, requires—new interpretations to fit new situations. . . . It too requires that we decide what we want it to mean. . . . It is what we want, not what the founders wanted, that counts." Shapiro, *Freedom of Speech: The Supreme Court and Judicial Review* (Englewood Cliffs, NJ: Prentice-Hall, 1966), p. 93.

36. They adhere to original meaning and take seriously the arguments and work of the framers of the Constitution. David Lowenthal explains why in *No Liberty for License: The Forgotten Logic of the First Amendment* (Dallas, TX: Spence Publishing Co., 1997), p. 60:

"To make subservience to the founding fathers not only necessary but admirable, we must lose our sense of superiority to them that has been sedulously cultivated during more than a half-century of the nation's intellectual life. The fathers of the Constitution were not ordinary men. As a collection of forty, their equal has not been seen since, and certainly cannot be culled from the groves of academe today. Their practical political thought, as it entered the Constitution, was powerful, original, and far-sighted. They had studied law and political philosophy deeply, and knew how to reason and write. . . . Moreover, they sensed themselves in a position of responsibility for the formation and preservation of a new nation, and constantly acted with this responsibility in mind. We who come after them are their heirs and beneficiaries, and by not shouldering that same responsibility we are often led to propose rash changes that can only harm rather than improve the system they created. To be sure, it is impossible to expect men raised under their system not to embody some of the same independence of spirit they exemplified. But independence does not require superficiality, vanity, or folly, and is perfectly consistent with an admiration for the founders best described as "rational reverence"—that is, a reverence that grows deeper the more their work is studied."

37. Quoted in Rossum and Tarr, *American Constitutional Law*, Vol I, p. 10. They seek not only to identify and preserve the Constitution's original meaning but also to defend it. See, for example, Thomas G. West's splendid new book, *Vindicating the Founders: Race, Sex, Class, and Justice in the Origins of America* (Lanham, MD: Rowman & Littlefield, 1997).

38. See Charles R. Kesler, "Separation of Powers and the Administrative State," in Gordon S. Jones and John Marini, *The Imperial Congress: Crisis in the Separation of Powers* (New York: Pharos Books, 1989), pp. 20–40; Edward J. Erler, "The Constitution and the Separation of Powers," in Leonard W. Levy and Dennis J. Mahoney (eds.), *The Framing and Ratification of the Constitution* (New York: Macmillan, 1987), pp. 151–166; Murray Dry, "The Congressional Veto and the Constitutional Separation of Powers," in Joseph M. Bessette and Jeffrey Tulis (eds.), *The Presidency in the Constitutional Order* (Baton Rouge: Louisiana State University Press, 1981), pp. 195–233; and Robert Scigliano, *The Supreme Court and the Presidency* (New York: Free Press, 1971), Chapter 1.

39. See Michael P. Zuckert, "A System without Precedent: Federalism in the American Constitution," in Levy and Mahoney, *The Framing and Ratification of the Constitution*, pp. 132–150, and Kenneth M. Holland, "Federalism," in Peter Augustine Lawler and Robert Martin Schaefer (eds.), *The American Experiment: Essays on the Theory and Practice of Liberty* (Lanham, MD: Rowman & Littlefield, 1994), pp. 57–76.

40. See Lane V. Sunderland, *Popular Government and the Supreme Court: Securing the Public Good and Private Rights* (Lawrence: University Press of Kansas, 1996), Gary L. McDowell, *Equity and the Constitution: The Supreme Court, Equitable Relief, and Public Policy* (Chicago: University of Chicago Press, 1982), and Ralph A. Rossum, "The Courts and the Judicial Power," in Leonard W. Levy and Dennis J. Mahoney (eds.), *The Framing and Ratification of the Constitution* (New York: Macmillan, 1987), pp. 222–241.

41. Herbert J. Storing, "The Constitution and the Bill of Rights," in *Toward a More Perfect Union: Writings of Herbert J. Storing*, edited by Joseph M. Bessette (Washington, DC: AEI Press, 1995), p. 122.

42. Robert A. Goldwin, *From Parchment to Power: How James Madison Used the Bill of Rights to Save the Constitution* (Washington, DC: AEI Press, 1997).

43. Helen E. Veit, et al. (eds.), *Creating the Bill of Rights: The Documentary Record from the First Federal Congress* (Baltimore: Johns Hopkins University Press, 1991), p. 118.

44. *Ib.*, p. 120.

45. See Ralph A. Rossum, "*The Federalist's* Understanding of the Constitution as a Bill of Rights," in Charles R. Kesler (ed.), *Saving the Revolution: The Federalist Papers and the American Founding* (New York: Free Press, 1987), pp. 219–233.

46. Storing, "The Constitution and the Bill of Rights," p. 118. (Emphasis in the original.)

47. See George Anastaplo, *The Constitutionalist: Notes on the First Amendment* (Dallas, TX: Southern Methodist University Press, 1971); Walter F. Berns, *The First Amendment and the Future of American Democracy*; Francis Canavan, *Freedom of Expression: Purpose as Limit* (Durham, NC: Carolina Academic Press, 1984); Harry M. Clor, *Public Morality and Liberal Society* (Notre Dame, IN: University of Notre Dame Press, 1996); Murray Dry, "Flag Burning and the Constitution," *1990 Supreme Court Review* (Chicago: University of Chicago Press, 1991); and David Lowenthal, *No Liberty for License: The Forgotten Logic of the First Amendment*.

48. See Walter F. Berns, *The First Amendment and the Future of American Democracy*; Michael J. Malbin, *Religion and Politics: The Intentions of the Authors of the First Amendment* (Washington,

DC: AEI Press, 1978); Gary D. Glenn, "Forgotten Purposes of the First Amendment Religion Clauses," *Review of Politics*, Vol. 49, No. 3 (1987), pp. 340–367; and David Lowenthal, *No Liberty for License: The Forgotten Logic of the First Amendment*.

49. Eugene W. Hickok and Gary L. McDowell, *Justice vs. Law: Courts and Politics in American Society* (New York: Free Press, 1993), Chapter 4; Christopher Wolfe, "The Original Meaning of the Due Process Clause," in Eugene W. Hickok, *The Bill of Rights: Original Meaning and Current Understanding* (Charlottesville: University Press of Virginia, 1991), pp. 213–230.

50. Bradford P. Wilson, "The Fourth Amendment as More Than a Form of Words: The View from the Founding," in Eugene W. Hickok, *The Bill of Rights: Original Meaning and Current Understanding* (Charlottesville: University Press of Virginia, 1991), pp. 151–171; Steven R. Schlesinger, *Exclusionary Injustice* (New York: Marcel Dekker, Inc., 1977); Hadley Arkes, *Beyond the Constitution* (Princeton, NJ: Princeton University Press, 1990), Chapter 8; and Ralph A. Rossum, "'Self-Incrimination': The Original Intent," in Eugene W. Hickok, *The Bill of Rights: Original and Current Understanding* (Charlottesville: University Press of Virginia, 1991), pp. 273–287.

51. Edward J. Erler, "The Ninth Amendment and Contemporary Jurisprudence," in Eugene W. Hickok, *The Bill of Rights: Original and Current Understanding* (Charlottesville: University Press of Virginia, 1991), pp., 432–451; and Walter F. Berns, "The Meaning of the Tenth Amendment," in Robert A. Goldwin (ed.), *A Nation of States* (2d ed.; Chicago: Rand McNally, 1974).

52. Hadley Arkes, *First Things: An Inquiry into the First Principles of Morals and Justice* (Princeton, NJ: Princeton University Press, 1986), Chapters XV–XVII.

53. Compare Richard G. Stevens, "Due Process of Law and Due Regard for the Constitution," *Politics in Perspective*, Vol. 13, No. 1 (Fall 1985), pp. 25–35, and George Anastaplo, *The Amendments to the Constitution: A Commentary* (Baltimore: Johns Hopkins University Press, 1995) with Michael P. Zuckert, "Completing the Constitution: The Fourteenth Amendment and Constitutional Rights," *Publius*, Vol. 22 (1992), p. 22.

54. See Edward J. Erler, "Immigration and Citizenship," in Gerald Frost (ed.), *Loyalty Misplaced: Misdirected Virtue and Social Disintegration* (London: Social Affairs Unit, 1997), pp. 71–90. Erler argues that illegal aliens are not "subject to the jurisdiction" of the United States and that Congress is therefore free to deny citizenship to their children who are born on U.S. soil.

55. See Judith A. Baer, *Equality Under the Constitution: Reclaiming the Fourteenth Amendment* (Ithaca, NY: Cornell University Press, 1983); Edward J. Erler, *The American Polity*, Chapter 5, and Ralph A. Rossum, *Reverse Discrimination: The Constitutional Debate* (New York: Marcel Dekker, Inc., 1980).

56. Michael P. Zuckert, "Congressional Power Under the Fourteenth Amendment—The Original Understanding of Section Five," *Constitutional Commentary*, Vol. 3 (1986), p. 123.

57. Berns, *The First Amendment and the Future of American Democracy*, x.

58. The words are from Chief Justice Warren's opinion in *Trop v. Dulles*, 356 U.S. 86 (1958). See Walter F. Berns, *Taking the Constitution Seriously*, p. 236: "The Framers . . . provided for a Supreme Court and charged it with the task, not of keeping the Constitution in tune with the times but, to the extent possible, of keeping the times in turn with the Constitution."

59. See Walter F. Berns, *For Capital Punishment: Crime and the Morality of the Death Penalty* (New York: Basic Books, 1977), p. 5, and Franck, *Against the Imperial Judiciary*.

60. Edward J. Erler, "Sowing the Wind: Judicial Oligarchy and the Legacy of *Brown v. Board of Education*," *Harvard Journal of Law and Public Policy*, Vol. 8 (1985), pp. 399–426; and Ralph

A. Rossum, "*Plessy, Brown*, and the Reverse Discrimination Cases," *American Behavioral Scientist,*Vol. 28, No. 6 (1985).

61. McDowell, *Equity and the Constitution*, pp. 128–129, and John Agresto, *The Supreme Court and Constitutional Democracy* (Ithaca, NY: Cornell University Press, 1984), p. 118.

62. Harvey C. Mansfield, "Foreword," in Lowenthal, *No Liberty for License: The Forgotten Logic of the First Amendment*, p. ix.

63. Lowenthal, *No Liberty for License: The Forgotten Logic of the First Amendment*, pp. xvii–xviii.

64. *Ib.*, p. xxii.

65. *Ib.*, p. xvii.

66. *Ib.*, pp. 272–273.

67. Anastaplo, *The Amendments to the Constitution: A Commentary*, p. 56.

68. Lowenthal, *No Liberty for License: The Forgotten Logic of the First Amendment*, pp. 196–197. Anastaplo supplies an important insight: "Although Congress cannot interfere at all with state religious establishments, it is evidently left free by the First Amendment to supervise state prohibitions of the free exercise of religion. Congress is kept from prohibiting the free exercise of religion, but it is not kept from correcting state interferences with the free exercise of religion. In this field, unlike that of religious establishments, the states need not be left alone by Congress to develop their local preferences in whatever way they choose." Anastaplo, *The Amendments to the Constitution: A Commentary*, p. 56.

69. See Berns, *The First Amendment and the Future of American Democracy*, p. 7; Anastaplo, *The Amendments to the Constitution: A Commentary*, p. 56, and Lowenthal, *No Liberty for License: The Forgotten Logic of the First Amendment*, p. 222.

70. Lowenthal, *No Liberty for License: The Forgotten Logic of the First Amendment*, p.222. As Lowenthal notes, the word religion "cannot be thought to include non-religion and irreligion—that is, belief as such. The freedom of religion is not a freedom of any opinion about religion, including atheism. For a religion is more than a belief or set of beliefs, even about some divinity. Religion presupposes a community of worshippers and a being (or beings) being worshipped." *Ib.*, pp. 198–199.

71. Michael J. Malbin, *Religion and Politics: The Intentions of the Authors of the First Amendment*, p. 15. See also Lowenthal, *No Liberty for License: The Forgotten Logic of the First Amendment*, p. 192.

72. Malbin, *Religion and Politics: The Intentions of the Authors of the First Amendment*, p. 14. (Emphasis in the original.) Both Malbin and Berns, *The First Amendment and the Future of American Democracy*, pp. 7–8, note that the First Congress reenacted the Northwest Ordinance of 1787, which set aside federal lands in the territory for schools and which justified that set aside as follows: "Religion, morality, and knowledge being necessary to good government and the happiness of mankind, schools and the means of learning shall forever be encouraged." They question how Congress could consistently promote religious and moral education while simultaneously banning all forms of assistance to religion.

73. 330 U.S. 1 (1947).

74. 406 U.S. 205 (1972).

75. 380 U.S. 163 (1965).

76. 398 U.S. 333 (1970).

77. They point out that the Court ignored the fact that Jefferson "did not think a 'wall of separation between church and state' prevented him from *requiring* the daily 'free exercise' of religion" at his University of Virginia. Lowenthal, *No Liberty for License: The Forgotten Logic of the First Amendment*, p. 189. (Emphasis in the original.)

78. Berns, *The First Amendment and the Future of American Democracy*, p. 60. See also pp. 65 and 75. See also Anastaplo, *The Amendments to the Constitution: A Commentary*, p. 57, and Lowenthal, *No Liberty for License: The Forgotten Logic of the First Amendment*, pp. 203–221. They all rely heavily on Tocqueville's arguments in *Democracy in America* and Washington's "Farewell Address" to support their argument that governments must collaborate with religious institutions to curb licentiousness and corruption and promote morality and common decency.

79. Anastaplo, *The Amendments to the Constitution: A Commentary*, p. 57. See also Lowenthal, *No Liberty for License: The Forgotten Logic of the First Amendment*, pp. 228–236.

80. Berns, *The First Amendment and the Future of American Democracy*, p. 38

81. Lowenthal, *No Liberty for License: The Forgotten Logic of the First Amendment*, p. 265.

82. While technically *Seeger* and *Welsh* involve statutory construction of the conscientious objector section of the Selective Service Act, and not constitutional construction of the free exercise clause, they are open windows into the Court's understanding of what constitutes religion.

83. Berns, *The First Amendment and the Future of American Democracy*, p. 78; and Malbin, *Religion and Politics: The Intentions of the Authors of the First Amendment*, p. 40.

84. Lowenthal, *No Liberty for License: The Forgotten Logic of the First Amendment*, p. 19; see also p. 156. See also Anastaplo, *The Constitutionalist: Notes on the First Amendment*, p. 115, and Anastaplo, *The Amendments to the Constitution: A Commentary*, p. 55.

85. "Criticism of the government, to keep it republican and working properly, begins with speaking and writing—the work of individuals—and culminates in *peaceable* assemblies and petitions—the work of groups. But here protected freedom ends. By the clearest implication, the First Amendment entitles no one, individual or group, to disobey, assemble riotously or violently, rebel, or replace republican government with some non-republican form of government." Lowenthal, *No Liberty for License: The Forgotten Logic of the First Amendment*, pp. 20–21. (Emphasis in the original.)

86. Berns, *The First Amendment and the Future of American Democracy*, p. 147.

87. 268 U.S. 652, 673 (1925). Lowenthal calls this "the single most disgraceful sentence in our jurisprudence." *No Liberty for License: The Forgotten Logic of the First Amendment*, p. 35. They also excoriate Holmes for his famous dissenting dictum in *Abrams* v. *United States*, 250 U.S. 616, 639, in which he declares that, according to "the theory of our Constitution," "the best test of truth is the power of the thought to get itself accepted in the competition of the market." As Walter Berns has pointed out, ideas that lose out in the competition of the market could "logically be suppressed. By the only relevant criteria—those supplied by the marketplace—they are false and, to say the same thing, unpopular; and to the extent that they are unpopular, they can be 'safely' suppressed. The more obnoxious they are held to be, the more unpopular they will be; and the more unpopular they are, the more safely those who hold them may be persecuted. It would seem, therefore, that the 'truth' that wins in the market provides a very good ground indeed upon which those who subscribe to it can 'safely' carry out their wishes, including a wish to extirpate the last vestiges of what the market has characterized as obnoxious 'thought.'" Berns, *The First Amendment and the Future of American Democracy*, p. 154.

88. Harry M. Clor, *Public Morality and Liberal Society*, p. 215.

89. Francis Canavan, "Freedom of Speech and Press: For What Purpose?" *American Journal of Jurisprudence*, Vol. 16 (1971), reprinted in McDowell, *Taking the Constitution Seriously*, pp. 305–343, 309. See also Canavan, *Freedom of Expression: Purpose as Limit*.

90. 403 U.S. 15, 26 (1971).

91. Harry M. Clor, "Obscenity and Freedom of Expression," in Harry M. Clor (ed.), *Censorship and Freedom of Expression: Essays on Obscenity and the Law* (Chicago: Rand McNally & Company, 1971), p. 108.

92. Anastaplo, *The Amendments to the Constitution: A Commentary*, p. 54.

93. Harry M. Clor, *Obscenity and Public Morality* (Chicago: University of Chicago Press, 1969), p. 97, and Berns, *The First Amendment and the Future of American Democracy*, pp. 121, 146.

94. Anastaplo, *The Constitutionalist: Notes on the First Amendment*, p. 54.

95. The words are from Justice Harlan in *Cohen v. California*, 403 U.S. 15, 25 (1971). See Berns, *The First Amendment and the Future of American Democracy*, p. 200: "Do we really live in a world so incapable of communication that it can be said that 'one man's vulgarity is another's lyric'?"

96. 378 U.S. 184 (1964).

97. See Berns, "Beyond the (Garbage) Pale," in Harry M. Clor (ed.), *Censorship and Freedom of Expression: Essays on Obscenity and the Law* (Chicago: Rand McNally & Company, 1971), p. 57: "Is it politically uninteresting whether men and women derive pleasure from performing their duties as citizens, parents, and spouses or, on the other hand, from watching their laws and customs and institutions ridiculed on the stage?"

98. Lowenthal, *No Liberty for License: The Forgotten Logic of the First Amendment*, pp. 102, 100.

99. Anastaplo, *The Amendments to the Constitution: A Commentary*, p. 54. See also Anastaplo, *The Constitutionalist: Notes on the First Amendment*, pp. 15–23.

100. Lowenthal, *No Liberty for License: The Forgotten Logic of the First Amendment*, p. 79. This is the rule that Justice Sanford applied for the Court in *Gitlow v. New York* (1925). Lowenthal argues that this was also the "accepted rule of the Supreme Court and all the courts of the nation" from the time of the founding until Holmes and Brandeis, "in an unjustified rupture" of our country's "long tradition," formulated the "clear and present danger" rule. *Ib.*, pp. 79, 27. See also pp. 74–78, in which Lowenthal catalogs ten specific defects of the "clear and present danger" rule.

101. Francis Canavan, "Freedom of Speech and Press: For What Purpose?" p. 334.

102. Berns, *The First Amendment and the Future of American Democracy*, pp. 158, 177.

103. Agresto, *The Supreme Court and Constitutional Democracy*, pp. 125, 131. See also Berns, *The First Amendment and the Future of American Democracy*, p. 53, and Lowenthal, *No Liberty for License: The Forgotten Logic of the First Amendment*, pp. 270–271.

104. Gary L. McDowell, *Curbing the Courts: The Constitution and the Limits of Judicial Power*.

105. Ralph A. Rossum, *Congressional Control of the Judiciary: The Article III Option* (Cumberland, VA: Center of Judicial Studies, 1988).

106. Lerner, "The Supreme Court as Republican Schoolmaster," p. 180.

24

Bureaucracy and America: Leo Strauss on Constitutionalism, the State, and Tyranny

John A. Marini

> Though we cannot acquiesce in the political heresy of the poet
> who says: 'For forms of government let fools contest—That
> which is best administered is best,'—yet we may safely pro-
> nounce, that the true test of a good government is its aptitude
> and tendency to produce a good administration.
>
> *Alexander Hamilton (The Federalist #68)*

Leo Strauss was an outspoken and influential critic of the discipline of Political
Science in the United States. Nonetheless, his work exerted considerable influence
on the way in which that profession has come to understand and evaluate American
politics and bureaucracy. Strauss's contribution to the study of American politics
was limited, partly as a result of his greater concern with the broader questions of
modern political thought which he called the crisis of the West. He was, however,
an ardent defender of constitutional government, who, more than any other contemporary scholar, revealed the dimensions of modern tyranny. Strauss's analysis
made it possible to distinguish the political science of the American founding, which
culminated in constitutionalism, from modern political thought which, after
Rousseau, culminated in the idea of the state.

It was Rousseau's critique of the modern doctrine of natural rights which
resulted in the destruction of nature as the standard for political right. In the political thought of subsequent thinkers, particularly Kant and Hegel, the rational mind
understood historically, replaced nature and nature's God. In Hegel, this rationality became tangible in the idea of the state. The state is the most rational and ethical organization. It is made possible by the reconciliation of the antagonism
between theory and practice, the universal and particular, and state and society.
Hegel noted:

we should desire to have in the state nothing except what is an expression of rationality.The state is the world which mind has made for itself; its march, therefore, is on lines that are fixed and absolute. How often we talk of the wisdom of God in nature! But we are not to assume for that reason that the physical world of nature is a loftier thing than the world of mind.As high as mind stands above nature, so high does the state stand above physical life. Man must therefore venerate the state as a secular deity, and observe that if it is difficult to comprehend nature, it is infinitely harder to understand the state.[1]

The differences between constitutionalism and the state have had profound consequences for the practice of politics in the modern world.The politics of the modern state culminates in bureaucratic administration because the practical problems of human life are to be solved by the technical "rationality" of science and social science. Indeed, rule itself is no longer understood in terms of politics, or consent of the governed, but in terms of expertise or knowledge.The institutional home of the knowledge required to administer the "rational" state is to be found in the modern university.The idea of the state presupposes the end of philosophy or history and, consequently, the end of politics.The result is, as Karl Marx noted, that "the government of men is transformed into the administration of things."

On the other hand, constitutional government must be understood from the perspective of nature, as perceived by the faculty of reason, itself natural. If man is a political being, it is because factionalism is sown into the nature of man.The fundamental problem of politics is tyranny, which is a problem coeval with political life.Thus, the primary necessity of constitutionalism is to limit the power of government. Moreover, the practice of government in a constitutional regime is dependent upon prudence, or common sense, not science, as fundamental for good administration. Prudence is the political virtue par excellence, the reasonable way of adjudicating means and ends.

Strauss's principled defense of the decent practice of politics led many of his students to devote their careers to the study of American politics. More than a few have taken an active part in political life. In addition, a number of the leading theorists of public administration have been students of Strauss or his students. One need only mention the names of Herbert Storing and John Rohr.There is no doubt that Strauss's students have been intelligent and influential defenders of American constitutionalism.At the same time, most have had few reservations concerning the problem of bureaucracy, or the modern state. Indeed, Storing looked to the bureaucracy as a remedy for certain defects within the Constitution, and Rohr has labored mightily to defend the legitimacy of the administrative state.[2] It remains to be seen whether Strauss's students have understood American bureaucracy in the light of his analysis of the state and modern tyranny.

THE BUREAUCRATIC PHENOMENON

In the twentieth century, bureaucracy has revealed itself as a pervasive and obdurate political problem, as well as a complex theoretical phenomenon. There is every reason to believe that the fate of contemporary man entails a growing dependence upon bureaucratic administration. This can be seen in the diminishing importance of the family, social groups, and communal associations. The trend toward bureaucratization is a consequence of the progressive displacement of the natural world by modern science, and the transformation of human—or social—associations into "rational" organizations. Max Weber, the most influential social scientist of our time, foresaw the manner in which the technical rationality of modern administration would result in bureaucratic domination.

> ·Joined to the dead machine, [bureaucratic organization] is at work to erect the shell of that future bondage to which one day men will perhaps be forced to submit in impotence, as once the fellahs in the ancient Egyptian state—if a purely, technically good, that is, rational bureaucratic administration and maintenance is the last and only value which is to decide on the manner in which their affairs are directed.

The growing dominance of bureaucratic structures in contemporary society raises important questions about the possibility of preserving constitutional government and a free society.

In Weber's view, modern bureaucracy must be understood as the historic and final form of the transformation of reason.[3] The universal or rational state provided the ground for the transition from theoretical to practical reason and with it, the dominance of rational organizations.[4] The progressive quantification or mathematization of knowledge and experience, which began with the natural sciences and attained preeminence through successful domination of nature, led to the victory of empiricism within the framework of the other sciences as well. Ultimately, the method of science was extended to control of the conduct of human life itself.[5] Indeed, Weber insisted that all Western forms of organization—including the economic—must be understood by the evolution of technical possibilities. "Its rationality is to-day essentially dependent on the calculability of the most important technical factors. But this means fundamentally that it is dependent on the peculiarities of modern science, especially the natural sciences based on mathematics and exact and rational experiment."[6] The result of the "rational" organization of social life was the consolidation of a universal, technically trained structure of officialdom, that would become the "absolutely inescapable condition of our entire existence."[7] The complete triumph of bureaucratic "rationality" would spell the end of self-government.[8]

Leo Strauss engaged the presuppositions of social science in his masterful analysis of Max Weber in *Natural Right and History*. In the process of examining

Weber's assertions, Strauss found that social science, far from providing any genuine guidance concerning political or social problems, could not even recognize the most profound human problems of our time. Furthermore, he showed that the Weberian "rationality" of the social sciences was in fact a repudiation of reason. In opposition to the implicit value-free nihilism of social science, Strauss did not hesitate to confront the gravest disorder of modern government. He supplied the most cogent analysis of tyranny in our time.

It has become clear as a result of Strauss's evaluation of tyranny, that modern administration must be understood in terms of its relationship to the political philosophy of the state.[9] The post-Rousseauian "idea of the state" presupposes the end of politics as well as the end of history, because man has solved the fundamental theoretical problems.[10] The state, which is understood to be the ethical organizational expression of the people's will, must be viewed as necessarily beneficent. It is the rational administration of progressive principles. Consequently, its power can not be limited. As Hegel noted, "The national spirit is the substance; what is rational must happen. . . . The contractual form of constitutional development is not in fact the rational, but merely a form of property. But the rational must always find a way, for it possesses truth, and we must cease to fear that bad constitutions might be made."[11]

In the wake of the acceptance of the idea of the state, and with it the triumph of rationality, the problem of tyranny almost disappeared from the vocabulary of political science. For Hegel and his successors, History, or progress, always moved in the right direction. Consequently, the traditional understanding of politics becomes problematic. The analysis of politics in terms of the age-old categories of regimes, (i.e., good and bad, or just and tyrannical) becomes almost meaningless. Rather, regimes must be understood to be either rationally progressive or politically reactionary. From a theoretical point of view, the fully developed rational state could not be tyrannical. Nonetheless, in the twentieth century, the political practice of the rational state proved to Strauss that tyranny was not a thing of the past.

Strauss was certain that modern despotism must be understood in light of the modern science of politics, or the theory of the state itself. He was fully aware that, although tyranny was not a thing of the past, modern political science could not provide a satisfactory analysis of it. It is within the rational state that the corruption of modern political thought has been shown in the practice of its politics. The political practice of the rational state tended inexorably in the direction of what Tocqueville called a centralized administration.[12] On the basis of Strauss's analysis, it becomes clear that the centralized administrative state, which in principle leads to the universal and homogeneous state, also leads to the subsequent loss of man's humanity.

Leo Strauss, unlike Weber, became a defender of the theory and practice of moderate or constitutional government. His defense of constitutionalism and limited government was a defense of reason rooted in nature. It presupposed rational expectations regarding the ends of politics and prudential judgment concerning the means. Moreover, Strauss supplied the philosophic critique which made it possible to recover an understanding of the theoretical roots of rational or prudential politics, which had been undermined by the victory of historicism. He knew better than most that the immoderate political practice of the twentieth century was a consequence of the utopian character of its political thought. In providing a defense of constitutionalism, and in laying bare the tyranny of the universal homogeneous state, Strauss provided the foundations for an analysis of modern life which could bring to light the deepest problems of bureaucracy.

BUREAUCRACY AND SOCIAL SCIENCE

Modern bureaucracy, which is dependent upon the methodology of the social sciences, was to be the rational administration of the affairs of society progressively discovered or invented by science and social science. Strauss criticized social science on two grounds: It had rejected reason as a means of understanding reality, and it was unable to evaluate politics in any meaningful way. In short, it could not evaluate the most flagrant abuse of power. It could not recognize tyranny. Modern philosophy had rejected nature in exchange for a philosophy of history which purported to have discovered rationality in the historical process.[13] That discovery culminated in the idea of the state.

There is an obvious connection between Hegel's "views and those of the greatest twentieth-century student of bureaucracy, Max Weber." The structure of bureaucracy advanced by Hegel "was almost identical with the Weberian ideal type."[14] Although Weber accepted the Hegelian framework of the state and bureaucracy, he rejected the rational character of history. In the process, he further undermined whatever pre-scientific rationality still existed in the social sciences which accompanied the modern state. Strauss suggests that Weber had "parted company with the historical school, not because it had rejected natural norms, i.e., norms that are both universal and objective, but because it had tried to establish standards that were particular and historical indeed, but still objective. Weber objected to the historical school . . . because it had preserved natural right in a historical guise, instead of rejecting it altogether." Furthermore, he rejected the assumption "that the history of mankind is a meaningful process or a process ruled by intelligible necessity."[15] In short, Strauss noted, Weber had rejected "both assumptions as metaphysical, i.e., as based on the dogmatic premise that reality is rational." For Weber,

the real is always individual. . . . To try to explain historical or unique phenomena by tracing them to general laws or to unique wholes means to assume gratuitously that there are mysterious or unanalyzable forces which move the historical actors. There is no "meaning" of history apart from the subjective meaning or the intentions which animate the historical actors. But these intentions are of such limited power that the actual outcome is in most cases wholly unintended. Yet the actual outcome—historical fate—which is not planned by God or man, molds not only our way of life but our very thoughts, and especially does it determine our ideals.[16]

Strauss suggests that Weber's primary motive in opposition to historicism was "devotion to the idea of empirical science." The idea of science led him to the realization that only science is independent of historical fate. Weber insisted upon the "notion of a 'value-free' or ethically neutral social science, which is "justified by what he regarded as the most fundamental of all opposition, namely, the opposition of the Is and the Ought, or the opposition of reality and norm or value." However, Strauss implies that:

> the true reason why Weber insisted on the ethically neutral character of social science as well as social philosophy was, then, not his belief in the fundamental opposition of the Is and the Ought but his belief that there cannot be any genuine knowledge of the Ought. He denied to man any science, empirical or rational, any knowledge, scientific or philosophic, of the true value system: the true value system does not exist; there is a variety of values which are of the same rank, whose demands conflict with one another, and whose conflict cannot be solved by human reason. Social science or social philosophy can do no more than clarify that conflict and all its implications; the solution has to be left to the free, non-rational decision of each individual.[17]

Moreover, Weber rejected the view that social science must be based on an understanding of "social reality as it is experienced in social life or known to 'common sense.'" Strauss suggests that for Weber, common sense, "is a hybrid, begotten by the absolutely subjective world of the individual's sensations and the truly objective world progressively discovered by science." Therefore, as Strauss noted, "not modern philosophy but modern natural science came to be regarded as the perfection of man's natural understanding of the natural world."[18]

For Strauss, by the end of the nineteenth century, it had become apparent that a distinction "must be made between what was then called the 'scientific' understanding (or 'the world of science') and the 'natural' understanding (or 'the world in which we live')."[19] He noted:

> It became apparent that the scientific understanding of the world emerges by way of a radical modification, as distinguished from a perfection, of the natural understanding. Since the natural understanding is the presupposition of the scientific understanding, the analysis of science and of the world of science presupposes the analysis of the natural understanding, the natural world, or the world of common sense. The natural world, the world in which we live and act, is not the object or the product of a theoretical attitude; it is a world not of mere objects at which we detachedly look but of "thing" or "affairs" which we handle.[20]

It is not surprising, therefore, that in Weber's view, science must administer progress. Nor is it surprising, as Strauss suggests, that "as long as we identify the natural or prescientific world with the world in which we live, we are dealing with an abstraction. The world in which we live is already a product of science, or at any rate it is profoundly affected by the existence of science."[21]

Weber was of the opinion, Strauss observed, that "scientific understanding consists in a peculiar transformation of reality. It is therefore impossible to clarify the meaning of science without a previous analysis of reality as it is in itself, i.e. prior to its transformation by science." The character of reality so transformed by science demanded, "that interpretive understanding be subservient to causal explanation." What is the character of reality prior to its transformation by science? In Strauss's understanding of Weber, "reality is an infinite and meaningless sequence, or a chaos, of unique and infinitely divisible events, which in themselves are meaningless: all meaning, all articulation, originates in the activity of the knowing or evaluating subject." Only the observing scientist can understand the meaning of the event that is observed. Consequently, Weber "did not even attempt a coherent analysis of the social world as it is know to 'common sense,' or of social reality as it is known in social life or in action."[22]

In Strauss's view, it is necessary once again to grasp the natural world, "as a world that is radically prescientific or prephilosophic." In order to do so, it is not necessary or sufficient "to engage in extensive and necessarily hypothetical anthropological studies." Rather, the use of "information that classical philosophy supplies about its origins suffices, especially if that information is supplemented by consideration of the most elementary premises of the Bible." In other words, not scientific "rationality," embodied in the idea of the state, but reason, and its relationship to revelation, would enable us to "understand the origin of the idea of natural right."[23]

SCIENTIFIC ADMINISTRATION: ECLIPSING PRUDENCE

The reasonable, or common sense, understanding of politics, culminated in constitutionalism. In a constitutional regime, public administration is dependent upon the determination of the proper relationship of practice and theory, or means and ends. The primary political virtue is prudence. Administration is subordinate to politics. On the other hand, bureaucratic administration, built upon the foundations of modern political thought, sought to appropriate the empirical methodology which had ensured the success of the physical sciences. Rational administration required an ongoing structure of scientific expertise to mediate progress. The bureaucracy is meant to replace politics.

The victory of modern science, and its autonomy, seemed to demand, in human affairs as well, the abandonment of the distinction between theoretical and practical science.[24] In political thought, as well, rationality had achieved a unity of theory and practice through the concept of will. By the end of the nineteenth century, the triumph of will had crystallized into the Hegelian "idea of the State" which sought to subordinate any natural standard of political right to the rationality of will. As Hegel noted, "Whether the state coheres on the basis of nature or of the freedom of the will is what forms the dividing line between constitutions. Every concept begins in immediacy, in nature, and strives toward rationality. Everything depends of the extent to which rationality has replaced nature."[25]

The technical rationality of the modern state had undermined nature and reason, and established a unity of theory and practice through the method of science. In his attempt to comprehend the foundations of modern thought, Strauss was forced to re-examine the basis of the distinction between theory and practice. In doing so, he was forced to reconsider the relationship of philosophy and politics. The politicization of modern philosophy had undermined the autonomy of philosophy, which had been understood as the quest for knowledge of the eternal, or the whole. It had abandoned the distinction between the "conditions of understanding and its sources, between the conditions for the existence and the pursuit of philosophy (specific kinds of societies, etc.) on the one hand, and the sources of philosophical knowledge on the other."[26] The result was the corruption of philosophy and politics, theory and practice. Moreover, modern philosophy, when politicized, had not brought about the best regime in practice. Strauss showed that it had become more difficult to achieve moderate political practice precisely because political theory had abandoned reason, at the point in which practice (or History) provided the ground for theory (i.e., had became rational).

> We have noted before that what appeared later on as the discovery of History was originally rather the recovery of the distinction between theory and practice. . . . The recovery of the distinction between theory and practice was from the outset modified by skepticism in regard to theoretical metaphysics, a skepticism which culminated in the depreciation of theory in favor of practice. In accordance with these antecedents, the highest form of practice—the foundation or formation of a political society—was viewed as a quasi-natural process not controlled by reflection; thus it could become a purely theoretical theme. Political theory became understanding of what practice has produced or of the actual and ceased to be the quest for what ought to be; political theory ceased to be 'theoretically practical' (i.e., deliberative at a second remove) and became purely theoretical in the way in which metaphysics (and physics) were traditionally understood to be purely theoretical. There came into being a new type of theory, of metaphysics, having as its highest theme human action and its product rather than the whole, which is in no way the object of human action. With the whole and the metaphysics that is oriented upon it, human action occupies a high but subordinate place. When metaphysics came, as it now did, to regard human action and its product as the end toward which all other beings or processes are directed, metaphysics became philosophy of history. Philosophy of history was primarily theory, i.e., contemplation, of human practice; it presup-

posed that significant human action, History, was completed. By becoming the highest theme of philosophy, practice ceased to be practice proper, i.e., concern with *agenda*. The revolts against Hegelianism on the part of Kierkegaard and Nietzsche, in so far as they now exercise a strong influence on public opinion, thus appear as attempts to recover the possibility of practice, i.e., of a human life which has a significant and undetermined future. But these attempts increased the confusion, since they destroyed, as far as in them lay, the very possibility of theory. 'Doctrinairism and existentialism' appear to us as the two faulty extremes. While being opposed to each other, they agree with each other in the decisive respect—they agree in ignoring prudence, 'the god of this lower world.' Prudence and 'this lower world' cannot be seen properly without some knowledge of 'the higher world'—without genuine *theoria*.[27]

As a result, the understanding of politics could no longer be derived from practical observation of the conduct of political life itself. Modern political science had become wholly theoretical but completely detached from the old metaphysics. Its authority was now derivative from the method of science. It had separated itself from philosophy and attained legitimacy through its neutrality as regards ethics. In returning to Aristotelian political science, Strauss pointed the way back to a theoretical defense of prudential politics.[28] Strauss was aware that "prudence is always endangered by false doctrines about the whole of which man is a part; prudence is therefore always in need of defense against such opinions, and that defense is necessarily theoretical." However, he knew that such a theory cannot be "taken to be the basis of prudence." Nonetheless, it was "the fact that the sphere of prudence is, as it were, only de jure but not de facto wholly independent of theoretical science," which makes understandable "the view underlying the new political science according to which no awareness inherent in practice, and in general no natural awareness, is genuine knowledge, or in other words only 'scientific' knowledge is genuine knowledge.' This view implies that there cannot be practical sciences proper, or that the distinction between practical and theoretical sciences must be replaced by the distinction between theoretical and applied sciences—applied sciences being sciences based on the theoretical sciences that precede the applied sciences in time and in order."[29] In Strauss's view, it was necessary to reaffirm the dignity of the political by returning to a natural, or prescientific, understanding of the political. In doing so, prudence could once again be seen for what it is.

CONSTITUTIONAL ADMINISTRATION

The most natural and reasonable political order is that founded upon a political theory of constitutionalism or limited government. The American Constitution created such a regime, based on modern principles of political thought. Strauss noted that "it would not be difficult to show that . . . liberal or constitutional democracy comes closer to what the classics demanded than any alternative that is viable in our age."[30] As Strauss noted, "According to the classics, the best constitution is a contrivance of reason, i.e., of conscious activity or of planning on the part of an individual or a few individuals. It is in accordance with nature, or it is a natural order, since it fulfills to the highest degree the requirements of the perfection of human nature, or since its structure imitates the pattern of nature."[31]

Strauss was aware that the political moderation of constitutional democracy was a consequence of a philosophy of government which was grounded in natural reason and the laws of nature. He contrasted the theoretical basis of constitutional government—a product of reason and nature—with that of the modern idea of the state, which is a product of history or the denial of nature. He became an ardent foe of the philosophy of history. Moreover, he questioned the legitimacy of the rational state. Philosophy of history had distorted the relationship between theory and practice: practice had provided the basis for theory, and theory subsequently distorted the understanding of practice. There could be no principled or autonomous ground in reason or nature from which to make prudential judgments regarding politics. As a result, the practice of politics could not be moderated by any standard whatsoever.

In its American origins, administration was understood to be subordinate to a political theory of liberal constitutionalism. A limited government, which distinguished the public and private sphere as well as the state and society, also maintained a distribution of power between the national and state governments. The practice of government was defined by its theory; the means were subordinate to the ends of republican government.[32] Consequently, administration was thought to be a function of prudence, not, as it came to be in the post-progressive era, an objective or general science, a product of the instrumental rationality of the modern state. But, prudence as a political virtue required the capacity to take into account actual circumstances in light of an end. In political life, as Madison insisted, the end is justice, or the best regime possible, in light of the conditions available. Political practice, in which prudence is the fundamental virtue, must be subordinate to, and informed by, a theory of republicanism.

The American founders understood political practice from the vantage point of reason or theory. Consequently, the practice of government was thought to be a reflection of its end or form. Liberal regimes had circumscribed the powers of government because the ends of politics were limited to the protection of the natural rights of man. That limitation was predicated upon recognition of the fact that the realm of the political did not encompass the whole range of human existence, as the previous religious regimes had claimed. The political triumph of Christianity, which universalized and politicized religious virtues, had tended to undermine the distinction between reason and revelation, and theory and practice. Religious rule had become more concerned with the earthly rather than the heavenly domain. It had resulted in the tyrannical rule of the Church and the priests. Religious rule was so comprehensive in terms of its claims on how men should live that it had become impossible to pursue moderate, or prudential, political practice. The rational solution required the separation of church and state, which necessitated a distinction between state and society, or the public and private sphere. An autonomous civil society in which individuals are free to exercise their natural rights made it imperative that the power of government be limited, for the same reason as that of religion. By limiting the purposes of government and creating a free society, it opened up the possibility that the ends of human life—understood through reason and not political or religious authority—could be freely pursued in civil society. It was only through limitation of the authority of the political that it would become possible to create the conditions necessary for the freedom of the mind in civil society. Only the separation of politics and religion could preserve the conditions necessary for the defense of both reason and revelation.[33]

In the American regime, the standard of right, understood by reason, was to be found in nature, or the laws of nature. The rational, or natural, standard dictated the principles of republicanism or self-government, which became the principles of constitutionalism. Constitutions create a structure for rational governance, but the practice of government requires prudence, the ability to relate means and ends. Decent practice in conformity with the republican theory would lead to good government. Thus, neither Adams nor Hamilton would deny that good administration is necessary for good government. Nonetheless, they were certain that good government is dependent upon the right form or theory of government. That theory is the product of a rational insight into the nature of man and of politics. Without a good form of government, there could be no good administration. They could not, therefore, acquiesce in the poet's political heresy, because they would not subordinate theory to practice, nor universalize practice by making it theoretical.[34] The attack on constitutionalism, by progressive intellectuals at the end of the nineteenth century, was animated by a theory of government radically at odds with the view of the American founders. It was rooted in the theoretical assumptions of the rational state, which had jettisoned the principle of republican government, and with it prudential administration as well.[35]

The political thought which laid the foundations of the modern state—and legitimized its political practice—is predicated on the denial of a natural standard of political right.[36] The standard in nature could not remain the justification for political right, once the human mind had made the discovery of the rationality of history. Thus, Hegel insisted that "the science of the state, is to be nothing other than the endeavor to apprehend and portray the state as something inherently rational."[37] The progressives in America accepted the Hegelian assumption that "the general dividing line between constitutions is between those that are based on nature and those based on freedom of the will."[38] Consequently, there can be no higher authority than the will of the sovereign people. The state, which embodies that will, claims to provide a resolution to the dilemma upon which constitutionalism is based. It claims to resolve the tension, once thought to be natural, between the public and the private sphere, the general and particular will, and the state and society.

In short, it claims to have solved the problem presented by modern liberalism, which Rousseau exposed, but left unresolved. That problem required nothing less than the necessity of turning individuals, or bourgeoisie, into citizens, or communal beings. In other words, the modern state was meant to replace constitutionalism, or limited government.[39]

The state, and modern social science, purports to have the capacity to institutionalize rationality in the service of will, through utilization of a universal class, the bureaucracy. Paradoxically, this rationality is to be achieved through the efforts of that class of persons who are devoid of a personal passion for power. Their very disinterestedness would ensure the kind of independence and objectivity necessary to carry out the will of the people. This universal class, the bureaucracy, "is the crucial link between the particularism of civil society and the universality of the state." As Hegel noted:

> the universal class has for its task the universal interests of the community. It must therefore be relieved from direct labor to supply its needs, either by having private means or be receiving an allowance from the state which claims its industry, with the result that private interest finds its satisfaction in the work for the universal.[40]

This class of civil servants, Sholomo Avineri noted, "is at the apex of the social pyramid." He has indicated the reason for the supremacy of a bureaucratic elite: "It is the only class of society, whose objective is *knowledge* itself, not nature, artefact or abstraction, as is the case with all other classes."[41] Lorenz Stein, an early Hegelian theorist of public administration who greatly influenced American progressives like Woodrow Wilson, pointed to the characteristics of this class of bureaucrats which overcome self-interest. He suggests that they "have the capacity to care deeply for the welfare of the whole and to subordinate to it any special interest. These men are therefore predestined to state service, to service on behalf of the idea of the state."[42] The American founders held no such view of public administration or the state.[43] The expectation that a class of citizens could devote itself exclusively to the public interest, or disinterested knowledge, would have been considered wholly utopian. Moreover, the title to rule, in a constitutional government, is not knowledge, but the consent of the governed. Public administrators, like other men, would be capable of reason, but, they would not be immune to the passions engendered by self-interest. Consequently, no class of men could be expected to be "predestined to state service." Nor could public administration be put into the service of "the idea of the State." Rather, administration must be subordinate to the principles of republican government, and the laws of reasonable majorities. The best that could be hoped for is prudent administration of reasonable laws, which derived their authority from the consent of the governed.[44]

The American founding was based on the attempt to solve the political-theological problem in a way that preserved the proper ground of both. The politicization of religion, in Europe, had undermined the truth of religion and destroyed the possibility of rational politics. Moreover, by grounding reason in the laws of nature and nature's god, the American founders resisted the trend which became irresistible in modern thought, the attempted "modification of the traditional belief in Providence." That modification, says Strauss, "is usually described as 'secularization.' 'Secularization' is the 'temporalization' of the spiritual or of the eternal. It is the attempt to integrate the eternal into a temporal context. It therefore presupposes that the eternal is no longer understood as eternal."[45] The American founders rejected the movement toward, what Strauss called, "the secularization of providence."[46] Consequently, in their view, the grounds of the distinction between good and evil could not be obliterated. Man must take his bearing by the laws of God and nature, which simply forbid man to do evil. Limited government is an indication that the human predicament is unchanging: evil cannot be eradicated. God, nature, and the eternal, cannot be transformed into History, being, or becoming.

In grounding political thought in nature and reason, the principles of politics are meant to be moral truths, and are understood to be permanent. Thus, progress is not possible in the moral realm. This view was still well expressed by Calvin Coolidge on the one hundred fiftieth anniversary of the Declaration of Independence. He noted, "If all men are created equal, that is final. If they are endowed with inalienable rights, that is final. If governments derive their just powers from the consent of the governed, that is final. No advance, no progress can be made beyond these propositions. If anyone wishes to deny their truth or their soundness, the only direction in which he can proceed historically is not forward, but backward toward the time when there was no equality, no rights of the individual, no rule of the people. Those who wish to proceed in that direction can not lay claim to progress. They are reactionary."[47]

The American founders thought reason was the means by which the "self-evident truths" were made intelligible. Nature gave man, as individuals, that capacity, which in turn informed them of their natural rights as human beings. The role of government was the protection of those natural rights of individual moral beings. Consequently, they understood politics, and practice, from the point of view of its ends, understood by reason, and its means determined by prudence, or in terms of justice and the common good. A common good was thought to be ascertainable because of a common denominator, which is the natural capacity of man to reason. Reason must be understood in light of the permanent truth of human nature, not the rationality of history. If the state could not become rational, will would not replace reason, nor administration replace politics. Nonetheless, the triumph of historicism, and with it the idea of the state and progressivism, led to the development of a science of politics and society. It is not surprising, therefore, that modern social and political science lost sight of the common good, and tyranny as well.

396 *John A. Marini*

MODERN TYRANNY

In Strauss's view, modern philosophy had corrupted the theory and practice of politics, destroying the possibility of moderate and prudent government. Moreover, the social science which accompanied the modern state showed itself to be incapable of making sound—or reasonable—judgements about politics. It could not even identify politics at its worst: tyranny.[48] Most importantly, the modern state and its science, although incapable of recognizing tyranny, opened up the prospect of the greatest tyranny of all. "We are now brought face to face with a tyranny which holds out the threat of becoming, thanks to 'the conquest of nature'and in particular human nature, what no earlier tyranny ever became: perpetual and universal."[49]

In his debate with Kojeve, Strauss noted that Kojeve's position depended upon the truth of the supposition that the universal and homogeneous state is the best social order. This universal homogeneous state presupposed the conquest of nature, as well as the end of work and fighting. In other words, the modern administrative state was predicated on the assumption that History had come to an end. Strauss denied the assertion that the end state could be the best social order. "The simply best social order," as Kojeve conceived of it, "is the state in which every human being finds his full satisfaction." A human being is satisfied, "if his human dignity is universally recognized and if he enjoys 'equality of opportunity,' i.e., the opportunity, corresponding to his capacities, of deserving well of the state or of the whole."[50]

However, Strauss wondered if humans could be satisfied in such circumstances. He noted that "this end of History would be most exhilarating but for the fact that, according to Kojeve, it is the participation in bloody political struggles as well as in real work or, generally expressed, the negating action, which raises man above the brutes. The state through which man is said to become reasonably satisfied, is, then, the state in which the basis of man's humanity withers away, or in which man loses his humanity."[51] Kojeve in effect confirms Strauss's doubt in a letter to Strauss where he described the character of this satisfaction in the end state. He notes, "the universal and homogeneous state is "good" only because it is the *last* (because neither war nor revolution are conceivable in it:—mere 'dissatisfaction' is not enough, it also takes weapons!). Besides, 'not human' can mean 'animal' (or better—automaton) as well as 'God.' In the final state there naturally are no more 'human beings' in our sense of an *historical* human being. The 'healthy' automata are 'satisfied' (sports, art, eroticism, etc.), and the 'sick' ones get locked up. As for those who are not satisfied with their 'purposeless activity' (art, etc.), they are the philosophers (who can attain wisdom if the 'contemplate' enough). By doing so they become 'gods.' The tyrant becomes an administrator, a cog in the 'machine' fashioned by automata for automata" (Kojeve's emphasis).[52] However, Strauss was confident that Kojeve had overestimated the tameness of man and from that he took hope. Strauss suggests, "there will always be men (andres) who will revolt against a state which is destructive of humanity or in which there is no longer a possibility of noble action and of great deeds."[53] In his view, nature and politics cannot be easily expunged from the earth.

The great thinkers of the nineteenth century, Strauss showed, had rejected nature as a standard. They had all, in one form or another, embraced the idea of History. In pointing specifically to the failures of Marx and Nietzsche, Strauss noted the importance of prudence and moderation in political life.

> But perhaps one can say that their grandiose failures make it easier for us who have experienced those failures to understand again the old saying that wisdom cannot be separated from moderation and hence to understand that wisdom requires unhesitating loyalty to a decent constitution and even to the cause of constitutionalism. Moderation will protect us against the twin dangers of visionary expectations from politics and unmanly contempt for politics.[54]

In the twentieth century, the rational administrative structures, which have become dominant in the modern state, are the product of "visionary expectations from politics." At the same time, they reflect in their neutral bureaucracies, an "unmanly contempt for politics," which is an indulgence that accompanies the belief that partisanship has ended, and rational rule has begun.

Constitutional government does not induce visionary expectations from government, nor is it contemptuous of politics. In its origins, constitutional or limited government is moderated by a rootedness in nature, which requires a reasonable and realistic understanding of the relationship of theory and practice, of ends and means. Consequently, prudence, not science, is the virtue which is paramount in terms of understanding political practice. But prudence is necessarily concerned with means. It presupposes the possibility of moral virtue, to direct men to the right—or good—ends. In America, the ends of republican government are good because they are in accordance with nature and reason. As a result, prudent administration becomes possible because of its relationship to those ends. It is the proper means to attain them. Without the ends, there can be no prudent administration.

CONCLUSION

Strauss's defense of constitutionalism struck a responsive chord in his students who devoted their careers to the study of public administration. However, most of those students, including Herbert Storing and John Rohr, seemed oblivious to Strauss's teaching concerning the state, and its relationship to tyranny. In attempting to legitimize the politics of the administrative state, they hoped to reconcile the practice of the modern state with the political philosophy which justified constitutionalism. But the practice of the modern state is dependent upon a theory which denies the truth of the natural necessities which require limited government. Rather, it presupposes a progressive solution to every human problem, in which case the power of government cannot be limited. Furthermore, the end of history and the coming into being of a rational society, rests on a denial of the fact that tyranny is a problem coeval with political life. But, Strauss showed that the modern state had not eliminated tyranny. Rather, his analysis of modern thought exposed the kind of tyranny that was inherent in the "idea of the State." He did so by making it possible to reestablish the theoretical ground of reason and nature as the standard for making that judgement. Thus, it became possible to understand the foundations of constitutionalism, and its dependence upon a reasonable understanding of man's nature, which Strauss distinguished from a philosophy of history that depends, ultimately, upon will and the progress of science.

Public administration in a limited government cannot be the same as that which is required in the "rational" state. Constitutional administration rests upon prudent administration in the service of reasonable principles of government. On the other hand, the form and structure of bureaucracy takes it shape from the idea of the state. The fully mature bureaucratic administration becomes completely dependent upon the expertise of the social sciences. Because it rests upon an "objective science," bureaucratic administration is contemptuous of politics, and self-government as well. It is predicated upon the assumption that the people must abandon their reason in order to allow the "rational" bureaucracy to fulfill their will.[55] In the modern state, Strauss noted, "the true public reason is the new political science, which judges in a universally valid, or objective, manner of what is to the interest of each, for it shows to everyone what means he must choose in order to attain his attainable ends, whatever those ends may be."[56]

Thus, the political theory of constitutionalism could not acquiesce in the heresy that "rational," or good, administration can replace the need for prudence in politics. This is so because man has not become fully wise concerning politics. Science cannot replace the necessity of justice. Hence, neither the most efficient nor enlightened bureaucracy could legitimately relieve the people of the responsibility of governing themselves. In a constitutional republic, unlike the theological regimes that preceded it, the title to rule is not divine knowledge. Nor can it be the rational, or scientific, knowledge implicit in the idea of the modern state. Indeed, such a rational bureaucracy would "create a will in society independent of the majority." It was precisely that which Madison rejected as "the method which prevails in all governments possessing an hereditary or self-appointed authority." Indeed, a "power independent of society," says Madison, could in fact become the height of injustice, because "it can be turned against the majority, the minority, or both."[57]

Political rule requires the necessity of consent, and just government requires that the only form of government compatible with consent is rule by majority. However, although majority rule is a practical necessity, the people's will is not sovereign. Thus, majority rule is not the same as Rousseau's general will. In Rousseau's thought, and those thinkers who embraced him, the general will replaced the transcendent natural law as a standard of political right. It provided the means of reconciling law and morality, the is and the ought. Thus the general will established the foundation for the absolute sovereignty of the people. The sovereign cannot err, because it is what it ought to be. As Strauss noted:

> Rousseau's concept of the general will which as such cannot err—which by merely being is what it ought to be—showed how the gulf between the is and the ought can be overcome. Strictly speaking, Rousseau showed this only under the condition that his doctrine of the general will, his political doctrine proper, is linked with his doctrine of the historical process, and this linking was the work of Rousseau's great successors, Kant and Hegel, rather than of Rousseau himself. According to this view, the rational or just society, the society characterized by the existence of a general will known to be the general will, i.e., the ideal, is necessarily actualized by the historical process without men's intending to actualize it. Why can the general will not err? Why is the general will necessarily good? The answer is: it is good because it is rational, and it is rational because it is general; it emerges through the generalization of the particular will, of the will which as such is not good.[58]

In the political philosophy which underlies the concept of the modern state, the general will is the source of right, which provides the ground of its legitimacy. On the other hand, in constitutional—or liberal—thought, majority will must be subordinate to reason and the laws of nature. Even though the will of the majority provides the basis for the legitimate use of power, it is not the source of right. It is for this reason that Thomas Jefferson would remind the people in his First Inaugural Address, that "though the will of the majority is in all cases to prevail, that will to be rightful must be reasonable."[59] The majority cannot give up its reason in the service of its will. Even the people themselves, although sovereign, said Jefferson, "are inherently independent of all but moral law."[60]

From its inception, the idea of the state presupposed the end of politics, and with it, the end of traditional morality, and, indeed, an end of constitutionalism. If however, history cannot replace nature, politics cannot be replaced by administration or technical expertise, however "rational" or efficient it may be. In a reasonable constitutional order, politics and administration must be understood in light of the moral basis of self-government. Thus, Hamilton could not "acquiesce in the political heresy of the poet," Alexander Pope, because he knew that the end, or the form, of government would determine the character of its administration. The best, or most prudential, administration would be possible only in the service of the principles of republican government. A good administration requires prudence, a political virtue, not efficiency, which becomes the hallmark of practice in the administrative state only because it is compatible with the technical rationality and neutrality of science. Nonetheless, on the grounds of practical necessity, or prudence, Hamilton, too, could "safely pronounce, that the true test of a good government is its aptitude and tendency to produce a good administration."

NOTES

The author thanks the Earhart Foundation for generous support of this project.

1. Hegel, G.F.W., 1942. *Philosophy of Right*, T. M. Knox, trans., London: Oxford University Press, p. 285.

2. See for example, Storing, Herbert J., 1980. "American Statesmanship: Old and New," in Robert A. Goldwin (ed.), *Bureaucrats, Policy Analysts, Statesmen: Who Leads?* Washington, D.C.: American Enterprise Institute, pp. 88–113; and Rohr, John A., 1986. *To Run a Constitution: The Legitimacy of the Administrative State*, Lawrence: University of Kansas Press.

3. The idea of the modern state follows in the wake of Kant's critique of reason. In Kant, practical or moral reason replaced theoretical or metaphysical reason, based on the assumption that moral law originates in human will. After Kant, practical reason is understood to be instrumental, or technical, reason. Technical rationality is a product of the theoretical unity of the state which is dependent upon recognition of the rationality of History. The rational state is committed to the progress of the natural and social sciences to subdue nature and rationalize society. The authority of natural reason and tradition was systematically undercut by the acceptance of the methodology and legitimacy of the sciences.

4. In Hegel, and especially Weber, instrumental rationality would replace prudence as the mechanism to mediate the relations between means and ends. Rationality, for human beings, is to be rooted in the social sciences. Its structural form is bureaucracy, which utilizes the systematic, empirical, and technical rationality of the social sciences as the means of solving every social, economic, and political problem. Social science provides not only the mechanism of solving every human problem, it provides the only authoritative means of evaluating the status or health of society.

5. The rational state is dependent upon an enlightened class of administrators to provide the technical expertise necessary to ensure its practical success. Rational bureaucracy is a new kind of organizational structure, based on a new kind of knowledge for the solution of human problems. It purports to replace those social or human structures and associations which are rooted in nature or tradition, and must be understood on the basis of common sense, passion, theoretical—or natural—reason.

6. See Marcuse, Herbert, 1968. "Industrialization and Capitalism in the Work of Max Weber," in *Negations*, Boston: Beacon Press. 1968.

7. Weber's Foreword to Vol. I, *Gesammelte Aufsatze zur Religionssoziologie*, cited in Marcuse, *op.cit.*, p. 204.

8. The administrative state becomes dependent upon a rational bureaucracy—or a social science—as the structural means of mediating practice. It provides the technical—or instrumental—rationality necessary to administer change or progress. In the rational state, the distinction between theory and practice ceases to have meaning. Practice, or action, provides the basis for theory, and politics becomes administration. The role of prudence as a political virtue ceases to have meaning. The triumph of administration, or the end of politics, is a consequence of the recognition of the end of philosophy, or the discovery of the rational character of History.

9. Strauss suggests that "modern philosophy, which is the secularized form of Christianity, created the idea of the universal and homogeneous state . . . the progress of philosophy and its eventual transmutation into wisdom requires the 'active negation' of the previous political states, i.e., requires the action of the tyrant: only when 'all possible active

[political] negations' have been effected and thus the final stage of the political development has been reached, can and will the quest for wisdom give way to wisdom." *On Tyranny*, Revised and Expanded Edition,Victor Gourevitch, Michael S. Roth, eds. New York:The Free Press,1991, p. 207.

10.The acceptance of the idea of the rational state has had profound consequences. Strauss noted that through the concept of the State, Hegel had solved the political-theological problem. "Hegel had reconciled 'the discovery of History'—the alleged insight into the individual's being in the most radical sense, the son or stepson of his time, or the alleged insight into the dependence of man's highest and purest thoughts on his time—with philosophy in the original meaning of the term by asserting that Hegel's time was the absolute moment, the end of meaningful time: the absolute religion, Christianity, had become completely reconciled with the world; it had become completely secularized or the *saeculum* had become completely Christian in and through the postrevolutionary State; history as meaningful change had come to its end; all theoretical and practical problems had in principle been solved; hence, the historical process was demonstrably rational." *The Rebirth of Classical Political Rationalism* (pp. 24–25).

11. Hegel, G.F.W., *Lectures on Natural Right and Political Science* (Heidelberg Lectures, 1817–1819).J. Michael Stewart, Peter C. Hodgson, trans., Berkeley: University of California Press,1996, p. 242.

12. See Marini, John. 1991. "Centralized Administration and the New Despotism," *Interpreting Tocqueville's Democracy in America*, Ken Masugi, ed., Savage, Md.: Rowman & Littlefield Publishers.

13. Strauss suggests that "historicism, . . . stands or falls by the denial of the possibility of theoretical metaphysics and of philosophic ethics or natural right." *Natural Right and History*, Chicago, University of Chicago Press, 1953, p. 29.

14. Both quotes from Werner J. Dannhauser, "Reflections on Statesmanship and Bureaucracy," in *Bureaucrats, Policy Analysts, Statesmen: Who Leads?* Robert A. Goldwin, ed., Washington, D.C.:American Enterprise Institute, 1980, p. 123.

15. *Natural Right and History*, p. 37.

16.The Strauss quotes are from *Natural Right and History*, pp. 37–38. Interestingly, the man Strauss called "the greatest social scientist of our century," would confirm only the technical, or scientific, rationality of a world which is socially constructed. It is not surprising, therefore, that in Weber's view, bureaucracy becomes a control instrument of the first order.

17. *Natural Right and History*, pp. 41–42.

18.All quotes in this paragraph are from *Natural Right and History*, pp. 78–79.

19. *Natural Right and History*, p. 79.

20. *Natural Right and History*, p. 79.

21. *Natural Right and History*, p. 79.

22.All quotes in this paragraph are from *Natural Right and History*, pp. 76–77.

23.All quotes are from *Natural Right and History*, p. 80.

24.The State provides a haven for science because their goals are compatible: knowledge of "objective truth." As Hegel noted: "the state is universal in form, a form whose essential principle is thought.This explains why it was in the state that freedom of thought and science had their origin. . . . Science too, therefore, has its place on the side of the state since it has one element, its form, in common with the state, and its aim is knowledge, knowledge of objective truth and rationality in terms of thought." Hegel, *Philosophy of Right*, 1942, pp. 172–173.

25. Hegel, *Lectures on Natural Right and Political Science*, p. 242.

26. *On Tyranny*, p. 212.

27. *Natural Right and History*, pp. 320–321.

28. Strauss noted that "the Aristotelian distinction between theoretical and practical sciences implies that human action has principles of its own which are known independently of theoretical science (physics and metaphysics) and therefore that the practical sciences do not depend on the theoretical sciences or are not derivative from them. The principles of action are the natural ends toward which man is by nature inclined and of which he has by nature some awareness. This awareness is the necessary condition for his seeking and finding appropriate means for his ends, or for his becoming practically wise or prudent. Practical science, in contradistinction to practical wisdom itself, sets forth coherently the principles of action and the general rules of prudence ("proverbial wisdom"). Practical science raises questions that within practical or political experience, or at any rate of the basis of such experience reveal themselves to be the most important questions and that are not stated, let alone answered, with sufficient clarity by practical wisdom itself. The sphere governed by prudence is then in principle self-sufficient or closed." "An Epilogue," in *Essays on the Scientific Study of Politics*, Herbert J. Storing, ed., New York: Holt, Rinehart and Winston, 1962, p. 309.

29. "An Epilogue," p. 310.

30. *On Tyranny*, p. 194.

31. *Natural Right and History*, p. 314.

32. John Adams understood administration in a wholly prudential way. He noted that "[Alexander] Pope flattered tyrants too much when he said, 'For forms of government let fools contest, That which is best administered is best.' Nothing can be more fallacious than this.... Nothing is more certain from the history of nations and nature of man than that some forms of government are better fitted for being well administered than others. We ought to consider what is the end of government before we determine which is the best form.... All sober inquirers after truth, ancient and modern, pagan and Christian, have declared that the happiness of man, as well as his dignity, consists in virtue.... If this is a form of government, then, whose principle and foundation is virtue, will not every sober man acknowledge it better calculated to promote the general happiness than any other form?" "Thoughts on Government"(1776).

33. See Harry V. Jaffa, *Original Intent and the Framers of the Constitution*, Washington, D.C.: Regnery Gateway, 1994; *American Conservatism and the American Founding*, Durham: Carolina Academic Press, 1984; and *The American Founding as the Best Regime, and Other Essays in Socratic Rationalism*, forthcoming.

34. The philosophical and political necessity of limited government, or constitutionalism, can be seen in the assumption, of Madison, that "factionalism is sown into the nature of man." Consequently, limitation upon the power of government is a practical necessity because the human problems are permanent and incapable of a universal solution. The tension between reason and passion, public and private, state and society, or individual and community, cannot be overcome. Because of man's imperfection, the power, the tasks, and the ends of government must be limited.

35. Surprisingly, Herbert J. Storing has argued that "in the most crucial sense, it can be said that, for the founders, the problem of government is a matter of administration." Storing implies that the founders accepted the progressive assumption of the primacy of practice over theory, or the rationality of History. This is baffling. The triumph of administration presupposes the end of politics, or a rational solution to all human problems. It is doubtful the framers

understood politics in this way. They assumed that tyranny was a problem coeval with political life. Like factionalism, it is sown into the nature of man. It is only on the basis of the theory of the state that the problem of tyranny is no longer the major problem of government. Thus, for the founders, politics could never become simply a matter of administration.

36. The progressives looked to history, or progress, rather than nature, as the standard for political right. Indeed, they viewed the modern nation state, and progress, in almost identical terms. As Herbert Croly observed, "nationality is a political and social idea as well as the great contemporary political fact. Loyalty to the national interest implies devotion to a progressive principle." Croly, *The Promise of American Life*, New York: Macmillan, 1909, p. 211.

37. *Philosophy of Right*, p. 11.

38. *Lectures on Natural Right and Political Science*, p. 242.

39. As Hegel noted: "Mind is actual only as that which it knows itself to be, and the state, as the mind of a nation, is both the law permeating all relationships within the state and also at the same time the manners and consciousness of its citizens." *Philosophy of Right*, pp. 178–179. In his view, constitutional government, which protects property, has not evolved from the natural to the rational stage of development. Consequently, the rights of individuals or property remain paramount. "If the state is confused with civil society," Hegel observed, "and if its specific end is laid down as the security and protection of property and personal freedom, then the interest of the individuals as such becomes the ultimate end of their association, and it follows that membership of the state is something optional. But, the state's relation to the individual is quite different from this. Since the state is mind objectified, it is only as one of its members that the individual himself has objectivity, genuine individuality, and an ethical life" (*Philosophy of Right*, p.156). In progressive thought, Rousseau's dilemma is resolved, full humanity is possible only within the framework of the state.

40. *Philosophy of Right*, p. 132.

41. Avineri, *Hegel's Theory of the Modern State*, London: Cambridge University Press, 1972, p. 108.

42. Robert D. Miewald, "The Origins of Wilson's Thought," in Jack Rabin and James S. Bowman, eds., *Politics and Administration: Woodrow Wilson and American Public Administration*, New York: Marcel Dekker, 1984, p. 20.

43. In contradistinction to the political science of the founders, the scientific study of politics grows out of the idea of the state. American political science, in its origins, not only presupposed the legitimacy of the modern state, the state itself provided a justification for the science of politics. As John Burgess, one of the first and most influential of American political scientists noted, "the national popular state alone furnishes the objective reality upon which political science can rest in the construction of a truly scientific political system"; Burgess, *Political Science and Comparative Constitutional Law*, Vol. I (Boston: Ginn and Co. 1891). It is for this reason that modern political science cannot critically analyze the politics of the modern state, it unconsciously shares its fundamental principles.

44. Hamilton expressed his distrust of utopian speculation in politics in a perfectly prudential way in a letter to Lafayette in 1788. "I dread the reveries of your Philosophic politicians who appear in the moment to have great influence and who being mere speculatists may aim at more refinement than suits either with human nature or the composition of your Nation." *Papers*, vol. 5, p. 425.

45. *Natural Right and History*, p. 317. Strauss insists that secularization "presupposes a radical change of thought, a transition of thought from one plane to an entirely different plane. This radical change appears in its undisguised form in the emergence of modern philoso-

phy or science; it is not primarily a change within theology. What presents itself as the 'secularization' of theological concepts will have to be understood, in the last analysis, as an adaptation of traditional theology to the intellectual climate produced by modern philosophy or science both natural and political." *Ibid.*

46. Strauss has observed that "secularization is the 'temporalization' of the spiritual or of the eternal. . . . It therefore presupposes that the eternal is no longer understood as eternal. . . . The 'secularization' of the understanding of Providence culminates in the view that the ways of God are scrutable to sufficiently enlightened men. The theological tradition recognized the mysterious character of Providence especially by the fact that God uses or permits evil for his good ends. It asserted, therefore, that man cannot take his bearings by God's providence but only by God's law, which simply forbids man to do evil. In proportion as the providential order came to be regarded as intelligible to man, and therefore evil came to be regarded as evidently necessary or useful, the prohibition against doing evil lost its evidence. Hence various ways of action which were previously condemned as evil could now be regarded as good"(Strauss, 1953, p. 317).

47. Calvin Coolidge, "The Inspiration of the Declaration" speech at Philadelphia, Pennsylvania, July 5, 1926.

48. Strauss noted: "Tyranny is a danger coeval with political life. The analysis of tyranny is therefore as old as political science itself. The analysis of tyranny that was made by the first political scientists was so clear, so comprehensive, and so unforgettably expressed that it was remembered and understood by generations which did not have any direct experience of actual tyranny. On the other hand, when we were brought face to face with tyranny—with a kind of tyranny that surpassed the boldest imagination of the most powerful thinkers of the past—our political science failed to recognize it" (1991, pp. 22–23).

49. *On Tyranny*, p. 127.

50. *On Tyranny*, p. 207. However, as Strauss noted, "if not all human beings become wise, then it follows that for almost all human beings the end state is identical with the loss of their humanity, and they can therefore not be rationally satisfied with it"(1991, p. 238).

51. *On Tyranny*, p. 208.

52. Letter to Strauss, September 19, 1950; reproduced in *On Tyranny*, p. 255.

53. *On Tyranny*, p. 209.

54. *Liberalism Ancient and Modern*, New York: Basic Books, 1968, p. 24.

55. See, Mansfield, Harvey C., Jr. 1986. "The Constitution and Modern Social Science," *The Center Magazine*, Vol. 19. Sept/Oct.

56. "An Epilogue," op. cit. p. 324.

57. Madison's quotes are from *Federalist* #51.

58. Leo Strauss, "The Three Waves of Modernity," in *An Introduction to Political Philosophy: Ten Essays by Leo Strauss*, edited by Hilail Gildin, Detroit: Wayne State University Press, 1989, p. 91.

59. *Writings of Thomas Jefferson*, Merrill D. Peterson, ed., New York: Library of America, 1984, p. 493.

60. Jefferson to Spencer Roane, September 6, 1819, *Writings*, p. 1426.

Part Five

Reflections from Practice

25

Leo Strauss and the World of Intelligence
(By Which We Do Not Mean *Nous*)

Gary J. Schmitt and Abram N. Shulsky

𝒯he topic must appear at first as a very strange one: what possible connection could there be between the tumultuous world of spies and snooping paraphernalia, on the one hand, and the quiet life of scholarship and immersion in ancient texts, on the other? However, intelligence isn't only involved with espionage and whiz-bang gadgetry; a large part of it deals with the patient piecing together of bits of information to yield the outlines of the larger picture. When one considers that this effort, called "analysis," often focuses on such major questions as the nature and characteristic modes of action of a foreign regime, then perhaps the juxtaposition of political philosophy and intelligence may seem less far-fetched. Indeed, in his gentleness, his ability to concentrate on detail, his consequent success in looking below the surface and reading between the lines, and his seeming unworldliness, Leo Strauss may even be said to resemble, however faintly, the George Smiley of John LeCarré's novels.

The trends in political science that Strauss polemicized against in his "Epilog" to *Essays on the Scientific Study of Politics*[1] also affected the world of intelligence. In a famous book, which laid out an agenda for the development of U.S. intelligence analysis in the post–World War II era, Sherman Kent, Yale history professor and former member of the World War II–era Office of Strategic Services (the OSS, forerunner of the CIA) argued that intelligence analysis should adopt the social science method which was then being elaborated in the academy:

> Research is the only process which we of the liberal tradition are willing to admit is capable of giving us the truth, or a closer approximation to truth, than we now enjoy. . . . we insist, and have insisted for generations, that truth is to be approached, if not attained through research guided by a systematic method. In the social sciences which very largely constitute the subject matter of strategic intelligence, there is such a method. It is much like the method of physical sciences. It is not the same method but it is a method none the less.[2]

This method was meant to be a means of predicting the future, specifically, predicting the future course of action of a foreign government. It was applicable to any government; in a uncharacteristic bit of whimsy, Kent describes the application of his method to forecasting the actions of "Great Frusina," an amalgam of the names of the other permanent members of the U.N. Security Council, as if to emphasize that it didn't matter whether one was dealing with a constitutional monarchy, a chaotic republic, a mature totalitarian tyranny or a revolutionary dictatorship.

Kent's faith in the power of this method was so strong that he disparaged the more traditional types of intelligence information, i.e., the types of secret or "inside" information that could only be gathered by spies able to penetrate the foreign government's inner circle and/or steal its documents, or by interception techniques and codebreakers able to listen in on its communications and decipher them. As he correctly pointed out, a Soviet spy who had full run of American secret documents in the first half of 1950 could not have found one that laid out U.S. plans to defend South Korea from invasion by the North, for the simple reason that the decision to do so hadn't yet been taken, and, in fact, wouldn't be until the invasion had already begun. But this example also highlights the extremely high standard that Kent was attempting to set for the "social scientific" method: in principle, it was to be able to predict decisions that hadn't yet been made and about which the very participants in the policy process were uncertain; with this method, one could understand the decision-making process better than the decision-makers themselves.

This ambition depended crucially on the idea that, however disparate political systems may appear, the underlying political processes were universal (rooted in human nature, as it were, although a proper 1950s social scientist would have been the last person in the world to use the term). As a result, they could be discerned by an empirical method that observed behavior, tallied it, calculated correlations between particular actions and particular features of the context in which they occurred, and so forth.

Another nontraditional feature of Kent's program was that it explicitly downplayed the importance of the possibility of deception. An atomic physicist needn't be concerned with the possibility that the particles he studies are attempting to mislead him into thinking that they behave otherwise than they in fact do; and, generally speaking, social scientists can have the same confidence in their data (although, it has been suggested that, in the 1996 Israeli election, some voters vented their anger at the media by deliberately misrepresenting how they had voted when questioned by those conducting exit polls.) Given that he thought that intelligence analysis should deal with fundamental issues (such as a nation's capabilities and interests) rather than ephemera (what one of its leaders said yesterday), Kent believed that intelligence analysts could be equally unconcerned with the possibility of deception on the part of the governments they were studying. (How, after all, could Truman have deceived Stalin about his intentions in Korea if, prior to the invasion, he didn't know them himself?)

While Strauss never, of course, addressed the question of intelligence analysis, it is easy to guess what he might have said about Kent's proposed methodology, since it was based squarely on the developments in social science that Strauss attacked. The primary point of attack would have been that it ignored the differences among "regimes" (or types of government and society) in its search for universal truths of social science. While Strauss was interested in understanding human nature, he understood from his study of the tradition of political philosophy—from Aristotle, most of all—that, in political life, universal human nature is encountered not in its unvarnished state, but as reflected through the prism of the "regime."

Because of the importance of the regime, it would be foolish to expect to be able to deduce theories of political behavior that would be universal, i.e., that would apply to democracies and tyrannies alike. With Tocqueville, Strauss would have argued that the regime shapes human political action in so fundamental a way that the very souls appear different. For this reason, among others, social science could never hope to be "scientific" in the sense of the natural sciences, which can be confident that the phenomena it studies do not vary from place to place.

The other issue raised by Kent's methodology—the general disregard of deception—is also tied to the tendency of modern social science to submerge clear differences between various forms of rule in favor of explanations that rest on the sub-political. Although it should be obvious that some regimes are more inclined to be "open" than others, Kent's reliance on the universal aspirations of modern social science seem to have blinded him to that fact. Combined with American intelligence's great confidence in its ability to collect intelligence by technical means (space-based photographic reconnaissance satellites, ground-based listening posts, etc.), Kent's willingness to downplay the issue of deception meant that American intelligence analysts were generally reluctant throughout the Cold War to believe that they could be deceived about any critical question by the Soviet Union or other Communist states. History has shown this view to have been extremely naive.

Strauss is of course famous for his doctrine (or, rather, his discovery) of "esoteric" writing, i.e., the idea that, at least before the Enlightenment, most serious writers wrote so as to hide at least some of their thought from some of their readers. Strauss was attacked for this doctrine on various grounds. Many critics argued that it gave license for fanciful and arbitrary interpretation of texts; once one asserted that an author's true views might be the opposite of those that appear on the surface of his writings, it might seem that the sky was the limit in terms of how far from the author's apparent views one could wander. However, the deeper reason for the unpopularity of this doctrine was different; after all, Strauss was a piker compared to the very popular (at least for a while) doctrine of deconstructionism which gave readers complete carte blanche when it came to interpreting texts, and which completely lacked the rigor Strauss brought to the problem of textual interpretation.

Rather, the dissatisfaction was political in origin; the notion of esoteric writing is clearly at odds with the main political tenet of the Enlightenment, i.e., that a good polity can be built on the basis of doctrines that not only are true but are also accessible: their truth can be "self-evident" (to quote the Declaration of Independence) to the average citizen. Even those post-moderns who no longer believe that it is possible to discover any truths at all on which a free polity might be based somehow still cling to freedom of speech, which was originally defended on the grounds that the propagation of anti-republican heresies can do no harm as long as pro-republican truths are left free to refute them.

Be this as it may, Strauss's view certainly alerts one to the possibility that political life may be closely linked to deception. Indeed, it suggests that deception is the norm in political life, and the hope, to say nothing of the expectation, of establishing a politics that can dispense with it is the exception.

On both of these counts, then, studying political philosophy with Strauss proved to be a valuable counterweight to the doctrines that were then prevalent, not only in the academy, but in intelligence analysis as well. By emphasizing the distinction among regimes as the basic political fact, political philosophy prepared one for a much better understanding of the world than did the "scientific" social science which sought to understand the various regimes in terms of universal categories.

As many observers have noted, a characteristic failing of American intelligence analysis is what is called "mirror imaging," i.e., imagining that the country one is studying is fundamentally similar to one's own and hence can be understood in the same terms. As described by Eliot Cohen,

> A far more serious problem . . . centers on the possibility that if policymakers read [estimative] intelligence, it will mislead them or reinforce inappropriate prejudices. The official school of intelligence writing seems to pay very little heed to problems of deception and concealment, a serious deficiency in view of the premium placed by many regimes . . . on such activities. But more pervasive, and even more pernicious, is the phenomenon of mirror imaging by intelligence analysts. . . . It is a varied and subtle phenomenon and can afflict those who pride themselves on their hardheaded realpolitik as much as it does those who take a sunnier view of international relations.[3]

This fault shows up in many ways. Cohen cites, for example, the use of the terms "moderates" and "extremists" to describe the various participants in Iranian political life in the 1980s. While there may well have been an internal struggle going on in Iran, use of these terms was misleading. For example, the term "moderate" would imply someone who wanted better relations with the West *and* who favored a relaxation of the rules enforcing strict religious practices; however, there is no reason why, in the Iranian context, someone holding the former view should also be expected to hold the latter. (Clearly, as Americans used the term, "moderate" meant nothing more than "more like us": but this is obviously a ridiculous category to use when trying to understand a very different society.) As Cohen points out, "That bloody 'extremist' Robespierre initially opposed a warlike foreign policy, as did the no less radical Lenin."[4]

Mirror imaging also affects the judgments of intelligence analysts concerning how foreign officials think about the strategic problems they face. Cohen cites a

number of cases when assuming that foreign leaders who think about these matters in the same way as Americans proved disastrous. The problem takes an almost
comic turn in the following defense of a 1962 intelligence estimate that incorrectly
assessed that the Soviets would not put missiles in Cuba:

> In that case, as Sherman Kent often said, his estimate of what was reasonable for
> the Soviet Union to do was a lot better than Khrushchev's, and therefore he was
> correct in analyzing the situation *as it should have been seen by the Soviets*.[5]

Many reasons are cited why this particular problem should be so deeply rooted in
American intelligence analysis: the failure of our educational system to teach foreign languages; a "universalistic" outlook which believes (not entirely incorrectly)
that others aspire to an American way of life; the "melting pot" tradition, which
suggests that, despite superficial differences of language, customs, etc., people are
fundamentally alike and want the same things. While these are all plausible contributors, the influence of American social science may be an even more important
and deeper cause. The study of political philosophy and its emphasis on the key
importance of the variety of regimes is an important antidote.

   Similarly, many critics of American intelligence have noted that it tends to ignore
"open sources," in particular, what foreign leaders say about their beliefs and intentions. While one must be alert to the possibility of deception, one must nevertheless
start with the "surface," as Strauss would have put it. The careful reading of what foreign leaders say would be an obvious beginning point for understanding what they
really think, even though the two should never be considered as simply identical.

   For example, at the time of the Iranian revolution in 1979, it appeared that
the intelligence analysts at the CIA did not have easy access to Khomeini's writings
about religion. In part, this reflected the standard social science view that, in a mod-
ernizing society such as Iran, religion was destined to play an increasingly minor
role. (A reading of Thucydides' account of the role that religious passion played in
causing the failure of Athens' Sicilian expedition would have sufficed to guard
against that particular mistake: Athens was clearly the most "enlightened" of ancient
Greek cities.) But it also reflected the view that one could assess the views of a
Khomeini from the outside, without having to try to understand him as he understood himself. Strauss's painstaking method of recovering the thought of thinkers
of previous times would have been applicable to understanding someone like
Khomeini, whose intellectual world was so different from our own.

   With the end of the Cold War, the struggle of ideologies has come to a close.
Some have foreseen an "end of history," in the Hegelian sense of the attainment of
philosophic self-awareness; others, a "clash of civilizations," in the sense of the conflict of what are ultimately mutually incomprehensible value systems. For those
brought up in the realist tradition, it will seem strange that theories of international
relations should have such philosophic origins and implications. Nevertheless, such
is the world we face; and the study of the classics of political philosophy with Leo
Strauss was a surprisingly good preparation for grappling with it.

NOTES

1. Herbert J. Storing, ed. (New York: Holt, Rinehart and Winston, 1962).
2. *Strategic Intelligence for American World Policy* (Princeton: Princeton University Press, 1949), p. 155. Kent's influence on the goals and methods of intelligence analysis in the United States was not limited to the fact that his book became the best selling book of its kind and a bible of sorts for those within American intelligence. After the U.S. was surprised by the invasion of South Korea in 1950, Kent was asked to join the Office of National Estimates (ONE), a new intelligence unit charged with producing comprehensive, forward-looking intelligence assessments, thereby hopefully precluding further surprises of this sort. Soon afterwards, Kent became the director of ONE—at the time, the senior analytic post in U.S. intelligence; he held that position for more than 15 years. As Bruce Berkowitz and Allan Goodman note, "ONE and the process of developing NIEs [National Intelligence Estimates] bore a strong resemblance to the principles for analysis Kent described in *Strategic Intelligence*." (*Strategic Intelligence for American National Security*, [Princeton: Princeton University Press, 1989], p. 5)

Kent's views on the application of the scientific method to intelligence analysis also influenced the institutional arrangements for carrying it out. Even before World War II had ended, Kent and other analysts within the OSS's analytic arm had reached the conclusion that the positivist approach to analysis—resting on Max Weber's fact-value distinction—should be reflected institutionally in a sharp division between intelligence analysis and policy-making organizations. Historically, foreign intelligence analysis in the U.S. and elsewhere had been located in government departments directly responsible for carrying out the key national security functions of war or diplomacy. Under the new ethos of social science objectivity, however, scholarly distance was essential for intelligence analysts. Thus, the CIA is not part of a policy-making department of government and is located geographically in the Virginia suburbs, away from the White House, the Pentagon, and the State Department.

Reflecting the general disillusionment among social scientists themselves with respect to the predictive capabilities of modern social science, scholars studying past intelligence "failures" began to question the assumptions and utility of Kent-like theories of analysis in the late-1970s. However, only in recent years has the intelligence community itself begun to challenge Kent's views and their hold on the practice of intelligence analysis. See, in particular, Douglas J. MacEachin's "The Tradecraft of Analysis" and Joseph S. Nye's "Estimating the Future" in *U.S. Intelligence at the Crossroads*, Roy Godson, Ernest R. May and Gary Schmitt, eds. (McLean, VA: Brassey's, 1995), pp. 63–96.

3. "Analysis," *Intelligence Requirements for the 1990s*, Roy Godson, ed. (Lexington, MA: D. C. Heath and Co., 1989), pp. 76–77.
4. Ibid., p. 77.
5. Discussant remarks of Ray S. Cline in Roy Godson, ed., *Intelligence Requirements for the 1980s: Analysis and Estimates* (Washington, D.C.: National Strategy Information Center, 1980), p. 77. Cited in Cohen, op. cit., p. 78, emphasis supplied.

26

Thoughts on Strauss and Our Present Discontents

Carnes Lord

There is little question where Leo Strauss stood on the major issues of the Cold War. Strauss understood Soviet Communism, as well as Nazism, as a recrudescence of barbarism in the contemporary era, reflecting the political and intellectual crisis of liberal democracy. Strauss' early concern with the question of tyranny, and the failure of Western social science to address it adequately, was probably his most important contribution to the debate over American policy toward the Soviet Union in the decades following World War II, and it was central in shaping the orientation of those students of his who were interested in security questions. More generally, Strauss' development of the theoretical issue of the "regime," and his emphasis on the fundamental differences among regimes, flew in the face of fashionable social scientific thinking during the 1960s and 1970s. It provided a vital intellectual anchor for those inclined to resist the notion that the West and the Soviet bloc were on a course of convergence as a result of economic and technological processes of modernization, and to understand Soviet actions during the Cold War as a function of deep imperatives of the Soviet system rather than as mere reactions to Western policy. At the same time, Strauss clearly viewed Western liberal democracy as the only viable alternative to the totalitarian temptation, and the closest approximation to the "best regime" of the philosophers that is possible under modern circumstances.

As the visible and accelerating erosion of liberal principles in the United States in the late 1960s and beyond made the ultimate outcome of the Cold War seem doubtful in spite of the manifest strengths of the postwar West, Strauss was increasingly sensitive to the need to mount an intellectual defense of the liberal polity, especially in its unique yet paradigmatic American version. At the same time, he was never sparing in his analysis of the vulnerability of the original liberalism embedded in the American experiment to the logic or the dialectic of modernity as such. World War II had been a great victory for liberalism, but Strauss worried that the victors, like other conquerors before them, would eventually succumb to the ideas of their defeated enemies.

The German ideas of greatest concern to Strauss—perhaps surprisingly, and in contrast to most American conservatives—were those originating not on the left but on the right, in what Strauss referred to as the "third wave" of modernity inaugurated by Friedrich Nietzsche. Historicism and positivism, now powerfully entrenched in American higher education and modulated to suit the egalitarian impulse of American political culture, threatened liberalism in ways more fundamental than Marxism, in spite of its continuing presence in intellectual life in the West. On the ideological battlefields of the 1960s, liberalism could more than hold its own against the Old Left; but it stumbled when confronted with the New Left, with its potent mix of liberationist, nihilist, and communitarian themes and a ready-made cause in the calamitous Vietnam War. With these developments, which profoundly demoralized the American political establishment and sent American education into a downward spiral from which it has yet to recover, Strauss' "crisis of the West" entered a new and acute phase.

For those arriving in Washington in the 1970s with direct or indirect exposure to the teachings of Strauss, the prospects for the republic could hardly have seemed bleaker. On the domestic front, the Watergate scandal had brought down an administration, and in the process wreaked incalculable havoc on the presidency as an institution. Internationally, the nation was reeling under the impact of the oil embargo and the final collapse of its position in Southeast Asia, while the Soviet Union was in the midst of an unprecedented military buildup. In the meantime, Congress and an increasingly countercultural press were vying with one another to discredit and dismantle elements of America's Cold War national security establishment, while successive administrations engaged in a series of rear-guard actions at home and abroad. The collapse of the American position in southwest Asia after the Iranian revolution and the Soviet occupation of Afghanistan, coupled with the national humiliation of the hostage crisis and the military failure at Desert One, the fraying of traditional alliance relationships, stagflation and "malaise" at home—all seemed to point to an America in retreat and decline.

How Strauss himself would have reacted to the political and cultural turmoil of the 1970s, the conservative revolution of the 1980s, the end of the Cold War, or the centrist presidencies of the 1990s, is impossible to say with any confidence. Strauss would certainly have welcomed the conservative resurgence that was already underway—thanks in no small part to his own efforts—by the time of his death in 1973. Yet there is little reason to suppose he would have felt comfortable with the fundamental outlook of the dominant elements in the conservative coalition that emerged in the 1980s. It seems highly likely that Strauss would have shared the cultural pessimism of Allan Bloom's *Closing of the American Mind*, rather than the optimism of Ronald Reagan himself or the liberal-democratic triumphalism of more recent years that has come to be associated with Reagan's legacy. Strauss always entertained a healthy respect for the American people, but he was never a populist. Loosening the shackles of government, desirable as it might be as public policy in particular cases, would not in his view automatically liberate the good sense and productive energies of ordinary Americans, since the moral character and the capacity for self-government of a given people is a fragile acquisition, not something that can be taken for granted.

Strauss has often been accused of being an elitist. Strauss believed, not of course that elites as such deserve to rule, or that elites of the philosophic or the right-minded deserve to rule without reference to the wishes of the people, or even (or perhaps one should say particularly) that intellectuals should have a leading role in politics, but rather that elites set the tone for the larger society, exemplifying a way of life and nurturing ideas and values—the deeper meaning of the notion of "regime" that Strauss found in Plato and Aristotle—that pervasively affect the character of the nation as a whole. Strauss never denied (as did the sociological tradition of elite theory stemming from Mosca and ultimately Machiavelli) the reality of democratic governance. But it is crucial to see that Strauss understood the crisis of liberal democracy as a crisis not of democracy as such, but of liberalism understood as the guiding philosophy and way of life of contemporary democratic elites.

There can be little question but that the ills we currently confront in virtually every area of national policy have a great deal to do with fundamental changes in the outlook of the American political class over the last thirty years or so. The liberalism of the early Cold War was pragmatic, tough-minded, sure of itself, and firmly rooted in the American political tradition. It was comfortable with the exercise of power and recognized the importance of political leadership and judgment in a democratic polity. At the same time, it was civic-minded. It looked on public service as an honor and a duty, while at the same time promoting civic education and greater popular participation in political activity. The liberalism prevailing in contemporary America is different in virtually every one of these respects. As Christopher Lasch has argued with only some exaggeration in his recent polemic *Revolt of the Elites and the Betrayal of Democracy* (1995), today's socioeconomic and professional elites increasingly see themselves as a free-floating global meritocracy of intelligence and achievement, with ties to local communities, fellow citizens, or the nation as a whole that are tenuous at best. To the extent that these elites carry intellectual baggage, it is largely of liberal provenance—but a decayed liberalism deeply influenced by the counterculture of the 1960s (also well analyzed by Lasch in his earlier *The Culture of Narcissism*) and its contemporary offshoots. The capture of the universities by the children of the counterculture, and the increasingly important role played by the academy in the public policy arena, are the key institutional developments in this story. The key intellectual development of more recent years is the marriage of the multicultural agenda of post-sixties radicalism with the philosophy of deconstruction. The infiltration of German and French nihilist doctrine into American intellectual life beginning in the 1970s has profoundly transformed academic study in literature and the social sciences in this country, in ways that are no doubt not yet fully appreciated in terms of their impact on our society generally. In particular, the notion, axiomatic in this body of writing, that social arrangements and forms of thought are no more than expressions of power relationships has unquestionably had a demoralizing and corrupting effect on the political behavior of elites; and it has spread increasingly into the popular culture thanks to the hold it has established on Hollywood and the national media. An unprecedented cynicism concerning the character and motives of politicians is today the conventional wisdom. Such attitudes undermine not only the incentives for civic responsibility but the very possibility of vigorous political leadership, with consequences that are only too visible in our current politics.

Let us return to the issue of national security policy. Remote as it may appear to be from these intellectual eddies and currents, national security is in fact as much exposed to their impact as any other policy arena, and in some ways perhaps more so. In spite of the public's appreciation of American military performance in the Gulf War, the legacies of Vietnam and Watergate continue to weigh heavily: generally speaking, government activities in the national security field are more scrutinized and contentious, their fundamental legitimacy more readily contested. In one sense, this is as it should be, given the expense and hazards of the instrumentalities of national security as well as the more benign international environment we now enjoy. Nonetheless, there is reason for concern. The declining legitimacy and the moral decay of our political and professional classes are not without their effect on the behavior of government officials; and recent developments (consider particularly the Ames espionage case) show that the nation's military and intelligence services in particular are by no means immune to it. The disappearance of their Cold War mission as well as the downward spiral of spending on these services have certainly contributed to the demoralization and drift that is so evident in them, as has the relentless effort of the current political establishment to use the armed forces to validate and advance the multicultural agenda. At a more fundamental level, however, one senses as well a steady erosion of the ethos of honor and national service that is at the core of military and intelligence professionalism. A number of factors seem to be at work here: the long-standing assault on traditional values in the popular culture, a civilian leadership that lacks credibility and authority, and a growing estrangement between the armed forces and the civilian world generally. Few would argue that civil-military relations in the United States are in a state of active crisis. But the trends are worrisome, and not only from the perspective of maintaining effective military forces. They have ominous implications for the long-term health of the republic.

Some have called recently for the reconstitution of an American conservatism that embraces the idea of a strong national government and promotes an ethos of national greatness and mission, arguing for (among other things) dramatic increases in defense spending and a more aggressive foreign policy designed to sustain democratic governance abroad. To try to address the merits of this project would take us beyond the scope of this discussion, but the simple point needs to be made that it is altogether doubtful that the moral or political preconditions for such an undertaking are currently in place. No political leader is in sight who could credibly articulate and sustain it; but perhaps more to the immediate point, there is no stomach for it among our political and cultural elites. What seems to be required at the present time is something different and more modest—not indeed isolationist retrenchment, but a refocusing of effort and attention on the home front in the broadest sense, with a view to (among other things) arresting the decline of American education, reviving a sense of citizenship and civic responsibility, and repairing vital national institutions such as the armed forces.

Like Shakespeare's Glendower, a future president may well find occasion to summon the nation's spirits from their present slumber; but will they come when he calls them?

27

The Charm of Competence:
A Straussian Looks at the Therapeutic State[1]

Susan Orr

I never had the opportunity to study with Leo Strauss. Nevertheless, I learned a great deal from him through the works he left behind as well as from those who studied under him directly. Spending time with great books, with either his work or his students to guide me, has given me an unusual advantage in the field of domestic policy. Viewing the human condition through the lens of political philosophy has led me to understand my work as a child welfare specialist from a distinctly different vantage point than most of my colleagues who come from the disciplines of sociology, psychology, education, and law.

What the public policy field known as "child welfare" constitutes is not self-evident. In politics, simply framing something as a "children's issue" has been used to champion various proposals from children's rights[2] to the right of all families to subsidized health- and day-care. In reality, child welfare encompasses public policy surrounding child abuse and neglect, foster care, and the adoption of state wards. In other words, child welfare concerns families in crisis, when the natural bonds are strained to the point of breaking. Despite its narrow-sounding scope, it is one of the most important areas within domestic policy, for it has everything to do with the relationship between the family and the regime.

The field of child welfare, resting on the foundations of social science, is plagued with the weaknesses inherent in that science. That deficiency, as Strauss tells us in his "Introductory Essay" to *Spinoza's Critique of Religion*, is a misunderstanding of all of nature and thereby, of human nature. Modern social science promised a lessening in suffering and a freedom from the constraints imposed by natural law. Its very application, however, leads to a collapsing of the possibilities of what it is to be human: neither virtue nor vice is given its due. Hence, the modern solution ends up causing more ruination than liberation. As Strauss's work reveals, "it is safer to try to understand the low in the light of the high than the high in the light of the low. In doing the latter one necessarily distorts the high, whereas in doing the former, one does not deprive the low of the freedom to reveal itself fully as what it is."[3]

It is through the light that political philosophy sheds that I have written the following reflections to illuminate the coming and necessary clash between the American experiment and the therapeutic state. The necessity for brevity has forced me to trace only the outlines of that conflict.

★ ★ ★ ★ ★

We live amid the ruins of the modern project, no longer certain of man's ability either to perfect himself or to triumph over nature. Indeed, those of a reflective nature have called this the "post-modern" age, suggesting that we are no longer enthralled with the promise of Enlightenment. The odd thing about the term "post-modern" is the inherent confusion and disarray it implies: an inability to go forward or to return. But, an equally important quality is that it is a faith shaken, not undone. It is essentially a crisis of confidence concerning our ability to overcome any obstacle by a combination of science and will. This current lack of confidence should not surprise us, given the fact that our century has seen much destruction from technological power harnessed for the sake of various notions of what constitutes progress.

While some take comfort in the downfall of the overtly oppressive Soviet empire and the derision with which the communist enterprise is now regarded, it is a cold comfort. Although vanquished on the political battleground, modernity's legacy, with its lure of power and progress, has not yet vanished. Instead, it is firmly entrenched in the realm of social policy. Its tentacles still have a firm grip upon American policy particularly as it relates to family life. It is all the more dangerous because it goes largely unnoticed.

Nowhere is the modern project so omnipresently apparent than in the realm of child welfare. The child welfare profession, as with many modern disciplines, stands upon the shoulders of the great moderns—Machiavelli, Bacon and Hobbes. It is particularly indebted to the Baconian promise to provide for the relief of man's estate through the application of science. The child welfare profession is predicated upon the two interconnected claims of modernity—the omnipotence of science and the infinite malleability of man. It is dedicated to improving the human condition through direct intervention at the smallest community level, the family. Most professionals, however, would not recognize their lineage, and some would even be horrified at the roots that are still discernible.

Everything about the enterprise is infused with the enthusiasms of modernity. Mirroring the science of modern medicine, child welfare professionals are trained to look at human behavior as a doctor would look at disease. Just as doctors strive to eradicate cancer, child welfare professionals work to end all strife within the family. Even the tools of their trade are couched in scientific terms. If someone beats a child, he is in need of treatment. Caseworkers use "risk assessment tools" to decide whether or not a child can safely remain in the home, as if by mere application of a checklist one could do more than guess who will choose to do evil. Such tools lessen the dignity of all involved: they fail to take into account, and in fact attempt to replace, the free will of the parent and the judgment of the caseworker. The profession continuously speaks of creating "systems of care" in order to protect children from the harm caused by bad parents, thus attempting to replace the natural family through social engineering. If a system fails, one simply needs to tinker with the machine, not find fault with the human beings involved. Finding fault is made more difficult because any agency intervention is cloaked under the secrecy of confidentiality laws; each intervention is treated as utterly private. Since child welfare agencies are lodged within the state, however, their actions cannot be private: citizens do not have a choice about when the agency enters into their lives.

Social service agencies that have the responsibility for child welfare are the most intrusive arm of the therapeutic state for these agencies have the authority to intervene in family life without a warrant, i.e., regardless of whether or not a crime has been committed. They have the power, in concert with cooperative courts, to disrupt or keep parents and their children together. Child protective services can remove children from their homes when the agency determines a child is "at risk" of being harmed. Because these determinations are done outside of the criminal courts, there are no due process requirements; the standard of evidence required for permission to remove a child from his home is consequently much lower. The judge must rely upon the judgment of the caseworker who files the removal order. If a parent thinks that he or she has been wrongly accused, there is no remedy outside of an administrative review, conducted by the agency itself. This combination of power without accountability is ominous.

That we decide to intervene in cases of abuse and neglect is not a problem in and of itself; rather, it is the manner in which such intervention is carried out. Child welfare professionals were long ago successful in persuading state legislatures to decriminalize child abuse and neglect. By forsaking the courts of criminal law, in which determinations of justice and injustice are made and punishments meted out, social work took on the much larger task of attempting to heal family members who have gone wrong. The therapeutic regimen is carried out by providing various services from things as simple as housekeeping to as complicated as residential drug treatment for both the drug-addicted mother and her children.

It is the essence of the therapeutic world that the professionals, the scientists of this Newer Atlantis, know best how to raise children. While the professionalization of everyday life has become more and more frequent, it is at its most intrusive in the field of child welfare. Motivated by compassion and an earnest desire to help children and families in trouble, the child welfare profession does not see the harm that such intervention, done under government auspices, can cause. Trapped within the framework of modern social science, the field of child welfare has cut itself off from the foundations of the regime.

How children are raised is always an inherently political question, for the most obvious reason that children constitute the perpetuation of the regime. A Spartan household does not resemble an Athenian one, and neither looks like an American one. While not the most elevated concern of political philosophy, it is a necessary one. Two examples from the ancients serve to illustrate the pivotal and permanent importance that the household plays upon political life, as well as to throw into sharp relief the modern view of familial relations.

In the *Republic*, Socrates constructs a city most in accord with the good. His perfectly just city requires not only the scientific regulation of procreation according to an arithmetic formula, but also the holding of women and children in common. Socrates maintains the necessity of eradicating all things private for the guardian class, particularly, that most private of institutions, the family, in order to bind the guardians' allegiance to the city. In this city without families where eros is completely regulated, what is one's own becomes identical with the city. But, the city in speech requires a self-forgetting and disregard for the limits inherent in having bodies, a forgetting that we are not completely immaterial. We are meant to be shocked by Socrates' proposition into considering the natural limits of politics. Eros cannot be completely controlled by the political realm without a resulting distortion in the human condition: eros and arithmetic are as one only in thought. As we shall soon see, the modern failure to recognize Socratic irony has led to the belief that we have complete control over how families are structured.

Aristotle's *Politics* begins in a similar fashion with a consideration of the beginnings of political life. He examines whether or not the family is simply a smaller version of the regime. In other words, does Socrates' city in speech conform to nature? To answer that question, Aristotle looks to the ends of both institutions. He determines that while the household exists for life, the *polis* exists for the good life. Family life on its own cannot provide for the highest element in man, although it provides a foundation by channeling our elementary desires. Mastering the household art requires more than mere self-preservation, but less than political rule. Thus, Aristotle disagrees with Socrates, insisting that statesmanship is not simply the art of the household writ large, but different in kind, a nobler and architectonic art, that allows for the grander virtues of magnificence, magnanimity and justice.

As the ancients understood, the family is that which is most one's own, the realm of the particular, as distinct from the common good. Family life is rooted in the nature of man, that he has bodily desires, but it is more than that. The family, at its best, is that community in which we begin to learn how to be good men and good citizens. In Leon Kass's *Toward a More Natural Science*, he suggests the following definition of the family that captures the subtleties inherent in that primary institution. Kass writes that the family is

> . . . that nest and nursery of humanity—private, intimate and vulnerable. Though its roots are the needs of bodily life—nurture, protection, reproduction, and then protection and nurture of the young—the household provides for more than the body. A richly woven fabric of nature and convention, it is established by law to nurture our nature. It is sustained by customs that humanize the human animal, engendering love and friendship, speech and education, choice and awareness, and shared beliefs and feelings.

This fragile network is protected by notions of the just and the shameful. Justice in the household is founded on clear demarcations of who belongs to whom, embodied first of all in the strict prohibitions against incest and adultery. Shame protects the intimacy and immediacy of family life—indeed, of all human relations.[4]

The family properly understood is a blend of nature and convention and because of that it stands in the almost sacred juncture between the public and the private world.

With the advent of modernity and the concomitant lowering of the ends of politics, the family loses it place as the wellspring of good citizenship. The public and private spheres become utterly disjointed. An interesting consequence is that the family becomes even more central to ordinary lives. It becomes, in Christopher Lasch's phrase, "a haven in a heartless world." At the same time, this necessary haven comes under continuous assault. With no natural standard to provide guidance, all goods become private; any choice becomes choice-worthy. The family is seen as a product of convention that arises only out of our original neediness; it is not understood as a permanent natural order in which human beings thrive. If the family is simply conventional, it is similarly infinitely variable. The family becomes just a group of individuals proclaiming themselves a family, in whatever form. And every formation must be granted equal status.

In the world of child welfare, it is the poor and marginalized citizens who are most hurt by such policy. Overcoming desperate circumstances requires good character, especially that virtue which is the foundation of all the other virtues: self-control. When virtue is not rewarded, but is, instead, one of many equally worthy, lifestyle choices, the poor are disproportionately harmed. When a poor person chooses badly, nothings shelters him or his children from the awful consequences of his actions. Middle-class and richer families have ways to insulate themselves from both misadventure and subsequent governmental intrusion, although they are not unaffected by it. And a glimpse into the current state of child welfare only confirms this dismal state of affairs.

Child protective agencies looked into the lives of over three million children in 1995 (the latest year for which we have data). In over one-third (36%) of the cases, a caseworker determined that a child had been hurt by his parents; of that number, less than half of those children (15%) were considered to be in sufficient danger to be removed from their homes and put into foster care.[5] That means that there were over one million cases of abuse and neglect were either substantiated or indicated.[6] Moreover, the numbers at all levels are increasing at an alarming rate. In the most recent national incidence study, researchers found that the number of abused and neglected children was two-thirds higher in 1993 than at the time of the previous study in 1986 and that the number of children seriously injured by their parents had quadrupled.[7] Moreover, as this study has consistently found, family structure is related to a child's risk of harm: children living in single parent households are at the greatest risk for harm.[8]

There are many reasons why the numbers are so high. But the pervading problem is the fact that the child welfare system is riddled with perverse incentives that undermine personal responsibility and reward destructive behavior. Social workers understand themselves as providing remedies in the guise of therapeutic treatment. Child abuse is not regarded primarily as a violation of justice, but as a symptom of illness. Parents, according to the social work model, harm their children as a result of the stress caused by living in harsh circumstances. Because abuse is seen as a disease susceptible to therapy, it is not surprising to find reluctance to ever pronounce any given parent incurable.

This model of treatment creates two perverse and contradictory courses of action: barely veiled force, on the one hand, and unjust behavior on the other. Social workers always hold the well-understood threat of taking away one's children if one fails to comply with agency desires. Conversely, the parent is given multitudinous chances to "improve" because abuse is not seen as a moral problem, which often places children in harm's way. The child welfare professional sees shameful behavior, such as abusing a child, as a symptom of mental stress caused by poverty or lack of education in how to be a good parent. Instead of looking for the answer in a malformed soul, i.e., in the possibility of vice, the profession looks for either an external answer, such as financial need, or an internal disorder like mental illness, because no one in their right mind would harm their own child. There is no public praising or blaming; there is only treatment, carried out in private by professionals. At its best, it treats humans as infinitely malleable; at its worst, it reduces them to solely material beings, whose character is completely dependent upon their economic conditions.

The alliance of relativism with the dynamic of the therapeutic creates a dangerous circumstance as the therapeutic makes demands without a real standard of what a good family ought to be. Ironically, with the elevation of private desires over public good, we have simultaneously allowed government to exercise ever more control over how we conduct our daily lives and shackled ourselves more severely to governmental authority.

Because of a belief in the healing power of science, the therapeutic state has continually extended its reach over the last several decades. Having begun by rescuing battered children from their parents, it now passes judgment on more ambiguous conduct such as emotional maltreatment and failure to seek psychiatric help for troubled children. Losing one's temper and yelling at one's children is certainly not good form, but hardly merits state intervention. Nor should a reluctance to seek therapy for a misbehaving child make one suspect. At the other end of the spectrum, an unwillingness to terminate the parental rights of truly degenerate parents has led to untold harm for too many children. Being beaten or neglected is not the worst thing that can happen to a child in his home: even conservative estimates suggest that 1,500 children die at the hands of their parents each year.[9] Four out of every five children murdered are three years old or younger.[10] Most of the families involved were already known to social service agencies.

On its own, the therapeutic state cannot make the necessary distinction between appropriate punishment and abuse, much less the difference between a bad day and a bad way of life. It cannot distinguish between what an older age called venial and mortal sin. Because the law no longer supports the natural order, the therapeutic state begins to intervene to impose its own order. Predictably, the results of such power in the hands of the therapeutic profession have been anything but helpful because the therapeutic profession has no standard to judge behavior other than what science tells it. Social science, in turn, can only speak in terms of child and family well-being, not happiness and the good life. Remember that the essence of social science is to deny an objective standard for making moral judgments. Social science, in fact, replaces moral law, bringing with it its own odd set of commandments. By clothing themselves in the raiment of science and technology, child welfare professionals avoid the appearance of making moral judgments about behavior while still allowing themselves to intervene in the lives of their fellow citizens. Having forsaken natural law, the ideal of physical health and emotional well-being becomes the closest thing to an objective standard of good and evil. Yet this vision of man necessarily skews our understanding of the human condition of man for it fails to account for the soul: human beings are not simply material.

In considering how the therapeutic state intrudes upon family life, we would do well to reflect on the following passage from G.K. Chesterton in *What's Wrong With the World?*, concerning the harm that governmental intervention can inflict upon those it wants to help. Chesterton writes:

> In most normal cases of family joys and sorrows, the State has no mode of entry. It is not so much that the law should not interfere, as that the law cannot. . . . Creatures so close to each other as husband and wife, or a mother and children, have powers of making each other happy or miserable with which no public coercion can deal. . . . The child must depend on the most imperfect mother; the mother may be devoted to the most unworthy children; in such relations legal revenges are in vain. Even in the abnormal cases where the law may operate, this difficulty is constantly found; as many a bewildered magistrate knows. He has to save children from starvation by taking away their bread-winner. And he often has to break a wife's heart because her husband has already broken her head. The State has no tool delicate enough to deracinate the rooted habits and tangled affections of the family; the two sexes, whether happy or unhappy, are glued together too tightly for us to get the blade of a legal penknife between them.[11]

The modern therapeutic state has managed to do everything that Chesterton counsels against. In thinking about the foundations of child welfare, we can begin to see why the enterprise has failed. We can also see why it is antithetical to the very foundations of American government.

The quintessential meaning of the proposition that "all men are created equal" is that human beings are capable of self-rule. There is no natural right for one person to rule another, without the other's consent because no one—no matter what profession they belong to—is so naturally superior to anyone else that he may rule another as one would rule an animal. The Declaration of Independence makes no distinctions between rich or poor, professional or citizen. But, to live in freedom requires the ability to rule oneself. Thus, the capacity for liberty must be nourished.

We first learn how to be free within the confines of family life. We grow in self-mastery by gaining control over our daily life, first and foremost, by having control over our own household. The therapeutic regimen turns the family over to the hands of professionals, which undermines the capacity for freedom. The charm of competence, however, is beginning to wear thin as we realize that we cannot medicate away our moral problems without a subsequent lowering of what it is to be human.

The dynamic of the therapeutic imposes an even "newer science of politics" than that proposed by Publius, one that contradicts that propounded by *The Federalist Papers*. It is a science of politics based upon compassion, rather than reason and choice, one that attempts to help families by alleviating the pain of moral failure through governmentally mandated compassion. Failing to learn how to be free, we drift toward more and more inhuman behavior. By forsaking justice, the therapeutic state brings misery to those it most wants to help. Children abused at their parents hands deserve more than what the therapeutic state can give them: they deserve to be treated justly.

NOTES

1. "The charm of competence bewitches completely first a few great men and then whole nations and indeed as it were the whole human race." Leo Strauss, *Thoughts on Machiavelli* (University of Chicago Press: Chicago, 1958), p. 297.

2. For example, the right of a minor to be sexually active regardless of the parent's concerns for protecting the child's health and morals.

3. Leo Strauss, *Spinoza's Critique of Religion* (New York: Schocken Books, 1965), p. 2.

4. Leon Kass, *Toward a More Natural Science: Biology and Human Affairs* (New York: Free Press, 1985), p. 237.

5. These cases broke down into the following categories: 53% were cases of neglect; 26% were physical abuse; 14% were sexual abuse; and 2.5% were medical neglect. U.S. Department of Health and Human Services, National Center on Child Abuse and Neglect, *Child Maltreatment 1995: Reports from the States to the National Child Abuse and Neglect Data System* (Washington, D.C.: U.S. Government Printing Office, 1997).

6. Indicated means that the agency did not have enough evidence to substantiate the case, but there were also grounds to suspect that abuse or neglect had occurred.

7. U.S. Department of Health and Human Services, National Center on Child Abuse and Neglect, *The Third National Incidence Study on Child Abuse and Neglect* (Washington, D.C.: U.S. Government Printing Office, 1996), p. xvii.

8. Children of single parents had a 77 percent greater risk of being harmed by physical abuse, an 87 percent greater risk of being harmed by physical neglect, and an 80 percent greater risk of suffering serious injury or harm from abuse or neglect than children living with both parents.

9. U.S. Department of Health and Human Services, National Center on Child Abuse and Neglect, *The Third National Incidence Study on Child Abuse and Neglect* (Washington, D.C.: U.S. Government Printing Office, 1996), p. 3-13.

10. U.S. Department of Health and Human Services, National Center on Child Abuse and Neglect, *Child Abuse and Neglect Case-Level Data: Working Paper #1* (Washington, D.C.: U.S. Government Printing Office, 1996) p. 5-1.

11. G.K. Chesterton, *What's Wrong with the World?*, in G.K. Chesterton's *Collected Works, Volume IV*, edited by James V. Schall, S.J. (San Francisco: Ignatius Press, 1987), pp. 67–68.

· *28* ·

A Student of Leo Strauss in the
Clinton Administration

William A. Galston

CORNELL DAYS

I had the good fortune to study with Allan Bloom during my undergraduate years at Cornell University. I came from a left-leaning family, and Allan never stopped struggling against what he regarded (with some justice) as my political naivete. Like most of Allan's students, I was enthralled by the thinkers of classical antiquity. At the same time, I believed that I was fortunate to live in a modern liberal democracy— that it would be hard to imagine (and unreasonable to expect) anything better. I was deeply perplexed about the connection between the Greeks and the American regime.

In the final semester of my senior year, Allan taught a seminar on Plato's *Republic*, which he was in the process of translating. Although it was thirty years ago, I vividly recall the excitement of weekly discoveries. As we worked our way through the book, a question began taking shape in my mind: if the rule of the wise is impossible, and if some tension between the demands of politics and freedom of the mind is inevitable, is it the case that this tension necessarily takes the same form (or reaches the same intensity) in all regimes? It seemed to me that Socrates' depiction of democracy as a "many-colored cloak" left room for the high as well as the low; Sparta would not have tolerated his activities for a day, let alone seventy years. During the final class, I raised my hand and asked whether by legitimizing dissent and restricting persecution, modern liberal democracies had not found a way of reducing the tension between philosophy and politics to a greater extent than any other form of government? Judged by the latitude afforded the philosophic enterprise (not the sole standard, admittedly), could one not conclude that liberal democracy was in fact the best regime?

It is testimony to the narcissism of the young that I cannot remember Allan's answer, though I do recall his complex amusement at my intervention. (The interpretive essay he subsequently published with his masterful translation of the

429

Republic indicated some sympathy with the underlying thrust of my question.) Today, three decades later, I see a more complex picture. From a legal/political standpoint, thought enjoys unprecedented freedom in liberal democracies. But liberal democratic society tends to deprive philosophy (and culture in general) of depth and significance. One sees signs of this in the laments of Russian and Central European intellectuals: under communism they were persecuted, but what they said mattered. Now it doesn't. Their activity no longer represents the struggle for forbidden truths or the vehicle of a nation's hopes; it is reduced to a commodity, or entertainment, or at best a conversation within a small group.

This is not to suggest that a brutal and repressive political order is somehow justified by the quality of the resistance it engenders; it is to suggest that the very safety of thought in a free society carries with it a kind of risk against which one must struggle. It is all too easy to see speech—philosophy, literature, cultural criticism—as a right without responsibilities, or as play without consequences.

THE UNIVERSITY OF CHICAGO

In the middle of my last semester at Cornell I was accepted for graduate studies in political science at the University of Chicago. Two weeks later I learned that Strauss was leaving the department, a grave disappointment. Nonetheless I had the opportunity to participate in his last Chicago course in the fall of 1967. The topic was Aristotle's *Politics*; it was for me a transformative experience.

To this day I do not know whether what I learned corresponded to anything Strauss intended to convey. What follows is a rough summary of what I took away from his memorable course:

There will always be competing claims about justice in politics and passions will run high, but no political order can function well without some agreement on justice and injustice. That agreement will be much harder to reach if the citizenry is sharply divided into the few rich and the many poor; the prospects for decent politics are greatly enhanced by a large, stable middle class. (One would, in Aristotle's terms, hope for such a class; in the terms of modern political economy, design policies to facilitate its growth and security.)

A political community's understanding of justice (whatever it may be) will serve as the basis of its institutional arrangements, within which decisions are made and competing claims balanced. But however wisely crafted, institutions cannot replace good citizens, whose virtues must be carefully and deliberately nurtured. Families have a role to play in this process, but the political community has a large stake in it as well. The conduct of education is a matter of collective concern. Religion can help nurture civic virtue and bolster respect for the principles of the regime.

Not everyone will attain the virtues of citizenship to the same extent; especially in a democracy, there will be an inevitable tension between the claims of equality and excellence, and between wisdom and consent—and therefore a democratic place for persuasive speech in the service of sound policies. But there is wisdom in the many as well as the few; democratic public deliberation can produce a whole greater than the sum of its parts.

Finally, no political community is comprehensive. Each encompasses a limited population and territory; the imperatives of self-defense should never be disregarded. Each community is morally limited as well; none is likely to embrace, or practice, a fully defensible understanding of justice. For that reason (among others), every set of institutional arrangements will be flawed, and every specific conception of the good citizen will stand in some tension with what it means to be a good human being simpliciter. The domain of politics is essentially limited, because political virtues and activities, though noble, are not the highest available to human beings; a zone of independence transcending politics must be acknowledged.

In short, the Aristotle I studied thirty years ago offered an understanding of government as both strong and limited: strong because legitimately involved in the material and moral well-being of its citizens; limited because not legitimately "totalitarian" regarding the life of the mind. It was possible, therefore, to imagine a kind of Aristotelian social democracy, and also a kind of Aristotelian liberalism, and to believe that an Aristotle returned to life in the twentieth century would not be wholly critical of modern liberal democracy—especially in view of the available alternatives.

Conversely, it seemed to me possible—indeed essential—to reconsider liberal democracy in the light of Aristotle's insights. For example, if there is a form of civic virtue suited to, and required for, each regime, then surely liberal democracy is no exception. The artful arrangement of constitutional institutions can take us only part way (as even the authors of the Federalist conceded). There must be specifically "liberal virtues," and the formation of liberal citizens must be a matter of common concern—even if the modern liberal understanding of limited government restricts the capacity of public institutions to inculcate civic virtue directly.

While this rethinking of liberal democracy in light of Strauss's Aristotle proved decisive for both my scholarship and practical political activities, I was left less satisfied by Strauss's more direct account of the origins of liberal democratic philosophy. There were two reasons for this. First, the anti-utopian, "low but solid" line of descent through Machiavelli and Hobbes to Locke seemed to give short shrift to the genuinely moral element in liberalism. Couldn't Kant's project be understood as an effort to uphold the possibility of human freedom, dignity, and distinctiveness in the face of the deterministic, homogenizing challenge of science? Wasn't Kantian morality and politics a doctrine of duties as well as rights? (My rigorous but generous advisor and lifelong mentor Joseph Cropsey allowed me to pursue these dissenting thoughts in a dissertation on Kant's historical essays.)

Second, it seemed to me that Strauss's official account of the rise of liberalism understated the extent to which it represented a response to the novel situation created by the rise of revealed religion. Strauss himself had explored with unparalleled profundity the tension between "Athens and Jerusalem," between reason and faith, between the pride of understanding and the humility of obedience. But what was to be done in practice when these two great sources of the West were copresent within political communities? Were institutions of faith to be allowed to repress the development of science and philosophy? Were the apostles of reason to be allowed to declare war on faith? And what was to be done when the unity of Christendom splintered and destructive religious passions spilled over into politics? Liberalism at its best tried, not to obliterate, but rather to domesticate, these differences in a manner that offered fair if not full liberty to the contending parties. I do not mean to suggest that liberalism solved the problem; no political dispensation could, and unresolved tensions manifest themselves in practical controversies down to the present. My suggestion is only that the liberal impulse on these matters is more capacious and more honorable than the anti-theological ire with which Strauss justly taxes Machiavelli.

Strauss reshaped my thinking, as he did for so many others, but his influence extended beyond scholarship. Though he was not a "conservative" in any of the American senses of the term, he sent large numbers of students on a path toward the conservative movement; I could not follow them. While I accepted Strauss's critique of utopian egalitarianism, I saw no contradiction between the broad thrust of his teaching and the best of modern liberalism (in the political rather than philosophical sense of the term). Unfortunately, as I pursued my graduate studies, American liberalism entered a period of degeneration and self-destruction. This posed a practical problem that has dominated my political endeavors ever since: the creation of a coherent alternative to both liberal excesses and a conservatism that, while not without strengths, proved too narrow and rigid to fully address the issues before us.

WANDERING IN THE POLITICAL WILDERNESS

Just months after I entered the University of Chicago, the worst year in modern American history began. The assassinations of Martin Luther King and Robert F. Kennedy presaged a breakdown of order and hope. As urban riots and anti-war demonstrations intensified, a fratricidal war broke out within the Democratic party. I instinctively took Hubert Humphrey's side against the partisans of the counterculture. I was not persuaded that the antinomian attack on all restraints was a basis for a decent society or politics. Nor could I accept the terms in which opposition to the Vietnam War was increasingly cast: the war might be tactically and strategically flawed, but I very much doubted that Ho Chi Minh was a misunderstood nationalist and social democrat. Four years later I found myself unable to support George McGovern's candidacy.

For much of the next two decades, as I wandered ineffectually through three presidential campaigns, I struggled to develop an alternative to the dominant tendencies in my party. My thoughts finally came together in 1989, when I published a political manifesto under the combative title, "The Politics of Evasion." In it I argued that the Democratic party could not hope—and did not deserve—to regain a presidential majority until it shifted its orientation in a number of respects. Americans would not support a party that they saw as lacking in realism and strength in matters of national defense, that espoused social policies at odds with the moral understanding of the middle class, and that pursued an economic strategy too concerned with distribution and class conflict at the expense of growth and opportunity. The electorate was rightly impatient with a politics drenched in sociological explanation; what they wanted was a politics of moral accountability in which social responsibility was matched by personal responsibility.

This broadside created a row within the party. It came to the attention of a young governor of Arkansas, and we had the opportunity to discuss it as his nascent presidential candidacy took shape. I advised the campaign and helped out during the transition, without expectation of anything more. On January 20, 1993 I was astonished to find myself entering the White House as Deputy Assistant to the President for Domestic Policy.

THE CLINTON ADMINISTRATION

One of my principal responsibilities was education. Bill Clinton had long believed that excellence in public education was the key to equal opportunity—that is, to a society in which individual merit would mean more than economic or racial background. As governor of Arkansas, he had challenged orthodoxy and key interest groups to push for more rigorous standards and testing. Now I was to represent the White House and work with the Department of Education to translate his approach into national legislation. Our proposal—the Goals 2000 bill—annoyed just about everyone. Conservatives opposed it on the grounds that it represented a large and unwarranted intrusion of federal power into traditional state and local prerogatives (it didn't). Liberals were skeptical because it focused on results rather than increased funding and because they feared that rigorous standards and testing would have a negative impact on poor and minority students (they wouldn't; just the reverse). After a legislative struggle that lasted more than a year and put the president at odds with the leadership of his own party, Goals 2000 was signed into law in March 1994. At the beginning of his second term, the President sought to reinforce this legislation by offering to share with the states a set of examinations in reading and mathematics, now administered to a relatively small national sample, for comprehensive testing of fourth- and eighth-grade students. This proposal remains mired in partisan controversy.

Goals 2000 was the flagship of the administration's education reform armada. I had the opportunity to work on the quinquennial redrafting ("reauthorization" in Washington parlance) of the Elementary and Secondary Education Act (ESEA), first passed during Lyndon Johnson's Great Society. We tried to replace long-established but ineffective "compensatory" programs for poor children with our broader strategy for improved educational outcomes. I was also able to use the ESEA as a vehicle to promote two of the President's other cherished ideas: charter schools, publicly funded but created, authorized, and run by educational innovators (parents, teachers, entrepreneurs) outside top-down, bureaucratized school districts; and a new emphasis on the promotion of school-based civic and character education nationwide. Other important efforts included national support for local initiatives to make schools safe, disciplined and drug free.

During the transition, I was asked to chair a working group charged with fleshing out the president-elect's proposal for a new national service program; as the administration began, I was asked to represent the Domestic Policy Council in the effort to translate this proposal into legislation. The core idea was simple: just as members of the armed forces who serve their country are eligible for a range of post-service benefits, so too young people who wish to serve as civilians should be able to do so and qualify for benefits that could be used to defray the costs of education and job training through a "domestic GI Bill." Underlying this idea was the principle of reciprocity: rather than getting something for nothing, these young people would contribute something of value to their country and receive something in return. Far from being an ad hoc contrivance to bolster a specific policy, this principle was at the heart of the president's effort to reconstruct domestic policy. Early in the administration he wondered aloud in my presence whether there should be any outright grants or subsidies for individuals who were capable of making some kind of reciprocal contribution.

Political considerations limited our ability to advance this principle on every front, but we did what we could. As in the case of Goals 2000, our draft national service legislation antagonized members of Congress across a broad political spectrum. Conservatives objected on the grounds that it would expand big government and that what they called "paid volunteerism" was an oxymoron (if so, we had better change the name of our "All-Volunteer Armed Forces"). Liberals feared that in times of fiscal stringency, this new venture would come at the expense of cherished social programs, and some of them were uncomfortable with its underlying principle, which they interpreted (correctly) as a critique of the welfare/entitlement state. After another prolonged struggle, the National and Community Service Act was signed into law. Although targeted for elimination after the Republican tidal wave in November of 1994, funding for the act survived with the president's unflinching support. As a result, tens of thousands of Americans have already had a chance to serve their country while expanding their educational and economic opportunities.

The national service program can be seen as part of President Clinton's effort to realign public programs with principles central to healthy liberal democratic life. The responsibility (if possible) to support oneself and one's family rather than becoming a permanent recipient of public assistance was at the heart of the President's welfare reform proposal, for which he took a great deal of heat within his own party. He proposed a simple new social contract: government will provide the kinds of temporary support (job training and placement, health and child care) needed to sustain the movement from dependency to employment; in return, individuals who are able to work must prepare themselves to do so and then accept available employment opportunities.

A similar conception undergirded the large expansion of the Earned Income Tax Credit (EITC) enacted in 1993. The principle was straightforward: if you work full-time, neither you nor your family should be living in poverty; if the market doesn't compensate your labor sufficiently to honor this principle, the public sector should step in to make up the difference. In many respects, after all, the social value of work exceeds its market value—for example, by giving children credible models of adult responsibility and by creating positive structures of community life. (William Julius Wilson has recently traced the social and moral catastrophes that overwhelm neighborhoods where work disappears.) Here again, the principle of reciprocal individual and public responsibility fell between the political stools: many conservatives denounced the EITC as a new form of welfare, while many liberals feared that its expansion would come at the expense of established social and economic policies.

It is not enough, obviously, for republican institutions and programs to rest on sound principles; especially in republics, the people themselves must have virtues that sustain these principles. Early on, my Aristotelian conception of civic virtue was nourished and rendered more concrete by an understanding (derived principally from Tocqueville) of the sources of civic virtue in the United States. I came to focus on three above all: the family, civil associations, and religion. Not entirely by chance, I had the opportunity to work on all of them during my White House years.

Starting in the mid-1980s, I had become increasingly concerned about the effects of family disintegration, not just on the economic status of children, but on their psychological, social, and moral development as well. I came to believe that trends such as the doubling of the U.S. divorce rate and the sixfold increase in the rate of out-of-wedlock birth since 1960 represented a clear and present danger to the health of the republic. I wrote extensively on these topics, to mixed reviews within my own political party. The President and the First Lady shared my concerns, however. I was overjoyed when the President accepted my advice and spoke out forcefully on teen pregnancy during his 1995 State of the Union address, catalyzing the formation of a national leadership coalition to address the problem. In her book *It Takes A Village*, Hillary Rodham Clinton surprised some of her supporters by expressing serious misgivings about the ready availability of divorce in contemporary America, especially when minor children are involved. The President subsequently reinforced this concern in heartfelt comments at the annual National Prayer Breakfast.

During 1994 I began discussing the condition of American civil society with Harvard professor Robert Putnam and examined his now-famous article "Bowling

Alone" while still in manuscript. Following an Oval Office meeting, the President asked me to assemble a group of scholars to advise him on his forthcoming State of the Union address. (I had a similar opportunity the following year, on the day of the great January 1996 blizzard in Washington.) I invited Putnam, Stephen Carter, and a number of other thinkers to Camp David for an extended discussion that involved the President and First Lady, Al and Tipper Gore, and a number of cabinet officers and senior White House staff. While the President was not entirely persuaded by Putnam's case that U.S. civil society is in decline, he instinctively understood the power of the public's belief that we are indeed in the midst of just such as decline. He went on to address that concern in a series of speeches, starting with the 1995 State of the Union and continuing through much of that year.

Beyond giving voice to this theme and offering moral leadership in events such as the 1997 Presidents' Philadelphia Summit on volunteerism, it is not immediately obvious what affirmative steps government can take to strengthen civil society. A place to begin is with a political variant of the Hippocratic oath: first, government should do no harm. Legal and regulatory strategies must be reviewed to ensure that civil activities and associations are not inadvertently impeded.

Just this issue arose early in the administration in the case of religion. In a much-criticized 1990 decision, the Supreme Court made it much easier for governments throughout the federal system to enact laws and regulations imposing burdens on the free exercise of religion. Groups representing the full spectrum of U.S. religious denominations banded together in a coalition to reverse this decision through a proposed Religious Freedom Restoration Act (RFRA), which would allow government to burden religion only in pursuit of a "compelling state interest"—a much more stringent standard. President Clinton strongly backed this legislation, enthusiastically signed it into law in the fall of 1993, and instructed us to monitor its execution. Subsequently, a White House team worked with executive branch agencies to ensure maximum feasible responsiveness to legitimate religious free exercise claims.

Throughout this process, we were aware that RFRA raised some important constitutional issues—in particular, whether this congressional action was consistent with its powers to enforce the liberty guarantees of the 14th Amendment. In June 1997, the Supreme Court ruled that Congress had exceeded that limit and that the constitutional separation of powers had been breached. Those who believe—as I do—that religious free exercise lies at the heart of a healthy civil society will continue to search for constitutionally appropriate remedies for the problem that prompted the enactment of RFRA. We must not allow overblown fears about the establishment of religion to impede efforts to guarantee the widest possible freedom of religion, consistent with the necessary and legitimate exercise of government authority.

CONCLUSION

During and after my White House years, I have often been asked what it is like for someone with training in political philosophy to serve as an advisor to the President of the United States. My standard response, offered in jest, is for the questioner to read Plato's Seventh Letter. A more serious response is that based on my experience it is difficult but possible for political philosophy to have an impact on practice, subject to constraints imposed by the democratic process.

To begin, a president is typically elected (especially to a first term) based on a set of policy proposals or at the very least a general orientation that is distinguishable from competing alternatives. Under normal circumstances, advice tendered to a democratically elected leader must remain within the four corners of the people's consent. The advisor has room to maneuver but is rarely free to counsel outright disregard of explicit democratic undertakings.

Advice is also subject to the limits of public explanation. If a policy that must be democratically approved cannot be set forth in terms the people can understand, then the president should be counseled to consider an alternative. Setting aside the (contested) merits of President Clinton's health care plan, its unfathomable complexity was a significant—perhaps decisive—argument against proposing it in the first place.

In a system of separated powers, the views of other elected and appointed leaders constitute an added constraint. Advisors should not lightly send presidents on fool's errands. If an otherwise meritorious proposal consistent with the president's promises stands no chance of acceptance, and if backing it diminishes the prospects of a second-best approach that is nonetheless preferable to the status quo, the advisor should think hard before urging the president to go for broke, let alone doing so without consultation in the president's name. (For purposes of long-term public education and negotiation with other branches, however, it is sometimes right to advocate policies that stand no chance of short-term approval.)

For me, the most challenging aspects of the advisor's role were psychological rather than philosophical or institutional. It is very difficult to advocate a particular course of action when every else in the room is counseling just the opposite—especially when the president seems to agree with the majority rather than the lone dissenter. Nor is it easy to be the bearer of bad tidings. Giving advice in the White House casts into high relief all the weaknesses of one's character. Reflection on such an experience in tranquility can be an important step on the road to self-knowledge.

Government Practice and the School of Strauss

Mark Blitz

$\mathcal{I}$ will divide my discussion of the implications of Strauss' work for government practice into three sections: conservatism, character, and constitutionalism.[1]

CONSERVATISM

Most people who served in government and also consider themselves "Straussians" worked in the Reagan Administration. This is more remarkable than it seems today, because when Strauss' students and their students began their studies twenty-five to fifty years ago, intellectuals generally believed that only liberals were open to ideas and that the term "conservative intellectual" was almost contradictory.[2]

Although several "Straussians" served under President Reagan, partisanship or personal attachment were not their prime motives. Several who served Reagan also served with Presidents Bush and Ford, and some have worked for congressional Democrats, or in the Clinton Administration. Students of political philosophy are, as such, not partisan and one can imagine circumstances under which Strauss' students would be more to the left than to the right. Nonetheless, to understand what students of Strauss bring to politics today, we must first come to grips with the elements in Strauss that prepared and allowed an affinity with conservatives. For without that affinity, and without the triumph of Reaganism, most would not have entered government in the first place, and the implications of Strauss' teachings for government service would be harder to discern. Even those who worked for Democrats are allied with that party's more conservative or, if one wishes, more traditionally "liberal" wing.

What, then, were the elements of what we learned or absorbed from Strauss, or, in my case, from his writings and his students, that, in retrospect, prepared the way for conservative politics? The first thing to mention is anti-communism, because the Russian threat was the dominant political fact from the end of the second world war to the end of the Cold War. Strauss' students were clearly anti-communist in a way that liberals were not, because they questioned in every way the life that communists promoted. The Soviet Union was a tyranny, and the Soviet goal was an expanded tyranny. Liberals were often hampered by the sense that socialism would in fact be more just than "capitalism" if only one could overcome the practical obstacles. They especially believed this for the "third world" of under-developed or developing nations. The strong liberal response to the Soviets that was originally so decisive in containing them began to weaken under the influence of this belief, and because of the conduct and outcome of the war in Vietnam. The uncompromising and unchanging understanding among Strauss' students that com-munism is tyranny therefore prepared an affinity with conservatives when they became the standard bearer of this understanding.

Connected to this was doubt about the efficacy and decency of the United Nations and other attempts at world federalism or a world state. Such institutions were either steps on the way to the universal homogenization of human beings, or foolish examples of our loss of confidence in our justice and power. Because the United Nations was the beacon of at least the rhetoric of liberal internationalism, to doubt it and its actions was to begin to become "conservative."[3]

Liberal internationalism also seemed to carry with it a bias against politics itself, a hope that universal agreement would replace political controversy. Liberalism generally seemed to treat politics merely as a means to social and economic ends, and not as a field of human excellence. One learned from Strauss and his students, however, to appreciate the magnificence of statesmanship, and to worry about the conditions that make it possible. Churchill and Lincoln were not conservatives nar-rowly speaking, although one was a Republican and the other a Tory at the time of his greatest actions. American conservatives mostly supported economic liberalism or nostalgic communalism rather than political excellence as such. Still, the empha-sis many conservatives placed on individual responsibility combined with the anti-politics of liberal internationalism to create an affinity between the love of the statesman's virtues and the possibility of becoming "conservative."[4]

Strauss and his students also emphasized the seriousness of America's founding and constitution. Natural rights were not historical artifacts, but, precisely, natural. The Constitution was not a mere contrivance resulting from selfish economic bargaining and acquiescence in slavery, but a form of government brilliantly considered, in the service of principles profoundly understood. Not Carl Becker and Charles Beard, but Jefferson, Hamilton, and Madison were the Americans worth studying.

This understanding could as easily have been liberal as conservative, but lib-erals had stopped using natural rights and constitutionalism to defend the American way of life. They no longer believed the principles of the Declaration and of lim-ited government to be true, and searched, instead, for newer constructions. The "Straussian" emphasis on the American founding became conservative both because it was an old fashioned return to old views and because conservatives more than liberals still talked in terms of constitutional politics and natural rights.[5]

Strauss and his students emphasized not just natural rights and liberty, but virtue as well. Virtue is once again an acceptable topic for political discussion and an acceptable name for human excellence. Thirty years ago, however, virtue was largely confined to special dispositions such as moderation in the direction of chastity, and few believed that anyone could say with conviction what constitutes good character and government's responsibility for it. To recognize thirty and forty years ago the importance of virtue and its connection to politics opened one to conservatism because liberals increasingly seemed to believe that liberty means satisfying any desire one wishes, in any way, place, and time, and at least some conservatives did not. One reason virtue is again discussed is the influence of Strauss' students on political opinion. But one should not underestimate in this regard the powerful support of common sense.[6]

The rehabilitation of virtue was connected to the general skepticism of Strauss and his students toward the new orthodoxy of moral relativism. Forty years ago relativism began to dominate the scene, not so much in the advanced forms of Nietzschean historicism as in the seemingly more benign form of an alliance with liberalism. Freedom meant doing as one pleased because no standards could say what it should please one to do. Doubting moral relativism went hand in hand with taking virtue and natural rights seriously. "Nature" is not primarily the earth and sky that surround our body, but the name from Plato through our Founders for the permanent and self-sufficient things that order and attract our mind. Perhaps, after all, there were true and natural standards that were valid everywhere and always. Because liberalism was the orthodoxy and moral relativism its leading practical dogma, to question the orthodox meant to be alive to the heterodox position called conservatism.

To dispute relativism and to take virtue and natural rights seriously meant that intellectual as well as political conventions were put in question. In some cases, perhaps even in most cases, the intellectual questioning preceded and largely caused the readiness for political change. The reigning intellectual masters of the 1950s and 1960s were Marx, Freud, and the existentialists. Strauss and his students questioned not just Marxism, but the power, depth, and evidence of Freud's understanding of the soul. They did not ignore Sartre's link with radical Marxists, nor Heidegger's with the Nazis. They did not shrink from considering religions in their own terms. Existentialism and, especially, Freudianism, were defining commitments of our leading academics and intellectuals, who were almost all liberal academics and intellectuals. It was a short step from questioning their masters to questioning their politics.

Strauss and his students also were among those who argued that the triumph of modern science and technology was not altogether good. The luster of material comfort was at least somewhat dimmed by the apparent decline in virtue and the ascendancy in most intellectual areas of positivism. At the least, the benefits of modern freedom were threatened by these tendencies. Access to central phenomena of human life was endangered by the threat of egalitarian leveling and by the strength of a social science that took its cue from utilitarianism and behaviorism. To question the contemporary in these terms was to take more seriously than any modernist could the concerns of romantic or "traditional" conservatives, even if immoderate traditional conservatism itself proves to be a variant of historicism and not a counter to it.

Questioning the modern, together with appreciating the power of America's old, originating, founding documents, meant that Strauss and his students paid attention to the dignity of the old as old. This conservative disposition was reinforced by the enormous emphasis on the great texts and authors of the West, that is, on the great books of the great tradition. That said, these books are studied as if they might be true. It is not age or the tradition but their natural power that makes them worthwhile. Similarly, our own founding documents are not merely our long-standing parchments. They are revolutionary, and speak from a natural right that vaults beyond any tradition. The old may be venerated as old, but in the last analysis its claim to deserve respect depends on its being good. This split between the old and the good is one of several that show why political philosophy cannot as such be conservative. The complexities in the relationship between virtue, natural standards, responsible liberty, and what is traditional also explain why conservatism itself is too varied to be the single and permanent vessel of the factors that allow Strauss' students to have an affinity for it. It was only because Reagan's conservatism emphasized some things more than others—anti-communism, natural individualism, comfort and even belief in the notion that the Declaration and Constitution proclaimed and instituted permanent standards—that it was politically attractive. And even then, its attraction was correlated to the decline of American liberalism after Truman, for liberalism has at other times stood for these very same "conservative" principles.[7]

Concern with great books belonged together with the view that the philosophic quest is the most important quest, and the philosophic life, or at least the life of genuine teaching, the most just life. To see this is to admit that all desires are not equal. Combined with an appreciation of virtue and statesmanship, this view of the dignity of philosophy meant that Strauss and his students were not simple egalitarians. In the context of current American politics, and especially American politics from Johnson through Carter, to challenge even the remotest region of egalitarian dogma directed one to conservatism. But it is important to recognize that the unequal qualities of mind and character that are defended are politically in the service of American equality of rights, properly understood.

Strauss and his students' exploration of philosophy led to the view that much as philosophers might support prudent politics, politics and philosophy stood in inherent tension. This is the political teaching of Plato's *Republic* and *Apology*. This understanding fit together with Strauss' discovery of philosophic esotericism, i.e., of the truth that some philosophers did not always say ostensibly what they meant in fact. This discovery is sometimes thought to be the heart of an "elitism" among "Straussians," and elitism is considered to be more conservative than liberal. But the grounds of disaffection with simple egalitarianism, and of support for a more subtle and complex natural standard, including a natural standard of equality, are the ones I discussed above. Esotericism is a consequence of the tension between philosophy and politics, not the cause of it. Philosophic esotericism, moreover, is in no way mysterious, open only to those initiated into arcane and irrational rites. It simply means that one must use one's reason rigorously in order to discover what really is being said. In this sense, there is nothing at all that is closed to anyone who uses our altogether common intelligence sufficiently.[8]

To recognize that the commerce between philosophy and politics requires prudent handling is to see the general necessity for prudence in politics. A final cause of the affinity between "Straussianism" and conservatism is the common questioning of utopianism and consequent appreciation of prudence. Practical wisdom means recognizing practical limits. Yet, this "Aristotelian" conservatism accords with, indeed it stems from, attention to the good and the right simply.

CHARACTER AND ANTI-COMMUNISM

I have emphasized the affinity between Reagan conservatism and "Straussianism" because the implications of "Straussianism" for contemporary political goals and policies flow fairly directly from this similarity. What Strauss' students did in office, and what they said in the battles of opinion that preceded Reagan's election, were well enough prefigured in the elements that permitted a conservative alliance in the first place.

One might sum up these policy directions in five ways: anti-communism (and not amelioration), the virtue of individual responsibility (and not excessive social welfare), equal rights (and not affirmative action or feminism), market competition (and not excessive regulation or quasi-oligarchy), and educational and artistic excellence (and not "politicization" or self-indulgence). People influenced by Strauss were directly and indirectly involved in each of these areas; naturally, their importance varied.

No useful end would be served by belaboring the obvious connection between these guides for policy and the general perspectives that "Straussians" and conservatives share. The relations are easy enough to see. Objections to the procedures, practices, and legal arguments that make up affirmative action, to take one example, follow visibly from attention to the proper understanding of equal natural rights. Changing government programs that restrict individual responsibility, to take another, follows from seeking to advance moral virtue and healthy initiative. It is also clear that there can be tensions among the different measures we use to try to secure these goals. The relevant point for now is that these purposes provided a standpoint from which to assess and develop concrete programs, suggestions, and activities. Without such a standpoint it is very difficult for anyone in Washington to step out from the bureaucratic fog.

In my own case, the substance of our efforts in the job where I had most control was directly related to what I had learned academically. I directed all our government's formal exchange programs with academics, and with future leaders in
politics and the professions. Much of this work involved finding common ground
for what our enabling legislation called "mutual understanding," and much involved
giving citizens of foreign countries a thoughtful sense of how America's constitutional democracy informed our political institutions and way of life generally. The
connection between the two tasks is that equality in natural rights and the tolerance associated with it, rather than excessive sentimentality toward unique mores
and distasteful doctrines, is the chief ground for truly mutual "understanding," as
well as the central element in the liberal democratic way of life.

Needless to say, my perspective, which argued that the success of America's
principles served a global good, was controversial, as were the policies and choices
associated with it. They are less controversial now that the Cold War is over. I doubt
that I would have approached things as I did without sharing in the affinity that I
discussed above, and I believe that anyone who had my job and shared this affinity
would have acted more or less as I acted. The views of other "conservatives" with
whom I dealt in "public diplomacy," however, would sometimes have led to different, and I presume they believe superior, results. Moreover, in some areas of policy,
monetary policy, for example, conservative economics professors usually had the
most to offer of immediate benefit. And, occasionally, the affinity I have outlined
gives direction that is either broad or subtle enough to accommodate or result in
reasonably wide differences in policy. Nonetheless, the general policy guidance that
stems from the areas of affinity between Reagan conservatism and "Straussianism"
was for the most part substantial and significant.

CONSTITUTIONALISM

I conclude with a brief mention of constitutional issues, by which in this context I
mean the form in which policies take place and by which they are shaped. Those
who study with Strauss and his students learn to admire our institutions and to
expect them to work in certain ways. Taking the founders seriously does not require
apolitical and naive institutionalism, of course, but in the nature of the case it means
respect for constitutional limits. To the degree that these limits are not self-enforc-
ing, how in practice does one live up to them? How much leeway does one have in
one's job, and how much should one take? When should someone else's imperfect
attempt justly take precedence over one's own (presumably) greater effectiveness?
How do the responsibilities of minor or major office at once embody the energy
through which they are executed and the limits through which they are checked?

To be aware of these and similar questions is sometimes to conduct oneself
peculiarly while in government, rather like a player who has special respect for the
game's founders and so conducts himself occasionally as if he were a referee. Politics

and government, of course, are not games, but though they are serious it is best that they not become deadly serious. Some moderation is necessary precisely as one presses ahead with one's own responsibility. Looking at politics from the outside even while one is looking around on the inside in order to do one's job can be a source of this moderation, even if a somewhat unusual one.

The distance from, or even levity about, day to day concerns that the kinds of questions I have mentioned engender is, surprisingly, not always as politically debilitating as it might seem. For, the questions are of a piece with the responsible affirmation of rights, or responsible self-interest, that inform the character of our government when character is at once our goal, our defining shape and order, and our motive force. Liberal constitutionalism seeks to engender the responsible individual character that elevates but is rooted in self-interest, and it tries to operate politically, economically, and socially through the mutual exercise and, therefore, mutual limiting, of such self-interested responsibility. So, to worry about protecting and educating this character is, in different degrees, a common concern both of our political observers and doers. This means that the observant doer is not always done in by others who are more immediately aggressive and effective.

While almost all political scientists will serve in government with their research eyes wide open, the issues that concern them are often alien to the purposes and procedures of governing. They come from methodology rather than being an extension of the perspective of politics itself. Too many political scientists are concerned, one might say, with the chemical composition of the chalk that makes up the sidelines, rather than with the game itself. Strauss' students are taught to look at the regime or character of our country. This sometimes means that one worries ineffectively about the sidelines rather than playing the game at hand. But at least they are the constitutional sidelines that help form the game, not sidelines "scientifically" understood. And, when affirmative action and equality of rights, moral and intellectual excellence, individual economic responsibility, and defending free government from communism are the chief issues of the day, the constitutional or even more formal problems that organize these issues are visibly, if hazily, in play. So, the glimpse of the deeper questions that study in the school of Strauss permits can serve one well in politics. Indeed, dealing practically with issues as they emerge in government can, for better or worse, affect one's understanding of these deeper problems themselves.[9]

NOTES

1. I will draw throughout on my own experience in government. From 1981–83 I was Assistant Director of ACTION, a federal agency which then encouraged private and volunteer approaches to social issues such as illegal drug use. After serving at the United States Information Agency, I became a senior staff member of the Senate Foreign Relations Committee from 1985–86, when Richard Lugar was chairman. I then returned to USIA as

Associate Director for Educational and Cultural Affairs, where I was the senior official in charge of our government's books, libraries, English language and exchange programs, including academic exchanges such as the Fulbright Program. I have also been a member of two federal boards.

2. See, for example, Lionel Trilling, *The Liberal Imagination*, Viking Press, 1950.

3. See Leo Strauss, *On Tyranny*, Cornell University Press, 1968.

4. See Harry V. Jaffa, *Crisis of the House Divided*, Doubleday, 1959; Harvey C. Mansfield, Jr., *Statesmanship and Party Government*, University of Chicago Press, 1965; and Herbert J. Storing et al., *Essays on the Scientific Study of Politics*, Holt, Rinehart and Winston, 1962.

5. See Leo Strauss, *Natural Right and History*, University of Chicago Press, 1953.

6. See Leo Strauss, *The City and Man*, Rand McNally, 1964, and Walter Berns, *Freedom, Virtue, and the First Amendment*, Louisiana State University Press, 1957.

7. The point of contact between Reagan conservatism and Straussianism is that each is, with different degrees of scope, power, and understanding, a revolutionary attempt to restore the primacy or, at least, the visibility, of what is naturally good in our own political and intellectual "tradition."

8. See *The Republic of Plato*, translated with notes and an interpretive essay by Allan Bloom, Basic Books, 1968.

9. See Mark Blitz, "The Character of Executive and Legislative Action in a Country Based on Natural Rights," in James W. Muller, ed., *The Revival of Constitutionalism*, University of Nebraska Press, 1988, and Mark Blitz, "The Problem of Practice—Foreign Policy and the Constitution," in Robert A. Goldwin and Robert A. Licht, eds., *Foreign Policy and the Constitution*, The AEI Press, 1990.

Notes on Contributors

George Anastaplo is Professor of Law at Loyola University of Chicago, Lecturer in the Liberal Arts at the University of Chicago, and Professor Emeritus of Political Science and of Philosophy, Dominican University. His most recent books are *The Thinker as Artist: From Homer to Plato & Aristotle*, *Abraham Lincoln: A Constitutional Biography*, and *Liberty, Equality, and Modern Constitutionalism: A Source Book*. The most recent addition to his exploration series is the 350-page "Law & Literature and the Bible: Explorations," 23 *Oklahoma City University Law Review* (1998).

Hadley Arkes is the Edward Ney Professor of Jurisprudence and American Institutions at Amherst College. He has written numerous articles and five books, among which are *First Things, Beyond the Constitution*, and *The Return of George Sutherland*. He has been a Fellow of the Woodrow Wilson Center and the National Endowment for the Humanities. He is a contributing editor to *National Review* and a monthly columnist for *Crisis* magazine. He is a frequent contributor to the *Wall Street Journal*, the *Washington Post,* and *Commentary.*

Larry Arnhart is Professor of Political Science at Northern Illinois University. He is the author of numerous articles in political philosophy and American government as well as *Aristotle on Political Reasoning: A Commentary on the "Rhetoric," Political Questions: Political Philosophy from Plato to Rawls*, and most recently *Darwinian Natural Right: The Biological Ethics of Human Nature.*

Laurence Berns has been teaching at St. John's College, Annapolis, since 1960. His writings include "Gratitude, Nature and Piety in *King Lear*" (*Interpretation*, Autumn 1972); "The Relation Between Philosophy and Religion: Reflections on Leo Strauss's Suggestions Concerning the Source and Sources of Modern Philosophy" (*Interpretation*, Fall 1991); "Aristotle and Adam Smith on Justice: Cooperation Between Ancients and Moderns?" (*Review of Metaphysics*, September 1994); "Our Political Situation: Good Government, Self-government and American Democracy," *The Great Ideas Today* (1997). He is completing a literal translation of Aristotle's *Politics.*

Mark Blitz is Fletcher Jones Professor of Political Philosophy and Director of Research at Claremont McKenna College. He has served as Associate Director of the United States Information Agency and as a Senior Professional Staff Member of the Senate Committee on Foreign Relations. He has been Vice President and Director of Political and Social Studies at the Hudson Institute. He is the author of *Heidegger's "Being and Time" and the Possibility of Political Philosophy* and of numerous articles in political philosophy, American politics, and foreign affairs.

448   *About the Contributors*

Aryeh Botwinick is Professor of Political Science at Temple University. He is the author of *Skepticism and Political Participation, Power and Empowerment: A Radical Theory of Participatory Democracy* (with Peter Bachrach), and *Postmodernism and Democratic Theory*. His most recent book is *Skepticism, Belief, and the Modern: Maimonides to Nietzsche*. He is currently working on two book-length projects: *Michael Oakeshott: Theory, Contingency, and the Political* and *Emmanuel Levinas: Reconceiving the Western Political Tradition*.

Eva Brann has been a tutor at St. John's College, Annapolis, since 1957 and was Dean from 1990 to 1997. Her books are *Late Geometric and Proattic Pottery from the Atheniae Agora, Paradoxes of Education in a Republic, The World of the Imagination, The Past-Present* and *What, Then, Is Time?* She has published articles on Plato's *Republic*, Thomas Jefferson, and Jane Austen among others. She is co-translator of Plato's *Sophist* and *Phaedo* and the translator of Jacob Klein's *Greek Mathematical Thought and the Origin of Algebra*.

Christopher A. Colmo is Associate Professor of Political Science at Dominican University, River Forest, Illinois. His most recent publication is "Alfarabi on the Prudence of Founders" in the *Review of Politics*.

Joseph Cropsey is Professor Emeritus in the Department of Political Science at the University of Chicago. Among his publications are *Polity and Economy: An Interpretation of the Principles of Adam Smith, Political Philosophy and the Issues of Politics*, co-editor *History of Political Philosophy* (with Leo Strauss), and *Plato's World: Man's Place in the Cosmos*.

Kenneth L. Deutsch is Professor of Political Science at SUNY Geneseo. He has published five books, *Political Obligation and Civil Disobedience, Constitutional Rights, Modern Indian Political Thought, The Crisis of Liberal Democracy: A Straussian Perspective*, and *Leo Strauss: Political Philosopher and Jewish Thinker*. He is presently working on a book dealing with German-Jewish refugees during World War II and their relationship to the American political experience.

Robert Eden is Professor of Political Science at Hillsdale College. His work includes *Political Leadership and Nihilism: A Study of Weber and Nietzsche* and articles on Franklin D. Roosevelt, John Dewey, Woodrow Wilson, Winston Churchill, Tocqueville, and Montaigne. His translation of De Gaulle's first book, *The Enemy's House Divided,* is forthcoming from University of North Carolina Press.

Murray Dry is the Charles A. Dana Professor of Political Science at Middlebury College, where he teaches political philosophy, American constitutional law, and American political thought. His publications include contributions to books and articles on the American Founding, federalism, and freedom of speech. He is currently working on a book on the First Amendment freedoms in political philosophy and American constitutional law.

Miriam Galston has a B.A. from Cornell University, a Ph.D. from the University of Chicago, and a J.D. from the Yale Law School. She is an Associate Professor at the George Washington University Law School, where she teaches corporations, bankruptcy, legal theory, and nonprofits. She has written in the areas of ancient and medieval political thought, tax policy, and legal theory. Ralph Lerner is responsible for her interest in ancient and medieval political thought and her commitment to teaching.

William A. Galston is Professor, School of Public Affairs, University of Maryland, and Director of the Institute for Philosophy and Public Policy. From 1993 to 1995 he served as Deputy Assistant to President Clinton for Domestic Policy. He is the author or editor of six books and numerous articles on political philosophy, American politics, and public policy. His recent publications include *Liberal Purposes: Goods, Virtues, and Diversity in the Liberal State; Justice and the Human Good*; and "Two Concepts of Liberalism," and "Political Economy and the Politics of Virtue: US Public: Philosophy at Century's End."

Gary D. Glenn has been a teacher of political philosophy and American political thought at Northern Illinois University since 1966. His publications include "Inalienable Rights and Locke's Argument for Limited Government," "Forgotten Purposes of the First Amendment Religion Clauses," "Cyrus' Corruption of Aristocracy," "Speculations on Strauss' Political Intentions suggested by *On Tyranny*," and "Partisanship and Neutrality in Teaching American Government: The Case of the Post-Behavioral Era."

Harry V. Jaffa is the Henry Salvatori Research Professor of Political Philosophy Emeritus at Claremont McKenna College and Claremont Graduate School. He is the author of numerous articles, and ten books, including his trail-blazing *Crisis of the House Divided*. His most recent book, *Storm Over the Constitution* (Rowman & Littlefield), is forthcoming. Also soon to be published is the first volume *Why the War Came* of his much anticipated *A New Birth of Freedom: Abraham Lincoln and the American Civil War*.

Charles R. Kesler is Associate Professor of Government and Director of the Henry Salvatori Center at Claremont McKenna College. He has written extensively on political philosophy and American politics, and is editor of *Saving the Revolution: The Federalist Papers and the American Founding* and as well of a new edition of *The Federalist* (Penguin-Putnam 1999).

Carnes Lord is John M. Olin Professor of Statecraft and Civilization at the Fletcher School of Law and Diplomacy of Tufts University. From 1989 to 1991 he served as Assistant to the Vice President for National Security Affairs. He has translated Aristotle's *The Politics* and is the author of *The Presidency and the Management of National Security* and editor of *Essays in the Foundations of Aristotelian Political Science*.

John A. Marini is Associate Professor of Political Science at the University of Nevada, Reno. He has written extensively in the areas of American politics, and administration, budgeting, and campaign finance. He is the author of *The Politics of Budget Control: Congress, the Presidency, and the Growth of the Administrative State* (1992) and co-editor of *The Imperial Congress: Crisis in the Separation of Powers* (1988).

Eugene F. Miller is Professor of Political Science at the University of Georgia. He is editor of David Hume's *Essays, Moral, Political, and Literary* and has published numerous scholarly articles on questions of political knowledge, on American political thought, and on the philosophy of Hume and other thinkers in the liberal tradition.

Will Morrisey is Executive Director of the Monmouth County Historical Commission in Freehold, New Jersey, and is Associate Editor of *Interpretation: A Journal of Political Philosophy*. He is the author of five books, most recently *A Political Approach to Pacifism*, and *Culture in the Commercial Republic*.

John A. Murley is Professor of Political Science at the Rochester Institute of Technology. He has written on the First Amendment, public opinion, and trial by jury. He is co-editor of the two-volume *Essays in Law and Philosophy: The Practice of Theory*. He is compiling *A Bibliography in Political Theory, American Politics and Other Areas*. He is co-editor of *The Political Thought of Willmoore Kendall* (forthcoming, which will include the correspondence between Willmoore Kendall and Leo Strauss).

Walter Nicgorski is Professor in the Program of Liberal Studies at the University of Notre Dame and concurrent Professor in the University's Department of Government and International Studies. He is chief editor of *The Review Of Politics*. His published scholarship concerns classical political theory, especially that of Cicero, as well as liberal and character education. He is co-editor of *An Almost Chosen People: The Moral Aspirations of Americans* (1976) and co-editor of *Leo Strauss: Political Philosopher and Jewish Thinker* (1994).

Susan Orr is Director, Center for Social Policy, the Reason Public Policy Institute. Previously she was with the National Center on Child Abuse and Neglect, at the United States Department of Health and Human Services. She received her Ph. D. from the Claremont Graduate University. She has written on women and equal rights and is the author of *Jerusalem and Athens: Reason and Revelation in the Works of Leo Strauss*.

Ralph A. Rossum is the Henry Salvatori Professor of American Constitutionalism at Claremont McKenna College. He is co-author of *American Constitutional Law*, 5th edition, (with G. Alan Tarr). His other publications include *Reverse Discrimination: The Constitutional Debate, Congressional Control of the Judiciary: The Article III Option, The American Founding: Politics, Statesmanship, and the Constitution* (with Gary L. McDowell), and *Police, Criminal Justice, and the Community* (with Alan Brent).

Gary J. Schmitt is Executive Director of the Project for the New American Century. He is Adjunct Professor at the Johns Hopkins University School of Advanced International Studies and has written extensively on national security affairs and American government. He is co-editor of *U.S. Intelligence at the Crossroads* and co-author of *The Future of U.S. Intelligence*. He is revising editor of the second edition of Abram Shulsky's *Silent Warfare: Understanding the World of Intelligence*. He has served as Executive Director of the President's Foreign Intelligence Advisory Board and minority staff director of the Senate Select Committee on Intelligence.

Abram N. Shulsky is a consultant on national security affairs to the Rand Corporation and to the Office of Net Assessment, in the office of Secretary of Defense. He is the author of *Silent Warfare: Understanding the World of Intelligence*. He has published numerous articles and reports on intelligence and arms control as well as contributions to *Essays on the Foundations of Aristotelian Political Science* and to *The Virtual Corporation* and *Army Organization*.

Gregory Bruce Smith teaches political philosophy at Trinity College, Hartford, Connecticut. A graduate of the University of Chicago, he has previously taught at Carleton College and the Universities of Chicago, Michigan, and Pennsylvania. He has written numerous articles on Strauss, Nietzsche, Heidegger, Derrida, and Plato. He is author of *Nietzsche, Heidegger and the Transition to Postmodernity* and is preparing a forthcoming book on Heidegger.

Ronald J. Terchek is Professor of Government and Politics at the University of Maryland. His most recent books include *Republican Paradoxes and Liberal Anxieties* and *Gandhi: Struggling for Autonomy*. His work has dealt with the problem of autonomy and rationality in liberal thought, the status of community, and citizenship in models of liberal democracy, and he is completing a book on the civic realist critique of contemporary liberal democratic theory and practice.

Michael P. Zuckert is Professor of Government at the University of Notre Dame. He has written *Natural Rights and the New Republicanism* and *The Natural Rights Republic*, the first two volumes in a tetrology directed to the American Founding. He is now completing the third volume, *A System Without Precedent: Political Science and the American Founding*.